A GRAY PLAYBOOK

A GRAY PLAYBOOK

OF LONG AND SHORT PLAYS FOR STAGE, PUPPET–THEATRE, RADIO & TELEVISION, ACTED BETWEEN 1956 AND 2009, WITH AN UNUSED OPERA LIBRETTO, A FILM SCRIPT OF THE NOVEL *POOR THINGS* AND EXCERPTS FROM THE PICTORIAL STORYBOARD OF THE NOVEL *LANARK* BY

ALASDAIR GRAY

Luath Press Limited

EDINBURGH

www.luath.co.uk

First published in Great Britain 2009

Published by Luath Press Limited, Edinburgh, Scotland

The publishers acknowledge the support of

Scottish Arts Council

towards the publication of this volume.

Typeset in 12pt on 14pt Baskerville
by Joe Murray of Glasgow.
This book was delivered in time for publication
thanks to the skilful last minute work of Richard Todd.

Printed and bound by CPI Antony Rowe, Chippenham.
The paper used in this book is recyclable.
It is made from low-chlorine pulps produced in a low energy, low emissions manner from renewable forests.
A CIP catalogue record for this book is available from the British Library.
Standard edition ISBN 978-1-906307-91-2
Deluxe Edition ISBN 978-1-906817-13-8

THIS BOOK IS DEDICATED
TO ALL MY HELPERS
INCLUDING
JOE MURRAY
Friend and Much Enduring Typesetter.

TABLE OF

CONTENTS

HOW THIS BOOK GOT MADE

AT AN EARLY AGE I grew so fond of using pens that my fingers could never master the keyboard of a typewriter. Editors, broadcasters and producers of plays will not read hand writing, so my manuscripts were typed out by my father at first, then by friends, then by temporary secretaries.

Mrs Flo Allan was a good secretary who typed for me in spare moments between working for the BBC. In the 1970s I visited her in the old Scottish BBC headquarters in Hamilton Drive, and saw I had entered an unexpected future. The typists were NOT clickety-clicking keys to make little levers stamp letters onto paper round a sliding drum. Behind their keyboards was a thing like a white plastic fungus, the stem swelling out into a half-globe with a screen in the flat surface facing them. Before that moment I thought, like most people, I was living in Modern Times. When word processors became standard writing tools, smart intellectuals started saying we are now living in Postmodern Times.

I still cannot master keyboard technology but have come to depend more and more on helpers who can. All my pages are continually revised, so time is saved when I can see them on the screen and dictate corrections without having each one retyped. Nowadays I revise work for publication while sitting beside a friendly secretary using a desktop computer. A file of the result is then passed to a typesetter, usually Joe Murray, with whom I design the final form of the book, so less time is spent correcting the printer's proofs. Joe has suffered me longest, for this is our ninth book together.

In 2002 the young novelist Rodger Glass became one of my temporary secretaries. He helped me finish a collection of stories, begin a novel, and start a website on which I put scripts of plays written in the late 1960s and early '70s. I had always hoped they would one day be published as a step toward to having them acted again, but no publishers I knew wanted that book. Rodger declared that publishers *should* want it, and got me writing urgent letters about it to my English literary agent and publisher in London. These led to nothing, so he persuaded me to ask Jenny Brown for help. Though Scottish, she is Rodger's literary agent and got his first novels published by Faber. Jenny got Luath Press of Edinburgh to publish *this* book. It is therefore dedicated to Rodger, and to Helen Lloyd who has now been my secretary and assistant for over three years, and to my wife Morag who read the proofs, and to Joe Murray.

I hope you are the kind of reader who enjoys enacting plays in the theatre of your mind. Most publishers (who would not last without knowing their own business best) think there are too few of you to make playbooks sell profitably. The plays of Shakespeare, Shaw, Singe, O'Casey, Pirandello, Brecht, Beckett and Friel are perhaps only profitable because schools and universities teach them. My novels are taught in some universities, which is why Luath Press thinks this collection of mostly forgotten plays may still pay for itself.

Readers of my novels and stories will find some of them here in their earliest form, though not in immature or clumsier forms. When staged or broadcast most gave pleasure to both the actors and audiences. But many will be new to you, having been acted in Scotland long ago and never turned into books. There is also a verse play, an opera libretto and a film script that have never been performed, but *not* (though this may be an author's vanity talking) because they don't deserve performance. In the 1890s the poet Yeats and Lady Gregory created the Abbey Theatre with the declared purpose of staging Irish plays *that had not yet been written*! Shaw and Oscar Wilde were then noted playwrights in London, but the Abbey wanted plays on Irish themes for Irish audiences, which led to an internationally acclaimed school of Irish playwriting. For most of the 20th century several brave Scots struggled to make theatres as successful in their own homeland, but with less success. But at last we have a National Theatre of Scotland, which may be heralding an improvement.

The plays are printed in chronological order with introductions telling how they were written and produced, thus amounting to an occasional playwright's autobiography. When a radio or television play was rewritten for the stage, the stage version is printed in hope that it may be staged again. Stranger things have happened. Shaw's success as a playwright led to the publication of his early rejected novels, which are far more mentally stimulating than fiction by all but the greatest novelists. If you find no such stimulation in this book you will be right to dismiss it as a vanity publication. But I cannot. On reading them again I was fascinated by how most, even the domestic dramas, reflect the political mood of the time they were written.

This cannot be said of the first and shortest, written in the last year of the Second World War when I lived with my family in the pleasant market town of Wetherby, Yorkshire. My father was manager there of a hostel for munitions workers between the town and its more famous racecourse. The hostel had a high wire-netting fence round it with gates through which the workers, over a thousand young women, were bussed to and from a factory where they made explosives. The gates were only locked at night and to me it had the character of a friendly concentration camp. There was a bungalow for the manager and his family, prefabricated dormitory blocks where the workers slept, a small hospital called The Sick Bay, administrative offices, a lounge, a library, a big refectory for breakfast and evening meals, also a concert hall where films were shown and plays presented by a band of actors paid by the government to entertain war-workers. My only previous experience of staged theatre had been pantomimes. In the hostel concert hall I saw *Night Must Fall* by Emlyn Williams (a modern murder play) and *Twelfth Night* – my first meeting with Shakespeare, in which I sympathised with Malvolio, disliked the heartless merrymakers who tortured him and have ever since regarded that play as his tragedy.

And sometimes my Dad helped people in the hostel to stage concerts in which anyone who presented themselves with confidence did turns. My mother (who had been in the Glasgow Orpheus Choir between the wars) sang *Weel May The Keel Row* or a song by Burns. I may have sung *Over the Sea to Skye* which was my main party piece – the name then given to a song or poem children were taught to sing or recite at family gatherings and domestic parties – but I certainly recited *Ten Little Houses* and another comic poem from a book for children by Gilbert Frankau. I must have been excited by performing on stage before a full audience but can now only remember taking it for granted. No doubt my parents were thus encouraging me to be a right little show off, but they reproved me for showing off at home or in private life. They only wanted me to get attention when I had something useful or interesting to say, show or give.

The primary school I attended was called The Church School, though I cannot remember receiving religious instruction there. I was generally happy with my classmates and teachers. The lessons never seemed too strenuous, and I enjoyed a practice never found in any later school attended or heard of. When our teacher had an official piece of business that kept her busy at her classroom desk, she invited any pupil who wanted the job to come to the front of the class and tell the rest a story. I was so eager for this job that I cannot remember anyone else doing it. Under the English class system I was perhaps treated as a privileged child – almost one of the big landowning class – because Dad was responsible to the Ministry of Munitions for employing a local staff of over two hundred. My parents once invited home for an evening meal my teacher, Miss Kershaw, something they would never have thought of doing in Glasgow. Miss Kershaw let me produce my first play in her classroom when I was nine.

I found the characters, scene and action in a child's prose version of Homer's *Odyssey* borrowed from Wetherby's public library, a story I found as fascinating as *The Wind in the Willows*, Thackeray's *The Rose and the Ring* and Kingsley's *Water Babies*, read about the same time. I copied the speeches straight from the book, only shortening them a little, and have never since written a play so fast or had it produced so swiftly, being myself the producer. For the part of Odysseus I chose a friend whose name I can no longer remember unless it was Raymond Daybell. I acted the most interesting character, Polyphemus. My dad typed the result and here it is.

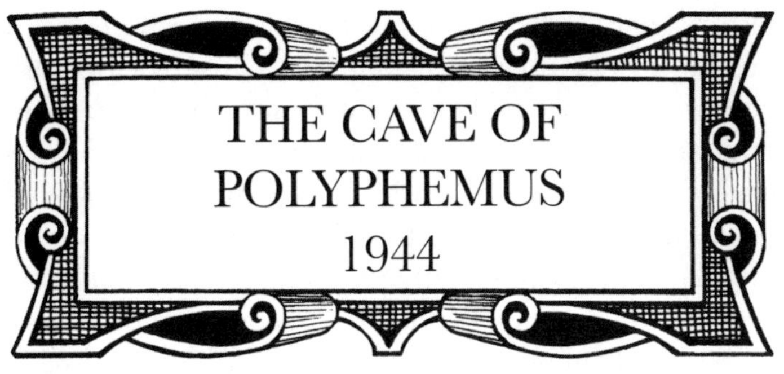

THE CAVE OF POLYPHEMUS 1944

CHARACTERS: **ODYSSEUS** and **TWO FOLLOWERS**
POLYPHEMUS and **TWO FOLLOWERS**
SHEEP and **GOATS**

SCENE: *Cave with cheeses hung on walls, bowls of milk against wall, fire on floor, and corner of cave hidden by partition, with shepherd's staff seen. Entrance on left. Enter* **O.** *and* **F.**, *former with skin of wine.*

O What strange place is this? It seems as if it were inhabited by some monster.

1ST F True Odysseus, but here is food and drink in plenty.

2ND F Let us eat our fill then go our way before the monster returns.

O: But that would be discourteous. We will wait for the monster's return and ask for the food.

Enter **POLYPHEMUS** *driving sheep and goats with much shouting*

1ST F Look, here comes the monster.

P Oh who are ye who enter the domain of the mighty Polyphemus?

O We are men from Troy who seek your hospitality. We are hungry.

P Where is thy ship?

O Alas our good ship has been dashed to pieces on the rocks.

2ND F We are the only survivors good Polyphemus.

P I also am hungry but I have a different way of satisfying my hunger.

O How is that?

P Thus.

P *throws* **1ST FOLLOWER** *into corner behind screen. There are hungry noises from corner, and* **P** *comes out after all falls quiet smacking his lips. During this* **O** *and* **2ND FOLLOWER** *cower and whisper.*

O Cruel giant, drink wine since ye have eaten of men's flesh (*holds out wine*).

P: Thanks little man, but tell me thy name that I may reward ye.

O No man is my name.

P [*after drinking the wine*] The wine is excellent no man, and thy reward, thou shall be eaten last, Ha Ha Ha.

P *yawns and lies down and goes to sleep at back of cave.*

2ND F Let us slay this monster. [*drawing his sword*]

O: No, if this giant is slain how can we escape? We can't remove the boulder from the mouth of the cave. It is too heavy.

2ND F Then what will we do?

O: Listen, I have a plan. You see that staff there. We will put its end in the fire then put it into the giant's eye.

2ND F That is a great plan indeed. Come let us get the staff.

Quietly the staff is obtained. Both hold it in the fire and turn it round for a few seconds then slowly approach the giant and stick it into his eye.

P Oh my eye, my eye. Comrades save me.

There are sounds of heavy feet running. They stop outside the cave.

1ST VOICE What ails thee, Polyphemus?

2ND V Why wake us from our sleep?

1ST V Does any man harm thee?

P: No man harms me. No man is killing me.

2ND V If no man harms thee it must be illness, and that we cannot cure.

1ST V (*to his comrade*) We will return to our sheep.

Footsteps fade away in distance.

P You shall not escape me. I know thou art still in this cave. I will find thee, never fear.

P *gropes his way around,* **O** *and* **F** *dodge him*

P I shall take my sheep and goats out to graze but thou shall not escape me.

P *gropes round cave until he finds animals. As he does this* **O** *and* **F.** *whisper then go to the mouth of the cave and wait.* **P.** *drives animals to mouth and moves boulder. As he does this* **O.** *and* **F.** *get beneath animals. As animals pass out* **P.** *feels back and sides of* **SHEEP** and **GOATS** *but not beneath them. After they pass out* **P.** *replaces the boulder and as he does this says.*

P Thou art still in the cave I know. I will call my comrades later and they will return and find thee. Fare thee well.

As he goes away he laughs and his Ha, Ha, Ha, fades away.

LIKE MOST BRITISH CHILDREN living in cities, or within easy reach of them, the first stage plays I saw were Christmas pantomimes based on well-known fairytales with happy endings. I loved the way these mingled comedy and melodrama with lovely women, grotesque clowns, songs and colourful scenery. I saw these pantomimes in big music halls – sometimes called vaudeville theatres – built in the 19th century and mostly destroyed by the spread of television in the 1960s. Oddly enough, the spread of popular cinemas in the early 20th century had done them no harm. They had been training grounds for all the great cinema comedians from Chaplin to Laurel and Hardy and the Marx Brothers. When sound came, Hollywood also drew on them for singing and dancing stars who, in their declining years, often toured the music halls where they were still sure of big audiences. These theatres had old machinery to create effects now only expected of films – demon traps letting actors leap up through the stage from under it or disappear into it, with or without claps of thunder, fireworks and clouds of steam. The Demon King often arrived and left that way. Nearly every pantomime had a *transformation scene* from the days before drop curtains were invented and audiences expected to see scenery changed. The Fairy Queen would wave a wand, the furniture of a royal palace slide away, trees and a lake slide in, the palace walls be drawn up to disclose moonlit hills under a starry sky and the audience would heartily applaud.

After World War 2 the Gray family often visited the Glasgow Citizens Theatre which I will say more about later. There we saw the late plays of James Bridie, Robert McLellan's *Jamie the Saxt* with Duncan Macrae playing the first king of all Britain, also a wonderful pantomime called *The Tintock Cup*, a grotesque parody of Scottish history. The Battle of Bannockburn was presented as a Scotland-England football match seen from the Scottish end, where Bruce and De Bohun, encumbered by chain mail armour, tackled each other for the ball under the eyes of the referee, a huge whistle-blowing spider lowered on a cable from above. This Christmas show was so popular that it ran for three months into the following year. Each year the D'Oyley Carte company brought a Gilbert and Sullivan opera to Glasgow which we usually attended. My sister Mora and I enjoyed *Iolanthe* so much that we borrowed a piano score of the libretto from Riddrie Public Library and I learned to sing the Lord Chancellor's Nightmare song to her accompaniment.

By that time our secondary school had introduced us to Shakespeare. I had the luck to read *Twelfth Night, Midsummer Night's Dream, Merchant of Venice, Macbeth* and *Hamlet* with teachers who enjoyed them. In 1944 we saw Laurence Olivier's film version of *Henry V* and in 1948 his *Hamlet*. The great soliloquies from the soundtrack were available on a record we bought and often played on our wind-up gramophone. But from a much earlier time the popular cinema was almost certainly the biggest part of my dramatic education – Disney, the Marx Brothers and Tarzan films, *The Wizard of Oz*, *Destry Rides Again*, *The Ghost Goes West*, *Hellzapoppin*, *It's a Wonderful Life*, and such odd British forerunners of the Ealing comedies as *Alf's Button*, *The Ghost Train*, *The Black Sheep of Whitehall* and George Formby films. And even more important than that was BBC Radio.

Nobody born after TV grew more popular in the 1950s can imagine the communal strength in Britain of BBC Radio. It is even less imaginable now as it competes with a flood of commercial channels, and the relaxed tone of BBC announcers has mostly become a rapid, attention-seeking advertisers' gabble that would have horrified John Reith, the BBC's first director. British politicians gave this obscure Scottish electrical engineer the job in 1922 because he had been a dependable British Army officer, and they did not think public broadcasting important. They realised its power during the 1926 General Strike, but also found Reith was a strong supporter of *things-as-they-are*. They trusted him so he held the job until 1938. But he was a Tory who disliked commercialism. The BBC mainly broadcast popular entertainment but Reith said it should also make the greatest cultural achievements available to "the labourer in his tenement and the crofter in his cottage". Though working in London he was the son of a Presbyterian minister, and had not noticed that outside Scotland labourers live in terrace houses and no farm workers are crofters. But he had the BBC broadcasting Mozart and Beethoven along with ragtime (the nearest thing to jazz the British then recognised) and Elizabethan plays along with 20th century West End successes. Throughout my childhood I enjoyed Children's Hour every evening from 5pm till 6pm between school and the evening meal. Half of it, broadcast from London, usually serialised a children's adventure story though I also remember the *Wind in the Willows* and an adaption of *The Old Curiosity Shop*. The rest would be songs, stories and comic poems from a local station so that children could hear the kind of accents spoken around them. Each station was introduced by an Uncle or Aunt. West of Scotland Children's Hour had Aunt Kathleen Garscadden, who once invited interested children to devise a five minute broadcast of their own. I got dad to type and send her puerile verses I had written and my version of an Aesop's fable. She invited me to the Glasgow Broadcasting House in Queen Margaret Drive where I read them over the air. The BBC paid for my tram fare there and back, and the glory of reading it more than compensated for lack of other payment. I was then eleven, and enjoyed my first illusion of embarking on a great career.

In 1946 the BBC started a third broadcasting channel which ran each evening from 6pm to midnight, and broadcast nothing that was not artistically or scientifically or historically educational, or avante garde. It was an open university for whoever enjoyed learning more than they could usually hear, so was denounced as elitist and finally scrapped as uncommercial in 1970. The Third Programme gave me the whole of Goethe's *Faust* in Louis MacNeice's translation, MacNeice's own poetic drama, *Child Roland to the Dark Tower Came*, Auden's *The Ascent of F6* with Britten's music, Wyndham Lewis's *The Childermass* and splendid dramatisation of Peacock's *Nighmare Abbey*.

Dad's Socialism had either made him a lover of Bernard Shaw's work, or Shaw's writing had converted him to Fabian Socialism. Among his books was a hefty volume containing all Shaw's plays written before the year of my birth, and Shaw's *Quintessence of Ibsenism*, and Ibsen's plays in the Everyman edition. By my seventeenth birthday I had soothed hours of adolescent insomnia by reading those 42 Shaw plays, which I enjoyed because most are truly playful – none of his characters end by being badly hurt, not even Joan of Arc. I also dipped into Ibsen, but *Peer Gynt* was the only play I could then appreciate, gladly identifying with the irresponsible hero whose wild imagination makes him an outcast at home before making him a corrupt millionaire in the world beyond. Unlike the hero of Goethe's *Faust* this does not lead to him being welcomed into Heaven; he loses everything and finally sees he only truly existed for the woman whose love he betrayed.

That was my experience of drama before the autumn of 1952 when I became a student at Glasgow School of Art. In those days the school hired buses each year to visit the College of Art in Edinburgh. A scratch football team there would play one of ours on The Meadows, then we were entertained with an amateur concert, a meal in their refectory, a dance to end the evening. We did as much for Edinburgh art students when they visited us in Glasgow, and I was one of several voluntary exhibitionists who wrote or acted revue sketches for the Glasgow concerts. This led to the school's Interior Design department asking me to provide entertainment for a party they were giving. The department head, Henry Hellier, had invited Joyce Grenfell, a popular actress and comedienne, so to win more public attention than usual I wrote a dismal symbolic drama, partly inspired by *The Ascent of F6*, called *To Hell with Everything*.

For years I hoped nobody remembered that play but I recently met Jennifer Campbell, illustrator and retired head art teacher of Dollar Academy, who reminded me that in Art School I had chosen her to play Peace. My hero, a kind of Everyman, returns to Peace at the end of World War 2, but she refuses to let him embrace her. He is also troubled by folk representing political forces I cannot now recall, though I painted them in a symbolic backdrop. I remember one looked like a giant anthropoid ape clutching a stone. The action took place before something hidden under a cloth that Everyman finally tears aside, showing a figure representing Science (played by Archie Sinclair of the Industrial Design Department) who blows everybody up. The play combined fear of my sexual unattractiveness with widespread fears of nuclear war. (Historical note: Britain was then the only nation after Russia and the USA to possess hydrogen bombs. Trade unions and local Labour parties had called on the British government to set other nations a good example by doing without them. The Tory government *and* parliamentary Labour party replied that Britain would be an unimportant nation without them, and could survive a nuclear war with the help of normal civil defence precautions. Meanwhile the government was building nuclear bunkers for itself and the civil service, while forbidding the BBC and newspapers to make this fact public.)

This poor play did not stop Miss Hamilton, head of the School's small Puppetry Department, asking me to write plays for her students. After one or two sketches performed at children's private parties I dramatized part of the Old Testament discovered through my love of William Blake. His engravings to *The Book of Job* inspired me to illustrate my own book of the Bible, and after searching through the shortest ones I had discovered *The*

"JONAH"
by
Alasdair Gray.
Incidental Music by Reid Moffat.
Sets by Alasdair Gray.

Scene I. An open space in a City.
Scene II. Deck of a Ship.
Scene III. An Interior!
IV. The Council Chamber, Nineveh.
V. A Desert near Nineveh.

Characters.	Carved By.	Operated By.	Spoken By.
Jonah	Monica Jamieson	(Duncan Shanks & (Andrew Stewart	Atholl Hill.
Mrs Jonah	Carolle McLaren	Robert Smyth	Vivian Simmons
Ship's Captain	George McCulloch		Arch. Sinclair
Grant, his Mate	Arthur Speirs	Arthur Speirs	Alastair Taylor
Customs Man	Robert Smyth	Robert Smyth	Malcolm Hood
King of Nineveh	Oonagh Walsh	Duncan Shanks	James Simpson
Chancellor	(Mae Fotheringham (Frank Bowles	Sandre Ogilvie	Arthur Speirs
Home Secretary	John Harvey	Vivia Barclay	Malcolm Hood
Chief of Police	Joyce Drummond	Gillian Macleod	Alasdair Gray
Sentry	Alastair Taylor	Alastair Taylor	John Campbell
Shepherd	Duncan Shanks	Duncan Shanks	John Campbell
Voice of God			Alastair Taylor

Management of Scenery & Properties: Gillian Macleod, Sandra Ogilvie and Vivia Barclay.
Lighting: Gerard Quail.
THE COMPANY WISH TO RECORD THEIR THANKS TO MR LAURIE
FOR USE OF HIS TAPE-RECORDER.

Book of Jonah. Only three chapters long, this book contains two miracles, one the most famous in the Bible because, after the creation of the world, it is the most unlikely. And unlike the Deluge, destruction of Sodom and Gomorrah, Egyptian plagues and trumpets blowing down the walls of Jericho, both miracles save a life instead of killing thousands. The true hero of Jonah is a reforming God using his power to persuade enemies, instead of slaughtering them. Jonah had inspired several of my pictures and the first play I think you may enjoy.

Directing it was good preparation for later productions of my plays. The puppeteers who carved and manipulated the little wooden actors listened carefully to my directions, seemed to accept them then ignored or forgot them. Scene 2 has Jonah in a cowardly state meeting the Captain and Customs Officer, so I wanted his sense of inferiority made evident by having the puppets playing them an inch or two taller. In Scene 4 he is confident enough to dominate the rulers of Nineveh, so I wanted the four of them to be an inch or two shorter. Nearly all the characters are types so I suggested historical individuals whose faces could be prototypes – the Commander of the Armed Forces, for instance, should resemble Bismark. When we came to rehearse the play I saw that the Commander of the Armed Forces had an elfin face, tip-tilted nose and merry smile. When I complained to Miss Hamilton she explained that the carvers were artists who had to be allowed to express themselves. However, by giving the Commander's head to the Sentry and swapping around some others, the speeches finally seemed spoken by faces that could utter them.

I got the voices completely right by taping them on one of the early reel-to-reel recorders, a heavy Grundig machine housed in a big squat portable case and lent by a painting teacher. I chose the speakers from student friends with appropriate voices. Jonah was not Jewish but Mrs Jonah was. The Captain was from the main sea port of Scotland's Western Isles. The Emperor of Nineveh had seemed pompous and insecure when I met him in our first year at Art School, but was now relaxed and confident, having started an art school choir which he conducted very well. Alas, a disease killed him after his happy marriage a few years later. The voices of the Home Secretary and God belonged to very close friends who died in 2005 and 2007. To interest carvers, manipulators and vocalists who still live, and perhaps the children or grandchildren of those who do not, see adjacent the programme of the one or two performances, presented in December 1956 before an audience containing students visiting us from Edinburgh College of Art.

At that time Britain's government was still encumbered with the large remains of an empire in the Caribbean, parts of Africa, Malaysia, Cyprus and Gibraltar. The Conservative Prime Minister Harold Macmillan had said "a wind of change" was blowing that would give all countries their own governments, but Britain was still fighting wars of occupation that, until 1961, enforced two years of compulsory military service on all healthy young males who did not conscientiously object. Being a Socialist who read his father's *New Statesman* and also a disciple of William Blake I thought all empires were criminal and no nation was right to invade others, another reason for the Book of Jonah providing a congenial theme as it showed God's politics and my own in harmony.

CAST

JONAH, A MINOR PROPHET	every scene
MRS JONAH	Scenes 1 and 5
THE VOICE OF GOD	Scenes 1, 3, 5
SHIP'S CAPTAIN	)
CUSTOMS OFFICER	) Scene 2
SHIP'S MATE	)
THE VOICE OF A BIG FISH	Scene 3
A SENTRY	)
GENERAL COMMANDING ASSYRIAN ARMY	)
CHANCELLOR OF EXCHEQUER	) Scene 4
KING OF NINEVEH	)
CHIEF CONSTABLE	)
AN ELDERLY GOATHERD	Scene 5

SCENES
1) Outside Nazareth in Palestine
2) The deck of small trading ship
3) Inside a very big fish
4) The King of Nineveh's council chamber
5) A hilltop overlooking the city of Nineveh

1: OUTSIDE NAZARETH

Backdrop shows a village of low white flat-roofed buildings among fields with date palms here and there. The sky is clear blue. **JONAH** *sits cross-legged on a grassy mound under a palm, head bent over folded arms, hand holding a short tobacco pipe. He is either meditating or asleep.* **MRS JONAH** *enters, over her head a shawl swathing the baby her left arm holds, in her right hand a hoe that she flings down. Jonah lifts his head. She points at him accusingly.*

MRS JONAH There sits a bone-lazy man who sits all day in the shade while I toil all day in the fields with his child on my arm! A dreamer! An idler! A parasite!

JONAH *knocks ash from his pipe and pockets it while saying calmly* –

JONAH I have told you before, Maggie, that some must work with their hands and some with their heads. My work is prayer and meditation.

MRS JONAH The result of my toil is in my purse – coins to buy food for us in the market. Where is the result of yours?

JONAH [*tapping his brow*] Here! I have been searching for God's being in words He gave to Moses, words I know by heart, then seeking Him in His designs as they appear in all things from the tiny dewdrop up to the mighty sun evaporating it.

MRS JONAH I asked for the result of your work.

JONAH I realised again that my spirit is too feeble for His pure essence, and until He seeks me, I must accept His dim reflection in both His words and His creation.

MRS JONAH No doubt I can make us a good meal out of that!

JONAH [*springing to his feet*] Woman! You are lacking in respect for a Prophet of the One and Only God!

MRS JONAH [*overawed*] I did not mean to be that, but ... but ... but ... [*she weeps and turns away*] What's the use of talking to you?

He goes to her.

JONAH [*tenderly*] Talking helps.

MRS JONAH But I've said it all before!

JONAH [*leading her to the mound*] I know – please say it again.

Sighing, she sits down beside him.

MRS JONAH When very young I felt different from other girls – their hopes and dreams seemed stupid and ordinary. I wanted my life to be special, but women can only be special by marrying a special man, and I didn't know any! Other girls were crazy about ordinary men with nothing but handsome faces, or money, or important jobs. I could only admire some skilled craftsmen, but their shop-talk bored me stiff.

JONAH [*preening a little*] Then you met me!

MRS JONAH Yes! Neither young, handsome OR rich, a poor scholar with no useful trade, but our Rabbi whispered that you might be a Prophet of the Lord.

JONAH [*firmly*] He was right.

MRS JONAH Who thinks that now apart from you? Why should I still believe it?

JONAH Because I am listening for God's word as patiently as when we first met, and can do nothing until He commands me. I was a child when the stories of Abraham and Joseph, Moses and Joshua filled me with knowledge that my life would be joined to theirs. I am now too old to help Israel conquer another land as Joshua did, or slay thousands like Saul or tens of thousands like David. I will be less wise than Solomon whose wisdom has been nothing but a list of proverbs since his followers split the chosen people's kingdom in two. I will also be less terrible than Elijah who was sometimes very cruel. I am glad that my book in our Scriptures may be the smallest.

JONAH *stands up. So does* **MRS JONAH**

MRS JONAH [*pleading*] But one day God **will** command you?

JONAH He must, and soon. I'm growing old.

MRS JONAH [*defeated*] I'll go and get your dinner ready.

JONAH [*absentmindedly*] You're a good wife, Maggie.

MRS JONAH *leaves.*

JONAH They also serve who only ... [*yawns and stretches arms*] ... only sit ... [*he looks at the bench, then sits on ground where he sat before ...*] only relax a little, while waiting.

JONAH *stretches full length and seems to sleep. The blue sky turns deep indigo. There is a faint flicker of lightning, then three seconds later a faint rumble of thunder. The sky goes black and at once a* **SOUND:** *thunder crash.* **JONAH** *sits up, staring upwards.*

SOUND: *organ note*

THE VOICE OF GOD Arise, Jonah, son of Amittai!

JONAH *leaps to his feet, still staring upward.*

THE VOICE OF GOD Arise, go to Nineveh, that great city, and cry against it; for their wickedness is come up against me.

JONAH [*gladly*] And what shall I cry against that great city?

THE VOICE OF GOD Words I will put into your mouth.

JONAH [*exultantly*] I will do it Lord! Yes, I have the strength to do it!

SOUND: *organ note.* **JONAH** *walks briskly up and down as the sky goes blue again. Enter* **MRS JONAH**, *running, child on arm*

MRS JONAH Jonah! Thunder and lightening on a clear bright day, was it? Was it? Was it ...

JONAH [*standing and nodding*] Yes, it was Him.

MRS JONAH You saw Him?

JONAH Most of Him! [*rubs his brow thoughtfully*] Some of Him ... perhaps only a small part, but enough. Yes, enough.

MRS JONAH What was He like?

JONAH Huge! The whole sky reflected His face like a mirror. Or part of His face. It was as big as all Israel.

MRS JONAH O!

JONAH No, He was bigger than that, so big that the whole world was like a wee midge buzzing in the cavern of His left nostril!

MRS JONAH Don't tell me such things, they confuse me. He had a command for you?

JONAH [*with a positive nod*] He did.

MRS JONAH What must you do?

JONAH I must arise, and go to Nineveh ...

MRS JONAH That great city? The capital of the Assyrian Empire?

JONAH [*suddenly thoughtful*] ... And prophesy against it. Their wickedness has come up before Him, you see.

MRS JONAH About time too! How will you do it?

JONAH I will go there, I suppose, and ... er, walk up and down the streets denouncing the place.

MRS JONAH [*thrilled*] Wonderful! They may cast you into a pit like Joseph, or into a lion's den like Daniel, or into a fiery furnace like Shadrach, Mechek and Abednego!

JONAH [*after a pause*] You've a hell of a morbid imagination, Maggie.

MRS JONAH But nothing can hurt you when you're doing God's will!

JONAH Abel did God's will and so did Job and look what happened to them. And maybe He made a mistake. I'm a kindly soul, it's not in my nature to go about cursing folk, that message should have gone to a different Jonah, son of another Amittai. They are both very common names.

MRS JONAH God doesn't make mistakes!

JONAH He's made a mistake about me. I'm leaving here. I'll go to a land where they have other Gods.

MRS JONAH The God of Israel is the only true God.

JONAH [*eagerly*] And Israel is His chosen nation, but since Judeah split with Israel it is no longer a powerful nation! And the false gods of other nations are at least strong enough to protect them! I'll go down to Joppa and take a boat to Tarshish – that should be far enough away.

MRS JONAH [*appalled*] You'll desert your God, your nation and – [*she gestures to the baby*]

JONAH [*wretchedly*] I'm just a silly weak old coward, Maggie. At least I'm leaving you among good people. [*he turns to go*] You'll have one less mouth to feed.

MRS JONAH Will you not give the child your blessing?

JONAH *turns back, raises hand above baby's head, speaks oracularly at first.*

JONAH In the name of God, Father of all Israel ... [*shakes head, almost whispers*] No. I cannot give the child my blessing.

JONAH *leaves.* **MRS JONAH** *sinks down on bench.*

MRS JONAH O Jonah, Jonah.

2: ABOARD SHIP

The raised afterdeck of a small trading vessel, with bulwark along the back, steering wheel at right angles to it, a stay-rope tied to it. The entrance is by gangplank sloping down in from left. An open hatch to the right has an invisible ladder down to the hold. Behind the bulwark a backdrop shows harbour wall and, beyond it, the buildings of a seaport at the foot of a cliff. The **CAPTAIN**, *pipe in hand, leans against the bulwark, smoking.*

SOUND *of seagulls, fading as the* **CUSTOMS OFFICER** *comes up through hatch, a notepad in one hand, pencil in the other.*

CAPTAIN [*affably*] Well, what did you find, Mr Thomson? No hidden wee bottles of contraband hootch or packets of expensive lace?

CUSTOMS Your bales and barrels correspond to the bill of lading, Captain MacPherson, but what about the human cargo?

CAPTAIN [*scratching his ear with the stem of his pipe*] What about what?

CUSTOMS The man not one of your crew.

CAPTAIN [*promptly*] No harm in him at all! A poor wee cowardly soul who came aboard this morning bound for Tarshish. He paid my fairly steep fare without a word of complaint, just as if he knew how honest I am.

CUSTOMS Cowardly? Why do you say that?

CAPTAIN He admits to being terrified of storms.

CUSTOMS That could be a cover for something. Have him up.

CAPTAIN [*shouts down the hatch*] Mr Mate!

The **MATE***'s head rises from the hatch.*

MATE Sir!

CAPTAIN Send up the passenger.

MATE Aye aye sir. [*he disappears*]

CUSTOMS [*pleasantly*] You'd take the Devil as passenger if he paid his fare, Captain MacPherson.

CAPTAIN Perhaps. Perhaps. But I'd see he behaved himself while he was aboard my vessel.

JONAH *comes up the hatch onto the deck. He is exhausted but keeps looking up at the sky in a dazed way. He answers most questions automatically, without thinking.* **CUSTOMS** *officer scribbles them on his pad.*

CUSTOMS Name?

JONAH Jonah, Son of Amittai.

CUSTOMS Nation?

JONAH Israel.

CUSTOMS Birth place?

JONAH Nazareth.

CUSTOMS Usual address?

JONAH Nazareth.

CUSTOMS Destination?

JONAH Tarshish.

CUSTOMS Why?

JONAH, *peering upward, seems not to hear.*

CUSTOMS [*louder*] Why are you going to Tarshish?

JONAH [*still peering up*] It's not in Israel.

CUSTOMS Why don't you like it here?

JONAH I've annoyed someone.

CUSTOMS The police after you?

JONAH [*shocked into paying some attention*] Certainly not! I have broken ... no ... human law! Not one. Ask anyone in Nazareth and they'll tell you I'm completely harmless.

CUSTOMS But you're running away because you've annoyed someone who must be pretty powerful. Who is it?

JONAH I refuse to name him. Our quarrel is a private matter.

CUSTOMS Political?

JONAH [*excitedly*] Yes yes! Exactly. This ... character I knew wanted me to take a political stance that is no business of a quiet family man like me.

CUSTOMS [*nodding*] So your former friend was an agent of the Israel and Judea independence movement?

JONAH [*drearily*] He's no friend of mine now.

He looks back at the sky.

CUSTOMS [*quietly to the* **CAPTAIN**] At last we're coming to the point. [*to* **JONAH**] Listen carefully, old boy. We Jews used to be a quarrelsome lot, always fighting each other, but Israel is now a peaceful part of the mighty Assyrian Empire. His Majesty in Nineveh requires nothing but law, order and regularly paid taxes. Everyone can worship their god in any way they like, short of human sacrifice. Some fanatics hate him for that, of course, but honest citizens have nothing to fear if they quietly inform the authorities ... Are you listening?

JONAH [*impatiently*] What are you talking about?

CUSTOMS About the secret underground terrorist organisation that has scared you shitless!

JONAH [*with a cackle of hysterical laughter*] Wrong wrong wrong! I don't give a damn for underground movements. It's not earthquakes I'm afraid of. [*looks apprehensively upward before appealing to the* **CAPTAIN**] Tell him to let me go below, I haven't slept for forty-eight hours.

CAPTAIN [*quietly to* **CUSTOMS**] Let him go, Mr Thomson. His trouble is all up here. [*taps his head*]

CUSTOMS Alright ...

JONAH *descends through the hatch.*

CUSTOMS ... but Captain, there's something more than insomnia wrong with that man. Tell my opposite number in Tarshish that the authorities should keep an eye on him.

CAPTAIN I will. [*shouts*] Tell the engineer to get his steam up, Mr Mate!

CUSTOMS *leaves by gangplank.* **CAPTAIN** *goes behind steering wheel and grasps spokes.* **SOUND** *of bell clanging, then a faint mechanical thumping starts.*

CAPTAIN [*shouting*] Raise anchor! Raise anchor and cast off!

End of gangplank withdrawn. **SOUND** *of rattling chains.*

CAPTAIN Full steam ahead!

SOUND *of louder engine thuds as backcloth slides left, bringing summit of lighthouse and tops of sailing boats in from right. These too slide off left leaving plain blue ocean horizon. The sky darkens. Distant.* **SOUND** *of low thunder.*

CAPTAIN [*loudly*] Mr Mate!

MATE [*head rising from hatch*] Sir?

CAPTAIN A storm coming up. Batten down everything you can.

MATE [*descending*] Aye aye sir.

SOUND: *wind and slapping waves. The horizon is hidden by crests of high froth-capped waves resembling Hokusai's. If the deck can be made to rock like a see-saw it increasingly does so: if not the wheel starts rocking as if the deck did. The captain clings to it. Louder* **SOUNDS** *of wind, splashing waters, thunder, then loud off-stage cries of terror.*

The **MATE***'s head appears.*

MATE [*shouting over the noise*] The crew are panicking, sir!

CAPTAIN [*wrestling with wheel*] Praying is the only thing they can do! This bloody wind's – hitting us – from every corner – of the compass – it's no canny! Order every man – to cry for help – to every God they have!

MATE's *head disappears.*

SOUND: [*offstage cries*] Adonai help us! Zeus forgive me! Dagon Dagon Dagon, spare me! O save us Poseidon! [*etcetera*]

MATE [*head reappears shouting*] Everyone's praying but the passenger, Captain!

CAPTAIN Why not?

MATE He's sound asleep and snoring!

CAPTAIN In this din? That's no canny either – have him up here!

SOUND: *more wind, thunder, cries of prayer.*

JONAH *struggles on to the deck, grabs the stay-rope for support.*

CAPTAIN Pray, damn you!

JONAH [*desperate*] Useless! God hates me! You'll all drown if you don't fling me overboard!

CAPTAIN We'll drown if I leave this wheel.

JONAH Please! Tell your men to do it!

CAPTAIN [*enraged*] Are you totally gutless?

JONAH [*gazing upward*] Help! O help!

He jumps into the sea. The waves subside. The wheel comes upright. **SOUND:** *thunder stops, wind fades. The* **MATE** *climbs on deck.*

CAPTAIN [*gruffly*] There you are. Take the wheel. I've never seen the like of that before.

MATE [*taking his place at the wheel*] I thought we were done for that time. Where's the passenger?

CAPTAIN He's certainly done for, but he wasn't a coward at the end.

3: A DARK INTERIOR

Total darkness.

SOUND: *faint regular thumps, enough to suggest a beating heart before human moaning starts.*

JONAH O ... O! O! O, what happened? Where am I? Not under water. Able to breathe, good, but oof, this place stinks of fish. Feel ... around. Floor ... not hard, not soft, not cold, not hot, not wet but not quite dry. How wide? ... Floor bends up into wall ... into ceiling. No room to stand, hardly room to move, but [*rapidly*] don't panic don't panic I am alive with room to breathe good good good so think! Think hard. [*with deliberate slowness*] I do not know where I am but the only thing wrong with the place is a fishy stink. And darkness. Faint sound like heart beats – submarine engine? And I got in so there must be a way out. [*sighs*] I wish I could see! Wait a minute, match box! Match box in waterproof tobacco pouch. Good ... Good, it is still here. So time to strike a light.

A mournful glutinous or bubbling voice with a slight echo is heard clearly, but as if from a distance.

THE FISH Don't dare do that.

JONAH Who are you? And why not?

THE FISH I am your host and I don't want my guts singed.

JONAH You mean I'm inside a – O! O! O! [*his moans start mounting to a scream*].

THE FISH Be quiet or I'll digest you.

JONAH [*after silence, sharply*] Why don't you digest me?

THE FISH He won't let me.

JONAH Who is He?

THE FISH Him who feeds me better meals, usually.

JONAH And made you save me? O God my God!

In a glad voice he chants –

I am cast into the deep in the midst of the seas:
Your floods surround me, billows and waves pass over
the head
of me in dark waters deep under the roots of mountains!
with weeds wrapped around my head,
yet you have saved my life from corruption, yes!

In the belly of Hell I remember the Lord my God
and my prayer is heard in your holy temple!
Those who reject your word forsake their own mercy!
I will do what I have vowed with hymns of thanksgiving!
Salvation is of the Lord!

SOUND: *rumble of thunder ending in musical chord.*

THE VOICE OF GOD Do you hear me, Fish?

THE FISH [*wearily*] Aye aye Captain.

GOD Vomit him out upon the dry land.

SOUND: *prolonged vomiting ending in a pop like cork leaving bottle.*

4: COUNCIL CHAMBER

An opulent council chamber with backdrop of open curtains, between which a balcony is visible with the tops of imperial buildings beyond them. An entrance on one side has the **SENTRY** *standing at ease beside it. Centre stage, a table has two chairs behind it facing the audience, and a chair at each end. The end chair near the entrance is throne-like. Enter the* **GENERAL** *and* **CHANCELLOR.**

GENERAL [*grumbling*] Well, here we are, first as usual. He likes punctuality in others but doesn't bother about it himself. [*sits in chair beside the throne.*] Why ain't the Police Chief here?

CHANCELLOR [*sitting beside him*] On the way to the palace I saw a crowd of oddly dressed people blocking the traffic between Royal Crescent and the Imperial Parade. He may be attending to it.

GENERAL An unauthorised public assembly, eh?

CHANCELLOR Looks like it.

GENERAL I know nothing about civilian business of course, but I've noticed a lot of them recently.

CHANCELLOR You will always find cranks drawing crowds around them in the slums. This is the first I've seen in a fashionable quarter since the last victory parade. [*sadly*] I had hoped that – just for once – we would have no domestic crisis to discuss. Sentry! I assume his majesty is still at breakfast?

SENTRY Yessir.

CHANCELLOR Do you know what he's having?

SENTRY [*after sniffing the air*] Fried liver, sir.

CHANCELLOR O dear. Prepare for storms, dear General. The King loves fried liver but it gives him indigestion. He is sure to accuse someone of ingratitude.

The **SENTRY** *stamps his feet, standing to attention as the* **KING** *enters.*

KING [*pleasantly*] Good morning gentlemen.

GENERAL and **CHANCELLOR** [*simultaneously*] Good morning sire.

KING [*settling into the throne*] What is keeping our Chief Constable?

GENERAL Can't say sire.

CHANCELLOR There are rumours, your Majesty, of an unauthorised public assembly.

KING This is not a public holiday!

CHANCELLOR True.

KING It must be a political demonstration!

CHANCELLOR Perhaps.

KING [*explosively*] What more does the public want? [*he stands and paces about*] I squander wealth on the citizens of Nineveh. The rich pay no taxes, the middle class has never been taxed more lightly, the labourers and unemployed are cheaply fed and entertained with bread and circuses and our empire pays for it all! Yet complaints and petitions and demonstrations are unending, I am sick of ingratitude!

The **CHANCELLOR** *shrugs mournfully.*

GENERAL The army's behind you to a man, sir. I can swear to that.

Enter the **CHIEF CONSTABLE.** *The* **KING** *resumes his seat, watching grimly as* **CHIEF** *goes to other end of table, faces him, salutes, places hands on tabletop and leans forward.*

CHIEF Beg to report, sir, special measures must be taken to deal with an unusual manifestation of –

KING Public discontent. I know. When did it start, how did it start, who started it?

CHIEF Two days ago a stranger arrived with nothing special about him except untidy hair, which is often the sign of some sort of enthusiasm.

KING He should have been arrested on the spot.

CHIEF Tidiness is not yet enforceable by law, sire. He also smelled strongly of fish.

KING Lord Chancellor, pass an Order-in-Council commanding all foreign fishmongers to have their hair cut or be registered as undesirable aliens.

CHANCELLOR I'll make a note of it, sire.

KING [*to Police Chief*] And then?

CHIEF He started talking to people in streets in districts where a lot of thriftless poor stand around. He was one of them Jewish preachers who only believe in one God, so was protected by Religious Toleration edict seven eight two six five zero D.

CHANCELLOR The empire wouldn't last a month if we tried forcing our faith on everyone.
GENERAL I worship Adad of course, but the army recruits regiments from every religion.
KING Foreign preachers, however, must not force their religion on us!
CHIEF What he said was so daft that at first policemen on the beat thought him harmless – unpolitical they told me this morning.
KING What did he say?
CHIEF "In six weeks Nineveh will be overthrown!"
KING, GENERAL, CHANCELLOR [*simultaneously jumping up*] Unpolitical?
KING Overthrown by what? A Babylonian revolt?
CHANCELLOR A barbarian invasion?
GENERAL Don't under-rate Persia.
CHIEF Had he mentioned other nations we'd have nabbed him for treason, but he said our sins would overthrow us.
The **CHANCELLOR** *smiles, the* **GENERAL** *laughs, both sit.*
GENERAL Ha ha! Is that all?
KING Why is that causing traffic jams? [*he too sits*].
CHIEF He hinted at natural calamities – storms, earthquakes, things insurance companies call "Acts of God". I only learned about it this morning when I found half the people believe him and are starting to panic.
GENERAL The Jews occupy a couple of tiny colonies. Why is a threat from their God frightening the world's biggest capital city?
CHANCELLOR Every religion has at least one supremely menacing God. It isn't idiotic to think Jehovah and Jupiter, Thor and Baal, Merodach and Adad are different names for the same big thunderer.
KING [*striking the table*] Chief Constable, have you jailed this troublemaker?
CHIEF No sire.
KING But you have ordered his arrest?
CHIEF No sire.
KING Why not?
CHIEF [*after a pause*] I never give orders that will be disobeyed.
KING Are you saying you cannot control your men?
CHIEF In this matter, sire, I have been overtaken by the speed of events. Constables on the beat heard Jonah preach when he seemed too daft to be arrested. He and his followers still haven't broken the law. They kneel publicly in bigger and bigger numbers, weeping and wailing and begging God to forgive them. Today they came out wearing sack-cloth prayer shawls. I find most of my constables are also wearing these. But they still patrol the streets and would certainly arrest brawlers, vandals and thieves, if criminal activity had not stopped along with most other businesses.
GENERAL [*standing up*] Then it is time, your majesty, to call out the army.
CHIEF [*sitting down*] If you can.
GENERAL Do you suggest, dammit, that my men are as mutinous as yours?
CHIEF Can't say. Ask the sentry.
The **GENERAL** *approaches the sentry who still stands to attention. The* **KING** *stands up to watch them.*
GENERAL At ease, my man. Private Mulligan, are you?
SENTRY [*saluting*] Yessir. Thank you sir. [*stands at ease*].
GENERAL I never forget a name. [*produces notebook, pen and writes as he talks*] You, Mulligan ... are in luck. You are probably about to earn ... rapid promotion. You will take ... this note to the guardroom duty officer ... He will send you out with a sergeant and squad of household guards ... to arrest a fish-smelling rabble-rouser ... you will probably find him speechifying [*to the* **CHIEF**] where?
CHIEF Try Central Park and Victory Square.
GENERAL [*to* **SENTRY**] You heard that? Now go. [*tears off note and holds it out*].
SENTRY Sir! Sir ... I'm not *fit* for this job!
GENERAL [*kindly*] Hardly anyone on earth is fit for their job, but you can't go wrong Mulligan, if you do what you're told. Here is my note ... Do you refuse to take it?
SENTRY *stands to attention, making inarticulate gargling noise.*
GENERAL [*fiercely*] Would you rather tell the duty officer that you are under arrest for disobeying a commanding officer?
SENTRY [*saluting smartly*] Yessir!
GENERAL So you are ready to be flogged to death through the ranks?
SENTRY [*saluting*] Yessir!
GENERAL [*softly*] Then go.
The **SENTRY** *marches briskly out.*
GENERAL [*to the* **KING**] One bad apple on top does not mean a stack of them is rotten. I will investigate, sire, and report back directly.
KING Do.

The **GENERAL** *leaves.* **CHIEF** *and* **CHANCELLOR** *watch the* **KING** *who strolls out onto the balcony and stands leaning on it, looking downward with interest.*

KING [*without turning*] Anything to say, gentlemen?

CHANCELLOR Your Majesty ... [*clears his throat*] ... The situation is surely not desperate if this preacher only wants people to weep and wail. They'll soon tire of that. You agree, Chief Constable?

CHIEF [*gloomily*] That depends on what happens forty days from now. Meanwhile, we have a general strike on our hands.

CHANCELLOR A strike for what? What does this Jonah want? A change of government? A change in the laws? Power? Gold? An invitation to the palace?

CHIEF He hasn't asked for anything.

CHANCELLOR Then he may have demoralised the people but is not a revolutionary. We have nothing to fear if this temporary suspension of business does not spread to the frontiers. I suggest that we – [*he breaks off as the* **GENERAL** *enters*].

GENERAL The prophet Jonah, sire, is downstairs requesting an audience with your Majesty.

KING [*without turning*] I'm expecting him.

GENERAL By your leave, I will bring him up.

KING [*turning his head*] Yes.

GENERAL *leaves.* **CHANCELLOR** *stands.*

CHANCELLOR [*eagerly*] Sire! This dangerous man has put himself in your power! We have him trapped!

KING [*shaking his head and entering the chamber*] I don't think so. Look outside.

He returns to his throne and sits with one leg thrown carelessly over the other and hands clasped behind head. **CHANCELLOR** *goes to balcony, looks down and groans.*

CHANCELLOR O dear.

KING What do you see?

CHANCELLOR [*still staring down*] A vast silent mob filling the palace yard and streets beyond. Most are wearing sackcloth. And there are policemen and soldiers among them.

KING [*with a chuckle*] You may also see many palace servants who have always been devoted to me.

CHIEF Is the mob kneeling?

CHANCELLOR [*re-entering the room*] No, they're standing and looking up here as if expecting something. [*He sits with elbows on table and head in hands*].

CHIEF [*gloomily*] An announcement, I expect.

KING I'm afraid the preacher has trapped us.

GENERAL [*entering*] The prophet Jonah, sire.

JONAH [*advances into the room and announces*] Yet forty days and Nineveh will be overthrown!

The **KING** *sits up with hands on knees, leaning forward.*

KING Who will do it?

JONAH God will do it.

KING How?

JONAH I do not know, King of Nineveh. God tells me to preach when, not how this city will be destroyed. God's power is infinite. With rainwater He once drowned everyone for their wickedness except one man and his family. He wrecked the first city of Babylon by confusion of speech, blasted Sodom and Gomorrah with fire and brimstone out of heaven, and when a hard-hearted Egyptian Pharaoh angered him, killed all the first-born of Egypt and their cattle with the last of ten terrible plagues.

KING My heart is not hard! I love my people! I will make any sacrifice to save them. Why does your God hate Nineveh? My government respects every god worshipped in my empire.

CHIEF Synagogues here get as much police protection as other temples.

JONAH Does that excuse your conquest of smaller nations?

KING A generation ago Nineveh was a smaller nation – Babylon ruled us. Led by my father we fought free of Babylon and kept our freedom by conquering it back – there was no other way.

GENERAL Right! Swallow or be swallowed.

JONAH Your wars did not end with the conquest of Babylon.

GENERAL Of course not. There are too many plains around here, no mountain ranges or natural frontiers to protect us, so the bigger our empire gets, the more enemies surround our borders. To prevent aggressive alliances we must whack them before they whack us!

CHANCELLOR [*eagerly*] And an expanding economy needs constant supplies of new slaves.

JONAH [*looking upward*] O God God God is there no limit to the selfish greed and stupidity and cruelty of people in power? Will great wealth always make them self-deluding and destructive? Must those whose work feeds, clothes and houses the rest always be poor and oppressed?

KING [*desperately*] We are no worse than others in our position.

GENERAL, **CHANCELLOR**, **CHIEF** [*simultaneously*] Not worse at all!
CHANCELLOR In fact we are better! Only Nineveh has a Royal Society for the Prevention of Cruelty to Slaves! Those too old and sick to work [*his voice begins to falter*] are given their freedom ... without even asking ... for it ...
JONAH Liars! Other lords enlarge their lands by grabbing fields from neighbours but none have grabbed more than Assyrian lords. Other employers get rich by destroying the work of others, but Assyria's destructions are endless. Other big nations crushed right with might in a race for empire but Assyria won that race. God now declares your success is finally unforgivable. Nineveh hangs like a fat rotten fruit, ripe for the hand of God to pluck and cast down into its proper dirt!
SOUND: [*silence in the room but from outside many voices chanting*] Jonah! Jonah! Jonah! [*are heard, faintly at first but growing louder behind the next speeches*].
KING General!
GENERAL Sir!
KING As Commander of the Armed Forces you will withdraw our troops from Israel and Judea and –
GENERAL Forgive me interrupting sire but that is enough at first! With your permission, I will proclaim in your name that Israel and Judea are raised from colonial to dominion status and then withdraw our troops. More cannot be done at once without provoking widespread revolt and total anarchy. By your leave I will go and implement your initial order.
KING Do it.
The **GENERAL** *leaves.*
KING Lord Chancellor!
CHANCELLOR Before Your Majesty says anything may I suggest –
KING You may not. As Minister for the Interior you have records of those enslaved in our last three campaigns?
CHANCELLOR Of course but –
KING Buy them back from their present owners at half their market value and –
CHANCELLOR Our Exchequer cannot afford that!
KING Then buy them at a third of the market value or a quarter or whatever the Exchequer can afford.
CHANCELLOR The upper classes won't stand that! We'll provoke a right-wing revolution!
KING Not if the police are on our side. Can I depend on them, Chief Constable?
CHIEF [*nodding*] I promise you can, sire.
KING Then see to it, Chancellor. And Chief Constable, see that he sees to it.
The **CHANCELLOR** *sighs and leaves, shaking his head, followed by the* **CHIEF**. *The* **KING** *stands.*
KING Come with me Jonah.
He goes out onto the balcony, **JONAH** *following. They stand together looking down and the* **SOUND** *of chanting stops.*
KING [*loudly*] People of Nineveh, Jonah stands beside me! Hear him!
JONAH Yet forty days and Nineveh will be overthrown!
KING I declare this to be a day of fasting. Let neither men nor women nor their beasts feed or drink! Let us clothe ourselves with sackcloth and cry mightily to God for forgiveness! Let each of us turn from our evil ways and the violence that is in our hands. Who can tell if God will repent of the evil he says he will do! Go home now, all of you, and pray to the supreme God there or in your temples, but not in the open streets.
SOUND *of a wailing multitude, fading as* **KING** *returns to the room followed by* **JONAH.**
KING What more can I do? What more does God want?
JONAH [*smiling and shaking his head*] God has not told me what He wants. He only tells me that in forty days Nineveh will be overthrown.

5: OUTSIDE NINEVEH

A bare hilltop where **JONAH** *sits cross-legged staring grimly at Nineveh in the distance, a walled city with many towers and domes. The sky is blue and cloudless.*
SOUND: *A distant cry of* Billy! ... Billy! ... Billy! *draws nearer*
Enter **GOATHERD** *with crook, wearing broad-brimmed straw hat*
GOATHERD Excuse me sir, but have you seen a goat with a silly lost look on its face?
JONAH No.
GOATHERD He must be somewhere near. If you don't mind I'll just rest to get my breath back. Yes indeed.
He sits down beside **JONAH,** *who ignores him.*
GOATHERD Excuse me for mentioning it, but you should cover your head to stave off sunstroke – ye ken? A handkerchief would do it.
JONAH *does not move.*

GOATHERD A stranger in these parts?

JONAH Yes.

GOATHERD [*gesturing*] And there you have Nineveh, capital of the world some call it. You've been there? [*a silence*] You must have been. [*a silence*] Did you like it?

JONAH I liked none of it.

GOATHERD Aye, a queer town Nineveh – especially recently. You know about that?

JONAH What?

GOATHERD What happened in Nineveh! You see, six weeks or forty-two days ago a stranger arrived, an elderly chap like us who stank like a rotten fish. [*he sniffs the air*] Excuse me sir, you've a bit of a pong yourself.

JONAH [*grimly*] Go on.

GOATHERD Well this man was one of these Jews who believe in only one high heid yin, one God alone. [*shakes head*] A poor religion yon. Not that I'm a polytheist like those Egyptians who have hunderds of gods, hunderds and hunderds, one for every animal and thing there is. Two gods are enough for me, Osram the Lord of Light and Ahriman the Prince of Darkness. What do you believe in?

JONAH The truth.

GOATHERD The truth! That's a god nobody worships. The Greeks have a Goddess of wisdom, but even they know it's stupid to tell the truth all the time. Anyway, this man walks into Nineveh, tells folk it's going to be destroyed in forty days, and the idiots believe him! [*chuckles*] They believe him, and wear sackcloth, and shut the pubs, and pour ashes on their head – even the emperor does that – and beg God to forgive them, and forty days later – nothing happens! [*laughs heartily*].

JONAH [*desperately*] But slaves were freed! Troops were pulled out of Palestine!

GOATHERD [*standing up*] And here's me thinking you knew nothing about all that. Well, I'll be looking for my billygoat, and do you put something on your bald old head. [*he leaves*].

JONAH [*after a silence, quietly*] There is Nineveh, God. Destroy it. Destroy it. [*silence*] You'll be two days late of course, but you'll still have time to stop me having been a total liar – me, the cowardly son of Amittai who at last did as you commanded and was believed! [*silence, then angrily*] Do you mean to destroy me with your silence? Do you pretend not to hear me, you who heard my voice from the belly of a fish?

SOUND *of faint rustling, and there uncoils from the hill behind* **JONAH**'*s back the stalk of a vine with large leaves that lean forward, casting a shadow over his head from a strong spotlight above.* **JONAH**, *glancing round, notices this, then speaks in a more friendly tone.*

JONAH A gourd plant! Making a shade just for me. A definite wee miracle. Thanks very much. But your greatest miracle was turning a feeble old cowardly scholar into the scourge of the greatest city in the world, why why why did you do it God if I am to go down in history as a dupe, a fool, a liar? Why did you repent of the evil you said you would do to Nineveh? Why did you let the King of that evil empire know your ways better than me, your chosen prophet? I do not ask for anything you have not done to bad cities long ago. [*loudly*] I only demand that you destroy Nineveh now! Here and now! At once!

SOUND *of a great wind rising, then thunder. The sky turns indigo, the vine collapses, the spotlight beats down on* **JONAH**'*s head. He stands up clutching it.*

JONAH [*weakly*] The heat. I can't bear this heat.

He falls down.

THE VOICE OF GOD [*sounding through the wind*] Are you right to be angry that I killed the gourd?

JONAH [*without moving, though loudly*] Yes I am right to be angry God, even unto death.

SOUND *of wind fading out behind* **GOD**'*s next words.*

GOD You have pity on a plant that grew and perished in a moment. Why should I not pity and spare Nineveh, that great city, where over six score thousand people live who don't know their right hands from their left, and also much cattle?

SOUND: *wind dies and strong spotlight fades as sky goes blue again.*

MRS JONAH's **VOICE** [*distant but drawing nearer*] Jonah ... Jonah ... Jonah!

JONAH *sits up rubbing his head, then dusting himself down. Enter* **MRS JONAH**.

MRS JONAH [*gladly*] There you are!

JONAH [*standing up*] Thank God for another miracle, His best miracle yet. [*he embraces her*] Where's our boy?

MRS JONAH With my mother.

JONAH How did you find me?

MRS JONAH When the Assyrian army pulled out of Israel we heard rumours about a Jewish prophet causing that, so I knew you had obeyed God after all! So I borrowed money and hurried here, but in Nineveh they said you had left this morning. And as I left too the sky turned the queer colour it was when He spoke to you back home – it was Him again?

JONAH Aye.

MRS JONAH What did He say this time?

JONAH Something so strange I can hardly believe it. Maggie, God is changing his nature.

MRS JONAH [*sternly detaching herself*] God never changes. God is eternal.

JONAH Then he wants us to change. My history will be one of the shortest in the Bible but one of the strangest – stranger than the stories of Abraham and Moses, Joshua and David! I thought I was an old-fashioned Jewish thunder-threatener, but was serving a God of mercy for all mankind. [*suddenly very cheerful*] Well Maggie, I'm glad I've at last done all I was ordered to do. [*he takes her by the hand*] Let's go home. Can you bear to live with a husband who's nothing special again?

MRS JONAH Of course, you idiot.

FOR AT LEAST half a century before Margaret Thatcher's administration, most Scottish pubs shut at 9.30pm. At that hour in the Hogmanay of 1954, outside The State Bar off Sauchiehall Street, I was being very drunk when I first met Robert Kitts with companions I knew. They took me to several parties in the homes of strangers, and as I sobered up we formed the kind of friendship only possible between a couple of imaginative young men who recognise each other's genius. We were both students of painting (he in the London Slade), were both writing novels based on our childhoods, were both enthusiasts for Kafka, Herman Melville, also Scott Fitzgerald whose *Tender is the Night* had been recently reprinted and recognised as a classic. The conversations started that night only ended when he returned to London, but on that night or the next we agreed that the natural outcome of our shared interest in visual and literary art was film making. Which Robert Kitts went on to do.

In 1963 I was a social security scrounger, recently sacked from my job as scene painter and supporting my wife and newborn son by drawing National Assistance benefit from my Sauchiehall Street labour exchange. One morning I received a telegram from Bob Kitts asking me to phone him at the London BBC, reversing charges. I did so from a street call box. He said he had almost persuaded his boss, Huw Wheldon, to let him make a documentary film about my work, but Wheldon wished to see me first. Could I come to the London Television Centre at noon, the day after tomorrow, which was a Thursday? I told Bob this was impossible: at 9.30am I had to collect my National Assistance from the labour exchange. (In those days unemployed labourers, tradesmen and professional folk all got their weekly state stipend in notes paid over the counter of the same office.) Bob told me to phone him back in an hour. I did, and he said that on Thursday I should take a taxi from the labour exchange to Glasgow Airport, where a seat would be booked for me on a 10.30 flight - if I kept a receipt for the taxi fare it would be reimbursed. When at London's Heathrow I would be met by a Hertz Car chauffeur, who would drive me to the television centre where Bob would introduce me to Huw Wheldon.

These were BBC Television's great days. After 1963 it had two channels, colour was still to come, and none of its producers thought commercial television worth competing with, so the quality of its productions were best in the world. Huw Wheldon, head of documentary and music programmes, was partly responsible for this. Like the BBC's founding governor, Lord Reith, he thought broadcasting should provide more than popular entertainment. Wheldon catered for what he called "the small majority" of folk who not only enjoyed the best art of the past, but innovative art now. His liking for new ideas started the careers of Ken Russell, David Jones, Melvyn Bragg and also Bob Kitts, who would have become as famous as the rest had he not worked to promote an obscure actress (his first wife) and obscure artists, one of them me. For a while I enjoyed the luxury of air flights, taxis, meals in posh restaurants and talking as an equal to Huw Wheldon. I had the heady experience of starting a grand new career in the London of 1960s television, which then seemed to welcome outsiders.

Before going to London I amused my wife by suggesting I would speak to Wheldon before he had time to open his mouth, saying "Before we proceed to the process of question and answer which is the purpose of this meeting Mr Wheldon, I must refer you to this stain on my jersey caused by *mince* which fell off a neighbour's fork as I was dining earlier today. It is not my fault, as I had no time to change. But explanations like this must seem like swatting midgies to a man of your wide experience. I notice a small but perceptible stain on your neck tie. Might that not be a bond between us?" This fantasy gave me the idea of a naïve, brazen, very pushy young Scot, one with limitless self-confidence because London was liberating him from a restrictive home life. The thought of this character persisted with me. A year or two after Bob's film had been made I was again a Social Security scrounger, but memories of the London experience began to supply ideas for his further adventures. On three occasions in Scotland total strangers had introduced themselves by saying, "Excuse me, but do you mind if I engage you in conversation?" Twice I had been in a café with friends who were also artists, as in those days our beards proclaimed. A married coal miner had needed to talk about his helpless love for a hospital nurse; he knew nobody who would sympathize, but thought artists might be able to. A younger man explained he had come to Glasgow from Greenock because he wanted to meet artistic people. That, I saw, was how Kelvin would introduce himself to an attractive girl in a Soho café. She – Jill – was based on Jane Mulcahy, a real English friend and for a while the partner of Alan Fletcher, an artist who had died young. I had once made notes for a play about someone like me attracting someone like her away from someone like him, but gave it up as a bad job. I now saw it was just the job for my Kelvin Walker.

I wrote the play quickly for television (no Scottish theatre existed to stage it) and either posted it to BBC Television Drama or sent it there via Robert Kitts. Not having a television set I did not know my play was half an hour too long to be accepted, but a BBC producer James Brabazon, wrote to say he thought it could be cut down to fifty minutes without damage; and should he come to Glasgow and discuss this with me? Of course! Once again I enjoyed the heady sensation of a splendid new career starting. When Mr Brabazon asked what actors I would like in my play I said I knew none, but would like Scottish actors in the Scottish parts.

The Fall of Kelvin Walker was networked in 1968 with Judy Cornwall as Jill, Harry Corbett as Jake Whittington the painter, Corin Redgrave as Kelvin Walker, and in the part of Hector McKeller, the Scottish businessman, a good English character actor whose name I forget. I also forget who played the small but crucial part of Kelvin's father. He had been chosen from a casting directory because his face looked right for a Presbyterian grocer, and his second name began with Mc. When I reached London for the rehearsal Mr Brabazon said, "You know you were especially keen to have a Scottish actor play the father? We thought we'd got one but he's Ulster Irish and can't sound like anything else. He's a bit of a disaster but it's too late to change him now." So the play, as a whole, was a success, apart from the end.

My new career as a dramatist began well. A crisis in the building of the Concorde, a faster-than-sound transatlantic airbus, provoked an emergency TV news film that postponed the broadcast of my play for over a year. Before it was networked Scottish BBC Radio commissioned a new play from me, and I had written a stage version of *Kelvin Walker* performed by a Glasgow School of Art drama club. I started sketching scenarios and fragments of dialogue for other TV films.

One was set in a future where an invention allowed every necessity or luxury people could want (except power over others) without expense of money or labour. Since everyone had access to these, towns, cities and national governments had vanished and the biggest communities had become the large homes of extended families like those described by Margaret Mead in *Coming of Age in Samoa*. Homes there were mainly run by women, men were free to do what they pleased, most joined teams that fought each other in battles organized like football games, battles for fame and attention, not territory or wealth. The only international organization was a broadcasting service that televised battles for world viewing and posterity; the only law was that battles never encroach on homes, families and personal property. The film would start in the thick of a future battle that seemed part of a new dark age before a swift victory showed winners and losers shaking hands before returning to their peaceful homes. The main character was a Hamlet-like warrior who, thinking men should have better things to do, reads the history of ancient revolutions when they thought they were fighting for better worlds, even though their wars killed women and children. James Brabazon liked the idea of this film, but said it would be too expensive to make.

An even more ambitious idea was suggested by a visit to Stirling Castle, no longer a British Army headquarters, when parts were being restored to their 14th century state when the castle was one of Scotland's royal palaces, the scene of many crises in the lives of the Stuarts. I did not watch television but knew that family sagas (the British *Forsyths,* the USA *Addams Family*) were popular. What if BBC Scotland AND England commissioned from me an eight part serial about the House of Stuart from its elevation after Bruce's victory at Bannockburn, to the reign of Queen Anne who signed the Union of Scotland's parliament with England's? My father at that time was lodging with me and my wife and willingly typed out a chronology of the Stuart dynasty's most striking episodes. Nothing came of this, but *The Fall of Kelvin Walker* stage version had a longer history.

Since the founding of the Glasgow Repertory Theatre in 1909 there had been several efforts to start a National Theatre of Scotland, the most successful being the Glasgow Citizens Theatre, started in 1943 by a rare group of arts-minded city councillors. Prompted by James Bridie, the only Scottish playwright since Barrie to have London West End successes, they gave their native city what most comparable cities in Germany had but few in Britain; a rates-subsidized professional theatre. Its aim was taken from the old Repertory Theatre's manifesto which said it should produce plays of international importance along with new plays by Scottish authors. Glasgow Citizens Theatre did that until 1964, when Giles Havergal became director. Giles was a master of exciting theatrical productions with only one local defect: he thought the Scots incapable of writing good dramas, so never produced any if we except (before his retirement in 2003) his company's version of Irvine Welsh's *Trainspotting.* The pre-Havergal Citizens had employed many fine Scots actors, initially drawn from Glasgow's left-wing Unity Theatre, thus giving them their professional start in life. Giles lived in London outside the theatre season, held his auditions there, so from the standpoint of Scots actors *and* authors the Citizens Theatre was a black hole. So some Scots whose enthusiasm for theatre was insufficiently backed by experience (most of them were journalists) started the Stage Company of Scotland in 1970.

My only contribution at first was to design the company's logo and letterhead. After two expensive productions in the former Partick Burgh Hall the Stage Company dwindled to a director-producer (Hugh Boyle) and four actors (Isabel Nisbet, Helen Mitchell, James Gillen, Robert Trotter) travelling in a van to perform in small far-apart Scottish theatres, performing plays with small casts, usually by my friend Joan Ure, though also by Cecil Taylor, Tom Gallagher and me. In the MacRoberts Centre, Stirling University, they successfully performed the greatly honed and improved stage version of *Kelvin Walker* that follows, apart from the end of the last scene. This received a concluding refinement by an improbably roundabout path.

In 1970 or 71 I received a phone call from a lady with a posh English voice who said her name was Frances Head, that she was a literary agent and had been told by James Brabazon that I was a worthwhile writer – would I like her to be my agent in London? Indeed yes, said I, having then a sixty minute play the BBC had paid me to write and then rejected. I posted it to her along with *The Fall of Kelvin Walker* and *Lanark,* a half-finished novel. She was a splendid agent, working hard for me, though I often disappointed her. She once phoned me in a buoyant mood because Binkie Beaumont was interested in staging *Kelvin Walker.* So was **** ******, who might direct it, and ****** ****, producer of the Swiss Cottage Theatre where *Kelvin Walker* might be put on before being shifted to the West End, if it succeeded as they thought it might. I cannot now remember who these asterisks were, but they and Binkie first wanted a word with me. I began to feel buoyant too. In London Frances took me by taxi to our conference in the producer's home, I think near Notting Hill Gate. She said, "You will find the atmosphere more relaxed than if you had met them in Binkie's place, which would be a little bit too grand." I asked who Binkie Beaumont was: she said, "He used to own the *whole* of the West End, and still has quite a big slice of it."

She left me in the less grand producer's flat with three pleasant, straightforward, unpompous English gentlemen. They praised my play for its characters, swift dialogue and plotting, then came to what they disliked – the end. My hero's ascent to the heights of London fame, power and publicity must not end (they felt) with him being dragged ignominiously hame by his daddy. I explained that, for me, no other end was possible, and after more discussion we parted without acrimony, though I insisted on taking the producer's copy of the script away with me. I went to Frances Head's home and place of work near Hyde Park and told her the situation while she thoughtfully walked up and down, smoking the cigarettes that eventually killed her. Then, without the faintest sign of annoyance, she discussed new endings that might please both me and Binkie. I owe to her and this discussion my final, greatly improved ending with Kelvin returning home, not dragged by his dad like a beaten dog, but with dad his ally in a campaign that will detach Scotland from the British Isles. This made *The Fall of Kelvin Walker* a Scottish version of John Millicent Synge's *Playboy of the Western World*. Alas, even that conclusion was too low-key for Binkie, who had said he would prefer Kelvin to end by marrying into the Royal Family – at that time the Queen's sister, Princess Margaret, had been divorced for several years. This ended my only chance of getting a play into London's great West End theatre district.

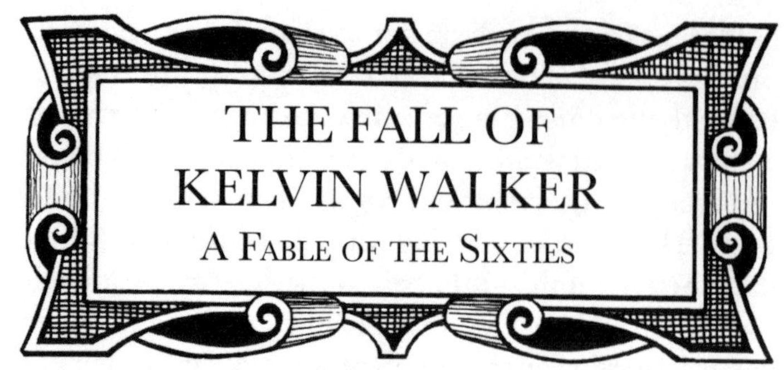

THE FALL OF KELVIN WALKER

A FABLE OF THE SIXTIES

CAST IN MOST SCENES

KELVIN WALKER – a Scotsman on the make
JAKE WHITTINGTON – an artist
JILL – Jake's mistress: a Bohemian girl

CAST IN THREE SCENES

HECTOR MCKELLAR – a Scottish media chief, Scenes 9, 13, 14
MRS HENDON – landlady, Scenes 7, 12, 13
MARY CRANMER – television interviewer, Scenes 9, 11, 14

CAST IN ONE SCENE

MIKE – wealthy bohemian, Scene 1
A WAITER – Scene 2
SIR GODFREY – captain of industry, Scene 4
SANDY BROWN – captain of industry, Scene 6
CLIFFORD DYKE – Prime Minister, Scene 11
MR WALKER – Kelvin's father, Scene 14

SCENE

1 a Soho coffee house
2 an expensive restaurant
3 Jake's studio
4 Sir Godfrey's office
5 Jake's studio
6 Sandy Brown's office
7 Jake's studio (evening)
INTERVAL
8 Jake's studio (morning)
9 Hector McKellar's office
10 Jake's studio, days later
11 a television studio
12 Jake's studio
13 Jake's studio, many days later
14 a television studio

NOTE: Wages and prices mentioned in the dialogue were right for the 1960s. A modern production might wish to modernise them.

1: SOHO COFFEE HOUSE

KELVIN *sits at a table copying addresses into a notebook out of the 'situations vacant' column of The Times. His coat is buttoned, he wears a hat, a suitcase stands beside his chair.*

MIKE *sits smoking a cigar at an adjacent table.* **JILL** *enters and goes over to him. She carries a coffee which she puts down on his table.*

JILL Hello.

MIKE Hello.

JILL [*slips into the seat facing him*] I believe I owe you an apology.

MIKE Oh I don't think so.

JILL Was I stinking drunk?

MIKE You were pretty pissed.

JILL And I don't suppose Jake helped much.

MIKE [*smiles*] You know Jake better than I do. How is he now?

JILL Still in bed. It was decent of you to get us home.

MIKE That's what the car's there for after all. How's the head?

JILL Oh better. I woke about dawn and was sick as a pig into a chair beside the bed. [*She giggles*] That helped quite a bit.

MIKE [*grins admiringly*] You're mad!

KELVIN *has been pondering the newspaper with the end of the pen pressed to his chin.* **JILL***'s statement startles him. He starts listening and frowning.*

JILL Did you undress me by the way?

MIKE Afraid not.

JILL Oh good. I must have done it myself.

MIKE Well, Jake certainly couldn't have done it. Look, I'm going now. You haven't forgotten tomorrow night have you?

JILL If you haven't changed your mind about us.

MIKE You know I'll always love you two no matter how alcoholic you get. See you about nine then shall I? [*he gets up*].

JILL Do we bring our own bottles?

MIKE Not if you're broke.

JILL That's good because we will be.

MIKE Do you want a loan? [*he puts his hand in his pocket*].

JILL Not now. I'll come to you when I'm desperate, shall I?

MIKE Yes. Yes do that. Well, have fun. [*he leaves*].

JILL Cheerio Mike.

She places her elbows on the table, sips some coffee, then sucks daintily at the tip of her thumb. **KELVIN** *briskly folds the newspaper and places it with the notebook in his pocket. He rises, comes across, takes his hat off and puts it down on the table and sits in* **MIKE***'s chair. His hair is parted at one side and carefully combed and haircreamed, like Hitler's. He puts his elbows on the table, interlocks his fingers and stares at* **JILL** *over the top of them. She appears not to notice. He speaks sharply in a clear, forthright Scots dialect.*

KELVIN Do you mind if I engage you in conversation?

JILL What?

KELVIN May I engage you in conversation?

JILL [*smiles*] Why not? I suppose we met at the party last night?

KELVIN No.

JILL Well I suppose it was some other party.

KELVIN [*shakes his head*] No.

A pause.

JILL I see. Well don't let it worry you. Engage me in conversation.

KELVIN [*starts talking eagerly*] Thank you, I will. I'd like to begin by being honest with you. I'm a stranger here. I arrived in London this morning. I know nobody in this city, and to be perfectly frank –

JILL You've no money.

KELVIN [*puzzled*] Why do you think that?

JILL In Soho most strangers who start by being perfectly frank and honest go on to borrow money.

KELVIN [*impressed*] Is that the case? I'm very glad you told me. That's a very handy thing to know. But [*he brightens*] as a matter of fact I have a great deal of money. [*takes a wallet from inner pocket and holds it towards her*] I think you'd be surprised at how much money I've got in this little wallet.

JILL [*nods twice*] I see. And you're looking for a girl who can give you a nice time.

KELVIN*'s mouth falls open. He stands up and starts talking in an ashamed, embarrassed, slightly stammering, almost tearful voice which is the reverse of his normal manner.*

KELVIN I ... I see I have pushed my company and c ... and conversation on to somebody who didn't want them. I hope you will believe though that I did ... I didn't mean anything insulting towards you, I'm really sincerely sorry for my rudeness.

JILL [*upset*] Oh hell. Look, do sit down. Please sit down!

KELVIN But ...

JILL No, please! I've just realised you're more foreign than I thought. I'll feel hellish if you go now.

KELVIN Are you sure of that?

JILL Yes, I promise I don't mind. I just didn't understand.

KELVIN [*sitting down and resuming at once his bright, eager manner*] Where was I?

JILL You were going to be frank about something.

KELVIN True. Well, I bought a copy of The Times, found some good jobs advertised in it, and 'phoned to arrange interviews for them, then I went for a walk, intending to acquaint myself with your city centre. After a while I found this café. I could see that, though not perhaps beautiful, it was definitely artistic. [*he looks around*] In a way. So I came in and overheard you talking to that man who went out a few minutes back, and it struck me from your conversation that you are the sort of person I've come to London to meet. You see I am from Glaik. Have you heard of Glaik?

JILL No. Tell me about it. Is it a small place?

KELVIN No, it's quite big. We manufacture fish-glue and sweaters and process a lot of cheese. A lot of folk think the Americans were the first people to process cheese. In a way that's true, but it was a Glaik man, Murdoch Stairs, who invented the process. And Hector McKellar, who does things on television, is a Glaik man. So you see that, geographically speaking, Glaik is more than a dot on the map. But culturally it lacks scope. It was the lack of scope that made me leave it. Have you heard of Nietzsche?

JILL Who?

KELVIN Frederick Nietzsche, the German thinker.

JILL No.

KELVIN But you've heard him discussed?

JILL Maybe, I'm not sure.

KELVIN That's queer. From your conversation I'd have sworn you read Nietzsche. Your conversation had what I could call a Nietzschean flavour to it. Anyway, I can talk to you about him, without embarrassment. It is no exaggeration to say that in Glaik there was [*taps table with forefinger*] – nobody I could discuss Nietzsche with. Nobody.

JILL [*sympathetically*] What do people discuss in Glaik?

KELVIN Sport. That's all. Sport. They have a few religious and political ideas but they never discuss them. They fight about them. There are no thinkers in Glaik, and no artists. Are you an artist?

JILL I'm afraid not.

KELVIN Funny. You look artistic. Do you know any artists?

JILL Well, my boyfriend is a painter.

KELVIN [*delighted*] I knew you had something to do with art! Is he a good painter?

JILL I couldn't say. I don't know much about painting. His friends think he's a rotten painter. Are you an artist?

KELVIN [*shocked*] Me? No! I have no artistic talent whatsoever I'm glad to say. But where there are plenty of artists people are generally open to new ideas, especially, Nietzschean ideas. And it is by these ideas that I mean to succeed.

JILL Succeed in what?

KELVIN The means are unimportant. I don't care how I begin. [*Taps the side of his brow with his index finger*] I've got it all worked out in here.

JILL [*puzzled*] What have you got worked out?

KELVIN [*suddenly smiles*] This conversation is taking us into dangerously deep waters. Do you mind if I ask your name?

JILL Jill.

KELVIN And your surname?

JILL I'd rather not talk about that. It's rather sordid.

KELVIN [*puzzled*] I don't understand. How can a name be sordid?

JILL [*without irritation*] Well if you must know, my mother got divorced and took back her maiden name and I had to take it back too because she couldn't bear to hear my father's name mentioned. Then she married again and made me take my stepfather's name to make me feel like one of the family. But I don't much like my stepfather so my friends just call me Jill.

KELVIN But ... that is *very* sad!

JILL Not really. Not now. What's your name?

KELVIN Kelvin Walker. [*He places a hand on her wrist*] Will you promise to do me a great and special favour? One which only you have the power to grant?

JILL [*smiles*] If I can.

KELVIN Will you allow me to go with you to the most expensive eating place in London and will you order for both of us the most expensive meal on the menu?

JILL [*answers seriously*] That's very sweet of you but can you really afford –

KELVIN Tonight there is nothing I cannot afford! [*produces wallet and holds it gravely above his head, rising to his feet*]

JILL Well I can't take you to the *most* expensive restaurant in London but I will take you to a *pretty* expensive restaurant if you're really keen.

KELVIN [*takes his hat and suitcase and they move out, talking*]. And you must tell me if I do anything wrong. My manners are clean, but perhaps not very polished as yet.

JILL Just be perfectly natural.

2: AN EXPENSIVE RESTAURANT

Strains of Viennese waltz music.

KELVIN *and* **JILL** *at a table, she leaning back to inhale the smoke of a cigar between her fingers.* **KELVIN** *leans forward opposite her to light his cigar from a candle in a branched candlestick in the table centre. A* **WAITER** *is removing the last of the cutlery and plates. When he withdraws, the white damask is blank except for the candlestick, menu, ashtray and near-empty wineglasses before* **KELVIN** *and* **JILL**. *An empty bottle lies in an ice-bucket at one side.* **KELVIN** *wears a tweed sports jacket, a fair-isle sweater and plus-fours. He leans back and exhales his own puff of smoke.*

KELVIN [*after a reflective pause*] What kind of cigar is this?

JILL A Corona.

KELVIN 's very nice.

JILL [*nods*] Mm.

KELVIN [*gestures to the audience*] Tell me, which ones in this lot are important?

JILL Important?

KELVIN [*nods*] Important.

JILL Well as we came in I saw Caradoc Smith.

KELVIN Caradoc Smith?

JILL [*nods*] The famous actor.

KELVIN But famous people aren't important.

JILL Would you mind explaining that?

KELVIN Not at all. Important people own and control and manipulate things. Famous people are mentioned a lot in the newspapers. Actors and writers and royalty are famous. But they aren't important.

JILL What about politicians?

KELVIN Some politicians are important. It depends on how they use their job. A few Prime Ministers have been important but the majority are just rank and file, no matter what the newspapers say.

JILL What about scientists?

KELVIN Tools, just tools. Tools employed by businessmen and politicians. An employee cannot be important. Not in the Nietzschean sense of the word.

JILL [*sips from her glass*] What about Jesus?

KELVIN [*sits up sharply, all alertness and suspicion*] Are you a Catholic?

JILL No. Why?

KELVIN [*relaxes, relieved*] In Scotland only Catholics and children refer to Jesus in that familiar way. No, Christ was not an important man. He had the chance to be, you may remember, when the Devil offered to make him king of all nations of the world, but he refused the offer, I think unwisely. He would have been a decent sort of king. He would have introduced reforms, and done people a lot of good. But no, he refused and left the world to folk like Nero and Attila and Napoleon and Hitler. Of course he became famous, and got a lot of publicity for his ideas, but who cares for his ideas nowadays? What important people have ever lived by them?

JILL What about the German you go on about?

KELVIN [*becoming grave*] Nietzsche?

JILL Was he important?

KELVIN [*hesitates*] N ... N ... No. No. When he was alive not many people paid attention to him and in the end he went mad. [*abruptly he strikes the table with his forefinger and leans towards her*] But now he is important! [*He rises slowly to his feet, saying to her as he does so*] Not the old mortal Frederick Nietzsche who died insane, but thc immortal and undying Nietzsche who lives on in me! [*slaps his chest and raises a hand dictatorially ceiling-ward. His voice has become very loud.*]

JILL *watches him with interest, tinged with alarm.*

A pause.

KELVIN [*cries loudly*] Waiter! [*the waiter rushes up*] Bring the young lady another bottle of what she ordered last time, please. [**JILL** *covers mouth with her hand to stifle giggling.* **KELVIN** *sits down. The waiter leaves.* **KELVIN** *says grimly*] I see I amuse you.

JILL I'm sorry, but, well you know you strike me as being absolutely mad.

KELVIN You are mistaken.

JILL [*worried*] Have I hurt your feelings? Christ, I didn't mean to ...

KELVIN [*sombrely*] Actually this has happened once or twice before. At the Glaik Free Institute Literary and Debating Society we have some women members and more than once I've found myself talking to one of them in the café over the road: talking, you understand, mainly for pleasure, but at the same time exchanging important ideas. The woman talks back, she seems to like me, there is an atmosphere of friendship and gaiety. Suddenly she says something that shows she is not amused by my words, but by my personality. She regards me as a freak. I had begun to think things were different in England.

JILL [*contritely*] Oh don't feel that! Hell, Jake and I are often called mad too ... [*she falls silent as the waiter appears, shows her the bottle and pours for her. She sips*] It'll do. [**WAITER** *leaves*].

KELVIN [*glumly*] Who taught you about cigars, wine, things like that? Your boyfriend?

JILL Jake? God, no. I picked it up from my stepfather.

KELVIN Is this the one you don't like much?

JILL That's the one. [*drinks*] Actually I used to like him quite a lot. [*a pause. She stares gloomily into her glass*] Then he made a pass at me. In fact several.

KELVIN [*inexpressibly shocked*] That was terribly wrong of him!

JILL So I had to leave, of course.

KELVIN How horrible for your mother!

JILL *She* doesn't know.

KELVIN You didn't tell her?

JILL [*exasperated*] How could I? She still loves the bastard!

Tears of maudlin pity appear in **KELVIN***'s eyes. He leans over the table and grasps* **JILL***'s free hand in both of his, speaking with heartfelt emotion.*

KELVIN I think we should get married!

JILL What?

KELVIN [*urgently*] I have no work or home yet, but in a week I'll have both. I won't insult you by telling you about the money I have, but I can honestly promise I possess all the qualities essential to a secure and happy married life!

JILL *manages to free her hand. She looks distractedly around for a* **WAITER**, *murmuring inattentively.*

JILL What qualities?

KELVIN Energy, intelligence and integrity.

JILL [*gives a brief, embarrassed smile*] Sounds like the motto of an insurance company. Waiter!

WAITER [*approaching*] Yes madam!

JILL The bill please.

WAITER Certainly madam. [*withdraws*].

JILL I think we should leave now, don't you?

KELVIN I suppose so.

He looks at the wine bottle and, seeing it still partly full, fills his glass from it, swigs it quickly back and fills and drinks till the bottle is empty. **JILL** *meanwhile rests her chin on her fist and moodily twirls the stem of her glass between her thumb and her forefinger.* **KELVIN** *puts the emptied glass down and addresses her defiantly.*

KELVIN I apologise.

JILL Don't.

KELVIN I was overcome by drink and emotion.

JILL I noticed that. Still, I enjoyed the meal and your company. Thanks very much.

KELVIN [*cheers up*] Not at all! It is for me to be grateful. I could never have ordered such a meal by myself. This evening has been both entertaining and instructive.

The **WAITER** *presents the bill to* **JILL** *who passes it to* **KELVIN**. *He takes it with one hand while drawing out his wallet with the other. As his eye takes in the price he presses his lips together, replaces the wallet and sets the bill on the table before him. He addresses the* **WAITER**.

KELVIN Will you leave us a moment?

WAITER *raises eyebrows, withdraws.*

KELVIN [*reads the bill with a pre-occupied expression, saying as he does it*] I have no wish to doubt anyone's honesty, but I am going to be obliged to challenge this bill. It cannot possibly come to twenty-two pounds and ...

JILL But you asked me to order the most expensive meal possible!

KELVIN I asked you to do that and I meant you to do that. But because I am Scottish I see no reason why they should charge six pounds for the oysters.

JILL They would have charged anyone who had as many helpings as we did. Here, read the menu.

KELVIN *takes the menu and glances to it from the bill once or twice. Then he speaks decisively.*

KELVIN Jill, I'm very glad to have known you. Now I want you to do me a favour. I wish to enjoy a coffee quietly, by myself. Please leave without me.

JILL [*horrified*] You mean you can't pay?

KELVIN That's not your business. Goodnight.

JILL [*voice rises*] But I thought you were rich!

KELVIN I thought so too. But I suppose riches are comparative. Waiter!

The **WAITER** *approaches.* **JILL** *and* **KELVIN** *speak simultaneously.* **JILL** *speaks loudest and* **KELVIN** *gives up first.*

KELVIN Waiter, I am going to be honest with you ...

JILL Waiter, waiter, waiter, we've changed our minds – two small black coffees please.

WAITER *stares and withdraws.* **JILL** *bites her thumb in furious thought, frowning into herself.*

KELVIN [*in a loud angry whisper*] I told you to leave!

JILL Shut up and let me think.

KELVIN My conscience is clean. I will simply explain to the management the situation and the circumstances which produced it. I've done nothing criminal. I refuse to feel guilty about this.

JILL For Christ's sake shut your bloody mouth. Things are bad enough without you getting all dignified and moral about them.

KELVIN *raises his clenched right fist towards her, one didactic forefinger extended, his mouth wrathfully open.* **JILL** *does not notice.*

JILL How much money have you anyway?

KELVIN [*subsides*] Twenty-four pounds.

JILL We need to borrow three more. Maybe Caradoc Smith will lend some. My mother knows him slightly. If not I'll phone Mike or somebody else who might come over with it. [*gets up*] For God's sake try to look casual.

She leaves. For a moment **KELVIN** *leans back with his arms folded and an expression of grim concentration, then almost compulsively takes the newspaper from his inner pocket, unfolds it at the 'Situations Vacant' page, takes out his notebook and continues copying out the underlined addresses. The waiter comes back with the coffees and puts them on the table.* **KELVIN** *ignores him. The waiter stands regarding him with an expression of scientific curiosity for a moment.*

KELVIN [*without looking up, or ceasing to write*] Well?

WAITER Anything else ... sir?

KELVIN Add the cost of the coffees to the bill. I will pay you when the young lady returns. Not before.

The **WAITER** *scribbles on the bill and withdraws to a little distance where he stands watching.* **KELVIN** *reaches out, grabs a coffee and swallows it without looking up. It is hotter than he expected, he clutches his throat but manages to suppress his urge to splutter, and continues writing. Looking up he sees the* **WAITER** *, seizes the other coffee, sips it this time and continues writing.* **JILL** *returns to the table with a set expressionless face and sits down, dropping a crumpled ball of money beside the notebook.* **KELVIN** *looks up. The* **WAITER** *moves instantly over to him. Looking at him sideways,* **KELVIN** *deliberately folds the paper up and returns it to his pocket, puts away the notebook, uncrumples the money and puts three pound notes one at a time on top of the bill, then brings out his wallet, removes four five-pound notes and places them one at a time on top of that. He stares the* **WAITER** *in the face.*

KELVIN I'll trouble you for a receipt. And remember the change. [*The waiter takes up the money with distaste and withdraws*] Jill, I'm going to repay this money much sooner than you expect.

JILL And where are you going to sleep tonight?

KELVIN I understand that the police do not molest people found sleeping on the banks of the Thames.

JILL [*wearily*] All right. Come home with me. Jake will put you up.

KELVIN *wants to argue.*

KELVIN I would be happier to accept these favours if I did not feel a certain contempt in your manner of offering them.

The waiter returns with a salver with a receipt and a lot of very small change indeed upon on it. He offers it ostentatiously. **KELVIN** *stands up and counts the money rapidly from the salver into his hand, then drops it in his pocket.* **JILL** *stands up and they move away, watched by the waiter.*

JILL Look, I just feel a bit drunk and just a bit disgusted with myself, see? I don't enjoy borrowing money from a man I only slightly know.

KELVIN I can only promise that I will repay you much sooner than you expect ...

3: JAKE'S STUDIO

JILL In here. Keep still a minute. [*She strikes a match to light an oil lamp and the studio is illuminated as she raises the wick*] We have electricity but it's worked by a slot meter.

The light stands on a table, extreme right. Also on the table is: A Primus stove supporting a saucepan; cans of soup; some plates and cutlery; a jar of paint-brushes; a palette; paint tubes; a bottle of turps; a lurid paperback. Beside the table, an easel holding a white board covered by ferocious black marks. Centre stage, a mattress on the floor heaped with blankets, sleeping bags, male and female clothing, towels, a hairbrush. Beside this mattress (hereafter called the bed) is an easy chair, covered with newspapers. Behind the bed, a folding draught screen. On the extreme left, a chaise longue or sofa. Conspicuous somewhere (perhaps pinned to the draught screen) are two large colour reproductions of Botticelli's Birth of Venus and Michelangelo's Creation of Adam from the Sistine Chapel. Any quantity of studio lumber may be piled around, including some frames and canvasses. **KELVIN**, *coat unbuttoned, hat on head, suitcase in hand, stands on the extreme right looking around him awkwardly. He registers shock when his glance falls on the painting.*

JILL [*lifts the lamp and carries it to the bed saying with faint annoyance*] Aren't you up *yet?*[*The snoring ceases.* **JILL** *squats down and places the lamp on the floor*] Are you *still* in bed?

An alert strong face appears at one end of the heap.

JAKE I'm not going to answer that. What time is it?

JILL After eleven.

JAKE [*peering at* **KELVIN** *who stands with case in hand between the two tables*] Do I know him?

JILL [*rising*] No. He's a wee Scottish laddie just arrived in London to take us all over. He's no money, no friends and nowhere to stay.

JAKE Is he hungry too?

JILL No. Actually we've both just eaten rather well.

JAKE I wish I had.

He stares at **JILL**. *She shrugs submissively and goes to the table. During the ensuing conversation she can be seen in the background lighting the Primus, opening a can of soup, pouring it into the pan, putting the pan on the Primus, picking up a lurid paperback from among the tins, sitting on the edge of the table and reading it.*

JAKE [*Beckoning* **KELVIN** *who comes nearer*] Wouldn't you like to sit down?

KELVIN [*nods*] Yes. [*does not move. There is a puzzled pause*].

JAKE Why don't you? [**KELVIN** *looks dubiously at the newspaper-covered chair and sits on the extreme edge of it, placing the case on the floor before him*] Relax! Take off your ... hat.

KELVIN [*removes his hat, puts it on top of the case and begins to speak very formally*] Thank you. I would like to start by saying how honoured I feel to be talking to you on my first night in London.

JAKE Why?

KELVIN Because it seems an honest and respectable way to start.

JAKE But why feel honoured?

KELVIN You are the first painter I've ever met.

JAKE But you don't know my work do you?

KELVIN I did not know it before walking into this room, but I've been using my eyes, and if you've no objection I'll mention a thing that puzzles me.

JAKE Go ahead.

KELVIN I cannot understand how someone able to paint that – [*points to Birth of Venus*] and that – [*points to Creation of Adam*] – should waste time painting that – [*points to painting on the easel*].

JAKE [*answers without rancour*] The first two are reproductions. The one on the easel is mine.

A sad, sincere look comes upon **KELVIN***'s face. He leans towards the bed, dismayed yet consoling, one hand raised like a clergyman at the bedside of a dying man.*

JAKE [*answering easily*] Don't let it upset you. Most people think that my paintings are a waste of time.

KELVIN Can I ask a question?

JAKE Ask away.

KELVIN [*points to easel painting*] What is that picture about?

JAKE It's about black and white.

KELVIN I think I understand you.

JAKE [*looks at him*] I think you're being polite.

KELVIN [*smiles*] True. I mean that picture there – [*points to Creation of Adam*] has a lot of blue and brown in it, but it's not *about* blue and brown.

JAKE You're damned right it isn't. It's about God creating man. The other is about the birth of Venus, Goddess of love and beauty. Nowadays nobody with education believes in anything except what they do for themselves. Personally the only thing I'm sure about is the marks I make on the canvas. So I paint black, on white.

KELVIN [*eagerly*] You don't believe God is important? Does that mean you're an atheist?

JAKE I wouldn't go as far as that. But I hardly ever think of Him. And I certainly don't believe in religion.

KELVIN Is that a common English attitude?

JAKE Pretty common. Are things different in Scotland?

KELVIN I cannot speak for the larger cities, but in the town of Glaik where I come from most people are for God or against Him.

JAKE Which are you?

KELVIN [*after a pause*] Against. I believe God is dead.

JAKE Didn't Nietzsche say that?

KELVIN [*excited*] You've read Nietzsche?

JAKE No. But I've heard people say Nietzsche said that.

KELVIN [*nods*] He did say that. If he had not said it I would not be here.

At the food table the soup boils over, extinguishing the Primus with a hiss and making a lot of smoke. **JILL** *drops her book, grabs the pan by the handle, finds it too hot to hold and drops it on the floor, spilling the rest of the soup.*

JAKE [*sitting upright and yelling at her savagely*] How often in Hell's name have I told you when you're doing something to give it your full attention!

JILL [*guiltily*] I'm sorry!

JAKE You'd better be! [*stares at her while she half-heartedly* *wipes up the mess before trying again. He pulls a face*] Women! Look, what has Nietzsche to do with you coming to London?

KELVIN Everything. Would you forgive a little of my personal history?

JAKE Carry on.

KELVIN My father is a Christian. In fact he's more than a Christian. He's a Session Clerk. He is the Session Clerk of the John Knox Street United Free Seceders Presbyterian Church of Scotland ...

JAKE What is a Session Clerk? A sort of bishop?

KELVIN [*smiles*] Dear me no. He's not a clergyman at all. He's an official elected by the congregation to correct the Minister when his preaching wanders from the true doctrine. As a result my father is very keen on God, and for as long as I can remember it was the custom for him and my five brothers and myself to go down on our knees in the living-room above the shop and pray for twenty to thirty minutes before going to bed.

JAKE What about your mother?

KELVIN She had the bad luck to die when I was four but I've several very favourable memories of her.

JAKE This praying: did you do it aloud?

KELVIN Each night someone would what was called *lead* the prayers by addressing the Almighty aloud while the rest accompanied them in their hearts. Usually my father did it, but when my brothers were studying to become ministers one of them would be allowed a fling.

JAKE Were these prayers always read from a book?

KELVIN Of course not! How can you pray from a book? A prayer isn't a poem or a formula. The point I want to make is this. If you had heard my father and brothers talking you would have sworn they were talking to something not quite human that was sticking to the ceiling just above our heads and ... watching. It's a small house and this made the place feel overcrowded. Another thing. I followed these prayers in my heart for many years but I never once felt that inhuman thing liked me. Not once! Naturally I said nothing of this. I was at a disadvantage already, being the youngest and having to help in the shop while the rest went to university. I grew up troubled and confused. I went for long, brooding kind of walks, but that didn't help: the thing came after me. I felt it flapping along in the air just over my head like an invisible vulture.

He stares apprehensively at the ceiling. **JAKE** *stares at him, fascinated and appalled.*

KELVIN [*smiling with sudden relief*] Then one day it started raining so I took shelter in a public library and there I discovered ...

JAKE Nietzsche?

KELVIN [*shaking his head*] I wasn't ready for Nietzsche. No. I discovered the sublime Ingersol.

JILL *comes over to the bed carrying a bowl of soup with a spoon in it. She hands it to* **JAKE** *and sits down on the bedding.*

JAKE [*taking a spoonful*] Haven't heard of Ingersol.

KELVIN Colonel Ingersol is an American atheist, unfortunately no longer living. He convinced me that when my father spoke to God he was only talking to himself. For the first time in my life I felt lonely. The relief was indescribable. But I'm boring you.

JAKE No, go on, I'm interested.

KELVIN Then I discovered Nietzsche, who went further than Ingersol. He showed me that since God was dead it was necessary to replace him. So this morning, without telling anyone, I lifted my savings and took the train for London.

JAKE [*frowns in a puzzled way and points his spoon at* **KELVIN**] I feel I've missed something. *Why* did you come to London?

KELVIN [*puzzled*] I've just told you why?

JAKE But what are you going to do?

KELVIN First I must find a job. I had meant to get a room first and then find a job, but as I have no money I'll have to get a job first.

JAKE You can stay here if you like.

KELVIN That's very kind!

JAKE Not very. We won't be here in a few days ourselves. The rent is overdue, and unless Jill borrows money from one of her rich admirers the landlady will throw us out.

JILL [*protests angrily*] I tell you I'm sick of borrowing money we can't pay back! Sick of it!

KELVIN *looks at her in a troubled way.*

JAKE [*coldly*] I wasn't hinting. I was stating facts. [*to* **KELVIN**]. What jobs are you looking for?

KELVIN *brings out the paper, unfolds it at the marked page and gives it to* **JAKE.**

KELVIN I'll try for these tomorrow. You'll notice I've underlined none whose Head Office is not in Central London and none whose starting salary is less than five thousand a year.

JAKE [*looks at the paper and raises his eyelids*] What's this?

[*reads*] 'Assistant Head of Department for the Ergonomics Department of London University'? 'Public Relations Officer for the Royal Society for the Prevention of Cruelty to Children'? 'Director of the Stereotype Promotions Branch of the Libido Canalization Corporation'? ... Look, where were you working in Glaik?

KELVIN In my father's shop.

JAKE What kind of shop is it?

KELVIN A small but highly remunerative grocery.

JAKE What kind of other work have you done?

KELVIN None. I said goodbye to that shop yesterday when I put the shutters up for the last time.

JAKE Then what do you think qualifies you for jobs [*taps the newspaper*] like these?

KELVIN My will to succeed!

JAKE *and* **JILL** *stare at each other questioningly.* **KELVIN** *smiles.*

KELVIN You think I'm mad, don't you?

JAKE Either mad or incredibly naïve.

JILL You can't walk into an important job just like that! You've to start at the bottom of the ladder and work up.

KELVIN That's not true! Nowadays the people who start at the bottom rung have retired before they reach the middle. Successful people all start climbing a few rungs under the top.

JAKE Yes, but ...

KELVIN Furthermore, the nearer you get to the top the less real qualifications matter. The Managing Director of a Chemical Corporation need know nothing of chemistry. A Minister of Transport need know nothing of drawing up rail timetables. The only qualities needed in a position of power are total self-confidence and the ability to see when the people under you are doing their jobs, and you can usually see that by the expression on their faces.

JAKE But let's be realistic Kelvin. Before they give you a job you have to be interviewed. Before they give you an interview you have to write them a letter giving your qualifications and experience. No qualifications, no interview. No interview, no job.

A pause in which **JILL**, *without taking her eyes off* **KELVIN**, *lifts a brush from among the bedding and starts stroking her hair.*

KELVIN Have you heard of Hector McKellar?

JAKE No. Yes! Wait a minute. It's one of those names you sometimes hear but can never remember why. He used to be a journalist. Is he with the BBC?

KELVIN And he's secretary of the Duke of Edinburgh Society for the Preservation of Local Culture. He's a Glaik man, though he left the place before I was born. Well, I'm going to take his name in vain.

JAKE What do you mean?

KELVIN *takes back the newspaper and folds it into his pocket. He speaks with sudden firmness.*

KELVIN I fear I am not at liberty to divulge.

JAKE [*slightly surprised*] You're not at liberty to divulge?

KELVIN [*definite*] No.

JAKE [*raises his eyebrows, purses his lips, nods*] I see. Perhaps you're not naïve. Perhaps you're fiendishly cunning.

JILL'*s position has become reminiscent of a mermaid on a rock. Both men contemplate her for a moment. She pretends not to notice.*

JAKE [*speaks rapidly*] Jill's too aware of how pretty she looks sometimes.

JILL What?

JAKE [*speaks as fast, but louder*] I said I'll take down your knickers and spank you if you're not careful.

JILL *resumes brushing. The two men watch. Suddenly an alarm clock starts ringing, muffled but loud.* **KELVIN** *stands up.* **JILL** *drops her brush.* **JAKE** *leaps out of bed and stands in a long shirt with dangling tail glaring wildly around.*

JAKE Where the hell is that coming from?

KELVIN From inside my case. I set it to remind me to go to bed at midnight.

JAKE Can't you stop it?

KELVIN *picks up his hat in one hand, his case with the other. The ringing stops by itself.* **JAKE** *and* **JILL** *are relieved.*

KELVIN If you could show me where I'll be sleeping tonight ...

JAKE Yes of course. [*he suddenly tugs at a sleeping bag from under* **JILL**, *tumbling her over. He tells her threateningly*] You'd better be here when I get back.

JILL *sticks out her tongue at him, readjusts herself and resumes brushing.* **JAKE** *takes the lamp and leads* **KELVIN** *to the chaise longue. He dumps the bag on it and places the lamp on the floor beside it, then shifts the draught screen between the bed and the chaise longue, so that the bed is in darkness.*

JAKE [*gestures expansively to* **KELVIN**] Pleasant dreams.

KELVIN Thank you.

KELVIN *puts his case and hat down on the chaise longue, opens the case and removes a pair of shoe brushes, a suit of pyjamas and the alarm clock.* **JAKE** *watches with his arms folded on his chest for* *warmth.* **KELVIN** *winds the clock up.*

JAKE What time are you getting up?

KELVIN Half-past six.

JAKE Do me a favour. Don't set that thing for half-past six.

KELVIN There's no need. I wake at half-past six automatically.

His back to **JAKE**, *he lays the suitcase on its side on the floor and places lamp, clock and brushes neatly on it.*

JAKE Why so early? You're not working in a shop tomorrow.

KELVIN So as to waste no time I'll be locating on a map the buildings where I'm seeking interviews and writing down on my notebook the quickest and cheapest ways of getting to them. This will take two hours. Then I'll go out and find a pawn shop. I need to raise a loan on two or three small objects of value which I happen to have with me. To do this before my first appointment I must rise at six-thirty. [*he pauses, facing* **JAKE** *blankly*].

JAKE [*slightly daunted*] The best of British luck! If we aren't up when you go out, take the key from the hook behind the door. I mean, we may not be in when you get back. We've been asked to a party.

KELVIN Thank you. Goodnight.

His manner is so coldly blank as to seem almost hostile. **JAKE** *suddenly feels the situation to be a humorous one. He grins, shakes his head and pats* **KELVIN** *encouragingly on the shoulder.*

JAKE Sleep tight, Kelvin.

KELVIN Goodnight.

JAKE *goes round the screen and gets down into the dark huddle of the bed.* **KELVIN** *stands staring at the lit side of the screen. There is a movement on the bed and* **JILL** *is heard to say in a laughing muffled voice.*

JILL Jake! You idiot.

KELVIN*'s face grows sad and lost looking. Abruptly he turns, stoops and switches the light off.*

4: SIR GODFREY'S OFFICE

A bulky man with a black moustache and brutal features sits behind a desk, telephoning; there is a chair in front of the desk.

SIR GODFREY No I'm sorry, Johannesburg is out, definitely out. Quebec, yes; Oslo, yes; but scrub Jo'burg. Totally. [*nods*] You've got it. [*puts down receiver*].

SECRETARY [*entering*] Mr McKellar is here, Sir Godfrey.

SIR GODFREY Wheel him in.

The **SECRETARY** *goes to the door, pauses and says:*

SECRETARY This way, Mr McKellar.

KELVIN *enters confidently. Exit* **SECRETARY**. **SIR GODFREY** *rises and indicates a chair before his desk.*

SIR GODFREY Good afternoon, Mr McKellar. Take a pew.

KELVIN Thank you. [*sits in a posture that is relaxed without being untidy*] Sir Godfrey, I'd like to begin by being totally frank with you. I am not Hector McKellar. I deceived you for the purpose of obtaining this interview, for though my qualities eminently equip me for your Head of Stereotype Promotions Branch, my qualifications and experience do not. You will see then that since it is in your own interest as well as mine that you employ me, the fraud whereby I gain the employment is morally justified. The end justifies the means. You are a business man so I need say no more on the matter. But before applying ourselves to the progress of question and answer which will constitute the main body of the interview itself there is a further irrelevancy which it would be well to clear from our minds. You have no doubt noticed a stain on my trouser leg above the right knee – [*taps it with his forefinger*] caused by mince. On my way here I visited a self-service restaurant for a snack. It was an overcrowded place and through no fault of mine the mince fell upon my knee from my neighbour's fork. [*genially*] But explanations of this kind must seem like swatting midges to a man with your breadth of vision. You, yourself, I notice, have a small but perceptible egg stain on your tie. Don't you feel this makes some sort of bond between us?

During this speech, **SIR GODFREY***'s face had been expressionless. At the mention of the egg stain it hardens into dislike. Now he leans forward and touches a switch on his desk. Sound – a low buzz.*

SIR GODFREY Show this ... *gentleman* out!

KELVIN *follows the* **SECRETARY** *to the wings, where he stops and turns.*

KELVIN Sir Godfrey, it is fortunate that we discovered so soon how impossible it would be for us to work together! But I want you to remember what has passed between us this afternoon. A moment ago I called you a man of vision. I no longer believe that. In less than a month you will realise how short-sighted you really are. Goodbye!

KELVIN *exits.*

SOUND: *a door is slammed.*

5: JAKE'S STUDIO, EVENING

The table is still on the right but the easel is now centre back, and the chaise longue is centre front with the sleeping bag neatly rolled, at one end. **KELVIN**'s *case lies beside it, with the clock and shoe brushes on it. The bed, tidily made, is extreme left with the draught-screen shielding it from the room and the chair, without newspapers, near the screen.* **KELVIN**, *wearing a floral apron, kneels beside the chair brushing it industriously with a hand-brush. Suddenly he pauses, listening. Loud voices are heard in the distance, coming nearer.* **KELVIN** *stands up as* **JAKE** *and* **JILL** *enter, talking simultaneously.*

JILL But what I can't understand is you pretending not to like her. I mean if you think it means nothing why pretend anything? I'd just like to know. Just out of curiosity.

JAKE [*at the same time*] All right! All right! All right! All right! All right! All right! All right! [*or more*].

A pause. **JILL** *walks straight past the chaise longue and sits down staring straight ahead with her hands clasped and pressed between her knees.* **JAKE** *lolls against the table and stares at her grimly.* **KELVIN**, *brush in hand, watches, fascinated.*

JAKE Have you finished? [*pause*] Or have you anything else to add?

JILL *continues staring miserably ahead.* **JAKE** *talks in a firm, bullying voice.*

JAKE Look if you want excuses you're going to be disappointed. By sheer accident I was sitting beside her on the floor. I was a bit drunk, so was she, we all were. Suddenly, she throws her arms round my neck and looks up at me wanting to be kissed. All right, she's a tart but she's an attractive tart, I felt like kissing her and I did. It's quite simple really. There's no need to build anything on it. For Christ sake I'm not in love with her. When I said I didn't like her I was telling the complete truth. Two minutes of her conversation would drive me up the bloody wall.

JILL But you could neck with her for twenty minutes. With me there. In a room full of people who knew us.

JAKE Look Jill, you'd better be careful! I'm warning you, you're beginning to make me feel trapped! I thought there was a good relationship between us, a decent relationship, both of us doing what we felt like doing, going our own ways when we wanted different things. But if you carry on like this, you'll make me feel trapped. I couldn't stand you then.

JILL *frowns sadly and speaks like a child repeating to herself a new and difficult lesson.*

JILL If I'm not careful ... you won't be able to stand me. I've got to be more careful in future, I see.

JAKE *strolls across to* **KELVIN**

JAKE [*with overstressed geniality*] How did you get on?

KELVIN Very well ...

JILL *springs up, grabs the shoe brushes and hurls them at* **JAKE**. *She misses. He leans elegantly on the back of the chair, flicks his shoulder with the fingers of his left hand as if removing dust.*

JAKE [*casually*] You don't mean you got a job?

KELVIN *glances uneasily at* **JILL.**

KELVIN No, but I had five interviews and arranged nine.

JILL *strides over to the easel, grabbing a knife from the table on the way. She raises it to the painting on the easel, glaring at* **JAKE** *as she does so.*

JAKE That's very good indeed. Do you think you made an impression on any of them?

JILL *slashes the picture and looks at* **JAKE** *as before.*

KELVIN Yes, but not for very long.

JAKE Did none of them send for the police?

JILL *knocks the easel down and then runs to the table and overturns it.* **KELVIN** *stares open-mouthed.* **JAKE** *shouts to him above the noise.*

JAKE It was decent of you to tidy the place up!

JILL [*rushing at him, clawing at his face and shouting in a sort of hysterical whisper*] Bastard! Rotten bastard!

JAKE *casually catches her wrist and spins her round so that she is bent over with her arm twisted behind her back. He takes a handful of her hair in his free hand and tugs it.* **JILL** *grunts.*

JAKE Call me master! [*he tugs hard. She cries aloud*] I said call me master!

JILL Master!

He lets her go and leans back casually. She stands and faces him calmly, rubbing her twisted elbow. **KELVIN** *stares at him in awe, dropping the brush on the chair.*

KELVIN That was a very wrong thing to do!

JAKE I'm sure Jill agrees with you.

JILL [*smiling contemptuously*] You filthy exhibitionist!

JAKE *nods gloomily.* **JILL** *picks up the lurid paperback from the floor, goes to the chaise longue, sits, crosses her legs and starts reading.* **JAKE** *speaks to* **KELVIN** *in a low urgent voice.*

JAKE Look, I can't do anything with her when she's in this kind of mood. Go and talk to her. Cheer her up a bit. I'm sure you can.

KELVIN *nods blankly.* **JAKE** *moves quietly around the room, deftly tidying up. When this is done he takes another canvas (perhaps a* *cheap reproduction of a Victorian masterpiece) and slowly begins to paint it black. From time to time he glances at* **KELVIN** *and* **JILL** *just to see how they're getting on.* **KELVIN** *goes to the sofa and sits beside* **JILL**, *who does not glance up from her book. After a moment, he takes an envelope from his apron pocket. It has the word* **JILL** *printed in small neat letters in the top right-hand corner. He lays it on the sofa between them and clears his throat.*

KELVIN Er ...

JILL [*coldly and monotonously*] Yes?

KELVIN Here are the three pounds you borrowed from the actor last night.

JILL You said you had no money.

KELVIN Nor had I, but I had a few old trinkets belonging to my mother and this morning I pawned them.

JILL Oh. [*pause*] You shouldn't have done that.

KELVIN But I needed money myself and I'll be able to redeem them in a week or two.

JILL Good. [*she turns a page*].

KELVIN [*clears his throat and speaks nervously and timidly*] You aren't angry with me for tidying the room up are you?

JILL Not a bit. [*a pause. Then she speaks bitterly, but still pretending to read*] I used to tidy it up myself before Jake made it clear that he didn't give a damn what I did.

KELVIN [*sympathetically*] It's hard to do a thing if nobody appreciates it. I did this tonight because I hoped it might please you. Since it does it will be easy to go on doing it. While I'm here, that is.

During this speech **JILL** *lets her book her droop, then puts it down and turns to face* **KELVIN**.

JILL [*in a low, tense voice*] You like me, do you? [**KELVIN** *nods. She pouts her lips and leans towards him. He smiles sadly and shakes his head. She grabs his hands in hers and says breathlessly*] Kiss me! Kiss me!

KELVIN No. You want to hurt him. [*nods to* **JAKE**] It won't hurt him because he will know why you are doing it. And it will hurt me because it won't mean anything and I'll want it to mean something.

JILL *suddenly sobs into her hands.* **KELVIN** *puts his arms around her kindly and speaks in a tender, reflective, almost musical voice.*

KELVIN I don't know much about love because I'm bad at it, but it seems an unnatural emotion. Those who should comfort us bring us pain instead. I would like to comfort you, give you things; a nice house, with a breakfast recess off the kitchen, and bright wallpaper, and a television set. But somehow that seems un-Nietzschean. [*he pats her shoulder*] Yes, you are right to love him and not me. Jake is a true adventurer, a bandit, an ... aristocrat. Compared with him not even Nietzsche can save me from being middle class, respectable and dull.

JILL [*sits up and starts tidying her hair, speaking in a hard voice*] Do you really think it's so aristocratic and adventurous to paint pictures nobody likes and live by scrounging from your parents and the National Assistance and kiss a prostitute at a party and twist your mistress's arm when she complains? And do you think it's so dull and middle class to arrive in London with no friends or qualifications, lose all your money on the first night and then try to bluff your way into a five-thousand-a-year job?

KELVIN [*staring gloomily*] Don't say those things. They encourage me.

JILL [*shakes her head*] You're not short of courage.

KELVIN Where you're concerned I've none at all.

JAKE *comes back to the sofa and leans genially over to them.*

JAKE Are you two lovebirds friendly again? Look, I've a suggestion. It's not late yet and Mike's party will have started to warm up nicely. Let's all go back to it.

JILL [*addressing* **KELVIN**] Would *you* like to go?

KELVIN No, I've nine interviews tomorrow and I need very regular quantities of sleep.

JILL [*addressing* **JAKE**] I'll stay too. I don't feel like a party.

JAKE *sits on the sofa back and speaks to her tenderly, caressing the lobe of her ear.*

JAKE Come off it, Jill. If Kelvin is going to bed it won't be much fun sitting reading by the fire. And if you go to bed with him he won't sleep and you'll ruin his chance of a job. Besides, you like parties. And this time I'll be a good boy. That's a promise.

JILL [*turns to* **KELVIN** *almost pleadingly*] Are you sure you won't come?

JAKE Yes, come on Kelvin, Jill would like you to come.

KELVIN Thank you, I prefer not to change my mind.

JAKE [*grins*] That puts us in our place. Come on. Walky-walky. [*he pulls* **JILL** *to her feet by one hand and walks with her to the door. Halfway there she stops and looks up into his face*].

JILL You think you can get me to do anything you like, don't you?

JAKE Of course. But only because you enjoy the things I enjoy.

JILL Take care. One day I'll want something you won't enjoy at all.

JAKE [*takes her chin gently between his thumb and forefinger*] I'll never tie you down, Jill.
SOUND: *the alarm clock rings*
JILL *clings in momentary panic to* **JAKE**, *who looks pained until* **KELVIN** *lifts the clock and switches it off.*
JAKE We'd better go, it's Kelvin's bedtime.
Chuckling, he draws **JILL** *towards the door. She looks back, calls:*
JILL Good night, Kelvin. [*she is also amused*].
KELVIN [*loud and cold*] Good night ... have fun, both of you! [*they leave*].
KELVIN'*s face goes blank. He repeats to himself in a puzzled voice.*
KELVIN Both of you. [*he bends down to replace the clock saying savagely*] The bitch! The bitch! The bitch!

6: MR BROWN'S OFFICE

A desk with an intercom panel, **BROWN** *sitting behind it writing and a chair in front.*
SOUND: *a buzz.*
BROWN *touches a switch on the panel.*
WOMAN'S VOICE Your visitor is here, Mr Brown.
BROWN Send him in Miss Waterson. [*his accent is Anglo-Scottish. He continues while* **KELVIN** *briskly enters. Then speaks without looking up*] Sit down.
KELVIN *sits.* **BROWN** *lays down his pen and stares at him, deadpan*
KELVIN Mr Brown, I want to begin by being honest with you. I am not Hector McKellar.
BROWN I'm aware of that. Hector McKellar and I were students together at Stirling University.
KELVIN [*interested*] Why did you allow me this interview?
BROWN Curiosity. I wanted to find out why you were taking my friend's name in vain.
KELVIN My reasons are basically praiseworthy. You are looking for a Co-ordination Controller for this city your firm is building north of the Wash. I am fitted for this job not by my qualifications, but by my qualities. I used Hector McKellar's name to obtain me an interview which an ordinary letter would not have obtained.
BROWN I see. Tell me, have you experience of local government?
KELVIN None.
BROWN Or Civil Service Administration?
KELVIN None.
BROWN Or Company Law?
KELVIN No.
BROWN Have you studied the problems of modern town planning?
KELVIN Never.
BROWN Have you a degree in Sociology?
KELVIN I have never been to a university.
BROWN Then what qualities can possibly equip you for a job like this?
KELVIN Energy, intelligence and integrity.
BROWN *regards* **KELVIN** *for a moment.* **KELVIN** *returns a blank unperturbed stare.*
BROWN Would you tell me your name?
KELVIN Kelvin Walker.
BROWN You have a high opinion of yourself, Mr Walker.
KELVIN I have not tried to hide that, Mr Brown.
BROWN True.
He leans back and regards **KELVIN** *with a thoughtful frown.*
KELVIN [*smiles and wags a finger at him*] You are wondering if I am mad, naïve or fiendishly cunning.
BROWN [*nods*] You're right.
KELVIN Let me demonstrate that I am just unusually intelligent. As Co-ordination Controller I would have departments under me responsible for things like local government administration, town planning, civil service liaison, and so forth. Is that the case?
BROWN It is.
KELVIN These departments will be staffed by qualified specialists who know their work thoroughly. My job will therefore be to make sure these specialists get on with their work, and decide disputes arising between the different departments. Is it not so?
BROWN Just so.
KELVIN In other words my job depends on my ability to judge character, to sense moods and use my common sense. Is this the case?
BROWN Largely, yes.
KELVIN Mr Brown, this is a job I could do well!
BROWN *is nettled at this.*
BROWN What reasons have you given me for believing that?
KELVIN No reasons! I am not asking you to accept me on reasonable grounds! Mr Brown, have faith in your heart, which is the divine part of you! Distrust your cowardly brain, which can only hobble about upon the warped crutches of reason and precedent as Adam before his maker on the first day of Creation! Does not

your heart *guarantee* that anyone who has approached you as I have approached you, and spoken as I have spoken, *must* be fit for this job?

BROWN *is desperate and protests desperately.*

BROWN No Mr Walker it does not! I have no wish to be offensive, but I suspect I am facing an abnormally self-assured confidence trickster with a-a-an almost inspirational gift of the gab.

KELVIN *stares at him for a moment like a child who cannot believe he has been struck. He rises to his feet, his face assuming expressions of horror and utter misery. He speaks in a quiet apologetic pleading voice.*

KELVIN Do you really think I am *that*, Mr Brown?

BROWN [*looks at his blotting pad, slightly ashamed of himself*] Mr Walker, please sit down. I really don't know *what* you are.

KELVIN [*pathetically*] Have I no chance of this job at all?

BROWN None. It concerns a government contract. Applicants are examined by a committee of Englishmen who were all educated at Oxford. In the long run they'll employ whoever I nominate, but only if he seems like the sort of person they'd have chosen themselves. Frankly I could not put you forward without weakening my position here.

KELVIN Mr Brown, yours is the first reason for not employing me that I have heard with respect. [*he rises*] I will take my leave.

BROWN *pushes a block of paper to* **KELVIN**'*s side of the desk.*

BROWN Write your address there. If I can recommend you to a position of power without jeopardising my own I'll certainly get in touch. It's hardly likely though.

KELVIN *writes.* **BROWN** *pulls the pad to his own side of the desk.*

BROWN One final thing. I positively forbid you to use Hector McKellar's name in this way again.

KELVIN *is thunderstruck.*

KELVIN Mr Brown! Without that name I have no plan, no strategy, no *reason* for being in London at all.

BROWN I bear you no ill will, Mr Walker, and this warning is a friendly one. If I hear of you using Hector's name again I will tell both him and the police.

KELVIN [*bitterly*] And of course you have my address.

BROWN *presses a button on the desk.* **SOUND:** *– a buzzing noise.*

BROWN Miss Waterson, take Mr Walker to the executive lounge and arrange a car to take him – home.

KELVIN *walks to the door looking dazed.* **BROWN** *calls after him.*

BROWN I can always get you a job as a sales representative!

KELVIN *looks round, appalled and nearly speechless.*

KELVIN I'll see you in Hell first!

KELVIN *leaves.* **BROWN** *sits looking thoughtful for a moment then picks up the phone.*

BROWN Get me Hector McKellar will you?

7: JAKE'S STUDIO, EVENING

The chaise longue has been shifted to the back and **JILL** *sits on it, reading. There is a bottle of whisky on the table.* **JAKE**, *looking bored, leans on the table being harangued by* **MRS HENDON.**

MRS HENDON I've been patient with you, Mr Whittington! Patient I am and patient I have been, but a fool I am not and a fool I never will be! Six pounds you owe in rent, and at the same time I notice over there a bottle of whisky which must have cost three at the very least.

KELVIN *appears in the doorway and stands there looking miserable and thoughtful. Nobody notices him. His coat is open and he wears his hat.*

JAKE Mrs Hendon, the whisky was a present. I know what I owe you. Give me another week and I'll pay the six pounds with interest if you like. As I told you last time, a client of mine is going to buy a painting. I've been expecting him for the past ten days, only he caught the flu, there's a lot of it going about you know ...

MRS HENDON I don't believe you.

JAKE Are you casting doubts on my honesty? I warn you, Mrs Hendon, I am a dangerous man to quarrel with –

JILL *stirs impatiently.*

JILL Come off it, Jake!

JAKE [*suddenly becoming quiet*] What do you mean?

JILL You know what I mean. Mrs Hendon knows what I mean. Christ, we *all* know what I mean so just come off it.

JAKE [*takes a step towards her, looking dangerous*] Now look ...

KELVIN *comes forward, producing his wallet as he does so. He addresses the landlady wearily.*

KELVIN Am I to take it Mr Whittington owes you six pounds?

MRS HENDON Eh? Yes he does.

KELVIN Here they are.

He hands over the notes, returns the wallet and speaks gloomily to **JAKE.**

KELVIN Sorry I couldn't come sooner, Whittington. I had a bad dose of the flu.

JAKE [*grins, folding his arms and chest luxuriously*] So you said in your card. Mr Walker is a buyer for the Scottish National Gallery, Mrs Hendon.

JILL, *who has been watching all this without amusement, snorts and resumes her reading.* **KELVIN** *sits down dejectedly beside her, elbows on knees and head in hands.* **MRS HENDON** *glares at him suspiciously then turns on* **JAKE** *again. She speaks more quietly.*

MRS HENDON Another thing, Mr Whittington. The noise.

JAKE Noise, Mrs Hendon?

MRS HENDON Sometimes it's parties but usually it's fighting.

JAKE Fighting, Mrs Hendon?

MRS HENDON The other tenants are tolerant people, Mr Whittington. They like you and your ... and the young lady here. But this is the last time I'm warning you. Next time you'll have to leave.

JAKE *raises his eyebrows and shrugs.* **KELVIN** *speaks drearily:*

KELVIN Mrs Hendon, our young friends have been financially insecure. Naturally they have lost their tempers on occasions. However, [*he sighs heavily*] I am sure the money you have received has not just paid for the roof over their heads; it will be a soothing balm upon their hearts. As Robert Burns says: 'Art thou troubled? Money will soothe thee.'

MRS HENDON I only hope Robert Burns was right, Sir. [*she goes to door*] For everybody's sake.

She leaves. **JAKE** *slaps his knee in delight, stands up and calls across to* **KELVIN.**

JAKE You know, you're quite an actor. That remote gloomy manner is distinctly impressive. [*he turns to the table*] By great good luck I removed from the party last night a means of celebrating the performance.

He uncorks the whisky and pours some into two glasses. **JILL** *throws down her book and speaks angrily:*

JILL How much money have you left now?

KELVIN Ten shillings ... A bit more than ten shillings.

JILL And how in the hell can you live on that?

JAKE Lay off him, Jill. Give him time to recover. [*he goes across and puts a glass into* **KELVIN***'s hand*] I'm sure you're as grateful to him as I am.

JILL I'm not grateful. Not at all. That he should ruin his chances to keep us idle absolutely sickens and disgusts me.

KELVIN [*putting the glass untasted on the floor*] *That* hasn't ruined my chances. I'll find work tomorrow.

JAKE [*sips*] How can you be sure?

KELVIN I'll get a job as a bus conductor. Big towns never have enough of them.

This is said with a gust of masochism. **JAKE** *and* **JILL** *stare at him. He leans his arms on his knees and looks between them at the floor. Then shudders and speaks with a kind of feeble wildness:*

KELVIN I've been undermined, a man called Brown undermined me. It wasn't that he threatened to call the police and so on, and if I stop using McKellar's name, who can I meet who matters? But he thought I was a confidence trickster and now I think he was right.

He covers his face and begins quietly crying. **JILL** *lays a hand on his shoulder saying gently.*

JILL Kelvin!

JAKE *knocks back his whisky, goes to the table, pours another glass, turns with it in his hand and delivers his great speech.*

JAKE Kelvin. Don't you understand? Haven't you got the point? All these chairmen and governors and directors and politicians, they're all confidence tricksters! Nobody believes for a moment that they're wiser or more virtuous than the rest of us. You've pointed out yourself that they don't even know more. Then how do they get up there? Because most people don't want to run their own lives, they want to be told what to do. So a gang of tricksters stand up and tell people what to do, and get very well paid for it. And what makes them successful? Their confidence. And how do they get it? By having the stuff ladled to them at home and at school and at university. I know what I'm talking about. My parents are rich. I've been to a public school. I'm a product of the ruling classes all right, but thank God I'm a decadent product. I'm just not interested in telling people what to do. Except Jill, when I'm in a bad mood. But you're different, Kelvin. Nobody had fed confidence into you. God knows where you get it from. And if you can only kick your way onto the ladder at the very top rung you'll show the whole racket to be as insanely arbitrary as it really is. Which is why I'm right there behind you cheering. You mustn't become a bus conductor, mate. It just wouldn't be right.

He drains his glass. **KELVIN** *has not been listening. His mouth hangs blankly open and towards the end of the speech he starts working nervously. He clenches his fists between his knees and looks like someone in a state of extreme terror.* **JILL** *leans towards*

him in alarm, he turns to her and cries in a fast high voice.
KELVIN I've lost my faith, Jill!
JAKE But you said you didn't believe in God!
JILL [*softly*] In yourself?
KELVIN I've nowhere to go, Jill!
KELVIN *puts his face in her lap and holds her round the waist, weeping hysterically. She lays an arm tenderly across his shoulders, looks sternly at* **JAKE** *and points to the door. He looks worried, pointing to himself with one hand and the door with the other in a gesture meaning – me? Leave? –* **JILL** *nods vehemently and frowns, pointing again to the door.* **JAKE**, *looking gloomily furious, tiptoes to the bed, takes an anorak from it, slips it on, takes a sleeping bag, bundles it untidily under his arm, then tiptoes to the door, grabbing the whisky bottle from the table on the way past. In the doorway he turns and seems about to shout something but she is holding the shuddering* **KELVIN** *in her arms and whispering in his ear.* **JAKE** *scowls, shakes his head and silently leaves.*

INTERVAL

8: STUDIO, MORNING

KELVIN *lies in the bed, his sleeping head and naked shoulders projecting from under the heaped clothes.* **JILL** *comes from the table with a mug of tea, places it on the floor and gently shakes his shoulder. He sits up, leaning on an elbow.*
KELVIN What time is it?
JILL After eight. [*she sits beside him*].
KELVIN How long have we ... how long have I slept?
JILL About twelve hours.
KELVIN That's strange.
JILL Not really. After all, you had something like a nervous breakdown. And I suppose it was the first time you did the other thing.
KELVIN [*looking at her uncertainly*] Yes. It was.
JILL Don't you want the tea I made you?
KELVIN Er yes. Thank you. [*He sips, looking over the cup*].
JILL How do you feel?
KELVIN Quite well. In fact very well.
JILL What are you doing today?
KELVIN Doing? [*introspective pause*] I think I'll phone and arrange some more interviews.
JILL [*sincerely*] I'm very glad.
KELVIN [*sits up*] It's queer that something as physical as love should be able to give a man courage. I thought only ideas could do that. [*He places his hand on hers and stares earnestly into his face. She smiles at him*] Only Colonel Ingersol and Frederick Nietzsche have done for me what you have done. [*she stops smiling*].
KELVIN [*after a pause*] Where's Jake?
JILL He probably spent the night with Mike. I expect he'll be here soon.
KELVIN How will we explain it to him?
JILL Explain what?
KELVIN The new arrangement.
JILL Have we arranged anything?
KELVIN Won't we have to?
JILL Kelvin, I love Jake.
KELVIN How can you?
JILL He's a decent sort of person.
KELVIN I've seen no sign of it.
JILL He may seem a bit of a bully to you but when it comes to sex he's very tender, totally unselfish and highly imaginative. And he does love me.
KELVIN Then why did he go away last night?
JILL Because he likes you. And I told him to go. He wasn't being a liar when he said he would never tie me down if I wanted something he didn't want.
KELVIN [*frowns*] Did all that happen last night ... just because you were sorry for me?
JILL [*shakes her head, slightly exasperated*] No! I wish you didn't want to put everything into words, it makes them different from how they are ... You see I like you an awful lot, and I thought you needed me. Look, you aren't going to get all moody about this are you?
KELVIN [*thinks for a moment, then says glumly*] I'm afraid not. A bit of me wants to get moody about it, but I still feel too well to give way to it. [*he leans forward suddenly and grabs her by the shoulders*] One last kiss, though, come on, one last precious souvenir of a night of madness! Just one!
JILL [*struggles, giggling*] Stop it you idiot! Let go! Now then, Fido, down bad dog! Bad, bad doggie ...
JAKE *comes in with the sleeping bag under his left arm and an envelope in his left hand.* **KELVIN** *lets* **JILL** *go and falls back on his elbow.* **JILL** *slides onto the floor and stands up, rubbing her arms.*
JAKE *has paused by the door.*
JAKE Still at it?

He throws down the sleeping bag and walks grimly up to the bed, watched apprehensively by the reclining **KELVIN**. **JILL** *strolls past him to the table where she lifts a brush and starts smoothing her hair.*

JAKE Good morning, sir. I trust you slept comfortably?

KELVIN Jake, I hope ...

JAKE Only one letter in the morning's delivery, sir.

He drops the envelope on the bed. **KELVIN** *picks it up, staring at* **JAKE** *as if he feared some kind of trap.* **JAKE** *stares grimly down at him.*

KELVIN It can't be for me. Nobody knows I'm here ... except Brown.

JAKE I would respectfully draw your attention to the fact that the envelope bears the insignia of the British Broadcasting Corporation.

JAKE *walks to the chaise longue and stands for a moment watching* **JILL** *brushing her hair.* **KELVIN** *opens the envelope and reads the letter.*

JAKE How is Florence Nightingale this morning?

JILL Come off it, Jake.

JAKE You've got a word for everything.

JILL You've a hangover, haven't you?

JAKE [*sitting down, clutching his head*] Oh God, yes.

KELVIN This is from Hector McKellar. [**JILL** *and* **JAKE** *stare at him*].

KELVIN [*reading aloud*] 'Dear Mr Walker, My good friend Sandy Brown has given me your name and suggested a meeting between us might benefit both. Kindly telephone my secretary and arrange an appointment. Yours faithfully, Hector McKellar, Director of Power Point.'

JILL He's found out you've been using his name! Don't phone, Kelvin, it'll be a trap.

JAKE If he was seriously angry he'd have sent the police, not just suggested an appointment.

KELVIN What is Power Point?

JAKE It's a programme which handles the political stuff. It televises Parliamentary debates, interviews politicians and businessmen and people like that.

KELVIN [*thoughtfully to himself*] I'll phone him. Yes, I'll phone him. [*he gathers a blanket round him and springs to his feet. The blanket hanging like a toga while he assumes a statuesque pose with right hand raised*] I have a premonition, an intuition, a conviction that the tide is about to turn!

KELVIN *with a magesterial gesture flings a fold of the robe across one shoulder.*

9: SIR HECTOR'S OFFICE

A desk with a telephone, a chair behind it, two chairs facing each other in front.

MCKELLAR [*stands in the wings saying*] Come in Mr Walker. [*He strolls over to the desk followed by* **KELVIN**] Sit down! [**KELVIN** *sits.* **MCKELLAR** *looks down on* **KELVIN** *for a moment, then sits on the edge of his desk*] And how is Glaik these days?

KELVIN As well as can be expected Mr McKellar, considering the general intelligence of the population.

MCKELLAR I know what you mean.

KELVIN I am seeking work with a starting salary of five thousand a year.

MCKELLAR [*raises his eyebrows*] Perhaps I should have asked what you can do for *me*.

KELVIN I am in your hands, Mr McKellar. I'll try whatever you put me into.

MCKELLAR [*strokes his chin*] And you have no qualifications.

KELVIN Quite so. If a clear, quick, vigorous tongue and brain are not qualifications then I have no qualifications.

MCKELLAR Well, we'll try you with the usual tests. Sandy Brown seemed to think your strong suit was your personality, and if you *have* a personality the tongue and brain will be no hindrance. [*he picks up the phone and dials three digits*] Hello. Is Mary Cranmer there? Send her in, will you? [*he puts the phone down, takes out a cigarette and lights it, watching* **KELVIN** *carefully*] And is your father still on the town council?

KELVIN No, he gave that up two years ago. He decided the world's business could be more efficiently managed by the agents of the Devil.

MCKELLAR Yes, that view also has much to be said for it.

MARY CRANMER *comes in. She has the smooth, shrewd, self-effacing promptness of a natural second in command.*

MCKELLAR Mary, this is Kelvin Walker, a fellow countryman of mine. He may be useful to us. I mean he seems fluent enough. Try him out, will you?

CRANMER Here and now, Hector?

MCKELLAR Why not?

MCKELLAR *goes behind his desk to watch.* **MARY CRANMER** *looks at* **KELVIN** *with her finger thoughtfully on one cheek and her head on one side.*

CRANMER Yes. First you must relax totally. If you can't do that, I can't begin.

KELVIN *adopts a torturous pose involving crossed legs and interlocked* *fingers.* **MARY CRANMER** *sits down facing him.*

CRANMER Are you comfortable?

KELVIN [*tensely*] Yes.

CRANMER Then imagine I am a Cabinet Minister, say the Minister of Smoke Abatement. On my advice the government have ordered twenty thousand smoke suppressors at a cost of a hundred pounds for use in the Nationalised Industries, but owing to an error in my office the suppressors are twice the size they should be and virtually useless. Hitherto I have been regarded as a popular Minister with considerable prospects, but now the newspapers are raising a bit of a stink. Think about this. When you're ready I want you to ask me some questions.

KELVIN [*pushes his hair back with one hand*] Ready.

CRANMER Go ahead then.

KELVIN *launches himself into the interview like a duck to water.*

KELVIN Mrs Cranmer, a lot of newspapers are implying that you are a fool. Why do you think you are not?

CRANMER That is a totally unfair question, I refuse to answer it.

KELVIN I'm sorry I'll phrase it differently. Why do you think the press is being unfair to you?

CRANMER For political reasons.

KELVIN But Mrs Cranmer, you are a politician!

KELVIN *is leaning ardently towards her, mouth and eyes wide open. She opens her mouth to speak, can think of nothing to say, so taps her cheek thoughtfully with her finger.* **MCKELLAR** *stubs out his cigarette.*

MCKELLAR Give him the disaster housewife, Mary.

CRANMER *produces a handkerchief and squeezes it nervously between her hands.*

CRANMER I'm a housewife who had seen a jet-liner crash into a row of houses killing almost all her neighbours. Think about that for a moment.

KELVIN I don't need to. What did *you* think, Mrs Cranmer, when you saw the plane was going to destroy these buildings which were so familiar to you?

CRANMER [*twists the handkerchief and speaks with a Lancashire accent*] I thought 'Oh dear, the plane's going to crash into the buildings'. And it did. It did.

KELVIN [*probing*] And what did you actually feel, Mrs Cranmer?

CRANMER I didn't know what to feel.

KELVIN The horror of the catastrophe must have numbed you to the core.

CRANMER Yes it did come as a bit of a shock.

KELVIN And what did you actually do Mrs Cranmer?

CRANMER I went and phoned me mother.

KELVIN Like a frightened child you ran to your earliest comforter. It must have been a great relief to confide in her.

CRANMER Oh yes a wonderful relief.

KELVIN And after that you got stuck into a good meal: something with plenty of meat and potatoes in it. Eating can be a wonderful resource.

CRANMER [*shocked into her ordinary voice*] Certainly not!

KELVIN [*piously*] Mrs Cranmer, your powers of endurance verge on the superhuman. Thank you for being so patient with me in your hour of loneliness and desolation.

CRANMER *looks at* **MCKELLAR** *who is leaning forward on folded arms.*

MCKELLAR Give him a bishop.

CRANMER Ancient or modern?

MCKELLAR Modern, of course.

CRANMER [*stares at* **KELVIN** *and says rapidly*] I am a bishop who has hit the headlines by consecrating pubs, discotheques and night clubs and holding communion services in them.

KELVIN [*without even stopping to think*] Why do you do these things, your grace?

CRANMER Because Christ should belong to publicans and sinners and *ordinary* people *everywhere.*

KELVIN That strikes me as a very condescending remark.

CRANMER [*worried*] It was not meant to be.

KELVIN Surely this unhealthy emphasis upon kindness and toleration is destroying the whole essence of the Christian message?

CRANMER [*shocked*] Surely not!

KELVIN But Christ's deliberate rudeness to his mother, his vicious treatment of the money-lenders, his brutality to the barren fig tree, all indicate a man with a touch of sadism in him.

CRANMER I can hardly agree with you there, though of course there is something in what you say ...

KELVIN I am suggesting, your Grace, that intelligent people would respect the Church far more if it were not so afraid of threatening, denouncing, dictating and horrifying us generally!

MCKELLAR [*stands up*] That will do, Mary. [*He comes to the front of the desk and leans on it. Mary Cranmer stands*] Are you thinking what I'm thinking Mary?

CRANMER I'm sure I am, Hector.

MCKELLAR [*nods*] Good girl! – Mary will take you to studio five for a proper screen test but you've no natural modesty so you'll have no trouble with it. Yes, we can use you.

KELVIN *stands and controls, with an effort, an urge to grin wildly.*

KELVIN What wage will I get?

MCKELLAR [*amused*] Heavens, I don't know. I know nothing about finance. What will they pay him, Mary?

CRANMER Well, if he starts with the usual trial period –

MCKELLAR No no! I want him tied by a firm contract from the start! I want no repeat of the O'Hooligan catastrophe!

CRANMER Then he'll start with something between five and six with six months salary in lieu of notice in case something goes wrong. If he's any good he can double it in three years. He'll have an expense account for research, wining and dining purposes. And of course the statutory increases to compensate for inflation.

MCKELLAR Does that seem fair to you?

KELVIN [*stoutly*] I am prepared to accept those wages. [*he allows himself a tight little smile and the briefest of faint laughs*] To be frank ... Hector ... this is happening faster than I expected.

MCKELLAR To be equally frank ... Kelvin ... the BBC is suffering just now from a dangerous personality deficiency: particularly in the field of dialect. [*begins to pace backwards and forwards, talking expansively.* **KELVIN** *and* **CRANMER***'s heads shift from side to side on their necks as they follow him with their faces*] I'm not talking about Southern English dialects – they're ten a penny. I'm referring to dialects which conjure a background of blackened smoke-stacks and abandoned mine-shafts, of tiny cottages in lonely glens. It's getting hard to buy those accents nowadays. I blame the educational system. It destroys the confidence of ordinary people and sends the smart ones to university where they end up sounding as unlike their parents as possible. Am I right, Mary?

CRANMER Quite right, Hector. My Daddy is a Lancashire spindle-polisher.

MCKELLAR The British viewer, you see, likes nothing better than seeing someone in a position of power being savagely grilled by an interviewer with an exotic lower-class accent.

CRANMER You always call it 'The British alternative to Revolution', Hector.

MCKELLAR [*not noticing the interruption*] I always call it the British alternative to revolution. Up till three months ago the commercial companies had Frisby Mallet and we had Nick O'Hooligan, but the independent companies lured O'Hooligan away by giving him a show of his own. Frankly, Kelvin, we've been looking for someone like you for several months; a simpleton, but a simpleton who asks, out of sheer naïvety, all the most pointed and devastating questions. You agree Mary?

CRANMER I was going to tell him the same thing, Hector, but less succinctly.

KELVIN I think I can play that part with the minimum of hypocrisy.

MCKELLAR [*stops and stares at* **KELVIN** *severely*] No! With the maximum sincerity! Hypocrisy is not a word used in television circles. Sincerity is. Do you watch television by the way?

KELVIN Never!

MCKELLAR Good. Don't. It could destroy your bloom.

KELVIN I'll bear that in mind, Hector, it's a good thing to know. Could you tell me how soon I'll get some money?

MCKELLAR Certainly not before you've signed the contract!

KELVIN You see the cost of living in London has been much higher than I anticipated. In a day or two I may be compelled to borrow money, and I need not tell *you*, Hector, how disagreeable that prospect is to someone with *our* background.

MCKELLAR [*stares at* **KELVIN**, *then at* **CRANMER**] Mary, are you free this afternoon?

CRANMER As free as you want me to be, Hector.

MCKELLAR Good girl, Mary. Take him for the screen test and if all goes well, take him to contracts and sign him up. Then take him to the finance department and arrange an advance of a thousand. [*Looks at* **KELVIN** *and asks ironically*] Will that be sufficient?

KELVIN I'll make it sufficient.

MCKELLAR [*suddenly becomes genial and rests a hand on* **KELVIN***'s shoulder*] When can we launch him, Mary?

CRANMER Tuesday night on Power Point, Hector. I thought of giving him a Nobel Prize winner.

MCKELLAR *moves* **KELVIN** *to the door.* **CRANMER** *follows.*

MCKELLAR Excellent! You'll have no trouble with one

of those, eh? [**KELVIN** *smiles and nods.* **MCKELLAR** *holds out his hand*] Good luck!

KELVIN And good luck to you Hector! You certainly deserve it.

10: THE STUDIO, DAYS LATER

The furniture is arranged as in Scene 8, except that the easel, with a few pictures on it, is back beside the table, and crowded by a new television set on one side, and a standard lamp on the other. A refrigerator stands at an awkward angle near the entrance, right.

Other luxuries: a pleated silk cushion on the chaise longue. A cloth and a vase of flowers on the table. The bed, neatly made, is covered with an eiderdown. **JILL** *sprawls on it showing a lot of leg and reading a paperback. Music comes from a small transistor radio beside her.*

The door opens and **KELVIN** *comes in. He wears a smart grey suit and waistcoat, and carries a briefcase and umbrella. He pauses to look with pleasure upon the refrigerator and tap it approvingly on the side with his hand, then he puts bowler, umbrella and briefcase on top, wandering about and glancing uneasily at* **JILL**'s *legs. She looks up, nods to him and returns to her book. He wanders into the studio part of the room and looks in a baffled way at the picture on the easel, which shows a headless female torso and a falling bomb side by side, painted in white on a black canvas. The bomb with a large 'H' printed on it, the woman with the words 'Fanny Adams' printed across her body below her waist.*

JILL You're early. Nothing on this afternoon?

KELVIN Yes. A rehearsal at five.

JILL You haven't much time, have you?

KELVIN I thought I might see you for a few minutes.

They are talking uneasily, almost evasively.

JILL Who are they giving you tonight?

KELVIN Dyke.

JILL Who? [*she reaches out and switches off the set*].

KELVIN Clifford Dyke – the Prime Minister.

JILL [*without interest*] They are pushing you.

She turns back to the book on the bed.

KELVIN *wanders disconsolately to the end of the room.*

KELVIN [*morosely*] I wish you were more impressed. [*he turns and stares at her, and adds venomously*] And I wish you wouldn't lie on the bed like that wearing a dress like that!

JILL [*turns angrily*] I'll lie where I like and wear what I damn well please!

KELVIN *goes and sits beside her, seizes her hand and presses the palm against his chest.*

KELVIN Do you feel anything?

JILL No.

KELVIN You don't hear my heart beating?

JILL No.

KELVIN [*lets the hand go and frowns*] That's queer. I feel it beating unusually loudly.

JILL It's your heart, after all.

KELVIN *stares glumly ahead.* **JILL** *suddenly flings her book down.*

JILL [*with exasperation*] Are you honest, Kelvin?

His mouth falls open. He stares at her and rises slowly to his feet showing every sign of guilty alarm.

KELVIN What do you mean, woman? What are you hinting at?

JILL [*perplexed*] I don't really know – are you honest about *life*?

KELVIN [*grins with relief and starts walking round the room*] Life! Oh yes, I'm fairly honest about life! I won't pretend I don't tell lies – you've heard me do it – but I'm always honest about the big things.

JILL Then why not get a room of your own?

KELVIN [*halts, turns to her*] Who would pay the rent here?

JILL I would. I'm starting work as a waitress the day after tomorrow. It's work I can do quite well – I've done it before.

KELVIN What's the wage?

JILL Five pounds a week plus tips.

KELVIN [*contemptuously*] You can't pay the rent out of that!

JILL Yes I can! And if I can't I don't care. It's not good for us to live like this! Before you came we often managed to pay the rent. Jake sometimes sold a painting, or his people sent him a cheque, or I would work for a week or two. If one landlord threw us out we stayed with friends till we found a room elsewhere. I mean, we managed. We had to manage. We had a kind of independence. Now we depend on you.

KELVIN [*eagerly*] I don't mind!

JILL But I mind! And Jake minds!

KELVIN He hasn't asked me to leave.

JILL How can he when he owes you – how much is it now? Twelve pounds? No. You paid the rent again this morning. It's eighteen.

KELVIN If he hadn't owed it to me he would have owed it to Mrs Hendon.

JILL And she would have thrown him out and he wouldn't have had to feel grateful to her. But now he feels grateful to you and it's bad for him. It makes him hate himself and he takes it out on me.

KELVIN *walks into the studio part of the room and stares at the canvas, then he turns and stands beside it and speaks brutally and desperately.*

KELVIN The reason I don't get another room is that I don't want to leave you. If Jake asks me to leave I'll refuse. If he throws me out I'll get Mrs Hendon to get me another room in the same house. If you shift house I'll hire detectives to find where you've shifted and I'll shift as near there as I can. Do you understand?

JILL But I don't love you.

KELVIN *steps quickly over to her and kneels before her, staring into her eyes.*

KELVIN How can you be sure of that? No, you *can't* be sure of that. [*he shakes his head*] You're *not* sure! [*he takes* **JILL***'s hand in his*] How can you be sure you don't love me when every bit of me is intent on you, intended for you? Jill, don't object to what I say, just listen to it, and don't listen to the sense, listen to the sound. Maybe I am dishonest, but if so it is because my words are false, so just listen to the music of them, not the meaning. Let my voice join the noise of my heart to the noise of yours, making it beat the same way.

JILL [*stares into his eyes. Fascinated, she says almost inaudibly*] Stop.

KELVIN How can you be certain you don't love me? Certainty is very difficult in a world as big and strange as this one. Listen, I can't leave you, and it's your fault. Surely if you didn't keep me here I could leave easily. But you keep me here, you know you keep me here.

JILL *shakes her head in a lost, frightened way.*

KELVIN Yes, you do it. You know you do it. Why do you do it?

JILL [*dreamily*] I'm not sure. [*she wakes up*] For God's sake Kelvin, come off it!

Defeated, **KELVIN** *rises and sits looking gloomily and lost upon the chaise longue. His knees apart, his elbows resting on them, his hands interlocked.* **JILL** *stands up, takes a brush and starts brushing her hair vigorously.*

JILL It's no use, Kelvin. You're here because you want to be here. You can't hypnotize me into believing anything else.

KELVIN I'll leave if you want me to.

Tears are moving down **KELVIN***'s left cheek.* **JILL** *puts the brush down and turns to him, open-mouthed, delighted, surprised, then slightly pitying.*

JILL Are you crying?

KELVIN *smiles and crookedly nods. She sits beside him, looking interestedly into his face.*

JILL So you are. But all the tears are coming out of your left eye. How odd.

KELVIN [*without violence*] I'm sick of my oddity.

JILL Kelvin, there's no need to be sad. We'll still meet a lot. Now you know the price of things you can take me out for meals you can afford.

KELVIN Yes.

JILL And let's face it, I'm the only girl in London you've spoken to. Now you're on television all kinds of gorgeous little dollies will be throwing themselves at your head.

KELVIN [*dryly*] I wish you'd stop consoling me. It's a bit condescending of you.

JILL [*more coolly*] I'm sorry.

KELVIN When will I leave?

JILL [*putting a hand on his shoulder*] There's no hurry Kelvin. Don't leave before you've found a proper place to go to.

KELVIN Thank you.

They look sideways at each other in a puzzled, enquiring way. The door opens and **JAKE** *comes in.*

JAKE Having fun?

KELVIN I've been trying to make Jill leave you.

JAKE *takes the grey bowler from the fridge, stares at it unbelievingly, sniffs it like a dog and replaces it.* **JILL** *rises, collects her book and sits down to read in the chair.*

JAKE Any luck?

KELVIN None.

JAKE Hard lines. [*Sudden double take*] God! It's a refrigerator!

KELVIN [*apologetically*] I ordered it to be delivered this morning to ... to ... to keep food in.

JAKE Can it be used for that too?

KELVIN [*stands up and speaks awkwardly*] I'd better go. There's a rehearsal at four-thirty.

JAKE Do you mean all these gloriously spontaneous interviews are rehearsed?

KELVIN Not exactly rehearsed, but people need a short time to get used to the atmosphere and start thinking along the right lines.

JAKE *feels venomous.*

JAKE I bet you're good at getting them thinking along the right lines.

KELVIN *is pleased and touched.*

KELVIN Yes, you're right, I am! How did you guess?

Daunted, **JAKE** *turns away from him, goes to the table and begins mixing paint on the palette.* **JILL** *takes up her book and sits reading it on the chaise longue.* **KELVIN** *shifts awkwardly from foot to foot.*

KELVIN Well, cheerio.

JILL [*looks up and smiles kindly at him*] Goodbye Kelvin.

JAKE [*does not look up*] Ta ta old ... fruit.

KELVIN *looks at him with a frown.*

KELVIN Yes.

He leaves. There is a pause. During the ensuing conversation **JAKE** *and* **JILL** *pretend to be reading and painting.* **JAKE**, *between stirring up colour on the paint table, tries to paint the word 'Sweet' above 'Fanny' but is unable to get more than the first three or four letters in the space. Each time this happens* **JAKE** *takes a cloth and scrubs out the lettering and tries again.*

JAKE I'm glad Auntie Kelvin remembered to tidy up today. I was afraid that being on the telly would put the good lady above domestic work.

Pause.

JILL I tidied up the place.

JAKE Why?

Pause

JILL I've realised I don't enjoy dirt and mess as much as you made me think. Any objections?

JAKE Why no! If you enjoy tidying up, tidy up. [*he rubs out 'Swee'*] I've never been an enemy of self-expression. [*he contemplates the cleaned canvas*] Be bold, be fearless, free, open, uninhibited. [*he grabs the vase of flowers, raises it to his nose and sniffs*] I hate to be critical but the water in this vase is starting to stink.

JILL *ignores him. He puts the vase down and resumes painting. She shifts her seat so that the back is towards him.* **JAKE** *goes to the paint table and stirs the brush in the paint.*

JAKE Did Mrs Hendon call this morning?

JILL Yes.

JAKE Did you open the door?

JILL No. Kelvin did.

JAKE I hope he paid the rent again.

JILL Of course. [*pause*] Did Mike give you anything?

JAKE Four quid.

JILL It's not enough, is it?

JAKE *has failed again to leave enough room for the final 'T'. He grabs the cloth and wipes the letters out with suppressed fury. His voice is carefully calm.*

JAKE You want me to get a job, don't you?

JILL I think you'd be happier if you got more money.

JAKE *cleans the cloth out, continues wiping and speaks between clenched teeth.*

JAKE So what do you want me to do? Become a bus conductor? And now we're on the topic, why don't you get a job?

JILL Actually I'm starting as a waitress at the Gay Crocodile on Sunday.

JAKE [*stands up and looks at her*] Good! Good! So what's the fuss about?

JILL [*turns a page*] I'm not fussing. Everything's lovely. [*pause*] Kelvin will stop paying for you and I will start so everything's lovely.

JAKE *throws the rag down, steps towards her then stops with fists clenched, breathing hard and staring at the back of her head. She does not move. Though her eyes stare across the book, not at it, and her mouth is apprehensively open. After a moment* **JAKE** *goes to the table and squeezes more colour out, speaking with quiet vehemence.*

JAKE Christ, this is going to be a good evening! This looks like being a really lovely evening.

JILL [*looking down at her book*] Doesn't it?

11: A TELEVISION STUDIO

Darkness, then a spot illuminates **MARY CRANMER** *standing left of stage.*

CRANMER Good evening. This afternoon, by an incredibly narrow majority, the government managed to get the South London Demolition Bill through its final reading in the House of Lords. This is a personal triumph for one man and one man alone: Clifford Dyke, leader of the British Co-ordination Party. We are fortunate enough to have him with us in the studio tonight. He will be interviewed by ... Kelvin Walker.

The spot disappears on **MARY CRANMER, KELVIN** *and* **DYKE** *are lit up, sitting on easy chairs, right, on adjacent sides of a low table.*

KELVIN One thing which puzzles many people Mr Dyke, is why you, as the leader of the Co-ordination Party, are pursuing a policy of Decentralization which you opposed again and again when the Decentralizationists were in power.

DYKE I'm glad you mentioned that, Kelvin. There's nothing puzzling about it really. The British Co-ordination Party is not against Decentralization as such; but it is opposed to unrestricted competitive Decentralization. True this Decentralization can only be efficiently and humanely and safely obtained by a government which is not afraid to co-ordinate, co-ordinate, co-ordinate; both where public and private industry are concerned.

KELVIN What about the British Bingo Board?

DYKE What about the British Bingo Board?

KELVIN When will you make it independent of the Arts Council?

DYKE When both bodies have been fairly co-ordinated by the new Ministry of Leisure and Pleasure. [*jovially*] Ask us another and make it snappy.

KELVIN Can I also make it personal?

DYKE You can try to, it's a free country.

KELVIN Are you not the only member of your Cabinet who has not been to university?

DYKE Quite right. I grew up during the depression. I had to leave school at fifteen to help my father with his milk-delivery business. I've not forgotten those years. I don't want to forget them. [*he stares straight out at the audience*] Some of those viewing tonight will know what I mean. [*he smiles at* **KELVIN**] No, I'm not a university man.

KELVIN Then what qualifies you to lead the country at a time like this?

DYKE You know, we British have always distrusted specialists. We need them, of course, but we need them doing things they know about, and two things a specialist will never understand are leading a party and governing a country. These things can only be done well on a sound basis of ordinary down-to-earth common sense. Right? Now if you ask me why my party chose me to lead them at a time like this and why the British people elected me to govern, I can honestly say I don't know but I hope –

A pause.

KELVIN Yes?

DYKE I hope it is because I'm not easily tired and can keep on at it when a lot of others have had to stop. I hope it is because I can tackle a problem on a basis of common sense rather than specialised prejudice. I hope it's because I'm not afraid to call a spade – or anything else – by its rightful name.

KELVIN To put in three words: your qualifications for Prime Minister are those of energy, intelligence and integrity.

A wave of delight starts to travel across **DYKE**'*s face but is overtaken and quelled by a wave of caution. He smiles lopsidedly and points.*

DYKE You're saying that, remember. Not me.

KELVIN Mr Dyke, thank you very much indeed.

The lights illuminate the whole stage and **DYKE** *leans back, relaxed and beaming.*

DYKE That went very well.

KELVIN [*composed, alert, casual*] I think so.

DYKE You asked me one or two things I hadn't quite expected, but I weathered them, eh? I weathered them.

KELVIN You weathered them.

DYKE New to this game, aren't you?

KELVIN Yes. I started here last Monday.

DYKE Where were you before?

KELVIN My father's grocery.

DYKE *stares at him.*

KELVIN I left school early because my brothers were studying to be Ministers.

DYKE What religion?

KELVIN United Seceders Free Presbyterian.

DYKE My own folk were Anabaptists. What are your politics?

KELVIN I've not had time to form political allegiances as yet. My main preoccupations have been philosophical.

DYKE Nietzsche I suppose?

KELVIN Yes! Yes! Do you read Nietzsche?

DYKE I used to, but he's a bit intoxicating for someone in the public eye. You should get down to something more solid. There's a little book I wrote myself some years ago: 'World Order in an Exploding Universe'. It's out of print, but if you like I'll send you a copy.

KELVIN [*producing a card from his waistcoat pocket*] This is my address.

DYKE *takes it and pockets it.*

DYKE Has Haversack contacted you?

KELVIN Lord Haversack? [**DYKE** *nods*] The newspaper owner? [**DYKE** *nods*] Why should he contact me?

DYKE He likes clever men. He's also looking for a rising name to attach to a new daily he's starting.

KELVIN [*delicately*] I thought you and he were opposed to each other – politically, I mean.

DYKE [*chuckles*] Yes, you've a great deal to learn, but you've no dogmas so you'll learn fast. [*He stands up*] I'll be frank with you, Kelvin. You are a very rare phenomenon, a clever uneducated man who can speak with confidence and conviction. We can use you.

KELVIN [*stands up*] Shall I join your party?

DYKE No, not yet. Take two or three months to get yourself established here, perhaps longer. In the past politicians had to be powerful before they got famous, but in a telly democracy it often works the other way round. Married, are you?

KELVIN N ... no. Not ... not yet.

DYKE Eye on someone?

KELVIN Yes.

DYKE Is she photogenic?

KELVIN Very.

DYKE Is she respectable?

KELVIN She would be if she married me.

DYKE Get her to do it. A respectable photogenic wife is an asset, publicity-wise. Do you play golf?

KELVIN No. But I'm willing to learn!

DYKE Good. We've too few golfers in the party. A Scotch golf-playing ex-grocery assistant with a photogenic wife and a strong TV personality will be worth jewels to us at the next general election. Jewels.

KELVIN And you'll remember to send that book?

DYKE Don't worry, I'll keep in touch.

12: JAKE'S STUDIO, NIGHT

Table, easel, standard lamp, television set, chair, screen and refrigerator are overturned and the floor strewn with bedding, clothes, paints and utensils. **MRS HENDON** *stands mid-stage shouting at* **JAKE** *who sits on the overturned fridge.* **JILL** *lies on the chaise longue, her face against the back of it, looking injured.*

MRS HENDON Tonight! You gotta leave tonight!

JAKE [*wearily*] Alright, we'll leave tomorrow.

MRS HENDON I said tonight! You leave tonight or I call the police! Come back tomorrow for your stuff, come tomorrow with a dustcart if you like, but you're not staying another night and that's flat.

JAKE Be reasonable, Mrs Hendon.

MRS HENDON You tell me to be reasonable! [*an aghast laugh*] That's good! Very good indeed! I'll tell you why I don't want you here tonight. It's the noise but not just the noise. I don't want murder done on my premises.

She goes over to **JILL** *and kneels beside her.* **JAKE** *is contemptuous.*

JAKE Don't be absurdly melodramatic.

MRS HENDON *shakes* **JILL**'*s shoulder gently, saying to her urgently and gently.*

MRS HENDON Are you alright? Is anything wrong Miss?

JILL [*with suppressed hysteria*] Please leave me alone. I'm alright. Please leave me alone.

For a while **MRS HENDON** *is the only person in the room who moves or talks. She rises from the sofa, turns and sees* **KELVIN.**

MRS HENDON Well Mr Walker, you see how matters stand. I gave him fair warning – you'll bear me out – fair warning more than once but he just doesn't care about others any more than a wild ravening beast. Well, he leaves tonight or I call the police. You can stay Mr Walker – and the young lady can stay if she likes, I'm not forcing her out but – [*to* **JAKE**] – You're going! Yes, you're going!

JAKE [*yawns, stretching his arms sideways*] What about the rent?

MRS HENDON *convulsively drags notes from a pocket and shoves them into one of* **JAKE**'*s outspread hands.*

MRS HENDON There's your rent!

Without moving his body or head **JAKE** *passes the money straight to* **KELVIN** *with a sweeping conjuror's movement. He accepts it blankly.* **JAKE** *folds his arms on his chest and observes the empty air in front of him.*

JAKE It's a wonderful feeling, paying a debt.

MRS HENDON Till midnight! You've got till midnight to clear out. After twelve I'm getting the police.

JILL *turns round and sits up, brushing her hair back with one hand and touching the left side of her face with the other. She has a black eye.* **MRS HENDON**'*s mouth and eyes open wide. She glares and points and shouts.*

MRS HENDON Look at her! Look at her face! [*to* **JAKE**] You bloody sadist! [*she leaves*].

JAKE You know I wish she was right Kelvin. If I was a real sadist I might get some fun out of life. Actually I find it a continuous wearying effort to keep Jill a few degrees more miserable than she makes me.

KELVIN *has been standing with the notes in his hand. He thrusts them into his pocket and goes to the chaise longue.*

KELVIN Jill ...

JILL *sits sucking her thumb, ignoring him, staring straight before her.* **KELVIN** *stands looking down at her.* **JAKE** *fishes a kitbag from among the debris and starts picking up and packing various articles of clothing, mostly his own. He talks as he does so.*

JAKE It had to happen sometime. We've been here too long. We've been here far too long. That's been the trouble. Come on, Jill, pull yourself together.

JILL *stands up, feels dizzy and almost collapses.* **KELVIN** *steadies her with a hand which grips her shoulder.* **JAKE** *does not notice. She shakes her head, shrugs* **KELVIN**'*s hand off and sinks down on the chaise longue holding her head.* **JAKE** *goes on talking.*

JAKE Well Kelvin, it's all yours, a room of your own at last. I think I still owe you, what is it? Eight pounds? Well you can have the furniture. It's not all as damaged as it looks. I'm sorry about the refrigerator and so on but Hell, we didn't ask you to bring it here. In fact you didn't ask us if you could bring it here. [*he pauses, squatting, and looks at* **JILL**] Come on, Jill. Get your things together.

JILL *rises and bends painfully to pick up a garment, still holding her head.*

KELVIN Are you really leaving with him?

JILL *pauses, crouching on her heels.* **JAKE** *looks up and then quizzically sideways.*

KELVIN I think you should stay here with me. In fact I want you to. I'm asking you to.

JAKE *grins and resumes his packing.* **JILL** *does not move.* **KELVIN** *turns his back to the room.*

JAKE Well, well, I'll say this for Auntie Kelvin, she's a trier. You've got to hand it to her. [*he glances at* **JILL** *and says gently*] Come on Jill. Bring your things here. I'll pack them.

JILL *stands up slowly, the blouse in her hand.*

KELVIN Yes. He knows when to be gentle.

JILL *pauses.* **JAKE** *bellows at her.*

JAKE I said bring them over here!

JILL [*flinging the blouse down and shouting*] Why the hell should I?

KELVIN *spins round to stare at* **JAKE**, *his face distorted by a vivid grin of soundless triumphant malignant laughter.* **JILL** *has her back to him and does not see.* **JAKE** *sees it and for the first time loses his assurance. He gapes at* **KELVIN** *with a look of almost terror, his hand shoots out to indicate him.*

JAKE His face! Look at his face!

JILL *stares at* **JAKE** *for a moment, then looks at* **KELVIN**. *His face has gone sad, but firm.*

KELVIN [*quietly, sincerely*] Stay with me Jill.

JILL [*staring at* **JAKE** *pleadingly*] Jake, let me stay here. Just for tonight.

JAKE [*staring at her, amazed*] Stay here with *him*!

JILL [*puts her hand to her bruised cheek and suddenly speaks hysterically*] I don't want to go out tonight! I don't want to see anyone!

She sits on the edge of the refrigerator and hides her face in her hands. **JAKE** *recovers his coolness and starts packing the bag again, wrapping the paint tubes in an old shirt before thrusting them into it.*

JAKE Please yourself of course. Where did I put those socks? Yes, Kelvin will be very pleased to have you. But after this I'm finished with you, you understand that don't you? [*he glances at her quickly*] Socks, brushes, shoes, paint ... ah, my flake white. I'm lost without my flake white.

He glances round the floor. **KELVIN** *picks up a paint tube and holds it out to him.* **JAKE** *pauses, staring blankly at* **KELVIN**'*s blank face.*

JAKE Thank you. [*puts it in the bag and looks at* **JILL**] Well Jill, are you coming? [*she doesn't move*] This is your last chance.

KELVIN *steps across the refrigerator and sits beside* **JILL**, *staring at her. She doesn't move.* **JAKE** *pulls tight the strings of the bag and knots them.*

JAKE By the way, Kelvin, there are a few things you ought to know about her. We've not been the only fishes in her little ocean. Ask her about her stepfather sometime.

JILL [*jerks her head up and shouts*] Shut up!

JAKE It's an interesting story –

JAKE *and* **JILL** *raise their voices to shout each other down.* **JILL** *bursts into tears before* **JAKE** *finishes talking,* **KELVIN** *holds her in his arms talking to her while* **JAKE** *finishes.*

JILL Shut up! Don't ... please. Shut up! Please, please, don't.

KELVIN *holds her.*

KELVIN Pay no attention, it doesn't matter, it doesn't matter at all.

JAKE [*at the same time*] Yes, while her mother was in hospital she slept with him. A man supposed to be her father. No wonder she's ashamed to meet her mother. Did you know she was too ashamed even to read her letters.

Silence. **KELVIN** *looks at* **JAKE** *over* **JILL**'*s shoulders, who clings to him, sobbing.*

KELVIN I think you should leave now.

JAKE'*s belligerent glare has disappeared. He takes the bag over his shoulder and moves to the door. He is beginning to feel horror at himself, in the doorway he turns.*

JAKE Jill, I ... I shouldn't have said that.

KELVIN Your feelings do you credit!

JAKE *stares at him dumbly and goes out.* **KELVIN** *rises and helps* **JILL** *over to the chaise longue.*

KELVIN Come over here. You'll be more comfortable. Jill, you'll be alright with me, Jill, I promise it. I promise it.

JILL *slumps into a corner of the chaise longue, her arm hiding her face.* **JAKE**'*s voice comes from outside as if he were shouting from a few yards away. His tone of voice is unemotional and ordinary.*

JAKE Kelvin! Come here a minute!
KELVIN [*looking up*] What is it?
JAKE I forgot to give you something.
KELVIN *gets up and goes to the door and disappears out of sight. A pause, then a scuffle, then a grunt, a crash, and the noise of feet running heavily downstairs and a distant door being slammed. After a silence low laughter is heard.* **KELVIN** *enters chuckling quietly. He holds a bloody handkerchief to his nose.*
KELVIN The bugger punched me! Ha ha ha! Can you beat it? [*approaches* **JILL**, *who has not moved, and still sobs into her arms. He grins at her delightedly and throws his jacket off, then bends and strokes her hair, shaking his head in wonder and delight*] Oh you're so bonny, so bonny! [*he walks away from her, grinning upward to the ceiling and saying cheerfully*] Oh God you're good to me! [*he goes back to her, wiping his nose and staring at her*] Oh Jill, how lovely you are, and to think, to think ... [*he walks away, tearing his tie off and staring ceilingwards*]. God you are grand to me, I approve of you. God, I approve of you! [*He turns and goes to* **JILL**, *laughing excitedly. She does not heed him. He puts an arm under her legs and round her shoulders and tries to lift her up. She lies as he holds her, hands covering her face and weeping. He grunts and carries her to the bed laughing and saying*] What a weight you are! God, what a lovely weight she is!

13: THE STUDIO, DAYS LATER

No trace of **JAKE** *remains: the room is totally suburban. The Venus print is replaced by a framed Tretchikov print of a green negress, the Adam print by a framed Peter Scott view of flying ducks. The chaise longue has bright cushions on it and stands front left with the standard lamp behind and a low coffee table in front. At back left is a television set faced by the easy chair, right.* **KELVIN**'*s jacket lies over the chair arm. On the wall nearby is a circular mirror embellished by gilt curlicues. At front right, a desk with a telephone and swivel chair have replaced the refrigerator.*
MRS HENDON *sits on the chair, her back to the desk, and scribbles in a shorthand notebook. Her clothes make some concession to her new role of secretary.* **KELVIN** *stands mid-stage and addresses the audience in strong, calm tones. He wears a sumptuous dressing gown open over exact collar, tie, waistcoat, well-creased trousers and splendidly polished shoes.*
KELVIN For the past century – except in time of war – our leaders have been content to drift with the current rather than set their face against it. How unlike the politicians of the Victorian times, the Shaftesburies and the Disraelis and Gladstones who were able to make Britain Great because they believed! Capital B at believed, exclamation mark , new paragraph. To those who seek to make Britain Great once more I suggest there is no hope at all in Marxism and Maoism and Gay liberation and Women's liberation and all the other isms and tions which bedevil the age. Belief there must be, but let us abandon mere earthly beliefs and believe once and for all in ...
The light goes out in his countenance. He bites his lower lip and walks thoughtfully round the room watched ardently by **MRS HENDON**.
MRS HENDON [*slowly prompting*] ... and believe, once and for all, in ... ?
KELVIN [*stops, frowns, then lifts an oracular hand*] But let us abandon mere limited earthly beliefs and believe, once and for all, in ... [*he frowns at his shoes then beams at the ceiling*] Belief, itself! Capital B at belief, exclamation mark, end of column.
MRS HENDON [*carried away*] Beautiful words, Mr Walker. Beautiful words.
KELVIN No, Mrs Hendon. Not beautiful words; true words, which are better.
MRS HENDON I stand [*she stands*] corrected. I'll get the girl to type this out and take it round to the Daily Leader by taxi.
KELVIN No need Mrs Hendon. Lord Haversack informs me that you can dictate it to the paper over the telephone. By the way, is our little typist coping?
MRS HENDON Well, barely Mr Walker. I drive her as hard as I can but you told her to use her imagination answering the fan-mail and imagination takes time. And this morning's delivery was twice what it was last week.
KELVIN Then we need an extra typist. Which suggests I must rent another of your rooms. The downstairs office is on the small side.
MRS HENDON All the other rooms are occupied, Mr Walker.
KELVIN By?
MRS HENDON The Irish and the Pakistanis.
KELVIN Get rid of the Irish. If I decide to refer to the racial question it will be useful to have coloured folk under the same roof, no matter which side I take.
MRS HENDON I don't think the Flanegans will go easily, Mr Walker.
KELVIN Is their room furnished or unfurnished?

MRS HENDON Furnished.

KELVIN Then I fail to see the problem. But we'd better avoid unpleasantness. Offer Flanegan thirty pounds to clear out and don't let him raise you over a hundred. I leave the details to you.

MRS HENDON I'll see to it, Mr Walker.

She goes to the door but before disappearing through it **KELVIN**, *standing mid-stage with hands in gown pockets calls out.*

KELVIN Mrs Hendon! [*she turns*] Mrs Hendon, without your secretarial experience and sound business head I would find life very very difficult. It weighs on my conscience that you are doing the work of three women and receiving the salary of one. I am shamelessly exploiting you: to do otherwise would curb my rate of expansion. But these are early days yet. Do you understand me?

MRS HENDON [*comes back into the room*] Oh I *do* understand you, Mr Walker, indeed I do! You see me mother's people were Scotch. From Glasgow.

KELVIN I've never been to Glasgow myself but believe my parents went there on some kind of honeymoon, to see the British Empire Exhibition of 1938. We have a picture of it at home with a picture on it of the Exhibition tower.

MRS HENDON [*seems to grow taller*] Shall I tell you something? On our side board we have an exactly similar tea caddy with an identical picture on it of that self-same exhibition tower.

KELVIN [*quietly musical*] Strange how differences of race and religion and outlook and income can dissolve before the magic of a humble tea caddy. [*he becomes solid and demanding again*] Which reminds me: this is my hour for tea. Instruct Jill to bring it in.

MRS HENDON At once, Mr Walker.

KELVIN *strolls to the desk, removing his gown as he does so. He drapes it over the swivel chair, picks up some letters from the desktop and looks slowly through them.* **JILL** *enters wearing a long gown and carrying a loaded tea tray. She glances at* **KELVIN**, *sees he is engrossed, goes to the coffee table and sets down the tray.* **KELVIN** *puts down the letters, goes to her briskly, takes her by the shoulders, glances up and down her with pleased approval and places a proprietorial kiss on her brow.*

KELVIN I want to buy you another dress tomorrow, a very, very, *very* expensive one this time.

JILL Why?

They sit down on the chaise longue.

KELVIN We've been invited to a garden party at the palace on Saturday.

JILL Buckingham Palace?

KELVIN *nods.*

JILL Will the Queen be there?

KELVIN Of course.

JILL *is excited,* **KELVIN** *calm.*

JILL Will she speak to us?

KELVIN We'll stand in a sort of queue and when we come in front of her she'll say how pleased she is to see us there.

He points to the tea pot. **JILL** *pours.*

JILL [*wistfully*] Aren't you *excited*, Kelvin?

KELVIN Not excited, no, but I'm satisfied. It's another step in the right direction. [**JILL** *sugars the tea*].

KELVIN [*very softly*] Jill, there is another matter that is weighing on my mind. It's hardly worth mentioning but it concerns the tea. I have told you I prefer two spoonfuls of sugar in my cup, and for the last three days you have given me one. I have not referred to it till now, in the hope that it was a temporary aberration, and as I mentioned, the matter is hardly worth mentioning ...

JILL So why mention it?

KELVIN Though not worth mentioning it is worth bearing in mind.

JILL *plonks another spoonful of sugar in and pushes the cup over to him, frowning. Suddenly she smiles and says cheerfully*:

JILL Oh, by the way, Jake phoned this morning. He's going to call in on us!

KELVIN [*stares at her*] You're glad?

JILL Of course! He's been my best friend for years. I like him. Don't you?

KELVIN I have never liked him. Why should I?

JILL Because he liked you! And if he hadn't let you stay with us on the night you arrived here I doubt you'd ever have –

KELVIN Oh I'm grateful to him but to pretend I liked him would be dishonest. [*sips tea*] I hope never to see him again in my life. [*thoughtfully*] Maybe this registry office wedding is a mistake.

JILL [*suddenly alert*] Do you want to postpone it?

KELVIN No, it's too late for that; we have to be married when we meet the Queen. [*he stands up*] But a Church wedding would be more suitable.

JILL Why? You don't believe in God and I don't believe in religion. Why?

KELVIN I never said I didn't *believe* in God. I used to say he was dead. [*matter-of-factly*] But he came alive again, on that night when I obtained you properly ... Do you remember that night?

JILL *puts her left elbow on the table and covers her eyes with her hand.* **KELVIN** *is too rapt in monologue to notice. He starts walking about.*

KELVIN I found myself talking to God in a mood of considerable appreciation, quite voluntarily, or rather involuntarily, because I didn't notice I was doing it at first. It wasn't like praying at home in Glaik, for though my prayer was greeted by silence, it was an attentive silence.

JILL I see.

KELVIN I asked myself, are you getting all this by the power of your individual human will? I didn't believe it. I am not naturally as irresistible and sublime as I became at that moment.

JILL No.

KELVIN *stands facing his reflection in the mirror. He smiles and speaks softly and smugly.*

KELVIN No. There was another power at work in me. From the very beginning I had been no more than a glove upon the hand of her out of whose womb came ice, and who engendered the hoary frost of heaven. [*he shakes his head piously*] It was a humbling experience.

JILL [*vehemently*] For Pete's sake Kelvin, come off it!

KELVIN [*turns on her, remarking mildly*] There are times Jill, when you say things that make you seem a million miles away from me. And it isn't necessary. Other people like me for my divine certainty. They're glad to live in a lawful universe once more, with a real ceiling over their heads. Two hours from now I will be defending God for the first time on BBC television. [*wistfully*] I wish you could come to the studio and see me on the job, Jill. It would do you an awful lot of good.

JILL [*through gritted teeth*] I hate religion and I'm beginning to hate television.

KELVIN [*sombrely*] I am appalled by the spiritual poverty revealed in that remark.

A faint knock. **MRS HENDON** *enters.*

MRS HENDON Mr Whittington is downstairs in the hall, Mr Walker.

JILL *rises gratefully to her feet.*

KELVIN Oh let him come up.

MRS HENDON *goes out.* **KELVIN** *paces up and down with his hands clasped behind his back.*

JILL [*anxiously*] Kelvin! I hope you won't ...

KELVIN Don't worry. I am not a violent man.

JAKE *enters dressed as a bus conductor and carrying a bunch of daffodils.* **KELVIN** *confronts him.*

KELVIN To be perfectly honest Mr Whittington, I don't like seeing you here. Common decency apart, I would have thought that ordinary self-respect would have kept you away. [**JAKE** *nods submissively*] However, my wife ... or she who is to become my wife ... would enjoy a few words with you for old times sake, so I feel reluctantly obliged ...

SOUND: *the phone rings.* **KELVIN** *turns and points an imperious finger at* **JILL**.

KELVIN Jill, do your secretary bit.

JILL *crosses over to the telephone and picks it up.*

JILL Hello? Yes it is ... I see. [*she looks at* **KELVIN**] The head of Amalgamated Independent Television wants to speak to you.

KELVIN [*rubbing his hands together*] The Head of Amalgamated Independent Television. Good ... I'll speak to him from the office.

JILL Hold the line please.

KELVIN [*walking to the door and confronting* **JAKE**] This call will last from ten to fifteen minutes. I hope you will be gone when I return.

He stares at **JAKE** *in the eyes.* **JAKE** *purses his lips gravely, nods, then stands aside to let* **KELVIN** *out.* **JAKE** *stares around the room. He begins to smile. His mouth shapes one or two words but at length he only says:*

JAKE Well, well.

JILL [*smiles ruefully*] Yes, it's all his now.

JAKE [*shrugs*] It's just as well.

JILL There's some warm tea in the pot. Would you like a cup?

She pours some tea into her own empty cup. **JAKE** *walks over to the table and lays the flowers on it.*

JAKE Actually, I just looked in to give you these.

JILL Why?

JAKE I heard you were getting married.

JILL [*passes the cup over*] No, he doesn't waste much time. The cup's dirty but it was mine.

JAKE *sugars and milks it.* **JILL** *takes the flowers and smells them.*

JILL These are lovely. Can you afford them?

JAKE I'm working.

JILL Do you hate it?

JAKE The work? No, I like it. I like any job for the first week or two. It's when I get used to it that I can't stand it. [*Drinks some tea*] Jill, I ... I hope you'll be very happy with him.

JILL*'s face lights up. She speaks breathlessly.*

JILL Do you Jake? [*he nods*] Then you do love me?

JAKE [*curtly*] There's no point in discussing *that*.

JILL *turns her face away to hide her delighted smile, and tries to speak casually.*

JILL I'm not going to marry him.

JAKE [*taken aback*] Why not?

JILL I'm afraid of him.

JAKE Why?

JILL Has it struck you that I'm the first girl he spoke to in London and this is the first house he visited?

JAKE What about it?

JILL I've started thinking that no matter what girl he spoke to first he'd have married her, no matter what house he'd visited he'd have got to own it.

JAKE Come off it, Jill, that's impossible; it's mad.

JILL I know, but when I'm with him the most insane things seem perfectly ordinary, that's what's so frightening. There's something wrong with his way of looking at the world. It wasn't too bad when he talked about philosophy, but now he's gone on to religion and it's worse, much worse. I don't think he's properly human.

JAKE Is anybody properly human? I know I'm not.

JILL Kelvin thinks he's the only one who is. And it makes him ... [*she hesitates*] ... horribly strong.

JAKE [*staring down at his shoes*] Jill, you know how hard it is for me to apologise. Well, when we had that last fight I said things ... did things ...

SOUND: *a knocking at the door.*

JILL Stay there Jake!

She takes a step towards the door. **MRS HENDON** *enters.*

MRS HENDON Sorry to interrupt but Mr McKellar has called to see Mr Walker ...

HECTOR MCKELLAR *strolls in.*

MRS HENDON Mr Walker will see you as soon as possible, but he hasn't much spare time these days, Mr McKellar. Works like a Trojan, he does.

MCKELLAR [*glancing around the room*] Yes I know that. [*to* **JILL**] Hello.

MRS HENDON *scowls at* **JAKE** *who has made himself comfortable on the chaise longue and goes out.*

JILL How do you do? Would you like to sit down?

MCKELLAR I would. I will. [*goes to the easy chair, sits down and lights a cigarette*] I take it you are Kelvin's fiancée.

JILL [*indicating* **JAKE**] We are both friends of Kelvin.

MCKELLAR Hm. How do you find him these days?

JILL I'm sorry?

MCKELLAR Have you noticed any changes in his mental condition?

JILL What a very rude question.

MCKELLAR I apologise. I was only wondering if he was as super-confident in private life as he has become in public.

JILL [*defensively*] Yes. He is.

MCKELLAR You must find it a strain.

KELVIN *enters, smiling quietly to himself. He lifts his eyebrows on seeing* **MCKELLAR**.

KELVIN Hello McKellar.

MCKELLAR I called in to take you over for the show.

KELVIN Quite unnecessary. I've ordered a taxi. But I don't doubt the thought was kindly meant.

MCKELLAR Not altogether. I'd like a ... private word with you first.

He glances at **JILL** *and* **JAKE** *who stand up.*

KELVIN Jill, go to the office, cancel the taxi and stay there. I must speak to you before I leave. [*he stares at* **JAKE**] Goodbye Mr Whittington.

JAKE [*comes over to him saying*] Kelvin I just want to tell you that ...

KELVIN *Goodbye*, Mr Whittington!

JAKE *goes out with* **JILL**, *smiling and shaking his head.* **KELVIN** *watches them go with a slight frown, then turns to face* **MCKELLAR** *who has stubbed out his cigarette and stood up.*

MCKELLAR You're going too fast for us, Kelvin.

KELVIN Who do you mean by 'us' Hector?

MCKELLAR In the narrow sense of the word I mean the British Broadcasting Corporation. In the widest sense of the word I mean the British public.

KELVIN But I'm not travelling too fast for the British public. Most of it is right behind me. You need have no fears for my popularity, Hector! After all, I'm only advocating a return to a few of the moral principles which almost everyone accepted up to twenty or thirty years ago.

MCKELLAR You're forgetting something. When you joined

the BBC I assigned you to a special role. You were to undermine the bigwigs but you were to do it irresponsibly, from no particular standpoint –

KELVIN That kind of undermining changes nothing Hector.

MCKELLAR Exactly! That's why I encourage it. But your column in the Daily Leader discloses a very definite standpoint. And your television appearances have begun to back it up.

KELVIN For example?

MCKELLAR Your interview last night with the Minister for Birth Control?

KELVIN Well?

MCKELLAR There was no call whatsoever to ask about her former marriage. It was irrelevant to the issue.

KELVIN I think not! It is a shame and a scandal that family planning should be under the guidance of one who has shown contempt for the Holy Institution of Matrimony. Making that plain isn't politics – it's common sense.

MCKELLAR What about your campaign to drive the body out of advertising?

KELVIN [*correcting him*] To drive the Divine Image out of advertising, Hector.

MCKELLAR I'm as Scottish as you are, Kelvin! I am perfectly aware that man and – to a lesser extent – woman, have been created in the image of God!

KELVIN Then it doesn't offend you, Hector, that this body – [*slaps his chest*] – The Image of the Creator! The finest thing we can know in the whole world! – is being degraded into bait for shopkeepers?

MCKELLAR Don't try to teach me about God! I'm second to nobody in my respect for Him. He's a good man in His rightful place: but drag Him down to the streets and He has us at each other's throats. He becomes a disaster and an embarrassment!

KELVIN Only to the Ungodly Hector! [*he points an accusing finger so near* **MCKELLAR***'s nose that he becomes embarrassed and moves towards his desk*] Women's liberation are with me on this as well as the Mary Whitehouse lot.

MCKELLAR And British Industry is against you!

KELVIN [*sits on the desk edge and speaks simply and kindly*] Industry is not sacred, Hector. It exists to give us coats, shoes and ovens and cars. If it cannot do so without trespassing on our most heartfelt instincts, I'm sorry, I must oppose it.

MCKELLAR [*stands erect and speaks loudly and formally*] I have been empowered to offer you a salary increase of five thousand a year: on condition that you down your column for the Haversack press, discontinue these public crusades, and content yourself with straightforward work as a BBC interviewer.

KELVIN [*nodding*] And of course you would make sure I interviewed no-one of importance whose ideas differed from my own.

MCKELLAR [*nodding*] That's right.

KELVIN [*bending his head to hide a smile*] I'm not in this game for money, Hector.

MCKELLAR [*relaxes, chuckles, and brings out a cigarette*] Good for you man. I told them you wouldn't be bought. [*he lights the cigarette*].

KELVIN [*puzzled*] If my services are embarrassing the BBC, Hector, I can always look for other channels.

MCKELLAR [*agreeably*] Of course you can! We'll discuss that another time: tomorrow perhaps. Tonight we're giving you a whole hour, a full hour of viewing time to speak out for your ideas. Do well tonight and there'll be no holding you ... [*he smiles*] ... Will there?

KELVIN Who's the chairman tonight?

MCKELLAR Me.

KELVIN You?

MCKELLAR Yes. It's years since I appeared on the box but after all, this is a special occasion. Remember, we're both lads from Glaik. I know how your mind works better than anyone else in these latitudes. [*he glances at his watch*] We'd better leave.

KELVIN *lifts the phone and dials one digit.*

KELVIN Come here, Jill.

He lays down the phone, goes to the mirror and straightens his tie and waistcoat. **JILL** *enters followed by* **JAKE.** **KELVIN** *calls over his shoulder.*

KELVIN Earlier this evening I asked you to come to the studio with me. You refused. Now I order you to come.

JILL *stares at him, half-amused and half-indignant.*

JILL Order me to come?

KELVIN Yes.

He picks up his jacket from the chair, slips it on and buttons it up before the mirror. **MCKELLAR** *moves to* **JILL***'s side.*

MCKELLAR [*quietly*] He may be glad of your company before the evening ends.

JILL What do you mean?

MCKELLAR The most successful of us sometimes need a little disinterested friendship.

He goes to the door. **KELVIN** *turns and stares at* **JILL**.

KELVIN Well?

JILL [*defiantly*] I'll come if Jake comes with us!

KELVIN [*stares from* **JILL** *to* **JAKE** *and then says shortly*] Suit yourselves.

He walks from the room followed by **MCKELLAR**. **JAKE** *and* **JILL** *face each other enquiringly. He offers his arm. She takes it and they walk out together.*

14: LIVE SPACE

A spot illuminates **MARY CRANMER** *extreme left.*

CRANMER [*feedback*] the television programme which examines the makers of television. The subject of our programme tonight is Kelvin Walker. Our chairman is: Hector McKellar.

The spotlight vanishes and lights an area mid-stage where three chairs stand round a low table, one at the back and one at each side. **KELVIN** *sits on the right,* **HECTOR MCKELLAR** *faces him on the left.*

MCKELLAR Good evening. A notable feature of the last few weeks has been the rise to public eminence of Kelvin Walker, partly through his column in Lord Haversack's Daily Leader, but mainly through his work as a television interviewer. In the studio tonight we have parents, teachers, psychiatrists, lawyers, clergymen and members of parliament, all keen critics of Kelvin's preachings, and in the course of the informal discussion I intend to call each one forward to give him a fair crack of the critical whip. But I want to begin myself by asking Kelvin to admit that the movements for which he speaks are all reactionary movements.

KELVIN [*purses his lips and shakes his head*] No. Oh no.

MCKELLAR [*raising an eyebrow*] You don't admit it?

KELVIN No. I insist upon it. When you say 'reactionary' you mean old-fashioned. It puzzles me that Victorian ornament and architecture have become popular again but people are ashamed of Victorian morality.

MCKELLAR So they should be. Victorian morality was a cruel and punitive morality.

KELVIN A morality that is unwilling to kill murderers and flog thieves does not deserve the name.

MCKELLAR Do you really believe that criminals can be reformed by corporal punishment?

KELVIN Of course not! But we don't punish the wicked in order to reform them – that's almost impossible – we do it to make the righteous feel more sure of themselves. Savage punishment is a way of asserting the difference between good and bad. By abandoning it we have come to feel that good and bad people are alike, so both sorts are less sure of themselves. The wicked accuse the good of treating them badly, the good beat their breasts and beg forgiveness. Bringing back the birch will restore the self-esteem of everybody.

MCKELLAR Are you suggesting that criminals want savage punishment?

KELVIN Indeed I am! People behave badly because they want to feel superior. A thief must feel very superior and cunning when he steals something. If you catch him and treat him as if he had a mental illness you rob him of his self-respect.

MCKELLAR Do you apply that rule to the education of children?

KELVIN [*nodding*] Of course. If children are never punished they never feel loved. My own father ...

He hesitates.

MCKELLAR [*softly*] Yes?

KELVIN My own father was, is, I mean, a very stern man. As a boy I was grateful for it. I have lived to be glad of it.

MCKELLAR [*raising a forefinger*] Let's just follow up this line of thought. Your father is with us tonight in the studio ... Will you come forward Mr Walker?

WALKER *comes into the circle of light wearing a black coat and hat like* **KELVIN** *in Scene 1. He also carries a black umbrella, and stares at* **MCKELLAR**, *ignoring his aghast son totally.*

KELVIN [*feebly*] Father!

MCKELLAR Sit down, Mr Walker.

KELVIN Father, I'm glad to see you!

WALKER *sits with the umbrella vertical between his knees and black gloved hands on the handle.* **KELVIN**'*s gestures are those of an anxious child, eager yet fearful, trying to attract a parent's attention.*

MCKELLAR Mr Walker, you have heard how highly your son esteems you. What do you think of him?

WALKER He is a hypocrite.

KELVIN I'm glad to see you father!

He is ignored.

MCKELLAR Indeed! Why do you think so?

WALKER I have seen him bend the knee at family prayers, and bow his head and pretend to murmur words with his mouth, and all the time there was nothing in his heart but emptiness and rebellion. I did not remark upon it for remark would have done no good, but if ever a man was outcast from the Godly and their ways that man was Kelvin Walker.

KELVIN Father, I've changed.

MCKELLAR What did you do about this, Mr Walker?

WALKER Naturally I did all I could for him in the circumstances. I deprived him of the education that would have given his viciousness scope. By giving him a shilling a week pocket money I prevented him visiting the billiard-saloons and picture houses and drinking dens to which his spirit would have naturally led him. Nonetheless he contrived to bypass these precautions by visiting a public library and battening upon God knows what pernicious rubbish. Then one day, in circumstances I am ashamed to mention, he left home without a word of warning. This was the last I knew of him till some days ago several customers congratulated me ... *congratulated* me on my son's appearance on television. But I had always known there was no good in the lad.

KELVIN Father!

He is ignored again and starts biting his nails.

MCKELLAR Mr Walker, what is your objection to your son appearing on television?

WALKER Am I right in thinking it may make him a powerful man?

MCKELLAR The signs point that way.

WALKER Power, Mr McKellar, can only be used well by men with faith. Understand me, I am not a bigot. Their faith need not be my faith. They can have the faith in the need to make a law or change a law, or fight a war or stop a war; if they have faith in something outside themselves they will only do the world the normal amount of harm. [*raises voice, jeering*] My son has only faith in his own desires! He is a hollow shell stuffed with nothing but self-conceit and driven onward by the winds of pride!

KELVIN [*driven to desperate insistence*] But father, I've changed. I'm not *wicked* any more!

A pause. Then **WALKER** *looks at* **KELVIN** *for the first time and speaks almost gloatingly.*

WALKER What about the twenty-five pounds you stole from me?

KELVIN [*eagerly*] I can repay it! I can repay it today!

WALKER [*barks harshly*] And the jewellery? The few poor trinkets that your mother treasured and that I treasured in remembrance of her?

KELVIN I have the pawn tickets here, in my wallet! I can redeem them anytime. Anytime.

WALKER [*turns and talks calmly to* **MCKELLAR**] Do you know, Mr McKellar, I have never been inside a pawn shop in my life? I have been poor, I came from a poor family. But my parents taught me to shun a pawn shop as I could shun a brothel. And yet my son, who had wanted for nothing in the way of food and clothing and warmth and a clean bed, is not ashamed to pass his mother's few poor trinkets over a pawn shop counter in return for ... how much money did they give you?

KELVIN [*crying wildly*] I needed that money. And my mother wouldn't have minded. She loved me. She would have given it to me.

WALKER [*thunderously*] I love you Kelvin! Why else am I destroying you like this? [*firmly, clearly*] To stop you destroying yourself! What right have you to power who neither fears God nor loves man? A grocer's assistant is all you're fit for. When you've learned humility you may try for something else. But not before.

KELVIN*'s mouth and eyes are wide open, the light on him grows unnaturally bright. He produces a moan by drawing air into his lungs and then, beneath* **MCKELLAR** *and his father's unblinking regard, presses his face down between his knees, folds arms tight around legs, and tries to compress himself into an egg. He succeeds as far as this is humanly possible.* **MCKELLAR** *stares, startled, then reaches out and touches the egg's shoulder.*

MCKELLAR Kelvin! ... Kelvin! [*no response. He bites his underlip, raises his eyebrows and faces the audience*] This comes as a shock. It appears that Kelvin, like many greater men, is less virtuous than he likes to pretend. But I am sure I speak for all of us that in losing our respect he has certainly gained our sympathy. [*he glances sideways at the egg*] It seems impossible – indeed unnecessary – to continue further. I suppose Presentation, with its usual thoroughness, will be able to fill in the remaining forty minutes with a little light relief. However, there will be a discussion of tonight's 'Feedback' on Late Night Line Up at 11.20 after the news. Good evening ladies and gentlemen.

The light goes up over the stage, revealing **MARY CRANMER** *standing to the right and* **JILL** *rushing forward from the left, followed more* *slowly by* **JAKE**. **WALKER** *remains seated, gravely regarding his son over the umbrella handle.* **MCKELLAR** *stands to confront* **JILL**, *who is nearly weeping.*

JILL You did that deliberately! You meant that to happen!

MCKELLAR Yes. And frankly I wish the job could have been done by somebody else.

JAKE You're a filthy bastard McKellar!

MCKELLAR [*nodding*] A necessary breed, Mr Whittington. [*He looks at* **WALKER** *and points to the egg*] You'll see to him?

WALKER [*nodding*] That's right.

MCKELLAR [*walks across and pats* **KELVIN***'s shoulder*] Never mind Kelvin. Those who live by the interview shall fall by the interview. The falling can be drawn out over years. In the long run you may feel grateful to me. [*He goes off left to* **MARY CRANMER** *as he nears her*] Well, Mary?

CRANMER [*as they disappear*] It was terribly embarrassing, Hector, but bloody good television.

WALKER [*stands, goes to his son and gently shakes his right shoulder*] It's all right son. They've done with you now

KELVIN [*his voice is a high, feeble and wild*] Who's there?

WALKER All but two of them.

KELVIN Which two?

JILL *kneels at his side.*

JILL It's us Kelvin! Don't *worry* Kelvin! Nothing *really* dreadful has happened.

Slowly **KELVIN** *brings his head up, stares at her blankly and then at his father.*

WALKER [*quietly firm*] You can come home with me. You ran away remember? I didn't turn you out.

KELVIN *stands up, biting his thumb.* **JILL** *rises with him, astonished.*

JILL Kelvin! You aren't going with *him?*

KELVIN *stares at her.* **JAKE** *comes to her side.*

JAKE Listen mate! You've been made a fool of and maybe you've lost your job. But that happens to everyone sometimes. You'll get other jobs.

He flicks the lapel of his uniform.

JILL Yes, stay here! Stay with us! What do newspapers and silly speeches on television matter? All that matters is freedom! What life will you have with that – [*points at* **WALKER**] – poisonous old man!

WALKER *grins.* **KELVIN** *stares from her to* **JAKE** *and back, the says coldly and quietly:*

KELVIN *You* don't love me.

JILL [*whispers*] I'm sorry.

KELVIN [*harshly*] Leave me. You understand *nothing.* Nothing at all!

She stares back, injured in the tenderest part of her: her wish to help. **JAKE** *takes her hand.*

JAKE Come on, Jill. There's nothing we can do.

He leads her out with a puzzled shake of the head at **KELVIN**, *who had begun to walk abstractedly up and down, snapping his fingers and muttering passionately to himself.*

KELVIN What did He mean by it? I could be happy if I knew what He meant by it.

WALKER He meant to drive you out of public life.

KELVIN Who are you referring to?

WALKER Your boss.

KELVIN Which one?

WALKER Hector McKellar of course.

KELVIN I was referring to God.

WALKER [*startled*] Kelvin! Are you telling me that you ... believe?

KELVIN [*stops, facing his father*] Have you not read my words in the newspapers?

WALKER Indeed! And they would have been greatly to my taste had I not thought them the words of a graceless hypocrite.

KELVIN You were wrong, father. Divine Grace was granted me with the first big success of my career. How else could I have done so well? Without faith I would have been as sounding brass or tinkling cymbal.

WALKER Without charity.

KELVIN What?

WALKER The apostle said a want of charity made us brazen.

KELVIN [*shaking his head*] I'm sure that is a mistranslation. Charity has very little practical value. But with faith we can move mountains.

WALKER *is struck by this.*

WALKER Kelvin! *I* have sometimes thought that.

They stare at each other. **WALKER** *strokes his chin.*

WALKER When I chose to assist in your public demolition I assumed you were still on your way to everlasting fire. I may have been ... hasty.

KELVIN You talk like a child father. You did not choose to demolish me: you were chosen to demolish me, by a superior power. Surely you! a session clerk! must *recognise* that. [**KELVIN** *steps away then turns*] Everything that happens in the world is part of a plan. Everyone in the world is labouring upon that plan. The ignorant labour unconsciously. But in every age a chosen few feel that plan in their very bones. For several weeks I have been the biggest bulldozer on the divine building site. Nothing could withstand me. Surely, *surely*, it is no part of the eternal purpose to bury this splendid piece of machinery – [*smites his chest with clenched fist*] – in the mud of a second-rate province like Scotland!

His father comes to him.

WALKER Kelvin! What if God has *work* for you in Scotland? [**KELVIN** *stares at him*] You call us a second-rate province but once, during the Reformation, we felt ourselves a chosen people. We had a leader, then.

Pause.

KELVIN [*thoughtfully*] A chosen people. [*he twice plucks his lower lip with his forefinger*] Father: remind me: what precisely are my assets?

WALKER Assets?

KELVIN *nods.*

WALKER Well, I suppose you still have your column in the Haversack press. And such is the corruption of the time that your performance tonight will make even more people keen to read it.

KELVIN Go on.

WALKER The BBC is determined to drop you but you have broken no contract so they will be obliged to make a fairly big settlement. Meanwhile your notoriety will shut no gates where other TV networks are concerned.

KELVIN [*sighs*] Then all is not lost.

WALKER [*severely*] But you will have to repent!

KELVIN I shall do it publicly, with heartrending thoroughness. Yes. The repentant sinner. There have been flimsier foundations to a new career. After all, John Knox began as a Roman Catholic priest.

WALKER Saint Paul was an orthodox Jew.

KELVIN Moses was an Egyptian prince.

WALKER All three started out by oppressing their own people.

KELVIN But they repented.

WALKER [*nodding*] Publicly.

KELVIN And if ... if I returned to Scotland, what would they think of me?

WALKER You would be welcomed. You've made a pile of money but you've also made a fool of yourself. The one will enable them to forgive you the other.

KELVIN And vice versa?

WALKER And vice versa.

KELVIN [*stares up into the air*] Father! I'm beginning to feel it in my bones again.

WALKER The plan?

KELVIN Yes. Yes I must return to Glaik and put my hand to the plough.

WALKER [*surprised*] Return to Glaik?

KELVIN It's as good a place to start as any: halfway between Aberdeen, where the oil is, and Glasgow, where the television is. [*he is struck by a thought*] I take it you are with me on this?

WALKER I am! If your intentions are those of a believer.

KELVIN I'll have no trouble convincing you on that score. I may even enter the ministry. Or perhaps not. It might impede me when I come to handle the Catholic question. Aye. And it may be necessary, later on, to make elbow room for ourselves by detaching Scotland from the British Isles.

WALKER [*worried*] Geographically?

KELVIN [*smiling*] No father. Politically. Don't worry. I haven't lost my grip on reality.

WALKER *strikes the ferule of his umbrella to the floor.*

WALKER There is one matter outstanding, however. I gather that while in London you've been living in a state of intimacy with a young lady, the same young lady you sent forth from this place with a flea in her lug. The past is the past, but you will get no support from me if you indulge any further in lawless liaisons.

KELVIN [*raises a self-deprecating hand*] It's all right! I've sufficiently plumbed the fickle depths of the female heart. I shall have no further carnal knowledge of woman before I have bound one legally to me. [*he stretches his arms*] So! My little adventure in London has been no more than a rehearsal, a sketch for the larger design to be executed in my native land. Well, I am not sorry I came here. I learned a lot by it. It will enable me to do ... [*looks upward*] ... Him ... a great deal of good.

For a moment **KELVIN** *and his father reverently contemplate an invisible something a few feet above their heads.* **KELVIN***'s expression changes for a moment from the smug assurance to the lost lonely look sometimes seen on his face earlier. His father speaks softly.*

WALKER Amen!

KELVIN [*pulls himself together and says briskly*] Come, father!

He marches out, his father following.

BEFORE KELVIN WALKER was networked in 1968 I received a letter from Stewart Conn, director of Scottish BBC radio drama, asking if I would write a half-hour play for a new series he was producing. My immediate reaction was, "Impossible!" I had never before written a play to order, did not think that I could, doubted that anyone could. This proved my ignorance of how imagination works. Before politely rejecting Stewart's invitation I remembered a domestic drama that unfolded when my wife and I sublet a room in our rented flat to the MacFees, a tinker family. The play was written fast, when I decided to make the landlords a kindly couple like my aunt and uncle. Stewart, having received it, posted it back with a letter saying he did not know if it was meant to be comic or serious, but would certainly broadcast it if I made some changes suggesting how it should be taken. This annoyed me. The gravest things, when I seriously consider them, strike me as also comic, an attitude that will always shape my art. Before writing a letter refusing to change *Quiet People* in any way, it occurred to me that Stewart had never read anything of mine before; perhaps he had been made uncomfortable by my unfamiliar style, but the style would be more familiar if he read the play a second time. So I changed two words, deleted a third, sent it back to him with a letter thanking him for his advice and hoping he would now find the play satisfactory. He did.

Between 1968 and 1977 I wrote six broadcast radio plays, five of them produced by Stewart Conn. Later I adapted some of these for stage and television performances, but *Quiet People* worked best as a radio play, and is printed here as one.

Footsteps on stairs. A baby whimpers.

MRS BROWN Wheesht John. Wheesht.

SOUND: *a doorbell chimes musically. Faint footsteps. A door is opened.* **MRS MITCHEL** *speaks briskly.*

MRS MITCHEL Yes?

MRS BROWN Is it you letting a room?

MRS MITCHEL [*cautiously*] Yes?

MRS BROWN Could I mibby see it?

MRS MITCHEL Well ... we had only thought of letting it to a single person ...

MRS BROWN It didn't say that on the postcard in the shop window.

MRS MITCHEL We did say it was a single room ...

MRS BROWN Could I see it then?

BABY Bah waw wah!

MRS BROWN Hush John.

MRS MITCHEL Oh certainly you can look at it.

Footsteps. A door is opened.

MRS MITCHEL You can see it's on the small side.

MRS BROWN But that's a double bed! ... My man would like it here. It would suit us just fine!

MRS MITCHEL I'm afraid a married couple and a baby is more than we bargained for. This is the first time we've ever let a room. My husband just retired you see ... We're very quiet people ...

MRS BROWN Oh we're quiet people ourselves ...

MRS MITCHEL But a family is more than we bargained for.

MRS BROWN Missus, I'll tell you the truth. We're staying just now in a basement in Garngash. And it's damp, terrible damp. For the baby's sake we've got to get out soon, you see, and nice rooms like this are that hard to come by.

MRS MITCHEL Well ... But you see ... [*she feels the matter beyond her and calls*] Tom! Tom!

A door opens.

MR MITCHEL What is it?
MRS MITCHEL This lady here ...
MRS BROWN Mrs Brown. Ruby Brown.
MRS MITCHEL She's called about the room, she's married with a baby you see ...
MR MITCHEL Oh that's too many ...
MRS MITCHEL But they're in a room just now, a basement that lets in the damp ...
MRS BROWN Honestly Mister when it rains the wet just streams down the wall, the baby is aye getting colds and when we complained to the factor he said if we didn't like it we could leave and now we've only two days to get another room and nobody wants you if you've a wean. Honestly mister this would suit us fine.
BABY Bah wah waw ...
MRS BROWN Quiet John hushushush.
MR MITCHEL Well. Since you're desperate ... [*pause*] Supposing we let you the room for a fortnight. That would give you time to find somewhere more suitable.
MRS BROWN Oh that's nice of you! Can we move in tonight?
MR MITCHEL Well ... [*pauses*].
MRS MITCHEL Yes I suppose so.
MR MITCHEL Until you find something more suitable.
MRS BROWN My husband will be that relieved. Honestly I don't think we'll ever find a place more suitable than this. We'll be back about seven then, so I won't say cheerio.
Door slams. A pause.
MRS MITCHEL She didn't ask to see the kitchen.
MR MITCHEL It's a small room for two people.
MRS MITCHEL I wonder what her man does?
MR MITCHEL Three, if you count the baby.
MRS MITCHEL I told her it was more than we bargained for.
MR MITCHEL Still, it won't be for more than a fortnight. I made that clear didn't I?
MRS MITCHEL I'm not sure she took it like that.
MUSIC BRIDGE. *A door is opened.*
MR BROWN Oh, Mr Mitchel!
MR MITCHEL Yes Mr Brown?
MR BROWN Would you step in here a moment? I'd like a word with you while the women are at the shops.
Door closes.
MITCHEL Well?
BROWN Sit down. Go on. Sit down there.
MITCHEL Well?
BROWN That's right. Now then.
Glugging of liquid poured from bottle.
BROWN There you are.
MITCHEL My my!
BROWN And one for me.
Glug glug glug.
MITCHEL I don't drink normally at this time of day Mr Brown ...
BROWN I'm called Sandy.
MITCHEL Well ... here's to you, Sandy.
BROWN And here's to you.
Clink of glasses.
MITCHEL You wanted a word with me?
BROWN Just a social word. We've been nearly two weeks here ...
MITCHEL Nearly three.
BROWN Three? So it is. Three. And the women seem to get on alright but when we two pass in the lobby we hardly nod to each other and that's been worrying me. I said to Ruby, is there something wrong with me? And she said no but you were a very refined sort of man ...
MITCHEL Oh but! ...
BROWN No no no! She's right enough, and I know I'm a rough diamond. But I'm not ashamed of it so today I said to myself, I'll ask Mr Mitchel in for a drink. And if he refuses, we'll leave.
MITCHEL [*mildly*] This is nice whisky.
BROWN Malt. It's all I drink. When I can afford it.
MITCHEL I take it you're a dealer in used cars Mr ... Sandy.
Brown is interested.
BROWN Why do you think that?
MITCHEL When you first came here you parked an old dormobile outside the close. Then it was ... I don't know the name ...
BROWN A Bentley.
MITCHEL And now it's a breadvan.
BROWN I mostly deal in scrap.
MITCHEL Do you work for a yard?
BROWN No, I work for myself. I travel all over. This morning I finished breaking up a tractor in a field near Lanark. I'd passed it a few times in the past year, it had a sort of abandoned look so a couple of days back I went

to the farmer and offered three pounds ten for it. It was no use to him.

MITCHEL And that was worth your while?

BROWN Not as much as I expected. There's more to breaking up an old tractor that you'd think. I'd to get my brother-in-law to help me. The most I ever made was at a factory near Kilmarnock. We'd been got in to strip it down and we tore out hundreds of feet of lead pipe and copper pipe and those big electric cables with the copper cores. And when we'd got it out I went to the manager and do you know what he said?

MITCHEL No.

BROWN "How much do I owe you." He expected to pay *me* for removing it, I expected to pay him for getting it.

MITCHEL What did you tell him?

BROWN I said "I think we'll just call it quits."

MITCHEL I suppose that was quite honest of you. So you're your own master.

BROWN Aren't you?

MITCHEL Yes, since I retired I suppose I am.

BROWN You don't look very old ...

MITCHEL Oh I'm not sixty yet. But I'd trouble with my heart so had to retire earlier than usual and don't qualify for the full pension. That's why we decided to let this room.

BROWN Will I tell you something?

MITCHEL Yes?

BROWN The wife and I have stayed in a lot of places, shifting around as we do. But the day after we came here I said to Ruby, since coming to the Mitchels I feel safe. For the first time in my life I feel safe.

MITCHEL [*after a pause*] It's hard not to take that as a compliment.

BROWN Well take it as a compliment!

MITCHEL I'll have to go now.

BROWN Have another glass.

MITCHEL No no no. My head's nearly humming with the first. But I'm glad you like it here. And my wife fairly dotes on your wee boy. So ...

Door opens.

BROWN By the way I meant to ask you something ...

MITCHEL Yes?

BROWN A wee favour. My brother-in-law, Jimmy, he was helping me on the tractor you know and he'll be helping me on other jobs. But he hasn't found a room yet. I was wondering, could we put him up here for a night or two? Just while he's looking around. He can sleep on the hearth rug. You'll hardly see him.

MITCHEL [*after a pause Mitchel speaks in a bleak dispirited voice*] I've a camp bed in the lobby cupboard. You can borrow it if it's just for the night.

BROWN That's very decent of you.

MITCHEL As long as it's just for the night.

BROWN Don't worry, he's a quiet bloke.

MUSIC BRIDGE *a door is shut abruptly. Mitchel speaks. He is agitated.*

MITCHEL Jean!

MRS MITCHEL Yes?

MITCHEL I've just come from the bathroom and I'm sure I saw that brother-in-law in the lobby ...

MRS MITCHEL Jimmy?

MITCHEL Yes. I'm sure I saw Jimmy listening outside their door. He stood up and went in when he saw me but I'm sure of it.

MRS MITCHEL Yes he often does it.

MITCHEL Often?

MRS MITCHEL Yes. Ruby was telling me he often listens outside the door before coming into the room to hear if they're talking about him.

MITCHEL Why?

MRS MITCHEL I don't think they like him.

MITCHEL No wonder. The room isn't twelve foot square and two men, a woman and a wean have shared it for a fortnight. It beats me where he sleeps. I lent him the camp bed and got it back next day with the canvas split down the middle ...

MRS MITCHEL He's a big heavy man remember ...

MITCHEL So where does he sleep?

MRS MITCHEL [*mildly*] It's none of our business Tommy.

MITCHEL [*calmed*] No. I suppose not. But why don't they tell him to leave?

MRS MITCHEL Well he's Ruby's brother. And Sandy employs him. And after all we've nothing to complain of.

MITCHEL No he isn't noisy or disorderly.

A sharp "rata tatat" on the door.

MITCHEL Who on earth at this hour ... ?

A door is opened. A slightly drink-slurred voice says:

JIMMY Canna come in?

Pause

MITCHEL You seem to have done it.

Jimmy is not offended.

JIMMY Canna sit down? Ooooh that's better. Good tae get the weight off yer feet. Ackshully I came to ask you a wee favour – what was it? – Oh yes, coulda buy a couple of fags off ye?

MRS MITCHEL [*cool*] Neither my husband nor myself smoke I'm glad to say. We cannae afford to.

JIMMY [*affably*] Still, I like your style of living. A three-piece suite! Television! Wall lights! Real plastic flowers! And a piano. That's nice. I like a good tune now and then. Would one of youse care to oblige?

MRS MITCHEL Neither my husband nor myself play I'm afraid. Tom, I'm going to bed now. I trust you will be following shortly.

Door opens and closes.

JIMMY My, your wife's a real lady. A real lady. By the way, have ye such a thing as a fag on you?

MITCHEL No.

JIMMY And she keeps ... the room ... she keeps ... the room lot bettern that slut my sister keeps hers. Credit where credit is due. Of course she's got space tae be a lady in. Ye need space. Look, I don't need a fag. Fag ends will do. Surely you've a few wee fag ends hid away in an ashtray somewhere? I could roll a fag myself out of them. "Give me the tools" I say, "and I will finish the job".

MITCHEL I'm sorry. I don't smoke. And now if you don't mind I'm going to my bed.

JIMMY Aye. It's late. [*wistfully*] Would ye mind atall if I mibby dossed down for the night on your settee here? [*he becomes crestfallen*] No. I can *see* ye would mind. [*he revives and becomes affable again*] So I'd better be on my merry way, eh?

MITCHEL Yes. Goodnight.

A door is opened.

JIMMY Goodnight!

A door is closed. **MUSIC BRIDGE**

A knock, firm but discreet, on a door. The door is opened after an interval. **MR MITCHEL** *speaks determinedly but quietly.*

MITCHEL I'd like a private word with you Mr Brown.

BROWN It's alright Tom. Come right in. He's not here just now.

MITCHEL I've come about your brother-in-law.

BROWN I was expecting this. Wasn't I, Ruby?

MITCHEL I'm afraid he'll have to leave.

BROWN And there's nobody more glad than I am to hear you say those words Tom. I don't know how you've stood him so long. Frankly, we're sick of him, aren't we, Ruby?

MRS BROWN Quite right. I'm his sister, Mr Mitchel, and he's my brother, but I'm not ashamed to say I'm ashamed to say it, and you can tell him to clear out any time you like.

BROWN And the sooner the better.

MITCHEL But ... I mean ... Why should I ask him to leave?

BROWN Well I think he'd take it more kindly from you Tom. He's a big strong man, even if he has put on a lot of weight and he used to be a professional wrestler, and after all you're quite old. If he cut up rough the law would be on your side and Jimmy isn't a fool.

MITCHEL Let's get this straight! You ask my permission to let your brother-in-law to stay the night – he stays a fortnight – you're afraid to ask him to leave and you expect me to do it! I'll be damned if I'll do it!

BROWN But Tom ...

MITCHEL Stop Tomming me! Your brother-in-law can stay here until doomsday for all I care. Goodnight!

A door is opened and slammed. Quick footsteps. A door is opened and shut. Sounds of **MITCHEL** *breathing deeply.* **MRS MITCHEL** *speaks calmly.*

MRS MITCHEL Did you tell them Tom?

MITCHEL Just ... let me ... get my breath. [*pause*] I told them.

MRS MITCHEL Were they upset?

MITCHEL Not they, they were glad! But they wanted me to tell him! Well I wasn't going to take that lying down. I lost my temper, I can tell you. I said he could stay here till doomsday.

MRS MITCHEL Why on earth did you say that?

MITCHEL I suppose ... I'm afraid of him too.

MRS MITCHEL Tomorrow I'll tell him to go. I'm not afraid of him.

MITCHEL No Jean! Let's consider it calmly. What have *we* against Jimmy? He called last night to cadge a cigarette.

MRS MITCHEL He came in without being asked.

MITCHEL Apart from that he was perfectly civil.

MRS MITCHEL Hmph!

MITCHEL So we're going to give him another chance. We'll pretend nothing's happened. And if we have the slightest extra trouble they'll all have to leave. Not just him, but all of them. And if they won't go we'll get the police.

MRS MITCHEL Just as you say Tom.

MUSIC BRIDGE: *A distant crash and commotion. A scream followed by footsteps rushing near and a door flung open.* **MRS BROWN** *cries out.*

MRS BROWN Oh Mr Mitchel! Stop them! Stop them, they're fighting!

A **BABY** *is wailing nearby.*

MITCHEL What?

MRS BROWN Oh mister stop them please!

Quick footsteps, then grunting, scuffles and thumps. **MR MITCHEL** *speaks loudly and firmly.*

MITCHEL Stop that! Stop that here and now!

Silence, but for the **BABY***'s wailing.* **MITCHEL** *speaks to it, gruffly tender.*

MITCHEL There there John. Shushushush Johnnie. Don't worry, it's alright.

The **BABY** *quietens.*

JIMMY Sorry Mr Mitchel, but this bastard owes me twenty pounds **...** He's cheated me and he'll try tae cheat you.

BROWN That's a lie. Tom knows about your sort so don't try anything.

MITCHEL It's perfectly simple! Four people are living in a room meant for one! That's the beginning and end of the matter! [*pause, then quietly*] Sorry Jimmy. But you'll have to leave.

JIMMY Oh don't worry Mr Mitchel I'm leaving. I've had enough. Where's ma jacket?

MITCHEL Is this it?

JIMMY Thanks. But I'm warning you, that Brown'll cheat you like he's cheated me.

BROWN And if he ever comes back Tom, send for the police. If you even see him hanging around the close, send for the police immediately.

MITCHEL The police have nothing to do with it. It's all the size of the room. Goodbye Jimmy.

JIMMY Goodbye Mr Mitchel.

Footsteps. A door opens.

BROWN On your way! Fighting man!

JIMMY [*off*] Next time you and I come together Sandy Brown, I'll disable you.

The door closes. A pause.

MRS MITCHEL Has he gone?

BROWN He's gone all right. Your man and I made short work of him. I appreciated the way you handled the situation Tom.

MITCHEL Aye. Well I need to sit down now.

BROWN Before you do, come into the room a minute. I want to show you something. You read books, don't you.

MITCHEL Yes?

BROWN Tell me, are these worth anything?

MITCHEL Hm. Where did you get them?

BROWN I was doing some removals yesterday for an old lady who's going into a home. She said she'd no use for them.

MITCHEL They're in good condition. Hm! Thomas Hardy. Maurice Walsh. "The Good Companions". Hm Hm Hm. You might get ten bob for the lot in a decent second-hand place.

BROWN Would you like them?

MITCHEL Well I **...**

BROWN Could you read them?

MITCHEL Yes but **...**

BROWN Take them. They're yours.

MITCHEL That's very generous!

BROWN Forget it chum. They cost me nothing. And now we'll have a drink.

MITCHEL No no! No drink for me!

BROWN Not just to celebrate the return to normality?

MITCHEL No no! We'll wait and see what normality is like first will we?

MUSIC BRIDGE: *A faint sound of snoring. In the distance the chime of the doorbell. This is repeated.*

MRS MITCHEL Tom! **...** Tom, wake up!

MITCHEL Wha? Whasat?

MRS MITCHEL The bell! There's someone at the door!

MITCHEL What's the time?

MRS MITCHEL Five past one.

MITCHEL My God! Where's my slippers and dressing gown **...**

Bell chimes again. A mattress creaks. A door is opened. The distant sound of a door being unchained and opened. Murmur, off.

MITCHEL [*distant*] All right, I'll tell her.

Distant knocking at another door.

MITCHEL [*off*] Mrs Brown! Mrs Brown!

Distant door opening. Mumble of voices, then nearest door shut.

MRS MITCHEL What is it Tom?

MITCHEL A boy with the filthiest face I've seen in my life. Would Mrs Brown give him a pair of trousers to take to Mr Brown at the Northern Police Station?

MRS MITCHEL Whatever for?

MITCHEL Well now. That's a question.

Snoring, as before. Distant chime as before, accompanied by heavy knocking which keeps on until the door is opened.

MRS MITCHEL Tom! Tom! There it is again!

MITCHEL Again? I see.

Movement, door opens and at once knocking is heard louder.

MITCHEL All right! All right!

Rattle of chain. Knocking stops. Door is opened.

BROWN Hullo Tom. I've got company.

MITCHEL So I see.

POLICEMAN Are you this man's landlord?

MITCHEL I am.

BROWN Come this way Sergeant. The wife's got her curlers in ...

Tramp of heavy boots followed by the slamming of a door. A door is closed quietly.

MITCHEL [*approaching*] It was Brown this time. And three policemen. They've gone into his room.

MRS MITCHEL Tom, this is terrible. I've never had police in the house in my life. What will the neighbours say? We'll have to do something. It's like living with an unexploded bomb. We never know what's going to happen.

MITCHEL We can do nothing till tomorrow.

MRS MITCHEL Why aren't you coming to bed?

MITCHEL I'm waiting till the police leave. [*pause*] I wonder if "trousers" was some kind of code word.

Tramp of boots across the lobby, muffled. Outside door slammed.

MRS MITCHEL They've left.

MITCHEL But have they taken Brown with them?

A faint tapping. Door opened.

MITCHEL Well?

BROWN I thought you might be worried so I'm looking in to tell you everything's all right. I ... er ... I had a slight accident with the van – nothing serious – and I'd left my driving licence at home. So naturally the police suspected the worst. But they've seen the licence now so it's all right. But there's another thing ...

MITCHEL We'll talk about it tomorrow.

Door shuts abruptly. **MUSIC BRIDGE.**

MRS MITCHEL [*jubilant*] Tom! Tom! I've been talking to Ruby in the kitchen – they're leaving.

MITCHEL Eh?

MRS MITCHEL Yes! Now! At once! They're all packed up and carrying things down to the van.

MITCHEL Well well well!

A door is opened.

BROWN Hullo! You've heard the news?

MITCHEL So we're losing you.

BROWN Aye. It must seem a bit sudden.

MITCHEL A bit sudden.

BROWN You see what happened was this ...

MITCHEL There's no need to explain ...

BROWN But I want to tell you. You see one day I was picking up a load of scrap from a factory and I'd got it into the truck, and the bloke went into the office for his account book or something like that. Anyway he didn't know who I was and there was nobody about so I just ... drove away. But he must have remembered my numberplate. Anyway it seems they're onto me so I'd better shift.

MITCHEL You shouldn't have done that.

BROWN You're right. Honesty is the best policy.

MITCHEL I'm sure, you know, if you contacted the factory and paid what you owed the whole matter would be dropped.

BROWN Aye, but I've no money you see. Hardly a shilling. And I was wondering if ... you remember you said those books were mibby worth something?

Pause. Crackle of notes brought out of wallet.

MITCHEL Here's two pounds.

BROWN My my. Were they worth all that?

MRS BROWN [*off*] Sandy! Where are you?

BROWN In here saying goodbye!

MRS BROWN [*approaching*] We're all ready Sandy ... Goodbye Mrs Mitchel. You and your man have been real kind, considering we havenae always seen eye to eye.

MRS MITCHEL Goodbye Ruby. Goodbye Johnnie.

BROWN You'll be glad to see the last of us, eh?

MITCHEL Not ... entirely.

MRS BROWN Sandy, we'd better go!

BROWN Well cheerio!

MITCHEL Goodbye Sandy, Goodbye Ruby.

MRS MITCHEL Goodbye Ruby, goodbye Sandy.

BROWN Cheerio Tom, cheerio Mrs Mitchel.

MRS BROWN Hurry up Sandy!

Slam then a pause.

MRS MITCHEL Oh Tom!

MITCHEL Oh Jean!

MRS MITCHEL Alone, alone at last.

MUSIC BRIDGE.

POLICEMAN But when did they leave?

MITCHEL Ten days ago.

POLICEMAN And you don't know where they went?

MITCHEL Look, this is the sixth time the police have called here asking the same questions and getting the same answers. The Browns left suddenly ten days ago. They drove off in an old dormobile or a Bentley or a breadvan, I don't know which. I don't know where they went but I do know they aren't coming back.

POLICEMAN Very good, sir.

Shuts door. Footsteps.

MITCHEL The police again.

MRS MITCHEL They must think we know something.

MITCHEL Yes.

MRS MITCHEL It's good to be alone isn't it Tommy? I never appreciated peace and quiet until they came.

MITCHEL Aye, it's good **…** What a way to live Jean!

MRS MITCHEL It wasn't our way.

MITCHEL No home but furnished lodgings. Never a month in the one place. Getting your money chancily from day to day. And the police after you! What kind of life is that for a man with a wife and child? How would the world keep going if we all lived like that? Look at me! Near thirty years with the one firm. The one firm!

MRS MITCHEL I've been thinking Tom. We don't really need to let a room. With care I could manage not too badly without these extra pounds.

MITCHEL Mind you, I didn't dislike them Jean.

MRS MITCHEL Oh no!

MITCHEL They were feckless, but there was life in them.

MRS MITCHEL I liked the wee boy.

MITCHEL I **…** don't think there'll be any harm in letting that room again. Whoever gets it won't be the Browns. And the two pounds were always useful.

MRS MITCHEL I'll write out the notice now.

MITCHEL There's a postcard behind the clock **…** I wonder why he needed trousers when he was at the police station.

MRS MITCHEL *speaks slowly to the scratching of her pen*:

MRS MITCHEL To let **…** furnished **…** single room **…** in good condition **…** two pounds a week with use of kitchen. Will I add "Single persons only need apply"?

MITCHEL No. No I think we'll just leave it at that.

Closing music.

IN 1969 I WAS invited to the London BBC television centre for a discussion with Shaun McLaughlin, drama producer. He told me he had been impressed by the father-son relationship which, only evident in the last scene of *Kelvin Walker*, explained all that had been shown before it. He said that hardly any English people wrote plays about fathers and sons, and asked if I could write a different one on that theme? "Yes," I said (now sure I could write a play on any given theme, if allowed to handle it in my own way) "But where do you want it set?" He told me that, alas, it could not be set in Scotland – statistics showed that the vast majority of British viewers in south Britain would switch to another channel if most people in a play sounded Scottish. But a change had come over English people since 1940 when southerners had insisted that Wilfred Pickles should not read the 6 o'clock news because they disliked his Yorkshire accent. Many new fictions and films made from them (*Room at the Top*, *Billy Liar*, *Saturday Night and Monday Morning*, *A Taste of Honey*) had made north English voices acceptable in the south, so my play could be set anywhere in Britain, as long as it was in England. I told Mr McLaughlin that my partly English childhood would let me easily give my hero's dad a Yorkshire accent. That was the origin of *Mavis Belfrage*.

The character of the dad was based on my own dad. Mavis was partly based on my first wife, who had induced me leave the house I shared with him, and partly upon Marion Ogg, a beautiful tall blonde woman of the sort too many men desire at first sight, which stops her finding one who contented her. The hero's character and dealings with Mavis were partly mine, though I gave him a Cambridge education, a steady job I would have loathed, and an imagination sublimated into toymaking. This play pleased and was accepted by Shaun

McLaughlin. However, it was rejected by another producer whose approval he needed. A few years later, in 1972, Frances Head, my London literary agent, got Granada TV in Manchester to broadcast it under the name *Triangles*.

CAST

MAVIS BELFRAGE One of those who wander hither and thither yonder upon the wastes of the waters – an attractive, haggard woman capable of loudly ominous silences. Her way of smoking shows ner nervous nature: she holds the cigarette near the tip, inhales in quick little drags, and stubs it out long before finishing. Otherwise she is completely self-possessed. Her accent is posh without affectation.

ERIC MUIR A young lecturer in educational theory at a teachers' training college. A Cambridge scholarship has left him confident within narrow limits he has set himself. Within these he is soberly definite, without nervous mannerisms. His nearly deadpan face conveys feeling with a minimum of change and under stress becomes immobile. His voice is curt and quiet, his accent like **MAVIS**'.

NORMAN MUIR Manager of electrical goods shop, a widower of fifty. He is a buoyant and firm person with a naturally loud voice, but never when angry or disturbed. He is intelligent and tolerant, can be broadly built or else small and dynamic. His accent is local.

BILL BELFRAGE A stoical boy, determined not to be excited or interested in anything. He becomes lively when involved in a game. He should not seem older than fifteen. A small actress could play him.

CLIVE EVANS A young Welshman with an irritating air of detached superiority – only in Scene 10.

DR. SCHWEIK A formidable Slavonic academic – only in Scene 8.

SCENES

1 Eric Muir's office
2 Mavis's bed sitting room
3 The Muir living room
4 The Muir living room, a week later
5 The Muir living room, a fortnight later
6 The Muir living room, very early morning
7 The Muir living room, a week later
8 The Muir living room, that night
9 The Muir living room, two days later
10 Clive Evans' lodgings
11 The Muir living room

1: ERIC'S OFFICE

A standing coat-hanger without hat or coat. A desk with a clean glass ashtray and thin sheaf of foolscap papers. A chair in front of the desk for visitors. Eric stands at the door.

ERIC Yes, please come in Miss ... er, Belfrage.

He walks to the desk and pauses beside it. **MAVIS**, *in plain blouse and skirt, with leather handbag hanging from shoulder-strap, follows him in and stops when he points to the chair.*

ERIC Please sit down.

MAVIS [*not sitting*] I won't be here long, will I?

ERIC [*he sits down in his chair*] The reason I want to speak to you is – [*he taps the desk thoughtfully with the fingers of one hand*] – not a professional reason.

MAVIS [*she nods*] You want to apologise.

ERIC [*surprised and amused*] No! Certainly not!

MAVIS Then why have you asked me here? [*she sits , opens her handbag, takes out a cigarette and, with a lighter, quickly, deftly, nervously lights it and inhales*].

ERIC During the past term you and I have got on rather worse than most students and tutors. You disliked my approach to the subject and told me so. Frequently. I've respected that, and of course I've defended myself. But I don't want you to think I gave you such abnormally low marks out of bad feeling.

MAVIS But you did!

ERIC No! [*he lifts the foolscap sheaf from the desk*] Let's take your paper one question at a time –

MAVIS [*interrupts swiftly and firmly*] There's no need! Did I write anything stupid in that paper?

ERIC No.

MAVIS Did I express myself badly?
ERIC You expressed yourself very well.
MAVIS Did I show I understood the subject?
ERIC You showed me that you understood it thoroughly.
MAVIS And you failed me.
ERIC Yes. You didn't answer my questions. [*he examines the paper*] I did not ask you to write about the flaws in Plato's educational system. I asked you to write about what Hoffman and MacKinlay regard as the flaws of Plato's educational system. I don't pretend Hoffman and MacKinlay's account is the only true account, or even the best possible account. On most points I preferred yours. But I had not asked for yours. The class has known for months that I would base my questions on Hoffman and MacKinlay. You knew it.
MAVIS Why are you so terrified of people's opinions?
ERIC [*on a surprisingly petty note*] They have nothing to do with me!
MAVIS I don't understand you. [*she stubs the half-finished cigarette in the ashtray*] But you want me to think you're an honest, decent, conscientious thick bloke. All right. I believe that is all you are. [*she stands*] Can I go now?
ERIC How ... did you get on in the other subjects?
MAVIS [*she smiles disdainfully*] Surely you've heard about that from your colleagues?
ERIC Yes. Why did you do so badly?
MAVIS [*for the first time she is on the defensive*] No-one can be good at everything. Anyway I didn't do so very badly. I was a borderline case. With reasonable marks in your subject I would have passed. Yours was the one paper in which I should have scored unusually high marks. You marked me as low as you could.
ERIC But you'll repeat the year?
MAVIS [*looks down and says in a low voice*] They won't renew my grant.
ERIC [*sitting on the edge of the desk*] I might help you there.
MAVIS [*doesn't look up*] What?
ERIC If you're a borderline case I can tell the Director the special character of your failure. He might be sympathetic.
MAVIS [*looks at the floor and shakes her head*] There would be no point. You see ... I'll never be a teacher. I can't stand children. Not roomfuls of them anyway. Their problems bore me. Their manners disgust me. That's why I failed all my practical subjects. I'm not even a borderline case. As for your subject, I could have passed easily if I'd wanted to, but I decided to sink with flags flying and the band playing instead of just – fading out. I suppose I did it to upset you. [*she looks at him with a smile*] I'm sorry.
ERIC What are you going to do now?
MAVIS Find a job – [*she shakes her head hopelessly*] – I don't know.
ERIC Would you let me take you out to dinner?
MAVIS [*stares, startled*] Why?
A pause. He shrugs slightly.
MAVIS When?
ERIC Tomorrow night.
MAVIS [*thinks about this*] Thursday would be better.
ERIC Will we meet in the lounge of the Three Feathers? Say about seven?
MAVIS Eight would be better.
ERIC [*stands up*] Goodbye, Miss Belfrage.
MAVIS Goodbye, Mr Muir.
They stand looking at each other.

2: MAVIS'S BEDSITTING ROOM

Two popular posters: "The Climax" from Beardsley's Salome sequence, and the photograph of a negress and white girl embracing. A table supporting: empty and half-full milk bottles, a jam pot, half a loaf, textbooks, a pile of aeroplane magazines, **MAVIS***'s handbag and some of her clothes. A bed with* **MAVIS** *in it, her face in profile on the pillow, a bare arm along the coverlet.* **ERIC***, in trousers, shirt and stockinged feet, sits beside her leaning on the headboard. His hands rest loosely on his thighs and his face is absent-minded. They have just made love and are more happy and relaxed than they expected to be.*
MAVIS You're quite a loverboy, aren't you?
ERIC [*doesn't look at her*] You led me on.
MAVIS You allowed me to. Some men are terribly assertive.
She shuts her eyes. He looks down and feels a strand of her hair between thumb and forefinger.
ERIC Have you known many men?
MAVIS Have you known many women?
ERIC [*he considers before answering*] Let's not discuss it just now.
A hand with accusing forefinger slides up from under the sheet and aims at him like a pistol.
MAVIS You're being secretive because you've got nothing to hide.

ERIC [*smiles, stands up and wanders from the bed*] I'm afraid I need you.
MAVIS [*shocked, she opens her eyes, lifts her head and says with a spontaneous pang of sympathy*] Oh, I'm sorry!
ERIC [*puzzled*] Why?
MAVIS [*shrugs, indifferently*] Nothing – it doesn't matter.
She sits up and starts tidying her hair with her hands. **ERIC** *contemplates her with his hands in his pockets.*
ERIC I want you to live with me.
MAVIS Oh?
ERIC Will you live with me?
MAVIS Why not? It'll be convenient, I'm terribly short of money.
ERIC [*comes over to the table*] Is that the only reason?
MAVIS [*drops her hands to her lap and looks at them*] No, Eric.
ERIC [*sits on the table edge*] You see, I'd like us to get married.
MAVIS [*purses her lips as if tasting sourness*] There's too much of that going on nowadays.
ERIC I'd like it all the same.
MAVIS Why?
ERIC I suppose ... I prefer things to be conventional.
MAVIS [*face lights up with sudden malicious, mischievous glee*] I'm married already.
ERIC [*shuts his eyes for a moment then opens them and scratches his head for a moment*] When did you leave him?
MAVIS Years ago.
ERIC Was he bad to you?
MAVIS No. He was nice. Only nice men fall for me.
ERIC Why is that?
MAVIS I suppose because I'm a bit of a bitch.
ERIC You're not a bitch!
MAVIS Nice men never believe I'm a bitch.
ERIC's *eyes fall on the stack of magazines. He lifts the top one up by the corner.*
ERIC [*warily*] Why are you so fond of aeroplanes?
MAVIS [*smiles sweetly*] They belong to my son.
ERIC How ... old is your son?
Note: *the least age the actor can represent.*
ERIC [*raises his voice indignantly*] That means you're quite old! I mean, I'm sorry, older than I am!
MAVIS [*coldly*] Had you not noticed?
ERIC No. I've always thought attractive women were my own age or younger. Where is your son?
MAVIS [*begins fumbling beneath her pillow with one hand*] He's staying with my sister tonight. Usually he sleeps here.
ERIC Where does he sleep?
MAVIS With me.
She brings out a cigarette case and feels below once more. **ERIC** *pauses and looks at her.*
ERIC Is that healthy?
MAVIS I don't know. *Where* is that lighter?
ERIC [*he sits down on the bed so as to face her and says simply, without pity*] You've a horrible life, Mavis.
MAVIS Do you really want me?
ERIC I need you. [*he smiles thoughtfully and lays a hand on one of hers*] You'll be happier with us. The boy can have a room of his own.
MAVIS Us?
ERIC My father and I. We took a house in Sandburn Park a year ago when I started teaching at the college. [*he turns her hand palm upwards and starts tracing lines with a fingertip*] We're buying it through a building society. He pays a third and I pay two thirds. I have the larger salary you see.
MAVIS What does your father do?
ERIC He runs a shop selling electrical equipment in the high street.
MAVIS [*withdrawing her hand*] Your posh accent isn't inherited then.
ERIC Acquired, I'm afraid. I hope you aren't disappointed.
MAVIS Will ... your Dad like me?
ERIC [*reaches down and takes his shoes from under the bed, saying cheerfully*] We never disagree about important things.
He begins to put on his shoes.

3: THE MUIRS' LIVING ROOM

Modern and open-plan. The lobby door is front right, a window with curtains beyond it, a bookcase beyond that. The bookcase supports a gramophone; a rack of records; and two plastic model aeroplanes, a fighter and a bomber, each resting on the box in which its parts were bought.

At the front of the stage, right, a low coffee table on a hearth rug supports: an ashtray, a cake-stand with cakes and sandwiches on it, a bowl of sugar lumps with tongs, a little milk-jug covered by a beaded cloth. The table has an easy chair on each side and a sofa and a standard lamp behind.

Left of centre, back, is a table almost covered by a structure of lego bricks suggesting a blend of Manhattan Island and a medieval castle. Some central pinnacles are over a yard high. A door to the kitchen is on the left.

NORMAN MUIR, *in flannels, knitted waistcoat and bow tie, with hands in pockets, stands staring out the window.* **ERIC**, *in dark trousers and pullover, is quietly clipping small windmills on towers on his city wall.*

NORMAN I don't like it. I don't like it. [*pause*] How long do you think she'll stay?

ERIC For the foreseeable future.

NORMAN And a kid in his teens. She's no chicken, Eric. [*pause.* **NORMAN** *turns and takes a couple of steps towards the table*] *Surely* you must have got her into trouble, Eric! She *must* be pregnant!

ERIC [*calmly, not looking up*] I've told you already. I've no practical reason for wanting her here.

NORMAN She's got a practical reason for coming though. No job. Living with her kid in a bed-sitter.

ERIC I've taken that into account. It doesn't matter.

NORMAN [*sighs, turns to the window, gazes out*] When we took this house, Eric, it was on my mind – I thought it was in yours too – that one day you'd marry and have a kid and there'd be room for all of us.

ERIC That's right. [*he looks up*] So what are you worried about?

NORMAN Well ... [*he grins*] ... it never struck me you might pick up a family second hand! [*he starts chuckling*] Is it cheaper that way, Eric? [*He turns round and becomes intimate and cajoling*] Eric ... Eric, listen! You don't need to take damaged goods! You deserve something better!

ERIC [*glares coldly*] Please keep your sales-talk for the shop.

NORMAN [*grin has been abolished by wonderment. He says quietly*] Christ, Eric, I take a lot from you! [*turns to the window again and* **ERIC** *resumes work on the windmills*].

ERIC You've never had to take anything from me. Before now.

Pause.

NORMAN Here's the taxi.

ERIC *crosses right and goes out.* **NORMAN** *follows. Sounds of opening front door, several "Hello's", a "Come in", a "Let me take those".* **NORMAN** *enters with two suitcases followed by* **BILL** *with a duffle bag.* **BILL** *wears jeans and a polo-necked sweater. He is sullenly determined not to enjoy anything.* **NORMAN** *puts the cases down near the door.*

NORMAN Drop your bag there, youngster.

BILL *does.* **MAVIS** *enters followed by* **ERIC.**

NORMAN [*to* **BILL**] You're called Bill – [*turns to* **MAVIS** *and smiles*] – and you're Mavis.

MAVIS [*gives a quick, tight smile*] Hello, Mr Muir.

NORMAN Better call me Norman, eh?

MAVIS [*another brief smile*] All right.

NORMAN [*points to the aeroplanes*] I hear you're fond of aeroplanes, Bill. What do you think of these?

BILL [*glances at them without interest*] They're all right.

NORMAN Have them. They're yours.

A pause.

MAVIS Say thank you, Bill.

BILL Thank you.

NORMAN Don't thank me – thank Eric. He bought them for you.

BILL [*tonelessly, to* **ERIC**] Thank you.

ERIC Don't mention it – I've plenty of money.

NORMAN [*rubbing his hands together*] Well now, before I show you round the house what about a nice cup of tea?

MAVIS I ... well, to be frank I can't stand tea.

NORMAN Coffee then?

MAVIS If it's no trouble.

NORMAN White, brown or black?

MAVIS Whichever's the least trouble – I mean black.

BILL *has wandered to the bookcase where he is pulling records from the racks, disgustedly examining the covers, and carefully avoiding looking at the aeroplanes.*

NORMAN Sure you wouldn't like white?

MAVIS Quite sure.

NORMAN What about you Bill? Some lemonade?

BILL [*does not look round*] Coffee please ... black.

MAVIS Pull yourself together Bill.

BILL Lemonade then, no, tea. I can't stand lemonade.

NORMAN [*heartily*] Three teas and one black coffee it shall be then.

He walks into the kitchen. **ERIC** *and* **MAVIS** *speak simultaneously.*

ERIC Cheer up!

MAVIS I shouldn't have come.

ERIC Don't worry.

She takes her cigarette case out and opens it. There is one cigarette left. She puts in her mouth.

MAVIS Oh God, I'm almost out.

ERIC You smoke this brand, don't you? [*He takes a packet from his pocket and drops it into her handbag. She lights her cigarette and inhales*].

MAVIS [*pathetically*] Eric, do you really love me?

He embraces her. She offers her mouth. Before their lips quite touch, **BILL**, *who has wandered to the castle table, calls out.*

BILL Mum! [*they move apart quickly.* **BILL** *stares up at the castle, becoming excited*] Mum! Come and see this!

MAVIS *goes to him, frowning, the cigarette in one hand.* **ERIC** *comes more slowly after her.* **BILL** *walks around, gazing and delighted, sometimes standing on tiptoes to see particular details.* **MAVIS** *also begins to smile.* **ERIC** *keeps a grave surface.*

MAVIS Who made this?

ERIC I did.

MAVIS Why?

ERIC It's my hobby. It's not finished yet.

BILL [*peers through an opening*] What is it, Eric?

ERIC It began as a city with a castle in the middle. But I was so keen to make a really safe city that I put the city inside the castle.

BILL A city like that wouldn't be safe nowadays. One Inter-Continental-Ballistic-Missile and –

ERIC [*quickly interrupting*] This city is on a planet where they haven't learnt to split the atom yet. They haven't aeroplanes either. Or motor cars.

BILL Why isn't it finished?

ERIC *pulls a switch on a battery case at the foot of the city wall. The windmill sails briskly revolve. He pushes the switch and they stop.*

ERIC I'm anxious to shift these windmills off the outside wall but I don't know where to put them.

In surveying the castle **MAVIS** *has become positively jaunty. She smokes relaxedly with a total indifference to her ash.*

MAVIS They look beautiful on the outer walls.

ERIC Yes, but if an enemy besieged the city it could easily destroy the sails with a cannon, and then the citizens would have no light or heat. The windmills drive their generators.

BILL [*is shocked into indignation*] How can a planet have electricity and not have cars or aeroplanes?

ERIC There is a reason but you'll have to discover it for yourself. I'll give you a clue though. Their ships and trains are powered by steam, not diesel.

MAVIS *places a hand on each of* **ERIC**'*s shoulders and smiles at him from arm's length. She feels motherly and loving. He stares back, obstinately ironically solemn.*

MAVIS Oh Eric!

NORMAN [*enters from the kitchen with the tray, the four cups, a teapot. He pauses to say warmly*] Get his mind off that nonsense, **MAVIS**, and you'll do us *both* a favour.

He continues on his way to the coffee table. **MAVIS** *and* **ERIC** *follow.* **BILL** *is left contemplating the structure with a frown.*

MAVIS But I'm delighted to find Eric has *one* touch of lunacy in him. In everything else he's so abnormally safe and sober ... Unless you count his feelings for me.

NORMAN [*grins and stoops to set down the tray.* **MAVIS** *sits on the end of the sofa nearest him and* **ERIC** *sits beside her*] Now on that point – [*he sits down in a chair*] For me to comment – [*He takes the ashtray from the table and stretches over to place it on the sofa arm beside* **MAVIS**] – Would be unbecoming to say the least. Have an ashtray.

MAVIS Thank you. [*she automatically stubs the cigarette in it*]

NORMAN [*calling out*] Ready for your tea, Bill?

BILL'S VOICE Not yet.

MAVIS Who keeps the house so beautifully tidy?

NORMAN We have a woman on Mondays and Fridays.

He starts to pour the tea for himself and **ERIC**, *afterwards adding milk to one and sugar to the other.*

ERIC Dad's being modest. He does practically everything. I'm no sort of housewife.

MAVIS Neither am I.

NORMAN [*while engaged with the cups*] I had to learn to be you see, when Eric's mum passed away. He was ten at the time and we hadn't much money then. But it's amazing what you can learn to take satisfaction in when you apply yourself. [*he looks up, smiling*] Even dusting a room!

NORMAN *and* **ERIC** *take their cups.* **MAVIS** *adds milk to hers.*

MAVIS It's the application that defeats me.

BILL [*approaching*] Eric.

ERIC Yes?

BILL Is it that they have no oil on this planet of yours?

He comes round to **ERIC**'*s end of the sofa and half-sits on the arm of the unoccupied chair.*

ERIC [*nodding in approval*] That's right!

BILL But they could have airships of the Zeppelin type, with steam-driven propellers.

ERIC Too dangerous. Sparks from the furnace might reach the gas –

BILL Not if we used helium. It's non-flammable. I've looked into it –

ERIC A steam-powered dirigible would be too heavy.

BILL I'm not so sure. The Germans were experimenting along those lines in the 1880s. I'll look into it. They may have come up with something.

ERIC [*raising a warning finger*] Look, Bill, if you're planning to destroy my city from the air you must expect me to fight back. I don't know how I'll do it yet but I'll think of something – rocket-carrying barrage balloons perhaps.

BILL [*flashing a sudden charming smile*] Oh that's all right. [*he turns and points to the model aeroplanes*] These are rather nice but you should have let *me* fit them together you know.

ERIC I meant to but I got carried away.

NORMAN Would you like tea now Bill?

BILL [*slips into the chair and sprawls low down with hands in pockets*] Yes please. But it's only fair to warn you that I take rather more sugar than I'm supposed to.

NORMAN [*pauses with half-raised teapot, contemplates* **BILL** *sternly for a moment*] I'm very glad you decided to be frank with me on that point Bill. It's going to make things a lot easier.

4: THE SAME, A WEEK LATER

The passage of time is chiefly indicated by **MAVIS**'*s clothes. She now wears fashionable slacks and shirt and sits reading and smoking in an easy chair near the lamp. There is an ashtray beside her but she ignores it.* **BILL** *sprawls on the floor drawing airships on sheets of paper on the coffee table. He uses colour fibre-tipped pens and a school geometry set. The castle table has been moved nearer the sofa. Some gas-filled children's balloons are attached by strings to outer walls and the base of a large new pinnacle rises in the centre.* **ERIC** *sits on the sofa with a teatray on his knees, constructing the summit: this has a revolving turret with gun-like protrusions. The standard lamp casts an area of light round the coffee table, chairs and sofa, for the curtains are pulled and the rest of the room is in darkness.*

NOTE: *All males are wearing carpet slippers.*

NORMAN *comes with stately steps from the kitchen, bending his arms by his shoulders and making an "Aaaaaeeech!" sound as if relaxing himself after worthwhile effort. A newspaper lies on the vacant armchair. He lifts it and sits down there, then takes a pair of horn-rimmed spectacles from his pocket and slips them on.*

MAVIS [*without raising her eyes from her book*] Norman.

NORMAN [*looks at her*] Yes?

MAVIS You know you didn't have to do the dishes.

NORMAN I don't mind washing a few dishes, Mavis.

MAVIS I would have done it myself later on. But after dinner I like to relax for a while.

NORMAN [*being friendly and reasonable*] It's a matter of temperament, Mavis. You can relax with a lot of dirty dishes nearby, I'm not able to. But don't worry about it. I've cleaned up after meals for the last fifteen years and I don't expect to stop just because *you're* here.

MAVIS [*gives* **ERIC** *a quick ominous glance but he is carefully engrossed in his toy. She looks down into her book saying coldly*]. Good!

NORMAN *reads his paper. The atmosphere is of calm activity, broken only by the nervous motions of* **MAVIS**'s *cigarette, on one occasion sending ash well past the ashtray onto the carpet.*

NORMAN [*from the depths of his paper*] Aye, aye! I see old Enoch's been shooting his mouth off again.

MAVIS [*after a brief silence*] He's a menace.

NORMAN A very clever man.

MAVIS The man's a menace.

NORMAN *smiles and lays down his paper, foreseeing an enjoyable debate. During this debate his voice is always good humoured and though sometimes too forceful, never really loud.* **MAVIS**'s *tone is sharply and coolly cutting, only rising in pitch when* **NORMAN** *touches her personally.*

NORMAN Now there I don't agree. After all, you, as an educated woman, you've got to admit that our cities are over-populated.

MAVIS The race issue has nothing to do with that. A third of the immigrants in this country are Irish. Another third are Europeans, whites from Australia and Canada and Africa. Only a third are black and brown and yellow.

NORMAN I'm not saying Powell is right on the race issue. I do say he's right on the immigration issue. Keep out the lot, I say – Irish, Australians, and ruddy Rhodesians included.

BILL I wish you two would be quieter – I find it very hard to concentrate.

MAVIS You forget that this country has exploited the coloured races for over two centuries. We owe them something I think.

NORMAN Who haven't the British upper classes exploited for the last two centuries? My father could have told you about exploitation. He was a docker in the thirties. It's only since old Clement Attlee started breaking the ruddy Empire up that the British worker has had a chance of a decent livelihood. And now you upper-class liberals start lecturing *us* about what *we* owe the coloured races!

MAVIS [*this is the one remark that gets under her skin*] I'm not upper class! [*she stubs out her cigarette furiously*].

NORMAN You've all the traits, Mavis.

MAVIS What traits?

NORMAN Well now, the first thing that springs to mind is the way you smoke cigarettes. You smoke them all the time but you never smoke more than half. If you'd ever known real poverty you'd smoke them to the tip like other people.

MAVIS *[in a dangerously quiet voice]* What's the second that comes to mind?

NORMAN *[under her glance, and now* **ERIC***'s, he says quietly]* Nothing Mavis, I'm sorry.

There is a pause in which **NORMAN** *picks up his paper,* **ERIC** *resumes work on the tower,* **MAVIS** *looks down at her book, but only to achieve calm and gather her forces. Suddenly she looks up.*

MAVIS Do you know how much money Britain has invested overseas?

NORMAN *[looks up from his paper. The question amuses him]* Sorry. Can't help you there Mavis.

MAVIS Over a thousand million; money which brings wealth to the whole country without anyone making anything, or doing anything but owning shares in foreign companies, most of them based in Africa and Asia. All this money doesn't just benefit the rich, you know. Our whole tight little island is floating, nicely and evenly, on an ocean of dark-skinned poverty. And as soon as a few of the exploited climb aboard we scream that we're being swamped.

NORMAN Are you a Communist?

MAVIS No.

NORMAN For someone who isn't a Communist you know a hell of a lot about foreign investment, don't you?

ERIC *[without looking up]* Dad.

Another silence, **NORMAN** *and* **MAVIS** *reading,* **ERIC** *tinkering, then* **NORMAN** *lays down his paper.*

NORMAN *[gently]* Mavis. *[doesn't respond. He calls cajolingly]* Mavis! *[looks up]* A thing I like about you is, you've got opinions. You and me have ideas about things, we can get a good brisk argument going with no holds barred. See my Eric? You couldn't start an argument with him to save your life. He's got opinions on nothing.

ERIC *rises and carries the completed pinnacle to the table behind the sofa where he leans across to clip it onto its foundation.* **MAVIS** *and* **NORMAN** *pay no attention.* **BILL** *jumps onto the sofa and kneels there with his arms folded on the back, watching.*

NORMAN He used to have. At school he was secretary of the debating society. He wrote a class magazine once. He marched to Aldermaston. He was even a member of that committee – what was it called? – Committee of a Hundred. We had some fine old argie-bargies in those days. *[he smiles reminiscently]* Remember those arguments, Eric?

ERIC *[in a tone that suggests his memories are somewhat less pleasant than his father's]* Yes.

NORMAN Then he got a scholarship and went to university, Cambridge no less. What did Cambridge do to you, Eric?

ERIC It educated me.

NORMAN And look at him now! No opinions. Won't argue. Doesn't vote. And spends his time playing games like a child of six.

ERIC *[delivers his apologia standing erect beside his structure, one hand resting on a tower]* I can't understand why people in this country feel their opinions matter. We never allow them to change anything. The Socialists refuse to frighten the stock exchange, the Tories refuse to fight the unions, the revolutionaries apply to the police for permission to demonstrate. Perhaps I should get angry about this but I can't. I'd hate a genuine fight with starvation and looting and machine guns fired from bedroom windows. All the people I meet seem decent and well intentioned. Their arguments are a harmless way of using up energy which might change things. Their opinions are a hobby, like mine. *[he glances with satisfaction at his city]* Exactly like mine.

MAVIS *[flings down her book and speaks out through almost clenched teeth]* Oh I would like to shake and shake you until you come alive!

ERIC *looks at her with a touch of obstinacy.*

BILL *[plaintively]* Don't talk like that Mavis, it gives me a headache.

MAVIS *lights another cigarette.* **NORMAN** *resumes his paper.*

BILL Precisely when am I allowed to attack your city, Eric?

ERIC *[with his eyes on the city]* When it is complete.

BILL *[discontented]* But you're always *adding* little bits. I don't mind spending a lot of time preparing an attack if I've a point to work towards. But you refuse to give me one.

ERIC *[turning to him]* All right then. The fifth of November. The war will begin on the fifth of November. That gives us nearly a month.

MAVIS Don't depend on it, Bill. We may not be here then. *[the three males stare at her.* **BILL** *sullen,* **ERIC** *shocked,* **NORMAN** *quizzical]* Anyway it's time you went to bed.

NORMAN *[he stands up]* How about some orange before you go, Bill? I'm going to have some.

BILL *[in a subdued voice]* All right. *[he lifts his drawings from the floor and lays them on the table, saying, as he looks from* **MAVIS** *to*

ERIC] Can I leave these here till tomorrow? [*Nobody answers. He lifts the drawings and follows* **NORMAN** *to the kitchen*].

ERIC What's wrong, Mavis?

MAVIS I'm leaving, Eric. I expected to live in your house, not your father's.

ERIC Two thirds of this house is mine!

MAVIS Only legally.

ERIC We ... must talk about this later.

MAVIS [*stands up*] Talk about it whenever you like. It will change nothing. [*shouting*] Hurry up, Bill!

BILL *comes in from the kitchen carrying his papers and a glass of orange and is very subdued. He is followed by* **NORMAN**, *also with a glass.*

MAVIS Upstairs Bill!

NORMAN Goodnight Bill.

ERIC Goodnight Bill.

BILL *goes out followed by* **MAVIS**. **NORMAN** *sits down, drinks from the glass and watches the glass very closely.* **ERIC** *leans glumly forward, elbows on knees and hands clasped between them. He sighs once or twice then looks to* **NORMAN** *ashamedly.*

ERIC We'll have to leave, Dad.

NORMAN Who's "we"?

ERIC Mavis and I. And Bill. You see ...

NORMAN Oh don't explain. Nothing needs explaining. But *you're* not leaving. [*he pauses and looks at* **ERIC**] I can't pay for this place on my own, you know.

ERIC I'd still pay my part of it –

NORMAN What! And the rent for somewhere else? And support a girl like Mavis?

ERIC [*obstinately*] I'll manage to do it. Mavis can take a job.

NORMAN And how will I feel living alone in a house this size? [*he sips his orange*] What I want is a couple of nice unfurnished rooms near the shop: a place I can shift my things into without over-crowding. Somewhere with a decent pub round the corner. I've missed the pubs since we came out here Eric. Tell Mavis not to worry. [*he puts the empty glass on the table and looks up. His son is gazing at him woefully.* **NORMAN** *grins and expostulates*] Don't look so tragic Eric! You're not driving a poor lonely old soul from hearth and home! I'm hardly fifty yet. I've got friends. Anyway I'll be visiting you if only to weed the garden and cut the lawn. I don't see you and Mavis doing it. I'll keep a key to the house so I can get to the tools. You won't get rid of me entirely.

ERIC [*smiles at him lovingly*] You're ... a very ... decent man, you know.

NORMAN [*grins with pleasure, then frowns thoughtfully*] And since I am leaving I'll make so bold as to ask a question I couldn't have asked otherwise.

ERIC [*becomes wary*] Yes?

NORMAN That Mavis – why don't you boss her a bit?

ERIC Boss her?

NORMAN Yes. I think she would be happier if you did.

ERIC If I ... bossed her she would leave me.

NORMAN And you're afraid of that?

ERIC [*smiling tightly*] I'm terrified.

NORMAN [*he stands up*] Can't help you there son. Goodnight.

ERIC Goodnight Dad.

NORMAN *goes out. A moment later* **MAVIS** *enters and crosses towards the kitchen. She pauses behind the sofa.*

MAVIS [*briskly*] I'm having a coffee. What about you?

ERIC No thanks.

MAVIS Still brooding?

ERIC I spoke to him.

MAVIS Well?

ERIC He's going to leave.

MAVIS [*flicks her index finger across the tip of her nose*] Won't that be very sad for him?

ERIC I think so. But he makes light of it.

MAVIS Well if you can accept it I suppose I can. He isn't *my* father. [*she goes into the kitchen*].

5: THE SAME, A FORTNIGHT LATER

It is early evening and the curtains are wide. The easy chairs are now at centre back with the coffee table between them and a bowl of huge flowers on the table. Another bowl of flowers stands on the bookcase. The table-fortress has been pushed against the kitchen partition. The sofa stands left at an angle so that **ERIC** *and* **BILL**, *sitting on it, face the entrance.* **ERIC** *is reading aloud from a book.*

ERIC Emboldened by Athene, who stopped her limbs from trembling, she checked herself and confronted him, while Odysseus considered whether he should throw his arms round the beautiful girl's knees and so make his prayer, or be content to keep his distance ... [*A door slams*].

BILL Here she comes.

MAVIS [*enters gaily swinging her handbag by the strap*] Hello! Have you noticed how late I am?

ERIC It's all right – I gave Bill his tea.

MAVIS [*dropping her bag on a chair*] I knew you would – I met Clive Evans when I was shopping. Don't you remember him? He was a student of yours once. It was nice meeting an old friend. He took me for a meal.

ERIC *passes the book to* **BILL** *who continues silently reading it.* **ERIC** *stretches his legs out in front and leans back, clasping his hands behind his head.*

ERIC Clive Evans. The Welshman?

MAVIS *moves around the room to employ an excess of energy whose conscious form is happiness. While talking she may rearrange flowers, turn almost dancingly, alter the position of a chair.* **ERIC** *contemplates her with pleasure.*

MAVIS Yes, it was fun, meeting him like that. He's a teacher now. Do I look as if I'm drunk?

ERIC You look happy, anyhow.

MAVIS I feel intoxicated. Do you know why? I've just impressed someone tremendously. Do you know that feeling?

ERIC [*shakes his head, smiling*] People don't admire me.

MAVIS [*goes over to* **BILL**, *saying*] Get them to do it. You should be able to. You're full of admirable qualities. [*she places a hand on* **BILL**'*s head, which is bent over his book, and peers at his neck*] Bill, you scruffy little tyke, go and have a bath.

BILL I had a bath last night Mavis!

MAVIS You need another. Upstairs now. Scoot!

BILL *sullenly departs.* **MAVIS** *continues wandering, though more calmly.* **ERIC** *looks thoughtful.*

ERIC I never liked Evans much, did you?

MAVIS In college, no. He was so clever and smug. Do you remember how he used to say "I think that sums it up"? But outside he's different, very gay and funny. Almost as big a surprise as you.

ERIC In what way?

MAVIS You know, in college you were suave, aloof, dominating. But at home you were mothered by your Daddy and played with a toy on the drawing room table.

ERIC [*is painfully struck by her comment but struggles to keep an even surface*] Anyway, you enjoyed yourself. That's good, Mavis.

MAVIS *slips into the sofa beside him – he is sitting up now – and takes his hand in hers. She becomes slightly childish and confiding.*

MAVIS Eric, I want to ask you a favour.

ERIC Yes?

MAVIS But before I do, promise you won't be angry.

ERIC Why should I be angry?

MAVIS I can't tell you before you promise not to be.

ERIC [*smiles*] All right.

MAVIS [*speaks slowly, looking down at his hands while paddling on the palm of one with her forefinger*] Eric, Clive, you know, would like an affair with me. And I would love one with him – [**ERIC**, *shocked, withdraws his hands. She cries in alarm*].

MAVIS You promised not to be angry, remember.

ERIC [*stands, steps away and turns. She lies against the sofa back, watching him alertly*] Do you want to leave me?

MAVIS No. I ... I think I love you Eric. You're the decentest man I know. You're my only friend. But I'll go if you like.

ERIC Look, why? What's wrong with us?

MAVIS [*more coldly*] Well frankly the sex thing isn't the fun it used to be, is it?

ERIC Isn't it?

MAVIS You know it isn't. You're very sweet and tender but you leave all the *work* to me. That's all right sometimes but not all the time.

ERIC You said you disliked assertive men.

MAVIS So I do, but there should be a middle way ... Oh Eric don't look so miserable! [*rises and comes over to him*] Look, order me not to do it then! Order me not to! I probably won't.

ERIC [*coldly*] I can't order you anything. We're not married. We've promised each other nothing. You can leave me when you like. I can ask you to leave when I like.

MAVIS Are you asking me to leave?

ERIC No. I need you.

MAVIS [*follows up her advantage*] And you're not angry?

ERIC Do you care how I feel?

They suddenly notice **BILL**, *who has appeared in bare feet and dressing gown.*

BILL Mavis!

MAVIS What is it?

BILL It's been weeks since you last scrubbed my back, you know.

MAVIS Get into the bath. I'll come in a minute.

BILL *leaves.* **ERIC** *faces her.*

ERIC Mavis, I don't want Bill to know about this. If he finds out, I'll ... we'd better separate.

MAVIS Why should Bill know? I'll always be home long

before he gets up. Oh don't look sad! I feel so happy and hopeful! I wish I could put half my feelings into you! I wish you could sympathise with me Eric!

ERIC *can think of nothing to say.* MAVIS *becomes brisk and sensible.*

MAVIS Look, I'll be back down in half an hour and we'll have a drink together and you'll see it all in perspective. Nothing terrible is going to happen!

But ERIC *feels it is. He sits on the sofa with hunched shoulders and hands clasped between his knees.*

MAVIS [*sits beside him asking sympathetically*] Are you very miserable? [*He bites his lower lip, not looking at her. She is struck by unexpected doubt*] Eric, am I hurting you a lot? [*with fear*] Am I being wicked? [*she feels for his hand, pleading*] Eric, please tell me I'm not wicked.

ERIC [*looks at her wearily*] It's all right, Mavis.

MAVIS [*stricken by total panic she caresses his face beseechingly*] Yes it is all right, isn't it? Make me believe it's all right!

Roused by her greater need he sits up and embraces her. She clings desperately.

ERIC Don't worry Mavis you're beautiful, you're a queen! Queens don't need to care – they can do what they like!

MAVIS Please say that again Eric! Please make me believe! Make me believe it!

6: THE SAME, VERY EARLY MORNING

The curtains are drawn. The standard lamp illuminates ERIC *in pyjamas, dressing gown and slippers, sitting on the sofa and rebuilding the central tower which stands with a coffee mug on the coffee table before him. There is a thermos jug on the floor in easy reach. He is concentrating so hard that his tongue protrudes and he doesn't notice* BILL *enter in pyjamas, dressing gown and slippers, comes quietly near and stands watching.*

BILL So you think that's an improvement?

ERIC *looks up startled and frowns. He is worried, and thinks a moment before replying.*

ERIC Yes I do. Why aren't you sleeping?

BILL Nobody can sleep *every* night of the year.

ERIC [*adds a piece to the tower, adding in a low voice*] I suppose not.

BILL This is the first time you've touched that city since Norman left.

ERIC Yes, I've had a lot on my mind, Bill. Please go back to bed.

BILL That tower will fall down if an enemy even whistles at it.

ERIC [*leaps to his feet and yells wildly*] Leave me alone! Get to bed will you!

He pauses, abashed by his loss of control and afraid BILL *has been frightened.* BILL *contemplates him with cool sympathy and at last remarks casually.*

BILL I find it hard to sleep too, when she's out all night.

ERIC [*sits down looking very woeful, rubbing his cheek with his hand*] It's depressing, isn't it? But one develops a certain tolerance.

ERIC [*reaches for the thermos, lifts, unstoppers, and pours into the mug*] Have some coffee Bill.

BILL [*sitting on the sofa*] Thank you.

He takes the mug, sips, pulls a sour face and puts it back on the table. ERIC *is putting the concluding bricks on the tower.*

BILL Our plan of attack has languished for some weeks hasn't it?

ERIC [*apologetically*] I really have been too busy you know.

He rises and carries the tower carefully to the city. BILL *turns to watch him.*

BILL Well is there any real point in waiting till the fifth of November?

ERIC [*fixes the tower in place*] You're right. There's no point in waiting. We'll destroy it now.

BILL Both of us? Aren't you going to defend it?

ERIC [*grimly*] Oh no! Oh no! [*begins to pace around the city with his arms folded behind his back*] This is an evil city, you see, which has grown powerful by conquering the weaker countries surrounding. But now she has sunk into decadence and corruption. Her defences are neglected. Her balloons are out of gas. [*he flicks one with the back of a hand, then faces the city, one arm behind his back, the other thrusting a Napoleonic hand inside his dressing gown*] This is our opportunity. [*turns to look gravely at the intrigued* BILL]

BILL Who are we?

ERIC [*ponders then walks briskly to the bookcase*] We are brilliant but neglected scientists who belong to one of the defeated nations. Carefully, in the secrecy of an abandoned coal mine, we have constructed two aeroplanes – [*he takes them from the book case and holds one out to* BILL].

ERIC This one is yours.

BILL [*comes over for it*] But there's no oil on this planet.

ERIC Quite. But the engines of these planes are fuelled by alcohol – distilled spirit; a brilliant discovery which only you, Herr Professor Bill Belfrage, could have hit upon!

BILL [*takes the plane, saying plaintively*] I think *somebody* should defend the city.

ERIC [*pulls from the book case six books of unequal size, all hard-covers*] Six good bombs should do the trick. Yes, yes. Three each. You will attack from the south, I from the north, and remember! We can only drop one bomb on each flight.

ERIC *takes the books to the end of the room near the entrance.* **BILL** *follows.*

BILL Will three be enough?

ERIC [*places three in a pile on the floor*] These three will be enough. Plato. Rousseau. And the most potent explosive known to the mind of man: "Hoffman and MacKinlay's Outline of Educational Theory". Down on your knees man! [*he points to the floor beside the pile*] Remain in hiding until I give the word.

BILL *goes down on one knee. Holding his plane on top of the pile,* **ERIC** *carries his books to the window, lays them on the floor with his own plane on top, then stands and draws back the curtains. Light floods in.*

ERIC It is nearly seven. [*he turns and contemplates the city Napoleonically*] The last dawn has broken over the doomed city as, weakened by a night of debauchery, she writhes in uneasy slumber. [*he raises a hand*] But already, beyond the horizon –

BILL Eric! Eric! Can't we have music?

ERIC [*pauses to consider*] Of course! [*he goes to the gramophone and moves his finger thoughtfully along the record in the holder*] Holst? Pooh! ... Wagner? Trite. Chopin? [*He takes out a record and places it on the turntable and swings the arm into the groove. The first bars of Chopin's "Revolutionary" are heard. He switches the record off and puts it back saying*] Trite also. Why should destruction be sombre and strenuous? It is building that is strenuous. Destruction should be gay! [*he takes out a record and puts it on the turntable*] Don't you agree Bill? All things built are knocked down again and those who knock them down are gay.

BILL [*is impatient*] Hurry up then!

ERIC All right, I'll see to the music and commentary while you begin the attack. Where was I?

BILL The debauchery bit.

ERIC Yes. [*solemnly*] Weakened by nameless debaucheries she writhes in uneasy slumber when hark! Beyond the horizon the distant sound, the *sound*, Bill, of the approaching enemy!

BILL Grooooan – grooooan – groooan – groan – [*He continues this noise*].

ERIC Louder grows the sound, louder and more ominous and now there rises slowly above the horizon – slowly Bill – the hitherto undreamed of shape – [**BILL** *lifts the aeroplane slowly above his head in his left hand then, taking the top book in his right, rises up till he is on tiptoe with the aeroplane as high as he can hold it*] – of a mighty aircraft. See! It approaches!

BILL *stalks menacingly forward on tiptoe in strides of increasing speed and begins circling the table.*

ERIC Approaches and attacks!

BILL, *aeroplane aloft, hurls his book into the central tower.* **ERIC** *lowers the needle into the triumphant clamant choral section of Beethoven's ninth.* **BILL** *and* **ERIC** *rush back to their piles for ammunition then converge on the city making explosive and crashing sounds with their mouths, skipping, leaping and hurling volumes with the rhythm and manner of children dancing round a bonfire. In an ecstatic mood* **BILL** *hurls into the collapsing structure not only the book but his aeroplane.* **MAVIS** *enters in time to see this. She halts to stare at them in amazement. Noticing her,* **BILL** *pauses and waits warily.* **ERIC** *steps across, lays his plane on the bookcase and switches off the record.* **MAVIS** *stands, one hand on hip, one holding the strap of her shoulder handbag. She is relieved and happy to see* **ERIC** *and* **BILL** *enjoying a game together, but hides this beneath a surface of school-mistress.*

MAVIS What are you two crazy infants playing at?

ERIC A war game.

MAVIS I'm not surprised at you Eric, but I thought Bill had some self-control!

BILL I couldn't sleep either.

MAVIS Hmm! [*she walks past them towards the kitchen*] And now I suppose you expect me to make you both a great big breakfast. [*she turns to look back at them*] All right! I will. *She enters the kitchen.* **ERIC** *contemplates the mess on the table with blank expression and folded arms.*

BILL [*reassuringly*] She's not angry with us you know. Will you build another city to knock down?

ERIC No. It takes too long. [*sits down on the sofa, clasping his hands*].

BILL What will we do then?

ERIC I'll have to think about that.
MAVIS [*calling from the kitchen*] Do you know what our trouble is, Eric Muir? We don't have enough fun together.
ERIC [*smiles slightly, then calls back*] I'm bad at fun.
MAVIS [*calling*] Well I'm going to teach you to be good at it. We're going to have a party.
She appears, wearing an apron, at the kitchen door.
BILL What a good idea!
MAVIS Don't fool yourself Bill Belfrage. This party will start when you're safe and sound in bed.
BILL *pulls a face.* **ERIC** *feels his chin.*
ERIC A party.
MAVIS Yes! You must have friends Eric.
ERIC I've a few friendly acquaintances. They work at the college.
MAVIS We'll invite them along and get them drunk on doped whisky. Some dull people become really entertaining when they're drunk.
ERIC It's an idea.
MAVIS And then there's your father. I bet he knows how to enjoy a party. And then there's Clive Evans. [**ERIC** *looks up, startled*] He's great fun, you must meet him ... I mean socially. [**ERIC** *is about to say something but glances uneasily at* **BILL**].
BILL Eric, you'll let me be there?
ERIC [*is almost angrily definite*] Certainly not!
BILL I had almost decided to regard you as a friend.
MAVIS [*returns to the kitchen, saying*] It seems strange, Eric, that we've never been to a party together. I used to go to so many.
ERIC *is too weary to respond in any way at all.*
BILL You act like a friendly sea-lion with some unexpectedly vicious traits. [**ERIC** *throws his head back and laughs. It is laughter without much vocal content, his head and shoulders shake*] You will let me come won't you?
ERIC [*sighing and nodding*] Probably.

7: THE SAME, A WEEK LATER

The coffee table is centre-front with a couple of tapering candles on and three plates of sandwiches. The sofa is behind it with **BILL** *sprawled in a corner reading a comic. An easy-chair is on either side of it with* **MAVIS***'s handbag on one.*
The bookcase has two candles and the surviving aeroplane on it. The former city table is covered by a cloth and plates of sandwiches, leafed oranges, bowls of fruit and nuts, glasses and a great vase of flowers.
MAVIS, *exotically dressed, arranges the flowers and hums to herself.*
ERIC *enters carrying a couple of carrier bags full of bottles of wine and spirits. He wears a fashionable startling waistcoat with his usual discreet suit.*
ERIC Sorry I'm late. I've been more extravagant than I intended.
MAVIS Eric! How funny!
ERIC [*goes to the table*] Hm! I meant it to be flashily impressive.
MAVIS It is!
ERIC [*unloads the bottles onto the table*] Then I won't grumble about the price of *your* party clothes. However much they cost.
MAVIS [*pulls a face and stretches her arms horizontally*] I hate money.
ERIC [*munches a sandwich*] These ... taste all right.
MAVIS [*making balletic gestures to left and right*] You like them? And haven't I made the house all neat and tidy? And won't your colleagues envy you for having such an efficient, loving, beautifully dressed, beautiful mistress?
BILL [*looks up for a moment*] Actually, I did all the cutting and spreading Eric.
ERIC *contemplates* **MAVIS** *who stands before him in an attitude of mock humility. He is nibbling the sandwich.*
ERIC You know, there dawns on me, waveringly, the notion that I will enjoy this party.
MAVIS Of course you will. And Eric ... [*she lays a hand on his shoulder and looks up at him with a little-girl front*] I've a favour to ask. [*he smiles, almost laughs at her*] What's so amusing?
ERIC Whenever you're extra gay and happy and then go on to ask me a favour it's usually something I hate to do.
MAVIS Is there anything you wouldn't do for me?
ERIC Probably not.
MAVIS [*puts her hands behind her back and says slowly*] Well, I thought, you and me and Bill would have a nice little dinner just now, and after that it'll be nearly seven, and then I wondered if you would drive into town to pick up Clive ... Evans you know. You see he hasn't a car, and this place is rather hard to reach by bus, and ... well, there'd be time for the two of you to have a drink together. Before the party. [*she says quickly*] Of course you needn't have a drink if you don't feel like one.
ERIC [*looks at her with a firmly closed expression*] No.

MAVIS [*the word had made her tense and quiet*] Why not?

ERIC Go and wash your hands Bill, we're having dinner in a minute!

BILL [*pulls a face and unwillingly lays down the comic*] Are you two going to have a boring emotional storm?

MAVIS Clear out Bill. [*He leaves*] Why not?

ERIC Mavis, I don't dislike Clive Evans because he is your lover. I sympathise with him there. I would like to be your lover. And I don't mind meeting him in company and saying the meaningless things people say to each other in company. But I'm not going to treat him as a friend to satisfy your convenience or, or, or your vanity.

MAVIS What a tiny, shrivelled, ungenerous ... [*she smiles at him mockingly*] ... *mind* you have! [*he stares at her, walks to the sofa and sits down. She walks about*] What do you suggest I do? I've told him to expect you. What do you suggest I do?

ERIC Phone him and tell him to come by bus.

MAVIS You do it! It's your idea.

ERIC No. [*to employ his agitation he picks up* **BILL***'s comic and stares blindly at the cover.* **MAVIS** *takes a few more aimless steps then turns and stands with folded arms*] I'll explain why I arranged for you to pick him up. He didn't want to come to the party. He thought you would dislike him because of me. I said you were above petty feelings of envy. I said you would prove it by bringing him here yourself.

ERIC [*in a low voice*] Then he understood my feelings, and respected them, more than you do. Please phone him and tell him you were wrong.

MAVIS Phone him and – ! What about the party? What sort of time will I have without Clive, with only you and your friends and your father to talk to? Nobody cheerful? Nobody who loves me?

ERIC [*speaks with the hard clarity of anger*] Our guests will be decent reasonable men and women!

MAVIS [*goes to the chair and picks up her handbag*] Give them a message will you? I may be rather late as I've gone to pick up a friend who's been delayed. [**ERIC** *jumps to his feet.* **MAVIS** *goes to the door and turns there*] There's a piece of meat in the oven. It should be ready now if it isn't burned.

ERIC Mavis, if you take the car you'll have plenty of time to get back before the guests arrive!

MAVIS I'll certainly take the car!

She goes out. **ERIC** *stands staring at the door, then unconsciously places his hand on his midriff.* **BILL** *wanders in.*

BILL I suppose I can come in now that it's quiet. [*He approaches* **ERIC** *and looks at him with interest*] Have you a pain there? [*surprised,* **ERIC** *nods and drops his hand*] It goes away when she comes back you know. Will I take the meat out of the oven?

ERIC [*walks towards the kitchen*] No. I will.

BILL [*follows him, saying*] You take some of her moods rather seriously I'm sorry to say.

8: THE SAME, THAT EVENING

The curtains are drawn but the candles unlit and the room bright. There are empty glasses on the coffee tables and two of the sandwich plates are empty. The easy chair on the right has been pulled back from the coffee table – **BILL** *sprawls asleep in it – and replaced by a plain chair from the kitchen on which* **ERIC** *sits without his fancy waistcoat. On the chair facing him sits massive* **SCHWEIK***, the only person present who can talk without conversing. During pauses in his speech* **SCHWEIK** *reaches forward and takes a sandwich, rams it in his mouth and ingests in one swallow.*

NORMAN*, on the sofa, watches* **SCHWEIK** *with mixtures of amusement, annoyance and boredom.*

SCHWEIK For years no-one has been a more radical critic of the system than myself. But an extended bureaucracy is no answer to the problem created by bureaucracy. I like these sandwiches. I regret that I have almost devoured them all. I regret too that everyone else left so soon. British intellectuals have very little staying power, I find.

Pause.

NORMAN Yes they did leave rather soon.

SCHWEIK These ego-powered rebellions change nothing but a few superficial details and leave us with even more unwieldy super-structures. You agree with me Eric.

ERIC I'm trying to keep an open mind.

Pause. **SCHWEIK** *eats.*

ERIC [*with effort*] Do you see any solution?

SCHWEIK I see no solution. I see no problem! Since Watt's invention of the steam condensation chamber, history has been a by-product of technological evolution, a process we all contribute to, whether willingly or not. What use is there in accusing and defending and complaining and campaigning? Technological progress is an exteriorisation of the only valid part of the human will.

NORMAN Do you know what you're talking about?

SCHWEIK [*glances at his wristwatch*] Unfortunately yes. And now I regret I can stay no longer. [*he places his hands on his knees preparatory to levering himself upright*] I had looked forward to seeing our charming Miss Belfrage again. In my psychology classes she always asked the most interesting questions.

ERIC I'm sorry. She had meant to be here a while ago.

SCHWEIK Who was it you said she had gone to pick up?

ERIC Evans. A friend of ours.

SCHWEIK Clive Evans?

ERIC Yes.

SCHWEIK I remember him. He used to sit beside **MAVIS** in my psychology classes. He also used to ask quite interesting questions. [*stands up. So does* **ERIC**].

ERIC There must have been some accident.

SCHWEIK Whatever the accident, it is nothing serious or you would have been contacted by telephone. Please give Mavis my regards. Psychologically speaking most trainee teachers are dead timber.

NORMAN Then why do you teach it to them?

SCHWEIK Ah, Mr Muir, we academics are permitted to question everyone but our paymasters! Would you like a lift into town?

NORMAN Thank you! [*he stands*] That's very kind. The last bus left twenty minutes ago.

ERIC Dad, I'll drive you in when Mavis brings the car back.

NORMAN We don't know when that will be, do we? [*he glances at* **BILL** *and says quietly*] Get the boy to bed. [*he squeezes* **ERIC***'s elbow. The three adults move towards the door*].

SCHWEIK For your sandwiches and your conversation, I thank you very much. And please to convey my regrets to our lost hostess.

They go out and their voices are heard off.

SCHWEIK Goodnight!

NORMAN Goodbye son.

The noise of a door slamming. **ERIC** *enters, goes to* **BILL** *and shakes his shoulder.*

ERIC Come on Bill.

BILL [*drowsily*] Is she back yet?

ERIC Not yet, but you've got to go to bed.

BILL [*not really awake*] Pull ... yourself together Eric, it's not as bad as ... you think.

ERIC Come on, Bill. Bedtime. Get up.

BILL [*opens his eyes, then sighs and stands*] Goodnight then. I suppose you'll be waiting.

ERIC Yes.

BILL Goodnight then.

BILL *wanders out.* **ERIC** *sits down on the sofa with hands clenched between knees and stares ahead. He does not move when, after a moment, the front door is heard to open and close and when* **MAVIS** *enters. She stands, watching him with cool sympathy.*

MAVIS Hello. [*pause*] How did it go?

ERIC Can't you guess?

MAVIS Yes. I suppose that's why I stayed away. You're brooding. You ought to be in bed. [*she drops her handbag on the chair.* **ERIC** *does not move or look at her*] If you want me to apologise I will. I'll even try to be abject. Will I apologise?

ERIC This can't go on.

MAVIS Probably not. Do you want me to leave?

ERIC No.

MAVIS Then I may as well go to bed. [*she looks towards the door and then looks back and says on a gentle note*] Come to bed Eric. I'll be nice to you. I can be, sometimes.

ERIC No.

MAVIS Well goodnight. I ought to feel guilty but I've worn that feeling out. I told you I was a bitch, Eric, at the very start.

ERIC Could you not change Mavis?

MAVIS Yes. One day I'll be old, and unattractive, and lonely. I think that really ought to satisfy you. [*turns to go*].

ERIC [*quietly*] Come here please. [*she comes over to him. He stands up and faces her sadly*]. That doesn't satisfy me. You see you hurt me tonight. Publicly. And there was no need to do it. So I must hurt you. I'll be able to rest then.

MAVIS [*screws her face up. She can't take this in*] What?

ERIC I must hit you.

He strikes her cheek with the palm of his hand, swinging from the elbow, then the other cheek with the other hand, swinging from the shoulder. The violent movement of his arms is emphasised by the stillness of his body and face. Her astonishment at the blows far suppresses her pain. She gapes at him, pressing her fists to her cheek.

MAVIS You ... ! You ... ! You ... !

She backs away slightly, reaching her hands towards his face as if to claw it. He smiles slightly.

ERIC [*warning her*] Better not!

MAVIS [*drops her hands, gasps for breath and manages to say quietly*] Are you happy now?

ERIC No.

MAVIS Was it as much fun as the books make out? [**ERIC** *shakes head*] Never mind. You've beaten a woman. In the long run it'll do your ego a world of good. [*thrusts her face at him yelling*] Would you like to do it again?

ERIC Twice was enough. [*she sneers at him and goes to the door*] I think we should go to bed now. [*she spits at him and goes out yelling*].

MAVIS Bill! Bill! Bill! Bill!

ERIC *goes to the sofa and sits on it, his head pillowed on his fist. There are noises of thumps and bangings.*

MAVIS [*off*] Yes now! Yes this minute!

More thumps. **BILL** *comes in holding a coat. He looks helplessly at* **ERIC** *then helplessly at the door.* **MAVIS** *enters carrying a suitcase and coat. She dumps down the first and struggles into the second.*

BILL [*petulently*] Where are we going Mavis?

She doesn't answer.

ERIC I think you should stay.

BILL Where are we going?

ERIC You can tell him. I promise not to follow.

MAVIS [*mumbling through clenched teeth*] I don't know where we're going. [*she lifts her case and points to her bag on the chair. she tells* **BILL**:] Bring that! [**BILL** *goes over and picks up the bag, looking at* **ERIC** *in a worried way with a slight shoulder-shrug*].

ERIC I still think you should stay. [*she picks up the suitcase and walks to the door.* **BILL** *follows.* **ERIC** *stands up*].

ERIC Goodbye.

MAVIS [*without turning her head, to* **BILL**] Say goodbye!

BILL Goodbye!

ERIC Goodbye Bill.

They go out. **ERIC** *watches. The door slams.*

9: THE SAME, TWO DAYS LATER

There is an air of untidiness. The flowers in the vase are withered, the curtains half drawn. **ERIC** *lies on the sofa in pyjamas and dressing gown, his head resting on a pillow, staring at the ceiling. A bottle of vodka, half full, with empty glass on the table beside him. Faint sounds from upstairs of thumping and banging.* **MAVIS** *enters wearing plain skirt and blouse, open coat, carrying a suitcase. She has a key in one hand and after a few steps is plainly surprised by the sight of* **ERIC**. *Her manner is brisk and sensible.*

MAVIS Hello! Shouldn't you be at work?

He says nothing.

MAVIS I came to get the rest of my clothes Eric. I promise I won't come again. I'm leaving the key this time.

She puts the case down, goes to bookcase, lays key on it, picks up the model plane and turns with a partly amused, partly contemptuous look.

MAVIS Are you drunk?

ERIC [*thickly*] Yes. Don' like it much.

MAVIS Anyway I'm taking this plane for Bill. You did give it to him. [*she kneels, opens case, takes some clothes out and wraps them round the plane saying*] Eric, I'm not angry that you hit me, please don't think that. I'm surprised you didn't do it sooner. But we've become bad for each other, I don't know why, and we'd better not see each other again.

She looks hard at him. He doesn't react. She puts the wrapped plane in the case and locks it, saying –

MAVIS You should send for your father – you need company. [*stands up holding the case*] You've enough clean underwear and socks in the bedroom to last you a fortnight ...

ERIC [*interrupting loudly*] I don't want in a day, or a week, or a fortnight, to find in a drawer the socks you cleaned and folded for me when we were happy.

MAVIS [*sensibly*] Then get Norman to come back here. I've left the key on the sideboard. Goodbye. [*starts to leave*].

ERIC [*calling*] Mavis!

She stops and looks at him. He sits up and speaks in a thick voice that tries to be reassuring.

ERIC Mavis whatever happens don' worry. We'd good times. Good things don' go bad because they sud'nly stop. Y're alright Mavis. 'Member that. Whatever hapns, you'n me were alright once – alrigh' now too!

She stares at him puzzled, shakes her head, hurries out. Sound of front door shutting. Long silence.

ERIC [*to himself*] Ev'ything alright really but too [*he yawns*] too tiring.

He sighs, stands, picks up pillow and goes slowly into kitchen. Faint sounds of thumps and a clatter then gentle, almost inaudible hissing. Time passes. Sounds of outside door opening, pause while someone removes coat and hangs it in lobby. **NORMAN** *enters, pauses, looks thoughtfully around the messy room, sees vodka bottle. Goes over, picks it up, shakes his head.*

NORMAN [*to himself*] Well well.

Puts bottle down: it clinks against the glass. Sound of oven door slamming in kitchen. **ERIC** *suddenly appears in doorway and stands holding pillow low behind him with one hand. Father and son stare at each other.*

NORMAN [*gently*] What's wrong son? Why aren't you at work? Why has nobody been answering the phone?

ERIC Headache.

He drops the pillow, goes to sofa and sits down.

NORMAN [*sniffing*] Faint smell of gas in here.

ERIC Pilot light in oven went out. S'alright. I lit it again.

NORMAN [*staring at him and nodding*] Is Mavis ... ? Has Mavis ... ?

ERIC Left me.

NORMAN Yes, you need a cup of coffee. [*goes towards kitchen then pauses, points forefinger, says urgently*].

NORMAN Listen son! When a thing like this happens to a man, the first thing he's got to do is cut his losses!

ERIC *stares at* **NORMAN**, *flings his head back, starts laughing almost silently, then the chuckles turn to almost silent sobs and he hides his face in his hands.*

NORMAN [*nodding*] Yes, you need a coffee.

10: EVANS' LIVING ROOM

A television set with sounds of a rugby match. A bowl of apples on the set. **EVANS** *watches thoughtfully from an easy-chair. At his feet* **MAVIS** *sprawls in a litter of Sunday papers, reading a colour supplement. There is a telephone on the floor beside her. Nearby, a bookcase.*

EVANS *rises and steps over to the set and switches off, then stands flexing his arms and tilting his head back.*

EVANS They should have won. I don't know who was most to blame – them, or the referee, or their opponents. But they should have won. [**MAVIS** *turns a page*] I'm going out now for an hour or two Mavis. I'll see you about eleven.

MAVIS [*looks up*] Where are you going?

EVANS The pub, where else?

MAVIS And I'm not coming?

EVANS [*balances with hands in pockets on the arm of the chair*] I'll be seeing Jack and Ernie Thompson, and Dickie Cunningham very likely.

MAVIS What about it?

EVANS Do you like them Mavis?

MAVIS I think they are bores.

EVANS And you don't hide your feelings do you? Frankly, Mavis you're an embarrassment in certain company. Why should you want to meet my boring acquaintances?

MAVIS [*looks down at the floor and says in a low voice*] I'm so lonely.

EVANS [*stands up and walks to the set, chooses an apple, bites a piece, and regards her thoughtfully*] That's a pity Mavis, but what can I do? I suppose I could kill the next couple of hours watching the telly with you or playing cribbage. That would make two people miserable instead of one. We'd end like these married couples who stop each other enjoying the things they can't both share so end up not enjoying anything, not even in each other's company. I enjoy meeting my friends. I won't stop because you don't enjoy meeting them and have no friends of your own.

MAVIS You explain everything beautifully.

The bitterness with which she speaks strikes **EVANS** *forcefully. He sucks in his lower lip, places the bitten apple back in the bowl, then lifts the bowl with both hands and carries it very reverently to* **MAVIS** *and lays it beside her feet as if offering them at a shrine.*

EVANS [*still stooping, speaking softly*] Look Mavis, a lovely bowl of apples for you, try one. They're delicious! [*stands up and points to the bookcase*]. Here's a bookcase, hardly a yard away from you. The finest minds in human history, Shakespeare, Milton, Edna O'Brien, Agatha Christie, have sweated blood to fill these shelves for you. Or here's the television, a window to the world, a choice of three windows, really. Hardly a night goes by without a view from one of them of people dying by bombs in Asia and starvation in Africa. Watch them doing it and feel privileged Mavis. Or do you want the sound of a friendly human voice? [**MAVIS** *looks up sharply*] Try the telephone! [*he points to it*] Dial the speaking clock and hear what the time will be on the third stroke. [*He loses his temper and thrusts his head towards her speaking in a low, almost hissing voice*] Do anything, Mavis, but try to shut me up inside your own depressing little predicament during the next two hours.

MAVIS [*cries out*] I wish I hadn't sent Bill away! He loved me!

EVANS [*soberly*] Kids have no choice, have they?

MAVIS *stares down at the carpet in silent misery.* **EVANS** *frowns. He regrets having lost his temper.*

EVANS Funny. I never suspected there was a cruelty in me. But when you start tightening your sullen screws on me the stuff comes bubbling out, doesn't it? [*she stares down, ignoring him*] Why don't you get a job, Mavis? You would have more things to think about then.

MAVIS [*glaring disdainfully*] What job? Nursing the sick? Wrapping biscuits in a factory?

EVANS Your trouble is you feel too good for the world. So you have to depend on people like me, who don't. [*he goes to the door and turns there*] I love you Mavis. I love you as much as you let me. I was very lucky to be around when you were getting tired of old Muir. I suppose we'll have another couple of months before you tire altogether of me. Let's pass them as pleasantly as possible, eh? [*He opens the door*] When I come back at eleven, I'll be a lot less ironical, you know.

EVANS *goes out.* **MAVIS** *sits for a moment as if listening to the reverberation of the slammed door, then moves some hair back from her face, gets up, sits down in the armchair with the telephone beside it, lifts the receiver and dials.*

MAVIS Hello, Eric?

TELEPHONE Croak croak.

MAVIS This is Mavis. Yes! No you never heard me on the telephone before did you?

TELEPHONE Croak croak croak.

MAVIS Do you hate me?

TELEPHONE Croak croak croak.

MAVIS Oh good. Eric, I would ... like to see you tonight, just to see you.

TELEPHONE Croak croak croak croak.

MAVIS I don't suppose you could pick me up in the car where I am?

TELEPHONE Croak. Croak croak croak.

MAVIS Sold it? I see ... Well I'll come out by bus if that's all right. I'll come right away. Unless ... Eric, is Norman with you tonight?

TELEPHONE Croak.

MAVIS Right, I'll set off now. At once.

TELEPHONE Croak, croak, croak croak. [*she puts the receiver down*].

11: THE MUIRS' LIVING ROOM

No utensils in the kitchen, no ornaments in the room, no curtains on the window. Easy chair with ashtray on the floor beside it stands left of centre. All the other furniture is piled back right. The books are piled centre front and **ERIC**, *wearing jeans and torn sweater, squats with scissors and string tying them into bundles. He seems paunchier than formerly and more relaxed. The doorbell rings. He rises, dusts his hands on his sweater and goes out. Sounds of door opening.*

ERIC [*off*] Come in, come in! [*enters, followed by* **MAVIS** *wearing her coat and handbag. She pauses and looks around*].

MAVIS You're leaving!

ERIC That's it.

MAVIS So I caught you on your last night in the old home?

ERIC Oh no! I'll be here till Tuesday. Then the furniture will be collected and sold and I'll stay for a fortnight at Norman's place. Then I go to Zambia.

MAVIS Why?

ERIC It might be ... more interesting. It might not, of course. Come with me and find out! [*he looks at her directly in the faced. She frowns, feeling lost*].

MAVIS Zambia!

ERIC Sit down over there. You won't mind if I go on tying these books up.

MAVIS *crosses to the chair and sits down, holding the handbag on her lap.* **ERIC** *kneels nearby and picks up a length of string, then looks at her.*

ERIC Life with Evans hasn't made you less beautiful, at any rate.

MAVIS [*smiling*] That's the only compliment you've ever paid me, Eric. You never used to refer to my looks.

ERIC [*smiling*] How's Bill?

MAVIS He's at a boarding school. [**ERIC** *stares at her, horrified*]. He's not a youngster, you know. His father decided to pay for him ... It's a good boarding school.

ERIC [*rises to his feet*] Perhaps you're a wicked woman after all! [*he addresses her urgently but with no hint of plea*] I think you ought to come back to me.

She feels increasingly lost and fumbles in her bag for a cigarette and lighter.

MAVIS I don't recognise you Eric.

ERIC [*looks down ruefully at his paunch, purses his lips and nods*] It's your fault. Whenever I feel lonely nowadays I go into a restaurant and eat. It seems to help.

MAVIS I'm not talking about your figure.

ERIC I love you.

MAVIS You don't seem unhappy.

ERIC The past few weeks have been the happiest in my life. I'm grateful, Mavis.

MAVIS I don't know what you mean.

She lights shakily a cigarette. He squats down on a pile of books opposite her.

ERIC Before I met you my life was completely shaped by my father, Mavis. The odd thing was, I didn't notice. He's such a decent chap I doubt if he noticed. Of course I'd been to Cambridge. Students at Cambridge are supposed to feel intoxicated and above themselves. But I worried about exams all the time and hardly made a single friend. I left Cambridge with nothing more than the qualifications for a nice safe job. Soon after that I met you. [*he smiles reminiscently*] I needed you, Mavis. I felt it here. [*he lays a hand on his midriff*] A definite physical ache sometimes. It wasn't lust, because lust comes and goes and this was nearly continuous. And then Dad left and *you* started shaping my life. Only you weren't tactful about it. And then – no wonder – you got tired of me and left.

MAVIS [*harshly*] And then began the happiest days of your life.

ERIC Not ... at once. I felt very tired at first, almost too tired to live. But dying needed a greater effort so I didn't, and then I discovered something strange. There was nobody standing over me pushing me around, and I was glad. I *am* glad. [*he smiles at her*].

MAVIS [*mockingly*] And you want me to emigrate with you!

ERIC Yes. I can live without you, we both know that, I don't need you any longer but I want you! You're beautiful and brave and clever and now I can love you like a man. It wasn't a man who used to love you, it was a ... [*he thinks, then smiles with amusement and distaste*] ... a dog shaped like a man.

MAVIS [*abruptly she leans forward and stubs her cigarette in the ashtray*] I'm afraid I don't know you Eric. [*she stands*].

ERIC [*stands and steps towards her saying with gay force*] All right I'm a stranger. Your life has been full of strangers. Come and live with this one. [*he lays a hand on her sleeve and stares brightly at her cold face*].

MAVIS You aren't the type of stranger I go for. [*he lets his hand fall. She adjusts the strap of the handbag upon her left shoulder, then looks at him*].

MAVIS I'm glad you're happy Eric. But you're the kind of man I detest most in all the world because the world is so full of you. All expert and smiling and damnably, damnably sure of yourselves! [*the smile dies on his face*] You used to be ... [*she looks down and says in a low voice*] ... not like that. I loved you then.

ERIC [*with a sudden flash of hatred*] Yes, you proved it didn't you?

MAVIS Well goodnight.

She goes to the door. He watches her go, his hand pressed to his midriff. Before she geos through he calls on a note of pain:

ERIC Mavis! [**MAVIS** *turns, faces him stolidly. He opens and shuts his mouth twice then smiles and says sincerely*] Good luck Mavis!

She smiles, raises her hand in farewell and goes out. The door slams. **ERIC** *turns slowly. His eye falls on the half-smoked cigarette in the ashtray. He goes across and picks it up and stands for a moment, contemplating it with a sad smile. At last he flings it into a corner and resumes tying up the books with business-like briskness.*

MY NINE YEARS as a busy playwright began in 1968. In the Glasgow Herald I read an article on Thomas Muir of Huntershill, and was so excited by this man so unfairly ignored by history books that I wrote a half-hour documentary radio play about his trial for sedition. This allowed me to dramatise *bon mots* of that corrupt and persecuting Tory, the High Court Judge Lord Braxfield, who enjoyed using the older Scottish speech in court. When a spokesman for electoral reform appeared before him on a charge of sedition, and pleaded that Christ too had been a reformer, in a snuffling chuckle Braxfield muttered audibly, "Muckle good that did *Him* – he was hangit an' a'." I have lost the script of that play, but after it was broadcast in 1970 I discovered that in the previous twenty-five years two other writers had independently written and broadcast forgotten radio plays about Muir of Huntershill.

Malcolm Hossick, producer of Scottish BBC Schools TV, commissioned five television plays from me, three of them in a series called *Today and Yesterday* about the differences between everyday life in Victorian and 1970s Scotland. To show that every difference was not wholly to the advantage of the present, I invented a 19th Century doctor of the sort who campaigned for pure municipal water supplies to abolish typhoid and cholera epidemics: he is pleased to hear 20th Century Britain does not have them, appalled to hear that the huge annual death toll by car accidents nowadays is so unimportant that we take it for granted. He also thinks warfare in Europe will never happen again, and when told of two world wars with Germany, fire-bombing and the Jewish holocaust, declares that the 20th Century will be a new dark age. I was happy with these three plays, sure they would lead to interesting discussions between Scottish teachers and their classes, and suggested Scottish BBC post a leaflet and questionnaire to local schools, drawing attention to it. Malcolm Hossick seemed to like the idea but left Scotland before the programme was produced. The new producer removed my references to 20th century warfare and genocide, thinking modern children should not hear of them. A main character in the series was a working class Victorian boy whose parents (I carefully explained) were not very poor – he went barefoot because his boots were saved for Sundays or unusually cold weather; and since tailor-made children's clothes were only bought by rich parents, his had been made by his mother cutting down and re-sewing his father's cast-offs, but she had done it well so he was not, by the standards of his time and class, badly dressed. On attending the first rehearsal I found the working class boy in a pink velvet suit with a frilled collar like Little Lord Fauntleroy. On protesting to the director (who had just joined BBC Scotland after working in commercial TV) he said that most Scottish pupils would have seen the *Forsyte Saga* on television, so could not be expected to enjoy a less opulent past. That ended my writing for Scottish BBC Schools Television.

Throughout this period Frances Head got me three hour-long and two short TV plays produced in England, four of them commissioned. She managed to arrange one meeting with Scottish producer, Pharic McLaren, who told me that Scottish plays seldom had strong parts for women and commissioned me to write one that did - *Sam Lang and Miss Watson*. This play was accepted, paid for and never produced. I made other efforts to get Scottish TV interested in me as a playwright. I was on friendly nodding terms with Tom Wright and Jack Gerson, the chiefs of BBC and Independent TV drama in Glasgow, but could not find anyone willing to discuss the possibility of me writing a play set in Scotland. Years later I met Peter MacDougall, author of fine plays about working class life in Greenock, *Just Another Saturday* and *Just a Boy's Game*. He had persuaded London BBC that Scotland need not be terra incognita in south Britain. They commissioned films from him that could only be made on Clydeside. The filming was arranged from a trailer parked outside the Scottish BBC headquarters in Queen Margaret Drive, because the Glasgow BBC bosses would not give it office room. Is Scotland the only country where officials have a distaste for local talent?

But Frances Head and Stewart Conn gave me no reasons to complain. By 1973 Stewart had broadcast four of my radio plays, three of which had also been staged: *Dialogue* by the Stage Company of Scotland, *The Loss of the Golden Silence* and *Homeward Bound* by the Poole Lunch-hour Theatre in Edinburgh. In one week, Granada TV broadcast *Mavis Belfrage* and London BBC my TV adaptation of *Dialogue*. I still think any three of the four following comedies could make a pleasant theatrical evening.

FOUR ONE ACT SEXUAL COMEDIES

DIALOGUE

1971

CAST

LEO A very conventional sales-representative of thirty-five.

SAM Like Leo, but younger. He speaks very few lines at the start of the first scene.

ELLA A nurse in her early twenties. She wears dull clothes and has the appearance of and manners of a nice young aunt.

WAITER Four lines in the middle of the play.

BEATRICE A woman of thirty wearing a vivid red dress. She has six lines at the end of the play.

SET

On the right of the stage is **LEO***'s flat: a modern sofa with a telephone on a coffee-table before it, and a large map on the wall behind. The map is made by joining together four Ordnance Survey maps. It is dotted with red flags on little pins and one isolated black flag on a brown patch near the centre.*

Left of stage is the lounge of the Waverley Bar: a table with two chairs, an ashtray, and a jug of water with the name of a whisky printed on it.

Between the two is **ELLA***'s room: a stool with a telephone on it.*

LEO*'s room.* **SAM***'s jacket lies on the sofa.* **SAM** *stands on the right adjusting a flamboyant necktie. There is the noise of a door slamming.* **LEO** *strides in, smiling in a jubilant, forced way.*

LEO Guess what Sam! I'm a free man!

SAM *swings round on him, forefinger commandingly pointed.*

SAM Hold it Leo! Just stand there!

LEO [*advancing*] But Sam –

SAM [*powerfully*] Stand there and look at me, Leo!

LEO *halts, staring at* **SAM***, who stares smugly back.*

LEO [*after a pause*] What at?

SAM [*incredulous*] You see nothing different?

LEO [*after a pause*] Is it the tie?

SAM [*patiently*] Yes Leo. Yes it *is* the tie.

LEO Oh very smart. Very good. A very nice fabric ... I'm a free man, Sam.

SAM [*putting his jacket on*] And there's nobody more pleased to hear that Leo, only just now I'm three minutes late for a little appointment and the girl may not be the patient kind, get me?

LEO Actually, I was ...

SAM Leo, I want to hear all about it, every last word, it's a fascinating topic but – [*walks past* **LEO**] Save it till later, eh?

LEO [*injured*] I'm not trying to keep you!

SAM Goodnight, Leo!

LEO *stands dejectedly until he hears the front door slam, then sighs and looks around. He sighs and walks up and down a little, snapping his fingers impatiently. Then he sits down, sighs again, picks up the telephone and dials.*

SOUND: *telephone, not ringing, but croaking loudly, as* **LEO** *would hear it. The croaking stops as* **ELLA** *picks up the phone on the left.*

LEO Hello, that you Margaret?

ELLA [*cautiously*] No, this is Ella, Margaret's room-mate.

LEO [*offhand and impatient*] Put me onto Margaret, would you?

ELLA She's gone out for the night with a friend. Who will I tell her phoned?

LEO *bites his lip, rearranges his thoughts, then speaks on a note of teasing intimacy.*

LEO What did you say your name was?

ELLA Ella. Ella Warner.

LEO Of course you are! You're Margaret's room-mate. Guess who this is?

A pause.

ELLA [*carefully*] I'm afraid I don't remember your voice.

LEO I'll give you a clue. We met at Margaret's party last week. You were wearing a ... a blue trouser suit.

ELLA [*flatly*] I was wearing a dress.

LEO [*nods*] That's right, a blue dress.

ELLA It's really more green than blue.

LEO Well, I got the colour right didn't I? This is Leo Spencer speaking.

ELLA [*after a pause*] Are you sure you're not thinking of someone else?

LEO [*very definitely*] Oh no. Oh no. You're Ella Warner, Margaret's room-mate. We met at the party last week. You wore a greenish blue dress and you think modern mothers allow their daughters too much freedom ...

ELLA [*surprised*] Did I say that?

LEO [*accusingly*] And you don't remember me!

ELLA [*defensively*] I hardly remember anybody there. It wasn't my party.

LEO Don't you worry Ella, you'll remember me when you see me. I'm coming round.

ELLA Don't be stupid!

LEO I'm taking you out for a meal.

ELLA I've just eaten.

LEO I'm taking you out for a drink.

ELLA I don't like drinking, usually I mean ... and I'm studying just now. I've examinations on Monday. [*nonetheless she is flustered*].

LEO You need a change, Ella, a break from routine, it'll help you concentrate on your studies, so I'll be round for you in half an hour, right?

ELLA I won't open the door if you do!

LEO *rubs the side of his face with one hand, glaring at the receiver in the other as if he would like to strangle it. Then he speaks flatly and glumly.*

LEO Have you been to The Waverley?

ELLA Well?

LEO It's a minute's walk from your front door. In half an hour I'll be having a drink in the lounge bar. I'll be smoking a rather unusual pipe. The bowl is carved to look like a bull's head ...

ELLA Oh!

LEO [*has a flash of hope*] Now do you remember me?

ELLA No, but I remember your pipe.

LEO [*returns to glum flatness. He has almost given up*] If you feel like a drink you might as well come along. Goodnight.

He puts the receiver back down and his room goes black. **ELLA** *stands for a moment looking at the receiver in her hand, then puts it down. Total blackness.*

Pub noises are faintly ahead, then we see the lounge bar of the Waverley Hotel. **LEO** *sits at the table glumly smoking his unusual pipe. There is a half-pint glass before him, one third full.*

ELLA [*enters shyly, hesitates, then goes quietly over to him*] Hello.

LEO [*looks up, surprised, then frowns and says without enthusiasm*] Oh. Hello. You made it. [*she sits opposite him. He attempts a lighter note*] What'll you have to drink?

LEO *lays his pipe in the ashtray.*

ELLA A ... a glass of cider.

LEO [*shakes his head*] Better not. The cider in here is pretty strong stuff. Better have whisky liqueur. [*he calls across to the waiter*] A whisky liqueur for the lady please!

ELLA But isn't that ...

LEO [*quickly interrupting*] Oh it's stronger, yes, but the glasses are so tiny it has no effect at all. [*he has grown sure of himself and ventures on the intimate note*] I bet you're wondering why I asked you here?

ELLA [*shakes her head*] No.

LEO Surely it's not every night an almost total stranger asks you out for a drink?

ELLA Over the phone it sounded like you wanted to talk to somebody. I thought you were lonely.

LEO [*indignantly*] Ella! How can you think so little of yourself?

The waiter arrives. He places the drink in front of **ELLA.** **LEO** *drops money on the tray without looking at him.*

LEO Keep the change ... Ella, since that party night and day I haven't been able to get you out of my head! I know we hardly exchanged two words, I know you don't even remember me but you've got to realise you've got qualities that men ... some men find impressive.

ELLA [*interested but not overwhelmed*] What qualities?

LEO Oh, your hair, your shade of lipstick, your conversation ... [*he feels he is not convincing her and concludes glumly*] It's less the pieces than the way they fit together.

ELLA I see. Are you sure you're not thinking of someone else?

LEO [*too quickly*] What do you mean?

ELLA I don't know.

LEO Well it's you I'm thinking about. [**LEO** *stares haggardly into his tankard*].

ELLA [*kindly*] Is something wrong?

LEO No.

ELLA One minute you're enthusiastic and the next you're flat and dull.

LEO I keep remembering a dream I had last night.

ELLA [*becomes enthusiastic*] I had a dream last night! Can I tell you about it?

LEO [*resignedly*] Go ahead.

As **ELLA** *speaks her face registers unexpected vivacity.* **LEO** *watches it closely but without pleasure.*

ELLA I was walking along a road in the country, it was a dull and ordinary day and I was worrying about my exams when suddenly I felt this warm golden light shining down on me from behind. I didn't dare turn and look but I knew, I knew a huge golden aeroplane was swooping after me in the sky and the warm happy feeling came from that. I knew the aeroplane was the Concorde.

LEO [*drinks from the tankard then looks at her*] Well?

ELLA That's all.

LEO Oh.

ELLA It left me feeling happy all day ... what did *you* dream?

LEO There was a stone head on the bedroom floor about six feet high, a piece of a statue of an Egyptian king. It should have been hollow but inside it was stuffed with dirty rags and I was trying to pull them out through the mouth with my hands. I dragged out these rags and dead leaves and rotten old newspapers and then I realised there was ... the corpse of some animal in the middle. I couldn't go on. I tried to cram the other dirt back in but it wouldn't go in. [*after a moment he says with vast indignation*] The room was an utter mess!

ELLA [*sympathising*] No wonder you're depressed.

LEO [*cheered by her tone*] Now I've told you that, I feel better.

ELLA [*thoughtfully*] I wonder if it means I'll pass my exams.

LEO What are you talking about?
ELLA The dream. My dream.
LEO [*strikes the table with his forefinger, solemnly definite*] Your dream means something more important than that. I've read psychology.
ELLA [*almost childishly interested*] Have you? What does it mean?
LEO Sex.
ELLA Oh no.
LEO Wait a bit. You're walking down a dull, dismal road worrying about your exams. That's ordinary life. Then you feel something warm and beautiful coming after you, something that you're afraid to face. It's called the Concorde and you know what Concorde is French for, don't you?
ELLA [*sees a way out*] Isn't Concorde a place in America?
LEO [*speaks like a kind, patient teacher to a difficult pupil*] Concorde is the French for togetherness, Ella. That dream is prophetic, Ella. It tells you what the future holds if only you've the courage to face it.
ELLA [*unwillingly impressed*] I see.
LEO I think that coming here tonight shows you *have* the courage to face it.
ELLA What does *your* dream mean?
LEO [*shortly*] I don't know.
ELLA Is *it* about sex?
LEO [*becomes brisk and breezy*] Shall we change the subject? What do you do? Are you a student?
ELLA I'm a nurse. But I'm studying to be a physiotherapist.
LEO Oh yes. Deep breathing. Physical jerks. I know about that.
ELLA The main thing is relaxation. [*unthinkingly lifts the liqueur and sips it, and pulls an agonized face*].
LEO Then you like hospital work.
ELLA Yes. It's useful.
LEO But the routine gets on your nerves sometimes.
ELLA No, I enjoy the routines.
LEO [*laughing tolerantly*] Don't try to give me that!
ELLA [*surprised into a bolder tone*] But I *do* enjoy the routines! They're sensible, they keep things decent. I wish there were more of them. Not in hospitals, I don't mean that, but outside.
LEO What are you talking about?
ELLA [*tone of an aunt giving a lecture*] Well, if you throw paper on the floor in a hospital someone comes to pick it up. If an old man wets his bed there's somebody to wash him and change the sheets. Or if somebody is in pain or dying, we have drugs to make him comfortable. Outside hospitals the only safe people are the rich people, but in hospitals nobody is neglected or starved or made to do work they're not fit for. There's always someone on duty, someone responsible in charge.
LEO [*accusingly*] Are you an idealist?
ELLA Why?
LEO You talk as if doctors and nurses were all hard-working and unselfish. But the medical profession is only a profession. People go into it for what they can get. The doctor who treated my father for rheumatism –
ELLA Oh some doctors are pretty bad. And nurses too. And even surgeons. I've worked with them. But at least they pretend to care for the patients. The routines make them. If they ignored ordinary routines they'd be discovered at once. But out here nobody need even pretend to help the weak and the sick and the lonely and all those millions and millions of children and I'm sorry, I talk too much.
Brief silence.
LEO [*defensively*] I'm something of an idealist myself.
ELLA Oh?
LEO Not much in my work (I'm a salesman) but in my ideas. [*struck by a thought*] I suppose physiotherapists are fairly well paid?
ELLA Better paid than nurses.
LEO [*waggishly knowing*] Aha! Aha! Aha!
ELLA [*timidly yet eagerly*] I think I might be ... good at it.
LEO Oh?
ELLA We have a little boy with really bad asthma. It's so bad they've had him on steroids, but of course they couldn't keep him on these for ever – they destroy certain glands if you do – and now he's as bad as he was before. Do you know, even in his worst panics, I can get him to breathe perfectly easily? I make him lie flat – it's almost impossible to get asthmatics to do that – and I make him breathe slowly and evenly and deeply, and in ten minutes he's in a perfectly normal sleep. I've tried to teach the boy's mother to do this for him but she can't. She loves him, she'd do anything to make him well, but when she talks to him or touches him his muscles tighten. He doesn't trust her.
LEO [*judiciously*] It's psychological, of course.
ELLA No, hereditary. His father has it.

LEO I mean you being able to help him is psychological.
ELLA No. Our head of department says it's a sort of hypnosis.
With an air of reckless desperation **LEO** *finishes his drink and glares at the air before him.*
ELLA [*softly*] Are you remembering that dream again?
LEO [*turning to her suddenly*] How old do you think I am?
ELLA I suppose ... about ... forty?
LEO [*slightly injured*] I'm thirty-four. [*he forges brightness into his tone*] But I've never been to hospital, and if I see a doctor once a year it's very unusual. I mean it's a very unusual year. That shows how fit *I* am.
ELLA But you're not relaxed, are you?
LEO Of course I'm relaxed.
ELLA Why do you breathe like that?
LEO Like what?
ELLA Quick and shallow, instead of deep and slow.
LEO[*feels shattered and speaks with sudden glumness*] I'm ... going through a phase. It'll pass. It'll pass.
ELLA [*pointing out conversationally again*] You've gone dull and flat again.
LEO [*turning savage*] Do you talk like this to everyone?
ELLA [*sadly*] I'm afraid so.
LEO You must find it pretty difficult to keep a boyfriend, then!
ELLA I do, yes.
LEO I'm trying to help you Ella, but God, you're making it hard for me! [*after a moment he says in an altogether dull flat voice*] My divorce came through today.
ELLA [*staring at him in wonder*] I never knew you were married!
LEO I'm not. I'm divorced. [*gently she slides her liqueur across the table to him. From now on her manner is one of thorough, professional sympathy*].
ELLA Would you mind finishing my drink?
LEO Don't you like it?
ELLA I'm sorry, I've tried to ... I'm sure it will do *you* more good.
LEO [*grateful*] Thanks!
As he drains it **ELLA** *asks timidly.*
ELLA Was it nasty?
LEO [*coughs and puts the glass down and speaks in a low voice without expression*] The proceedings were perfectly straightforward. There was no unpleasantness whatsoever. As my lawyer pointed out, it was a formality devoid of tragic voices. We've been separated for almost two years.
ELLA I see.
LEO [*speaking out bravely*] Ask me anything you like.
ELLA But I –
LEO No no no! Ask away. Ask me anything. [*sighs profoundly*] You'd be astonished how uninterested most people are in this kind of thing.
ELLA Well ... [*tries to think of something to ask*] Well, was ...
LEO [*interrupting*] If you want to know if she was unfaithful to me or was I unfaithful to her the answer is no. In both cases. As far as I'm aware.
ELLA Then why did you separate?
LEO We were incompatible.
ELLA I see.
LEO She kept telling me I got on her nerves and after a while this got on my nerves.
ELLA It must have ... why did you get on her nerves?
LEO To answer that I'll have to explain about my work. Do you mind?
ELLA No!
A note of considerable weight and dignity enters **LEO***'s manner. He is speaking of what he knows better than anybody else. He desires to set it forth clearly.*
LEO I am a sales representative for Quality Fabrics. Quality Fabrics have divided Scotland, you see, into twelve basic zones: North North; North East; North West; North South; Middle North; Middle East; and so on. Each of these zones is divided into five districts: North, Middle, East, South and West. Well, the man facing you at the present moment, Ella, is the traveller entirely responsible – [*strikes the table between them with his finger*] – for the whole South North West and South North Middle. Excluding Glasgow.
He stares at her challengingly. She responds with a slight strained smile which suddenly becomes bright as she thinks of something to say.
ELLA You must pass through some lovely scenery!
LEO So they tell me.
ELLA But surely –
LEO Ella, I'm one of the best drivers I know. In ten years I have not once been involved in an accident that could even remotely be traced to my own negligence. While driving I keep my eyes on the road and my mind on – not just the car ahead of me – but the car in front of the

car ahead of me. In my time I've travelled as far north as Thurso, as far east as Arbroath, as far south as Berwick. And for all the scenery I've enjoyed I might have been driving backwards and forwards through the Clyde Tunnel.

ELLA That's terrible!

LEO [*is cheerily definite*] And there you are wrong!

ELLA But if you don't enjoy the scenery ... and most of your time is spent driving ... then you can't be ... you must be ...

LEO I must have a pretty ghastly life?

ELLA Yes!

LEO It hasn't struck you that a man can enjoy driving for its own sake?

ELLA No it hadn't!

LEO Well, I enjoy driving for its own sake. That's why I'm a good driver. You can enjoy scenery or enjoy driving, but if you try to enjoy them together you're a bad driver and a public nuisance. A good driver is constantly achieving and reconciling two things – maximum speed and maximum safety. This is an achievement which absorbs the whole personality. [*he drops his didactic tone and remarks glumly*] It was an achievement my wife refused to recognise.

ELLA How?

LEO When I got home at night I was exhausted! Damn it, I averaged about three hundred miles a day! I was doing the work of two men! And she benefited because I got whacking big bonuses! Quality Fabrics appreciated what I was doing, why couldn't she?

ELLA You haven't told me what was wrong.

LEO When I got home I was exhausted. I wanted nothing but a meal and an hour by the fire with the newspaper and then, perhaps, a spot of television. That was natural, wasn't it? After all that driving I needed to relax. But she insisted on talking. Telling me things. Asking me questions. And she insisted on being answered. A simple "yes" or "no" or "that's nice" wasn't good enough for her, she wanted detailed discussions. What did I know about hats and shoes? Why should I care whether the new wallpaper should be pink to harmonise with the hearth rug or green to contrast with it? Life is too short.

ELLA But she hadn't seen you all day. Perhaps she wanted to talk to you because she was lonely.

LEO If Beatrice had waited a couple of hours I'd have been able to talk to her. As it was she kept driving me out of the house. To pubs in fact, though I'm not a drinking man. A couple of half-pints is *my* normal limit.

ELLA Did you talk to people in the pub?

LEO Of course. Talk is easy in a pub. It comes to you mechanically. You don't have to think. Before I married Beatrice I talked to her all the time in pubs. But a public house and a private house are different things and if a marriage has any depth it should let a couple be silent together, for a change. I remember reading one of these articles on "how to make a success of your marriage", and one thing it said was "never let your wife feel you take her for granted". That made me laugh. If you can't take your wife for granted then who *can* you take for granted? Everybody else you meet – especially the women – you've to be polite and entertaining to, you've to exhibit yourself and sell yourself to them by talking, just as I exhibit Quality Fabrics to a potential buyer. A wife should be beyond that. Don't you *think* so?

ELLA [*purses her lips and frowns like a doctor considering a case, then looks at him accusingly*] Had you any children?

LEO No.

ELLA You should have adopted some.

LEO [*sighs*] Ella, I have noticed that you are heavily pre-occupied with the mercy and kindness approach to life, and it makes you hard and cruel sometimes. I know there are plenty of helpless and unloved children in the world but do you think it would be fair to get one in, like a paperweight, to stop an unlucky marriage from blowing away?

ELLA [*stubborn on this point*] These children are dying from a lack of love and your wife had more of it than you could take. And if you had begun to love the child too – and you would have, when it grew older – then you both could have talked about it when you came home in the evenings.

LEO [*resignedly*] You're a hard woman, Ella, a hard woman.

ELLA [*contrite*] I'm very sorry – I know you're right because I've been told so before. I just think that most things which upset people would vanish if they tried to be more useful.

LEO *plumbs the depths of self-abasement. He stares tragically at the empty glasses.*

LEO You think I'm useless. Maybe I am.

ELLA [*flustered*] Oh no! I'm sorry Leo, I didn't mean that!

LEO [*looking up at her*] You called me by my first name. This is the first time you've done it.
ELLA Is it?
LEO [*lays his hand on hers. His voice becomes softly urgent*] Come home with me, Ella. I really do want to talk to you. I feel we're on the verge of saying something really meaningful ... But it's hard to say it here. A pub is no place for genuine ... concorde.
ELLA Oh! Well I ... all right, just for an hour, but it mustn't be any longer, Leo.
LEO [*turns and calls loudly to the waiter behind the bar*] Waiter! Waiter! Two whisky liqueurs!
ELLA [*shocked into a louder tone than normal*] You just said –
LEO [*interrupting angrily*] You pity me, don't you? That's why you're ready to come back with me. I'm one of your orphans!
ELLA [*speaks in a fierce near-whisper*] Please talk more quietly, people are looking. And I don't want a whisky liqueur.
LEO [*bitterly*] You can give it to me out of the goodness of your heart like you did the last one.
ELLA [*almost indignant*] Why don't you like pity and kindness?
LEO [*dogmatically*] Because they're insulting to a man's essential nature!
ELLA What's a man's essential nature?
LEO [*snarls*] I don't know!
ELLA You want me to be nice to you as if you were doing me a favour!
LEO [*wildly*] I want to be admired! Is that *too* much to ask?
ELLA Admired for what?
LEO [*cries out in desperation*] If you see nothing else in me you might at least notice I am made in the image of God!
The **WAITER** *moves purposely towards them.*
LEO [*slumps down into mere glumness, remarking lamely as he does so*] If you had a religion you might.
ELLA *has lost all notion of the subject of the conversation.*
ELLA Have *you* a religion?
LEO No.
WAITER [*respectfully stern*] Excuse me, Sir, I think you'd better leave.
LEO [*astounded*] What?
WAITER You're making too much noise. And the swearing upsets the ladies.
LEO I didn't swear! I was discussing religion.
WAITER That can lead to trouble, Sir, I think you'd better leave.
LEO [*grabs his pipe from the ashtray, stands up and moves round the table*] All right! Don't worry! I'm leaving!
ELLA *rises also.* **LEO** *pauses, stares at the waiter, pockets his pipe and moves to the left, pausing to remark over his shoulder.*
LEO I'd like to point out that, while you are not losing a regular customer you might be losing someone who might become a regular customer.
ELLA, *who has come up beside him looking worried and concerned, suddenly starts to giggle. He stares at her.*
LEO You think that was funny.
ELLA I'm sorry ...
LEO [*with finality*] Goodnight.
He turns to walk away.
ELLA [*asks timidly*] Would you like me to come with you?
LEO [*stares at her, amazed*] Of course I would!
He looks into her kind, friendly face, then offers his arm. She takes it. As they walk off she can be heard saying:
ELLA Just for half an hour, I can't stay late, you know ...
Blackness, then a door is heard to slam. We see **LEO***'s room. After a moment he enters followed by* **ELLA**. *She looks around.*
LEO I share this place with a friend – he's out this evening.
ELLA You keep it very tidy.
LEO [*is complacent about this*] I can't stand mess.
ELLA [*sees the map and goes towards it*] What a huge map!
LEO I made it by joining together four survey maps. It gives an astronaut's view of my whole territory at present. The white flags show the positions of the Quality Fabrics stores. But it's only for decoration – it's useless otherwise.
ELLA [*points at it*] Here's a black flag – what does that stand for, Leo?
LEO [*gaily*] Aha, now the black flag is useful. It serves as a reminder and a warning. It marks the spot where I was once seduced by Mother Nature – I suppose you want to hear all about it?
ELLA Oh yes!
She sits on the corner of the sofa with legs curled up and chin upon fist. **LEO** *leans across it to trace lines with his finger.*
LEO One Saturday I was driving along the coast from Stranraer – just about here. I do a lot of weekend work. They give bonuses for it. The day was hot and the road was busy, I'd had an exceptionally hard week, so instead of driving up to Ayr, I turned inland just north of Ballantrae. This line marks a third class road. You can see

why I thought it would be a shortcut. Anyway, I ran up this twisting sort of valley, and passed some old farms and came onto these moors. There was a gate across the road (it's not marked) – I suppose to keep sheep from wandering. So I had to leave the car. Otherwise nothing would have happened.

He turns from the map and scratches his head. He is talking in a perplexed way, more to himself than to **ELLA.**

LEO You see the air wasn't just warm, you had little fresh breezes blowing through it and I could hear of those birds going poo-ee-poo-ee in the distance ... What do you call them?

ELLA Lapwing?

LEO No. Curlews. That's the name. Curlews. Anyway, I shut the gate behind me and drove on for a mile or two and reached a second gate, where the flag is. But instead of just opening it and driving through I lay back on a bank of heather for a puff at the old pipe. There was not a human being, or a telegraph pole, or another car than my own in sight, only heather and farms and this hill opposite, with an old house among some trees at the foot of it. Everything was warm and ... brilliant, and calm. I could hear a cricket nearby, in the grass ... [*looks accusingly at* **ELLA**] You know what I did?

ELLA No.

LEO [*on in a rising note of astonishment and indignation*] I fell asleep! I fell asleep and woke up ninety minutes later with a splitting headache and a fit of the shivers! I was totally behind schedule. I got to Dalmellington all right but I was too late for Kilmarnock and Strathaven. That little nap of mine cost Quality Fabrics as much as fifty pounds worth of business. It was a lesson to me. [*glares at* **ELLA** *angrily*].

ELLA [*softly*] Were they annoyed?

LEO [*puzzled*] Who?

ELLA Quality Fabrics.

LEO [*laughs briefly and begins to walk about the room*] Oh no! That loss is my estimate, not theirs. And it would need more than one accident of that kind to damage a man with a record like mine. But it showed I was human, like the rest. If I hadn't pulled myself together I could have gone to pieces entirely. Men do, in my business.

ELLA [*sympathetically*] No wonder you can't relax.

LEO [*stops and looks at her*] Ella, you haven't understood what I've told you. I *can* relax, but I've chosen not to. You like routine but I'm an individualist. Office work would be the death of me. As things are I drive my own car, I choose (within limits) my own times, I like my work and I'm well paid. I am a free man, Ella. But the price of freedom is eternal vigilance. Beatrice, Beatrice never understood this. In our three-and-a-half years of married life she never once sympathised with what I was doing for her.

ELLA You were doing it for her?

LEO Don't ask me *questions*, Ella. [*he sits glumly beside her*].

ELLA I'm surprised you haven't got an ulcer.

LEO [*looks at her alarmed*] Do you think I have an ulcer? I do have stomach-pains after meals these days. And ... there's a kind of swelling. [*he puts a hand to his stomach*].

ELLA [*sits up. Staring at him, her voice is sharp*] You should have seen a doctor.

LEO I told you. I never visit doctors. It's her ...

ELLA [*professionally interested*] Would you mind letting me feel it?

LEO Please do ... I'll just loosen my waistband.

He pulls up his jersey and unloosens his waistband. With a frown of professional concentration she inserts her hand and feels. **LEO** *leans back with his eyes, an arm along the sofa behind her.*

ELLA [*explores the solar plexus area*] Can't feel anything.

LEO Further down and more to the left.

ELLA [*frowning with concentration*] I still can't feel anything.

LEO What firm, soft fingers you have. Neither hot nor cold.

She pauses and looks at him. He opens his eyes and smiles. She smiles and says, almost inaudibly.

ELLA Aren't you cunning?

He puts his arm round her shoulder and pulls her close to him. She fits in easily. They lie together for a moment, **LEO** *gently feeling the side of her neck. She shuts her eyes.*

LEO *You* aren't tense.

ELLA Did you think I would be?

LEO That talk about being useful to the suffering masses made me think you were more ... rigid.

ELLA Yes.

LEO Like me?

ELLA I like ... this.

They kiss and lie clasping each other.

LEO [*murmurs dreamily*] Woman ... is the downfall of the weak man, but the relaxation of the warrior.

ELLA Who said that?

LEO Napoleon.

ELLA You feel Napoleonic.

LEO Tonight I do ... Josephine.
ELLA Don't be naughty.
LEO I feel ... good.
They kiss.
LEO Can I see you tomorrow?
ELLA Yes.
LEO And the day after?
ELLA Yes.
LEO And the day after that?
ELLA I've examinations then ...
They kiss.
LEO [*with sudden passion*] Beatrice, you're beautiful, Beatrice!
ELLA*'s eyes open fly open disbelievingly. She gapes at him, then slaps his face and springs to her feet.*
ELLA You aren't thinking about me! You aren't thinking about *me* at all.
LEO *sits on the sofa, staring straight ahead of him.* **ELLA** *tugs at her clothing straight and straightens her hair, becoming less indignant as she does so.*
ELLA I'm sorry I hit you, Leo, but you've been thinking about someone else all night! [*he does not move. She stares at him*] I'd better go, hadn't I? It's quite late. [*he does not move*] I ... I'm sorry I hit you Leo, but I really must study now. [**LEO** *does not move.* **ELLA** *goes to the left but pauses before entering the darkness*] I'm sure you'll feel a lot better tomorrow ... [*She tries to think of something else to say*] I admire you Leo. I really do. [*truth and the silence compel her to add*] In some ways ... just a little. Goodnight!
She leaves. A door slams. He does not move. After a moment, in a vacant, mechanical way, he reaches for the telephone receiver and dials a number. His face is expressionless. The dialling tone is heard. It stops and a spotlight left shows **BEATRICE** *lifting the receiver.*
BEATRICE [*briskly*] Hello? This is Hampden 6732.
LEO [*in an unfamiliar voice, quiet and hesitant*] Hello Beatrice ... I was wondering ... I was thinking that, after the court business today, perhaps you were feeling rather lonely ...
BEATRICE [*after a pause, in the same brisk tone*] I'm sorry Leo, I just can't help you any more. It's too late. I'm sorry you feel lonely but it's really too late. Goodnight Leo. [*a pause*] Goodnight Leo!
She puts the receiver down and the spot goes out. After a moment **LEO** *puts his receiver down, then feels in his jacket pocket and brings out a tobacco pouch. From the other pocket he produces the usual pipe and slowly begins to fill the pipe from the pouch, without looking at what he is doing. The light on him narrows and goes out.*

HOMEWARD BOUND
1971

CAST

ALAN	A thirty-year-old bachelor with the innocent babyish expression of a man who has always been spoiled by women. He wears neat, expensive, casual clothes and sandals.
VLASTA	A tall, striking thirty-five-year-old Slav. She wears a white blouse, long black skirt, fur coat and histrionic jewellery.
LILLIAN	A pretty little girl in her early twenties. She talks with a chirpy local accent.
THE METER MAN	He wears a plastic raincoat, trilby hat, carries torch and notebook and speaks two lines.

SET

The ideal set would have a moss-green fitted carpet, white woodwork and pale grey walls, and an oriole window where two walls meet: a window with dark green floor-length curtains and a view of treetops. On the right-hand wall, low shelves which incorporate a record player near the window and a hearth with burning coal fire in the middle. The lower shelves would be hidden by louvre-board shutters, but along the top, starting beside the record player, would stand a record rack, then a china shepherdess, then two modern terracotta figurines of the female nude, then (above the fireplace) a clock with a revolving spring pendulum under a glass dome, then sherry glasses and decanter.

The hearth would have a polished brass fender, a tall brass scuttle and Victorian fire irons. There would be an old-fashioned high-back armchair to the left of the fireplace, a small easy chair to the right, a chaise longue opposite.

Against the left-hand wall would be a low double bed or very deep sofa with thick blue cushions and a framed print or drawing above it, and deriving an air of invitation from a low coffee table nearby. On the table lies a salver of apples, peaches and grapes; a board supporting a chicken, oatcakes, a pat of butter, a salt cellar and knife. Left of the bed, the door. When opened it would show a minute hall with the door opposite.

The room would contain nothing more than this. What was not expensively bleak and contemporary would be expensively Victorian and ornate. The print above the bed could be Picasso's 'Minotauromachie' series.

ALAN'S APARTMENT

SOUND: *an Incredible String Band record, "The Hangman's Beautiful Daughter", is singing "The Minotaur Song" ending with the words –*

"I'll do wrong as long as I can."

ALAN *is frowning closely at the clock face. It is 2.45. He glances at his wristwatch, sighs, strolls to the window and gazes glumly out, hands in pockets.*

SOUND: *The song ends. The record switches off with a click.*

ALAN *turns and goes broodingly towards the record player.*

SOUND: *A doorbell softly chimes.*

ALAN*'s head jerks up, grinning brightly. He straightens his tie, steps to the door and opens it.*

SOUND: *The doorbell chimes again.*

He steps into the hall, opens the front door, pauses, then speaks on a surprised note:

ALAN Vlasta.

VLASTA Can I visit you?

ALAN Come in.

He stands aside to let her through. She enters the room quickly, head bowed and biting her lower lip. Her coat swings open and she clutches a handbag. She goes to the large chair and sits down. **ALAN** *closes the doors behind him then stands watching her alertly. She opens the handbag without looking at him and takes out a handkerchief.*

ALAN I'm glad you came.

She bows her face into her handkerchief and bursts into sobs that shake her whole body but don't make much noise. He watches a moment with no change of expression then tiptoes to the coffee table, lifts it, places it near **VLASTA***'s right elbow, selects an apple from the plate, sits down in the small chair facing her, and starts quietly eating. A moment later the sobs diminish. She takes a mirror from her handbag and wipes off tear-traces, taking care not to damage her make-up.*

ALAN [*softly*] Eat something. It helps, sometimes.

VLASTA You are always very sweet to me. [*she restores handkerchief and mirror to handbag, snaps it shut, tears a wing from the chicken, bites a piece and swallows*] Half an hour ago I threw out Arnold.

ALAN [*decisively*] You're well rid of him.

VLASTA [*smiling sadly*] You are so nice Alan. [*she bites and swallows more chicken*] He did not want to go – I had to call the police. He was drunk and violent – he cracked my tortoise, Alan.

ALAN You were right to call the police.

VLASTA He was sweet to begin with – just like you. And then he went bad on me. Eventually they all go bad on me – except you. [*glancing around*] Are you expecting someone?

ALAN [*smiles sadly*] Expecting someone? I only wish I was.

VLASTA But why this food? ... And the room ... surely you do not always keep it so spick-and-span?

ALAN I do nowadays. Since you left me I've become a real old woman, dusting the clock, hoovering the carpet – I've even grown cranky about food. I don't eat regular meals any longer. I keep plates of fruit and cold meat beside me and have a nibble whenever I feel like it.

VLASTA How odd! But you have no little girlfriend? No mistress?

ALAN Afraid not. [*throws his apple core ruefully into the fire*] I could have, I suppose. I know plenty of women. I've spoken to them ... hundreds of them. And some of them responded, a little. But I couldn't keep it up. After you they were all so insipid.

VLASTA [*emits a triumphant cry*] Ah, I knew it! I knew it! When I left you I told myself, I am destroying this man. All his confidence comes from me and now I am leaving him his confidence will go too. He'll be incapable of anyone else – in fact, I'm castrating him. But I had to do it. You were nice but ... oh so deadly dull. No imagination. And so I had to leave. [*she bites the chicken*].

ALAN But it was agony!

VLASTA [*speaking with mouth full*] I know. I was sorry for you. [*she swallows*] But I needed excitement. I will take my coat off. This room is far too warm.

VLASTA *lays down the bone and stands.* **ALAN** *jumps to his feet, goes behind her and helps with the coat, murmuring tactfully as he does so.*

ALAN I hope you'll take off more before you leave.

VLASTA I am in no mood. This room is too warm. [**ALAN** *lays the coat on the chaise longue, goes to the bed and sits on the foot, watching her. She stretches her arm sideways and yawns*] I am a dreadful woman. I destroy men, Alan. Arnold kept shouting that while the policemen led him away.

ALAN [*assuming the posture of Rodin's thinker, elbow on one knee and brow on clenched fist*] God it's agony leading this ... destroyed life.

VLASTA Think of Wilfred Jenkins, old before his time and drinking like a fish.

ALAN He was a fifty-year-old alcoholic when you met him.

VLASTA He's worse now.

ALAN Please sit beside me. I am very lonely.

VLASTA [*sits*] I saw Angus pushing his baby up the street in a pram in the park yesterday – an abject slave to a woman too stupid to understand him.

ALAN [*looks up*] He seems pretty contented to me – we play snooker sometimes.

VLASTA [*smiling at his naïvety*] You are so naïve. Have you forgotten all I taught you? Below the surface of these calm lives, all kinds of hideous evil things are happening: spiritual incests, rapes, tortures, murders, suicides. And the calmer the surface the worse what lies beneath.

ALAN [*smiles and pats her hand*] I love the way you make life into an adventure, an exciting, idiotic adventure.

VLASTA [*stiffening dangerously*] Idiotic!

ALAN No no no, that was a slip of the tongue, a ... subconscious device by which my conventional bourgeoisie hypocrisy attempted to defend itself.

VLASTA [*placated*] Hm. I see you remember some of the things I taught you. [*yawns*] I am so tired. It is exhausting work, explaining life to thick policemen.

VLASTA *lies back on the bed with eyes closed and hands under her head.* **ALAN** *takes off his tie, drops it on the floor, unfastens the top button of his shirt, pauses, then leans over and tweaks open the top button of her blouse.*

VLASTA [*without opening her eyes*] I told you I was in no mood.

ALAN Sorry. [*resumes the Rodin's thinker pose*].

VLASTA [*opens her eyes and says lazily*] I love you for being so easily discouraged. [*she sits up and begins briskly to unbutton her blouse*] Dear Alan, I can refuse you nothing. [*he jumps up and begins unbuttoning his shirt. He is absolutely straight-faced. She laughs a little*] You are like an ugly old neglected sofa I can always fall back upon.

ALAN [*bows and remarks mildly*] Always at your service.

SOUND: *the doorbell chimes.*

ALAN [*with sudden huge annoyance*] Damn! Damn!

VLASTA What is the matter? [*suddenly suspicious*] Were you expecting someone? Do you know who that is? [*she stands up*].

ALAN It doesn't matter. I mean no, of course not. [*He tries to embrace her*] Ignore it. Ignore it, Vlasta.

SOUND: *the doorbell chimes.*

VLASTA [*evading him, fastening her blouse*] On the contrary, I shall answer it. [*she hurries to the door, still buttoning her blouse. He rushes over and stands in front of the door buttoning his shirt*]

ALAN [*pleading*] Be sensible, Vlasta.

VLASTA [*in a loud voice*] Open that door or I will scream!

ALAN [*through clenched teeth*] Listen! That might be, just might be a young lady I greatly admire and respect. She must not be upset! Do you hear? She must not be upset!

SOUND: *the doorbell chimes.*

VLASTA [*coolly*] Then open the door!

He stares at her then opens the door and the front door behind it. A stout ugly man stands outside wearing a plastic raincoat and a trilby hat.

MAN 'Tricity board. Can I see your meter, Sir?

ALAN Yes. Yes you can.

He stands back to let the **MAN** *in, shooting a haunted glance at* **VLASTA**, *who folds her arms and frowns. The* **MAN** *flashes a torch at the meter dial behind the ajar door.* **LILLIAN** *edges into the hall.*

LILLIAN Sorry I'm late, Alan.

ALAN [*nodding glumly*] Yes.

LILLIAN [*goes past him into the room. Seeing* **VLASTA** *she smiles and says*] Hullo! I'm Lillian Marsh.

VLASTA Good! Good!

VLASTA *walks away.* **LILLIAN** *stares, startled. The* **METER MAN** *scribbles in his notebook and then snaps it shut.*

MAN Disturbing weather we're having, sir. Sunshine one minute, thunderstorms the next.

ALAN Yes. Goodbye.

ALAN *closes the front door, enters the room and closes the room door.*

VLASTA, *hand on hip, leans against the shelves by the fireplace.* **LILLIAN** *stands looking thoughtfully at the crumpled bed and the necktie on the floor beside it.*

ALAN Lillian. This is Vlasta, Vlasta Tchernik. Old friend. She called unexpectedly.

LILLIAN Did she?

ALAN Yes.

VLASTA [*ignoring him*] He was seducing me when the meter man called. He had my blouse off.

LILLIAN [*looking at* **ALAN**] Is that true?

ALAN [*nodding*] Yes.

LILLIAN Oh Alan!

Both feel very depressed. She sits on the chaise longue and he on the large armchair. There is a pause while **VLASTA** *glares from one to the other.*

ALAN [*pathetically*] I wish you had come up when you said you would. I had given you up.

LILLIAN I'm only forty minutes late! I've been punctual up to now.

ALAN Yes. So I thought that ... well, you'd suddenly tired of me.

LILLIAN Why did you think that? We got on so well the last time we met ... Didn't we?

ALAN Oh I enjoyed myself. But did you?

LILLIAN Of course! I told you I did.

ALAN Maybe you were just being polite. A lot of women are polite at those times. After I'd waited fifteen minutes I thought "She was being polite when she said she enjoyed herself." And when I'd waited twenty minutes I thought "She's not coming, she's met someone more interesting."

LILLIAN *stares at him.*

VLASTA He has no self-confidence. None at all. He is a weakling, a coward, and a cheat. And dull. Oh so terribly dull.

LILLIAN Nonsense. He says very clever things sometimes.

VLASTA Give me an example!

LILLIAN Well ... [*she frowns*] Well, we went a walk last Sunday, and he said "The country looks very green today. But I suppose that's what it's there for."

VLASTA He was quoting me. And I got it from a book.

LILLIAN [*to* **ALAN**] Were you quoting her?

ALAN Yes.

LILLIAN [*to* **VLASTA**] Well ... clever remarks aren't important. He says very sweet sincere things sometimes.

VLASTA Oho! [*goes over to the chaise longue*] This really interests me. Tell me about these sweet sincere things. [*she sits beside* **LILLIAN**].

ALAN [*standing up sharply*] Would you ladies like me to make a ... pot of tea? ... A glass of sherry? [*they ignore him. He drifts towards the shelf with the decanter on it*].

VLASTA Tell me just one of these sweet sincere things.

LILLIAN I'd rather not.

ALAN *wanders uneasily over to the fireplace.*

VLASTA Then I shall tell you one. Let me think. [*she taps her lower lip with a finger*] Yes. When you get into bed together, does he stretch himself and say in a tone of, oh such heartfelt gratitude: "Thank God I'm home again"?

LILLIAN *is too impressed to speak. She nods several times.*

VLASTA I thought so!

ALAN *seizes a glass and bottle from the shelf, hastily pours himself a glass and swigs it back.*

VLASTA [*accusingly*] You are trying to give yourself Dutch courage.

ALAN I'm trying to anaesthetise myself.

LILLIAN [*stands up, goes to him and says quietly*] Give me the sherry, Alan. [*he takes the glass from the shelf and is about to pour when she reaches for the bottle*] I'll pour it. [*He hands her the bottle. She lobs it down to smash in the hearth. He stares at her, aghast. She shakes her head and says faintly*] You don't deserve anaesthetic. [*she wanders away from him, clenching her hands and trying not to cry. He stares at her back, deploringly*].

ALAN Lillian! Lillian! [*he sighs, stares down at the mess, then takes shovel and hearth broom and kneels to sweep up the glass.* **VLASTA**, *who has been staring awestruck at* **LILLIAN**, *goes after her*].

VLASTA That was magnificent. You were wonderful. People think I am very fierce and violent because I am outspoken but believe me I never, never break things. I am too timid!

LILLIAN [*harshly*] What other nice things did he say to you?

VLASTA [*smiling*] Well ... !

ALAN Stop! [*he puts broom, shovel and broken glass into the coal scuttle and comes over to them, saying in firm tones*] Vlasta, please leave. We're as miserable as you could want us to be.

VLASTA But I am enjoying myself! I shall not leave.

ALAN Lillian, I've been stupid, very, very stupid. I hope you'll ... soon ... be able to forgive me. But this is an indecent situation and I'd like you to clear out of it. I'd like you to leave before she hurts you any further.

LILLIAN She didn't hurt me. You did. And I have no intention of being hurt any further. [*nods at* **VLASTA**] "Thank God I'm home again." What else did he say?

ALAN [*loudly*] I get no pleasure from this conversation! You two may, I don't. I know it's rude and unhostly but I'm going to leave. Vivisect me all you like – behind my back. I'm spending the night at my mother's house. [*he walks to the door and turns*] The outside door will lock when you close it behind you. Goodbye. [*he opens the door*].

LILLIAN [*to* **VLASTA**, *in a high, clear voice*] He's very houseproud, isn't he? [*he hesitates, looking back. She steps across to the clock and lays a hand on the glass dome*] How much do you think this cost ... Vlasta?

VLASTA Oh, a great deal of money. Are you going to smash that too?

ALAN [*goes over to* **LILLIAN**, *greatly agitated*] Lillian, that has a Mudge Pirouette triple escapement. It's only wound up once a year and keeps perfect time if the balance isn't upset. Please don't jar the movement.

LILLIAN [*retreats along the shelf from the clock, seizes a figurine and holds it high above her head, smiling forcedly*] What about this?

ALAN Take *care* for God's sake! That's a terracotta by Shanks! By Archibald Shanks!

VLASTA Strange how much he cares about things being hurt and so little about feelings being hurt.

ALAN In the first place I haven't tried to hurt people's feelings. I've simply tried to, to, to enjoy myself. In the second place, of *course* things are more important than feelings. We can all recover from hurt feelings – if we aren't children. But destroy a well-made clock or statue and a certain amount of human labour and skill and talent goes out of the world forever. Please Lillian. Put that figurine down.

VLASTA [*hissing*] Break it!

There is a pause. **LILLIAN** *has been slightly impressed by* **ALAN**'*s speech. She cradles the figure in her arms and pats its head.*

LILLIAN Don't worry little statue: I won't hurt you. But your owner will have to act like a sensible adult and not keep running off to his mummy whenever life gets tough for him. [*she walks over to the chaise longue and sits down*] Sit down Alan. Sit down Vlasta.

VLASTA Certainly!

ALAN, *with a defeated look, slumps down in the large armchair, tries to comfort himself by tearing a drumstick off the chicken and gnawing it.* **VLASTA** *walks over to the chaise longue and sits beside* **LILLIAN** *who sits with an absent-minded sad look, cuddling the figurine like a child comforting herself with a doll. Once again* **VLASTA** *plucks her lower lip.*

VLASTA What ... shall ... I ... tell you ... next?

LILLIAN Anything you like.

VLASTA Have you noticed how he plans his seduction scenes always with food nearby? [**ALAN** *stares haggardly at the drumstick in his hand*] Obviously sex and eating are very much mixed in his mind. I haven't worked out what that is yet. Something nasty, anyway. [**ALAN** *puts the drumstick back on the plate and rests his brow on the palm of his hand*] Then again, he's not a very passionate lover physically.

LILLIAN [*surprised*] Isn't he?

VLASTA Oh I'm not pretending he gives no pleasure. But he relies too heavily on words. It is strange, I have known men, very passionate, physical types, very athletic, who could be thrown totally off their stroke by a single frank remark. I like frankness so this always surprises me. But Alan is all the other way. He keeps whispering these little monologues ... you know what I mean?

LILLIAN[*subdued*] Yes.

VLASTA Fragments of erotic dramas. At first this is very exciting ... [**ALAN** *puts his fingers in his ears*] ... he can get you very worked up by it. But when he nears the climax he just lies back and leaves the effort to the woman. After a few months this becomes very dull. How long have you known him?

LILLIAN A fortnight.

VLASTA [*looks at* **ALAN** *and shouts*] Take your fingers out of your ears!

LILLIAN [*holds out the figurine at the angle of a Nazi salute. She says loudly*] Remember the talent and labour and, and skill that went into making this statue Alan!

VLASTA Do you want them destroyed because you're afraid to hear a few ordinary truths?

ALAN *withdraws his fingers and resumes, in earnest this time, the pose of the Thinker. The women consider him a moment, then* **LILLIAN** *restores the figurine to the safety of her arms.*

VLASTA [*to* **LILLIAN**] Which monologues has he used on you?

LILLIAN [*shortly*] The king and queen one.

VLASTA [*frowning*] I have not heard that one.

LILLIAN He pretends we are a king and queen making love on the top of a tower in the sunlight. There's a little city below us with spires and red roofs and a harbour with sailing ships going in and out. People can see us for miles.

VLASTA Hm. The scene is oddly familiar to me ... Ah, I remember now. He got it from a picture in a book I lent him, Jung's "Psychology of Alchemy". It is poetic rather than erotic. But what do you feel about the perverse monologues?

ALAN [*stands up, looking stunned*] Would no-one like a cup of tea? *Chinese* tea? [*the women look up without looking at him*].

LILLIAN I haven't heard those yet.

VLASTA You've never had to pretend you were Miss Blandish?

LILLIAN Can't say I have.

ALAN *strolls in a dazed way slowly towards the bed, snapping his fingers to himself. The ladies follow.*

VLASTA I forgot. You are a novice. "No Orchids for Miss Blandish" was a sadistic American thriller which made a great impression on him when he was ten or eleven. It is a pity there are no state-inspected brothels in Britain. So many adolescents are initiated into sex through books and films and it gives them queer ideas that mark them for life. Alan is such a milksop that I expected his perversion to err on the masochistic side ...

ALAN *flings himself down on the bed, face staring at the ceiling, arms outstretched and ankles crossed in the posture of the crucifixion. The ladies sit on opposite corners of the bed-foot and converse across his toes.*

VLASTA No such luck. He compensates with sadistic fantasies. I suppose that ties in with his feeling for food. Yes! Of course! Insufficient breast-feeding in infancy has turned him into an oral sadist. At the same time his crazy feeling for objects is part of the anal-retention syndrome.

ALAN, *without moving, emits a not loud but perfectly sincere scream.*

ALAN Aaaah!

VLASTA End of round two. The enemy flat on the canvas. [*She addresses* **LILLIAN** *on an intimate note*] I enjoyed that. Didn't you?

LILLIAN No. It was horrible. [*she puts the figurine down on the floor beside her*] You know, when he said those things to me I felt so *special*, so unique ...

VLASTA And now you find you have been to bed with a second-hand record player.

ALAN [*with difficulty*] If ... I said ... the same things to both of you ... it was because you both ... both sometimes made me feel the same way.

VLASTA [*to* **LILLIAN**] Perhaps every woman makes him feel the same way. How many others has he said these things to? [*tears start rolling down* **LILLIAN**'*s cheeks.* **VLASTA** *says to* **ALAN** *in a low hiss*] She's weeping! You made her weep!

ALAN I'm sorry.

VLASTA [*leans across his shoes to lay a hand on* **LILLIAN**'*s shoulder*] Yes, weep little Lillian. It is good for you. I wept when I came here tonight. [*she looks vindictively at a recumbent* **ALAN**] *You* haven't wept yet tonight!

ALAN [*suddenly determined*] And I'm not going to! [*he sits up, leans towards* **LILLIAN**'*s back and says awkwardly*] Lillian, I haven't had the time to tell you this before but ... I love you. I love you. [**LILLIAN** *raises her head. He looks at* **VLASTA**] I don't love you. Not one bit. But since you don't love me either I don't understand why you're trying to crush me.

LILLIAN [*in a sad, faraway voice*] You deserve to be crushed, Alan.

ALAN [*wriggles near her, pleading*] I honestly don't think so! I've been selfish, greedy, stupid and I've told lies but I honestly don't think I've been wicked. I haven't tried to hurt anybody: not even for fun. My main fault is trying to please too many people at the same time. And none of this would have happened if only you'd been punctual! Believe me Lillian ...

He stands up and shatters the figurine underfoot. **LILLIAN** *rises and the two of them gaze, horrified, at the fragment between them. He kneels down, picks up the two biggest pieces, holds them unbelievingly at eye-level and lays them carefully on the floor again, his mouth turning sharply down at the corners. He lies face down on the bed.* **LILLIAN** *sits beside him, supporting herself by an arm across his body.*

LILLIAN Alan, I'm sorry that happened ... I didn't mean it to happen.

VLASTA [*scornfully*] Are you *sympathising?*

LILLIAN [*apologetically*] I'm afraid so. He's crying.

VLASTA Do you think those tears are real?

LILLIAN *touches his cheek with a finger, licks it, touches the cheek again and holds the finger out to* **VLASTA.**

LILLIAN Yes, they are. Taste one.

VLASTA *takes* **LILLIAN**'*s hand to her mouth, licks a finger tip but does not let it go.*

VLASTA What beautiful fingers you have ... so soft and small and shapely.

LILLIAN Oh?

VLASTA Yes. I'm more than a little butch, you know. How

else could I have given myself to a thing like – [*nods at* **ALAN**] – that?

LILLIAN Then I suppose I'm more than a little ... what's the opposite of butch?

VLASTA [*taken aback*] I don't know.

LILLIAN Neither do I ... [*suddenly impatient, she withdraws her hand*] ... I don't *want* to play this game. [*bends over* **ALAN**, *gently lays her hand on his neck and says softly in his ear*]. Alan, I'm sure Archibald Shanks has made hundreds of little statues – you can always get another.

ALAN [*in a muffled voice*] 'Snot just that ... I've ruined everything between you and me! You and me!

LILLIAN [*lies closer to him*] I don't hate you, you know.

VLASTA [*watching them with an ironic smile*] I used to be told the British were cold and lacked emotions. The loss of your Empire seems to have done you a lot of good! [*they ignore her. She frowns and says to herself*] What perplexes me is that ... I have an urge to ... help her resurrect him, so to speak. Am I feeling pity? [*she glances at them and shakes her head*]. No. I despise pity. I *love* destroying men, especially the confident ones. But I suppose, when you've destroyed one, you've got to set him up again before you can knock him over a second time. Just like skittles ... [**ALAN** *has a free hand lying near her – the other is softly caressing* **LILLIAN***'s shoulder.* **VLASTA** *pats the hand experimentally*] Strange how the strongest desires lead us to practise the most abject virtues. Here is my hand, Alan ... don't be afraid of me!

His hand rises and clasps her wrist, then softly begins patting a way up to the shoulder. There follows a gently busy silence, then **ALAN***'s voice is heard to say in a tone of heartfelt gratitude:*

ALAN Thank God I'm home again.

The women look at each other, not very startled.

SOUND: *the Minotaur song comes in.*

LOSS OF THE GOLDEN SILENCE

1973

CAST

HE Older

SHE Younger

SET

An impersonal bed-sitting room.

SCENES

One: The room soon after breakfast.

Two: The room at teatime.

PRODUCTION NOTE

Stage directions in this play have been kept to a minimum.

Actors and directors will naturally introduce some other movements.

None of these should be highly demonstrative.

1: SOON AFTER BREAKFAST

A bed-sittingroom, neither fashionable nor squalid. The bed has a coverlet that comes to the floor all round. There is an armchair and, facing it, a sofa with cushions on it. A dressing table has cosmetics on top and a clock with hands at seven-past-nine. Below is a row of shoes, two third women's, one third men's. A table has the remains of breakfast-for-two on it – a teapot and cups, decapitated eggshells in egg cups. The room lacks any ornament or suggestion that its tenants have tried to make it interesting, though it may contain such impersonal hints of prosperity as a telephone on a coffee table, a standard lamp, a television set. There is also a tall wardrobe. The only visible book is being read by a young, attractive woman flamboyantly dressed, who sprawls on the floor beside the sofa. The door suddenly opens and a man enters and glances abstractly round. **HE** *is some years older than the woman, and wears a dark coat over a dark suit. The woman swiftly thrusts her book under a sofa cushion and lies back watching him expressionlessly.*

HE [*in a preoccupied tone*] I've come back for my wallet. Forgot my wallet.

SHE It's on the chair beside the bed.

HE *goes to the chair.*

HE So it is. [*lifts it and turns, putting it in his pocket*] What did you hide under that cushion?

SHE I beg your pardon?

HE When I came in you hid something under the sofa cushion.

SHE I didn't.

HE Don't be silly.

SHE I hid something private under that cushion.

HE *walks to the sofa, puts his hand on the cushion, then hesitates.*

HE Mind if I look?

SHE I can't stop you. It's your cushion. It's your room.

HE [*pushes the cushion aside*] All right then! [*lifts book*] I see. A book. The Pursuit of the Millennium: A Study of Revolutionary Anarchism in the Middle Ages. [**HE** *sighs profoundly*] So you're intelligent!

SHE [*defensively*] It has nothing to do with you!

HE *lays the book down, walks to the chair, sits with hands clasped and elbows on knees, staring haggardly before him.*

HE I'm puzzled. We've been living together for more than a week –

SHE [*standing up*] More than a fortnight. [**SHE** *sits on the sofa*]

HE How did you fool me for so long? You must be very proud of yourself. [*Pause*] Or could you not have kept it from me a few weeks longer? We were getting on so well.

SHE [*crisply*] You went out this morning as usual at nine o'clock and came back three minutes later. Don't blame me for lifting that cushion. [**SHE** *picks up the book and looks into it*] You'd better hurry up or you'll be late for the office.

HE [*surprised*] What office?

SHE Wherever it is you work.

HE Listen, you know *nothing* about my private life ... Or have you been reading my letters?

SHE You don't get any letters.

HE Good. From the moment I go out that door I become a mystery to you. Perhaps I have a private income and don't need to work. Perhaps when I go out in the mornings I visit my mistress. My other mistress!

SHE [*resuming reading*] Well you'd better hurry up or you'll be late for your other mistress.

HE [*coldly*] Where have you hidden the rest?

SHE [*putting the book down*] What are you talking about?

HE Don't play the innocent with me! That isn't the only book you've read, where have you hidden the rest?

SHE [*coldly*] In my suitcase under the bed.

HE *strides to the bed, kneels, lifts the coverlet to expose a large case, then looks at her over his shoulder.*

HE [*uneasily*] Do you mind if I have a look?

SHE [*exasperated*] Oh look if you want to!

HE *drops the coverlet and stands.*

HE [*sighing*] No need. It doesn't matter.

HE *wanders towards the chair.* **SHE** *stands up to confront him.*

SHE [*brutally*] Shall I tell you what's in that case? [**HE** *stares at her stonily*] Sidney's Arcadia. A Study of Renaissance Psychology. A Short History of Scientific Ideas. Burton's Anatomy of Melancholy. And six exercise books full of notes for a doctoral thesis on the British Epic.

HE Good.

HE *sits down.* **SHE** *folds her arms.*

SHE Listen, if living with an educated girl depresses you, why not forget it? *I* don't want to talk about it.

HE I'm not depressed because you're educated. I'm depressed because now I know the sort of things that go on in your head. Next time we're eating breakfast and I see you frowning thoughtfully, I'll think "Damn! She's worried about her doctoral thesis".

SHE Why damn?

HE Eh?

SHE Why will that annoy you?

HE Because I'll feel I have to say something cheerful and reassuring about it.

SHE Do you really resent having to make ordinary friendly remarks over the breakfast table?

HE Yes!

SHE What a selfish attitude! Anyway, you couldn't reassure me about my thesis on the Epic. You're too ignorant.

HE For the first time in a fortnight I tell you what I'm thinking and at once you call me selfish and ignorant. That's very matrimonial of you.

SHE I'm sorry.

SHE *sits down on the sofa, picks up the book and starts reading.* **HE** *rises and wanders about disconsolately with hands in pockets.*

HE [*plaintively*] Why do you think I'm ignorant?

SHE [*speaks without looking up*] You've no books. You never read.

HE How do you know? You only see me in the evenings and weekends. During the day I may be working as a librarian, a journalist, a schoolteacher, a lecturer on medieval literature or some other esoteric balderdash.
SHE [*still seems to be reading*] You used to read. Once.
HE How can you possibly tell?
SHE You said esoteric balderdash without even smiling. [**SHE** *looks up*] What do you work at?
HE I won't tell you.
SHE *throws the book down on the sofa beside her.*
SHE In the last five minutes our relationship ... has gone badly downhill. And I certainly can't blame myself. [**SHE** *folds her arms*].
HE And if I tell you what I do during the day you'll guess what I'm thinking about most of the time. And then you'll start to despise me.
SHE Why?
HE Because familiarity breeds contempt.
SHE Not always.
HE Yes always! I was married once. [*sits at the breakfast table*].
SHE I knew that of course.
HE Why "of course"?
SHE In our fortnight together you've said almost nothing but "pass the jam" and "see you later" and "let's go to the cinema". Only a married man could be so laconic.
A pause in which **HE** *lifts an empty eggshell from a cup and seems to study it.*
HE I have also paid you ... some tender and heartfelt compliments.
SHE In bed, yes. That doesn't count.
HE It is the only time language counts. [*carefully returns the shell to the cup*] Apart from then it's a weapon people use to shove and claw and disqualify each other. Listen to us!
SHE You started.
HE Yes, guilty. Guilty. I broke first. And now we're nagging each other like a married couple.
SHE I'm tired of people complaining about marriage. If it was as bad as moaners make out it would have been abandoned years ago.
HE [*sighs*] Were you ever married?
SHE No, but my parents were.
HE Being born into a marriage doesn't count. That accident happens to most of us. The horror only dawns on you when you choose it for yourself.
SHE What horror?
HE *stands up and wanders about restlessly.* **SHE** *is watching him with interest now.*
HE The lack of privacy. You begin by sharing a room and bed and meals and the money you earn – that isn't too bad. It can even be fun. But you end by sharing your thoughts, your hopes – even your moods. Have you noticed how cheerful I am at breakfast?
SHE I'm not very observant at breakfast. But I've heard you singing in the bathroom while I was frying the eggs.
HE Were you irritated?
SHE A little. But I could ignore it.
HE My wife couldn't. She was always cross and grumpy when she got up, and she took it as an insult if I wasn't as depressed as she was. If I sang or whistled or even hummed, she said I was giving her a headache. [**HE** *sighs*] So I crushed the melody in my bosom and did become as depressed as she was.
SHE [*amused*] You exaggerate fantastically. It's very entertaining ... So your wicked wife kept forcing you to share her moods?
HE I was just as bad. Sometimes I came home from work and found her brooding about something. It was very strange, I knew if I left her alone she would cheer up eventually, but I couldn't do that. I couldn't stand her not feeling as happy as I was at that moment. So I tried to nag her into feeling happy. I would ask what was wrong, and then explain how unimportant it was, and we would end up irritated with each other. Whenever we weren't equally happy or equally sad, we nagged each other till we were equally irritated. All our conversations became wrestling bouts.
SHE All?
HE Yes. What else could they be?
SHE [*crisply*] Speech, at its best, is a way of sharing ideas.
HE I know. But when a couple have been conversing night and morning for a month they've no ideas left to share. Each knows what the other thinks and feels and can recite backwards the other's pathetic little stock of jokes and reminiscences. The sharing has been completed. The daily conversations have destroyed all the mystery which makes strangers attract each other. I'm *sick* of words.
SHE But you're pouring them out!

HE [*sits down beside her*] Yes indeed. I'm like an alcoholic who can go for weeks without liquor, but if he once takes a single sip, can't stop drinking till he's flat on his back. I started telling you about my wife. Now I'm telling you about my bad habits. That will lead inevitably to childhood, schooling and how I make my money ...

SHE [*laughing in a friendly way*] Yes but ...

HE [*pats her hand*] Wait a minute! When I've finished – when I've cut myself into little pieces and handed them to you on a tray – you'll start talking.

SHE [*shortly*] I don't like talking about myself.

HE Perhaps not, but I'll get you doing it. I won't be able to stop myself. I'll worm out your father and mother, your adolescence, your love-life and your emotional difficulties. After a week has passed – a fortnight if you're unusually stubborn – you'll no longer be the lovely stranger I met at a party, the mysterious woman who shares my bed and breakfast. I'll have turned you into words. You'll be like me: a cluster of problems with a trite little history behind it.

SHE [*after a pause, in a low voice*] Do you really find me ... lovely and mysterious?

HE I've managed it till now. When I saw you at the party that evening, across a crowded room, I thought ...

SHE Fly to her side, and make her your own, or all through your years you will dream on alone. [*pause*] Have I hurt your feelings?

HE [*in hurt tones*] Oh no no. What you just said is, is really very witty.

SHE [*slipping an arm round his shoulder and saying kindly*] I do want to know what you thought when you saw me that first evening.

HE [*sighs*] You see we met in a house I'd never seen before in my life. I'd been talking to a stranger in a pub who said he knew where there might be a party with plenty of unattached women. When we got there I was dismayed to find that I was by ten years the oldest person in the room – all the women looked like silly, chattering little girls: except you. You weren't much older than them but you stood against the wall looking splendidly lonely and self-possessed, as if you owned the place and despised it.

SHE [*lightly kisses his cheek*] I did own it. At any rate I rented it.

HE *straightens and stares at her.*

HE [*surprised*] Really?

SHE I shared it with two of the chattering little girls.

HE Have you given it up yet?

Pause.

SHE Finish what you were saying about me.

HE You were the only woman I wanted to speak to and I foresaw the conversation at once: a discussion about film and politics to show we were intelligent, then remarks about work and hobbies to show we had money but were keen on other things too, then stories about friends and places we visited to show we were very human and interesting and capable of friendship. I saw it coming and felt sick before I started. So many dishonest speeches when all I wanted was –

SHE [*lightly kisses the corner of his mouth*] Sex.

HE [*shocked*] What a crude little word!

SHE It's the right word.

HE No! What I wanted wasn't crude or little. I wanted to, to bathe my unique maleness in your unique femaleness, to dissolve the fused hard bead of my separate identity in the dark flame of –

SHE [*stands up impatiently*] You've read too much D.H. Lawrence.

HE [*with dignity*] A man can *never* read too much D.H. Lawrence.

SHE *wanders about the house with a slight frown between her eyebrows, pausing at times to attend the monologue which* **HE** *seems to be saying more to himself than to her.*

HE The point is, I stood beside you and offered you a cigarette. You accepted it. We danced a few times, I asked you home with me ... and you came. When I went out next morning you were asleep, or pretending to be. I was sure you'd be gone when I came back but I left the key on the dressing table beside your hat, just in case. And you *had* gone when I came back, but ten minutes later you entered with a suitcase and half a pound of sausages which you fried in the most touchingly natural way in the world. Since then we've lived together without explanations, accusations, excuses or a single cross word. You've been better than little Moggy.

SHE Who?

HE A cat who visited me once when my wife took the children to the seaside. I developed mumps at the last moment and couldn't go. For three or four days I lay in bed reading, listening to records, only getting up to feed out of tins. The privacy was wonderful. On the second day a cat ran in when I opened the door for milk. She was a neat little thing with a smooth black coat, but hungry, so I fed her. When I went back to bed she came and curled in the hollow behind my knees. I liked to stroke and pat her – she was so graceful and ... and suave. When she wanted out she patted the door with her paw, and I let her out, but she came in again next morning with the milk. We kept company for more than a week, and never exchanged a word or bullied each other in any way at all. We weren't bothered about each other. Before I met you that was the most purely happy friendship in my life: but our friendship has been better.

SHE *sits beside him, chin on fist and elbow on knee.*

SHE [*thoughtfully*] That's what the last fortnight has been to you – an exciting friendship.

HE Of course! Surely you have felt that too?

SHE To be perfectly honest – [*pauses*].

HE Yes?

SHE *sits up and faces him.*

SHE To be perfectly honest, what you've said against talking makes sense. It's eccentric but it makes sense.

HE You think so?

SHE Yes. I think we should switch on silence again. We're still fairly mysterious to each other. All you know about me is that I'm intelligent. All I know about you is you were married once. I see you've an almost drunken desire to reveal yourself but I'm sure I can help you conquer it. The thing to remember is, I'm not interested in you when we aren't making love. [**SHE** *stares at him.* **HE** *is daunted*].

HE Oh. Good.

SHE Shall we try it then?

HE Yes but –

SHE [*laying a finger on his lip*] Shhh! [**SHE** *stands up. So does he.* **SHE** *says in a whisper*] Off you go to wherever it is.

HE Yes but –

SHE [*laying a finger to her own lip*] Shhh! Shhh!

HE *sighs and goes slowly to the door where* **HE** *turns and raises a hand to speak.* **SHE** *again places a finger to her pursed lips. Defeated,* **HE** *goes out, closing the door quietly behind him.* **SHE** *sits down on the sofa and picks up The Pursuit of the Millennium.*

2: THE ROOM AT TEATIME

They sit at the table near the end of their evening meal. Neither is an epicure. They are finishing off fried egg, pies, peas and potatoes. There is also a sauce bottle, a two-tiered cake-stand with sliced bread on the lower tier, and two wrapped chocolate biscuits and two garish icing cakes on the upper. On her side of the table is a teapot with a cosy and a jam dish. **HE** *lays down his fork, takes a slice of bread onto his side-plate and says:*

HE [*curt and quiet*] The jam please.

SHE [*passing it*] Here.

HE Thanks.

HE *spreads it on his bread.* **SHE** *continues eating for a moment.*

SHE How did you get on today – oh, I'm sorry. [**HE** *glares at her until she resumes eating. So does he. After a moment she looks up*] I didn't mean to say that – it slipped out – I'm sorry. [**HE** *glares at her with compressed lips until she shrugs and resumes eating.* **HE** *bites the bread. Suddenly she lays knife and fork down firmly on her plate*] I'm sorry but I want to talk to you! [**HE** *stares down at his plate*] Maybe we should be – will be – silent again, but only when we know each other a little better.

HE [*in an odd, strained voice*] You might find yourself knowing too much about me. [**HE** *sighs, stands up, takes a few steps from the table and turns*] Have you heard of ... Bible John?

SHE Yes ... wasn't he a sort of Glaswegian Jack the Ripper?

HE [*with a Glasgow accent*] Aye, that's right.

SHE I seem to remember identikit photographs in the papers. He always looked different but he always had the same funny smile.

HE [*smiling funnily*] That's right – hen. [**HE** *walks behind her saying quietly*] I'm coming behind you ... I'm going to put my hands round your neck. [**SHE** *raises her eyebrows, startled, but does not turn.* **HE** *puts his hands round her neck*] ... I'm beginning to ... squeeze it ... [**HE** *does, but not very perceptibly*].

SHE [*sensibly*] Have you finished?

HE [*glumly, in his usual voice*] Yes. [**HE** *releases her neck and walks across the room, grabbing a cake as he passes the table.* **HE** *bites it, swallows and tells her accusingly*] If I'd have put on that act yesterday I could have had you crouching in that corner in an agony of terrified apprehension.

SHE Perhaps, but now it's too late. Please sit down and listen, you make me nervous wandering about like that. [**HE** *sighs and sits at the table*] ... I've been thinking all day about what you said this morning. It's completely changed my notion of you. I thought you were a stupid, pitiable man who couldn't talk because he had no clear ideas. So of course I didn't *want* to speak to you. But you are intelligent. And you talk well, even if your language is shot through with out-of-date romantic clichés ...

HE Eh?

SHE ... All that business of crushing the melody in your bosom and me frying sausages in a touchingly natural way. By the by, I'm sure I know what you work at. You write copy in an advertising agency.

HE Wrong!

SHE Oh. Never mind. Come to think of it, your clichés would be too sentimental for a successful firm. [**HE** *groans*] I'm not criticising you – I enjoy the way you talk. And I'm amazed by the different way you see things. For example, us living together for the past fortnight was an exciting adventure for you. To me it was just – convenient. [*Pause*] That hurts you of course. All afternoon I've been thinking "He doesn't want us to talk because he can't stand the truth. He likes me mysterious – why tell him how uninteresting I am?"

HE Nonsense!

SHE [*fiercely*] I am! ... I can attract men physically, I know that, but so can any woman under thirty who knows how to dress and carry herself. I'm also intelligent, so I've always despised girls who think some sort of love is the only reason for living. That kind of girl bores and irritates me, and there are so many of them. Trouble is, I don't find men much better. I've never lacked invitations, but whenever I wasn't locked in a steamy clinch I almost always found the boy dull and uninteresting and obviously he felt the same about me. My subject was the British Epic. His was sport or motor cars or films. We couldn't interest each other at all. I did meet a few who pretended to like books but were astoundingly ignorant. Some of them had university degrees too, but if I tried to discuss the Epic Time with them they grunted and stared and grunted and nodded like sleep-walkers. So I stopped talking about what interested me. My mind was *my* business and nobody else's.

HE Then why talk?

SHE Words do one thing well, if used by honest people: they clear up misunderstandings. I detest being thought something I'm not and I am *not* a suave little cat with arms, legs, etcetera – the whole human works, as you put it. Before today I didn't give a damn about what went on in your head, but now I know you – a little – and I refuse to be an object you can project fantasies onto, like one of those horrible plastic women they advertise in men's magazines. I'd rather bore you as the uninteresting person I am than excite you as the wonderful person you imagine.

HE [*gasps*] You ... are ... wrong! Wrong about me (which I expected anyway) but most of all wrong about yourself!

SHE All right. Stalemate. Have some tea. [*lifts the teapot*].

HE No thanks. A question. Why have you lived for a fortnight with a man you thought pitiable and stupid?

SHE [*puts the pot down*] I was in a tight corner. You were a way out.

HE Go on.

SHE I met a man who one day didn't bore me. He was keen on politics, but not like these boys who talk about the evils of this and think themselves very dangerous because they read radical newspapers and quarrel with their daddies. This man stood in picket lines, carried collecting-boxes and pestered MPs and town councillors. I've seen him at a street corner lecturing an old-age pensioner, an unemployed navvy and a four-year-old child sucking a lollipop. They arrested him for it. Most people found him laughable and annoying. They hated being reminded how horribly most people are treated in this world. I hated it too, except when I was with him. You see, he knew the remedy.

HE Ha! Revolution!

SHE [*loudly*] He wanted the hungry to fight for food, the poor to fight for wealth, the homeless to fight for houses! And he helped them do it. I've seen him find rooms for homeless families. I've helped him. Until you've done the same you're in no position to despise him. [**SHE** *becomes more thoughtful*] My work didn't interest him at all. He thought Epic Poetry was a luxury of the exploiting classes, like owning a private park. He was wrong, but I never bothered to argue. He was very nervous and vital, he kept thinking and feeling about things all the time, and when I was with him. I had to do it too. I enjoyed that at first – it made a change. As you've noticed, I'm a rather calm person. But after a while I saw what he really wanted to have me feeling and thinking about him. In public life he was brave and independent – he really could stand alone. In private he was a glutton for adulation. He was good at sex – better than you, I suspect – but I had to keep telling him so, which eventually made it rather depressing. Each time we made love he wanted to be told how much more wonderful it had been than the time before, and if I didn't tell him that he'd insist on starting again, even if neither of us felt very enthusiastic. If I'd been more of an actress I could have kept him, I suppose. But I hate having to pretend. [*pauses then sighs*] I dried up in the end. Not one syllable of approval, not one gasp of pleasure could he squeeze out of me, no matter how cleverly he talked or how lovingly he behaved. He started hinting that I was frigid and I retorted by becoming ironical and withdrawn. In the end he threw me over for the sort of inexperienced young girl who could admire him without reservations – one of my flatmates actually. I was amazed at how much I resented that. He really was a very interesting man. If only he'd been more sure of himself. Then I met you at the party.

HE [*hopefully*] A totally different type? Not brilliant, perhaps, but self-assured? And silent?

SHE You looked worried and withdrawn. But you were clean and the right age and knew nothing about me – I couldn't have stood being comforted by a friend. And I really did want to leave that house behind me. They were both in it, you see. [**SHE** *sighs and looks round*] I've liked living here. You're not a selfish man and I've had peace and quiet to get on with my work.

HE Until now. [**HE** *gets up and wanders to the sofa, hands in pockets, turning, he asks on a low note*] You said an odd thing. You said you suspected he was better at sex than I was. Why don't you know?

SHE I once met a man who would eat a meal and tell you he hadn't tasted such good mutton since the third of October, 1963, when he dined with the Professor of Marine Biology at Aberdeen University. But the peas were ghastly. The only chef outside France who understood peas was working at a Blackpool boarding house. I find remarks like that hard to believe. I enjoy most kinds of food when I'm hungry, and though some meals are definitely better than others I just cannot remember the taste afterwards. Sex is like that – I remember last week's sex as little as last week's dinners. Of course I know sometimes I'm disappointed and sometimes I'm unusually pleased, but I'm never sure why. Maybe the man's been unusually virile, or unusually sensitive to my mood. Or perhaps I'd just got over a cold and felt more fresh and open than usual. Or maybe I'd been working too hard and *passionately* needed distraction. But usually sex is just ... daily bread. Don't you feel that?

HE [*sits down and sighs*] Not yet. Sexually speaking my wife and I got on very badly. With you it's all been good.

SHE Yes, I thought there might be more wrong with your marriage than too many conversations. [*stands up*].

HE Tell me about your work.

SHE [*quickly*] It wouldn't interest you.

HE You're very protective towards it, aren't you? Sit beside me. [**SHE** *does*] When my thesis is complete it will be read by a committee of academics. Half of them will like it because they don't really understand it. The other half will understand and hate me for it.

HE [*fascinated*] You must tell me more.

SHE [*sighs*] Well, do you know what an Epic is?

HE A very long poem.

SHE Not nowadays. Since Gibbon's Decline and Fall most Epics have been prose: even if we accept Wordsworth and the Brownings, Doughty and The Dynasts.

HE Look, you'll have to stop using names. I'm educated. I've *heard* of these people. But I haven't read them. Just tell me what an Epic is – don't give me examples.

SHE [*sternly*] An Epic is a work which gives a complete map of the Universe as far as a civilisation is able to understand it. Most poetry describes the isolated human soul. Novels, dramas, histories, describe men in society. Science describes the structure of the world and its place among the stars. But a true Epic shows all these together like themes in a great symphony. I believe that English has lacked the Epic dimension since Ulysses, and I have grave reservations about that book. Of course we've many specimens of the comic Epic, but in spite of the resolution of the old Vitalism – Mechanism controversy nothing really serious has emerged. Sometimes I think Einstein's failure to solve the Unified Field Equation means that a modern Epic is unwriteable. And then I wish I was dead.

HE But you're not trying to write an Epic! You're writing *about* them.

SHE [*eagerly*] I'm not a creative writer, no, but creative writers find scholars more useful than you think! I have this fantasy that the next true Epic will be written by a woman. I imagine my thesis being published and a copy lying in a neglected corner of an obscure public library. A wretched, pimply, uninteresting little girl comes along, but she has great soul – a sort of female Alexander Pope –

and she reads my book and discovers her mission in life: to write a modern Divine Comedy relating particulars to universals in a synthesis which draws upon Marx and Freud just as Dante drew on Aristotle and Christian Neoplatonism!

HE I haven't the faintest idea of what you're talking about! Nobody can have read all these writers! Anyway, from now on no first class artist will bother with a book. Fifty years from now almost everybody will be illiterate. Nobody will study literature but television script-writers with no ideas of their own.

SHE [*on a note of low, barely compressed fury*] Don't you dare say that to me! Don't dare!

SHE *bursts into tears: he is distressed and tries to embrace her.* **SHE** *shrugs him off.*

HE What's the matter?

SHE That's what I'm afraid of! What you said is ... what I'm afraid of! Sometimes the fear of it keeps me awake at nights!

HE [*awed*] Cor! ... I never knew anyone take their work as seriously as you take yours ...

HE *puts an arm around her shoulder and pulls her gently to him.* **SHE** *submits.*

HE What's your name by the way?

SHE [*sniffing*] Kate.

HE Kate ... please cheer up. I'd like to help you. I'd like to help you!

SHE What's your name?

HE You've seen it on the front door.

SHE Yes, your surname. All I know of your Christian name is that it starts with a Q.

HE I won't tell you my first name.

SHE Why not? [*separates herself*].

HE It's a ridiculous name. I'd rather forget it.

SHE Quentin?

HE No.

SHE Quintus? Quintilian?

HE No, let's change the subject.

SHE Quilp? Quagmire? Quoop?

HE [*testily*] Stop fantasising, Kate.

SHE Stop Kateing me ... Quoop!

SHE *emits a brief burst of hysterical laughter.* **HE** *stands up.*

HE I've never met anyone whose mood changed so rapidly ... [**HE** *walks away and turns to speak.* **SHE** *hears him with downcast eyes*] Listen though! Please listen. I don't understand you, but I see one thing, clearly. You have a great soul, a really great soul, and you're *right* to keep it bottled inside you – put into words only a professor could understand it. But because you keep it inside don't think it doesn't show. It shows in your silences and your movements. It shows in your way of frying sausages, don't laugh. It would exist if you'd grown up among people who couldn't write – they'd have turned you into a priestess or something like that.

SHE [*stands up and says coldly*] You're doing it again. Stop.

HE [*comes to her*] What am I doing?

SHE Imagining me something I'm not.

HE Why are you afraid of admiration?

SHE It's so filthily personal – excuse me while I pack my things.

They stare into each other's eyes. At last he says in a low voice.

HE All right.

SHE *goes to the bed, drags out the case, lays it on the bed, opens it and, while he talks, stacks the books inside into a block at one side, to make space.*

HE [*loudly*] Let me put my admiration into words you might accept. I think you're glorious, but as you say, that's only personal. Had I been a different man – had I been a stronger, more vital man – I might have found you repulsive. My eyes could only have seen glory in –

SHE [*going to the dressing table*] The coming of the Lord?

HE [*forcefully*] In one of your silly inexperienced flatmates!

SHE *opens a drawer and stacks it methodically on the dressing table top, afterwards picking up her shoes from beneath and wrapping them in a towel. Meanwhile he is saying more quietly.*

SHE The truth is, everyone is glorious. Without speaking – without acting – merely by existing – men and women are as splendid and uniquely coloured as hillsides, trees, and elephants. I mean, nobody who uses their eyes thinks a tree ugly or uninteresting. They can admire even small ordinary things like a sparrow or a seashell. Any sparrow! Any seashell! But when it comes to human beings we only seem able to admire the ones we want to imitate or sleep with. Our vision of humanity is buggered up by our desires.

SHE [*at a distance*] Hare Krishna! Hare Krishna! Have you seen my hairbrush – Quoop?

HE [*patiently*] Under the bed.

SHE *carries the things to the bed and packs them carefully into the case.*

HE The thing is, when we admire a thing we won't let it alone. We see glorious elephants so we kill them to hang their heads on a wall. We see splendid forest so we cut motorways into them and chop down trees to make car parks. We see a fine woman so we force her to admire us. I honour your old boyfriend for his political decency but he sounds a bastard. You loved him – could he not have helped you to like yourself? To be liked, just to be liked, is the basic right of *every* human being –

SHE [*poms the American National Anthem*] Pompy pom pom pom pom! Pompy pom pom pom ...

HE [*firmly*] You can't hurt me, Kate. Twelve years of unlucky marriage have immunised me against merely deliberate insults ... [**SHE** *picks a hairbrush from under the bed, packs it into the case, locks it, goes to the wardrobe, opens it, takes out coat and hat and puts them on*] I suppose a parent was to blame. I've been a parent, so I know how they work. Some parent felt it was wrong of you to like yourself much so he – or she – discouraged all your girlish little tricks by persuading you they weren't interesting. So you said, "All right, I'm uninteresting, so I'll build something great that has nothing to do with me". So you put your energy into building this fantastic mind – and believe me it is a fantastic mind. And now, because I insist your mind is part of you, and I'm fascinated – why, you're running away. You would have stayed here if I'd agreed to find you as uninteresting as you found mc. Isn't that true?

SHE [*comes over to him saying sensibly*] I haven't the faintest idea what you're talking about. Here's your key back.

HE *takes it, and then says after a moment in a tired voice:*

HE Thanks. Where will you stay tonight?

SHE My old room. I haven't given it up.

HE What about ... that man and your flatmate?

SHE Oh she was just a one-night stand. He left, the day after the party. I found that out a week ago.

HE [*thoughtfully*] A week ago!

SHE *goes to the bed, picks up the suitcase and turns towards him.*

SHE [*in a low voice*] There's one thing I want to confess. Most of what I told you about the Epic wasn't original. I got it from a book by Tillyard. When I finish my thesis it will be no more than an extended footnote to the work of Tillyard: who, of course, is a man.

HE [*nodding*] Chopping down your size again – very praiseworthy. But I'm not impressed.

SHE [*with real fury*] You devil!

SHE *goes to the door.* **HE** *follows.*

HE I'm not. I want to meet you again. Soon.

SHE *turns and holds her hand out and says coldly*:

SHE Goodbye!

HE[*shaking it but not letting go*] What about seven tomorrow night? The lounge of the Blue Lion. Neutral territory.

SHE Goodbye. [**SHE** *pulls her hands free and half turns to the door*].

HE Will you come tomorrow night?

SHE I ... I honestly don't know.

HE [*laying his hands on her shoulders and saying softly*] Kate ... Kiss me before you go. If you don't I won't be able to sleep tonight.

SHE *puts down her suitcase and they embrace.*

SHE [*murmuring*] Poor old Quoop.

HE [*murmuring*] If you come I'll tell you my name and occupation.

SHE Certainly that's an inducement.

HE Must you ... leave?

SHE Yes. You know me too well.

They sigh and separate. **SHE** *lifts the case.* **HE** *opens the door.*

SHE [*on a friendly note*] Well ... Goodbye!

HE Goodbye – goodbye.

HE *shuts the door behind her and wanders back into his room sighing and murmuring.*

HE Damn. Damn damn damn damn damn damn damn.

HE *sighs again then looks down and sees a book on the sofa. Thoughtfully he picks it up.*

HE Hm ... The Pursuit of the Mm ... She forgot her book.

With sudden excitement.

HE She forgot her book! [**HE** *rushes to the door, tears it open and rushes out shouting*]. Kate! Come back Kate! You forgot the Pursuit of the Millennium!

SAM LANG AND MISS WATSON
1973

CAST

MISS WATSON Any age between 25 and 35. She is attractive but not conventionally attractive.

SAM LANG A big, well-dressed, self-made businessman of 40. He has modelled himself so ostentatiously on executives in cheap American films that it takes a while to notice his intelligence.

MRS MILDREN a middle-aged efficient office manager.

TEDDY A brisk assistant manager of 25.

MRS LANG A pretty, faded, fashionably dressed, nervous woman, only in Scene 3. Her accent and manners indicate a more genteel background than her husband.

SET

SAM LANG*'s office. A large desk stands against a large decoration of Chinese dragons in red, black and gold. The desk has two telephones and a Chinese statuette of an old man with long whiskers. In front of the desk are three low easy chairs around a low coffee table. There are two doors, one of them the entrance, the other leading to a small cloakroom-toilet. The play is in four scenes over a six-month period. From Scene 2 onward a small secretary's desk with typewriter and 'in' and 'out' trays stand near the entrance at an angle towards the large one.*

1: THE INTERVIEW

LANG *leans back with his heels on his desk, telephoning, and watched by* **MISS WATSON** *who stands patiently to the right, one hand gripping the strap of a shoulder bag, and by* **TED**, *who stands to the left.*

LANG That's where I stand Mr Cockport. The ball's in your court now. I've checked my side of the correspondence so check yours. Goodbye. [*He sets the phone saying*]. Anything else Ted?

TED Yes. The storage racks in the loading bay. The head-joiner still wants overtime.

LANG The hell he does! [*picks up the telephone*] Put me through to the loading bay. [**MISS WATSON** *stirs impatiently*]. **TED** *eyes her with interest.* **LANG** *grins at her*] Not much longer, Miss, er ... Hello, MacAfferty? Listen, you said you'd have the job finished in three weeks, so what's the trouble ... Christ Jimmy you're not going to tell me those men of yours are working are you? I've got eyes in my head ... Tell you what I'll do. After the racks in the loading bay you're supposed to be shelving the basement ... Well I'll pay you right away for the hours you've done so far and you can clear out. Otherwise you'll finish the job for the price you stated and then go to the basement. Right? Alright ... that's alright then. [*puts down the receiver, leans back, flexes his muscles, then swings round suddenly and faces* **MISS WATSON** *with an air of discovery*] Miss Watson I've been a bad boy leaving you standing here all this while. One thing though, you stand beautifully: relaxed, not stiff. Doesn't she stand beautifully Ted?

TED [*with a quick smile*] Yes ... you sorted out the joiner Sam?

LANG That's right. And by the way, better get onto another firm about the basement job. We can't depend on anything this lot say.

TED Right. [*he leaves*].

MISS WATSON [*patiently*] I've come about a job, Mr Lang.

LANG Of course you have. [*he lifts a letter from his desk*] This letter from the agency tells me all about you. [*he glances at it*] Linda Watson. Hm. Well Linda; you've had some experience but in a receptionist experience counts a lot less than style ... [*he looks at her*]. You look alright. You know how to dress. You stand well and I bet you walk well. [*Leans back*] Try it anyway.

MISS WATSON [*puzzled*] What?

LANG Let me see you walking Linda.

MISS WATSON Where?

LANG Just around the room.

She stares at him for a half second, then strolls in a casual circle back to where she stood before. Her face is quite impassive.

LANG [*nodding*] Good! [*glances back at the letters*]. It says here you've done book-keeping.

MISS WATSON I did some for my last employer. Nothing complicated. He was a dentist.

LANG Now that could be useful to us. [*lifts the phone*] Mrs Mildren? Yes, could you come here a minute? [*To* **MISS WATSON**] You see receptionists always have time on their hands. And simple accounting could fit in very nicely.

[*The door opens and* **MRS MILDREN**, *a neat middle-aged black-dressed lady enters*] Come right in, Mrs Mildren. I want to ask you about our Rina. What does Rina do all day? She's not lazy is she?

MRS MILDREN No, Mr Lang. But I haven't the work to keep her occupied.

LANG I thought so. You see Linda here – she's maybe going to be our new receptionist – she's done book-keeping. And as receptionist her hands won't be full *every* minute of the day. I mean, how many hours a day would she need not do if we give Rina the heave?

MRS MILDREN [*frowning reflectively*] Two hours would be enough.

LANG Two hours! What do you say Linda?

MISS WATSON If it's work that requires concentration –

MRS MILDREN Oh it won't need that. You'd just be keeping a record of invoices and receipts.

LANG That's alright then Mrs Mildren, I know this isn't the hour but let's have coffee all round. I *feel* like it. How do you take yours Linda?

MISS WATSON Black. One sugar please.

MRS MILDREN *goes out.* **MISS WATSON** *pushes her hair back from her brow with one hand in a troubled-looking gesture.* **LANG** *sits back and lights a cigarette.*

LANG Cheer up Linda. I've only one more hurdle to put you across and that's the matter of overtime. What's your attitude to overtime? We pay well for it, there isn't a lot of it, but it's erratic.

MISS WATSON If you could give me a day's notice ...

LANG Ah but I couldnae ...

MISS WATSON [*after a moment*] Well if I had *some* notice –

LANG Couldn't guarantee it. What do you think of all this – [*flaps a hand to all the dragons*] – this décor.

MISS WATSON *looks around the walls and a small smile twists one corner of her mouth.*

MISS WATSON It's colourful.

LANG *lies back and roar with almost soundless laughter, then stands and walks to a wall and turns and faces her from between two dragons.*

LANG Bet you think it's ghastly. Come on. Admit you think it's ghastly. [**MISS WATSON** *nods. He nods*] It's like me. Vulgar, powerful, and you can't ignore it. Right? [*She nods again*] I always wanted an office like this. You should have seen our last place. Three dirty little rooms you could hardly swing a cat in. Now, suddenly, boom, we've arrived, it's all happening. Want to know why? Why even big firms like to buy equipment through me?

MISS WATSON Government subsidy?

LANG [*slightly taken aback*] Well this *is* a low-development area so I got *some* help that way, but the real reason is that firms can order from me at short notice and have delivery on the dot. They can phone me at five-to-five on Friday and ask for thirty gross of two point two millimetre needle lenses and they'll have it on their doorstep next morning. [*He has strolled back to the desk and edges a haunch and places a hand affectionately on the bald skull of the statuette*]. See this old bloke? He's the Chinese God of Wealth. I sometimes burn jossticks in front of him.

MISS WATSON Mr Lang it would be very hard for me to work overtime without some notice –

LANG You got a kid?

MISS WATSON You've nothing to do with my private life!

LANG [*grins*] Quite right! Quite right! But ten minutes notice is all the time I can promise. Enough time to make a few phone calls anyway. [*He returns to his seat and tilts it back to her*].

MISS WATSON [*looking at the floor, almost inaudibly*] Alright.

LANG Good! [**MRS MILDREN** *comes in with three mugs on a tray*] You've a new colleague, Mrs Mildren.

MRS MILDREN *places a mug on* **LANG***'s desk, then holds the tray to* **MISS WATSON**, *who takes one.*

MRS MILDREN Glad you're joining us.

MISS WATSON Thank you.

She sits down abruptly. **MRS MILDREN** *lays the tray on the low table and sits down also.* **LANG** *has a two-woman audience. He expands.*

LANG When can you start, Linda?

MISS WATSON Tomorrow.

LANG That's the spirit; but you'd better make it Monday. Mrs Mildren, put the bullet into Rina for Monday will you. And I personally will see to Alice. Alice, our leetle receptionist. Yes, you know it wasn't so much her refusing overtime that decided me to get rid of her. I can forgive a girl a lot if she's decorative. But Alice is fat. I came in yesterday and I said to myself, No! No! This isn't what we want for Lang Photomatics Ltd. We want something svelte and nubile. She's dumpy!

MISS WATSON [*suddenly swallows some coffee, lays the cup on the table and stands up with an air of decision*] Mr Lang, I am not taking this job.

These words freeze the others in an attitude of staring. **LANG** *is completely taken aback, but manages to inject into his query a vaguely academic note.*

LANG Why?

MISS WATSON [*giving him a sudden, spontaneous, lovely, mischievous smile*] Personal reasons. [*She walks out coolly*].

LANG [*suddenly puts his mug down, stands, strides after her and shouts*] Linda! [*He halts right and calls more quietly*]. Miss Watson I mean ... Please! [*On a cajoling, friendly note*]. Please hear me ... for just one minute!

MISS WATSON [*off*] Why?

LANG I'd sincerely like to talk to you ... come on, I won't eat you! ... [*playfully*] Are you afraid of something?

MRS MILDREN *stands and gathers the mugs onto a tray as* **LANG** *strolls back, followed by* **MISS WATSON**.

LANG Leave the coffee, Mrs Mildren – we haven't finished it yet.

MRS MILDREN Certainly, Mr Lang.

LANG [*going to the desk*] And would you check the order from Newcastle? We should have heard from them by now.

MRS MILDREN Certainly, Mr Lang.

MRS MILDREN *goes out carrying her own mug, and exchanging an "oh these men" glance with* **MISS WATSON** *on the way.* **LANG** *sits on the edge of his desk.* **MISS WATSON** *sits down, coolly crosses her legs and watches him.*

LANG Linda –

MISS WATSON [*interrupting him quietly*] We aren't on first name terms Mr Lang.

LANG [*nods*] Right ... I won't ask why you walked out like that. You think I'm a bastard.

MISS WATSON [*nodding*] I know it.

LANG Right. That's how I get things done, Miss Watson. By being a dirty pressurizing bastard. It really is effective.

MISS WATSON I don't like working for bastards.

LANG Ah, but I'm a clever bastard. I wouldn't pressurize you. It wouldn't work with you. You've shown me that.

MISS WATSON Why do you want me? Especially?

LANG I need a receptionist. And you'd be a good one. And I think you need the money.

MISS WATSON [*interested*] Why do you think that?

LANG You'd have walked out a lot earlier if you hadn't.

MISS WATSON *smiles and nods thoughtfully.*

LANG So what about it then?

MISS WATSON I'll take the job if you don't fire that other girl – whatsername – Rina.

LANG Alright, Rina stays. But you've got to do overtime when I say so. That still stands. It's essential.

MISS WATSON [*nodding*] I can put up with that.

LANG Good. Do you want an advance on your salary?

MISS WATSON No. I'll manage.

LANG Good.

He sits on a chair on her level. They both sip coffee.

MISS WATSON You're right – I'll be a good receptionist. I can handle people.

LANG I'm surprised you're not onto something better.

MISS WATSON I don't know shorthand and my typing's horrible.

LANG Go to nightclasses. You'd pick it up in no time.

MISS WATSON [*shaking her head*] I hate learning anything that bores me. And since we've decided to be honest I'd better tell you – I may stay here as long as a year. But you can only depend on me for six months.

LANG [*astounded, admiring, amused*] You little bitch!

MISS WATSON Please don't swear ... you do understand, don't you?

LANG Don't think I do.

MISS WATSON There aren't many interesting jobs open to women in office work. If you stay anywhere more than a year you get taken for granted. But if you can't change your job you can always change your employer. There are a lot of women like me nowadays.

LANG [*pointing a finger at her*] You're going to be here longer than you think.

MISS WATSON Oh?

LANG [*he stands and moves around the room*] Lang Photomatics isn't one of your steady, plodding, boring firms. We're new, vital, expanding. Six months ago I had a staff of eight. Now I've twice that. What'll we be like in *another* six months? You've hit us at the right moment. You'll work bloody hard but you won't be bored. And I'm sorry, you'll have to get used to the swearing.

LANG *stands, hands in pockets, facing the window.*

MISS WATSON Yes, it's a dangerous time for you. [**LANG** *swings round and stares at her*]. Quite a lot of successful small firms go bankrupt when they try to expand. I worked in one. It's easy for a boss to manage a small staff personally. A big staff is different. Unless you learn to delegate responsibility you go under. You can't be everywhere.

LANG Can't I though? [*grins crookedly, then chuckles*]. I must be mad ... but you're such a bloody little know-all that I want to tell you everything. Can I trust you? With a secret, I mean?

MISS WATSON Well. [*frowns*].

LANG Alright alright. Don't answer that. I *do* trust you so come over here. [**LANG** *goes behind his desk.* **MISS WATSON** *stands up, puzzled, and goes to him.* **LANG** *raises a forefinger*]. When you said a boss couldn't be everywhere you were reckoning without the miracles of modern science ... come round here. [**MISS WATSON** *does. He slides out what seems to be a drawer*]. What do you think of that?

MISS WATSON What is it?

LANG You should know. You've read about them in the papers. What'll we try? Reception hall? Accountancy? Stores? Loading bay? Right, Loading bay.

LANG *presses a switch.*

SOUND: *a sawing noise.*

JOINER'S VOICE You know what the accountants call him?

OTHER'S VOICE Naw?

JOINER'S VOICE The Great I Am. Christ, I hate that bastard.

LANG Good. They're sawing at any rate. [*He turns the device off, sits down in his chair, tilts it back and chuckles heartily*].

MISS WATSON [*glaring at him*] What a cheap, nasty trick!

LANG [*good-humouredly*]. Cheap? The wiring alone cost two hundred. Go on, say it. I'm a bugger!

MISS WATSON [*really distressed*] I feel like walking out of here.

LANG [*seriously*] But you're not doing it. You're interested.

MISS WATSON That's really sickening. [*She sits down*].

LANG [*leans forward over the desk, frowning to himself, and after a moment says in a low voice*]. You're right – this is a dangerous time for me. I've been bankrupt before, and pretty much for the reasons you've mentioned. I hate delegating responsibility; I don't trust people, and why should I? By and large they're a gang of lazy, unimaginative cowards. Without me to bully and pressurize them they'd achieve nothing. I load all I can onto them and they're afraid to tell me when they can't manage. So suddenly, without warning, they walk out on me. [*He frowns*].

MISS WATSON I'll give you plenty of warning when I leave – a fortnight at least.

LANG Don't be in such a hurry. The next six months is going to be crucial and your experience might be very useful to Lang Photomatics; and I don't mean just as a receptionist. [*He touches a switch on the intercom panel*] Ted? Can you spare ten minutes?...Then bring in the Cockport file, we'll go over it in detail. [**MISS WATSON** *stands. He glances at her*].

LANG Right, Miss Watson, five-to-nine Monday sharp.

MISS WATSON Goodbye.

LANG Right. Goodbye. [*As she leaves he is in his busy executive act*].

2: A MONTH LATER

There is a new desk in the office, smaller than **LANG***'s and facing it at an angle.* **MISS WATSON** *sets a tray on the low table: it holds teapot, milk, a bowl of sugar lumps, three cups on saucers, a plate of chocolate biscuits. She lifts the teapot and is filling the cups when* **MRS MILDREN** *enters followed by* **TED**. *The chairs are arranged round the table.* **MRS MILDREN** *and* **TED** *sit down,* **TED** *taking the chair which allows the clearest view of* **MISS WATSON.**

TED [*in a low voice*] Good-good-good-good.

MISS WATSON *puts down the teapot and sits while* **TED** *deftly sugars the cups – one lump for* **MISS WATSON** *and* **MRS MILDREN**, *three for him – and* **MRS MILDREN** *milks them.* **MISS WATSON** *doesn't take milk. They take cups and saucers and a quietly tinkling silence follows.*

MRS MILDREN [*addressing* **MISS WATSON**] Have you heard from The Great I Am yet?

MISS WATSON Yes. He'll be back in the morning.

TED Did he get the orders?

MISS WATSON I don't really know. He phoned from a cafeteria on the M1. I gathered he'd driven four hundred miles, contacted four firms and had less than four hours sleep. Something like that. He did sound rather tired. I didn't ask questions, I congratulated him on his stamina.

MRS MILDREN [*tartly*] He's got stamina alright.

TED If he's in one of his martyr-to-industry moods he's probably done quite well. He puts on his best manners when he's disappointed or in a tight corner.

MISS WATSON [*thoughtfully*] When you think about it, that's rather admirable.

A thoughtful pause.

TED I wish he was more of an idiot ... He's such a gassy big balloon that he *ought* to be an idiot. But he's a good boss, in some ways.

MRS MILDREN Not around the office! There's only one way of running an office properly and once you've found it you should stick to it. He just couldn't leave well alone.

Every day he'd come snooping around with suggestions. [*looks at* **MISS WATSON**]. He's improved since he promoted you.

TED [*nodding*] It's the same in the stores and in the loading bay. When he sees someone doing nothing he gives them a job, and it doesn't matter *which* job. You get van men painting radiators and store men sweeping out the vans. So when their real work arrives they're in the wrong place at the wrong time.

MISS WATSON [*puzzled*] Why has this firm done so well?

TED He's a good salesman.

MRS MILDREN Yes. He's good with buyers and suppliers.

TED Keep him busy with outside appointments, Linda.

MISS WATSON [*smiling*] I'll try. [*takes a biscuit and sighs*]. But I wish we could find a different topic of conversation.

MRS MILDREN So do I!

TED [*fervently*] So do I!

MRS MILDREN We've enough of him when he's actually here.

A long, thoughtful pause. **TED** *considers, not too obviously,* **MISS WATSON***'s legs, then clears his throat.*

TED Has he er ... ever made a pass at you, Linda?

MISS WATSON [*calmly*] No.

TED Funny.

MISS WATSON Why?

TED That's why the last two receptionists left. He couldn't leave them alone.

MISS WATSON Oh?

TED Funny he hasn't made a pass at you, Linda.

MRS MILDREN He respects her. That's why.

MISS WATSON What's his wife like?

MRS MILDREN What you'd expect.

TED Yep. Just what you'd expect ... Linda?

MISS WATSON Yes Teddy?

TED Do you think I have a future in this firm?

MISS WATSON Sam trusts you, Ted.

TED No, I mean, has the *firm* a future? I've been here three years, and suddenly we're in bigger premises with more staff, but he hasn't raised our salaries. His line is, we've expanded the plant, but we've to go carefully till we've a clearer view of the future.

MISS WATSON [*frowning*] It depends on whether he's able to learn.

MRS MILDREN I hear footsteps.

They raise their heads alertly. The door opens and **LANG** *enters. He carries a briefcase, wears a light overcoat, unbuttoned, and has the preoccupied look of a tired man nobly bearing the burdens of great office. He goes towards his desk.*

LANG [*dully*] When the cat's away the mice will play.

MISS WATSON [*crisply*] Some tea, Mr Lang?

LANG Tea? No, not tea ... [*He drops the briefcase on the small desk, goes to his own, sits down, crosses his ankles on the desk, lies back and sighs*]. I am shagged out. Utterly and completely shagged out ... don't mind me. Eat your biscuits. Nibble biscuits all day if you like. In ten minutes I'll be off home to my kip and that's the last you'll see of me till nine – [*pause*] – sharp – [*pause*] – tomorrow.

LANG *closes his eyes. The others exchange glances.*

TED [*lifts his cup and says mildly*] Did you get the orders, Sam?

LANG What orders? [*he opens his eyes*] Of course I got the orders. Did *you* get through to old Cockport?

TED Well actually –

LANG No no no, tell me tomorrow. Give me time to recover.

LANG *closes his eyes again, then* **MRS MILDREN** *puts the cups on the tray.*

MRS MILDREN [*quietly to* **MISS WATSON**] I'll see to these.

She carries the tray out, followed by **TED**, *who shuts the door behind them.* **MISS WATSON** *stands smoothing down her skirt and considering* **LANG** *for a moment, her head on one side.*

LANG [*speaking without opening his eyes*] Linda?

MISS WATSON Yes?

LANG Pour me a whisky. Please!

She goes round to his desk, opens a deep drawer, removes a glass and whisky bottle, pours a measure of one into the other, and places them both within reach of his hand.

MISS WATSON There.

LANG Thanks. [**MISS WATSON** *goes to her own desk and leans on the edge, watching him. He sits up, sips the whisky, sighs deeply and looks at her*]. Well?

MISS WATSON There's been nothing special in the correspondence. The orders for Barclay, Colquhoun and Clugston Shanks went through as planned.

LANG Good.

MISS WATSON A last minute order from Laird and Urquhart caused a minor strike from the only available van driver. Ted sorted it out.

LANG Good lad.

MISS WATSON I've a suggestion to make about the van drivers ...

LANG [*interrupting*] I've missed you, Linda.
MISS WATSON [*smiling*] Have you, Sam?
LANG I have, yes.
MISS WATSON Oh.
LANG I've missed you a lot.
MISS WATSON All the same, you're probably going to fire me.
LANG Why?
MISS WATSON I've had your bugging system unwired.
LANG Why???
MISS WATSON In the first place, because I found it tempting. I kept wanting to use it. In the second place, it was useless. Everyone knew about it.
LANG How could they? The only people I told were you – [*dire suspicion crosses his mind*] – and Ted?
MISS WATSON What about the electricians who installed it?
LANG They installed it before we moved in!
MISS WATSON Were they a local firm?
LANG Of course not! I'm not exactly an idiot.
MISS WATSON Then they probably had a drink in the local pub. You can't keep a thing like that secret, Sam. It made you ridiculous.
She is still leaning on the desk. **LANG** *walks up and down.*
LANG I don't care! I don't mind them finding me ridiculous as long as they do what I say. That system worked even if they *did* know about it. Perhaps it worked better! [**LANG** *stands facing her.* **MISS WATSON** *listens, open-mouthed*]. The fact that they had to keep their mouths shut or talk about me in sign language made them feel I was always there, always listening to them, it kept me in their thoughts ... like God!
MISS WATSON Like God?
He embraces her. They kiss and become lost in each other. After a moment she says again.
MISS WATSON Like God?
LANG [*humbly*] Like a small, local God ... God I like you Linda. [*They kiss*]. Do you like me?
MISS WATSON I'm not sure ... I ... I like this though.
LANG [*wonderingly*] I know nothing about you. Nothing.
MISS WATSON I'm a very ordinary person, Sam. [*playfully*]. Sexy Sam.
LANG Do they call me that?
MISS WATSON I do.
LANG [*turning away from her to avoid becoming too excited*] Look I ... I've got to go. This is neither the time nor the place. [*He goes to the desk, drinks what's left of the glass and turns to face her*] We must meet somewhere else, right? [**MISS WATSON** *looks back at him thoughtfully*]. We'll discuss it tomorrow. Right?
MISS WATSON Alright. [*He goes to her and they embrace again. She says softly.*] Sam.
LANG Mm?
MISS WATSON You're paying Ted too little.
LANG [*softly*] I know. [*He kisses her hair*] He puts up with it.
MISS WATSON [*stroking his cheek*]. He'll leave if you don't pay him more.
LANG Good to know. [*They kiss*] I'll pay him more. The papers in the briefcase ... [*He nods to it*].
MISS WATSON Mm?
LANG You'll see to them?
MISS WATSON Mm!
LANG Good. [*They kiss, separate, tidy their clothing. He goes to the door, turns and says in a more normal voice*]. You shouldn't have ripped out those wires, Linda.
MISS WATSON Yes I should, Sam.
LANG [*sighs and scratches his head*] Anyway, I'll see you tomorrow.
MISS WATSON [*nods*] Right. Nine. Tomorrow. Sharp.
LANG [*points at her accusingly*]. You! Are developing! A sense of humour!
LANG *leaves.*

3: A FORTNIGHT LATER

MISS WATSON *stands arranging flowers in a vase on her desk.* **TED** *is sprawling in one of the chairs.*
TED I won't pretend I've told him straight but he knows what I think. Casual labour's cheaper in the short run and dearer in the long run because you can't depend on it.
MISS WATSON Yes.
TED Every week there's trouble with these drivers. *I* can't *always* sort it out. And he isn't always here.
MISS WATSON I'll tell him. [*She stands back to examine the effect*].
TED I'd be grateful if you would. I bet he sometimes makes passes at you, Linda.
MISS WATSON [*smiling*] Why, Ted? [*She carries the bowl over to* **LANG***'s desk and sets it there*].
TED He's different when you're around. More relaxed and human. I'd be careful if I were you.
MISS WATSON [*lightly*] But Teddy, he's too old.

TED [*rises and goes to her*] Oh yes, you think that. But *I* understand how he feels.

MISS WATSON Now, Teddy!

TED [*trying to embrace her*] Come on, Linda, be a little more friendly!

MISS WATSON Now Ted, let's not spoil a wonderful relationship. [*She fends him off, laughing a little*] Go away!

TED Please Linda! Let me –

MISS WATSON No, certainly not!

The door is suddenly flung open by **MRS LANG** *who stands blinking brightly at them. A pause in which* **TED** *shows every sign of guilty embarrassment.* **MISS WATSON** *is merely amused.*

MRS LANG O Hello.

MISS WATSON Hello.

MRS LANG I should have knocked. But I thought my husband was in here.

TED He's ... er ... downstairs Mrs Lang, sorting out a dispute with van drivers. I'll tell him you're here –

MRS LANG O no, I don't want to interrupt his work. His work must always come first, mustn't it? Sit down, you look uncomfortable and that makes me nervous.

MISS WATSON *sits quietly at her desk and starts working with a letter from her "In" tray.*

TED I was just going to my own office, Mrs Lang.

MRS LANG Of course. Yes.

TED *escapes.* **MRS LANG** *lights a cigarette with a lighter from her handbag and circles the room, pretending not to be examining* **MISS WATSON**. *She pauses before the flowers, then turns.*

MRS LANG [*suddenly*] You'll be the famous, Miss ... [**MISS WATSON** *looks up*]. You're the famous Miss ... [**MRS LANG** *taps her brow*].

MISS WATSON [*quietly*] I'm called Linda Watson.

MRS LANG I don't know why I forgot your name. It's never off his lips.

MISS WATSON I find that hard to believe.

MRS LANG You're right of course. He never mentions you. But you're always on his mind.

MISS WATSON Why?

MRS LANG Oh, you're part of his work and his work always comes first. [*She moves somewhere else*]. I knew you'd be – not pretty – you aren't very pretty – but I knew you'd be attractive. His receptionists are always attractive.

MISS WATSON [*nodding*] Yes, they would be.

MRS LANG He runs through them rather fast.

MISS WATSON So I gather.

MRS LANG Of course, you're not a receptionist, you've been promoted.

MISS WATSON I've been his secretary for over a month.

MRS LANG I was shopping in town and thought I'd pop in and see his ... er ... décor. [*She glances round*] I knew it was Chinese but I hadn't expected such big dragons. Can you work among all these dragons?

MISS WATSON [*smiling*] I shut my eyes to them.

MRS LANG *I* couldn't do that ... It's been a lovely summer. I hope you got out of the city at weekends. As often as you could!

MISS WATSON Sometimes.

MRS LANG Last weekend was perfect for the seaside, don't you agree?

MISS WATSON I didn't go to the seaside last weekend.

MRS LANG Sam went to Aberdeen. On business, of course. He said that anyway. What business do they do in Aberdeen on Sundays!

MISS WATSON I don't know!

MRS LANG [*cries out desperately*] Miss Watson, I am not a silly woman!

MISS WATSON *stands up and stares at her in wonder and pity.* **MRS LANG** *sits down suddenly.*

MRS LANG [*in a tremulous voice*] I mean I am not ... always ... as silly as this.

MISS WATSON [*coming over to her*] Of course you're not silly, Mrs Lang. Please let me make you a cup of tea. Or would you like coffee?

MRS LANG [*she puffs the cigarette in one hand then dabs her eyes with a small handkerchief with the other*] You look quite kind ... but I had four cups of coffee before I came here, to give me courage you know. It's foolish of me to get emotional. Or it would be if I didn't feel so much better afterwards.

MISS WATSON I know what you mean.

MRS LANG [*shaking her head*] I don't think you do. Sam and I get on rather well, really. We've been married for fifteen years. [*She stands*] Have you a toilet?

MISS WATSON [*pointing*] Through there –

MRS LANG Thank you. You are very kind. [*She goes out*].

MISS WATSON [*greatly distressed, wandering round the room shaking her head and murmuring*]. No! Oh no!

LANG *enters looking thoughtful.*

LANG Is my wife here?

MISS WATSON [*coldly*] In the toilet.

LANG [*going to his desk*] Chatted a bit did you?

MISS WATSON Not much.

LANG [*sitting on the edge of his desk*] Quite a character, isn't she?

MISS WATSON I found her a very straightforward person.

She sits down at her desk and resumes work.

LANG [*a little surprised*] Oh? [*A pause. He takes a more jovial note*] Well, I sorted out the drivers.

MISS WATSON [*without looking up, indifferently*] Congratulations. You'll have to sort them out next week too if you don't start hiring dependable men at decent rates.

LANG Are you annoyed about something?

MRS LANG *enters. She is brighter and more sure of herself.*

MRS LANG Hello Sam.

LANG Having a look round, eh?

MRS LANG Yes, I wanted to see your ... your décor.

LANG Like it?

MRS LANG Very cheerful, yes. I like Miss Watson too. She's very attractive and kind. I'm glad she's got a boyfriend.

LANG [*warily*] Has she?

MRS LANG Yes. In this office.

LANG Oh?

MRS LANG *stares at him. He frowns back.* **MISS WATSON** *looks up from a document she has been seeming to read.*

MISS WATSON When Mrs Lang came in Ted and I were fooling about a bit.

LANG O Ted! Yes, Ted's quite a lad. It's time you were off Betty. We've a lot to get through. [*He goes over and lays an avuncular hand on his wife's shoulder*].

MRS LANG [*pleading*] I only looked in for a *minute*, Sammy!

LANG Fine. You'll see me again at six. [*He leads her to the door*].

MRS LANG Yes, unless you have one of your ... last minute orders. [*She tries to look at* **MISS WATSON** *over her shoulder*].

LANG In which case I'll phone. Off you go, Betty. [*He opens the door and kisses her quickly on the brow*]. Bye bye.

MRS LANG Goodbye ... goodbye Miss ... Linda Watson!

MISS WATSON *looks up haggardly and mouths "Goodbye" as* **LANG** *firmly closes the door. He walks over to his desk shaking his head.*

LANG What a woman! [*He sits down, tilts the chair back, puts his feet on the desk and says in a small voice*]. Linda, for God's sake give me a whisky.

MISS WATSON [*distinctly*] The bottle and glass are in a drawer on your left hand side.

LANG [*opening his eyes*] Eh? You're right. I'm not a baby. [*sits up, opens the drawer, pours himself a whisky and sighs*] What a woman! [*sips*]. You're mad about something. Spell it out will you?

MISS WATSON [*with cold fury*] Have you ever tried to imagine what it's *like* being married to you?

LANG 'Course not. What do you take me for? A poof? [*chuckles and sips*] You're sorry for Betty, eh?

MISS WATSON She wasn't like that when you married her.

LANG [*nods and speaks very seriously*]. No! She was a nice wee thing then, full of all kinds of pretty tricks. It's a pity she didn't marry someone else. Someone like Ted.

MISS WATSON What's wrong with Teddy?

LANG Nothing! A decent, dependable bloke. He's on the make, like the rest of us, but he'll never take risks. His wife will have a nice house, and every five years he'll shift her to a bigger one, and he'll mow the lawn at the weekends, and every morning over breakfast he'll grumble to her about his nasty boss. [*sighs*]. Betty would have been happy with him, because she's no ideas either. [*stands and moves round the room*]. I've got ideas. I like taking risks. I want to *do* things, so her life with me makes her feel second rate. It would have been different if we'd had kids. Maybe. But there was a miscarriage with the first and ... after that she didn't want to take risks. I don't blame her.

MISS WATSON You make me sick!

LANG [*goes to her, saying in a low, intense voice*] Linda, I have lived with that woman [*points to the door*] – that wreck! – for all of fifteen years, when I haven't actually been working or ... er ...

MISS WATSON [*rises to face him*] Or enjoying dirty weekends with the office girls?

LANG Right! [*They glare into each other's faces. He grips her shoulders*] Do you think it's fun being me?

MISS WATSON You make me s...

She hesitates and stares at him open-mouthed. They kiss.

LANG [*murmuring*] I need to see you tonight.

MISS WATSON Not tonight, Sammy!

LANG Tonight.

MISS WATSON[*separates herself from him and sits down, shaking her head*] No. Tomorrow.

LANG [*shrugs*] Alright. Tomorrow then. [**LANG** *sighs, goes to his desk, sits, runs a hand through his hair*]. Christ, what a mess. [*He sighs, straightens his tie and asks on a glum note*] Alright. Where are we?

4: LATER STILL

MISS WATSON is alone, typing at her desk. She does this with sucked in underlip and frowning concentration, then mutters "Damn" and stops to eliminate a mistake. The door opens and LANG enters, grinning smugly and waving a form.

LANG Linda!

MISS WATSON Yes?

LANG You still trying to type that apology?

MISS WATSON Yes.

LANG Tear it up.

MISS WATSON [*startled*] What?

LANG Look what I found in the basement – the original order from Cockport and Co. It was them that made the mistake – not us! [*He chuckles*].

MISS WATSON [*smiles at him and leans back*] Sam!

LANG It was in an old box file. I must have mislaid when we shifted. [*He lays it on her desk*].

MISS WATSON I'll get it photocopied. [*rips the sheet out of her typewriter.*].

LANG [*goes to his desk*] That little discovery has saved Lang Photomatics nearly two thousand quid. [*He sits on the edge of his desk*].

MISS WATSON [*crumpling the sheet and bending to throw it in the wastepaper basket*] Sam, by the way ... [*sits up*]. Do you remember when I came here?

LANG Yes?

MISS WATSON I said you could depend on me for six months.

LANG [*cheerfully*] And I said you'd be here longer than you expected.

MISS WATSON Yes. Well I want to leave quite soon now.

LANG What?

MISS WATSON There's no hurry of course. I'll take two or three weeks teaching someone else to take over, you won't be inconvenienced.

LANG [*staring at her*] What's wrong, Linda?

MISS WATSON Nothing. I'm just tired of the job.

LANG [*looks at her worriedly, then his face clears and he starts to chuckle*] Blackmailer!

MISS WATSON [*puzzled*] What?

LANG Alright alright. How much do you want?

MISS WATSON What for?

LANG To stay.

MISS WATSON I don't want to stay. I need a change.

LANG [*suddenly grave*] Linda! I'll pay you sixty quid a week starting from now. How about that?

MISS WATSON Oh! ... Well, if you think I'm worth it, do. And I'll make sure the next girl really knows her job thoroughly.

LANG For God's sake! [*He walks around the room*]. You're talking as if we're nothing but a boss and a secretary. What about our weekends together!

MISS WATSON [*eagerly*] They were wonderful, Sam. I enjoyed myself. It's the work I'm tired of. [*She sees he is distressed and becomes slightly distressed herself*].

LANG What other work can I give you?

MISS WATSON *I* don't know! [*smiles suddenly*]. Of course you could make me your business partner – that would certainly induce me to stay.

LANG [*staring*] You're out of your tiny mind if you expect me to –

MISS WATSON Of course I didn't expect you to make me your business partner! If this firm were Watson Photomatics I wouldn't want you for a partner.

LANG [*bites his under lip, rubs the side of his face and speaks very quietly*] Perhaps I haven't been as honest as I should have been. I haven't made it clear just how much I like you. I've thought of saying this before, really I have. I put it off because it didn't seem necessary! No! [*fiercely*] That wasn't the reason! I put it off out of cowardice! But I mean it, Linda!

MISS WATSON Mean what?

LANG I'd like us to get married.

MISS WATSON [*she stands up, startled*] What?

LANG [*goes to her*] Yes, I'm married already, alright! But you know what my home's like, I need someone hard and independent, someone who stands up to me, someone like you Linda! We need each other, because we're the same kind of person!

MISS WATSON [*eagerly*] But I'm not hard and I'm not like you! I've had to act hard, of course, or you'd have trampled on me, just as you trample on others. But I'm quite gentle when I'm with gentle people, Sam. You only see me when I'm with you. I'm different when I'm with private boyfriends.

LANG Private boyf ... Who are you talking about?

MISS WATSON Friends of my own age. With all this overtime I'm in danger of losing touch with them. What I need now, for a few months, is a quiet, ordinary, nine-to-five receptionist's job with no overtime.

He slumps down in the seat behind his desk. She stares at him, wanting to be understood.

LANG [*quietly*] Go away, Linda.

MISS WATSON [*surprised*] What?

LANG I don't want to be in the same room as you. Clear out.

MISS WATSON That's silly!

LANG Don't worry – you'll get a fortnight's salary in lieu of notice. But you'll get it through the post.

MISS WATSON [*concerned*] Sam, I didn't mean to hurt you ...

LANG [*fiercely*] Don't talk – walk!

MISS WATSON [*she looks at him and at last says coolly*] May I collect my coat?

He doesn't answer. She goes into the toilet.

LANG [*suddenly bellows*] And if you want a reference I'll tell anybody at all that you're hardworking, efficient, good in bed, and can't be depended upon for more than six months!

MISS WATSON [*she comes out wearing a coat and carrying her shoulder-bag*] That sounds reasonable.

LANG [*bitterly*] Bitch!

MISS WATSON Please don't swear at me, Sam.

LANG Bitch! Bitch!

MISS WATSON And you, of course, are a bastard. You told me so the day I arrived. A clever bastard I think you said. [*More kindly*] Goodbye Sam.

She stares at him. He says nothing. She leaves. He sits for a moment then raises a clenched fist.

LANG [*through clenched teeth*] The little b…

LANG *stops, lies back, and is gradually mastered by his sense of humour. He smiles, then chuckles, then laughs quite loudly, ending by scratching his head and giving a couple of theatrical groans. Then he pulls himself together, sighs and lifts the phone.*

LANG Hello, reception? Put me on to the Buchanan Employment Agency.

IN THE VERY EARLY SEVENTIES some people in London BBC decided to show interest in a few other British cities with a series of semi-documentary films. They rented an empty building in each and sent a London TV crew there to film local entertainers and others discussing the state of the place before a local audience. Part of the entertainment would be a play by a local writer. I was commissioned to write the following play for Glasgow. I based it on a meeting in the street with an old man who asked me to change his electric lightbulb. At that time our city council had modernised Glasgow for the benefit of the motor industry by building a multi-lane ring-road that ran very close to its heart, thus destroying several local communities and separating others almost as firmly as a high-security fence. To accommodate folk rendered homeless by the destruction of solid four-storey tenements, multi-storey blocks were being built of a sort that their architects jokingly called *prole-stacks*. Cities in the USA had discovered this cheap way of housing many people was also a bad way, and had started knocking their prole-stacks down before Glasgow finished putting hers up. Billy Connolly had a part in the programme singing, "Ye cannae fling a jeely piece from a twenty-storey flat, twenty-thousand hungry weans will testify tae that."

Though my play also reflected some civic disgruntlement it pleased the producer, Naomi Capon. She commissioned me to write another Scottish play, and also carry out research for a documentary on how art was being fostered in three new towns: Glenrothes in Scotland, and two I visited in England with names I don't remember. My report was detailed, conscientious and showed several ways of making towns finer places, but nothing came of it. Ms Capon accepted the second play she had commissioned, *In the Boiler Room*, calling it, "another moving miracle." It was never produced because she left the BBC soon after.

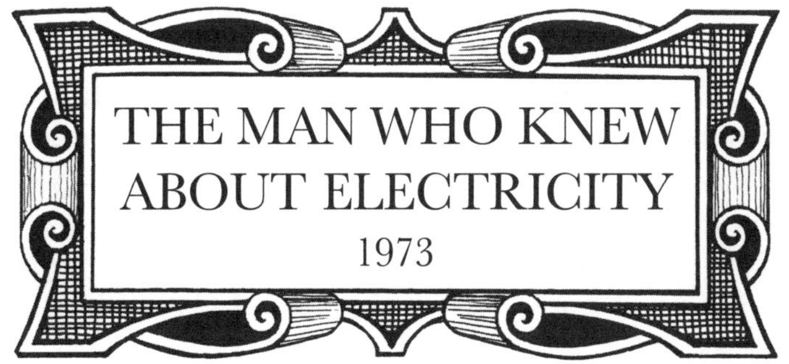

THE MAN WHO KNEW ABOUT ELECTRICITY

1973

CAST

OLD MAN

Character: Brisk, cheery, self-obsessed and slightly deaf.
Appearance: Sixty to sixty-five, small, dry, light and quick and always grinning as if at a secret joke.
Clothes: Black boiler-suit; dirty cloth cap; brand new tweed jacket rather too big for him, the right sleeve hanging empty because the arm is in a sling and the hand swaddled in grubby bandages.
Accent: Glasgow.

STUDENT

Character: Confident, conventional, good-natured and unintelligent. He can pass examinations by working very hard so he works very hard.
Appearance: Eighteen, sturdy, clean and well fed. A short-back-and-sides haircut.
Clothes: Expensive and conventional. He carries a shining leather briefcase stuffed with books and wears a university scarf.
Accent: Middle-class Scottish.

WOMAN

Character: Uneducated and tense, resigned rather than bitter. As her life allows no scope for intelligence it is impossible to know if she is intelligent. She is the same age as the student.
Appearance: At first sight too dumpy and sluttish to be attractive, but her plumpness is the womanly counterpart of the student's sturdiness and she carries it well. When she has been seen clearly there should be no doubt about her physical attraction. She wears no make-up.
Clothes: A housecoat over a nightdress, her feet in slippers, hair in curlers.
Accent: Glasgow.

IRISHMAN

Character: Sly, calm, clever and alcoholic. He would never use or threaten violence but deploys a formidable appearance.
Appearance: Massive, slow-moving, about forty. Walking, standing and sitting demand all his concentration so he disguises his sickness by a deliberate manner, and like the woman's attractiveness, it dawns on the viewer slowly.
Clothes: Tennis shoes, baggy flannel trousers, pin-stripe waistcoat, crumpled raincoat, grubby collar and tie.
Accent: Irish.

While the producer may not get actors to fulfil all these directions, the costumier should be guided by the clothing notes.

SETS

The telecine or outside filming shots show upward views of new multi-storey blocks, panning down to a busy street. The main action is in the room and kitchen, divided by a lobby, of a street level flat.

1) Busy Glasgow Pavement
2) Lobby in Condemned Tenement
3) The Old Man's Room
4) The Kitchen
5) The Lobby
6) The Kitchen
7) Busy Glasgow Pavement

****

TELECINE *Three or four quick stills of the tower-blocks of Strathclyde University, seen beyond half-demolished and condemned tenements. Focus on the summit of one such block [suggestion: The Livingstone Tower] and pan down to the pavement of a busy street. [Suggestion: George Street]. The* **OLD MAN** *can be seen soliciting passers-by, who ignore him. This shot could be taken from the pavement opposite, the* **OLD MAN** *being glimpsed between passing traffic.*

1: BUSY PAVEMENT

The **OLD MAN**, *grinning, speaks to a businessman who hardly pauses to listen.*

OLD MAN D'ye know anything about electricity Jimmy?

The businessman walks away. The **STUDENT** *passes. The* **OLD MAN** *falls in step beside him.*

OLD MAN How are ye doing Jim?

STUDENT [*brusquely*] Fine thanks and I'm not called Jim.

OLD MAN That's great Jim. D'ye know anything about electricity?

STUDENT Quite a lot. [*stopping*] What about it?

OLD MAN Then you'll know how to change a bulb?

STUDENT A bulb?

The **OLD MAN** *produces a light bulb in cardboard container from pocket.*

OLD MAN One of these. Twenty-five pence this cost.

[*anxiously*] D'ye think it was worth it Jimmy?
STUDENT What happened to your hand?
OLD MAN [*holds the bandaged hand up and says eagerly*] Flaming paraffin, flaming paraffin all over it but the doctor isnae worried, in fact he's delighted. [*chuckles*] No there's nothing the matter wi' me. Ye'll change that bulb Jimmy?
The **STUDENT** *frowns at his watch.*
STUDENT Well ...
OLD MAN Ye won't lose by it Jimmy! Nothin' for nothin', I know the score.
STUDENT Listen, I'm catching a train at Queen Street in fifteen minutes, where do you live?
OLD MAN This way Jim, just round the corner ...
They move on together.
... and ye'll be quiet about it? Nice and quiet? My landlady's a woman, ye see, and she gets funny notions ... [*taps side of his head*] ... she's full of these funny notions.

2: TENEMENT LOBBY

About the size of a cupboard, one wall has only room for the front door and a fuse-box beside it. In a left wall is the door to a kitchen, in the right the door to the **OLD MAN***'s room. A dirty fanlight window above the front door admits daylight from the street. The front door is stealthily unlocked from outside and the* **OLD MAN** *enters cautiously, followed by the* **STUDENT** *who frowns in a puzzled way. The* **OLD MAN** *shuts the front door quietly, winks and presses his finger to his lip, points to the kitchen door, taps the side of his head, unlocks his room door [it is fastened by a padlock and staple] and ushers the* **STUDENT** *in.*

3: OLD MAN'S ROOM

A window has the curtains drawn and [since they don't quite meet] pinned together with two safety pins to prevent anyone outside peeping in. A sideboard has many egg cartons stacked on it, two modern transistor radios and an alarm clock. There is a single bed whose covering seems to be nothing but overcoats, a tall wardrobe with egg-cartons stacked on top, a very solid table in the centre with a light socket hanging above it. Plugged into this is a cluster of adaptors, from which a light bulb protrudes obliquely. The cluster is the centre of a web of wires running to a bed-warmer under the heap of coats, an anglepoise lamp on a chair by the bed, an electric radiator on the floor, two new radios on the table beneath. The table also supports a mug, a plate and a pile of egg cartons. The **STUDENT** *stares open-mouthed at the light fixture, while the* **OLD MAN** *carefully shuts the door behind them.*
STUDENT [*pointing*] Haven't you a wall socket?
OLD MAN Of course! Of course! But it gives off sparks and shocks and things. [*chuckles*] Don't worry, there's no flies on me.
STUDENT But that light fixture's overloaded, your landlady could be prosecuted for it.
OLD MAN It would only upset her. Women are like that.
The **STUDENT** *lays down his briefcase and climbs onto the table saying:*
STUDENT If you'd pull the curtains we could see a bit better.
OLD MAN Whit? This is a ground-floor flat. These wirelesses are valuable Jimmy. [*pats one and chuckles*]. No no, I wasnae born yesterday.
The **STUDENT**, *standing on the table, looks closely at the knot of adaptors and the bulb.*
STUDENT Is this switched off?
OLD MAN It's no working is it?
The **STUDENT** *points to a radio beside his feet.*
STUDENT Turn that on.
The **OLD MAN** *obeys.*
SOUND: *Number one on the hit parade very loud, with hoarse static crackling through it.*
OLD MAN [*shouting*] Would ye like to buy it Jimmy?
The **STUDENT** *points to the wall switch by the door and bellows above the noise.*
STUDENT Switch that off!
The **OLD MAN** *obeys.*
SOUND: *Fades quickly out.*
STUDENT [*unscrews old bulb saying*] Now give me the new one.
The **OLD MAN** *hands up the new bulb. The* **STUDENT** *bends to take it then hands him the old. The* **STUDENT** *tears off the carton, drops it on the table and screws the new bulb into the socket while the* **OLD MAN** *shakes the old bulb questioningly against his ear.*
STUDENT Switch on the light.
The **OLD MAN** *trots over to the switch and presses it down. The bulb lights up.*
SOUND: *The radio blares out.*
OLD MAN [*shouting*] You've done it Jimmy! You've done it!
The **STUDENT** *jumps down to the floor. The light goes out.*
SOUND: *The radio fades out. A door is flung violently open somewhere outside, and a baby is heard beginning to scream.*
The door of the room is shoved open and the **WOMAN** *violently enters.*

She wears slippers, housecoat, and has her hair in curlers.

WOMAN Whit the hell's goin' on in here? [*to the* **STUDENT**]. Who are you? Whit're ye up tae?

STUDENT [*calmly*] Changing the bulb.

She faces the **OLD MAN** *who is grinning in an embarrassed way, and nervously shaking the old bulb beside his ear again.*

WOMAN I warned ye! I warned ye about visitors yes a did! [*to the* **STUDENT**] Clear out! Clear outa here this instant! And get that fuse mended first.

STUDENT Will you relax a minute.

WOMAN [*more quietly*] Listen, I've a wean in there that cannae *sleep* with the light off! How can I relax?

STUDENT You attend to the kid and I'll attend to the light. Have you fuse wire?

WOMAN [*sullenly*] In the box behind the front door.

STUDENT Good.

He picks up his briefcase and walks coolly past her into the lobby. The baby is still yelling.

4: THE KITCHEN

A window in the wall opposite the door has a sink and draining board in front of it. There is only one tap, but a small gas water-heater above this. The window is curtain-less but for a strip of dirty lace curtain across the bottom, and a blind has been pulled down to this. There is a very old gas cooker loaded with kettle, frying pan and pots; an upright cupboard or press with shelves loaded with plates, cups, nearly empty packets and tins, and an out-of-date electric iron. Near the back wall is a carrycot pram from which the yelling comes. In the middle of the room is a kitchen table with a drawer in it, and a chair at each end. Nearby is a worn armchair. On the wall by the sink hangs an old-fashioned shaving mirror. Otherwise the walls are decorated by several cheap religious prints, notably a Madonna and Child.

PS *There is an electric wall socket on the draining board side of the window.*

The **WOMAN** *enters, goes to the pram and pushes it gently back and forth, saying in a low voice:*

WOMAN Come on Theresa, pack it in. There there. Pack it in now. You're *alright*. You're *alright*.

The baby's cries lessen. The **STUDENT** *appears at the door holding fuse and wire in one hand, briefcase in other.*

STUDENT Have you a screwdriver?

WOMAN A had but a lost it.

STUDENT Have you a nail-file?

WOMAN Naw.

STUDENT Have you a tea-knife?

WOMAN There's knives in the table drawer, and hurry up. This one'll no' sleep if the light's no' on.

STUDENT Why not?

He steps to the table, lays the briefcase on it and opens the drawer.

WOMAN Nobody likes the dark.

STUDENT [*rummaging*] Then let the blind up – it's broad daylight outside.

WOMAN This is a ground floor flat and I've had enough trouble with nosey-parkers. Whenever anyone as much as looks in here some rotten thing happens.

STUDENT Like what for instance – I've found your screw-driver, by the way.

He sits on the table edge and starts to repair the fuse with deft efficient movements, peering closely in the dull light and talking without looking up.

STUDENT Like what, for instance?

WOMAN [*still pushing*] Well, when the old boy burnt his hand the S.S. came to see him ...

STUDENT S.S.?

WOMAN Social Security. Anyway they looked in here and they cut my allowance right out. Just like that.

STUDENT Why?

WOMAN [*in a low voice*] Nothin' to do with you.

Pause. The **STUDENT** *works away quietly. The* **WOMAN** *steals a glance at him.*

WOMAN Where do *you* come from?

STUDENT Helensburgh.

WOMAN One of the nobs, eh?

STUDENT Not really.

WOMAN Are you a student?

STUDENT First year technical. I think ... that's ... just about ... right.

He lays down the screwdriver, stands, steps to the door then turns on a sudden thought and reaches for the briefcase.

WOMAN [*impatiently*] Ach leave it! A'll no steal yer books. He frowns, leaves the briefcase and goes out through the door saying –

STUDENT Well, keep your fingers crossed.

A moment later the light comes brightly on. The baby's slight cries cease. The woman steps away from the pram and faces the door. The **STUDENT** *enters briskly. He goes to the table and lifts the briefcase.*

STUDENT That might hold for a few days longer but unless you mend the wall socket in the old boy's room you'll have another fuse on your hands. That light fixture's overloaded.

WOMAN You know about electricity?

STUDENT I'm studying to be an engineer.

WOMAN D'ye think you could mend an iron? This one here –

She steps to the cupboard and lifts the iron.

WOMAN It conked out three weeks ago and I really need it for dryin' the wean's nappies. I mean she's gettin' a rash.

She lays it on the table. The **STUDENT** *sighs and glances at his wristwatch.*

STUDENT Well I've missed my train so I suppose I can spare twenty minutes.

He lays down the briefcase, pulls a chair up to the table, takes the screwdriver and begins unscrewing the iron's plug.

WOMAN You're a pal.

She turns to the mirror and begins removing her curlers, laying them on the draining board of the sink. She speaks without turning, raising her voice a little.

WOMAN Sorry I yelled at ye through there.

STUDENT Didn't worry me.

WOMAN You see I've had enough trouble with that auld bastard – excuse the language.

STUDENT [*smiling at the plug*] I've heard worse.

WOMAN I suppose you think I'm ... I suppose you think I'm a bad lot.

STUDENT No. Why?

WOMAN Living here. Like this.

STUDENT Don't suppose you can help it.

WOMAN I can't. That's right.

She lays down the last of her curlers, shakes her head and starts wandering nervously about the room.

WOMAN [*abruptly*] Do you believe in God?

STUDENT Now and again. Nothing wrong with the plug. [*sighs*] Let's look at the connection.

WOMAN Life can be Hell sometimes, can't it?

STUDENT [*easily*] Everyone has their ups and downs.

WOMAN I believe in God but he doesnae help much.

She pauses near the table, close to the **STUDENT** *but not facing him. She clenches her hands and sucks in her lower lip. The* **STUDENT** *is engrossed in opening the iron. She says in a low quick voice.*

WOMAN Would you ... Would you care for a short time?

He glances in a perfunctory way at his wristwatch.

STUDENT Thirteen minutes past five.

He opens the iron and she walks away from him looking defeated. Suddenly he looks up.

STUDENT What did you say?

WOMAN [*bitterly*] Not a thing.

She sits in the armchair, folding her arms under her breasts and crossing her legs. He looks at her wearily. For the first time his voice has an uncertain note.

STUDENT Did you ... did you ask me the time?

WOMAN Right! Right!

He stares at her legs. She cries out bitterly.

WOMAN Something the matter?

He shakes his head slightly.

STUDENT No! Not really.

He glances down at the iron, clears his throat and says in a quiet, embarrassed voice.

STUDENT I'll ... I'll need something with a thin end. Like a needle.

She stands up and plucks thoughtfully at her lower lip.

WOMAN [*quietly*] Would a kirby do?

STUDENT What?

WOMAN A hairpin.

She takes a hairpin from her pocket and holds it up. He stands and faces her saying tensely:

STUDENT Yes I think so.

She goes over to the table, eyes and mouth open in a vacant, hunted expression. She lays the pin on the table before him.

STUDENT Thanks.

He raises his hand to her. A door is heard to bang open. They turn, startled. The **IRISHMAN** *stands balefully in the doorway.*

IRISHMAN [*flatly*] I'm interrupting you.

STUDENT No you're not.

WOMAN He's mending the iron.

She goes back to her chair and sits.

IRISHMAN [*fiercely*]I say I'm interrupting!

He enters the room, slams the door behind him, goes to the table and sits slowly down in the chair facing the **STUDENT** *who stands staring at him, tensed for fight or flight.*

IRISHMAN [*softly*] Sit down young fella. Carry on with what you were doin' ... don't mind me!

The **STUDENT**, *not altogether reassured, sits and fiddles with the hairpin.*

STUDENT I don't mind you. The old boy got me in to replace a bulb for him then she asked me in to do this.

He starts poking at the connection.

WOMAN [*offhandedly*] He knows about electricity.

IRISHMAN Yes there's big futures in electricity.

He takes a flat bottle with no label from his coat pocket, uncorks it, is about to take a swig then pauses and says to the **STUDENT**:

IRISHMAN You'll not be offended if I offer you none? This stuff is alright for the likes of me, in fact it's indispensable. But it wouldn't do for a young fella who still had his health ... Make the man a cup of tea Mary!

The **WOMAN** *rises, fills kettle, puts it on cooker etc. The* **IRISHMAN** *swigs from the bottle, coughs, puts it down, wipes mouth with his sleeve.*

IRISHMAN I trust I amn't upsetting you? I'm a disgusting spectacle, that's true. Well, I'll go in a minute.

STUDENT [*working*] You don't disgust me.

IRISHMAN Still, judging by your clothes you don't often sit in a room with a coupla cases like us.

STUDENT It might interest you to know that my father's father was a riveter with Harland and Wolf.

IRISHMAN Indeed! So you feel a degree of solidarity with the working classes?

STUDENT [*looking up*] I think I can say that.

The **IRISHMAN** *raises a triumphant forefinger.*

IRISHMAN Good for you! But you see, we're not working class. We're ... how could I put it ... we're *casualty* class.

STUDENT There's no such thing.

He devotes himself to the iron.

IRISHMAN No? [*sighs, lifts the bottle but on second thoughts lays it down untasted*] You know, this was a working class district. Casualties lived here too, but the majority were decent hardworking labourers and tradesmen. Not the sort of people I normally see eye-to-eye with, though many of them were Irish, like meself. One day the area was scheduled for redevelopment – somethin' to do with the ringroad or the university, I don't rightly recall which. So the landlords stopped repairin' the properties and the working class were given expensive homes in posh districts like Castlemilk, and Drumchapel, and Easterhouse. Of course the casualties could not afford the higher rents, so they stayed behind. And now the whole area – the part not knocked down I mean – is populated by casualties, unemployed people, and old-age pensioners, and moral casualties like me, and sentimental casualties like [*he points accusingly at the* **WOMAN** *who stands by the cooker with her hand on the handle of the kettle, waiting for it to boil*] ... like her.

WOMAN Now don't you start on me!

IRISHMAN Sorry Mary, sorry. I was led astray by the exuberance of my verbosity. [*to the* **STUDENT**, *on a matter-of-fact note*] But she is sentimental. She could have had a job in a Bridgeton lemonade factory at seven pounds a week but she didn't want to give up the child.

STUDENT [*roused*] Oh but surely –

The **IRISHMAN** *interrupts with upraised forefinger.*

IRISHMAN I know! I know! I told her meself! The child, I said, will be happier without you for a mother. If you really love her you'll get her adopted or shoved into a home and it'll give *both* of you a break. But she would not see reason. She is one mass of utterly disreputable primitive instincts.

WOMAN For Christ's sake hold your bloody tongue! [*to the* **STUDENT**] Pardon the language.

IRISHMAN [*quietly*] We'd be lonely people if it wasn't for my tongue Mary.

The **WOMAN** *pours the water into the teapot. The* **STUDENT** *has stopped working and listens thoughtfully, elbow on table and chin on palm of hand. The* **IRISHMAN** *notices this and concludes briskly.*

IRISHMAN But I was sorry when they working classes cleared out. As I say, I didn't always see eye-to-eye with them but they added tone to the district. And a lot of them were good neighbours.

STUDENT The old man through there – is he a casualty?

IRISHMAN N ... No. Not yet. That burnt hand of his is temporary. He usually pays his way. Works as a nightwatchman. Of course he's nearly seventy and won't be able to live here forever. This building's condemned, sooner or later they'll have to knock it down, and when he loses his job he'll be hard put to finding a place to stay. Why, I'm told that even quite prosperous people are finding it difficult to discover new houses.

STUDENT Well, my parents aren't exactly prosperous, but when they moved into a new house recently they had to pay twice what it cost ten years ago.

IRISHMAN [*pleased*] Exactly! Exactly! You understand then that it's equally difficult for the likes of us ... Strange, isn't it, the vast improvements we've seen in recent years – more cars and roadways and bigger buildings – yet all the time the casualty class gets larger and larger. Do you think there's a connection?

STUDENT Couldn't say.

IRISHMAN Well, we're part of Europe now. I'm sure it'll help.

The **WOMAN** *sets a cup of tea before each of them. The* **STUDENT***'s cup has a saucer.*

WOMAN Sorry there's no biscuits.

She walks away.

IRISHMAN Mary, you're a lovely girl. Look at her, son, isn't she a lovely girl? Look at the way she walks.

The **STUDENT** *gives he a quick glance then sips his tea.*

STUDENT She's not bad.

IRISHMAN Hear that Mary? The gentleman thinks you're not bad! Now when a laconic fellow like him says that about a woman it's better than a whole cargo of compliments from the like of me.

The **WOMAN** *turns and shouts.*

WOMAN You're a pimp! You're a pimp!

IRISHMAN [*strongly*] Well if I am I'm the worst-paid pimp in Glasgow!

They glare at each other. The **STUDENT** *abruptly seizes the screw-driver and goes to work on the connection. The* **WOMAN** *sits down in the armchair, arms folded and legs crossed. The* **IRISHMAN** *picks up his bottle, looks at it, sets it down and sips his tea, remarking thoughtfully to the* **STUDENT***:*

IRISHMAN She doesn't really think that. Actually I'm not a pimp. Pimping is a middle-class occupation. A pimp, you see, is a kind of employer, and I haven't the necessary dynamism, the get-up-and-go to employ a girl like Mary. My feelings for her are fatherly ones. But women, you know ... ? [*he taps his brow*] They take these notions. Why do you think she lets me come here?

STUDENT Don't know.

IRISHMAN Well she feels *safer* with a man in the house, an undemanding kind of man who doesn't lose his temper and can be trusted with the baby if she needs a night out. I'm alcoholic you see, but I am *not*, and have never been, a drunkard. No no, I can control myself. Liver, lights, stomach, genitals, circulation – they're crumbling, slowly and surely. But the brain is in full working order. I'm confident that me brain will stay intact for another coupla years ... [*he shakes his head in a puzzled way*] What was I talkin' about?

STUDENT Why you live together.

IRISHMAN We both need company, you see, and we're the best we can find in the circumstances. In spite of what she called me a minute ago there is no financial bond between us. None at all. And would you believe it, her social security money was cut off a fortnight ago because someone decided she was cohabiting with me. Whatever that means.

He stares at the **STUDENT** *who is screwing the iron together.*

STUDENT [*crisply*] Bad luck.

IRISHMAN [*enthusiastically*] That's it in a nutshell! Bad luck! That, is what a Frenchman, would call the *mot juste*. Education has certainly given you a way with words young fella. But I don't know why I'm boring you with all this. Tell me, have you a girlfriend?

STUDENT Yes.

IRISHMAN Going steady?

STUDENT Nearly a year.

IRISHMAN But you live with your parents?

STUDENT Yes.

IRISHMAN Who does the girl live with?

STUDENT [*crisply*] Let's not talk about her, eh?

IRISHMAN You are a gentleman Sir, and I apologise. It's just, I have a theory you see, that a lot of nonsense is talked in the papers about the permissive society. You'd think to read them, sir, that young people below the age of twenty-five were indulging in all sorts of startling practices. Now I think that most young people are just as respectable and cautious, and discreet, and unadventurous, and miserable, as we were in my young day. Here a minute. [*beckons the* **STUDENT** *and leans towards him. The* **STUDENT** *cocks an ear in his direction*] Mary there – nineteen – been to bed with a young fella nearly twice in her life, and *that* was more than a year ago. *And* little good it did her. So when I came in and saw the pair of you – well I misunderstood the position entirely and for a moment I felt ... hopeful you might say. I like her. I like her. And she needs a bit of healthy appreciation from someone in her own age-group. She's a fine strong girl you see. She needs ...

WOMAN [*desperately*] I need money! Money for rent! That's all *I* need!

IRISHMAN [*reproachfully*] Oh Mary you need a lot more than that ... don't be put off by her rough tongue mister. That's a consequence of superficial economic tensions. (She's afraid of being chucked out into the streets.) Solve these tensions and you'll find her the most docile creature imaginable. [*In a low beguiling voice*] You'll be able to do anything you like with her.

The two men at the table are seen past the **WOMAN***'s profile. She is sucking her lower lip, trying not to cry. The* **STUDENT** *briskly rises and carries the iron towards her. And past her. He plugs it into a wall socket.*

STUDENT Just testing.

He lounges against the wall, regarding her thoughtfully.

STUDENT How much do you need?

WOMAN [*in a low voice, not looking at him*] Six pounds.

STUDENT That old boy next door – can he not help? If you lose this place he'll be homeless too.

WOMAN He'd paid three weeks in advance. I still need six pounds.

The **IRISHMAN** *in the background is swigging from the bottle. He sets it down, saying in a remote voice:*

IRISHMAN Not a bad old fella really.

STUDENT Well ... [*he takes out his wallet and lays two pound notes on the draining board*] ... at the moment this is all I can spare. Sorry.

WOMAN [*stonily*] Thanks. I'll make up the rest somehow.

STUDENT Good.

He bends, pats the iron, unplugs it and sets in on the draining board. A close-up of the iron, the hair-curlers and two Scottish pound notes.

STUDENT'S VOICE The iron's working.

WOMAN'S VOICE [*sincerely*] Thanks mister.

The **STUDENT** *walks to the table, picks up the briefcase and goes to the door. The* **IRISHMAN** *rouses himself with an effort and forces himself to his feet.*

IRISHMAN You're surely not leaving?

The **STUDENT** *turns at the door and says to the* **WOMAN** *awkwardly:*

STUDENT Goodbye.

IRISHMAN But you'll be back? It's a lonely life here by herself all day – she'll always be glad to see you ...

STUDENT [*flatly*] Will you please shut up?

The **IRISHMAN** *does, and sits down, defeated. The* **STUDENT** *looks at the* **WOMAN**. *He hesitates, wanting to say more than he can, and at last says:*

STUDENT Well. Goodbye Mary.

WOMAN [*sincerely*] Thanks a lot.

They look at each other. He hesitates, opens the door and steps out.

5: THE LOBBY

The **STUDENT** *is confronted by the* **OLD MAN** *who has opened his door and stands in it grinning and chuckling.*

OLD MAN You did it Jimmy! [*he holds out a ten-penny piece*] Here, catch this!

STUDENT [*staring*] What's this for?

OLD MAN Ye changed the bulb didn't ye? Nothin' for nothin' – I know the score! Here, take it!

STUDENT No! No!

OLD MAN Take it, ye've earned it.

The **OLD MAN** *drops the coin into the* **STUDENT***'s breast pocket then skips backward and slams the door. There is the sound of a bolt being shot. The* **STUDENT** *stares, baffled, then knocks on the door.*

STUDENT Open up! This won't do! It's silly! I don't need ... [*hesitates then says in a louder voice*]. Listen, I tell you what I'll do, I'll mend that wall socket! I'll come back tomorrow and mend that wall socket!

6: THE KITCHEN

The **WOMAN** *and the* **IRISHMAN** *sit where they did at the end of Scene 4, impassively listening.*

STUDENT'S VOICE I'll be back tomorrow! The afternoon, say about two-thirty! ... Don't forget, two-thirty! ... Remember, I'll be back!

SOUND: *footsteps and the front door slammed.*

The **IRISHMAN** *looks at the* **WOMAN** *and frowns. She stares straight before her. He sighs and starts to stand up.*

IRISHMAN [*kindly*] I think, Mary, you need a cup of tea.

WOMAN No.

IRISHMAN Oh yes you do. I'll make it.

7: BUSY PAVEMENT

Tracking shot, from in front, of the **STUDENT***'s head and shoulders as he walks down the street. His face frowns sternly then slowly relaxes into a sly smile which widens into a grin of triumphant anticipation. Freeze frame.*

TELECINE *The grinning head is imposed on the stills the film began with: modern tower blocks over old condemned tenements.*

IN THE EARLY 1970s Frances Head got me two major commissions from Granada Television. For a series called *Queen Victoria's Scandals* I wrote about Henry James Prince, an Anglican priest who, from being an extreme puritan, founded a breakaway sect that worshipped him as the incarnate Holy Ghost and let him make all his sexual wishes come true. My researches in London took me to the library of the old British Museum where I read his published diaries, pamphlets and accounts by those who had known him; then to the Colindale Newspaper Library for reports of his scandalous Abode of Love in the London Times. From Somerset House in London I got copies of marriage certificates proving that Hepworth Dixon, his fairest and most intelligent biographer, was wrong in an important detail. I was so pleased with the factual material I dramatised that I imagined publishing it one day as Ben Jonson had published his tragedy *Sejanus*, with footnotes giving the historical sources of every episode. The play was accepted but production was delayed by a discovery that the Granada TV studios were insulated with asbestos tiles now recognised as health hazards.

While these were replaced I was commissioned to write a play for a series about religious trials called *For Conscience Sake*, so chose the trial of Socrates because I was tired of twisted Christian consciences. Plato's account of the trial is the best and longest, but one-sided. Socrates appears in it as wise, calm, humorous, good, and repugnant to a majority of his fellow citizens *because* he is wiser and more virtuous. I believed the philosopher's enemies must have had some good reasons for thinking him dangerous, reasons Plato ignored because he disliked democracy. I read all I could about 5th Century B.C. Athens, discovering such a host of uniquely interesting folk that I conceived a three-act play called *Democracy* in which the trial of Socrates would be the culminating scene. And I departed from historical truth by having two former friends of Socrates and enemies of the Athenian people summoned as witnesses, though witnesses were not called in Athenian trials, and those I presented had been killed before the trial took place. I was happy with these two plays, believing the producers who had accepted my scripts would stick to them.

There were no signs that my career as a televised playwright was coming to an end. I was interviewed in London by a smart young BBC director who wanted me to write something about Scottish radicalism between the World Wars. He became highly excited when I told him of John Maclean, the Marxist Glasgow school teacher who helped the 1915 Clydeside housewives' rent strike, which forced Lloyd George's government to stop landlords raising rents for the duration of the war. Dismissed from his post, he started the Scottish Labour College, giving free classes in socialist economics to working men. In 1917 he was made Britain's first Soviet consul because Lenin believed the British Communist revolution would start in Scotland. Maclean disagreed, later rejecting the British Communist Party becasue it was controlled from Moscow. He founded the Scottish Workers' Party, and before 1929 was jailed six times for sedition and incitements to strike – imprisonments that destroyed his health and at last killed him. I refused this producer's commission to write a documentary drama about Maclean because many who knew him were still alive, including Nan Milton, his daughter. Though believing in his greatness, I knew I could not be true to the facts of his life without months of research.

I was glad when years later my friend Archie Hind had his play *Shoulder to Shoulder* produced in Cumbernauld's Cottage Theatre. It is almost wholly based upon letters written by, to, and about Maclean. I preferred writing plays that sometimes allowed me the freedom of fantasy.

Then in 1974 Frances told me of a London TV producer planning a series of modern plays based on popular nursery tales. *Goldilocks and the Three Bears*, for instance, became the story of an innocent young social worker who visits an unemployed family and just manages to escape alive. Like most first proposals this did not attract me until suddenly I imagined the Aladdin story with the hero a junior civil servant, wicked uncle Abanazer a senior one, and the magic lamp a secret government paper giving its owner unlimited powers of blackmail. The TV producer rejected the idea so I made of it a radio play that Frances sold to London BBC. Directed by my old friend Shaun McLaughlin, *McGrotty and Ludmilla, or The Harbinger Report* was broadcast on the 18th of July 1975. I give the date to show that, though a shameless plagiarist, I did not plagiarise the Whitehall comedy series *Yes Minister*.

Twelve years later, long after my TV career ended, Michael Boyd, director of Glasgow's Tron Theatre, asked me to consider writing a modern version of Gogol's play *The Government Inspector*, about a silly fool mistaken for a highly placed official by the equally foolish bureaucracy of a town he visits. Instead I interested him in commissioning this stage version of *McGrotty and Ludmilla*. It was produced in February 1987 with this cast:

Producer and Director	Mike Boyd
Mungo McGrotty	Kevin McMonigle
Arthur Shots	Russell Hunter
Ludmilla	Julia St. John
Ms Panther, Mrs Bee, Mary Fox	Vivienne Dixon
The Minister	Sandy Neilson
Aubrey Rose, American artist	Bill Murdoch
Charlie Gold, Harbinger	Sean Scanlan
Set Designer	Peter Ling

It was my first chance since Art School days to be personally involved in the production of a play. I wanted, like Bernard Shaw, to read my play to the cast before the rehearsals started, a 19th century custom common in France and Britain when actors often only learned their own speeches and cue phrases from other actors that stopped or started them. Mike reminded me of Miss Hamilton by explaining that the actors must first find *themselves* in their parts before I explained my interpretation, so let me read them my version a week after rehearsals began. Despite my intrusions the production was so well acted, well produced and well attended that afterwards I was told it had been the Tron's most successful production to date. This may or may not have been true. Everyone in theatre shines as flattering a light as possible on things they produce together – they could not persevere otherwise. But I sincerely believed that a Swiss Cottage production would have persuaded Binkie to transfer it to the West End (of London) but alas, he had died fourteen years earlier. And, even alaser, Frances Head died of lung cancer in 1976, ending (though at first I did not notice this) my first and busiest spell of playwrighting.

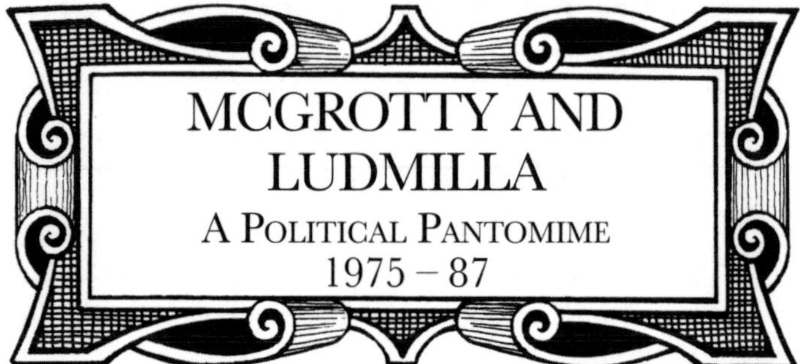

CAST

MUNGO MCGROTTY – A raw Scottish Aladdin
SIR ARTHUR SHOTS – A wicked uncle
MISS PANTHER – The perfect secretary
LUDMILLA – The icy debutante
THE MINISTER – An ageing fusspot
MRS BEE – An ordinary secretary
CHARLIE GOLD – A civil service Guildenstern
AUBREY ROSE – A civil service Rosencrantz, Scene 4
A CLUB SERVANT – Scene 4, one line
HARBINGER – A very sick man, Scene 7
MISS KAY – A secretary, Scene 7, four lines
AN AMERICAN ARTIST – Scene 12
A NICE OLD LADY – Scene 12
A SERVANT – Scene 12, three lines
THREE DISTANT VOICES – Scene 12, one line each
A WAITRESS – Scene 19, two lines
A WELSH MP – Scene 21
PARLIAMENTARY VOICES – Scene 21

SCENES

1 A MINISTRY CORRIDOR
2 SIR ARTHUR'S OFFICES
3 THE SAME, SOME TIME LATER
4 A LONDON CLUB
5 THE MINISTER'S OUTER OFFICE
6 SIR ARTHUR'S INNER OFFICE
7 HARBINGER'S OFFICE
8 SIR ARTHUR'S INNER OFFICE
9 THE MINISTER'S INNER OFFICE
10 MCGROTTY'S LODGINGS
11 THE MINISTER'S INNER OFFICE

INTERVAL

12 THE MINISTER'S PRIVATE HOUSE: DINING ROOM
13 THE MINISTER'S PRIVATE HOUSE: CONSERVATORY
14 LUDMILLA'S STUDIO
15 A STREET
16 THE MINISTER'S INNER OFFICE
17 SIR ARTHUR'S OFFICES
18 A STREET
19 A CAFÉ

20 SIR ARTHUR'S OFFICES
21 THE HOUSE OF COMMONS

SET
The corridors of power are indicated by a backdrop of Roman-Imperial-Renaissance-Victorian columns. Through arched windows between them are seen the tops of Big Ben, the Royal Hilton Hotel, The Dome of St. Paul's Cathedral, Telecom Tower, Nelson's Column, Broadcasting House and the Winged Victory. A central door frame at right angles to the backdrop indicates a division between the two rooms. On the left is an opulent desk and a ponderous old safe; on the right is a sofa, low table and cocktail cabinet. Other props and flats required by the pantomime may be stacked on each side in view of the audience.

CASTING
The parts of McGrotty and Shots cannot double with others, but two women and four men can act the play if Ludmilla doubles with Miss Kay; Miss Panther triples with Mrs Bee and the Gracious Old Lady; Charlie Gold doubles with The Minister; Aubrey Rose quintuples with Harbinger, the American, the Waitress and the Welsh MP. The spare Servants and voices can be done with whoever is available. A cast of three women and three men could perform the play in a different combination using drag.

PROPERTIES
An office desk, preferably opulent; a sofa; a low coffee table; a drinks cabinet; some cans of lager, preferably Tennent's Superlager; four chairs; two telephones; a modern metal briefcase; a cardboard folder; a pile of box files; a large official envelope.

FLATS
The front of a ponderous old safe, with openable door.
A small crowd of life-sized distinguished contemporaries holding glasses.
A long narrow table with the above sitting at it.
A large urn of ferns on a pedestal. (If modelled on the Warwick Vase, the ferns may be omitted).
A smart car seen from the side.
The House of Commons front bench.

CLOTHING
McGrotty needs at least two suits: one ill-fitting pin-striped double-breasted two piece, with tartan necktie, and one better-fitting grey three piece with a large pocket in the lining. An ideal production would also give him an impressive suit of tweed plus-fours, and a final garment in which he looks indistinguishable from any Conservative cabinet minister born to the job.

1: A MINISTRY CORRIDOR

SOUND *Big Ben striking the Westminster chimes, but the hours are struck by three notes of a cuckoo clock.*
At a leisurely pace **SIR ARTHUR SHOTS** *and* **CHARLIE GOLD** *enter through the audience and mount the stage, conversing.* **MUNGO MCGROTTY**, *who has not learned to carry himself properly, later shambles across the stage front carrying an unwieldy pile of box files.*
SHOTS Every organisation needs a great deal of corruption, of course, to stop it becoming rigid, callous and inefficient. Look at the old Polit-bureau.
GOLD Yes it's very upsetting.
SHOTS But even corruption can be carried too far. Everybody knows the Foreign Office is a pretty sinister show. You and I know that it's an innocent babe in arms compared with the RSPCA.
GOLD Yes it's very very upsetting.
SHOTS Poor Harbinger.
GOLD Why poor?
SHOTS He's on the verge.
GOLD Verge?
SHOTS Brink.
GOLD Brink?
SHOTS Verge of crack. Brink of breakdown.
GOLD Well I find that very, very –
SHOTS *notices* **MCGROTTY** *is likely to collide with them.*
SHOTS Mind where you're going! [**MCGROTTY** *recoils into him*]. Aaaargh! My ankle you clumsy fool!
MCGROTTY [*managing not to drop the files and retreating from him sideways*] I didnae do that deliberately you know. All the same, I'm sorry. I mean, I really am sorry! I mean, if you want me to grovel I'll grovel but honestly, there's no point! No point at all! [*Exit* **MCGROTTY**].
GOLD A hopeless fellow that. Been with us a fortnight.
SHOTS Hopeless is he? Hm. [*They separate.* **SHOTS** *enters Scene 2*].

2: SIR ARTHUR'S OFFICES

Formidably immobile, **MISS PANTHER** *sits at her desk in the outer office, hands folded on it. Her voice is quiet and distinct.*

PANTHER Good morning, Sir Arthur.

SHOTS Anything afoot, Miss Panther?

PANTHER I'm afraid not, Sir Arthur. Somebody's secretary phoned but said there's nothing doing.

SHOTS I can wait. [*hitches a thigh familiarly over a corner of the desk*] You and I have seen a great deal of foul weather together Miss Panther. Remember the Loch Ness oil leak? And the call-girl credit squeeze? And the scandal over the rogue virus shares which nearly put the whole nation in quarantine? Material has lain upon this desk – [*thumps it*] – which could have provoked revolutions, overturned administrations, and made you a very rich woman Miss Panther. But I have never once had cause to doubt your loyalty. You are discretion itself.

PANTHER Thank you, Sir Arthur.

SHOTS I mention this because I intend to question you on a matter so seemingly trivial that you might mention it casually to someone and I want that not to happen.

PANTHER Then it shall not happen, Sir Arthur.

SHOTS [*he strolls away from the desk, then turns*] Who is the new young fellow with the Scots accent and the disgusting necktie?

PANTHER He is called Mungo McGrotty.

SHOTS Clever is he?

PANTHER I gather not, Sir Arthur.

SHOTS Surely he shows *some* signs of low animal cunning?

PANTHER I gather not even that, Sir Arthur.

SHOTS How did he get here?

PANTHER Our last minister was criticized in the House for employing nobody but Etonians, so we sometimes take on people with no kind of background in order not to seem elitist, Sir Arthur. We prefer them to be fools because clever ones don't always do what they're told.

SHOTS [*deliberately*] Miss Panther, I want to know more about this young fellow. Fetch me his file and anything else you can – discreetly – discover. [*He turns to go*].

PANTHER Sir Arthur! [*He looks back. She takes a manilla folder from a drawer, stands and holds it out to him*]. I believe this contains all you could wish to know about Mungo McGrotty. [*He is surprised but not greatly. He takes the folder.*]

SHOTS Thank you, Miss Panther.

He walks to his inner office, sits on the sofa, spreads open the folder on his knees and reads the contents. **MISS PANTHER** *has resumed her seat. The lights dim.*

SOUND: *Half of the Westminster Chimes.*

The lights come up.

3: THE SAME, LATER

SOUND: *A door is clumsily knocked.*

PANTHER Come in.

Enter **MCGROTTY,** *holding a sheaf of paper.*

MCGROTTY This is for Sir Shots – it's meant to be sort of urgent. Anyway that's what old Charlie says.

PANTHER Give it to me. [*takes it, then points*] Now walk in that direction until you arrive in the next room.

MCGROTTY [*alarmed*] Eh? Oh!

He hesitates. She continues to inexorably point. He goes miserably in the indicated direction. **SHOTS** *does not look up from the folder on his knees until* **MCGROTTY** *gives a miserable little cough.*

MCGROTTY Honest, it wasnae deliberate.

SHOTS I beg your pardon?

MCGROTTY I didn't bash into you deliberately, you know.

SHOTS I'm glad you did it. [*lays the folder on the low coffee table and stands up*] It compelled me to notice you and I was struck by ... something in your face. [*Loudly*] Isolate us, Miss Panther, Mungo and I must not be disturbed!

MISS PANTHER *presses something on her desk. All but the area surrounding* **SHOTS** *and* **MCGROTTY** *are at once in deep darkness.*

SHOTS [*intimately*] I've been looking through your file. It confirmed what I suspected. Your father was the best friend I ever had. Sit down. [*He points to the sofa*].

MCGROTTY My father? But he ... he ...

SHOTS Died before you were born. I know. Sit!

MCGROTTY [*He sits*] But he was a ... he was only a ...

SHOTS Sergeant in the Pay Corps. And I was a colonel in the REMC. All the same, three days after the Normandy landing he saved my life.

MCGROTTY [*astounded*] Really?

SHOTS You need a drink. Have you a preference?

MCGROTTY I could do with a can of export.

SHOTS Here's a gin ... and tonic. I don't want this tête-à-tête smelled afterwards upon your breath. I suppose you've read all about it? The war in France, I mean.

MCGROTTY No, I don't read books.

SHOTS I'm glad to hear it, they can be terribly misleading.

Take a cigar. Have a light. [*presents a box and lighter.*]
MCGROTTY [*Puffing and coughing*] Thanks.
SHOTS I'm going to tell you the full story so listen carefully. [*paces about, pausing at moments as the spirit moves him*] In the late autumn of '44 I was reconnoitring some miles in advance of the front line. My men didn't like it, the top brass didn't like it, but it kept me on my toes. Picture a gleaming blackness punctured by the kapow! kapow! of the howitzers and the staccato whine of the tracers. In the middle stands a sinister geological formation with a crevasse in the side. The Mexicans call them arroyos. My instinct told me to give it a miss. My duty was to investigate. I was about to enter when I was prevented by a hand placed flat on the centre of my chest. It belonged to a weazened little runt of a fellow, one of those twisted, wretched splinters of humanity which our industrial slums spew forth in such abundance. North of the Tweed I believe you call them bauchles. [**MCGROTTY** *looks puzzled*] The Germans call them poison dwarfs, but of course they are the salt of the earth. In a gesture more eloquent than any words, the wee chap just ... pointed. [*An impressive pause.* **MCGROTTY** *stares open-mouthed*] My foot. Had been about to descend. Into a heap of Blitzlichtpulverum, the beastliest booby-trap in the whole hellish arsenal of the Hun. That *bauchle*, Mungo, was your father. [*More casually*] That was the last I saw of him. A fortnight later I heard that, ironically enough, he had got himself wiped out by the same boche booby-trap in the battle of the Bulge. Please don't drop ash on the carpet.
MCGROTTY, *much moved, lays down cigar and drink.*
MCGROTTY [*tearfully*] I never realised my dad was that kind of bloke.
SHOTS *gives him time to recover, then sits beside him.*
SHOTS Like working here?
MCGROTTY [*off-handedly*] The money's all right.
SHOTS Made any friends?
MCGROTTY No, but it doesnae bother me. I'm used to not having friends. At home nobody liked me because they thought I was stuck up. Here nobody talks to me because I'm not stuck up enough.
SHOTS Good. I will befriend you. The debt I owe your father shall be repaid, with interest, to you. I am going to have you promoted, and rapidly; but Mungo, I will toil for you *behind* the scenes. No word of this *special* connection between us must get about. I make that a test of your loyalty. Your father's loyalty knew no bounds. Does yours?
MCGROTTY [*puzzled*] Eh?
SHOTS [*patiently*] Will you keep your mouth shut about ... us?
MCGROTTY Yeah. Sure.
SHOTS You should find it easy to be discreet. You have no friends. Don't make any. You are used to being uninteresting. Stay uninteresting and I'll make it worth your while.
MCGROTTY [*tearful again*] Sir Shots, you're being very nice to me and I don't know what to say ... could I phone and tell my Mammy the good news?
SHOTS [*fiercely*] Not even your ... hm. Mammy. Never trust a woman, McGrotty. [*He stands up*]. Trot off now. People will be wondering what's happened. Mungo is leaving, Miss Panther!
The rest of the stage becomes visible. **MCGROTTY** *stands, wanders towards the outer office, then turns.*
MCGROTTY Could I call you Uncle Arthur, Sir Shots?
SHOTS [*kindly*] Just call me *Sir* Arthur, McGrotty.
MCGROTTY Thank you, Sir Arthur.
Exit **MCGROTTY** *past the impassive stare of* **MISS PANTHER**.
SHOTS *comes to the edge of the outer office.*
SHOTS I want, as soon as possible, to talk to Charlie Gold, Miss Panther.
PANTHER I have taken the liberty of sending for him, Sir Arthur.
SOUND: *A brisk knock.*
SHOTS That?
PANTHER Will be he.
SHOTS [*enthusiastically*] Come in Charlie! Come in, come in, come in! [*Enter* **GOLD**]. How good to see you! Come in, come in, come in! [*They enter the inner office*] A drink?
GOLD Not at the moment.
SHOTS Have a seat. [**GOLD** *sits on the sofa.* **SHOTS** *talks while mixing an elaborate cocktail*] This is in the strictest confidence, Charlie.
GOLD Something to do with Harbinger?
SHOTS No no. If Harbinger digs deep enough to implicate himself we have nothing to worry about. No, I want to confess something, Charlie.
GOLD Oh?
SHOTS I believe in fair play.
GOLD You do?
SHOTS Yes. I don't like judging people by their first

impression. You know that young fellow who bumped into us yesterday? The one with the Scotch accent and the disgusting necktie? Perhaps you saw him leaving here as you arrived.

GOLD McGrotty?

SHOTS I had a word with him this morning. Bit of a rough diamond but ... he interests me, strangely.

GOLD Oh.

SHOTS Don't you think he's wasted, as a messenger?

GOLD It ... hadn't occurred to me.

SHOTS Frankly I ... wouldn't mind encountering him in something closer to our *own* sphere, if you see what I mean.

GOLD Yes.

SHOTS [*expansively*] Anyway I leave him in your hands, Charlie. He has depths, that youth. Someone ought to plumb them.

He drinks. **GOLD** *stares glumly before himself.*

4: A LONDON CLUB

This consists of two easy chairs. **AUBREY ROSE** *sits on one, reading The Times. A servant has approached him.*

SERVANT Would you like to order dinner now, sir?

ROSE I believe you've got something I killed in the larder. See if it's ripe will you?

Exit **SERVANT**. *Enter, very breathless,* **CHARLIE GOLD**.

GOLD There you are Aubrey. Listen to this. [*sits down*] Listen to this. Bloody Arthur Shots saw me today and – I can hardly believe it. You know that horrible new youth they've given me?

ROSE McGrotty?

GOLD Arthur is interested in him. Wants me to promote him.

ROSE Impossible! He isn't even pretty.

GOLD [*helplessly*] I know.

ROSE It's the young girls Arthur's always gone for. Wasn't there something between him and the Minister's daughter?

GOLD He's getting on, of course. He called McGrotty a rough diamond with depths which ought to be plumbed.

ROSE [*calmly*] I'm not doing it.

GOLD Who will?

ROSE Kick him upstairs.

GOLD Eh?

ROSE Give him to Granny.

GOLD Give him to the Minister? How can I?

ROSE Tell Granny what Arthur told you, rough diamond with depths etc. Tell him we can't afford to be elitist nowadays. Elitist is still quite a fashionable word.

GOLD I know the Minister is thick, but is he thick enough to swallow bolshy old rot like that?

ROSE Yes.

GOLD Well that's a weight off my mind.

5: THE MINISTER'S OFFICES

MCGROTTY *sits behind a desk, elbows on it and hands supporting face. He is gazing, fascinated, at an exchange of words between* **LUDMILLA** *and the Minister's secretary.*

LUDMILLA I must see Daddy at once.

MRS BEE The Minister is engaged at present.

LUDMILLA Then tell him I must see him at once. [*Exit* **MRS BEE**.]

LUDMILLA [*to* **MCGROTTY**] Hullo! I've never seen you before.

MCGROTTY [*dazzled*] I've seen you. Often.

LUDMILLA What a nasty tie! Surely you can afford a nice one.

MCGROTTY I'm bad at choosing things.

LUDMILLA Then get someone with an education to do it for you. And while you're about it, get a proper suit. Off-the-peg stuff lets down the tone of the office dreadfully. I know Daddy's a very new Minister but you ought to make an effort. People notice.

MINISTER [*appears at a door clutching a letter*] Ludmilla, the Prime Minister's on the phone, I can't see you now.

LUDMILLA You must. Mummy sent me. [*She walks past him through the door*].

MINISTER I wish people would support me more. Here McGrotty, take this letter to Arthur Shots and get *him* to answer it or something. I just haven't the time these days. The whole place is a menagerie, no peace, no support ...

MCGROTTY *proceeds indolently to Scene 6, reading the letter as he goes, shaking head, shrugging shoulders.*

6: SIR ARTHUR'S OFFICES

MCGROTTY *stands at the door.* **SHOTS** *almost runs to greet him.*

SHOTS Welcome, Mungo. Welcome! Welcome!

MCGROTTY Hullo. Granny wants you to do something about this. He's climbing the wall back there.

He hands over the letter. **SHOTS** *barely glances at it.*

SHOTS How are you doing, my boy?

MCGROTTY [*indifferently*] Apart from folk making remarks about my clothes it's all right really. I mean the extra money comes in handy. I suppose I've got you to thank.

SHOTS Don't mention it. Your career is only just beginning. In a year or two, or a month or two, or in as little as in a few days, a chance may arrive for me to do you some *real* good. Your salary could be doubled. Or would you prefer a lump sum? Ten thousand, tax free say? Think about it.

MCGROTTY [*overwhelmed*] In a few days?

SHOTS It is possible.

MCGROTTY But how ... ?

SHOTS Shh! When the time comes I will ask you to do a very simple, easy little thing, something that won't take more than a minute. And when you have done it Miss Panther will hand you a packet wrapped in pale blue paper containing ten thousand pounds in notes and we'll have another discussion about your future. Meanwhile here is the card of the only tailor in London worth cultivating. [*He hands over the card*] Phone him today. Make an appointment. Say I recommended you and leave the rest to him.

MCGROTTY Can I sit down ... ? You see there's this girl ... A girl I would like to ...

He sinks down into the sofa. **SHOTS** *comes nearer him.*

SHOTS [*softly*] There may be a tiny element of risk.

MCGROTTY [*worried*] Risk?

SHOTS A tiny element. But you have placed your future in my hands so if you obey me nothing really bad can happen. If you disobeyed me I would let you go and you would smash. You wouldn't like that. It would be letting your father down, and he had such hopes for you ...

MCGROTTY But he died ...

SHOTS [*impatiently*] Before you were born, of course, of course, but he suspected something like you was on the way.

MCGROTTY [*moistly*] I can't help feeling you have taken his place, Sir Arthur.

SHOTS Quite right, quite right, but there's no need to blub about it. Off you go now like a good fellow.

MCGROTTY *rises and goes.*

SHOTS [*suddenly*] Oh Mungo!

MCGROTTY [*at the door*] Sir Arthur?

SHOTS Have you read that delightful book by Orwell, 1984?

MCGROTTY I sat my A-levels on it.

SHOTS Do you remember the amusing interview between O'Brien and Winston when O'Brien holds up three fingers?

MCGROTTY Yes.

SHOTS How many fingers am I holding up Mungo? [*raises three*].

MCGROTTY [*worried*] Three, Sir Arthur?

SHOTS What would you say if I told you the actual number was four?

MCGROTTY I would say ... I would say there was something wrong with my seeing, Sir Arthur.

SHOTS Haha! You'll do. Off you trot.

Exit **MCGROTTY**. **SHOTS** *takes a few thoughtful paces about his office before clenching his fist and speaking with terrifying intensity.*

SHOTS By thunder, he'd better do!

He deliberately crushes the letter into a ball.

7: HARBINGER'S OFFICE

A desk with a telephone and a large sealed official envelope on it. Nearby is an easy chair on which **HARBINGER** *sits hunched in a state of dreadful contemplation. He does not react to the sound of a distant telephone.*

SOUND: *A distant telephone rings twice.*

Enter **MISS KAY**.

MISS KAY The Minister is on the line, Mr Harbinger.

HARBINGER [*sighs*] Oh dear.

Exit **MISS KAY**. **HARBINGER** *goes drearily to the desk, sits down, lifts phone. We suddenly see the Minister some distance away in spot light, speaking into a phone.*

MINISTER Harbinger! When am I getting your report?

HARBINGER Well Minister, you see –

MINISTER The Prime Minister's been on to me about it, the Foreign Office has been on to me about it, all kinds of people are nag-nag-nagging me and you do nothing but procrastinate.

HARBINGER I'm not very well, Minister.

MINISTER [*without sympathy*] Well I'm sorry you aren't well. Why aren't you well?

HARBINGER I'm distressed by my report. It incriminates so many decent, public-spirited, necessary people. Famous people. Some of the highest and best-loved names in Britain.

MINISTER I don't care how distressing the report is, *I'm* paid to suppress the facts, not you. When can I have them? When? When?

HARBINGER Today?

MINISTER Really?

HARBINGER The envelope is here, on my desk.

MINISTER Good. I won't be in today, I'm on my way down to Wales to open the Rhondda Valley nature reserve. But send it round at once and I'll read it first thing tomorrow morning. Goodbye Harbinger.

HARBINGER Goodbye Minister. If ... if anything happens, tell them I tried.

MINISTER I don't follow you Harbinger. If anything happens to what, tell them you tried what? I suggest you send over the report, take an aspirin and go to bed.

He puts down the receiver and vanishes. **HARBINGER** *puts down his receiver as if laying it to rest forever.*

HARBINGER [*quietly, after a profound sigh*] Tomorrow, and tomorrow, and tomorrow, life's but a walking shadow, told by an idiot. [*Loudly*] Miss Kay!

Enter **MISS KAY**.

HARBINGER [*loudly*] Miss Kay, take this envelope marked "Extra Top Secret and Confidential". Dispatch it at once by special messenger to the office of the Minister of Social Stability and then – [*quietly*] – put out the light and then put out *thy* light.

MISS KAY [*puzzled*] Sir?

HARBINGER Tell me when you've sent it off.

She leaves with the letter.

HARBINGER The evil men do lives after them. Their virtues we write in water, with a bare bodkin ... [*He rises and wanders distractedly about*] ... I remember ... the house where I was born. I believe ... in God the Father Almighty, Maker of Heaven and Earth, and in Jesus Christ his only Son our Lord, the rough male kiss of blankets, good strong stupefying incense smoke, and jellies smoother than the creamy curd. My head ... [*touches it*] ... my head knows too much ... [*yells aloud*] ... Pantocratoraphorbia! [*pulls himself together and whispers*] Everybody is going to hate me! [*covers his face with both his hands*] If thy head offend thee ... pluck it. [*uncovers face*] Offer it to one who will understand. [*begins to feel strengthened and comforted*] I believe ... in the Fellowship of the Holy Ghost, the Holy Catholic Church, the Communion of Saints, the oppressor's wrongs, the proud man contumely, the insolence of office and the spurns which patient merit of the unworthy take. But trailing clouds of glory do we come from ... our home beside the lake, beneath the trees, fluttering and dancing in the bee-loud glade. And I shall have some peace there.

Enter **MISS KAY**.

MISS KAY The report has been sent off, Mr Harbinger.

HARBINGER [*bravely*] I'm glad. [*wistfully*] I've done the state some service in my time, Miss Kay.

MISS KAY Are you ... all right, Mr Harbinger?

HARBINGER Yes.

Exit **MISS KAY**. **HARBINGER** *sits down at the desk and opens a drawer.*

HARBINGER [*casually*] Out, out, brief candle.

He lifts a revolver and shoots himself through the head.

LIGHTS: *Instant darkness.*

SOUND: *A telephone rings, then another more distant, then both are overlapped by a third, sounding very near and extra loud. Then all is suddenly cut.*

8: SIR ARTHUR'S OFFICES

SHOTS *stands firm with feet a little apart and hands clasped behind his back. An official envelope lies on a nearby chair or table.* **MISS PANTHER** *speaks to him from the door.*

PANTHER Mr Harbinger's secretary phoned, Sir Arthur. The Report has been sent over.

SHOTS Good. Good.

PANTHER And Mr Harbinger has shot himself.

SHOTS Good. Good.

PANTHER And I have sent for Mungo McGrotty.

SHOTS Excellent!

A brief pause.

PANTHER Here he is.

Enter **MCGROTTY**, *wearing new suit. Exit* **PANTHER**.

SHOTS [*calmly genial*] Come in and congratulations Mungo! A certain pale blue packet awaits you on Miss Panther's desk. It will be yours when you leave the building tonight.

MCGROTTY But what ... what am I supposed to? To?

SHOTS Do. Look at this envelope marked "Extra Top Secret and Confidential". [*holds it up*] Is it familiar to you?

MCGROTTY A minute ago Mrs Bee the secretary put one just like it in our office safe.

SHOTS Put this one into the large poacher's pocket in the lining of your brand new, made to measure, Saville Row suit.

MCGROTTY *takes it and tries it.*

MCGROTTY [*astounded*] It fits exactly!
SHOTS Now listen carefully, Mungo. You will return to the office at precisely one minute past five. The Minister's secretary will be impatiently waiting for you, the other staff will have left. You will tell her you have to read and memorize the secret oxygen famine plans for an emergency meeting tonight at the Air Ministry –
MCGROTTY But that's not true!
SHOTS [*louder*] She will take you to the inner office, open the safe, hand over the plans and hover nearby while you read them. Suddenly the telephone rings in the outer office. It is her job to answer that phone. It is also her job to be present when the safe is open. She decides to trust you, and goes out to the telephone, but Mungo! You are not the harmless idiot she supposes! You step to the safe and switch the envelope inside with the one in your pocket. The operation takes four seconds. A minute later the secretary returns. You hand back the oxygen famine plans and return here, to me. Six months later your name appears in the New Year Honours List. *[Pregnant pause].*
MCGROTTY But that's stealing.
SHOTS I am surprised Mungo, to hear you use such an unscientific word. You will not be "stealing" the document in question. You will simply be transferring it, from one office to another, as cautiously as possible.
MCGROTTY But why?
SHOTS [*very gravely*] Mungo, the United Kingdom will be in terrible danger if that document falls into the wrong hands. It contains information that self-seeking unscrupulous men want very much to get hold of, and the Minister's safe is not burglar-proof. The fact that you will bring the envelope here tonight demonstrates that. For years I have prayed for this chance of exposing the inadequacy of our security arrangements. Will you help me Mungo?
MCGROTTY There's something about this I don't get, Arthur.
SHOTS [*fiercely*] Then I over-rated your intelligence! I thought you were clever enough to know there were things you could *never* "get", Mungo, things you must leave to me. Well, I was wrong. You are an unpatriotic donkey with the guts of a louse and not the faintest notion of which side your bread is buttered! [*He flings himself down on the sofa with an air of abandoning everything, before at last speaking quietly*] Please go away, Mungo.
MCGROTTY [*troubled*] I don't like disappointing you Sir Arthur.
SHOTS That shows there are sparks of decency in you. Unluckily they are feeble sparks. I'm not angry, Mungo, but I had so looked forward to rewarding your loyalty. Ten thousand pounds is very little money nowadays, but it would have been a start. Leave me Mungo, I ... can't pretend I'm not ... wounded.

MCGROTTY [*gasping and swallowing*] I'll do it.
SHOTS [*he jumps to his feet*] We'll drink to that. And while waiting for five o'clock ... [*He goes to the drinks cabinet*] ... I'll tell you a tale of your father's loyalty. I was crawling through a minefield at the head of my battalion one evening when ...

9: THE MINISTER'S OFFICES

A desk and a large safe. A lady's handbag is on the desk. **MRS BEE** *is opening the safe.* **MUNGO**, *looking horribly guilty, stands awkwardly beside her.*
SOUND: *creaking hinges.*
MRS BEE I must tell the janitor to oil the hinges. [*She partly vanishes behind the ajar door*] Here they are – the secret neutron-flex umbrella plans. [*She reappears and hands* **MCGROTTY** *a manilla folder*].
MCGROTTY I ... actually asked er ... for the secret oxygen famine plans.
MRS BEE Granny keeps them in the same folder. We're running short of folders.
SOUND: *a telephone next door.*
MRS BEE Who can that be at five past five? I'll be back in a jiffy, Mr McGrotty.
Exit **MRS BEE**. **MCGROTTY** *half-vanishes behind the ajar door and starts frantically fumbling.*
MCGROTTY [*mumbling*] Transferring, not stealing. Transferring, not stealing. Transferring, not stealing. Transferring, not stealing. Transferring –
Enter **LUDMILLA.**
LUDMILLA Hullo funny one!
MCGROTTY *recoils from the safe with a shriek.*
LUDMILLA What's the matter with you? What are you doing? Stealing state secrets or something?
MCGROTTY [*sullenly straightening his jacket*] Of course. That's what they pay me for isn't it? Why are you here anyway? Your dad's in Wales.
LUDMILLA I left a handbag yesterday with lots and lots of money in it. [*Humming carelessly, she goes to the desk*].

MCGROTTY Why did you call me funny one?

LUDMILLA Because you're funny. You wear funny clothes.

MCGROTTY This suit cost nearly three hundred guineas! It was cut for me by the only tailor in London worth cultivating!

LUDMILLA Yes I can see it is a good suit, but on you it looks funny. It's your basic shape that's wrong.

MCGROTTY You're no oil painting yourself if it comes to that!

LUDMILLA [*sweetly*] If you mean I'm not attractive why can't you take your eyes off me?

MCGROTTY *gasps as if punched in the stomach. Enter* **MRS BEE**.

MRS BEE [*irritably*] Someone kept telling me to hold the line then said they'd the wrong number. Do be quick Mr McGrotty, this is my bridge night.

MCGROTTY I can't take any more! I can't! It's too much! Awahahoooo!

He rushes out, weeping. The women stare at each other.

LUDMILLA Well, well!

MRS BEE I only told him to hurry up!

LUDMILLA [*giggling*] He *is* funny!

Enter **SHOTS**, *casting badly disguised glances in every direction.*

SHOTS [*with forced geniality*] Good evening ladies.

LUDMILLA Uncle Arthur!

SHOTS Where's the young McGrotty? I'm giving him a lift to the Air Ministry.

LUDMILLA I made him hysterical and he ran away. Take me out to dinner, Uncle Arther.

SHOTS [*hysterically*] Ran away? Ran away with, my God! Urgent business Ludmilla! Oh what if he – [*runs out crying*] – No, it's too horrible! Oh poor bloody Britain!

Again the women stare at each other.

LUDMILLA I wonder if men are suited to the strains of a political career.

10: MCGROTTY'S LODGINGS

MCGROTTY, *in shirt sleeves and stockinged feet, sprawls horizontal along a sofa under a framed Tretchikoff print of a green Chinese girl. There are some lager cans on the floor beside him. He is holding one and softly singing "I Belong to Glasgow". There is an easy-chair nearby.*

SOUND: *a door rapped hard.*

MCGROTTY [*silence*].

Door opens and **SHOTS** *enters.* **MCGROTTY** *does not move.*

SHOTS [*tensely*] Where is it McGrotty?

MCGROTTY Sit down Arthur, I thought you'd drop in. Have a canna lager.

SHOTS Where is it McGrotty?

MCGROTTY Sorry I can't offer you spirits – spirits go to my head.

SHOTS [*shouting*] Give me the report McGrotty! Now! At Once! Do you hear me?

MCGROTTY [*sits up and speaks calmly but frankly*] I'll tell you what I hate about London, Arthur. Everybody tries to bully me here ... Actually it was just the same in Scotland. My mammy bullied me, my teachers, my bosses ... I like you Arthur, because you've talked to me like an equal.

SHOTS *sits down to get on the same level.*

SHOTS [*quietly*] Mungo. The report. Please. Where is it?

MCGROTTY [*encouragingly*] That's better! Now, [*hands him a can*] take a suck at your lager, [**SHOTS** *is so distracted that his hand automatically takes it*] and stop looking around the room because the report isn't here. Ludmilla! [*chuckles*] ... She's a warmer, isn't she? I love that girl. [*sings*] ... "She's as pee-yoor as the lily in the dell ... " When I ran out of the Ministry tonight I wasn't avoiding you Arthur. I was going to drown myself. But as I stood on Waterloo Bridge at midnight, and stared down at the oily black waters, I thought "Why spoil my expensive suit when I've a vital Government paper in the pocket?" So I wandered about a bit and then came back to the hotel. Don't worry, Arthur, the report's perfectly safe.

SHOTS More money. Is that what you want?

MCGROTTY No. I want Ludmilla.

SHOTS You can't have her.

MCGROTTY [*deliberately*] Then sod everything, Arthur.

SHOTS [*jumping up*] I can't *give* her to you, McGrotty! She isn't mine!

MCGROTTY I know, Arthur, but you could help me become the kind of man she's keen on – suave, popular, the life and soul of Royal Garden Parties. Rich, too, if that's any help. And quoted in the papers and on television. [*wistfully*] I've always wanted to be quoted.

SHOTS Mungo, that letter ... How can I explain. It's political dynamite. It's political dynamite of the first water. I won't try to frighten you by saying that, improperly used, it will mean the end of civilisation. That's done for anyway, because we find it too inhibiting.

I'll tell you this however. If the information in that document leaks out, every piece of money in the world, every dollar, rouble, yen, pound-sterling, credit card and cheque book will become worthless paper. Do you realise what this means?

MCGROTTY [*he puts his feet up on the chair*] I think so, Arthur. It means the Minister won't mind me seeing a bit of Ludmilla every now and then.

SHOTS For God's sake work with me Mungo! Only I have the knowledge, the contacts, the finesse to handle something on this scale!

MCGROTTY Yes, I can see you'll be a lot of help to me, Uncle Arthur. But first I want you to call on the Minister at ten sharp tomorrow when he comes in for the Report. Tell him the score. Put him in the picture. [*Yawns*] Ooohah! ... Sorry I'm a bit tired. I'll drop in before eleven and we'll work something out.

SHOTS *stares at the lager can in his hand as if it contained his whole horrible future.*

SHOTS In plain words, you are not simply using the Report to blackmail the Minister, you are blackmailing me into blackmailing the Minister.

MCGROTTY [*admiringly*] That's right, Uncle Arthur! And you don't think you can do it! You're the most persuasive talker I've ever heard! That tongue of yours has had me doing things a kick from my Mammy's wellies wouldn't make me do. Never under-rate yourself Arthur ...

11: THE MINISTER'S OFFICES

MRS BEE *is arranging some flowers in a vase on the desk. Enter the Minister.*

MINISTER [*very brisk and cheerful*] Good morning, Mrs Bee.

MRS BEE Good morning, sir. How did the opening go?

MINISTER Oh very well. I'm fond of animals, especially the stuffed sort, and a building in the middle had lots of those. Have you any goodies in the safe for me this morning?

MRS BEE Only the report from Mr Harbinger. I was sorry to hear that he had shot himself.

MINISTER [*gravely*] Yes, indeed. He was a poor golfer, but they say he owned the finest collection of Florentine incunabula outside the British Museum. I always meant to ask him what incunabula were and now – [*sighs*] – I suppose I'll never know. [*brightly*] Well, at least he finished his report. Open the safe, Mrs Bee. [*She does*].

SOUND: *hinges creak.*

She takes out and hands him an envelope. He sits down at his desk with it.

MINISTER [*gloating*] "Extra Top Secret and Confidential". It always thrills me to get an envelope with that on it ... Now, paperknife.

He opens the envelope and pulls out a sheet of almost blank paper.

MRS BEE *is shutting the safe.*

MINISTER [*after a pause*] Mrs Bee? [**MRS BEE** *looks round*] I'm rather puzzled. There's nothing in this envelope but a sheet of paper on which are typed the words "This is not the Harbinger Report", I mean, if this isn't, what is?

SHOTS *enters.*

SHOTS Sorry to barge in Bill –

MINISTER Thank goodness you're here Arthur. Look what Harbinger sent me. He must have been off his chump.

SHOTS [*He examines the sheet*] Please leave us, Mrs Bee.

Exit **MRS BEE.**

SHOTS [*clearing throat*] I ... I can explain that cryptic message Bill. The explanation *will* come as a shock, but when you've had time to absorb it, you'll understand that things could be much, much worse.

MINISTER What do you mean?

SHOTS Two weeks ago you obliged Charlie Gold by taking a young Scot into this office.

MINISTER I ... did it to oblige you. Charlie said McGrotty was a particular boy-friend of yours.

SHOTS [*indignant*] Charlie told you that? And the bounder was my fag once. There's no loyalty nowadays. None. None.

MINISTER Do come to the point, Arthur.

SHOTS Well I admit that I once thought McGrotty was a clean potato, but he's turned out to be a rotten egg. He has stolen the Report and ... er ... hidden it.

Pause.

MINISTER Oh dear.

SHOTS Quite.

MINISTER We must put one of the Special Branches on to him.

SHOTS No. They would get back the report all right, but what Special Branch officer could resist reading a document marked "Extra Top Secret and Confidential"? And then the Special Branch would be in a position to take over the running of the country.

MINISTER That would never do.

SHOTS You see, with all his faults, McGrotty's ambitions are comparatively limited. He only wants ... er ... Ludmilla.

MINISTER [*overwhelmed*] But does he really think he can make me prostitute my daughter by holding the country to ransom? He's as bad as the coalminers.

SHOTS Not quite as bad Bill. He only wants to meet her socially, to impress her with his prospects in life ... I suggest we explain the matter to her and get her to wheedle the document out of him. She'd enjoy the Delilah bit.

MINISTER Haha, yes! And then she'd read it, and likely tell her pals in the Women's Lib. We'd be giving her the power to plunge us all into a dark new age, and Ludmilla would never resist a temptation like that. The whole thing's a nightmare ... By the way Arthur, how are you involved?

SHOTS [*briskly*] Well you see Bill – [*pause, then says gravely*] What happened you see was this – [*pause, then lamely*] It's a very complicated story, Bill.

MINISTER Yes, I see. You, Arthur, are not just a bad hat. You are an *utter rotter.*

SHOTS [*pleading*] It takes all kinds to make the world, Bill.

Enter **MCGROTTY**. *It is clear that he is now at ease in this world.*

MCGROTTY Sorry to barge in Bill, but has Arthur told you the score?

Pause

MINISTER Yes, McGrotty.

MCGROTTY So what do you suggest?

MINISTER [*coldly, after a pause*] I'm having a small gathering tomorrow night, just the family and a few intimate friends. Poor Harbinger's death had reduced the guest list to thirteen. Drinks at seven, dinner at eight.

MCGROTTY It'll be a start, socially. What about the career?

The Minister stands up and speaks with uncharacteristic force, mainly to **SHOTS**.

MINISTER Tomorrow it will be announced in The Times that Arthur Shots, on grounds of age and ill health, has resigned his post as Head of the Criminal Disablement Department ...

SHOTS Oh steady on!

MINISTER I shall offer the post to you, McGrotty.

MCGROTTY Thanks, Bill.

SHOTS Now Bill, you can't possibly –

MINISTER If you resist me in this Arthur, I will lay the whole business in the lap of the Prime Minister. *She'll* know how to handle you. [*more quietly*] I also expect you to resign from the National Repeal Club. I don't ever want to bump into you again.

Short pause.

SHOTS So be it, Bill, but you're making a mistake. I may be pretty foul but my kind of foulness does no damage at all to things as they are, and in the long run I'm the only poison strong enough to deal with weeds like McGrotty here.

MCGROTTY Sticks and stones, Sir Shots, may break my bones, Sir Shots, but I am immune to nasty names.

He demonstrates his sense of immunity by sitting on a corner of the Minister's desk.

MINISTER Leave us, Arthur.

SHOTS [*from the door*] I promise I cherish no hard feeling, Bill.

Exit **SHOTS**. *The Minister sits down on his desk beside* **MCGROTTY**.

MINISTER McGrotty, a week from now I must present Harbinger's Report to the Cabinet. When can I have it, McGrotty? Please?

MCGROTTY Call me Mungo.

MINISTER Mungo.

MCGROTTY Bill, a week can seem like ages, and we need a few days to adjust to each other. The situation is novel for both of us ... [*he squeezes the Minister's knee*] ... we're still feeling our way, Bill ...

INTERVAL

12: THE MINISTER'S HOUSE

A partition with a door seperates a roomful of guests from a conservatory, indicated by a couple of chairs in front of a fat baluster urn from which fronds sprout. In the main room the available actors play at being as many as possible. They are helped by a cut-out free-standing flat of public people, with glasses in their hands, behind which is a long dining table. **SOUND:** *the Westminster chimes, ending with a shrill cock-crow, which gives way to the hubbub of nice people enjoying pre-dinner drinks. When the light goes up* **MCGROTTY**, *who has just arrived, is being received by the Minister. Further off* **LUDMILLA** *is talking enthusiastically to an American. A servant circulates with a tray of drinks.*

MINISTER [*sighing*] So you've arrived.
MCGROTTY Yes, Bill. This is a nice big room, Bill.
MINISTER I won't introduce you to anyone. You know a few from the office and the rest from their appearance on television. Excuse me ...
He drifts away.
SERVANT Whisky or sherry, sir?
MCGROTTY No thanks.
He goes over to **LUDMILLA**.
AMERICAN No no! No no! No, I've been arranging my exhibition of Pop Panic at the South Bank.
LUDMILLA [*greedily*] I want to know all about that.
MCGROTTY Hullo Ludmilla!
She ignores him.
AMERICAN We take the public upstairs in an old-fashioned ghost train, and they come out in an open space where ... broom-baroom ... four Hells Angels on motorbikes come riding round them in a ring that gets smaller and smaller till they have to escape by jumping down a hole in the floor.
LUDMILLA What a *fantastic* mind you have. Where does the hole take them?
AMERICAN Down a chute to the exit.
MCGROTTY This is a nice big room, Ludmilla.
LUDMILLA But what if someone has a stroke?
MCGROTTY, *discouraged, turns away.*
AMERICAN The Arts Council will pay for the damage.
SERVANT Sherry or whisky, sir?
MCGROTTY No thanks.
DISTANT VOICE (1) I was disappointed in Vesuvius.
DISTANT VOICE (2) Why don't you buy another island?
GRACIOUS OLD LADY Hello, you look rather out of things. Let me introduce myself. I'm Mary Fox. Dame Mary Fox. I'm an actress.
MCGROTTY [*bitterly*] I don't go to pantomimes.
OLD LADY I'm not surprised, nowadays. Are you in Bill's Ministry?
MCGROTTY Head of Criminal Disablement.
OLD LADY Ah! Then I have a bone to pick with you. I am a part-time secretary of a charitable organisation called Kleptomaniacs Anonymous. Why won't your department answer our letters?
MCGROTTY New to the job, excuse me ... Hey! Give me a drink you!
SERVANT Of course, sir.
MCGROTTY *grabs a glass in each hand and immediately swallows the contents of one.*
GOLD Hello Mungo. Reaping the fruits of your enterprise, eh?
MCGROTTY [*empties the second glass and says loudly*] Plucking.
SOUND: *instant silence.*
GOLD I'm sorry?
MCGROTTY Fruit is plucked. Not reaped.
GOLD [*moving away*] Good.
DISTANT VOICE I feel I've exhausted the Pacific.
SOUND: *the hubbub resumes.*
MINISTER [*loudly*] Dinner's ready now. Shall we sit down?
Someone carries the flat of standing celebrities to the side. Backstage is a long table with cut-outs of seated celebrities round it, a seat for the Minister at the top, and three places, facing the audience, for **MCGROTTY**, **LUDMILLA** *and the* **GRACIOUS OLD LADY**.
SOUND: *when the actors are seated the hubbub reduces to a murmur and a tinkle of cutlery.*
MCGROTTY I'm glad I'm sitting next to you Ludmilla.
LUDMILLA You've someone on your other side too, and so, thank God, do I.
She turns away from him.
OLD LADY Ah we meet again Mr ... I'm sorry, I didn't catch your name.
MCGROTTY Oh hullo there. [*suddenly indignant*] What are these beetles doing in my horse dewars?
OLD LADY They're not beetles, they're prawns.
MCGROTTY I'm not eating muck like this. [*loudly*] Hey Ludmilla! These are very nice knives and forks Ludmilla! They're a queer shape but I like them Ludmilla!
SOUND: *total silence.*
LUDMILLA [*coolly*] What am I supposed to say to that?
MCGROTTY [*gasping for breath*] You talk as if I was keech, the only keech in this room! Well I've got proof to the contrary! *Documentary* proof!
LUDMILLA [*standing up and talking through gritted teeth*] Come with me!
She walks to the door. **MCGROTTY** *scrambles after her. The* **MINISTER** *says in a loud, desperate voice:*
MINISTER An unpolished gem, but brilliant in his own field, of course.
LIGHTS: *Cut off in the dining room.*
MCGROTTY *and* **LUDMILLA** *arrive before the urn.*
LUDMILLA Sit down and cool off.
She sits with arms grimly folded. **MCGROTTY** *plumps down beside her.*

MCGROTTY [*brightly*] Well now, what shall we talk about?

LUDMILLA We have nothing to talk about. You have just ruined a rather enjoyable dinner party.

MCGROTTY Aren't you curious about my hold over your Daddy?

LUDMILLA Not at all. It probably has to do with the asphalt shares he picked up when he was under-secretary for motorways. I'm bored with this sordid politicking.

MCGROTTY Animals then.

LUDMILLA What do you know about animals?

MCGROTTY [*smugly*] When I was eleven I taught a mouse to waltz.

LUDMILLA Nonsense. How could you?

MCGROTTY I played him tunes on my mouth-organ at mealtimes and made him stand up and beg for his cheese and sugar. Eventually he waltzed in circles whenever he heard the music.

LUDMILLA [*through clenched teeth*] Pavlov did that sort of thing to dogs and Pavlov was a bastard.

MCGROTTY No Ludmilla! Wee Jimmy got to like the waltzing. He would do it between meals, round and round the kitchen table. The other kids paid me twopence a skull just to see him. Then [*sighs*] one day he waltzed too far. He fell off the table. The cat got him.

LUDMILLA Oh poor little chap!

MCGROTTY [*solemnly*] Jimmy was my first and last pet.

LUDMILLA [*quite kindly*] You see Mungo, animals take naturally to some human activities – like horses to fox-hunting – but no animal should *ever* be asked to stand on its hind legs. Promise not to do that again.

MCGROTTY I promise ... You know, I behaved disgustingly tonight. I've got not no savwar fare Ludmilla, but ... I'm a fast learner! Listen, I don't want to interfere with your social life, but surely you could spare me a few afternoons? Show me the sights. Teach me the moves. Tell me what to wear. [*stonily*] I might tell you your Daddy's secret. It's actually more interesting than asphalt shares. Go on – give me one afternoon.

LUDMILLA Tomorrow.

MCGROTTY Tomorrow?

LUDMILLA I want to get it over as soon as possible.

MCGROTTY [*stands up and speaks quietly*] Goodnight. I won't pester you again. And tell your Dad not to worry. I'm sorry I acted like that, and I'm not going to any more parties for a long, long time.

LUDMILLA Do you know the way out?

MCGROTTY Don't worry. I've a good memory.

Exit **MCGROTTY**. **LUDMILLA** *looks thoughtfully after him. A moment later she hears a queer noise behind the urn.*

SOUND: *Pssst! Pssst! Pssst!*

LUDMILLA [*not alarmed*] Who's there?

SHOTS *emerges, glancing furtively around.* **LUDMILLA** *is delighted.*

LUDMILLA Uncle Arthur!

SHOTS Quiet Ludmilla! Quiet! Nobody else must know I'm here.

LUDMILLA Why ever not? I've been reading in The Times how sick and old you are.

SHOTS [*He sinks beside her, mopping his brow with a handkerchief*] Yes I'm in a jam. So's your father. And you know who's to blame don't you?

LUDMILLA I *did* notice Daddy's even more flustered than usual. But he keeps muttering about you.

SHOTS Ha! Blames me does he? Well, I'm not surprised. He's fallen into the claws of the most Machiavellian snake in the Western hemisphere.

LUDMILLA How exciting!

SHOTS Listen Ludmilla, I'm convinced that you can save us. Your father doesn't agree with me, of course, but I *know* you can save us. Because you're British. Yes, the little girl I used to dandle on my knee is British to the core ...

LUDMILLA Cut the patriotic cackle, Arthur, tell me what's happening.

SHOTS I'm glad you're a tough cookie, Ludmilla, for I'm about to disclose facts which have already robbed one man of his life and sanity. Listen closely.

They bend their heads together.

13: THE CONSERVATORY

MCGROTTY *stands at the door talking to* **MISS PANTHER**.

MCGROTTY Miss Python?

PANTHER My name is Panther, Mr McGrotty.

MCGROTTY Come in here anyway.

She comes in. He sits on the sofa and contemplates her for a moment.

MCGROTTY Hm. How long have you been in this job?

PANTHER Twelve years Mr McGrotty.

MCGROTTY So you understand the department better than anyone else.

PANTHER Quite so Mr McGrotty.

MCGROTTY Then I'm leaving all the work to you. I know

I'll have to sign papers, and attend the odd meeting, but you'll tell me when and how. Right?

PANTHER It's the usual arrangement, though seldom so clearly stated, Mr McGrotty.

MCGROTTY Fine. And I'll try to find a fiddle for raising your wages. I haven't discovered the limits of my powers yet, but Arthur Shots offered to put my name on the honours list, so I suppose I can do the same for you, if you're keen.

PANTHER Thank you Mr McGrotty.

MCGROTTY Let me tell you about me Miss Python. [*stands up and walks about*] To others I appear the dour, hard, silent, practical Scot of legend, and of course I am that basically; but I am also a man of passions, and even instincts. Don't mistake me, I'm no mad rapist, but this afternoon I want to negotiate – purely for my own satisfaction – a piece of private business. Can you get me a suitable shorthand typist? An intelligent widow of thirty-five say, or an empty-headed wee lassie of eighteen? Even you, Miss Python, are not, in my eyes, totally without charm if you feel equal to the job.

PANTHER [*faintly after a pause*] I will find you somebody, Mr McGrotty.

MCGROTTY Good girl. See to it then.

Exit **PANTHER**

MCGROTTY [*he sings quietly*] Scots wha hae wi' Wallace bled, Scots wham Bruce has oftimes led, Welcome to your gory bed, Or to ...

Enter **MISS PANTHER**

PANTHER The Minister's daughter has arrived, Mr McGrotty. She says she has an appointment.

MCGROTTY Does she? Python ...

PANTHER I shall retard the typist.

MCGROTTY Good girl, Python.

Exit **MISS PANTHER**. **MCGROTTY** *rubs hands, straightens shoulders, and adopts the posture of a man prepared for anything. Enter* **LUDMILLA**.

LUDMILLA [*brightly*] Mungo!

MCGROTTY [*warily*] Hullo, Ludmilla. What do you want?

LUDMILLA Didn't I arrange to go out with you this afternoon?

MCGROTTY No.

Pause.

LUDMILLA You see I've been brooding about you. It's struck me you may not be the wholesale disaster I assumed.

MCGROTTY Go on.

LUDMILLA You see you can't help shambling and slouching, so ordinary good tailoring looks second hand on you. But trendy or hippy gear would be even worse, because it has a joie de vivre quality that your whole manner contradicts. What you need are shaggy tweeds; the best quality of course, and tremendously well cut in something like the style of an Edwardian gamekeeper. That would make you look quite sexy in a Hunchback of Notre Dame way.

MCGROTTY [*awed*] Ludmilla, my grandfather was a gillie on the Earl of Home's estate!

LUDMILLA [*triumphantly*] There you are then!

MCGROTTY Ludmilla, I'm going to telephone my tailor and tell him lies and bluster and threaten till he agrees to see me within the hour. And you'll come and give him the orders, right?

LUDMILLA Right.

MCGROTTY And in return I want to buy clothes for you, oh yes, a complete outfit of the most devastatingly expensive ... expensively glamorous ... [*pulls himself together*] ... In fact, a complete outfit, but I want to see you choose it.

LUDMILLA I'll cost you a packet if you do that.

MCGROTTY A dawdle! A dawdle!

LUDMILLA A dawdle?

MCGROTTY [*airily*] Spending is a principle of mine. Ordinary men invest their surplus income but I encourage the workers by consuming the products of their toil. At heart I'm a socialist.

LUDMILLA Aren't we all? I've a studio just off Bond Street. If we go there afterwards I'll rustle us up a little snack.

MCGROTTY I didn't know you were an artist.

LUDMILLA I'm not but a studio always comes in handy. An aunt gave me this one for my birthday.

14: LUDMILLA'S STUDIO

MCGROTTY *and* **LUDMILLA** *are on a sofa with its back to the audience so that we mostly see the top of their heads. There is a scattering of garments nearby, and a telephone on a low table in reach of* **LUDMILLA**'*s hand.*

MCGROTTY Ludmilla, I've never visited a girl who had a complete library of pornography before!

LUDMILLA Is there anything you'd like to borrow?

SOUND: *a cork pops.*

LUDMILLA Isn't it lucky I had a crate of champers left over from the last party?

MCGROTTY I don't want any more champers.

LUDMILLA Then what, exactly, do you want?

MCGROTTY You know very well what I want. You see, for the first time in my life I feel thoroughly at home. Can I ...?

They embrace intimately.

LUDMILLA I suppose you can ... Mmmm.

MCGROTTY Mmm.

LUDMILLA Mmmmmmungo, you said if I went out with you, you'd tell me Daddy's secret. And I don't think I can go further out with you than this.

MCGROTTY I'm sure you can.

LUDMILLA Where's the Harbinger Report Mmmmmungo?

MCGROTTY You'll have to seduce me thoroughly before I tell you that. Since I was able to read I've dreamed of being seduced by a cool, lovely, selfish utterly depraved upper-class English girl. Mm.

LUDMILLA [*without anger*] You scheming little rat.

MCGROTTY You like animals.

LUDMILLA Not rats.

MCGROTTY In that case ... [*starting with a low growl far back in the throat he builds up to a roar*] ... Mmmmmrrrrr aaaaawwwrrr!

Their heads sink out of sight.

LUDMILLA Ooooh! Ooooh! Ooooh! I like that!

MCGROTTY Mrawr! Mrawr! Mrawr!

LUDMILLA Ooh! Ooh!

MCGROTTY Mwar. Mwar.

LUDMILLA Ooh!

MCGROTTY Mwar.

LUDMILLA Oooh!

MCGROTTY Mwar.

LUDMILLA Ooooooh!

A pause.

LUDMILLA Mmmmmmungo, would you like anything else?

MCGROTTY [*dreamily*] Thank you, Ludmilla. Not at the moment.

LUDMILLA Where have you hidden the Harbinger Report, Mungo?

MCGROTTY [*still dreamily*] In the safe in your Dad's office.

LUDMILLA What? [*Her head appears*].

MCGROTTY There's a metal tray on the bottom shelf with rubber stamps in it. I shoved the envelope underneath.

LUDMILLA You only pretended to steal it?

MCGROTTY Yeah.

LUDMILLA That's brilliant!

MCGROTTY [*sitting up*] No, spur of the moment. Anyway, you can tell your Dad ... I suppose you've finished with me now.

LUDMILLA I'm not *entirely* sure.

SOUND: *phone rings.*

LUDMILLA*'s hand reaches for the receiver.*

LIGHTING: *distant spotlight.*

SHOTS *appears with receiver in the spotlight.*

SHOTS Ludmilla!

LUDMILLA Wait there a minute. [*stands up, adjusting a wrap around herself*] Mungo, a sugar-daddy wants to whisper sweet nothings. I'm taking the phone where you can't hear me.

MCGROTTY [*resignedly*] Aye, all right.

She carries the phone to one side. When she talks **MCGROTTY** *appears to dress himself.*

LUDMILLA Arthur, at the bottom of Daddy's safe there's an old tray that hasn't been shifted since the Boer War.

SHOTS Well?

LUDMILLA The report is underneath.

SHOTS [*gasps*] But ... that's intelligent!

LUDMILLA He must be pretty smart if he managed to throw the blame on you. You said so yourself.

SHOTS Of course. Er ... Ludmilla! Ludmilla, I'm sorry the Report is in the safe.

LUDMILLA Why?

SHOTS Now we'll never get a chance to read it, and it's full of delicious filth about all kinds of top people, filth the Government will never let out in a million years.

LUDMILLA Oh, Daddy's sure to allow me a peep. After all, I found it for him.

SHOTS You'll be disappointed, Ludmilla. He's terrified of you reading that Report. That's why he never told you it existed. He doesn't trust you. So now we'll never know why the Pope shot poor Kennedy.

LUDMILLA How *bloody* unfair.

SHOTS I agree.

LUDMILLA Listen Arthur, when Daddy's in his office the safe is always open and I sometimes leave my shopping in it. Tomorrow I'll pretend to do that and borrow the Report while his back is turned.

SHOTS Splendid. I'll collect you and take you to my place, and oh Ludmilla, what an afternoon we'll have eh?
LUDMILLA Have the car outside at eleven sharp.
She replaces the receiver.
LIGHTING: *the spot goes out.*
LUDMILLA *returns to the sofa where* **MCGROTTY** *stands awkwardly awaiting her. She has almost forgotten him.*
LUDMILLA Hello. Are you still here?
MCGROTTY [*miserably*] Just leaving.
LUDMILLA Remember to shut the door.
She turns her back on him.

15: A STREET

A flat of a parked car with **SHOTS** *behind the open window.*
SOUND: *traffic noises.*
Enter **LUDMILLA** *with envelope. She pats it triumphantly.*
LUDMILLA Got it, Arthur.
SHOTS Good. Hop in the back.
LUDMILLA I can't ... the door's locked.
SHOTS No, just jammed a little. Give me that thing and use both hands. Thanks. [*takes the envelope*].
SOUND: *clutch let in.*
LUDMILLA [*tugging*] I'm sure – this door – is locked.
SHOTS It is, yes. I'm afraid, Ludmilla, I agree with your father. You're too young to read this Report.
LUDMILLA Arthur!
SOUND: *engine roars.*
SHOTS [*over it*] I'll phone tonight and apologize!
LIGHTS: *instant darkness as the car shoots off.*
LUDMILLA [*screaming*] Arthur! Arthur! ... *Arthur!*

16: THE MINISTER'S OFFICE

He sits with elbow on desk and face propped on hand. **MRS BEE** *is at the door.*
MRS BEE Sir Arthur Shots, Sir.
MINISTER [*does not move*] Oh.
Enter **SHOTS**.
SHOTS [*very genial*] Good morning, Bill! Heard the good news from Ludmilla? We've got the Harbinger Report!
MINISTER You have the Harbinger Report.
SHOTS And you have my hearty sympathies. How is Ludmilla, by the way?
MINISTER Still smashing things in her bedroom.
SHOTS Poor kid! Tell her I'll pay for the damage.
MINISTER Arthur, I have to show the Report to the Cabinet on Friday.
SHOTS Most unwise. They're all mentioned.
MINISTER [*aghast*] All?
SHOTS All except you. So tomorrow I'm taking the Report to the Palace.
MINISTER [*thunderstruck*] Palace?
SHOTS Britain is a monarchy Bill. The Queen – who happens to be a distant cousin of mine – possesses certain prerogatives which the report may persuade her to exercise. Our only problem is, er ... [*He points at the Minister*].
MINISTER [*not really surprised*] Me?
SHOTS Yes. I can see your seat on the front bench had become an embarrassment to you. And no wonder! Modern politics are a rat-race. A man of principle like yourself is well out of them.

17: SIR ARTHUR'S OFFICES

MISS PANTHER *at her desk.* **SHOTS** *sitting on his sofa. Enter* **MCGROTTY**.
MCGROTTY [*sighing*] Hullo there, Python. It's a rotten morning.
PANTHER My name is Panther, Mr McGrotty.
MCGROTTY That doesn't matter, it's still a rotten morning. Ever been disappointed in love, Panther?
PANTHER [*with a grim little nod*] Just once.
MCGROTTY No no no, I mean *really* disappointed. Have you ever had your wildest dreams come true and then ... phut! Nothing! You are left clutching a handful of withering memories.
Pause.
PANTHER Do you wish me to dredge you something out of the typing pool?
MCGROTTY [*shocked*] Python! What has got into you? This is *not* the remark of the perfect secretary! Sex is no cure for a bleeding heart, Python. Work is the cure. Hard work. I am going to make Criminal Disablement the strongest branch of the Ministry for Social Stability. I am going to give social stability sharp jaggy teeth and claws, Miss Python. So send the mail through to my office, and a nice cup of tea, and see if you can get me a pocket-sized vernacular translation of Mein Kampf ... [*strolls through to the inner office*].
MCGROTTY Arthur!

SHOTS [*quietly*] Come in my boy. No, you aren't dreaming. I really am back in my old place. [*stands up*] I didn't *need* to see you this morning but it was a luxury I could not refuse myself.

MCGROTTY Arthur ...

SHOTS You are too sentimental for a political careerist McGrotty. Your three days of giddy power ended yesterday in your orgy with Ludmilla. You were fool enough to trust a woman, McGrotty!

MCGROTTY Arthur, I didn't trust her! I told her where the Report was because she'd been nice to me!

SHOTS Petit bourgeois poppycock! I had you promoted McGrotty because I thought that, stupid, ill-mannered and badly dressed though you were, you were capable of the unfashionable quality of loyalty. But you have bitten the hand of the goose that laid the golden eggs and I mean to make you squirm. There are thirty-seven branches of Her Majesty's Security Service and I am going to have you investigated by every one of them in rotation.

MCGROTTY But there's nothing! I mean, nothing for them to –

SHOTS Nothing to find out. Exactly. But they won't know that. Just think! For the rest of your life every employer who gives you a job, every landlord of every dwelling you try to hide in, every man, woman and child who is fool enough to befriend you, will be visited and questioned by sinister officials with the full backing of the British Government. They will be pestered again and again for details of your finances, feeding habits and sex life. How long do you think you'll be able to last, McGrotty?

MCGROTTY [*with dignity*] Sir Shots, you are not just trying to depress me. You are being deliberately unkind.

SHOTS [*shouting*] Clear out! Clear out!

18: A STREET

MCGROTTY *slouches down it, to be pursued suddenly by* **LUDMILLA**.

SOUND: *traffic and pavement noises.*

LUDMILLA Mungo! Mungo! ... Mungo, where are you going you *utter fool!*

MCGROTTY [*wearily*] Leave me alone, Ludmilla.

LUDMILLA [*grabbing his arm*] You stupid, stupid idiot! Why didn't you warn me against Arthur Shots? Why didn't you tell me everything?

MCGROTTY Leave me *alone!*

LUDMILLA Oh no, you're not going to escape as easily as that. Come in here. [*drags him into Scene 19*].

19: A CAFÉ

A table with two chairs and a waitress. **LUDMILLA**, *with a policewoman's grip, leads* **MCGROTTY** *firmly past the waitress.*

LUDMILLA Two very strong, unsweetened coffees please.

Exit waitress. **LUDMILLA** *places* **MCGROTTY** *in one chair and sits opposite.*

LUDMILLA Well? What have you to say for yourself?

MCGROTTY I told you what you asked me to tell you! I thought you knew everything else! [*snivelling*] Please don't be nasty to me.

LUDMILLA Stop snivelling or shift your chair where people can't see.

MCGROTTY I don't care when other people are nasty to me because I don't like them. But you were so nice to me yesterday! I can't bear it!

LUDMILLA [*impatiently*] It's ridiculous getting emotional before we've worked out what to do.

MCGROTTY [*in a new tone*] We?

LUDMILLA Yes. You're desperate, I hope? I mean, *really* desperate?

MCGROTTY Oh yeah!

LUDMILLA Good, then you'll do something. Daddy isn't desperate, he's just hopeless. Arthur's taking the Report tomorrow to the Palace. The Queen will send for the Prime Minister who will either announce an unexpected Cabinet reshuffle or a general election. Arthur will become the new Minister for Social Stability or Leader of the Opposition, and poor old Dad will be kicked into the Lords. He's mooning around the house moaning that Arthur's too clever for him. Arthur isn't really clever. He just has an unusual quantity of cunning for his breed.

MCGROTTY What breed is that?

LUDMILLA The political breed. You see there are political people and financial people and art people and animal people. I'm animal with a smattering of art; but it's recently struck me that politics could be fun if treated like a blood sport. You haven't any breeding of course. You're nothing.

MCGROTTY Nothing?

LUDMILLA You belong to the class that have to take the

first job they can get. With a bit of the right push you could become anything. [*thoughtfully*] Anything at all.

MCGROTTY [*glumly*] We'll never get that Report back from Arthur.

LUDMILLA Our only hope is to find out what it says. There must be *somebody* who knows.

MCGROTTY [*off-handededly*] I know what it says.

LUDMILLA You do?

MCGROTTY [*off-handededly*] I was hanging around your Dad's office for a couple of days while Arthur moved out of his. Nobody knew there was anything in the safe but the ordinary secret papers, so I was able to take out the Report for something to read when I went to the lavatory. There were some rare laughs in it.

LUDMILLA What does it say?

MCGROTTY [*sighing*] Well ... it involves the mafia of course, and the World Monetary Fund, and a European Necrophilia ring and the CIA ... Not the American CIA, the Chinese CIA. The American CIA is in it too, but it doesn't know it's in it. The link is a prominent member of the British Government.

LUDMILLA [*thrilled*] Not ... Daddy?

MCGROTTY No, it's actually ... [*whispers to her*] ... but who will believe a thing like that? Without the Report we can't prove it.

LUDMILLA Tell me more but keep your voice down, people are looking.

MCGROTTY [*whispers some more*].

LUDMILLA Everlasting life?

MCGROTTY Unluckily a week's supply uses up fifty tons of wheat and a quarter of a million barrels of petroleum.

LUDMILLA Heads of state are actually getting this stuff?

MCGROTTY Why do you think the energy crisis happened fifteen years ahead of schedule? Why do you think the grain shortage happened twenty years ahead of schedule?

LUDMILLA How unfair! *We* must get some. Why did Harbinger shoot himself?

MCGROTTY He found he was the ring-leader of an organization he was investigating. He had thought he was the ring-leader of a different organization. He was an honest man in his way. However, the Head Rabbi kept his mouth shut, the Falklands War was organized to distract attention, and the public suspect nothing.

LUDMILLA Yes, it all fits. [*jumps up*] Mungo, can you type that out exactly as you've told it to me?

MCGROTTY Easy! [*stands*] Folk seem to think I got Civil Service promotion because I'm an idiot. Actually it's because I've a filing cabinet memory. I forget nothing I've read, if it's official.

LUDMILLA [*embraces him, and says ecstatically*] Oh Mungo, you give me such dizzy feelings of power! You know so much, yet you're such putty!

Enter **WAITRESS**, *with tray.*

WAITRESS Two Turkish coffees, Madam.

LUDMILLA You kept us waiting for hours and we don't want it now.

20: SIR ARTHUR'S OFFICES

SHOTS *is on the sofa, a brandy glass in one hand and the Report in the other. He is reading and shaking his head in grave astonishment. Beside him is an open metal briefcase.*

SOUND: *the Westminster chimes, ending in one mighty stroke. When the stroke dies away* **SHOTS** *has briskly downed his brandy, put the Report in the envelope, locked the envelope in the briefcase, and stands ready to leave. Enter* **MISS PANTHER**.

PANTHER The Minister and his daughter have just arrived, Sir Arthur.

SHOTS Indeed?

PANTHER With Mungo McGrotty.

SHOTS Indeed! I hope you told them I can see nobody just now. I am on my way to the Palace.

PANTHER I did tell them that. The Minister's daughter said you would change your mind if I mentioned just one word to you, Sir Arthur.

SHOTS [*puzzled*] Word? What word?

PANTHER I believe it was ... pantocratoraphorbia.

He drops his briefcase.

SHOTS [*screaming*] Pantocra?

PANTHER toraphorbia.

SHOTS No no! Don't say it! You don't know what it means!

He acts like a man in whom all thought has suddenly become a form of torture.

PANTHER Do you really *wish* to receive your visitors, Sir Arthur?

SHOTS [*frantically shakes his head and whimpers*] Yes.

MISS PANTHER *withdraws, then pauses.*

PANTHER Shall I ... put Her Majesty off, Sir Arthur?

SHOTS [*frantically shakes nods his head and whimpers*] No.

Exit **MISS PANTHER**. *Enter* **LUDMILLA**, *thoroughly in charge of things,* **MCGROTTY**, *thoroughly at home, the* **MINISTER**, *thoroughly depressed.*

SHOTS [*pleading*] Ludmilla! Oh Ludmilla!

LUDMILLA Shut up and sit down, Arthur. It's not as bad as you think, we intend to be quite kind to you. You sit down too Daddy. I do realise that all this has come as a bit of a shock.

MCGROTTY *goes casually to the drinks cabinet and pours himself a whisky and soda.* **LUDMILLA** *lights a cigarette and surveys them.*

LUDMILLA Firstly, I want you to know that Mungo and I are getting married. The engagement will be announced in tomorrow's Times.

SHOTS [*looking at the Minister*] Mmm?

MINISTER Mnya.

LUDMILLA Secondly, we four in this room are the people who know the contents of the Harbinger Report, so for a long time to come we'll be in an absolutely unique position.

SHOTS But ... but ... but ...

MINISTER [*timidly*] Arthur has arranged to show Her Majesty the Report, Ludmilla.

LUDMILLA Mungo has an idea about that. Tell them, Mungo.

MCGROTTY Arthur, er ... I'm sure it would be unwise to show Her Majesty the whole Report. It would only distress her, and I think we should keep something for ourselves. Give her the dirt on the United Kingdom, but hold on to Australia, Europe, Asia, Africa and the Americas.

SHOTS I, er, had meant to give her Australia too.

MCGROTTY [*firmly*] Not Australia. We deserve some recompense for our trouble, Arthur.

LUDMILLA Anyway it's clear we'll have to work together, so there can be no question of booting Daddy into the Lords.

MINISTER Actually, Ludmilla, I want to go into the Lords. Politics have become too strenuous recently. In the old days we thought nothing of a spot of fraud or a discreet phone call to our stock-broker, but outright blackmail and treason were comparatively rare.

LUDMILLA Good. That leaves just Arthur and Mungo. Well, Arthur, what do you suggest?

SHOTS [*sighs*] Well, I suppose he can stand at the next by-election.

LUDMILLA Only if it's a thoroughly safe seat.

SHOTS And once he's in the House his experience will qualify him as Under-Secretary for Social Stability.

LUDMILLA Minister for Social Stability.

SHOTS [*pleading*] Please don't force the pace, Ludmilla! I can get him into the Cabinet as soon as I'm in Number 10 but not before.

LUDMILLA Good. You can discuss the details on your way to the Palace. Mungo is coming with you ...

SHOTS [*wailing*] Oh no! How can I possibly justify ...

MCGROTTY Tell Her Majesty she can trust me, Arthur. Say I'm your right-hand man.

LUDMILLA Tell her Daddy, the only honest Minister in her government, insisted on Mungo accompanying you. You don't mind us using your name do you Daddy?

MINISTER You can do what you like but please, please tell me as little as possible.

LUDMILLA So you see Arthur, there's nothing to worry about.

MCGROTTY Let's hit the trail. [*finishes his whisky and sets down the glass*] Walkie walkie Arth.

SHOTS, *in a dazed way, rises to his feet like a very old man and points a shaking finger at the briefcase.*

SHOTS ... rereport ... rereport ...

MCGROTTY *lifts the case.*

LUDMILLA Mungo, remember to –

MCGROTTY To remove the crucial paper as soon as we're in the car. See you later. [*blows her a kiss*] So long Bill. Come on Arth. Don't worry about a thing. If you dry up I'll do the talking. I like Royalty. You're safe with me.

He leads **SHOTS** *out.* **LUDMILLA** *twirls delightedly round.*

LUDMILLA Oh Daddy that was glorious! Mungo has the makings of a really blasé political bully! He and I are going to go up and up and up! Oh Daddy I can't wait for the day when I sit in the Visitors' Gallery and see him rising in the Commons and refusing to answer his first question!

The Minister has hidden his face in his hands.

21: THE HOUSE OF COMMONS

A flat of the Government front bench: a row of seated two-dimensional dummies with **MUNGO** *sitting solidly near one end. The rest of the cast are now dispersed through the audience. One rises to speak from the very back:*

WELSHMAN [*loudly*] ... and what about the Harbinger Report? It is seven months since the Government promised to lay the facts before the House. Since then nothing has emerged but rumours, excuses and prevarications. When will the people of Britain be told the truth?

VOICES IN THE AUDIENCE Hear hear! Shame! Shame! Yes, the truth! Resign! The truth! The truth! The ruth!

MCGROTTY The honourable member for Tonypandy is clearly living in the past. It is many months since the main findings of the Harbinger Report were laid before this House. It was then freely admitted that two or three public servants had weakly and foolishly put private gain before the general welfare. The main culprit – Harbinger himself – chose to pay the supreme penalty. The others were severely reprimanded. To do more at this point in time would be barbarous vindictiveness. I suggest that this House has important matters to debate! Drug abuse. The fight against inflation. Local government dictatorship, the insensate greed of the trade unions, Lesbian resistance to the Defence of our Realm and international terrorist conspiracies to destroy law, order, freedom, democracy and common decency both abroad and here! Here! Here in Britain. [*His accent becomes a little more Scottish*] The people of Britain have elected us to help and protect them. That's our job. Let's do it! There are many more issues than this storm in a Civil Service teacup!

VOICES IN THE AUDIENCE Hear hear! Shame! Shame! Hiss hiss! Well said! Well said! Boo boo! Resign! Resign! Resign! [*etc*].

SOUND: *the human uproar has the chattering of apes added to it, then the barking of dogs, the braying of a donkey, and finally the deafening cries of a vastly amplified cuckoo.*

AFTER ATTENDING THE RECORDING OF *McGrotty and Ludmilla* in Broadcasting House, London, I came home by train and for the first time heard over a loudspeaker the voice of someone who claimed to be the driver. He told me where and when the train would arrive, some features of the landscape we were passing through, and the opening times of the restaurant and buffet cars. This was eighteen years before British Rail was privatized, yet it had begun imitating the little talks by which pilots of commercial airlines reassure flight passengers. I thought this very funny. Before reaching Glasgow I had imagined most of *Near the Driver*, my best and last radio play, which I wrote and posted to Stewart Conn soon after. He told me he would need permission from London to produce it (he had never mentioned needing that before) and a few days later told me London had said " No."

I will explain later my perplexed efforts to get it broadcast, and how that was finally achieved.

NEAR THE DRIVER

A One-Act Play for Voices

1975

SOUND: *Railway station noises. Footsteps. Driver's voice heard over loudspeaker: loud, distant, blurred.*

DRIVER The 2041 Aquarian from Bundlon to Shaglow will leave platform 79 calling at Bagchester, Shloo, Spittenfitnay and Glaik. The 2041 Aquarian from Bundlon to Shaglow will leave platform ...

SOUND: *Carriage door slams blurring other sounds.*

TEACHER [*hopeful, polite*] Excuse me, is this seat beside you being kept for someone?

FIREMAN [*forbiddingly*] No.

TEACHER I wish to sit on it. Please remove your newspaper.

FIREMAN That's an empty window-seat over there.

TEACHER True, but it's on the right side of the carriage and I always travel on the left. Here's your newspaper. I notice it is a communist publication. I'm sure you understand my feeling.

MR DEAR [*distant*] Politics. They twist everything into politics. What has right and left to do with rail travel?

MRS DEAR [*distant*] Nothing dear. Sh.

MR DEAR [*distant*] Face the engine and your left is on one side, face the guard's van and it's on the other. Why *bother* about it?

MRS DEAR We shouldn't bother dear. Sh.

TEACHER [*conversationally*] Of course there were plenty of left hand window-seats near the guard's van. But I feel safer when I'm near the driver.

MIRIAM My father feels that way too, though he won't admit it. Will you, Dad?

FIREMAN Shut up, Miriam.

MRS DEAR [*distant*] I feel that too, dear.

MR DEAR [*distant*] I know you do dear, please shut up.

TEACHER In most railway accidents the train is struck in the rear, isn't it? So statistically speaking we *are* safer near the engine.

CHILD That's stupid!

FIREMAN Shut up, Patsy.

MIRIAM [*on top of her father*] Don't be rude, Patsy.

TEACHER [*eagerly*] Oh, please. I'm a teacher! Retired! But I know how to handle difficult children. Why is what I said stupid, Patsy?

CHILD Because in a collision the front of one train always hits the front or back of another. So the safest place in a train is always the middle.

FIREMAN [*brief chuckle*].

Pause.

TEACHER [*deliberately*] Patsy! Here is a bright, new, silver-looking four pound piece. I am giving it to you because what I said was stupid and you were right to correct me.

MIRIAM [*shocked*] Do you call that handling a difficult child?

TEACHER I do. Yes.

MRS DEAR [*distant*] Dear, could we move further down the train, in America last week ...

SOUND: *Musical chime. Driver's voice on loudspeaker.*

DRIVER Good day. This is Captain Rogers, your driver, welcoming you to the 2041 Aquarian from Bundlon to Shaglow. The Aquarian leaves at the end of this announcement, arriving in Bagchester exactly forty-one minutes later. Tea, coffee, sandwiches will be served at half twenty-three hours, and in accordance with the latest stockmarket reports tea will be twenty-one pounds, coffee twenty-six. The price of sandwiches is unchanged since yesterday, and expected to remain stable for the duration of the journey. The bar is now open, and Britrail trust you will have a comfortable trip. Thank you.

SOUND: *Musical chime.*

CHILD [*excited*] We're moving, we're moving, we're moving!

FIREMAN Disgusting! Twenty-one pounds for a cup of tea!

MIRIAM I feel that too, Dad.

TEACHER But I'm glad they warned us. What is half twenty-three hours? It's a terrible thing for a retired teacher to admit but I can't grasp this new way of telling the time.

MIRIAM [*uncertainly*] Half twenty-three is eleven and a half. Half past eleven, isn't it?

TEACHER A.M. ?

MIRIAM Yes, isn't it?

FIREMAN [*abruptly*] Don't be daft, Miriam. Half twenty-three hours is twelve from twenty-three and a half which is eleven and a half is half past eleven PM.

CHILD No! No! Our headmaster says –

FIREMAN Shut up, Patsy!

TEACHER Oh, please let me hear what your headmaster says, Patsy!

PATSY He says we shouldn't think about time in twelves any more because of demicilation –

TEACHER Decimalisation.

CHILD Yes. So half twenty-three hours is half past twenty-three.

TEACHER [*sighing*] I wish they had let us keep the old noon with the twelve hours before and after it. But even the station clocks have changed. Instead of a circular minutes round the edge, past and future, we have a square window with nothing in it but the moment we're at now. Nothing eight hours twenty minutes twelve seconds. Then flick! and it's nothing eight hours twenty minutes thirteen. It makes me feel trapped. Trapped, yet pushed at the same time.

CHILD Our headmaster says railway timetables are worked by computers nowadays. And computers don't like counting in twelves.

TEACHER I'm sure they could be trained to do it, I'm told some of them are quite intelligent. And I hate that little flick when one second becomes the next.

MRS DEAR [*distant*] I hate it too, dear.

MR DEAR [*distant*] Please shut up, dear.

FIREMAN [*quietly threatening*] Patsy, if you interrupt me just once more you are going to feel the whole weight of my hand on the side of your jaw.

TEACHER Time and money: so much disappeared so suddenly: the little farthings with Jenny Wrens on them, thick brown three-pennies, silver sixpences, the old ha'penny. Did you know, Patsy, that ha'pennies used to be one inch in diameter, the size of the modern tuppeny?

CHILD What is an inch?

TEACHER Two point five three nine nine nine eight centimetres. And the old pennies were lovely huge lumps of copper, two hundred and forty to the pound, we shall not see their like again, with Britannia ruling the waves between a small battleship and the Eddystone lighthouse. Britannia was a real woman, you know. Not many people realise that. She was copied from a ... girlfriend of the Merry Monarch, not Nell Gwyn. The old pennies had room for so much history on them. They were history! Even in the sixties you still found coins with young Queen Victoria's head on them. We called them bun-pennies because her hair was gathered in a bun at the nape of her neck, and the old Queen was so common we took her for granted. Just think! Every time we went shopping we were handling coins which had clinked in the pockets of Charles Dickens and Doctor Pritchard the poisoner and Isambard Kingdom Brunel. [*sighs*].

MR DEAR Excuse me for interrupting you, Madam, but I could not help overhearing you –

TEACHER I fear that my voice *is* rather penetrating –

MR DEAR Yes indeed. And it might interest you to know that the weight of a modern penny, subtracted from a pre-decimal penny, leaves enough copper to construct circuits for thirty-nine pocket television sets.

TEACHER Oh.

MR DEAR [*distant*] I just thought you'd like to know that.

TEACHER [*lamely*] Thank you.

FIREMAN [*violently*] But is it?

MR DEAR I beg your pardon?

FIREMAN You said that the copper saved by switching to decimal currency could be used to make cheap sets. But was it?

MR DEAR Quite likely. At any rate it was used for –

FIREMAN I'll tell you what it was used for! It was used to build the circuits of an electronic nuclear defence system that cost the British taxpayer eighty-three million pounds and was obsolete two years before completion.

MR DEAR I have no wish to discuss politics with you, sir. [*distant*] Or with anyone.

FIREMAN I believe you ... Stop jiggling about, Patsy. Where's my paper?

MIRIAM Here you are, Dad.

SOUND: *Rustling newspaper.*

CHILD Can I go for a walk, mum?

MIRIAM Well ...

CHILD Please Mum! I promise not to stare hard at people!

MIRIAM All right then, if you promise not to stare hard at people you can go to the buffet and buy a biscuit with the four pounds the nice lady gave you.

CHILD [*fading*] Thanks Mum!

TEACHER What sex is your little child?

MIRIAM [*reflectively*] I feel there's too much sex nowadays.

TEACHER Oh so do I. But is Patsy a girl or a boy?

MIRIAM We're trying not to influence.

TEACHER Is that wise? I feel children are often happier for a little guidance.

MIRIAM [*helplessly*] I don't know, really. But that's the modern way, isn't it? You see, we think – [*she pauses*] We think [*she pauses*].

FIREMAN Mobility.

MIRIAM What's that, Dad?

FIREMAN Mobility.

MIRIAM Yes, we're thinking of the future. People talk as if men and women will always do the same sorts of job but Dad and I don't agree. We believe women will always be expected to do *some* things better than men, and vice ... vice ...

FIREMAN Versa, Miriam.

MIRIAM Versa. But since nobody can predict what these will be nowadays we'll let Patsy choose her sex himself when she leaves school. What I say is, if the child learns proper manners and how to tell right from wrong, why bother about sex. My mother never mentioned it.

TEACHER Nor did mine.

MIRIAM Anyway, I'm quite sure Patsy won't become one of these dreadful women's lib ladies. Or a teddy boy.

FIREMAN A cat.

MIRIAM What's that, love?

FIREMAN Teddy boys were fifties. Beatniks sixties, then came Hippies, Punks and Goths. And now they call themselves Cool Cats.

TEACHER Are you sure? There have been so many strange names for young people – mods, skinheads, ravers, bobby-soxers, flappers, knuts, mashers and macaronis – that I've started thinking of them as youths. The police news always calls them youths.

MR DEAR [*distant but fierce*] And quite right too!

MRS DEAR [*distant*] Sh, dear, sh.

SOUND: *Musical chime: loudspeaker.*

DRIVER Good afternoon. This is Captain Rogers, your driver speaking. The 2041 Aquarian from Bundlon to Shaglow is making excellent time. On your left you can see the partly reforested bings of the Outer Bundlon slag depot, and on our right we are just leaving the soya fields of the British Golliwog Jam Corporation. I regret to announce that a special stockmarket newsflash has obliged us to raise the price of coffee by two pounds a cup ...

TEACHER Oh dear!

MIRIAM [*nearly simultaneously*] That's twenty-eight pounds!

MR DEAR This is intolerable!

FIREMAN [*nearly simultaneously*] Bloody disgusting!

DRIVER ... regrettable, but tea and biscuits are still expected to remain stable for the duration of the journey. Passengers with an interest in transport will not need to be told that today is rather a special one for Britrail. In one and a half minutes it will be twelve-forty-two hours precisely, and the hundred and fiftieth anniversary of the exact moment when Isambard Kingdom Brunel...

TEACHER [*over*] Brunel!

DRIVER ... tapped the last ceremonial rivet into the Grand Albert Royal Tennine Suspension Bridge, the first broad-gauge box-girder suspension bridge in the history of engineering. To honour the occasion we will now play you a recording of "The Railways of Old England", orchestrated and sung by Sir Noel Coward. Through the length and breadth of Britain, in trains trundling through the lonely pass of Killiecrankie or thundering across the Stockport viaduct, passengers are rising to their feet to hear Sir Noel Coward sing "The Railways of Old England". [*softly*] Twelve, Eleven, Ten ...

SOUND: *People shuffle to their feet.*

FIREMAN [*over*] Bloody rubbish.

MR DEAR [*over*] Excuse me, sir! Are you not going to stand?

FIREMAN [*over*] Don't move, Patsy!

DRIVER ... Six, Five, Four, Here, It, Is.

MUSIC: *Railways of Old England: Under.*

MR DEAR [*over*] [*loudly*] Excuse me, sir! Are you not going to stand?

FIREMAN [*over*] No!

MRS DEAR [*over*] [*distant*] Sh, dear! Please!

MR DEAR [*over*] Please shut up dear, I will not sh. I gather, sir, from your newspaper that you are a communist and would prefer to travel on a Chinese train. Well, Britrail has no harsher critic than myself. I'm glad Beeching axed it. I'm glad they privatised it. But with all its faults our railway system was built by a combination of Irish brawn, Scottish engineering and English financial daring which made us the foremost steam railway empire in the universe. Does this mean nothing to you?

FIREMAN [*over*] Don't talk to me about Britrail. I worked all my life for Britrail. I was a fireman from the old L.N.S. days to when they brought in bloody diesel...

MR DEAR [*over*] That's quite enough.

FIREMAN [*over*] Britrail was destroyed by people like you, bloody stockbrokers and lawyers and retired admirals on the board of directors ...

MIRIAM [*over*] Stop, Dad! Stop it!

MR DEAR [*over*] That's ludicrous.

FIREMAN [*over*] Shut up, Miriam! When they nationalised us the government said "Britrail belongs to the people now!" But who did we get on the new board of directors? Platelayers? Stationmasters? Footplatemen? Did we hell! We got the same old gang, retired admirals, company lawyers, civil servants with posh accents ...

MR DEAR [*over*] I am not listening to you!

FIREMAN [*over*] ... The gang that eventually sold us out to the car manufacturers, the building societies and the oil corporations.

MR DEAR [*over*] I am not listening to you!

FIREMAN [*over*] I never thought you would.

MUSIC: *Ends on a final sounding phrase.*

MIRIAM You shouldn't get excited, Dad.

SOUND: *Shuffle of people sitting down.*

TEACHER [*confidently*] Excuse me.

FIREMAN Mmm?

TEACHER I was entirely on your side in that little exchange, even though I was standing. I like the tune, you see. Though the words are inaccurate. Our railways are British, not English.

FIREMAN Mm.

MIRIAM I wonder where Patsy is?

Pause.

PATSY [*distant*] Mum! [*nearer*] Mum!

DRIVER Good day, good people. Does this small person belong to one of you?

MIRIAM Patsy, where *have* you been?

PATSY Mum!

DRIVER Wandering far too near the engine for anybody's good, I'm afraid.

PATSY Mum!

MIRIAM How very naughty. Thank the nice man for bringing you back.

PATSY Mum, there's nobody driving this train. The driver's cabin's empty. I looked inside.

Brief pause.

MIRIAM Patsy, that's not a very nice thing to say, not with that accident in America last week. Apologise at once.

PATSY But Mum, it really was empty –

MRS DEAR Dear, I'm terribly worried.

MR DEAR Don't be stupid, dear. The kid's obviously gone the wrong way and blundered into the guard's van by mistake.

TEACHER But this gentleman says he found Patsy near the engine –

MR DEAR The child knows nothing about mechanics, who does nowadays? It wouldn't surprise me to learn that modern trains are driven from an obscure cabin somewhere in the middle.

FIREMAN [*violently*] It wouldn't surprise *me* to learn that modern trains have no drivers at all.

MRS DEAR Oh!

MR DEAR [*almost simultaneously*] Pay no attention, dear.

DRIVER [*also almost simultaneously*] Excuse me!

FIREMAN You needed a driver in the days of steam, two of them, counting the fireman, tough men, strong men who knew the engine and could clean it themselves, and grasped every valve and stop-cock like it was the hand of a friend, who felt the gradient through the soles of their boots and heard the pressure in the thrusts of the piston. But nowadays! Nowadays it wouldn't surprise me if the driver of this so-called *train* ...

DRIVER Excuse me!

FIREMAN ... wasn't lying back with a glass of brandy in a London club, watching us on a computer screen and half-sloshed out of his upper-class over-educated skull!

DRIVER You're wrong, I'm afraid.

FIREMAN Who the hell are you?

MIRIAM Dad! That's not nice!

DRIVER May I, er, sit with you for a moment?

MIRIAM Of course!

MRS DEAR [*almost simultaneously*] Of course!

DRIVER You see, it embarrasses me to say this, but it's a free country, you're entitled to know –

TEACHER [*suddenly*] You're the driver! I recognise the voice?

DRIVER Well ... yes ...

Brief pause.

DRIVER [*continues*] So you see, I'm not lying back in a London club, I'm sitting here, with you. I really am one of you.

MIRIAM [*dazzled*] But you sounded so different on the ...

MRS DEAR [*dazzled*] Dear, I feel so safe ...

MR DEAR [*importantly*] Excuse me, sir!

DRIVER Yes?

MR DEAR I have said harsh things about Britrail in my time.

DRIVER [*genially*] Of course you have!

MR DEAR But I never doubted that our trains are the safest in the world and our drivers second to none – if the unions would stop confusing them by promising them the moon.

DRIVER Thank you.

MRS DEAR Dear, this is ... wonderful.

MIRIAM Stop scowling, Dad. It isn't polite.

TEACHER Train driving seems to have changed in recent years. Could you tell me ...

DRIVER Excuse me, madam, I'll be glad to answer any questions you care to put after I've ... I've, er ... [*he is confused, but pulls himself together*] You see, it isn't every day I've a chance to speak to John Halifax.

FIREMAN Eh?

DRIVER You *are* John Halifax? The last of the steam men? Who took three whole minutes off the Bundlon to Glaik run in the great railways race between L.M.S. and the L.N.E.R. in 1934?

FIREMAN [*wonderingly, after a pause*] You know about that?

DRIVER You are a legend in railway circles, Mr Halifax. Or may I call you ... ?

FIREMAN Yes, yes, call me John, but how did you know I was on the train?

DRIVER Aha! I'm not supposed to tell passengers certain things. But to hell with security. The truth is, the ticket-office clerks aren't the ignorant gits the public sometimes assume. They keep me informed. So I used your grandchild's escapade as an excuse to seek you out. And here I am!

FIREMAN I see ...

DRIVER I hope you won't get cross but I need to ask you a terribly personal question. About the last great Railway Race.

FIREMAN Carry on.

DRIVER Do you remember stoking the Spitfire Thunderbolt up the Devil's Kidney gradient with only three minutes to reach Beattock summit or you would lose the whole race?

FIREMAN [*softly*] Oh, I remember, yes!

DRIVER Were you, on that heroic drive, exhausting yourself, torturing yourself, pressing out every ounce of your energy and intelligence merely to advertise the old L.M.S.

FIREMAN No, I was not.

DRIVER Then why did you do it? I know it wasn't for money.

FIREMAN [*after a pause*] I did it for steam! For British steam!

DRIVER [*triumphantly*] I knew you would give me that answer.

MR DEAR Excuse me! I ... want very much to ... You see, Mr Halifax and I kick, you might say, with opposite feet – he's left and I'm right. And I didn't realise before now that we really are different parts of the same body. Captain Rogers has made me see that for the first time. Mr Halifax, I am no toady. So when I offer you my hand I am merely demonstrating my respect for you as a man. I am apologising for nothing. But here ... is ... my hand. Will you ... ?

Pause.

FIREMAN [*emotionally*] Put it there.

DRIVER And there – please.

FIREMAN [*chuckling*] Why not?

MR DEAR And there, Captain Rogers!

DRIVER Thank you, thank you!

The three men chortle happily.

TICKET INSPECTOR [*distant*] Tickets, please. [*nearer*] Thanks, tickets please.

MRS DEAR This is so nice!

MIRIAM Yes, isn't it.

TICKET INSPECTOR Ticket, please.

DRIVER [*coldly*] I'm your driver, you fool.

TICKET INSPECTOR [*after a brief pause*] So you are! Hahahahahahaha! [*recedes, laughing louder as he does so*] So he is! Hahahahaha. So he is! Hahahahaha –

SOUND: *Distant slammed door cuts laughter.*

DRIVER [*regretfully*] A very rough diamond. I'm sure they weren't like that in your day.

FIREMAN [*tolerantly*] Oh, we had them too.

TEACHER Perhaps Captain Rogers will now tell us why he isn't with his engine.

DRIVER I'm afraid, madam, the heroic age of engine driving went out with steam. The modern engine (we call them traction units nowadays) only requires my attention from time to time. Our speed and position are being monitored, at the present moment, from headquarters in Stoke-on-Trent. It's a perfectly safe system. All Europe uses it. And America.

TEACHER There was a recent accident in America –

DRIVER Yes, through a fault in their central data bank at Detroit. These big continental systems are all far too centralised. The British, er, branch of the system has enough autonomy to prevent such accidents happening here. So you see, although I am not drinking brandy in a London club (I never touch alcohol – doctor's orders) I look more like a Piccadilly lounge-lizard than like the legendary John Halifax here. My main task is to keep down the buffet prices and stop passengers bickering with one another. And I'm not always successful.

MRS DEAR I think you succeed splendidly.

MR DEAR Hear hear!

TEACHER You're certainly good with passengers ...

FIREMAN You aren't the fool I took you for, I'll give you that.

DRIVER [*gratefully*] Thank you, John.

SOUND: *Musical chime: voice on loudspeaker.*

DRIVER [*on loudspeaker*] Good afternoon, there is no cause for alarm. This is your driver, Captain Felix Rogers, speaking. Here is a special message for Captain Felix Rogers. Will you please proceed to the traction unit. Please proceed to the traction unit. Thank you.

PATSY He's talking to himself, Mum!

MIRIAM Don't be rude, Patsy.

FIREMAN [*knowledgeably*] Pre-recorded, of course.

DRIVER Of course. If the traction unit is empty when a message comes from HQ, the graphic printout activates that announcement and – duty calls! I'm sorry I have to return to my cabin. I'll probably find a rotten stock-market report that forces me to raise the price of tea. I hope not. Goodbye, John.

FIREMAN Goodbye, er ...

DRIVER Felix.

FIREMAN [*solemnly*] Felix.

DRIVER [*solemnly*] Thank you, John. [*heartily*] Stay where you are, everybody. Goodbye! Goodbye!

MR DEAR Goodbye sir!

MIRIAM [*almost simultaneously*] Goodbye ... sir!
FIREMAN [*almost simultaneously*] Cheerio.
MRS DEAR What a nice man!
MIRIAM Yes, wasn't he?
MR DEAR He was informed – and informative.
TEACHER But the situation he laid before us was not reassuring.
MR DEAR What do you mean?
TEACHER Nobody is driving this train.
MR DEAR Utter rubbish! There's a ... there are all kinds of things driving this train, data banks and computers and silicon chops all ticking and whirring in the headquarters at Stockton-on-Tees.
MRS DEAR I thought he said Stoke Newington.
MR DEAR Shut up, dear. The town doesn't matter.
TEACHER Well, I find it disturbing to be driven by machines which aren't on board with us. Don't you Mr Halifax?
FIREMAN I ... I might have done if I hadn't met the driver. But he's an educated chap. He wouldn't take things so casually if there was any danger, now would he?
MR DEAR Madam, we are actually far safer being driven by a machine in Stoke Newington. No thug with a gun can force *it* to stop the train, or divert us into a siding where terrorists threaten our lives in order to blackmail the government.
TEACHER [*firmly, after a pause*] You are both perfectly right. I have been very very foolish.
SOUND: *Musical chime, voice on loudspeaker.*
DRIVER [*on loudspeaker*] Good afternoon. There is no need for alarm ...
MR DEAR [*over*] What did I tell you?
MRS DEAR [*over*] Ssh, dear!
DRIVER [*on loudspeaker*] This is your driver, Captain Rogers. We are cruising above the Wash at a speed of two hundred and three kilometres per hour, and the Quantum-Cortexin ventilation system is keeping the air at the exact temperature of the average human skin. So far our run has gone very smoothly and I deeply regret that I must now apologise for a delay in the anticipated time of arrival. An error in our central data bank has resulted in the 2041 Aquarian from Bundlon to Shaglow running on the same line as the 2042 Aquarian from Shaglow to Bundlon. The collision is scheduled to occur in exactly eight minutes thirteen seconds ...
EVERYBODY [*over driver*] Oh! Oo! No! Ah!
DRIVER ... at a point eight and a half kilometres south of Bagchester. But there is absolutely no need for alarm. Our technicians in Stoke Poges are working overtime to re-programme the master computer and may actually manage to prevent the collision. Meanwhile we have ample time to put into effect the following safety precautions ...
CHILD [*over driver*] Mummy!
FIREMAN [*over driver and almost together with* **CHILD**] Shut up Patsy!
DRIVER Please listen carefully. In the back of your seats you will see slight metal projections. These are the ends of your safety belt. Pull them out and lock them round you. That is all you need to do. The fire prevention system is working perfectly, and shortly before impact steel shutters will close off the windows to prevent injury from splintered glass. At the present moment television crews and ambulances are whizzing towards the point of collision from all over England, and in cases of real poverty Britrail have undertaken to pay the ambulance fees. I need not say how much I personally regret the inconvenience but we're in this together, and I appeal to the spirit of Dunkirk ...
FIREMAN [*snarling*] Nnaaaargh!
DRIVER ... that capacity for calmness under stress which has made us famous throughout the globe. Passengers near the traction unit should not attempt to move to the rear of the train. This sound –
SOUND: *Distant swish and thud.*
DRIVER – is the noise of the sliding doors between the carriages sealing themselves to prevent a stampede. But there is no need for alarm. The collision is not scheduled for another, er ... seven minutes three seconds exactly, and I will have time to visit your compartments with my personal key and ensure that safety precautions are being observed. This is not goodbye, but au revoir. And fasten those belts.
SOUND: *Musical chime.*
MIRIAM [*moaning*] What can we do, Dad?
FIREMAN Attend to the child, Miriam.
CHILD I don't want to be tied up.
MIRIAM Just pretend we're in an aeroplane, dear –
SOUND: *Zip-zip clunk.*
MIRIAM And look – Grampa's doing it, we're all doing it.
SOUND: *Three overlapping zip-zip clunks.*
MRS DEAR [*whispering*] Dear, I – I'm terrified.
MR DEAR [*tenderly*] It's a bad business, dear, but we must make the best of it. I'll strap us in.
SOUND: *Two zip-zip clunks.*

MIRIAM And now we're all [*fighting hysteria*] safe as houses!
MR DEAR Madam?
TEACHER Yes?
MR DEAR I owe you an apology. This rail system is more inept, more inane, more ... altogether *bad* than I thought possible in a country like ours.
FIREMAN You can say *that* again.
PATSY [*sulkily*] I want to get *off* this train.
TEACHER [*suddenly*] The child is correct. We should slow the train down and jump off.
THE MEN No but – Yes but –
TEACHER I *know* our speed is controlled by wireless waves or something but the motor – the thing which makes the wheels turn – is quite near us, in the traction unit, could we not –
FIREMAN [*interrupting*] By heck, it's worth a try! Let me get – [*gasp*] Just let me get to the [*gasp*] This bloody belt won't unlock!
MR DEAR [*gasping*] Neither ... will mine!
TEACHER [*forlornly*] I suppose they call this security.
FIREMAN [*straining, with gritted teeth*] I won't – let – the bastards – do it!
SOUND: *A rending noise.*
CHILD [*excited*] Grampa! Grampa! The belt's tearing!
SOUND: *A door slides open.*
DRIVER [*coldly and quickly*] What seems to be the problem?
FIREMAN Quick, Felix. Get me out of this seat and into your cabin. I want a crack at the motor. I'm sure I can damage it with something heavy. I'll shove my body into it if that will let some of us off!
DRIVER Too late for heroics, John. And I cannot possibly allow you to damage company property.
FIREMAN [*aghast*] You – are – insane!
DRIVER No, John Halifax, *you* are insane. I have this gun to prove it.
MRS DEAR [*screaming*] Help! Help! Help! Hel-
SOUND: *A sharp bang. Pause.*
FIREMAN [*softly*] You bastard. [*loudly*] You bastard!
SOUND: *Rending noise terminated by another bang.*
MR DEAR You've k ... You've k ...
DRIVER I have not killed them. This is an anaesthetic gas pistol developed for use against civilians in Ulster. In this emergency the train comes under martial law and my title of Captain ceases to be nominal. Does anyone else want a whiff? Saves emotional stress. A spell of oblivion and with luck you wake up in the ward of a comfortable, crowded hospital.
TEACHER [*icily*] Thank you. I prefer to face death with open eyes, however futile and unnecessary it appears.
TICKET INSPECTOR [*distant, shouting*] Captain! Captain!
DRIVER [*shouting*] Yes?
TICKET INSPECTOR [*distant, shouting*] Three and a half minutes, Captain.
DRIVER Goodbye, good people.
MIRIAM [*desperately*] Sir, where are you going?
DRIVER The guard's van. I have to survive the wreck to report it at the official enquiry.
MIRIAM Sir, please unlock Patsy and take him with you, she's only a *little* child.
CHILD [*shouting*] No, Mum. I'm staying with you, Mum. He's nasty, nasty, nasty!
DRIVER [*quickly*] Goodbye, good people.
SOUND: *A sliding door is slammed.*
CHILD [*interested*] Are we going to die, Mum?
MIRIAM [*quietly and kindly*] You know "The Lord is my Shepherd", Patsy? Let's say it, shall we? The Lord is my shepherd –
MIRIAM and **CHILD** I shall not want. He maketh me down to lie in green pastures. He leadeth me beside the still waters.
SOUND: *The sliding into place with a clang of metal sheeting. After this a faint rhythmical throb is heard which lasts till near the end of the play.*
TEACHER There go the shutters.
MR DEAR Pitch, pitch dark. They haven't even allowed us light.
MIRIAM and **CHILD** [*very softly*] He restoreth my soul. He leads me in the paths of righteousness for his name's sake ...
They recite 23rd Psalm very slowly and quietly, returning to the start and continuing till the crash.
TEACHER Do you remember when every train had a communication cord which *any* traveller could pull, and stop the train?
MR DEAR [*almost amused*] Yes! Penalty for improper use, five pounds.
TEACHER Once upon a time every small boy wanted to drive a train when he grew up. And in many communities the station master played bridge on Sunday evenings with the headmaster, the banker and the clergyman.

MR DEAR I remember signal boxes with pots of geraniums on the sills.

TEACHER I remember a bright spring morning on the platform at Beattock. A porter took a wicker basket from a guard's van and released a whole flight of pigeons.

MR DEAR We had a human railway then. Why did it change?

TEACHER [*firmly*] We did not stick to steam.

MR DEAR Eh?

TEACHER We used to depend on coal, our own British coal which would have lasted for centuries. Now we depend on expensive, dangerous, poisonous stuff produced by foreign companies based in America and Arabia and ...

MR DEAR You're wrong. These companies aren't based anywhere. I've shares in a few. The people running them have offices in Amsterdam and Hong Kong, holiday homes in the Bahamas, bank accounts in Switzerland ...

TEACHER So that is why we are driven from outside. None of *us* is in charge of us now.

MR DEAR Some of us pretend to be.

SOUND: *Distant train siren approaching rapidly.*

TEACHER [*loudly, to be heard above it*] But nobody is really in charge of us now! *Nobody* is in charge of us.

SOUND: *Very great explosion followed by a clatter of subsiding wreckage. Then complete silence for three seconds.*

CHILD [*drowsily*] Mum ... Mum ...

MIRIAM [*on a wondering note*] I think ... Patsy ... we're going to be ... all right.

SOUND: *A greater but more abrupt, final explosion.*

IN THE 1970s the musicians John Purser and Wilma Paterson, also Stewart Conn were my near neighbours. Both Wilma and I liked George MacDonald's magical novella, *The Golden Key*, and discussed this allegory about human life and aspirations until she decided that I should make a half hour radio play of it, for which she would write music. After a dinner party in her home she bullied Stewart into commissioning me to write that play.

George MacDonald (1824–1905) was a Congregational Scots clergyman who wrote many magical tales for children. His imagination resembled that of Charles Kingsley, the Church of England Socialist who wrote *The Water Babies*. The Christianity of both was liberalised – perhaps liberated – by a knowledge of Buddhism. The heroes and heroines of *The Golden Key* and *The Water Babies* have several purifying adventures after dying on earth, adventures in which they pass more than once through water. These stories were linked in my mind with *Child Roland to the Dark Tower Came*, a line flung out by Edgar in *King Lear* when he was mimicking insanity. It had inspired Browning to invent a poem about Child Roland, the last of a company who had sought to destroy the Dark Tower, an ultimate source of evil. The poem has Roland, late in life, cross a wasteland as horrid as T.S. Eliot's and at last confront the Tower, knowing that to die defying it is the best anyone can do. A century later Browning's poem inspired Louis MacNeice to write verse drama for radio with the same name. In my teens I heard his Roland overcome 20th century temptations on the BBC Third Programme, and also Auden's wonderful verse play *The Ascent of F6*, with music by Benjamin Britten. With these in mind and Wilma's (imagined) music, I turned MacDonald's prose into rhyme.

The BBC had then a radiophonic department that specialised in sound effects suggesting strange mental states and unusual surroundings. With these and suitable music I think this would still be a good sound play, though the BBC rejected it. However, I received payment because it had been commissioned.

THE GOLDEN KEY

A 30-MINUTE RADIO VERSE PLAY

1975

CAST

VOICE 1: Mild, female, made supernaturally clear through radiophonic treatment.
VOICE 2: Cool, male, radiophonic like **VOICE 1**.
TANGLE: A little girl, older girl, old woman then young girl
NURSE: Shallow and genteel.
BUTLER: Coarse and pompous.
AERANTH: A female singing voice.
THE WOMAN: Rich, mild, mature, same as **VOICE 1**, but natural – not radiophonic.
TEACHER: A clever old man.
MOSSY: A boy, young man, old man, then young again
DOVE: Moaning female
SPARROW: Chirpy male
THRUSH: Female singer
CUCKOO: Male mocker
MOLE: Slow, pedantic male adviser
SQUIRREL: Rapid, scolding female adviser
BEES: Monotonous females
FOX: Suave aristocrat
OLD MAN OF THE SEA: Mature and strong, like **VOICE 2,** but sounding natural
THREE FISH: Male lecherous voices, radiophonic treatment.
OLD MAN OF THE EARTH: Young and cheerful.
OLD MAN OF THE FIRE: A chill voice, female, radiophonic.

THE GOLDEN KEY

MUSIC: *very brief introduction ending in special fading chord.*

SCENE 1

Two supernaturally clear voices converse: radiophonic treatment.
VOICE 1 Tell me what *you* see through this dirty window.
VOICE 2 A great kitchen where two servants play a bad game.
VOICE 1 Who sits in the corner?
VOICE 2 A wild little girl.
VOICE 1 What is she trying to do?

SCENE 2

TANGLE *reads softly to herself, very near.*
TANGLE As Gol-den hair. Lay in bed. Per-tending to sleep. She heard the soft. Tread of the three. Bears. Com-ing up-stairs.
The servants talk loudly, but far off, with a faint echo suggesting a great room.
NURSE The queen of hearts. Beat *her* if you can.
BUTLER I do, with a big black spade.
NURSE Ooh!
TANGLE [*near*] Bears treading softly upstairs and... Growing? No. Growling.
NURSE You've taken all my little diamonds. What can I do?
BUTLER Give me your big ones too.
TANGLE [*distant, but loud*] Growling!
NURSE [*very near*] Mr Trimmer, what can I do? You're grabbing all I've got and that wild child deafens me by growling.
BUTLER Go to bed, Tangle! You are an eyesore.
TANGLE [*distant*] Can I have a candle?
NURSE No. They're dear and dangerous. Beside, the moon will rise soon.
BUTLER You heard what I said Tangle! Go to bed!
NURSE And shut the door.
SOUND: *Distant door shuts.*
NURSE [*sighing*] We neglect that child, Mr Trimmer. I can't bear to look at her thin legs, ragged clothes, nose always in a book. You and I are too few for the huge amount of scolding we have to do.
BUTLER Thirsty work, Miss Partridge. Yes.
SOUND: *Wine poured.*
BUTLER More claret?
NURSE How kind.
SOUND: *Wine poured.*
BUTLER Brandy for me.
NURSE What will we say? ... [*she sips*] if the master returns and sees his house and child in a dreadful way?
BUTLER [*comfortably*] Ours is a lonely house – [*swallows*]. with no neighbours to tell tales. The master's bank pays our bills. His cellar – [*swallows*] – holds a century of wine. I don't think he will return in *my* time.
NURSE A lonely house, yes. With rustling and stirring in every shadow.
BUTLER [*slyly and very near*] Noises like voices. The forest outside the window grows nearer when it's dark.
NURSE Oh, Mr Trimmer, you scare me! You know you do!
BUTLER Yes, Miss Partridge. It is my way of snaring you.
They giggle.

SCENE 3

MUSIC: *Starts with soft, single instrument sounding behind the radiophonic voices.*

VOICE 1 This house is a great shame. Nothing inside it is clean.

VOICE 2 See the small girl climbing the stair to bed. What forest beast has hair as rat-tailed and tangled as her hair?

VOICE 1 Don't blame her.

VOICE 2 I never blame. Her faults are not her fault. They are sickening, just the same. And she is the weakest one here. Drive her out and the filthy servants will disappear, and the house cave in and stop poisoning the air. We will frighten her away after the moon has risen.

MUSIC: *Two quiet instruments in rising cadence.*

VOICE 1 In a big dark room she undresses,
Stands naked on a chair, pulls a nightgown
over her head
Then clambers onto the heavy four-poster bed.
Peeping from under the quilt she sees
The moon float into the sky from behind
the forest trees,
And silver the ivy round the window,
silver the floor
And silver the reflection in the mirror
behind the door.

VOICE 2 So I take a shape like an ape and look out of the mirror!

MUSIC: *Stops.*

VOICE 2 [*gibbering*] Cheecheecheechee He He He Tanglee! I beckon you! I beckon you!

TANGLE [*aghast*] No! ... Nurse please! ... Oh!

SOUND: *Many little gibbering cries.*

VOICE 2 [*talking over them*] Now each carved head on the wardrobe winks and glares and the chairs start to dance. Stir your stumps, show your legs, you chairs!

SOUND: *Wooden clatter to a polka rhythm.*

TANGLE [*laughing*] How funny! Funny! [*claps her hands*].

SOUND: *Total silence.*

VOICE 1 [*quietly*] Let the chairs go back. I made a mistake.

VOICE 2 She is too wild a child to fear what is only strange.

VOICE 1 I will use something she knows. What book was she reading?

VOICE 2 Goldenhair.

VOICE 1 Good. Now comes a noise from the stair.

SOUND: *Soft heavy footsteps come steadily upstairs, accompanied by low conversational growling.*

TANGLE [*frightened whisper*] As Goldenhair ... lay in bed she ... heard the soft tread ... of the three bears coming upstairs and ... [*loudly*] No!

SCENE 4

MUSIC: *Starts, very agitated.*

VOICE 2 She leaps to the floor –

VOICE 1 Runs to the window –

VOICE 2 Flings it up and slides –

VOICE 1 Down through the –

VOICE 2 Down through the –

VOICE 1 Down through the ivy to the ground

VOICE 2 And she runs –

VOICE 1 She is running –

VOICE 2 She is running the wrong way –
She is going astray!

VOICE 1 She is running into our wood.

VOICE 2 She should run towards the town
with her tangled hair, her filthy gown.

VOICE 1 She thinks the forest less dangerous at night.
She is right.

VOICE 2 She is wrong. Ferns are whipping her,
brambles rip, tripping her.
A tree bars her way.
Branches sway down gripping waist, gown, wrist.
Twigs and leaves twist in her hair,
and roots have bound
her feet to the ground!

MUSIC: *stops.*

SCENE 5

SOUND: *Thrashing leaves and branches.*

TANGLE [*sobbing with effort*] Help! ... Help! Please help me,
someone

MUSIC: *Distant harp with the* **AERANTH'S** *distant voice singing. Both come steadily nearer.*

AERANTH Io lilla
Heara lollo
Callo lilla
From a willow

Io lilla
Heara lollo
Callo lilla
From a willow.

TANGLE [*wondering*] A fish with shining feathers swimming through the air. With a small round face like an owl's – [*cajoling*] Help me, airfish! Please help me with these –

SOUND: *Rustling.*

TANGLE – these branches.

AERANTH Io lilla
see a little
Tangle in a
twisted willow.
Bend away
the willow branches –
[*whispering*] with my beak!

SOUND: *Creaking, rustling.*

TANGLE Thank you. Now this one.

SOUND: *Creaking, snapping.*

TANGLE The tree's letting go. Thank you airfish. I'm free. Could you help me some more? I can't go home, the house is full of bears. Could you take me somewhere safe?

AERANTH [*whispering*] Follow me.

[*singing*] Leave behind the twisted willow,
wade across the ferny floor,
rustle over leafy floor,
tiptoe on the mossy carpet
down an aisle of stately silver
elmtrees standing in the moonlight,
to a cottage thatched with branches –

TANGLE A cottage with an open door. Can I go in?

AERANTH Follow through the open door.
to a room where firelight flickers,
firelight flickers, water bubbles –

SOUND: *Boiled water bubbling.*

MUSIC: *A soft plunging chord.*

SCENE 6

TANGLE [*distressed*] *Oh!*

WOMAN Hullo.

TANGLE The airfish swam into the pot of bubbling water on your fire! I can see it resting on the bottom.

WOMAN Then I'll put on the lid.

SOUND: *A clink. The bubbling stops.*

WOMAN I'm glad you've come. What is your name?

TANGLE The servants call me Tangle.

WOMAN Ah, that was because your hair was so untidy. And it was their fault, the silly people. Still, it's a pretty name, I'll call you Tangle too.

TANGLE What is your name, please?

WOMAN Grandmother.

TANGLE Is it really?

WOMAN Yes indeed. I never tell stories, even in fun. If I did they would come true. How old are you?

TANGLE Ten.

WOMAN You don't look it. Are you certain?

TANGLE I was ten when I left the house.

WOMAN But it is three years since you ran away from the bears. So you are thirteen now.

TANGLE How old are you?

WOMAN Thousands of years.

TANGLE You don't look it.

WOMAN I think I do. Don't you see how beautiful I am?

TANGLE But when people live long they dry up. At least, I always thought so.

WOMAN I'm too busy to dry up, my work won't allow it – but I cannot have my little girl so untidy. There are stains all over your face.

TANGLE [*defensively*] A tree made me cry.

WOMAN I'll wash you clean. And then you will sleep.
And then we can eat the fish.

TANGLE But!

WOMAN I know what you mean. You don't like to eat the messenger who brought you home. But it is the kindest thing you can do for him. He was afraid to go out until he saw me put on the pot and heard me promise he would be boiled when he came back. You remember how fast he flew into the pot, don't you?

TANGLE Yes –

WOMAN So open that door in the wall and tell what you see.

SOUND: *Click of a lock opened.*

SCENE 7

MUSIC: *Water cadences mingle with* **AERANTH** *harp.*

TANGLE A deep tank.

WOMAN A tank of clear water.

TANGLE A tank of fishes –

WOMAN – of fishes with shining feathers –

TANGLE – and walled with green plants.
WOMAN Tall irises with blue and yellow flowers.
Take that nightgown off.
Step down into the clear spring
Where the fishes sing.
The **MUSIC** *makes a soft plunging sound.*
WOMAN And now she lies bare,
and water untangles her hair.
Her body floats and blooms.
Fish slide by her side,
their feathers washing her clean.
TANGLE [*drowsily*] I love this feeling.
WOMAN You are lovelier than you know.
Now fishes! Pillow her head, support her knees
and float her up out of the water please!
Float her upstairs to my bed.
TANGLE Don't – [*yawns*] – give up your bed for – [*yawns*] – me, Grandmother.
WOMAN I never sleep, my bed is for the guest.
Lay her gently down. Cover her up.
Now she will rest.
MUSIC: *Stops.*

SCENE 8

TEACHER Name the colours of the rainbow.
MOSSY Violet blue green yellow orange and red.
TEACHER And the seventh colour is?
MOSSY Nameless?
TEACHER Quite right. And where the rainbow ends there is, if you can find it, a golden key.
MOSSY What is it the key of? What will it open?
TEACHER Nobody knows.
MOSSY Being gold, I suppose I could get a good deal of money if I sold it.
TEACHER The pragmatists would agree. The Platonists say, better never find it than sell.
MOSSY Did you ever know anybody find it?
TEACHER Yes. Your father found it, I believe.
MOSSY What did he do with it, can you tell me?
TEACHER He never told me.
MOSSY What was it like?
TEACHER He never showed me.
MOSSY How does a new key always come to be there?
TEACHER Origins are not my field.
Pause.
SOUND: *Distant bird noises, very faint.*
MOSSY Can you tell me about the forest outside the classroom door?
TEACHER There are more things in it than are dreamed of by philosophy. The linguistic school doubt if it's real.
MOSSY [*almost to himself*] I saw the end of the rainbow in it once. Far away among the treetrunks, under the branches. [*louder*] The strange thing is, sir, I couldn't see it in the sky.
TEACHER I envy you. And now go home. Goodbye.

SCENE 9

SOUND: *Bird noises: dove, sparrow, thrush and distant cuckoo, and then rustling footsteps.*
MOSSY The forest is full of voices. My father used to talk to them, they say. The trees have very few branches low down, which is why I can see into it for such a long way.
MUSIC: *The rainbow music begins among the bird notes, which fade as it grows louder.*
MOSSY Oh, the rainbow end! I can see it,
far off among the trees.
Every colour I know is shining there,
shade after shade.
I must go to it, I must go,
though when near it will fade …
No! No, the nearer I get the more shining
and real it seems and
now it is only two trees away!
Delicate colours, distinct, all combining,
silently burning up into the blue sky,
oh where is the crown of that arch?
It rises so high, each colour is like the
the column of a church with
lovely forms in them rising
as though ascending a winding stair,
but not regularly! Now one goes up,
now many, now several, now none!
Men, women, children, all different, all beautiful,
up they go to … to …
I can't see where,
and now the colours soften, desolve
fade into the blue air.
MUSIC: *ends.*

SCENE 10

MOSSY [*disappointed*] Faded into air. Faded. [*sighs*].
SOUND: *faint birdsong.*
TANGLE [*a girl now*] Hullo. Have you lost anything?
MOSSY [*preoccupied*] Nothing at all.
TANGLE Why are you searching the ground?
MOSSY I'm looking for something. A key. Ah!
MUSIC: *A low ringing key note.*
MOSSY Here it is, on this cushion of moss.
TANGLE It looks like a jewel to me. What will you use it for?
Pause.
TANGLE [*insisting*] What will you use it for?
MOSSY [*defensively*] Who are you?
TANGLE I'm called Tangle. What is your name?
MOSSY Mossy.
TANGLE Is it really?
MOSSY [*loftily*] Names are never real. Only things are real.
TANGLE [*puzzled*] Is that clever?
MOSSY [*ashamed*] No, it's stupid. I said it to make you admire me.
TANGLE Why?
MOSSY Because you are a beautiful girl.
TANGLE Not a child?
MOSSY No. A girl.
Pause.
TANGLE Would you like to come home with me?
MOSSY Yes, but –
TANGLE [*hastily*] It's no distance. This is the cottage, here.
MOSSY It looks like a wigwam to me. Or an igloo made of leaves.
TANGLE Grandmother lives inside, won't you come in? She won't mind.
MOSSY Are you sure?
TANGLE Yes, I ... think she sent me to find you. I'll open the door.

SCENE 11

SOUND: *Door opens, then faint bubbling sound.*
MOSSY [*shyly*] Hullo.
SOUND: *Bubbling fades.*
WOMAN What is that in your hand, Mossy? May I look?
MOSSY Yes, certainly!
MUSIC: *The key note.*
WOMAN [*respectfully*] Oh please take my chair!
MOSSY [*laughing*] No!
WOMAN *Please* let me serve you!
MOSSY I can't, you are a great splendid beautiful lady!
WOMAN Yes, but I always work, it is my pleasure. And you will have to leave me so soon!
MOSSY How you know that, Madam?
WOMAN You have the golden key.
MOSSY I don't know what it's for! Tell me what to do!
WOMAN You must look for the keyhole, that is *your* work. I cannot help you.
MOSSY What kind of box will it open? What is inside?
WOMAN [*sadly*] I dream about that, but I don't know.
MOSSY Must I go at once?
WOMAN No, first have some food. Sit down too, Tangle. The fish is nearly cooked.
SOUND: *Fade in bubbling very loud, which suddenly stops.*
MUSIC: AERANTH *cadence fades into distance.*
SOUND: *Tinkle of knife and fork; voice over, then fade.*
TANGLE [*cheerfully*] The fish tastes as delicate as cream.
MOSSY [*glumly*] I wish I didn't need to travel alone.
WOMAN Tangle will go with you.
MOSSY Oh I'm glad!
TANGLE No Grandmother, no! I want to live always with you!
WOMAN I'm sorry to lose you, Tangle, but I'm never allowed to keep my children long. Even the fish can't stay for ever in the tank. If you meet the Old Man of the Sea, ask him if he hasn't got more for me. My stock is getting thin.
TANGLE But I don't know this young man!
WOMAN You need not go with him unless you please, but you must go some day, and I'd like you to go with him. No girl need fear a youth with the golden key. You will take care of her Mossy, will you not?
MOSSY I will. Yes.
Pause.
TANGLE [*shyly*] Then I want to go.
WOMAN Good. I will open the door.
SOUND: *Door opens.*

SCENE 12

Musical voices blend and overlap at various distances.
DOVE Coooooo, I love looooove. Ooo, I love loooooove.

SPARROW Cheerup sweet. Cheerup sweet.
THRUSH Song song song song song song is territory,
song song song hedges the glade
where my eggs are laid, song song song –
DOVE Coooooo, I love loooooove.
SPARROW Cheerup sweet.
CUCKOO [*remote*] Hoo hoo! I had you, I had you!
MOSSY The forest voices are making sense.
WOMAN And if you should lose each other as you go through the – the – I never can remember the name of that country – don't be afraid but go on and on. Goodbye Mossy.
MOSSY Goodbye Grandmother.
WOMAN [*tenderly*] Goodbye Tangle. Let me kiss you. Don't cry. Goodbye!
TANGLE [*almost crying*] Goodbye!
DISTANT SPARROW Cheerup sweet.
SOUND: *Door closes. The musical bird voices sound faintly in the distance.*
MOSSY [*decisively*] We must walk away from all the places we know.
DISTANT THRUSH Song song song song –
MOLE The profound mole knows the right way to go. He understands the ground and is expert in the whole.
SQUIRREL Spade fists! Spade fists! Nuts are the goal, skip all over the tree. Pick nuts, slip to a branch and bank them quick.
MOSSY Thank you for your advice.
SQUIRREL Bank nuts. Bank nuts. Have a nut.
TANGLE Thank you squirrel.
DISTANT DOVE Loooooove love.
DISTANT CUCKOO I had you!
BEE 1 Bzzyourgoal –
BEE 2 Bzzyourgoal –
BEE 1 Bzzyourgoal should be –
BEE 2 Bzzzshares –
BEE 1 Bzzzshares –
BEE 2 Bzzzshares in corporate gold.
TANGLE I like honey.
MOSSY Will you give us some?
BEE 1 Bzzyou do not obey our queen –
BEE 2 Bzzzand charity beginzzzz –
BEE 1 Beginzzz –
BEE 2 Beginzzz at home:
FOX Yet they've killed every drone in their hive.
MOSSY Fine day Mr Fox.
FOX Sir Fox, if you please. I am the landlord here. I catch and eat the lot: bird-eggs, moles, squirrels and honeycomb. But not people. So you're trespassing. I'm afraid you will have to leave.
MOSSY We're looking for a path.
FOX [*voices fading behind*] You'll find one beyond the trees.

SCENE 13

TANGLE The forest is behind us now.
MOSSY The path rises through rocks.
TANGLE Jagged rocks. And the way is ... [*panting*] ... very steep.
MOSSY Give me your hand. I see a doorway ahead.
TANGLE Doorway?
MOSSY A rough one, cut in the rock.
TANGLE [*worried*] Stop!
MOSSY A long gallery like a coalmine.
TANGLE Black as night.
MOSSY If we don't go in we'll have to turn back. Come on.
TANGLE [*sadly*] Alright.
SOUND: *Footsteps, not loud, but echoing. Voices echo slightly too.*
TANGLE [*fearfully*] Oh Mossy, is it your hand I'm holding? I can't see.
MOSSY Of course. There's nothing to fear.
TANGLE Is it your voice I hear?
MOSSY Of course!
TANGLE You sound angry. Are you really a friend?
MOSSY The echo makes us both sound strange. But I can see light at the end.
SOUND: *Footsteps lose their echo, then stop. A wind is heard faintly. It fades.*

SCENE 14

A silence. When **MOSSY** *and* **TANGLE** *speak they are a grown man and woman.*
MOSSY On this high precipice the wind dies.
TANGLE There is no sound at all from the wide plain below.
MOSSY The mountains on the far side tower to an awful height.
TANGLE The plain is dim and smooth, is it moving or still?
MOSSY A path winds down to it, difficult and steep. Come. We'll see.

MUSIC: *Starts distant and vague, then comes nearer.*
TANGLE Yes, I must see. Is it a deep lake?
MOSSY No sound of water.
TANGLE The surface shifts, rippling with shadows like a field of grain.
MOSSY Yet without a wind.
TANGLE I've never seen a space look like it. No colours, but such rich tones.
MOSSY Moving tones.
TANGLE Moving, shadows – the shadows of beautiful leaves, innumerable leaves, floating, shaking in a breeze we can't feel. Dip your foot in them, Mossy.
MOSSY The plain is smooth sandstone beneath.
TANGLE No forest on the mountain behind, no trees to be seen, yet shadowy leaves, branches, stems cover the valley as far as the eye can reach. And now I spy flowers, and the shadow of a bird with open beak, its throat stretched in song.
MOSSY They're shallow shadows. We can wade through if we keep our eyes on the icy pinnacles on the far side –
TANGLE We can wade knee-deep in this lovely shadow-lake. Where do the shadows come from?
MOSSY Nothing above but bright white mist.
TANGLE In places the shadows heap up as if cast on a thousand planes of air.
MOSSY They are growing thin here – the ground is almost bare. Look!
TANGLE Look, a shadowy form floats across, half bird, half human with outspread wings –
MOSSY A Titan strides grandly through the wind-tossed leaves.
TANGLE A sweet female shape follows children who skip and leap.
MOSSY Wild horses gallop across, running a free race.
TANGLE [*awed*] The profile of a beautiful face.
MOSSY [*moved*] The profile of my father's face. Fading.
TANGLE But the shapes I love most of all – the loveliest shapes – [*desolate*] There are no names for these at all. I need to sit down, Mossy.
MOSSY Do ... Tangle, we must find the country from which the shadows fall.
TANGLE You feel that too? [*excited*] What if the key –
MUSIC: *The keynote sounds.*
TANGLE What if the key in your hand were the key to *it*?
MOSSY That would be ... [*pause*] grand!
TANGLE Let's go on!
MOSSY No, we must rest a bit, if we want to reach the far side before night.

SCENE 15

MUSIC *seems to recede and continue faintly.* **TANGLE** *and* **MOSSY** *are very old now.*
TANGLE Mossy, how long ... have we been ... on this plain?
MOSSY Why?
TANGLE Your hair is streaked with white.
MOSSY You have wrinkles on your brow.
TANGLE I thought so ... It is almost night. Are we near the far side?
MOSSY I don't know –
MUSIC: *stops.*
MOSSY – Please don't let go my hand. Tangle, where are you?
TANGLE [*calling in the distance*] Mossy, where are you?
MOSSY Tangle, I can't hear you!
TANGLE [*nearer*] Mossy, I can't hear you!
MOSSY [*distant*] Tangle, where have you gone?
TANGLE [*near*] Mossy, I'm all alone!
MOSSY [*distant*] I'm alone, Tangle! Alone!
TANGLE [*distant*] Alone! [*nearer*] Alone! [*near*] Alone. [*sighs deeply*].
MUSIC: *Returns faintly.*
TANGLE Silly of me to weep. Grandmother said if we lost each other we should go on. And Mossy has the key, no harm will come to him, I believe. I have been too long with shadow on this plain. It's good to reach the far side.
MUSIC: *ends.*

SCENE 16

TANGLE A path – [*sighs*] – rising – [*sighs*] – through rocks. To a rough door in the mountain. [*sighs*] I thought so! A long dark gallery like a coalmine. [*peevishly*] I *can't* go in there alone! It's not fair to expect an old lady to go underground, they can scold all they like, I don't care, I won't!
The **AERANTH** *is heard in the distance, getting nearer. His voice is more vigorous.*

AERANTH Io lilla
Heara little
Lady by a
Hollow tunnel.

Io lilla
Heara little
Lady crying by a tunnel.

TANGLE [*pleased*] My airfish!

AERANTH [*singing*] Not a fish now!

TANGLE But I ate you!

AERANTH [*singing*] You ate my husk. This is a better husk, I hope you agree.

TANGLE You are like a lovely boy with shining wings.

AERANTH [*singing*] Sparkling wings. Follow me!
You'll be able to see,
And the tunnel won't be long.

The **AERANTH** *song takes an echoing quality.*

AERANTH Io lilla
Lead a little
Lady down a hollow tunnel.
Underneath the icy mountain,
Underneath the mountain range
To the shore where she will know
A sea change ...

Fade **AERANTH** *song.*

SCENE 17

SOUND: *Waves beating regularly on a shore.*

TANGLE [*a girl again*] Excuse me sir, is that the ocean?

MAN OF THE SEA Yes, beautiful lady. Haven't you seen it before?

TANGLE Never. Am I really beautiful?

MAN OF THE SEA Very.

TANGLE I'm glad. I want to be like my grandmother. Why do you lean on a stick twined with green and white buds?

MAN OF THE SEA These are flowers which grow under the sea.

TANGLE Are you the Old Man of the Sea?

MAN OF THE SEA I am.

TANGLE Then grandmother says, Have you any more fishes ready for her?

MAN OF THE SEA We will go and look, my dear. My house is over there.

TANGLE It seems a steep rock – or a stone ship upside-down.

MAN OF THE SEA The sea can make anything stone.

SOUND: *Door opens.*

TANGLE Your door is a huge old rudder.

MAN OF THE SEA Step through.

SOUND: *Door closes. Wave sound stops.*

MAN OF THE SEA We have entered by the top-floor.

SCENE 18

MUSIC: *Descending notes.*

TANGLE [*over music*] Are we going very deep?

MAN OF THE SEA [*over music*] Sufficiently. [*pause*]. This will do.

MUSIC: *Stops.*

MAN OF THE SEA Here is my snug little locker. Let's see about these fishes for my daughter. I wonder if you'll like the view.

TANGLE What view, please?

MAN OF THE SEA Push aside that shutter.

SOUND: *Sliding noise.*

MUSIC *begins. Undersea music mixed with faint peculiar vocal gurgles.*

TANGLE [*wondering*] The heart of the great green deep ocean – I can see for miles and – what odd ugly creatures, all mouths and feelers.

MAN OF THE SEA The unctuous lump sucker, the spinous shark, the twisted squid squirting ink into the dark. I'll tap the glass to call them near.

SOUND: *Two taps on a window.*

The sly oily voices in the music grow distinct, then louder. There need be only three, but they overlap and are eventually multiplied into a great hubbub.

FISH 1 Yoo hoo!

FISH 2 Google boggle gobble isn't it a nice little piece –

FISH 3 Plump little bit –

FISH 1 Wouldn't mind a slice of –

FISH 2 Yoo hoo!

FISH 3 Google boggle gobble isn't it a nice little piece –

FISH 1 Plump little bit –

FISH 2 Wouldn't mind a slice of –

FISH 3 Yoo hoo! [*etcetera*]

MAN OF THE SEA [*sternly*] Silence!

The hubbub continues.

SOUND: *Glass rapped.*

MAN OF THE SEA [*loudly*] Silence all of you!

The **FISH** *are silent. Only the submarine music is heard.*

MAN OF THE SEA [*sighing*] I'm afraid none of these are ready yet.

SOUND: *Sliding noise ending in click.*
MUSIC: *Stops on click.*
MAN OF THE SEA [*sighing*] They were talking about you and they talk such nonsense!
TANGLE So can't you send grandmother more fishes?
MAN OF THE SEA I'll send them when I can. My work needs more time than hers. [*gently*] But can I do something for you?
TANGLE Can you tell me the way to the country from where the shadows fall?
MAN OF THE SEA No, but I'll send you someone who may. The Old Man of the Earth is older than me and lives further down this stair. Come over and see.
TANGLE The stair is dark.
MAN OF THE SEA Is it really?
TANGLE [*discovering*] Not as dark as I thought. In fact I see the way quite plain.
MAN OF THE SEA Your eyes cast a light of their own, now. You need never fear darkness again. Goodbye!
TANGLE Goodbye! Thank you. Goodbye!

SCENE 19

MUSIC: *Descending cadence at first with* **TANGLE***'s voice over it.*
TANGLE I go into the earth in search of a country in the air, and if I find it, oh I hope Mossy is there.
MUSIC: *The descending stops. An opening out is indicated, merging into plain of shadow music, which fades away slowly behind the voices.*
TANGLE Excuse me, Sir ...
MAN OF THE EARTH [*cheerful, pre-occupied*] Yes?
TANGLE Why are you smiling into that silver mirror?
MAN OF THE EARTH I am delighted by what I see. It isn't me. Yet.
TANGLE You look no more than twenty. Can you be the Old Man of the Earth?
MAN OF THE EARTH I am.
TANGLE Can you tell me the way to the country from which the shadows fall?
MAN OF THE EARTH No, though I see its shadows sometimes in my mirror. The Old Man of the Fire will know, he's much older than me.
TANGLE Where does he live?
MAN OF THE EARTH I'll show you his door. Help me lift this stone from the floor.
SOUND: *A grating noise.*
MAN OF THE EARTH Now what do you see?
TANGLE A hole that goes plumb down.
MAN OF THE EARTH What do you hear?
MUSIC: *Fade into rushing sound.*
TANGLE The sound of a great river, far below.
MAN OF THE EARTH That river flows down to the wisest man of all. I would like to go and see him, but I must mind my work. Goodbye.
TANGLE There are no stairs!
MAN OF THE EARTH Throw yourself in. There is no other way.
TANGLE Throw myself?
MAN OF THE EARTH Or go back. Or stay here.
Pause.
TANGLE [*loudly, suddenly*] Goodbye!

SCENE 20

MUSIC: *The river noise swells up into turbulent loudness.*
TANGLE [*high and quick*] Stream streams, water scalds, I don't want to bear it!
MUSIC: *A great plunge.*
TANGLE [*as before*] It is too sore, I don't want to bear it any more!
MUSIC: *A greater plunge.*
TANGLE [*despairing*] A fall down a boiling cataract over a burning wall!
MUSIC: *ends.*
TANGLE [*sobbing*] I don't want to feel, to feel, to feel any more.

SCENE 21

SOUND: *The plink-plonk of water dripping steadily in a cave.*
TANGLE Coolness. [*pause*] Cool dripping in a cave with mossy walls.
MUSIC: *Crystalline tappings, erratic yet harmonious, begin faintly to blend with the plink-plonks. They grow a little louder.*
TANGLE [*bewildered*] Little boy! Little baby, what game are you playing with these crystals and coloured balls?
The **MAN OF FIRE***'s voice is inhumanly clear and piercing.*
MAN OF FIRE The best game. I arrange and change, so things can grow and disappear.
TANGLE All things?

MUSIC: *Two brief taps.*

MAN OF FIRE Yes. And those who see the game don't feel time pass. How long have you been watching me?

MUSIC: *Three brief taps.*

TANGLE Less than a minute?

MAN OF FIRE More than a year.

SOUND: *A final crystalline tap.*

TANGLE Is that why you look youngest though you are the oldest of all?

MAN OF FIRE Yes, I can help you. I can help everyone.

TANGLE Can you tell me the way to the country from where –

MAN OF FIRE [*overlapping*] – from where the shadows fall? Yes, I go there sometimes. I will show you how to go.

TANGLE Don't send me into that great heat again!

MAN OF FIRE No need. Let me touch your heart with my cool hand ... Now you may walk through the world's flaming core and not feel sore. When I open this gate, go forward!

SOUND: *Loud thunder gives way to:*

MUSIC: *A hot blaze of sound, going on for a while and receding, rather than fading, into the shadow-plain music which also fades.*

SCENE 22

SOUND: *Dragging, limping footsteps, drawing closer but not getting very loud.* MOSSY*'s old voice is heard, punctuated by pauses.*

MOSSY A steep path. Rough door. A tunnel ... I seem to have passed this way before ...

SOUND: *Footsteps echo, but not the voice, which is too low.*

MOSSY If this ... tunnel leads ... to a forest ...
I have spent ...
Half my life returning the way I went.
What sound is that?

SOUND: *Footsteps stop. Faint sea-storm noises.*

MOSSY Wind among leaves? ... No.

SOUND: *Footsteps continue. Storm gets louder.*

MOSSY No, it is wind and waves ... another door.
And now it is evening ... [*raising voice*]
Evening on the stormy shore.

SOUND: *Storm of wind and waves.*

MOSSY [*loudly*] Sir!

MAN OF THE SEA [*loudly*] Yes?

MOSSY [*loudly*] I am looking ... for the Old Man ...
of the Sea!

MAN OF THE SEA [*loudly*] I am he.

MOSSY But ... I see a strong kingly man ...
in middle age.

MAN OF THE SEA [*loudly*] Your sight is better than most,
young man!

MOSSY [*in a low puzzled voice, in a lull*] Young?

MAN OF THE SEA [*loudly*] In such a storm you had better
rest in my house. It is just here.

SOUND: *Door opens.*

MAN OF THE SEA Step inside.

SOUND: *Door shuts, storm stops.*

MAN OF THE SEA You must bathe. Let me help you
undress.

MOSSY Thank you Sir. These rags soon come off.

MAN OF THE SEA Come through this arched door.

SCENE 23

MUSIC: *Very restful – the music of* TANGLE*'s bath.*

MAN OF THE SEA Climb down three steps.
Rest on the bath's sandy floor.
Lie at length in the best water of all.

MOSSY [*drowsily*] I lie between tall flowers, green and white. This water spreads through me like sleep.

MAN OF THE SEA What do you clutch in your hand?

MOSSY Mm? [*amused*] I'd forgotten that. Look!

MUSIC: *Key note.*

MAN OF THE SEA [*with respect*] The Golden Key!

MOSSY [*sadly*] Yes. But I never could find the lock.

MAN OF THE SEA How do you feel?

MOSSY Very old. And my feet ache.

MAN OF THE SEA Do they really?
Pause.

MOSSY [*young and surprised again*] No! They don't.
I feel no pain.
I feel calm and strong.

MAN OF THE SEA You are young again.
You have tasted death. Is it good?

MOSSY It is better than life!

MAN OF THE SEA No, it is only more life. [*at a distance*]
I will leave you to sleep.

MOSSY Is it right to sleep in a bath?

MAN OF THE SEA [*at a distance*] In this bath, yes.
Goodnight.

MUSIC: *ends.*

SCENE 24

SOUND: *Fade in of brisk waves on shore, with wind. The voices of* **MAN OF THE SEA** *and* **MOSSY** *fade in, both of them vigorous and brisk.*

MAN OF THE SEA It looks like another stormy day.

MOSSY I like that rough sea.

MAN OF THE SEA What is forming on the dark horizon?

MOSSY The rainbow!

MUSIC: *Distant chords of the rainbow tune are heard among the wave noises.*

MOSSY From a patch of glittering waves on the dark horizon, the rainbow curves up to a blue flaw in the sky. Can that be the other end of the rainbow that gave me the key?

MAN OF THE SEA Why not walk over and see?

MOSSY Can I?

MAN OF THE SEA Your feet will make no holes in the water now.

MOSSY Will you come too?

MAN OF THE SEA I'll stroll with you part of the way.
Step out!

MUSIC: *Wild water, like* **TANGLE***'s plunging river, but brisk rather than terrible, and more regular.*

MOSSY [*laughing*] This is a strange feeling ...

MAN OF THE SEA Like walking on the back
of galloping horses. You seem to have the knack.
We are moving too fast to sink in the sliding waves.

MOSSY Why don't we reel in this buffeting air?

MAN OF THE SEA We're too solid.

MOSSY Our eyes are not blinded by spray!

MAN OF THE SEA We see too clear.

MOSSY But we get no nearer.
Horizon and rainbow recede.

MAN OF THE SEA It's a habit they have. And look!
That little black rock!

MOSSY A black rock in the waves before the rainbow foot.
It grows as we draw close,
it is a mile, it is many miles high!
It is a mountain shutting out the sky!

MUSIC: *The plunges of* **TANGLE***'s boiling river are heard, but plunging up, rather than down.*

MAN OF THE SEA The sky and the rainbow too.

MOSSY Can we walk round it?

MAN OF THE SEA You can't. You must walk through.

MOSSY [*sighing*] Through.

MAN OF THE SEA Above where the breakers rise and fall,
do you see a narrow ledge?

MOSSY Barely.

MAN OF THE SEA Do you see something else
on that dark rock wall?

MOSSY Nothing but a sparkle of blue.

MAN OF THE SEA Sapphires, round a keyhole edge.

MOSSY [*alert*] Keyhole?

MAN OF THE SEA [*kindly*] That's right. Up you go!

MOSSY Can I climb so high?

MAN OF THE SEA Let a breaker lift you up.
Step onto the ledge before it begins to drop.

MOSSY [*determined*] Right! Goodbye *good* friend!

MAN OF THE SEA [*far off*] Goodbye!

MUSIC: *A long breaker rises to a dizzy height, and stops.*

MOSSY [*loud and firm*] Now! ... The ledge.
The keyhole and! The key!

MUSIC: *Keynote sounds.*

MOSSY [*voice over*] I turn it. And!

MUSIC: SOUND: *Keynote ends and hollow rumble starts.*

MOSSY [*voice over*] The rock wall falls back before me!

SOUND: *Hollow rumble ends in bang, but too loud. Echoing footsteps start, not too loud.*

MOSSY [*voice over*] I cross ... an arched ... porch.
I enter ... a long hall, like a church.

SOUND: *Footsteps stop.*

SCENE 25

MOSSY A line of seven columns upholds the vaulted roof.
On the pedestal of one a woman sits,
with face resting on knees.
Her hair has grown to her feet,
it ripples like golden water ... Excuse me, please,
may I see your face? ...
[*awed*] How beautiful you are, Tangle!

TANGLE [*gladly*] Am I? I've waited for you so long.
And you are like the strong man of the sea.
No! Like the old man of the earth.
No! Like the oldest man of all,
and yet you are my young Mossy!

MOSSY And you are like your Grandmother, noble and tall.

TANGLE [*tenderly*] Do you still have the key?

MOSSY Yes! Tangle, it's getting dark. There are no windows. The rock door has shut.

TANGLE [*calmly*] Then the moon will soon shine through the columns. They are hollow and lead to the sky.
MUSIC: *Rising moon music, going on to the end.*
MOSSY Yes. They begin to glow. One violet. One blue.
TANGLE Green, and yellow –
MOSSY Orange –
TANGLE Red –
MOSSY And a nameless colour, most beautiful of all!
MUSIC: *Moon music mingles with ascending rainbow music.*
TANGLE Delicate colours, distinct, yet all blending –
MOSSY Silently burning –
TANGLE Lovely forms in them rising
as though ascending a winding stair.
MOSSY This is the real rainbow end.
Look there at the nameless colour column!
TANGLE Sapphires gleam round a little slit.
MOSSY I am putting the key in, and turning it.
MUSIC: *Key note.*
TANGLE The key vanishes. An open door appears.
MOSSY Give me your hand. We climb –
TANGLE – Climb through the roof,
up the rainbow into the sky.
MOSSY The earth spreads below like a carpet –
TANGLE woven with sea and land –
MOSSY like a moist and blue green ball!
TANGLE Like a jewel!
MOSSY We are climbing to the country –
TANGLE and **MOSSY** From where the shadows fall.
MUSIC: *ends, having blended rainbow and shadow-music triumphantly.*

ANNOUNCER And I think by now they will have reached the country from which the shadows fall. The play of the Golden Key was adapted from etc by etc with music specially written by Wilma Paterson, and produced by etc etc.

IN 1976 I RECEIVED the production script of *my* play for Granada's *Queen Victoria's Scandals* series, but it was not quite my own play though my name was given as the author. Prince's diaries describe his dealings with a Welsh labourer's wife dying peacefully, because she is a Christian, and her parson has told her she will go to Heaven. Prince persuades her she will go to Hell unless she discovers Christ through *him*. My dramatization of this terrible scene had been made more lurid. An addition had the woman's husband (who had never actually intervened) threaten Prince who recoils, falls, pierces his hands "on an agricultural implement," then stands up displaying them like The Crucified One. Other, smaller changes for the worse had been made, all of them against the terms of my contract with Granada arranged by Frances Head. This declared that no changes could be made to the original script without consulting its author. Alas, Frances was dead, so I wrote a polite letter to Michael Cox, the producer.

It said that production delay had led to the script reaching me in a distorted form that needed more work on it; however, we were both intelligent men and would soon sort things out through discussion. Having received the script on Friday morning I wrote my letter in the afternoon, signed it but before posting read the production schedule. It told me that the first rehearsal would be held on the coming Monday morning at 9 o'clock in London – too late to discuss correcting the script. If I borrowed money from one of my friends, bought a weekend train ticket to London and turned up at the rehearsal, I could only make myself uselessly unpleasant to a producer, director, many actors and a large team of camera, sound and continuity experts who only wished to earn their living by starting their usual job. That I would be legally right to interfere was irrelevant. The producer had certainly breached the contract, but getting a lawyer to threaten Granada with a court case would lead to a huge expense of emotional energy and time, whether I won the case or not. If Frances Head had not died I could have left the matter to her. All I did was add a postscript to my letter, congratulating Cox on his political acumen in sending me the script so soon before the production, and threatening Granada with a law suit if it advertised me as the author. I ended by saying: "Before signing this letter I called you intelligent. I no longer believe that. You may have the cunning to prosper in your chosen trade, but you lack the intelligence to do well in it." In 1976 it was possible to send from any British post office things called *telegrams*, short messages that couriers would deliver by hand within an hour of being sent. I made sure that both producer and director would be handed telegrams on Monday morning, repeating that my name must not be attached to this play. I knew this would make my future as a TV playwright unlikely, but would have felt worse had I not done it. Martin Green was given as the author's name when *Belovèd* was finally televised.

With no more work from Scottish BBC Radio or from English television I had to find another source of income. Labour Exchanges were now obsolete, so I applied to a local Job Centre and before the end of the year became head of the Glasgow Arts Centre's painting department. The Centres had started in the 1960s when several teachers of music, drama, crafts and painting decided that too many children lacked artistic opportunities, and decided to provide these without being paid. On Saturday mornings and a weekday evening they held classes in a central Glasgow school and two outer ones. Parents and teachers with cars gave lifts to children from districts with bad bus services. This kindly organisation was busy, popular and publicised. Firms and foundations donated money. So did Glasgow District Council. In 1973 it also gave a former school beside the Kingston motorway bridge for use as headquarters. In that year the Glasgow Arts Centres Trust was formed, a limited liability company and registered charity, and therefore untaxed. One of the music teachers became a full-time salaried director. My son had attended that place in 1973 when, as a visiting parent, I found it muddled, noisy and cheerful. The other parents I met were professional folk like me, so I assumed that children of needier parents were still being given art classes in housing scheme schools. When I was employed by the Trust, all teaching was now confined to the building intended as headquarters.

This now had two arts directors. The first was now solely responsible for organising musical festivals and tours abroad, and his wife (who had no teaching qualifications) was the salaried director of all other art teaching. I and seven new teachers taken on at the same time cost the Trust nothing – our wages were paid by a government Jobs Creation Scheme devised to reduce unemployment, of which there was much. If a boss persuaded a civil service inspector that more employees would do socially useful work, extra staff would be paid by the government. Our first staff meeting at the Centre was a merry one. The arts director told us she regretted being unable to provide a staff room or much in the way of equipment, but was sure that our skill and enthusiasm would compensate for lack of them. She said that with more money she would willingly give us, not only a staff room, but a rumpus room like those some Japanese firms provided. In the rumpus room dissatisfied employees were encouraged to relieve frustrations by battering effigies of their bosses with clubs.

In the next few days I and the rest of the new staff were puzzled by an absence of much to do. I and my staff of two had an afternoon art class for retired folk, one evening class for older local schoolboys, a Saturday mixed class for school children and nothing else. I painted signs for a vegetarian restaurant held in one of the schoolrooms and painted scenery for a Christmas pantomime produced by our director. Pleased with the scenery, I suggested that the teacher of photography make a record of it. He told me that would cost his department money he could ill afford, and the next day a note from our director told me I should not give orders to people outside my own department. Most of the departments seemed as underemployed as mine. Robert Lacey, music teacher, gave occasional piano lessons to single pupils, one being the son of Sir William Gray, Glasgow's Lord Provost and Labour Party chief. Robert knew I had been a playwright. After our first staff meeting he approached me and on a mysterious note murmured, "I give you the subject of an opera – *The Rumpus Room*!" I thought this a strange and shallow idea, but in the following weeks it took root. Scottish industries were closing faster and faster, usually after asset-stripping by managements who were shifting their industries down to England or overseas. I discussed the opera with Robert in lunch breaks, and also on visits to Heatheryhaugh Cottage where he lived with his wife Marion among fields near the upper windings of the Clyde.

Early in 1977 someone told me that my Socratic play *The Gadfly* was advertised that week in the *Radio Times*, with the poet Christopher Logue in the part of Socrates. I decided to watch it on a friend's television set, discovered it was not being shown in Scotland, so never learned how close it was to my original script. I left Glasgow Arts Centre soon after, finding that payment for idleness was bad for me. I survived by painting a mural in a restaurant in return for meals until Elspeth King, curator of the People's Palace Local History Museum, got me an honestly earned Jobs Creation wage by making me Glasgow's official Artist Recorder. By then Robert Lacey had also resigned from the Glasgow Arts Centre, in order to complete our opera.

When the libretto was finished to both our satisfactions Robert contacted interested musician friends in the Scottish National Orchestra, then he and I met John Baraldi, American director of a drama group for young people in Bridgeton, by Glasgow Green. This group later supplied most of the actors for Bill Forsyth's first film, *That Sinking Feeling*. Baraldi took a copy of the libretto, said he would seek funding to allow Robert time to compose the music, and we heard no more from him. Robert's wife grew pregnant with their first child so he gave up all thought of a musical career and became a social worker for the Red Cross.

CAST IN ORDER OF APPEARANCE

THE UNION A chorus wearing overalls, the women with headscarves

SHARD A shop steward – bass baritone
Dynamic, radical, wearing blue suit under khaki dust coat.

JENNIE CLARK An orders clerk – soprano
A plain, quiet girl who asks questions. She wears a simple skirt and sweater in black, white or grey, with no jewellery.

STANLEY ORGER An orders manager – tenor [high]
A worried ageing family man wearing a knitted waistcoat.

BILL PRODMAN A production manager – tenor
A dynamic manager wearing a plain white shirt and blue tie.

MRS ADHEAD Head accountant – alto
Mature and sceptical. She is fashionably dressed, perhaps spectacled.

HENRY DICTOR A managing director – high baritone
Aristocratic, relaxed, ageless.

GLENDA Dictor's secretary – light soprano
JENNIE's age, but sexy and highly decorative.

SINGLE SET

On the right a staircase, broad at the base, narrows upward to the platform which is **DICTOR***'s office. This contains* **DICTOR***'s desk, with telephone and potted flower on it,* **GLENDA***'s desk, with telephone and typewriter, a coatstand with* **DICTOR***'s coat, hat and scarf on it, and a low easy-chair for visitors.*

On the left, but hidden by a curtain when the opera opens, is the rumpus room – a floor strewn with large cushions surrounding a seven or eight foot dummy of **DICTOR***, with a weighted hemispherical base which lets it rock when pushed. There is also an open tea-chest containing nine coloured cudgels like baseball bats, and four revolvers with gunbelts and holsters.*

At the back, on a slightly raised dais, are the Orders and Accountancy offices. Orders is two desks, edge to edge and side by side, a telephone and In and Out tray on each. Accountancy is a single desk with telephone.

The **CHORUS** *start and end the opera sitting in the front row of the stalls. Seven or eight have lunch-boxes under their seats. They must be able to move easily on and off stage.*

ACT 1

A section of **CHORUS** *begins softly, without orchestra.*

CHORUS 1
Blunka blonka, blunka blonka, blunka blonka, sweev-zoop!
Blunka blonka, blunka blonka, blunka blonka, sweev-zoop!
Blunka blonka, blunka blonka, blunka blonka, sweev-zoop!

CHORUS 2 [*joining in*]
Slup! Gob! Slup! Gob! Slup! Gob! Churrrrge.
Slup! Gob! Slup! Gob! Slup! Gob! Churrrrge.
Slup! Gob! Slup! Gob! Slup! Gob! Churrrrge.

CHORUS 3 [*joining in*]
Idellybidelly idellybidelly idellybidelly *tok*!
Idellybidelly idellybidelly idellybidelly *tok*!
Idellybidelly idellybidelly idellybidelly *tok*!

SHARD *addresses the* **CHORUS.**

SHARD Listen brothers!
Don't get alarmed, but your jobs are threatened.
There's a cut-back in production
and redundancies are threatened.
A ban on overtime is the sensible solution –
You trust me, don't you?

VOICES FROM CHORUS No! Yes! No!

SHARD Of course you trust me!
Don't get angry yet, the Union
Is doing all it can, but it isn't easy.

JENNIE *and* **ORGER** *sit facing each other across their desks, each with a telephone receiver in their left hand,* **JENNIE** *with a pencil poised above a pad in her right.*

JENNIE How much? When?
[*nods and writes*]
Yes we can ... How much? When?
[*nods and writes*]
Yes, certainly we can ...
How much? When?
[*nods and writes*]
Yes we can ...

ORGER I regret however, a union dispute
has delayed the last consignment.

JENNIE Yes we can –

ORGER I regret an unexpected breakdown
has delayed the last consignment.
Not for long of course. How long?

JENNIE I'm *sure* we can.

ORGER Can't say how long. No.
I'm sorry. No, it isn't easy.

JENNIE Yes, I'm told we can.
How much?

ORGER I'm sorry. No. It isn't easy.

MRS ADHEAD *sits at her desk listening sceptically to* **PRODMAN** *who sits on the edge of it, discoursing to her.*

PRODMAN We must buy more space, more time
And tell the housewife what we have to give.
We must buy more space, more time
And tell the nation what we have to give.
We must buy more space, more time and tell the universe –

MRS ADHEAD [*interrupting*]
It isn't easy. Time and space cost money.
The budget can't afford it.

PRODMAN No it isn't easy.

ORGER [*on phone*]
Sorry. No. I'm sorry no.

JENNIE [*putting phone down*] I don't see how we can.

PRODMAN *stands and addresses the world.*

PRODMAN To expand, to expand,
We need more markets to command, to expand.

MRS ADHEAD We must create a new demand, to expand.

ORGER [*on phone*]. A union dispute
has delayed the last consignment.

SHARD Redundancies are threatened.
A ban on overtime is the sensible solution.
You trust me don't you?

VOICES FROM CHORUS No! Yes! No!

SHARD Of course you trust me!
The Union
Is doing all it can, but –

ORGER [*loudly on phone*] I'm sorry, no. I'm sorry no!

MRS ADHEAD Time and space cost money.
The budget can't afford it.

PRODMAN [*running hand through hair*] No, it isn't easy –

ORGER [*slamming phone down*] Isn't easy –

SHARD [*pointing at the chorus*] It isn't easy –

PRODMAN, **ORGER**, **SHARD** [*slowly and loudly*]
It's bloody difficult!

The three men slump despondingly, chins on fists. The women quietly write. The highest level is illuminated where **DICTOR***, in leather gloves, stands refreshing the potted flower on his desk from a* *toy watering can. His back is towards* **GLENDA** *who is typing, silently and balletically, her fingers not touching the keys.*

DICTOR [*thoughtfully watering*]
I'm not blind. I'm not deaf.
Things are not quite what they should be.
I'm not deaf. I'm not blind.
Glenda!

GLENDA Sir?

DICTOR Is there someone I should see?

GLENDA The production manager
Has asked for an appointment.

DICTOR I am not Napoleonic,
But send for him at once.

GLENDA [*standing*] You're mistaken Sir.

DICTOR [*looking around at her*] Oh?

GLENDA [*ardently*] You *are* Napoleonic Sir.

DICTOR [*smiling*] Perhaps I am Napoleonic,
So send for him at once.

GLENDA *steps to the head of the stairs and claps her hands twice.* **PRODMAN** *looks up. She beckons, then returns to her desk.* **PRODMAN** *ascends briskly.* **DICTOR** *sets down can, removes gloves, and graciously shakes hands.*

DICTOR Hello Bill!

PRODMAN Hello Henry, there's a crisis in the –

DICTOR Have a seat!

PRODMAN No thanks Henry, I think better on my feet.
We've an urgent problem with the –

DICTOR [*offering case*] Cigarette?

PRODMAN No thanks.

DICTOR Mind if I do?

PRODMAN Not at all. We've trouble with the union.

DICTOR [*sitting on the edge of his desk*]
You'll give yourself an ulcer Bill!
Learn to relax. Sit down!
Sit down and tell me all about it.

PRODMAN *sits reluctantly down.* **DICTOR** *lights cigarette.*

PRODMAN A strike is threatened.

DICTOR Of course. Of course.

PRODMAN The shop steward called a meeting and –

DICTOR No details please. I manage things much better when I don't quite know the details.

PRODMAN The orders manager tells me that –

DICTOR [*raising a finger*]
What people tell you doesn't matter.
It's what they do that matters.

PRODMAN Orders have been cancelled!
The advertising budget is –

DICTOR [*stands*] No details Bill! I am not Napoleonic
so don't bother me with details.
I want you to relax –
you're quivering with tension. Breathe slowly!
Think of what you have to say, and then –
in just one sentence – put me in the picture.
He looks admiringly at his flower.

DICTOR Take your time – there's no hurry.

PRODMAN *drops his face into his hands.*

CHORUS 1 [*softly*] There's no hurry, there's no hurry,
there's no hurry ...

DICTOR *flicks a speck of dust from a leaf.*

DICTOR Are you ready?

CHORUS 2 Are you ready? Are you ready? Are you ready?

PRODMAN [*not lifting head*] Yes.

DICTOR Well?

PRODMAN [*looking up*] If something isn't done quickly
the firm will fall to pieces.

CHORUS 3 Fall to pieces! Fall of pieces! Fall to pieces!

DICTOR I see –
Complete silence from **CHORUS**

DICTOR – we need a rumpus room.

PRODMAN [*startled*] *A* what?

ALL THE CHORUS A rumpus room! A rumpus room!
A rumpus room!

PRODMAN [*loudly, over chorus*] A rumpus room?

DICTOR A rumpus room!

CHORUS [*crescendo*] A rumpus room! A rumpus room!
A rumpus room! A rumpus room!
A rumpus room! A rumpus –

LOUDSPEAKER [*interrupting*] Hoot! Hoot! The sixty-minute
lunch-break is starting in ten seconds.

TABLEAU *Everyone stands frozen. A five second chime sounds.*

LOUDSPEAKER Hoot! Hoot! The sixty-minute lunch and
recreation break begins precisely – [*pause*] – Now!

SOUND: *a long gone note.*

A pause, then the **CHORUSES** *stand and stretch, take lunch boxes from under their seats, then in twos and threes climb onto the stage. Some sit on the foot of the stairs, others stand chatting for a moment. Perhaps someone switches on a transistor radio.*

Meanwhile **SHARD** *strolls over to* **JENNIE** *and begins a gallant conversation.* **ORGER** *puts heels on desk and reads a newspaper.* **MRS ADHEAD** *stands and begins a narcissistic little dance.* **GLENDA** *makes up her face from a compact.* **DICTOR** *takes* **PRODMAN***'s arm and leads him downstairs and across the stage to the curtains, pausing to give an affable word to anyone he encounters. They respond uneasily.*

PRODMAN [*before the curtains, shrugging*]
I'm sorry Henry. I don't understand.
DICTOR Don't worry Bill. I'll show you.

He snaps his fingers. The curtains part. **PRODMAN** *gazes at the dummy. Gradually the rest stop what they're doing and gaze too.*

PRODMAN I still don't understand.
DICTOR Then wait till I explain it to the others.
I am not Napoleonic, but I never say things twice.
Please dispose of this. [*hands* **PRODMAN** *cigarette*].
DICTOR *addresses the company.*
DICTOR Ladies and gentlemen –
Or may I call you fellow workers?
I interrupt your hard-earned hour of recreating
But to enrich it with an innovation.
This entertaining doll if vigorously handled,
May give amusement to us all.
Exercise too!
He pushes the effigy. It rocks.
Almost a portrait, isn't it?
ORGER [*shocked*] Oh no Sir! It's not a bit like you!
DICTOR [*gravely*] I hope that isn't true.
It's meant to be like me.
ORGER [*hastily*] On second thoughts, it is a bit like you.
Almost a portrait!
PRODMAN I still don't understand.
SHARD What use is it?
DICTOR Mr Shard, this is a bad time for our firm.
SHARD That isn't news to me.
DICTOR How could it be?
Computerization has not made us more efficient
Or entry into Europe more competitive.
Decimalization did not lower our costs.
Besides, the work is boring and repetitive.
At every level there's a feeling of frustration.
Is that not so?
ORGER No!
SHARD Yes!
PRODMAN, JENNIE, ADHEAD Yes!
CHORUS Yes!
ORGER [*uncomfortably*] Well, just a bit.
DICTOR Yet our product is a thing the whole world needs
– It's safe, quick, cheap and strong.
It used to be a household word,
So what went wrong?
Don't answer right away.
Pause. Relax. Reflect.
Then tell me in one word, or maybe two,
What strikes you as the cause.
Part-song for five voices and **CHORUS.**
GLENDA Inflation.
ORGER Taxation.
ADHEAD The administration
Has lost all connection with the real situation.
PRODMAN Our machines are old fashioned
And should be renewed.
SHARD The wages are too low
And must be reviewed.
GLENDA Because of inflation!
ORGER Because of taxation,
Inflation, taxation and red infiltration!
PRODMAN Our machines are too slow –
SHARD – And our wages too low.
CHORUS 1 And our wages too low.
CHORUS 2 And our wages too low.
CHORUS 2 & 3 And our wages too low.
WHOLE CHORUS And wages and wages and wages too low!
End of part-song.
DICTOR [*raising his hands*] I know! Believe me, I know!
Let me put the question in another way.
There's someone in the firm you ought to blame.
Who is that? We're all friends here, I hope.
Please don't be afraid to say the name.
People look at each other suspiciously, then **PRODMAN** *points at* **SHARD**.
PRODMAN Him!
DICTOR No.
SHARD [*pointing at* **PRODMAN**] him!
DICTOR Oh no.
ORGER [*worried*] You surely don't mean me?
DICTOR Of course not. *I* am he.
Half my work is to be blamed for everything.
Don't you agree?
SHARD [*scratching head*] Well, it ought to be.
DICTOR But blame is not enough! It needs expression.
[*He waves at the effigy*]
This indoors game provides release
For everybody's feelings of aggression.

JENNIE What indoor game?

DICTOR I call it knock the boss. Pass these round.

He lifts the sticks from the box and gives them to **GLENDA** *and* **MRS ADHEAD**, *who distribute them among the* **CHORUS** *and* **SOLOISTS**, *excepting* **DICTOR**. *Some examine the sticks frowningly, some wield them experimentally like golf-clubs or baseball bats.*

SHARD [*grinning and waving his stick*] This is kids' stuff!

DICTOR We're all children at heart. The rules are simple.
Choose partners and divide in two groups,
half to the right and half to the left. Come now,
choose your partners and Knock the Boss.

Amused and good-humoured, the company pair off, **ORGER** *going for* **MRS ADHEAD**, **PRODMAN** *for* **GLENDA**, **SHARD** *for* **JENNIE**. *They group themselves for a dance in which each couple – or a partner of each couple – has a turn at whacking the effigy in time to the music.* **DICTOR** *stands to one side like a master of ceremonies. Perhaps he climbs the stairs a few steps.*

DICTOR Are you ready?

DICTOR*'s hoedown, with* **CHORUS** *and interruptions*

DICTOR It used to be
a basic right
to knock the boss
when he wasn't in sight.

CHORUS It used to be
a basic right
To knock the boss
when he wasn't in sight.

DICTOR Things are better now –
I'll tell you why!
You can knock my image
with me standing by!

CHORUS Things are better now –
he's told us why,
We can knock his image
while he's standing by!

SHARD [*bawls cheerily*] All thanks to the Unions, of course.

DICTOR [*saluting* **SHARD** *cheerfully*]
White collars and machine hands
share this game.
It's easy to be friendly
with a boss to blame.

CHORUS White collars and machine hands
share this game.
It's easy to be friendly
with a boss to blame.

DICTOR If you can make me touch the ground
you get the chance of another time around.
Everybody enjoys a strike,
so strike strike strike
as hard as you like!

CHORUS Everybody enjoys a strike,
so strike strike strike
as hard as you like!

PRODMAN [*shouting*] Our favourite sport!

ADHEAD [*shouting*] Watch it on television every weekend!

The rhythm of the dance increases.

DICTOR Now the money you earn buys less and less,
you wife's on valium, your home's a mess,
your home's a mess and your children smoke
and seem to think you're some sort of joke.
The street where you live is far from clean,
the graffiti on the wall get more obscene,
the Government claims it's doing its best
but that doesn't help so you feel depressed.
You feel depressed, you want to scream,
you must find some way to let off steam:
only a criminal likes knocking other men so
knock my image!
Knock my image!
Knock my image!
Batter it again!

CHORUS Knock his image!
Knock his image!
Knock his image!
Batter it again!

DICTOR Now everybody feels just great –
we can all be cheerful with a boss to hate.
Smash it into bits if you can –
I can always replace a plastic man!

CHORUS Smash it into bits if we can –
He can always replace a plastic man!

End of Hoedown.

The **CHORUS** *attack the image altogether, pulling it onto its side, holding it down and hitting it, with much laughter. The soloists stand watching.* **ORGER** *calls to* **DICTOR**.

ORGER No hard feelings, Mr Dictor.

DICTOR [*joining them*] None! It's this kind of give-and-take that keeps Britain stable. Perhaps the game will be more fun if some of you pretend to defend. Who would like to lead a defence?

ADHEAD Isn't that your job Mr Dictor?
DICTOR No no. I'm neutral. What about you Mr Shard?
SHARD [*grinning*] Not me. I lead the opposition.
DICTOR Excellent! What about you Bill?
PRODMAN Not today Henry.
DICTOR Never mind. Stanley is officer material. He'll stop them scratching my paint – eh Stanley?
ORGER [*pleased*] Certainly sir – if you think I'm up to it.

DICTOR *goes with* **PRODMAN**, **ORGER**, **ADHEAD** *and* **GLENDA** *to the properties box.* **SHARD** *goes to the* **CHORUS** *round the effigy.* **JENNIE** *stands mid-stage by herself looking worried.*

SHARD Break it up comrades! Break it up. We're going to use different tactics. Barricades!
Come on, I want a barricade along here.

The effigy is released. The **CHORUS** *pile cushions into a barricade. Some crouch behind, holding the sticks as if they were rifles. Those round the box take out pistols with holsters and put them on.*

SHARD [*shouting across*]
Over here Jennie. You're on our side aren't you?
JENNIE No!
ADHEAD [*holding up a pistol*] Come here Jennie, this is yours!
JENNIE No! ... Mr Dictor!
DICTOR, *helping* **GLENDA** *arm, seems not to hear.*
ORGER Don't be a spoil-sport Jennie.
JENNIE Mr Dictor!
ADHEAD It's only a game.
JENNIE [*very loudly*] Mr Dictor, you said ...
Everyone stops and stares at her.
JENNIE You said half your work was to be blamed for everything!
DICTOR Well?
JENNIE What is the other half?
SHARD [*coming beside* **JENNIE**] She's right! You're giving us a laugh. Is that all you mean to do?
Everyone looks at **DICTOR**.
PRODMAN Henry, what he says is true.
That can't be all you mean to do.
DICTOR [*looking at him*]
Et tu Brute?
It seems you all intend to recall me to my duty.
Glenda! Back to the office.
DICTOR *follows* **GLENDA** *towards the foot of the stairs.* **SHARD** *intercepts him.*
SHARD Back to the office? That's no answer!
What are you doing there?
DICTOR I don't need to answer that question –
CHORUS Oh! Oh! Oh!
DICTOR [*loudly*] – but an answer!
Silence
DICTOR But an answer seems only fair.
My main task is finance.
The only way our firm can regain health
is by a gigantic increase in everybody's wealth!
ORGER That's true!
The only way the firm can regain health
is by a gigantic increase in everybody's wealth!
JENNIE [*interrupting*] How will you get that?
SHARD Answer her!
DICTOR If you wish. [*climbs a step and turns*].
DICTOR*'s aria, with interruptions.*
DICTOR To some of you I seem aloof and far away.
Many people here have never seen me till today.
but please don't think my life is
just a round of idle play.
I'm waiting for a call from Copenhagen.
SHARD How will that help?
DICTOR The firm needs money. We all need money –
I know that you agree.
But who can raise that money?
Can you? Can they? Can she?
No. It must be someone the banks trust,
and that leaves only me,
leaves me waiting for a call from Copenhagen.
PRODMAN Why Copenhagen?
DICTOR Finance is international. Its links are very long.
African coffee is controlled
from an office in Hong Kong.
The world today is like a single vast machine
forged with Pittsburgh steel and fuelled
by oil from Aberdeen.
Every man's a brother,
we depend on one another.
I'm depending on a call from Copenhagen.
He climbs more steps then turns.
In my lonely office at the top I telephone. Dictate.
I am not Napoleonic. I don't feel very great.
But we also serve who only sit and wait –
Faithfully wait – hopefully, lovingly
wait for that call from Copenhagen.
He climbs to the top.

ORGER [*emotionally*] God bless you, Mr Dictor Sir!
DICTOR [*smiles down on them, says*] I'm afraid I'm keeping you off your lunch. [*sings*]

Things are in a mess just now and,
yes, the problem's mine.
I don't ask for your sympathy, I only ask for time,
time to organize assistance
which is coming down the line,
The line that links my desk to Copenhagen.
End of aria.

DICTOR *sits at his desk and gravely contemplates the telephone. From her own desk,* **GLENDA** *watches him adoringly.*

LIGHTS: *fades on the office as* **ORGER** *calls:*

ORGER Don't worry sir! We won't rock the boat!
[*to the rest*] Does nobody feel hungry?

SHARD [*to* **CHORUS**]
We're wasting time brothers. I'm going to eat.

SHARD *walks off quickly followed by* **ORGER**. **PRODMAN** *follows, scratching his head.* **MRS ADHEAD**, *unstrapping her gunbelt, goes and drops it in the bin. Amused, she says to* **JENNIE**:

ADHEAD Did you notice?
The two men forgot
to remove their weapons?

JENNIE There's something –
peculiar –
about this rumpus room.

They look at each other. The **CHORUS** *have settled down with their lunch boxes.*

INTERVAL

ACT 2

The **CHORUS** *sit round the stage, eating from lunch-boxes, smoking, or reading papers. One or two, on their feet, idly rock* **DICTOR**'*s image, but stop this when the action onstage becomes interesting.* **SHARD** *enters quickly through the audience, ignoring* **ORGER** *who hurries behind him.*

ORGER I don't care what you think Shard!
You're prejudiced.
Thank goodness for the boss, I say.
Thank goodness we still have men like him,
smooth but tough – a real commander!

SHARD A commander? [*to* **CHORUS**]
This idiot thinks the boss is a commander!
CHORUS *Some jeering.*

SHARD [to **ORGER**] The boss isn't a commander.
He isn't tough. He's just ... slippery.
PRODMAN *enters, wiping his lips with a napkin.*

PRODMAN He wasn't always like that.
He used to be a commander.
Remember those days?

SHARD [*nodding grimly*] Yes, I remember those days.
Trio for **PRODMAN**, **SHARD**, **ADHEAD**, *and* **CHORUS**

PRODMAN Once he was tough –
SHARD – Oh he was tough.
PRODMAN He told us what to do, in those days.
CHORUS In those days, in those days ...
PRODMAN [*to* **SHARD**] In those days he made mincemeat out of you.
SHARD That isn't true!
He gave hard knocks but
he could take them too – the bastard!
Me and the men knew how to fight them –
CHORUS In those days, in those days –
SHARD – Not now. Not now. He's too ... slippery.

MRS ADHEAD *and* **JENNIE** *quietly enter during this verse.*
MRS ADHEAD *steps forward.*

ADHEAD [*wistfully*] I was a young girl, in those days.
SHARD Loved him, did you?
ADHEAD [*nodding*] He was an easy man to love,
in those days.
CHORUS In those days, in those days.
SHARD [*accusing*] You liked the iron hand
inside the iron glove.
ADHEAD I loved his eagle eye, his habit of command.
His temper was appalling.
When you angered him
you felt the sky was falling.
He was all a boss should be.
He could frighten me –
CHORUS In those days, in those days –
ADHEAD Not now. Not now. He's too ... evasive.
PRODMAN [*passionately*] And the firm did well!
SHARD Not all that well –
PRODMAN [*aggressively*] Yes very well!
Although he gave us hell, in those days ...
CHORUS In those days, in those days –

PRODMAN Our merchant fleet sailed everywhere.
We owned a bank in every port.
When our goods moved into China
the Royal Navy sent a gunboat for escort.
CHORUS – in those days.
PRODMAN He commanded us –
CHORUS – in those days.
SHARD Me and the men knew how to fight then.
ADHEAD He was all a boss should be,
even though he frightened me.
PRODMAN He would never, never have suggested
a rumpus room –
CHORUS [*softly*] – in those days, in those days.
JENNIE [*softly*] Is there nothing we can do?
End of trio.
ORGER [*violently*] I'm sick of all this moaning!
SHARD You're sick all right.
ORGER If we stopped complaining and worked harder
things would improve and we'd earn more pay!
No wonder the boss isn't strong.
He can trust nobody –
[*to* **PRODMAN**] not even you!
And that's what's wrong.
PRODMAN Not true – I'm his man! [*thumps chest*]
But I can't trust him!
He seems to have no policy, no plan.
He'll hint at what we ought to do
but not support me when I put it through,
so all our schemes have failed.
He should be jailed – he's so evasive.
ORGER I'm sick and tired –
ADHEAD [*to* **JENNIE**] He does look rather tired.
ORGER I'm tired of pessimistic rot. [*waves paper*]
Read the firm's newsletter.
Things are getting better.
This month we've shown a profit.
ADHEAD No we've not.
ORGER It says so here!
We're half a million in the clear.
ADHEAD The firm has sold our factory in Spain
and the head office in Park Lane.
It's actually a loss, although it looks like gain.
ORGER [*unconsciously crumpling paper*] Loss?
JENNIE, **SHARD**, **PRODMAN** Loss – loss?
CHORUS [*standing up*] Loss?
EVERYONE How can a loss be a –
How can a loss look like a –
How can a loss be a gain?
ORGER [*flinging paper away*]
That doesn't mean a thing.
The old lion's in a corner,
but he's drawing back to spring
He's bought us time!
JENNIE But how is he using the time he's bought?
SHARD [*jeering*] He's waiting for phone calls!
He's built a rumpus room!
He might as well be boozing.
PRODMAN Mrs Adhead, you're the accountant.
How long can we last like this?
ADHEAD If nothing is radically changed
we'll be bankrupt in three weeks.
ORGER [*appalled*] Bankrupt!
SHARD [*maliciously*] Un ... Em ... Ployed.
ORGER Surely not the administration?
ADHEAD Everyone.
ORGER But we'll get compensation – won't we?
ADHEAD No. Reading between the lines –
OTHER SOLOISTS Yes?
ADHEAD – it seems to me –
OTHER SOLOISTS Yes?
ADHEAD – that we are faced –
OTHER SOLOISTS Yes?
ADHEAD – with total liquidation.
ORGER, *dazed, turns towards the dummy and appeals to it.*
ORGER Mr Dictor, Sir!
[*The dummy rocks towards him*]
You won't let that happen – will you?
SHARD [*coming beside* **ORGER**] Will you, Mr Dictor Sir?
[*The dummy rocks towards him*]
Yes, he'll let that happen.
ORGER *collapses face in hands.* **SHARD** *points to the dummy.*
Trio **SHARD**, **PRODMAN**, **ADHEAD**
SHARD He's an old man now.
He's made his pile.
He doesn't need to care –
if we go down the drain.
PRODMAN He can sit up in
his office building
castles in the air –
while we go down the drain.

ADHEAD He's forgotten where
our product's sold
and the buyers who take it.
SHARD He doesn't know, now,
how it's made,
or the workers who make it.
PRODMAN He won't support
a decent plan of
re – org – anization.
ADHEAD His one resort is
post – pone – ment and
pre – var – ication.
In fact it's clear – Mr Orger,
ORGER *looks up*
PRODMAN the firm would do better – Mr Orger,
SHARD if he wasn't here – Mr Orger.
ORGER [*hopelessly*] Then what can we do?
The **CHORUS,** *gathered round the stage in their three groups, face inward. Ignoring the soloists they sing "What Can We Do"* ***1st*** *verse.*
CHORUS What can we?
Can we do something?
Can we do nothing?
What can we?
What can we?
What can we do?
What can we do?
They continue chanting behind the soloists.
ADHEAD Unemployment stares us in the face!
SHARD I would call a strike meeting, but a strike
would hardly meet the case.
ORGER [*on his knees*] I'm not a young man anymore –
I was due for promotion.
Is this my reward,
for twenty-five years of devotion?
SHARD Yes, that's your reward
for twenty-five years of devotion.
He contemptuously flings a cushion at the image.
ORGER *collapses again.* **JENNIE** *goes to comfort him.*
2nd *"What Can We Do" verse.*
CHORUS Can we do nothing?
Can we do something?
Can we do anything, what?
anything, what?
Is there anything to do?

PRODMAN *approaches* **SHARD.**
PRODMAN I don't trust you, Shard.
SHARD Thanks. I don't trust you.
PRODMAN But if we worked together,
there might be something we could do.
SHARD You're paid too much to work along with me.
PRODMAN The situation's desperate.
It's hard today
to get a new job at my level,
unless you emigrate.
We two might just save the firm,
if we co-operate.
SHARD How can we co-operate?
They move towards the stairs, conferring, then climb to the first level office. **SHARD** *sits at a desk,* **PRODMAN** *sits on it, talking to him.* **SHARD** *sometimes nods, sometimes shakes his head.*
MRS ADHEAD *helps* **JENNIE** *lift* **ORGER** *up.*
3rd *"What Can We Do" verse.*
CHORUS How can we?
How can we?
When can we, what can we do?
What can we do?
ORGER I was never
unemployed in my life –
How will I tell this
to the wife?
ADHEAD Don't be such a small man, Stanley.
ORGER I know I'm small –
which makes me more than some
who think they they're so tall.
He said – [*points to dummy*]
– he would restore us, to health
by an increase in our wealth.
JENNIE Bosses often say that.
ADHEAD It's not new.
CHORUS But what can we do?
How can we, when can we, what? What? What?
What can we do?
End of "What Can We Do."
ORGER *breaks away from the women, points to the dummy.*
ORGER [*shouts*] I'll tell you what to do – Knock the boss!
The **CHORUS** *look at him.*
SOME CHORUS VOICES Knock – knock? Boss – boss?
ORGER Knock him right out of the game!
OTHER CHORUS VOICES Knock the boss?

WHOLE CHORUS Knock the boss!

ORGER *and a section of* **CHORUS** *grab clubs, and start battering the dummy, watched by the rest, some of them amused, some excited and encouraging.* **SHARD** *and* **PRODMAN**, *who are drafting a paper, pay no attention.* **MRS ADHEAD** *watches sardonically.* **JENNIE**, *horrified, clings to her side.*

Start of Fight with the Dummy.

ORGER Take that! You're selfish!

A STRIKER Greedy bastard! Take that!

OTHERS And that! And that ... And that and that.

ORGER You're stupid! Dense!

A STRIKER No more brains than a block of wood! No sense!

ORGER Take that!

ONLOOKERS Hooray! Hooray! Hooray! ...

A STRIKER He's ... not cracking. Take that!

OTHER STRIKERS Not cracking!

ONLOOKERS Put in the boot! Put in the boot!

A STRIKER Right! Here goes!

ONLOOKERS Hooray! Hooray!

STRIKER Yargh! Yarrooh! My foot! My foot!

He hops about, holding it. The **ONLOOKERS** *are amused.*

ORGER Stand back! Everyone stand back! I'm going to shoot!

ORGER *draws his revolver and aims it with both hands.* **MRS ADHEAD** *goes to him. The* **STRIKERS** *round the dummy scatter.*

ADHEAD Careful, Stanley – You'll hurt yourself.

ORGER [*desperately*] I'm a grown man!
Keep back! Here goes!

He fires. **JENNIE** *claps her hands to her ears.* **SHARD** *and* **PRODMAN** *stand up, staring.*

A STRIKER *advances, grabs* **ORGER**'*s free hand, and raises it above his head like a boxing referee.*

STRIKER Ladies and gentlemen – the winner! Hip! Hip! ...

CHORUS Hooray! ... Hooray! Hooray! ... Hooray!

The Fight with the Dummy ends

SHARD *grabs the pistol from* **PRODMAN**'*s holster and fires it over his head. The noise is much louder than* **ORGER**'*s pistol. Everyone turns and stares at* **SHARD**, *still holding aloft the smoking pistol.*

SHARD [*in a tremendous voice*]
Brothers!
Brothers, what's got into you all?
Playing at commandoes? [*he points*]
Shooting at a doll?
That's what the boss wants you to do!

ORGER [*waving his revolver*]
That's true! We should attack the man himself.

PRODMAN You're a fool, Stanley – be quiet.

PRODMAN *unstraps his holster.* **SHARD** *steps forward.*

SHARD Our job is to take the firm over –
not waste time on a riot.

SHARD *flings his pistol down on the floor.*

JENNIE, **ADHEAD** Take-over? Take-over?

VOICES FROM CHORUS Take-over? Take-over?

ORGER *drops his pistol and joins the* **CHORUS** *who cluster round* **PRODMAN** *and* **SHARD**, *who have gone mid-stage.*

Duet with Interruptions **PRODMAN** *and* **SHARD**

PRODMAN Please hear the proposals
Brother Shard puts to you –
to prevent the firm closing
there are things we must do.

SHARD Our director is a dummy
and so it's quite clear,
that the knowledge to run the business is
not up there but down here.
To dismantle a dummy
a gun is no good.
Take a screwdriver to it –
we've a use for the wood.

Some of the **CHORUS** *set about dismantling the dummy in a workmanlike way. A Marxist in the* **CHORUS** *raises his hand.*

MARXIST [*stammering*] Cocococomrade Shard,
a cucucucuquestion!

PRODMAN He hasn't finished yet.

SHARD To get some support
in attacking this mess,
we must tell the T.U.C.,
our M.P. and the press.

PRODMAN Mrs Adhead – Jennie – will you see to that?

ADHEAD *and* **JENNIE** *go to desks on stage 1, mime telephoning.*

MARXIST [*straining for attention*] Cocococomrade,
Cucomrade Shard, a cuquestion.

SHARD [*ignoring him*] And now brother Prodman has
something to say.

PRODMAN Our product's good, and not too dear
and if we supply it
fast enough to the consumer
the consumer will buy it.
To keep us all working
and get the work done
we must move very quickly
and all move like one.

VOICE FROM CHORUS How will you manage that?
SHARD The thing which prevents men
behaving like brothers
is that some of us are paid
a lot less than the others.
VOICE FROM CHORUS You can say that again!
PRODMAN We haven't time.
SHARD And so, to eliminate
envy and blame,
we propose, for the takeover,
that we're all paid the same.
OTHER VOICE Same as who?
MARXIST [*hand raised*] A cuquestion!
ORGER I've been here longest!
OTHER VOICE My needs are greatest!
PRODMAN The same, within limits.
OTHER VOICE What limits?
SHARD [*conclusively*]
We'll work that out later.
The problem is not
who will earn more than who,
but to stop us all joining
the unemployment queue.
ORGER That's true! That's true!
The problem is unemployment!
VARIOUS VOICES Unemploy – employ – unemployment
– ployment.
CHORUS The unemployment queue.
End of Duet.
MARXIST And now may I ask my cucuquestion?
JENNIE *and* **MRS ADHEAD** *put down their phones and stand.*
SHARD Go ahead.
MARXIST When will you kukick out
the dececadent
cucrypto-fascist cucucapitalist hyenas
from the cocommanding height of the ececec –
ecececececececececec –
VOICES FROM CHORUS Economy! When will you grasp
the economy?
SHARD Now. Lift that thing up.
He points to the dismantled dummy, whose head has been pulled out on the end of a long pole. **ORGER** *hurries across to help raise it like a standard.*
Ascent March: Marseillaise plus Blake's Jerusalem.
SHARD Arise, arise ye sons of industry!
JENNIE, **ADHEAD** Arise, arise ye sons of industry!
SHARD, **PRODMAN** Arise, arise ye sons of industry!
whose labour feeds our land,
who work with lever or computer,
with pencil or spanner in hand –
SHARD, **PRODMAN**, **JENNIE**, **ADHEAD**
With pencil or spanner in hand!
SHARD Why should some people at the top
decide that industry should stop?
PRODMAN When management becomes an idle show
We starve under it – or else we make it go!
SHARD, **PRODMAN** Arise arise! Seize control!
JENNIE, **ADHEAD** Arise! Arise!
SHARD, **PRODMAN** Why should we, not they, be on the dole?
JENNIE, **ADHEAD** Arise! Arise!
CHORUS Bring me my bow of burning gold!
JENNIE, **ADHEAD** Arise! Arise!
SHARD *and* **PRODMAN** *lead everyone upstairs in a series of stylised Soviet-poster-like tableaux. The dummy's head, carried by* **ORGER**, *is in the middle of the group.*
CHORUS Bring me my arrows of desire,
JENNIE, **ADHEAD** Arise! Arise!
SHARD, **PRODMAN**, **ORGER** When management's an idle show,
CHORUS Bring me my spear. Oh clouds unfold!
JENNIE, **ADHEAD** Arise! Arise!
SHARD, **PRODMAN**, **ORGER** We starve under it or make it go.
CHORUS Bring me my chariot of fire.
JENNIE, **ADHEAD** Arise! Arise!
SHARD, **PRODMAN**, **ORGER** Why should some people at the top,
CHORUS I will not cease from mental fight,
JENNIE, **ADHEAD** Arise! Arise!
SHARD, **PRODMAN**, **ORGER** Decide that industry must stop?
CHORUS Nor shall my sword –
JENNIE, **ADHEAD** Arise! Arise!
SHARD, **PRODMAN**, **ORGER** Arise! Seize control –
LOUDSPEAKER – Hoot! Hoot! The 60 minute recreation break
JENNIE, **ADHEAD** Arise! Arise!
SHARD, **PRODMAN**, **ORGER** Why should we,
not they be on the dole?
LOUDSPEAKER Is stopping in 10 seconds.
JENNIE, **ADHEAD** Arise! Arise!
SHARD, **PRODMAN**, **ORGER** March on! March on!
All hearts resolved –
Light shows **DICTOR***'s office. He sits, as we last saw him, gravely contemplating his phone, with* **GLENDA** *balletically typing.*

LOUDSPEAKER Hoot! Hoot! The 60 minute lunch, and
recreation break ... Ends exactly now.

CHORUS Nor shall my sword
Sleep in my hand
Till we have built –

JENNIE, **ADHEAD** Arise! Arise!

SHARD, **PRODMAN**, **ORGER**
All hearts resolved to build, to build –

SOUND: *gong*

CHORUS, **SHARD**, **PRODMAN**, **ORGER** Je – ru – sa – lem –

JENNIE, **ADHEAD** Je – ru – sa – lem –

EVERYONE In –

The phone rings on **GLENDA***'s desk. Instant silence.*

SHARD *and* **PRODMAN** *have reached the top. The phone rings again.* **GLENDA** *stops typing and picks it up.*

GLENDA [*to the phone*] Yes he is ... [*to* **DICTOR**] A call from
Copenhagen, Sir.

DICTOR [*standing up*] Put it through.
[*sits on the corner of his desk, pompomming the last line of Jerusalem, then lifts the phone.*]
Yes, hello ... Good. Yes ... Good. Yes ... Yes.
Good. Goodbye.
[*stands and smiles at* **SHARD** *and* **PRODMAN**.]
Please go on singing!
"Till we have built Je-ru-sa-lem in ..."
How does it go?

SHARD [*handing him the paper*] Read that list of demands.

PRODMAN The whole firm will back it.

DICTOR [*reading*]
Ah! ... Workers' control ... profit sharing. I see.
The usual thing. But it no longer concerns me.
While you were busy with your recreation
my share in the firm – a controlling share –
was bought by the Danish subsidiary
of a gigantic American corporation.

CHORUS [*to each other*] Corpor – orper – ation – ation?
Americation?

SHARD What difference will that make?

DICTOR I hope it gives the firm a new lease of life –

ORGER [*enthusiastic*] It must! With Americans in charge!

DICTOR Maybe not. They may close the factory down,
[*indicates the revolutionary* **CHORUS**.]
when they recognize the position.

JENNIE Why buy a factory then close it down?

DICTOR It reduces competition.

SHARD [*blustering*] We'll stage a work-in if they try to close us!

DICTOR Yes. A bit of old-fashioned socialism
might save the day.
Try it. [*hands back paper*]
I wish you all the best,
but I'm retiring from the fray.

DICTOR *goes to the coat-stand where* **GLENDA** *starts to religiously enrobe him in scarf, coat and hat.* **SHARD** *casts a worried glance at his following, who are looking at each other.*

UNRULY VOICES What are we doing? Shut down.
Work in? Now? Corporation-ation.
Good? Bad! When? What? How?

PRODMAN [*to* **SHARD**] The problem has acquired a
completely new dimension.

MARXIST Cucucomrade Shard, a cuquestion!

SHARD [*shouting over them*] Your attention brothers, please!
Your attention!

VOICE When do we seize control?

ORGER How long must I stand here
holding up this pole?

SHARD We can't seize power before we meet the new
People we're seizing it from.

VOICES Why not? What do we do?

SHARD We'll have to wait a bit.

VOICES Boo! ... Boo! ... Boo!

ORGER *lowers his pole. The* **CHORUS** *turn their backs on* **SHARD** *and leave the steps, muttering to each other.*

SHARD [*desperately*] The union cannot fight
the new bosses before we are able to
confront the new bosses.
Am I right?
Of course I'm right.

JENNIE [*desperately*] Then we've done nothing.

SHARD Don't say that –
the people showed their strength.
We moved as one, didn't we?
Yes, we moved as one.
[*suddenly sits down on the top step and covers his face with his hands.*]

CHORUS [*sombrely*] But nothing has been done.

DICTOR, *in scarf, hat and unbuttoned coat, addresses everyone sympathetically.*

DICTOR'S *solo with* **CHORUS** *"Nothing Done"*

DICTOR Ladies and gentlemen –
or may I call you fellow-workers?

Since I am leaving I would like to say
how favourably I have been impressed
by your conduct here today.

CHORUS But nothing has been done.

DICTOR As Shard –
as brother Shard has said,
you moved as one.
Nobody lost his head – [*points to dummy*]
except me, and that was just in fun.

CHORUS And nothing was done.

DICTOR Meanwhile, until you're new
director comes I'm leaving one of you
in charge. Bill Prodman here. Gooooo
dbye Bill! Do nothing I wouldn't do.
[*shakes* **PRODMAN***'s head, and retains it.*]

CHORUS Nothing was done. Nothing done.

DICTOR [*intimately*]
And Bill!
When everything here falls flat,
you'll have no trouble getting another job –
if you keep your nose clean.
I promise that.

PRODMAN [*shaking* **DICTOR***'s hand*] Thank you Henry.

He sits down soberly in **DICTOR***'s chair behind the desk.* **DICTOR** *pulls on his leather gloves and lifts the potted flower.*

The **CHORUS** *stand about the stage in groups of two and three.*

CHORUS [*muttering*]
A bastard ... a thorough bastard ...
Will he get away Scot free? ...
I'd like to give him something he'd remember ...
Do it! ... Give it to the bastard.
Perhaps I will. Let's see ...

DICTOR *descends the stairs, pausing beside* **SHARD**.

DICTOR Gooooooooodbye Shard. May I shake your hand?

SHARD No.

ORGER Shame! Shame!

DICTOR [*enthusiastically*]
It's not a shame! I respect a man with principles.
[*Passing* **ORGER**]
Good officer material, Stanley!
[*He passes* **MRS ADHEAD** *and* **JENNIE**]
Goodbye Mrs Adhead. Goodbye, er, Jennie?
Is that your name?
[*He threads his way through the* **CHORUS**, *who stand like statues stonily staring at him*]
Why, old Jock is it?
Still with us? I remember you
when I was so high ...
We're all Jock Tamson's bairns of course ...
Keep your noses clean ...
A man's a man for a' that ...
Gooooodbye ...

He stops before two stout young men with folded arms blocking who are the exit.

Er ... should I remember you?

ONE OF THE MEN [*grimly*] No. We're new.

DICTOR Delighted to have met you all the same.
Please give this to your wife.
[*hands him the potted flower, then turns to the company as if remembering something.*]
One final word!
I'm enough of a socialist myself
to sympathise with your fight for better things,
and when the country's economic plight
improves, I'm sure that everything
will be put right
meanwhile –
excuse me.

He turns and dodges out swiftly between the two men. Everyone gapes after him.

SHARD [*looking up with a bitter jeer*]
He's beaten us!
He's beaten us!
He's got everything he wanted.

CHORUS And we've done nothing, nothing.
Nothing has been done.

JENNIE [*to* **SHARD**] But why?
We all reached the top together as you planned –
Why didn't you take command?
Why did we stop?

SHARD Can you tell her, Prodman?

PRODMAN [*reasonably*]
The factory now belongs to people
too strong and far away for us to fight.
It's possible they'll stop it closing down
if we show them we can work all right.
By the way, the lunch break's over.

ORGER Thank goodness. I'm exhausted.

ORGER *and* **MRS ADHEAD** *descend the stairs and return to their desks.*

GLENDA *lays some papers before* **PRODMAN**, *who starts signing them.*

MARXIST [*hand raised*] Cucucucucucomrade Shard!
Cucucucucucomrade Shard!

SHARD [*roughly and loudly*]
Don't shout at me! I'm sick to death of questions.
If something new crops up I'll call a meeting.
Why not get back to work?
You want to work don't you?
Work is what it's all about.

The **CHORUS** *collect their lunch-boxes and leave for the stalls.* **SHARD** *remains sitting despondently on the steps.* **JENNIE** *has descended to the stage and stands in a puzzled way between fragments of* **DICTOR***'s dummy.*

SHARD [*glumly to himself*]
Yes. He won everything he wanted.
The men who manage money can do anything.
They're too deep for us,
too deep for us.

Suddenly **JENNIE** *sings.*

JENNIE A farmer is a deep man.
All of him knows the ground we live on,
draining, fencing,
seeding, breeding,
how grain and cattle, how food grows;
why it comes, where it goes,
all day and all night.

SHARD *looks at her and* **ORGER** *says:*

ORGER Come on Jennie. We've had our fun.

Again **JENNIE** *sings.*

JENNIE An engineer is a deep man.
All of him knows the metal we live by,
Mining, smelting,
Forging, welding,
The tools that make our clothes and houses
That heat and light
Our rooms and roads
All day and all night.

SHARD *stands up and sings with her.*

SHARD A financier's the deepest man of all!
JENNIE Not very deep.
SHARD He knows the money we live by ...
JENNIE Phoning banks, phoning brokers,
SHARD What fields go under concrete ...
JENNIE Phoning banks, phoning brokers,
SHARD When factories will close ...
JENNIE Signing cheques, phoning brokers,
SHARD Why a city grows, and withers ...
JENNIE Phoning councillors and brokers,
SHARD And nations decay ...
JENNIE Reading small print very closely,
SHARD And wars begin ...
JENNIE Transferring capital to Switzerland –
SHARD, JENNIE All night and all day.

CHORUS [*softly*] All day, all night. All day, all night.
All day, all night.

PRODMAN [*looking up briefly*] Lunch break's over, Jennie!

ORGER [*plaintively*] Help me Jennie!

CHORUS 1 [*softly*] All day, all night. All day, all night.
All day, all night.

JENNIE *goes to her desk and* **SHARD** *descends the stair talking broodingly to himself.*

SHARD The men who own the money own the folk
who make things.
Has it always been this way?

JENNIE [*sitting down*] No. It hasn't.

SHARD Will it always be this way?

CHORUS 1 All day, all night. All day, all night.
All day, all night.

CHORUS 2 Will it always be this way?
Will it always be this way?
Will it always be this way?

CHORUS 3 [*louder and louder*]
No it can't be! No it can't be! No it can't be!

The first two choruses gradually join the third until their chanting overwhelms the theatre, though the **SOLOISTS**, *except for* **JENNIE**, *continue their clerical work as if unconscious of this.*

FOR OVER TEN YEARS my playwriting became a thing of the past, and a friend I had not seen for a while asked, "What became of you Alasdair? You were once nearly famous." I also met Jefferson Barnes, now principal of Glasgow Art School, who said, "You're becoming quite famous Alasdair." I asked why. After a thoughtful pause he said, "I really don't know."

I will enlarge this introduction with gossip about dealings with the British Broadcasting Corporation.

Years after London refused Stewart Conn permission to broadcast *Near the Driver* I learned that Shaun McLaughlin now worked for Bristol BBC and sent him a copy. He replied that he was glad I remembered him, that he liked the play but must do "some wheeling and dealing" before London would let him produce it. Shortly after he returned it because London BBC censorship had rejected it.

In 1981 my novel *Lanark* was published and received more acclaim than an author's first book usually gets. My friend Bernd Rullkotter translated it for publication in Germany and his German translation of *Near the Driver* was accepted by West Deutsches Rundfunk – West German Radio. It was broadcast in 1983 under the title *Beim Zugführer*. Then came a year when Stewart Conn had a holiday from Scottish radio drama and was temporarily replaced by James Runcie, son of Canterbury's Archbishop. He wrote to me saying he greatly liked *Lanark*, and hoped he could commission another half hour play for Scottish BBC. I sent him *Near the Driver*. He wrote back expressing delight with it. Days later came another letter saying "the self-elected London cognoscenti" had rejected it, and the BBC would clearly never let it be broadcast.

My friend Joy Hendry is editor of *Chapman*, the longest-lasting of Scottish literary journals. In 1986 she printed the play in *Chapman*, and shortly after I was contacted by Jane Noakes, producer of Scottish BBC Schools Radio, asking if she could produce it. I told her, "London won't let you broadcast it." She said, "London doesn't censor Scottish Educational Radio." So *Near the Driver* was broadcast to Scottish schools in the spring term of 1989.

Each schools broadcast was 20 minutes long so the half hour play was split in two and broadcast two days running. Since the second broadcast lasted ten minutes, Jane got me to fill the other ten minutes with a short talk about the play which follows:

FANTASY AND REALITY
A Postscript for Schoolchildren to Near the Driver 1989

I hope you were amused by my fantastic play about an impossible train journey, even though the ending was horrible. Horror stories are always popular with many people, I think because imagining impossibly bad things makes it easier to like the real world we live in, but I have always most enjoyed the fantastic stories that have people in them who strike me as real. Alice in Wonderland is a sensible small girl in a land of daft but believable adults. She meets a mother who thinks crying babies should be spanked – treatment which turns her own baby into a pig. Badly treated children *are* inclined to become as nasty as those who hurt them. She also meets a red queen with the manners of a Communist or Fascist dictator, who forces Alice to run as fast as possible in order to stay in the same place. Dictatorial bosses often force underlings to do a lot of work that changes nothing, as some of you will find when you go to work.

Another great political fantasy is *Gulliver's Travels*, first printed in 1726, two hundred and sixty three years ago. Gulliver is an English sailor shipwrecked on an island peopled by six inch high men and women. They are a civilised nation ruled (as England was then ruled) by a set of politicians chosen by their king. He chooses them by getting them to walk along a tightrope, like circus acrobats. Those who fall off are sacked, unless they are fit enough to climb back on again, and the more tricks a politician can perform on a tightrope, the more powerful he gets. The Prime Minister is so smart that he can turn complete somersaults on the political tightrope. The first readers of *Gulliver's Travels* enjoyed it as a funny but convincing picture of their own Britain, where people in power did things they had previously denounced as wrong. Eight or nine years ago something made me think Britain is still partly ruled by such people.

You all know about the Russian Chernobyl disaster that happened in 1986. In 1979 a similar accident started happening to a nuclear power station at a place called Three Mile Island, in the USA, an accident that governments with nuclear energy programmes say will never happen. A large nearby town was evacuated and for two days an explosion was feared that might have destroyed the life of a whole state. Experts, however, got the accident under control. While this was happening, of course, government spokesmen from other nations with nuclear power appeared on television explaining why such an accident could never happen in *their* country. The British Cabinet minister responsible for atomic energy explained that the American power station was using a gas-cooled system which was far less safe than the water-cooled system we British used, so we had nothing to fear. I will not tell you whether he belonged to the Labour or Conservative party because it does not matter – both our largest political parties want atomic energy for Britain, so no matter which party was in power the politician responsible for energy would have said the same thing, because part of his job was stopping people like you and me from feeling worried. A few months later the same minister announced that the British nuclear power stations were changing to a new gas-cooling system to be bought from an American corporation, because the American system was safer and cheaper.

If you think about it, you may find other similarities between fantastic stories and the world in which we live.

Jane Noakes was English, yet prepared to ignore the opinions of London BBC censors. It is a tragedy for Scottish radio that she died in a car accident a few months after the broadcast.

In 1983 I met the film director Sandy Johnson and producer Iain Brown. They wished to make a film of my novel *Lanark*, an idea I thought impractical. Good films have been made from good books – Dickens' *Great Expectations*, Gunter Grass' *The Tin Drum*, Henry James' *The Europeans* – but not often. Most good films are made by directors finding a story that pleases them and paying someone to write a shooting script along lines they dictate. If they don't like the result they pay other authors for a rewrite. In *Casablanca* the script was revised while the film was shot up to the very last scene. Half of my television scripts had been produced without distortions, but the chance of a film company using a script of mine as I wished were a 100 to 1 against. But Iain and Sandy were young and Scottish and their professional careers were just starting. They really wanted me to write the *Lanark* film script. So Iain Brown bought the film rights and paid Sandy and me to write a shooting script that would satisfy the three of us. Two years later, through close discussions, without fuss or disagreement, we achieved one.

Lanark is two stories about one man. The central tale shows a boy called Thaw growing up and dying in 1950s Scotland; this is framed in a longer narrative about his afterlife as a man called Lanark, who has adventures in a surreal modern purgatory. We decided that the Thaw narrative should be filmed in black and white, on the old-fashioned small academy size of screen, but with a difference. From childhood onward Thaw makes pictures, starting with crayons and working up to painted walls. In the Thaw part of the film the pictures he made would have colour within them but the surrounding world, including the painter's hand, would be black and white. (This idea came from an adolescent dream I remembered in which I saw myself painting a richly coloured picture in a world where everything, including myself, was shades of grey.) His afterlife as Lanark would be widescreen and highly coloured, like Dorothy's life after the hurricane sucks her up out of grey dust-bowl Kansas and deposits her in technicolour Oz. The film began with a credits sequence showing Thaw's suicide by drowning. This was presented in split screen panels that prepared viewers for the variety of colour we would use later. Showing three or more views of the same action simultaneously on one screen was a device we had learned from Abel Ganz's *Napoleon*, and was used elsewhere in the *Lanark* tale. To show these devices convincingly I drew the storyboard.

Money to make this film has still not been raised, because those who finance big productions judge their fitness by reading nothing longer than one or two page summaries. Here are extracts from the *Lanark* storyboard.

Title: white on black

sound: faint wind on a moorland hilltop.

Triptych credit sequence in black & white: credits in centre; left & right, clouds ascending from left to right. Sound: faint wind & bird calls.

Left low angle close-up of triangulation pillar against sky. Right pillar & some of hilltop from distance with Lanarks head rising into frame. Sound: faint sound of drum rythmically swished.

Left: crow glimpsed in flight. Right Lanark, scare-crow-like, with tired jerky movements climbs into view, skirts of coat flapping in wind.

Left & right: He leans to rest on pillar a moment, in close-up to the left. Sound: melancholy piano blends with percussion (Perhaps Saties Interlude?) continues till credits end.

In both frames Lanark pulls himself erect and descends past pillar.

A MAN WHO DIES,

Left: long shot of him descending hillside track with pillar highest on hilly skyline. Right: close-up with summit beyond right shoulder.

AND GOES TO HELL,

Left: Close up of full figure descending steep road through wood. Right: Long shot of same on road bridging a rocky stream.

AND FINDS IT VERY

Left: Long shot of him on road, staring across stony beach at loch in foreground. Right: Close up of him doing the same.

LIKE THE PLACE HE

Left: Long shot — he crosses beach and wades into loch. Right: Close-up of his legs doing the same.

Left: medium distant view of him wading toward camera, knee deep

Right: High angle view of him, waist deep

Left. high angle view—

Right: close up— head and hands

Left: head, hands go under.

Right: one upflung hand.

End of Triptych – full screen view of hand submerging.

Sound: music stops.

Sound: water lapping. Perhaps far islands & Ben Lomand is glimpsed before—

Long shot underwater of sinking body, arms spread to suggest flight. Sound: Heartbeat. cut to—

cafe interior, crowded, in colour, red dominent, the Sludden clique prominent. Balcony is empty. Sound heartbeat. Cut to—

Black & white: medium underwater shot of body floundering. Sound: conversation gabble: "I dont know why we come here:" "A hellish place—" cut to—

cafe interior, colour, empty but for Gloopy behind bar. Sound: gabble of busy conversation "lets start a new ism"— cut to—

underwater close-up, black & white, corpse of Lanark on loch floor. Sound: heartbeats stopping.

In same clothes as in credits, but now neat & clean-shaven, Lanark sits on cafe balcony, his right hand now in a thick glove. The café seems empty now apart from Gloopy behind counter.

Lanark finds that hell is a 1960s espresso café in a city without daylight, where people mysteriously arrive and disappear. He joins a cliqué controlled by Sludden, who he dislikes, and is strongly attracted by the film's heroine, Rima, who invites him to her lodgings after a party.

RIMA'S ATTIC

A DOWNWARD CLOSE-UP OF TWO BLUE-STRIPED MUGS ON BARE FLOOR-BOARDS. EACH CONTAINS BLACK COFFEE ESSENCE AND BROWN SUGAR. BESIDE THEM IS A SUGAR BOWL, A BOTTLE OF CAMP COFFEE ESSENCE, A HALF-FULL BOTTLE OF BRANDY. RIMA'S HAND POURS BOILING WATER FROM A SMALL ELECTRIC KETTLE INTO EACH MUG, SETS THE KETTLE DOWN, LIFTS THE BRANDY AND ADDS SOME TO BOTH.
PULL BACK TO SHOW—

AN ATTIC WITH SO LOW A CEILING THAT ONE CAN ONLY STAND UPRIGHT IN THE CENTRE. A MATTRESS MADE UP AS A BED COVERS A QUARTER OF THE FLOOR. LANARK'S SHOES, PULLOVER AND TIE ARE BESIDE THE BED. HE LIES ON IT WITH BACK ON THE PILLOW, SHOULDERS AGAINST WALL, WATCHING RIMA WHO SITS ON THE BED-FOOT WITH HER BACK TO HIM. HER DUFFEL-COAT HANGS ON A HOOK ON THE DOOR IN THE WALL BEYOND HER. A CHEST ON THE FLOOR LEFT OF THE DOOR HAS A TABLE LAMP ON IT BESIDE TWO OLD DOLLS: A CHINA BABY AND CLOTH DUTCH MAN. A SWISS PENDULUM CLOCK, CHALET-SHAPED BUT HANDLESS AND MOTION-LESS, HANGS RIGHT OF THE DOOR AND A STRINGLESS GUITAR LEANS IN THE CORNER. ON THE WALL FACING THE BED A ROW OF HOOKS SUPPORT HANGERS WITH RIMA'S OTHER CLOTHES ON THEM. HER SHOES ARE IN A ROW ON THE FLOOR BENEATH. ELSEWHERE THE WALL HAS SMALL CHILDISH CRAYON SKETCHES OF GREEN HILLS AND BLUE SEAS PINNED TO IT.

A TWO-BAR RADIATOR WITH CURVED REFLECTOR SHIELD IS PLUGGED INTO THE SAME WALL-SOCKET AS THE KETTLE.

DESPITE THE POVERTY OF THESE PROPERTIES THE APPEARANCE IS COSY AND PLEASANT. RIMA ALMOST SMILES AS SHE TURNS TO HAND LANARK A MUG, SAYING:

RIMA: You probably wont refuse to drink it.

LANARK: Thanks.

HE SIPS. SHE TURNS HER BACK TO HIM, NURSING THE MUG ON HER LAP. HE STARES AT HER.

LANARK: You're kind to me. (SHE DOES NOT MOVE.) Did you come to this city long ago?

RIMA: (DRILY) What does "long" mean? (SHE SIPS.)

LANARK: Were you small when you came here?

SHE SHRUGS. HE PUTS DOWN THE MUG, GOES TO HER ON HIS KNEES, LAYS A HAND ON HER SHOULDER. HER ONLY REACTION IS TO CLOSE HER EYES.

LANARK: (TIMIDLY) Do you remember a time when days were long and bright?

A TEAR TRICKLES FROM UNDER ONE OF HER EYELIDS. LANARK CANNOT SEE IT. HE PUTS HIS OTHER HAND ON HER OTHER SHOULDER.

LANARK: (SOFTLY PLEADING) Let me undress you?

SHE DOES NOT MOVE. HE UNZIPS THE DRESS AT THE BACK AND DRAWS IT DOWN TO HER WAIST. HER SHOULDER-BLADES, UNDER THE BRA-STRAP, ARE GREEN WITH SCALES AND PRICKLES.

LANARK: (DELIGHTED) You've got dragonhide! Your shoulder blades are covered with it!

RIMA: (STILL NOT MOVING, AND WITH CONTEMPT.) Does that excite you?

LANARK: I have it too! Here!

HE SHOWS HIS GLOVED HAND. SHE FACES HIM.

RIMA: (HARSHLY) Do you think that makes a bond between us?

HE PLACES A FINGER ON HIS LIPS, PLEADING FOR SILENCE, AND CONTINUES UNDRESSING HER.

A SHORT SEQUENCE OF CLOSE-UPS SHOW RIMA'S HEAD AND SHOULDERS AS, WITH OPEN EYES, SHE ENDURES, NOT SHARES HIS LOVEMAKING. IT SOON ENDS. HE COLLAPSES FLAT BESIDE HER AFTER A FINAL GRUNT OF RELIEF.

LANARK: (GASPING) Thanks! Oh thanks!

SHE STANDS UP AND LOOKS DOWN AT HIM.

RIMA: Well? Was that fun?

HE GAZES AT HER, CONFUSED, THEN DEFIANT.

LANARK: Yes! Great fun!

RIMA: How nice for you.

TALKING, SHE TURNS AWAY AND PULLS ON JEANS AND A SWEATER. THE CAMERA CONCENTRATES ON LANARK AND HIS GROWING HORROR.

RIMA: You're not much good at sex, are you? I suppose the best I'll ever get is Sludden.

LANARK: You told me.... you didn't .... love.... Sludden.

RIMA: I don't, but I use him, sometimes, just as he uses me. He and I are very cold people.

LANARK: Why did you let me come here?

RIMA: You wanted so much to be warm that I thought you perhaps were. You're as cold as the rest of us, really, and even more worried about it. I suppose that's what makes you clumsy.

LANARK COVERS HIS EYES WITH HIS UNGLOVED HAND.

LANARK: You're trying to kill me.

RIMA: Yes, but I won't succeed. You're terribly solid.

DRESSED NOW, SHE BENDS AND SLAPS HIS CHEEK BRISKLY.

RIMA: Come on. Get up. Get dressed and get out.

HE STARES AT HER THEN STANDS AND ADJUSTS HIS TROUSERS AND SHIRT, NOT LOOKING AT HER AT ALL. SHE HANDS HIM HIS TIE, WHICH HE STUFFS INTO A POCKET, AND PULL-OVER, WHICH HE PULLS ON. THE SHOES ARE THE SLIP-ON SORT. HE PUTS HIS FEET IN THEM. RIMA GOES TO THE DOOR, TAKES HER DUFFEL COAT FROM THE HOOK, OPENS THE DOOR AND STANDS BESIDE IT, HOLDING UP THE COAT FOR HIM TO SLIP HIS ARMS IN. HE STARES AT HER.

RIMA: (IMPLACABLY) Goodbye, Lanark.

HE WALKS STRAIGHT PAST HER OUT OF THE DOOR.

THE STAIRS

A LOW-ANGLE SHOT FROM MIDWAY UP. LANARK, STONE-FACED, DESCENDS BLOCKING ALL VIEW OF THE TOP.

RIMA'S VOICE: Lanark! (A PAUSE) Lanark!

HIS HEAD DESCENDS OUT OF VIEW, REVEALING HER AT THE STAIRTOP, COAT IN HAND.

SOUND: THE STREET DOOR IS OPENED.

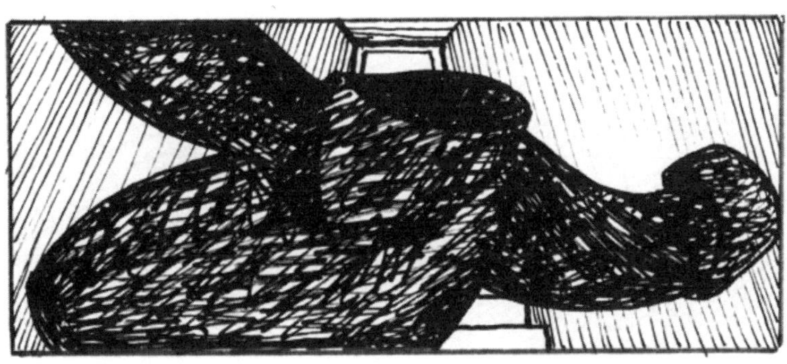

RIMA: Lanark, take this!

SHE FLINGS COAT INTO THE CAMERA: BLACKNESS.

SOUND: STREET DOOR SLAMS.

FOG & SNOW

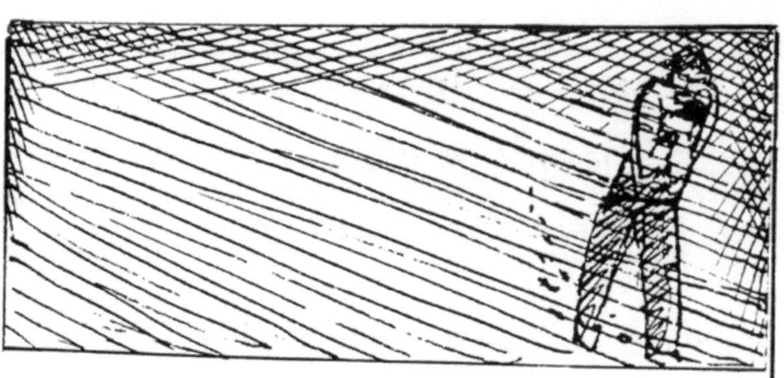

SOUND: FOOTSTEPS IN FROZEN SNOW.

A DIM HUNCHED FIGURE EMERGES ON THE RIGHT AND BEFORE VANISHING OFF RIGHT WE RECOGNIZE LANARK, COATLESS, CLENCHED GLOVED HAND PRESSED TO CHEST, OTHER HAND CLUTCHING WRIST OF IT.

SOUND: THE DRONE OF AN APPROACHING TRAMCAR.

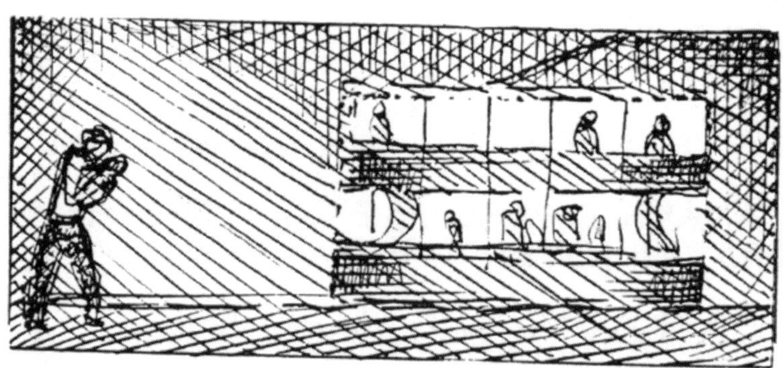

DIM HUNCHED LANARK TRUDGES IN PROFILE FROM LEFT TO RIGHT WHILE THE REMOTER SILHOUETTE OF TRAMCAR PASSES RIGHT TO LEFT. LANARK CLENCHED HAND SHAKES SPASMODICALLY, AS IF TRYING TO BREAK THE GRIP OF THE OTHER HAND.

SOUND: WOMEN TITTERING.

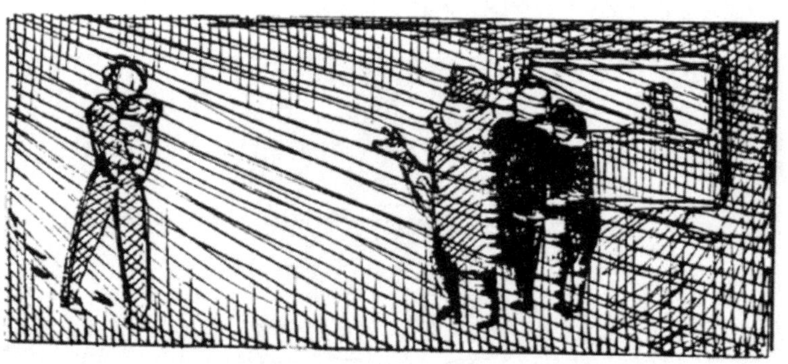

FOG THINS RIGHT TO SHOW 3 WOMEN WITH A COFFEE-STALL BEHIND, ONE OLD AND FAT, ONE OLD AND WIZENED, ONE YOUNG IN FUR COAT AND HAT.
SOUND: FOOTSTEPS IN SNOW.
LANARK EMERGES LEFT. THE YOUNG WOMAN WAVES AND CALLS.

GAY: *Lanark!*

HE HALTS, STARING. TRACK TO THEM AS SHE APPROACHES SAYING:

GAY: *Lanark, where have you been? Sludden's been looking everywhere for you. He wants to tell you something.*

LANARK STARES AT HER. HIS GLOVED HAND SQUIRMS. HE TIGHTENS

HIS GRIP. IT GOES INERT.

GAY: (SMILING SLYLY) I know why you're wearing a glove, I've got one too! (HE STARES AT HER) I'll show you my disease if you show me yours. (HIS MOUTH OPENS.) Everyone has a disease

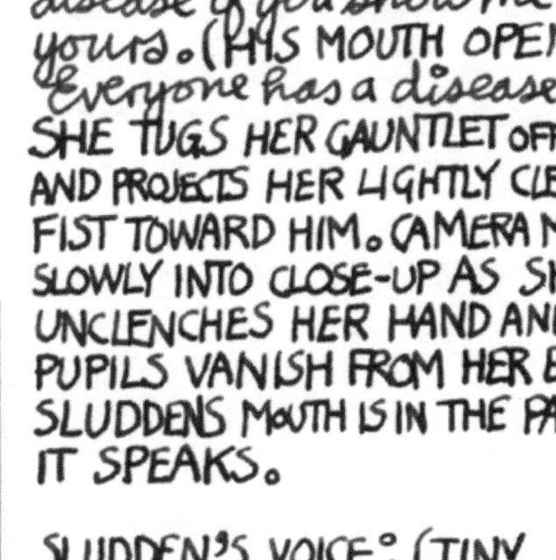

SHE TUGS HER GAUNTLET OFF AND AND PROJECTS HER LIGHTLY CLENCHED FIST TOWARD HIM. CAMERA MOVES SLOWLY INTO CLOSE-UP AS SHE UNCLENCHES HER HAND AND THE PUPILS VANISH FROM HER EYES. SLUDDENS MOUTH IS IN THE PALM. IT SPEAKS.

SLUDDEN'S VOICE: (TINY AND CLEAR) You're far too serious, Lanark.

LANARK: Oh. Oh God.

SLUDDEN: You worry too much.

CLOSE-UP OF GAY'S HAND AND FACE.

LANARK'S VOICE: Oh this is Hell.

GAY'S MOUTH FALLS OPEN. SLUDDENS VOICE COMES OUT OF THAT TOO, BUT DEEP AND HOLLOW.

SLUDDEN'S VOICE: But you're trying to understand life and that interests me.

SOUND: LOW SOLEMN ORGAN CHORDS CORRESPOND TO BACK-TRACKING FOOTSTEPS.

CAMERA BACK-TRACKS UNTIL GAY APPEARS HANGING IN THE THINNING FOG LIKE A PUPPET, HER TOES A FEW INCHES ABOVE THE SNOW.

SOUND: STRONG ORGAN MUSIC.

ZOOM BACKWARD TO PASS, THEN SHOW FROM IN FRONT, LANARK RUNNING BLINDLY TOWARD THE CAMERA LIKE ONE NEAR THE END OF HIS EMOTIONAL & BODILY POWER.

THE NECROPOLIS

THE CAMERA ZOOMS BACK BEFORE HIM THROUGH THE STONE PILLARS OF A HUGE OPEN WROUGHT IRON GATE. LANARK SLOWS TO A HALT BETWEEN THEM AND, BREATHING DEEPLY, GLANCES BEHIND HIM FOR THE FIRST TIME. NOTHING IS VISIBLE THERE BUT

SOUND: ORGAN MUSIC, SOLEMN AND EERIE.

HE TURNS AND THE CAMERA TURNS WITH HIM, KEEPING HIM CENTRAL AS HE SURVEYS A SNOW-COVERED HILLSIDE OF BLACK MONUMENTS, THE TALLEST AND MOST CLOSELY CLUSTERED ON THE SKYLINE. THE WEIGHT OF THE GLOVED HAND MAKING IT HARD FOR HIM TO KEEP BALANCE. HE NOTICES THIS AND LIFTS THE HAND CURIOUSLY TO HIS FACE.

SOUND: END ORGAN MUSIC.

CUT TO CLOSE-UP.

THE HAND HAS SWOLLEN. CLAWS PIERCE THE ENDS OF THE GLOVE FINGERS.

WITH AN INDRAWN CRY LANARK THRUSTS THE CLAW AS FAR FROM HIM AS HE CAN, PRESSES HIS FACE WITH THE HUMAN HAND, STUMBLES TO THE GATE PILLAR AND CRIES THROUGH CLENCHED TEETH —

LANARK: *Let me out God, Let me out God, God let me out.*

— STRIKING THE PILLAR WITH HIS BROW EACH TIME ON THE WORD OUT. THEN HE DROPS HIS ARMS, LEANS BACK ON THE PILLAR. HIS BROW IS BADLY GRAZED, HIS EXPRESSION UTTERLY HOLLOW.

SOUND: A DISTANT MELODIOUS BELL CLANGS RESONANTLY ONCE.

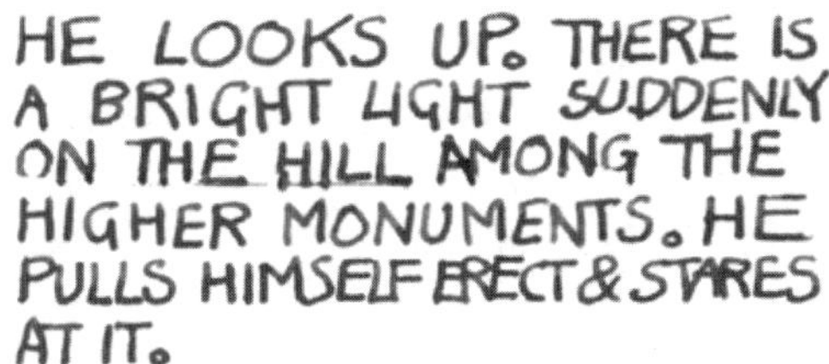

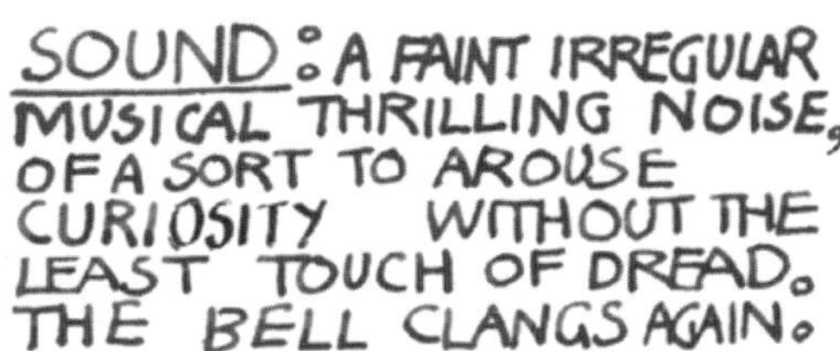

LANARK WALKS TOWARD THE LIGHT, CUT TO —

LANARK CLIMBS A STEEP PATH TOWARD THE LIGHT. CUT TO—

HE ENTERS A SPACE SURROUNDED BY OBELISKS. THE LIGHT COMES FROM THE FAR SIDE OF A MONUMENT IN THE CENTRE.

SOUND: THE TRILLING SOUNDS CLOSER; NOT LOUDER, MORE INTIMATE.

HE PROWLS ROUND THE MONUMENT, SEEKING THE SOURCE OF THE LIGHT, AND SEES ON A BRIGHT SURFACE WHAT SEEMS THE SHADOW OF A GREAT BIRD, THE BODY STATIC BUT THE WING TIPS TWITCHING. HE GLANCES UP TO SEE WHAT CASTS THE SHADOW.

SOUND: THE TRILLING STOPS. A LOW BELL-CLANG.

THE SHADOW BECOMES A DISTINCT MOUTH.

MOUTH: I am the way out.

LANARK: What do you mean?

THE MOUTH CLOSES AND DESCENDS TO THE SNOWY EARTH, PASSING LIKE A COLOURED SHADOW OVER THE PROJECTIONS OF THE MONUMENT BASE. IT STOPS AND OPENS JUST IN FRONT OF LANARK'S FEET, AND OPENS. HE PEERS IN. AN UPDRAUGHT MOVES HIS HAIR.

LANARK: Where will you take me?

THE MOUTH SHUTS AND STARTS FADING.

LANARK: (DESPERATELY) Stop! I'll come.

THE MOUTH GROWS DISTINCT.

LANARK: (HUMBLY) How should I come?

MOUTH: Naked and head first.

LANARK: I'll come how I can.

HE PULLS OFF PULLOVER AND SHIRT, TEARING THEM ON THE SCALES AND SPINES WHICH COVER HIS RIGHT ARM AND SHOULDER.

HE SITS ON THE HARD SNOW, PULLS OFF HIS SHOES, AND DROPS HIS LEGS INTO THE MOUTH OVER THE UNDERLIP.

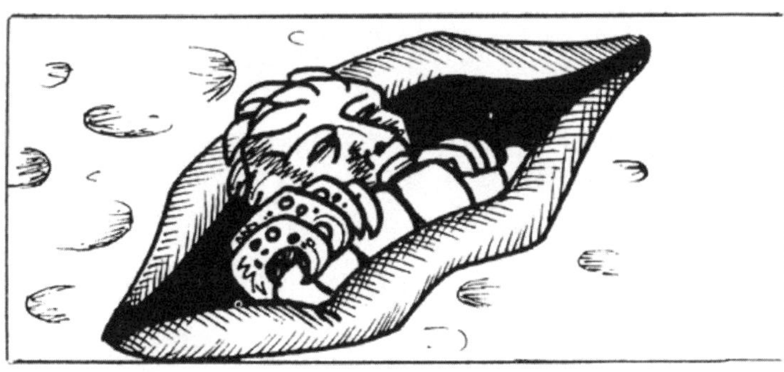

HE LEANS FORWARD, GRIPS THE TEETH OPPOSITE AND SLIDES DOWN TILL HE HANGS FROM THEM. SUDDENLY THE HUMAN HAND LOSES HOLD. IT AND HIS HEAD FALL FROM SIGHT. CUT TO—

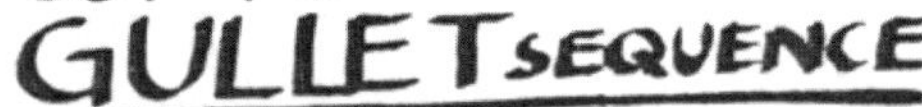

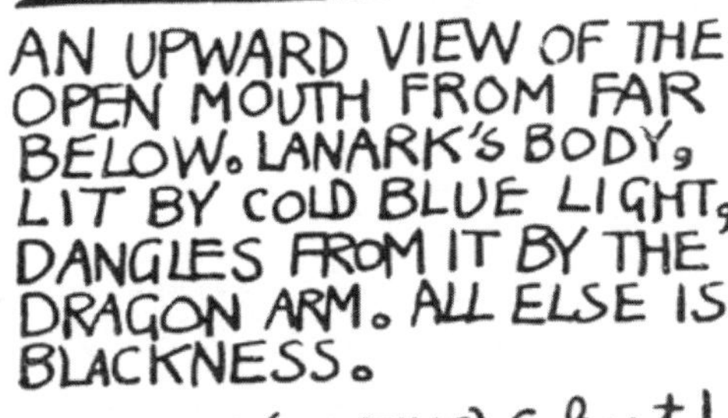

THE MOUTH SHUTS.

IN COLD BLUE LIGHT HE FALLS THROUGH BLACKNESS, LEAVING THE SCREEN BOTTOM RIGHT.

CUT TO—

DOWNWARD SHOT OF HIM, LARGE, FALLING INTO THE FRAME FROM THE BOTTOM EDGE AND

DIMINISHING TO NOTHING IN THE CENTRE.

CUT TO—

OBLIQUE UPWARD SHOT OF HIM SOMERSAULTING DOWN INTO CLOSE-UP FROM TOP LEFT. BEFORE LEAVING THE SCREEN BOTTOM RIGHT HE IS SUDDENLY CAUGHT BY A HUGE INVISIBLE HAND, THE LIGHT ON HIM GOES HOT ORANGE RED AND

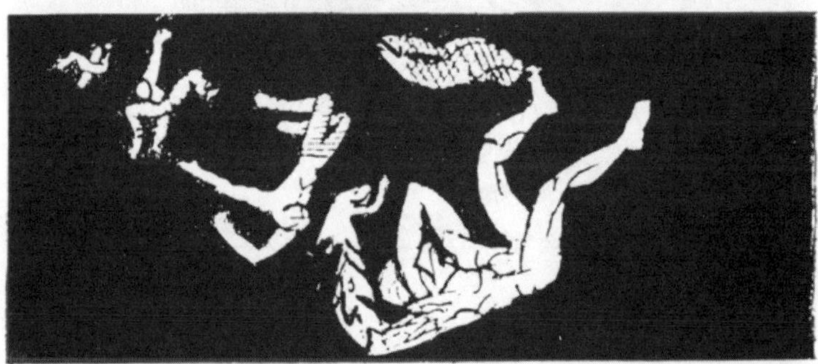

<u>SOUND</u>: HARSH BUZZING

THE INVISIBLE HAND TIGHTENS, SQUEEZING HIM INTO A PAINFUL KNOT.

HE FIGHTS THE PRESSURE AND MANAGES TO STRAIGHTEN HIS ARMS. LIGHT ON HIM GOES COLD BLUE AND —

SOUND: BUZZING STOPS

HE FALLS AGAIN. CAMERA KEEPS HIM IN FRAME FOR $2\frac{1}{2}$ SECONDS UNTIL —

SOUND: HARSHER BUZZ

IN HOT ORANGE LIGHT THE HAND CATCHES HIM AGAIN AND SQUEEZES TIGHTER. THE SPINES ON ARM AND SHOULDER ARE FLATTENED AND SNAP. WITH HUGE EFFORT HE JERKS ONE LEG STRAIGHT —

SOUND: $\frac{3}{4}$ SECOND OF SILENCE.

HE FALLS IN BLUE LIGHT TILL CAUGHT AGAIN —

SOUND: STILL HARSHER BUZZ, AS

IN RED LIGHT HE IS SQUEEZ-ED TIGHTER STILL UNTIL —

SUDDEN BLACKOUT. SILENCE.

SOUND: BUZZ.

MEDIUM CLOSEUP. INTENSE PRESSURE IN A DIFFERENT POSITION, IN A DARKER LIGHT, EXCEPT THE DRAGON ARM WHICH GLOWS BRIGHTER.

CUT TO—

BLACKOUT
SILENCE

CUT TO—

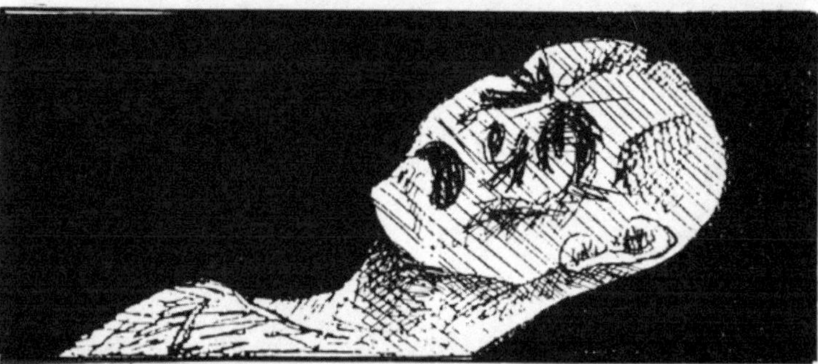

SOUND: BUZZ.
CLOSE-UP OF FACE IN DARK CRIMSON LIGHT, DISTORTED BY G-FORCE PRESSURE, THEN SOUND AND IMAGE FADE INTO—

TOTAL BLACKNESS FOR FIVE SECONDS.

SOUND: SCISSORS FAINTLY SNIPPING, THEN SILENCE.

THE BLACKNESS PALES TO DOVE GREY WITH CREAMY BRIGHTNESS AT THE FOOT OF IT LIKE A CLEAR DAWN SKY. THIS IS THE CEILING OF—

THE WARD IN THE INSTITUTE

SOUND: SNIPPING. GIRLISH GIGGLE AND WHISPERS.

TILT DOWN PAST DIAL OF A 25 HOUR CLOCK AND ARCHES. COLOURS ARE ALL WARM WHITES APART THE REVOLVING SCARLET SECOND HAND OF THE CLOCK AND AZURE SKY BEHIND CLOUDS BEYOND THE ARCHES.

P.O.V. SHOT OF LANARK'S LEGS AT THE BOTTOM OF A HOSPITAL BED, NAKED AND APART, YOUNG NURSES CLIPPING HIS TOENAILS AND GOSSIPING.

LANARK'S RIGHT HAND, HUMAN AGAIN, RISES INTO CENTRE OF SCREEN FROM THE BASE OF IT. THE LEFT HAND RISES TO TOUCH IT. THE NURSES NOTICE.

LEFT NURSE: Feeling better, Bushybrows?

LANARK: (AFTER PAUSE) Yes. (OTHER PAUSE) Why do you call me Bushybrows?

THE LEFT NURSE LIFTS AN OCTAGONAL MIRROR AND HOLDS IT CENTRE SCREEN.

LANARK'S FACE IN IT IS OLDER AND MOUSTACHED, WITH BUSHY EYEBROWS.

LANARK: I see. (PAUSE) How old do I look?

LEFT NURSE: (REMOVING MIRROR) A bit over thirty.

RIGHT NURSE: No chicken, anyway.

THEY ROLL THE SHEET DOWN FROM HIS STOMACH AND TUCK IT IN. LANARK FOLDS HANDS ON STOMACH.

LANARK: A short while ago I was a bit over twenty.

LEFT NURSE: Well Bushybrows, that's life, isn't it!

MUNRO HAS ENTERED RIGHT, AND COMES TO THE BED-FOOT.

HE IS A THIN MEDICAL MANDARIN WITH HALF-MOON SPECT CLES, WHITE COAT, BLACK WAISTCOAT, STRIPED TROUSER COLLAR, TIE. HE STANDS AT THE BED-FOOT, HIS GRAVE EXPRESSION NOT QUITE HIDING A SENSE OF HUMOUR.

MUNRO: Remember me?

LANARK'S VOICE: No.

MUNRO: Three days ago you punched me, just here– (HE TOUCHES A SMALL PIECE OF PLASTER ON THE SIDE OF HIS CHIN) Oh yes, you came out fighting. I've just delivered someone else, but he's not in as good a shape as you are.

HE LOOKS LEFT. PAN LEFT ROUND A CORNER INTO THE WARD QUIETLY CHATTERING ORDERLIES PUSH A BED WITH THE SKELETAL AND UNCONSCIOUS BRIGADIER ON IT, AND A TROLLEY HOLDING OXYGEN CYLINDERS AND A DRIP-FEED SYSTEM. THE CAMERA FOLLOWS THE BED TILL WE SEE IT PLACED BESIDE LANARK'S, ON THE FAR SIDE OF HIM.

THE ORDERLIES GO OUT TO THE RIGHT. NURSES LINK THE DRIP-FEED TO THE BRIGADIER'S ARM. PROPPED HIGH WITH PILLOWS, HIS SKULL-LIKE HEAD IS IN PROFILE MID-SCREEN, CONTEMPLATED BY LANARK LEANING ON HIS ELBOW RIGHT, AND MUNRO STANDING LEFT.

LANARK: I met that man once. He was a soldier.

MUNRO: Then you can help us. If he recovers consciousness, talk to him. You'll find it excellent practise.

LANARK LOOKS AT HIM.

LANARK: Practise?

MUNRO: Good medical practise. You'll soon be one of us, you know – a doctor. You'd better get dressed.

Lanark's afterlife adventure is interrupted by a long flashback explaining how and why he came to drown himself. For this narrative the wide screen shrinks to the early cinema small screen, mostly in black and white but not entirely. Lanark is shown growing up into an artist whose pictures are shown in colour although the world around him is not. The flashback starts from a young child's point of view, shown as follows.

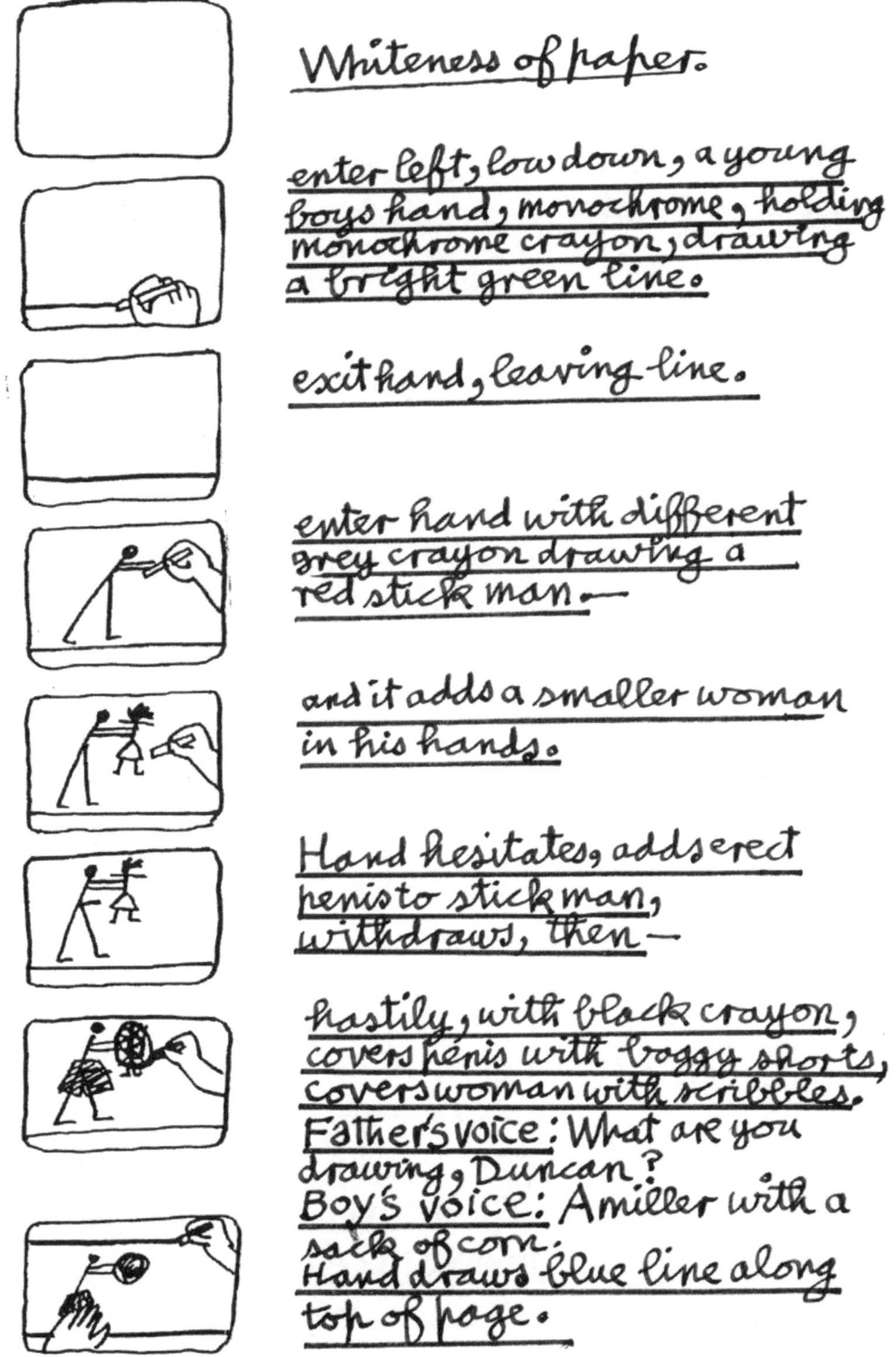

Fathers hand descends, finger on blue line.

Father's voice: What's this meant to be?

Boy's voice: The sky.

Left and right his hands press the paper.

Tabletop with drawing fills half lower frame, father fills top right quarter, left quarter has livingroom fireplace & chair

Father: Do you mean the horizon?

(Boy obstinate) It's the sky.

Father: (reasonable) The sky isn't a straight line Duncan!

Boy: It would be if you saw it sideways.

Father: Wait a minute.

Father departs, revealing mother seated, knitting top right. Only movement is her needles, the coal-fire flickering.

Father's hands place on the table an electric lamp.

Father's voice: Look here, Duncan.

Camera tilts up to show close-up of father holding a golf-ball near the lampshade.

Father: The world is round, like this ball. This lamp – [switches it on] is like the sun. The side of the world away from the sun is dark, when night comes. The bright side is day. The present time is Sunday afternoon so you and I are roughly here!

He points triumphantly to the brightest part of the golf-ball.

Close up of ball and pointing finger.

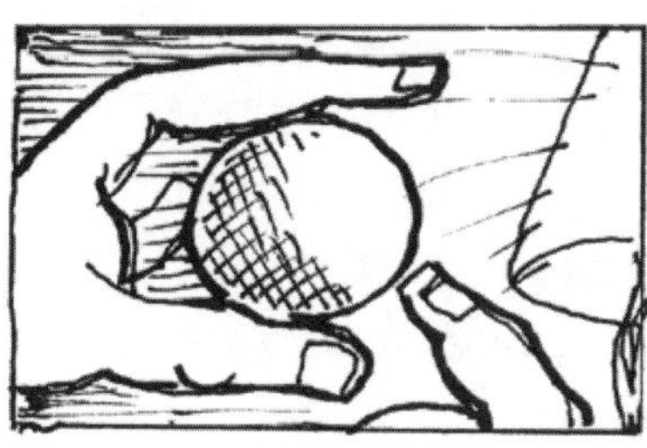

Boy's voice: Why don't we fall off?
Father: We're kept on by gravity.
Boy's voice: What's gavty?
Father: Grrrrravity keeps us on the world's surface. Without it we would fly up into the air....
Boy's voice: and come to the sky?
Father: No no no no!
Close up of solemn, spectacled boy seen from fathers viewpoint.
Father's voice: There is nothing above us but empty space!
Boy, not convinced, strengthens the blue skyline with his crayon.

Near the end of this flashback life story Lanark's frustrated intercourse with a prostitute causes a widescreen hallucination in black, white and limited areas of strong red.

Lanark's voice: It's only eczema— neither infectious or contagious—
Woman: (moving back so that the lamp lights her face) In my job we cannae afford to take chances.
SOUND: Subsonic organ note cuts out all other sounds.

The womans head, seen from neck up, is silently talking as camera tilts sideways. Her face freezes, immobile, and behind all turns pure red, which trickes sideways to fill the area of the wide screen. The following sequence is in red, black and white, the red confined to some background areas, the sun, some womens garments and lips.

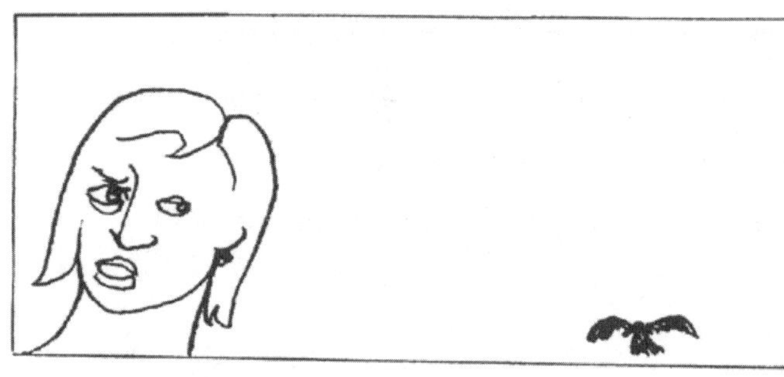

SOUND: This become the squawking of a crow which rises from the base of the frame near the right corner, and flaps its way diagonally upward across the red screen, enlarging and followed by the head & shoulders of Lanark, also enlarging as he nears and drawing behind him a sharp black-and white collage of Glasgow buildings. The crow, very big, flies off screen behind woman's head, not touching it. As Lanark reaches her she vanishes and—

SOUND: of organ chord as sky goes black, leaving a large red sun two thirds of way across the screen.

Thaw turns to watch as with solemn, discordant organ blasts, the city re-arranges itself in two masses under the solar disc, whose outline tensely vibrates.

Between the two masses slides up the Knox monument on top of the Necropolis, Cathedral, Royal Infirmary. The statue strikes across the solar disc. <u>SOUND</u> is cut, then a skittish chirping & giggling is heard distantly, but coming nearer. Lanark turns, is on Jamaica Street gazing across tramlines at far parapet with the railway bridge beyond. A locomotive emitting clouds of steam crosses slowly, silently as a horde of women, led by Rima, dressed like the prostitute but in bright red, run left to right along the far pavement, the crow ahead of them. As the running women beckon and wave to Lanark, from left and right an old Glasgow tramcar enters, the far one full of revelling art students in party clothes, The nearest, driven by the classics master in green drivers uniform, is full of Lanarks 12 year old classmates, his parents being the only adult passengers with Lanark as a schoolboy beside them. Adult Lanark, desperately waves to draw their attention but only his younger self waves back, the rest give no sign of seeing him.

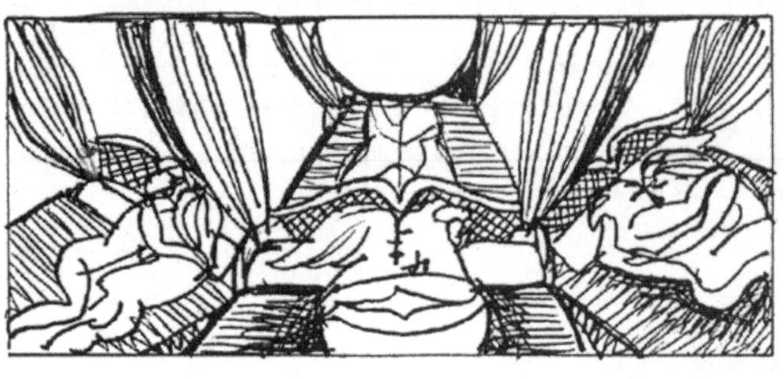

As the tram departs he sees his sister Ruth, as a girl, on the rear platform, waving to him. He starts to wave back, then sees in a shop entrance across the road the beckoning figure of Rima. He goes to her. She wears the red prostitute dress, shoes, lipstick as do dummies resembling her in the shop windows. Other colour is black + white. She embraces him. Discordant waltz music. They dance up the entrance into a yard full of women in whorish undress dancing orgiastically with his former teachers and church helpers. In a far wall is a wide doorway to a bed chamber, on one side a pulpit from which the old wino beggar is declaiming, on the other an eagle lectern at which the Minister stands, making admonishing gestures to Rima & Lanark as they waltz past him after the crow, who settles on a red-upholstered four-poster bed with red chinese lantern above. Suddenly naked, they fall embracing on the bed where they are reflected by mirrors all round.

Close-up of their upper bodies, their movements suddenly frozen.

Sound: cut organ music.

Rima: What's that?

The screen behind them goes red, with a small black dot that expands rapidly from near Lanark's shoulder to become the crow.

Lanark: Eczema! It's neither contagious nor infectious.

Prostitutes voice: Sorry! I cannae afford to take chances.

Sound: final, dire organ chord. Rima & crow vanish, Lanark's shoulders are clothed as red background bleeds back to academy size screen and — early morning light. Downward shot of Lanark, head in hands, squatting on stair-foot.

Move into close-up. He sighs, starts to stand up.

Medium shot of top half of entrance to stairway. Lanark rises shakily into it, glances down, the with a sudden, fearful expression, staggers. Righting himself he looks down again, sighs, then walks out toward camera.

SOMETHING ASTONISHING happened in 1985. Tom Kinninmont, a Scottish BBC producer, asked me to write a television play for him! Canongate Books were about to publish *The Fall of Kelvin Walker* as a novel. Tom had received an advance copy and thought it would be wonderful on TV with Bill Paterson in the main part. (Bill Paterson is a fine actor and in those days every TV producer thought he would be good in a Scottish part). I told Tom that the story had been televised by London BBC eighteen years before and he said, "Oh dear! London won't let us do it again." I asked why not? Hardly anybody now remembered the 1966 production, which had a badly flawed ending. It would be new and adventurous for BBC Glasgow to televise a play with a London setting – did he *need* London's permission to televise a story he liked? It seemed that he did. He told me later that London had definitely said No, but would let him commission a new play from me based on *The Story of a Recluse*. This had just been published by Jonathan Cape in *Lean Tales*, a collection of short stories by Agnes Owens, James Kelman and me.

The Story of a Recluse was only partly mine. The first two and a half pages were from a volume of incomplete fiction by Robert Louis Stevenson, the greatest part being *Weir of Hermiston*. The shortest piece breaks off at a tantalising moment when the young hero, son of a strict Edinburgh clergyman, gets drunk and unconscious for the first time in his life and wakens wearing a woman's nightgown in a strange bedroom. I published this wonderful beginning among other stories of mine, not trying to complete it, but using it to introduce an essay about ways he might have continued it, and opting for the most probable. I easily dramatised Stevenson's beginning for Tom, but how could I show more than one way the story might have gone? I decided to make my hero an old man at the start of the Second World War telling someone how, as a young medical student, he lost the only woman he loved. His story becomes a series of flashbacks to 1890s Edinburgh, sometimes showing what he feared was going to happen, sometimes what he hoped would happen. These developments were always interrupted by his account of what *really* happened, taking the story back to an earlier point then going forward differently. My script was accepted, and paid for, and a year went by.

Then Tom Kinninmont invited me for lunch at the Ubiquitous Chip with himself and the film director, Alastair Reid, who is sometimes confused with Alastair Reid the poet. Through every course of the meal we gossiped cheerfully about everything except our reason for being there. Since production and rehearsal dates had not been fixed they were obviously going to ask me to make changes. When the brandies came I opened the business, saying I was prepared to spoil my good script in any way they wanted, if the BBC would pay me half as much again as I had been paid already. Alastair Reid looked questioningly at Tom Kinninmont who said, "Yes, that's alright." So I was bribed into writing something they thought more entertaining. My unreliable narrator was changed to me, Alasdair Gray, the writer acting myself. At tense moments in the drama the actors froze and I appeared among them (once emerging from under the heroine's dressing table) and told viewers why the play would go back a minute or two then carry on different. That was not the only change they wanted.

I am sure *The Story of a Recluse* was the most expensive fifty minute TV film ever made in Scotland. Hardly any of the same length made in England can have cost more. My heroine was originally an American of Irish extraction, but the heavy villain who kept her had made a fortune in San Francisco, so Tom and Alastair decided she should be of Spanish extraction. They flew to Madrid, auditioned several Spanish actresses and cast a beautiful one who spoke English badly. For the villain they got Stewart Granger, an American film star who had played handsome heroes in the 1930s and 40s. He had the right presence but found it so hard to remember lines that accuracy was not insisted upon. Instead of, "Better take your friend away, he has not a cool head" he said, "Get your friend out of here, he's out of his mind." Producer and director got me to add three spectacular scenes. The Forth Railway Bridge was shown under construction by being filmed through a glass painted to eliminate the central spans, while on the shore many extras dressed like Victorian labourers moved about, with a horse pulling a cart of girders, while I stood lecturing the viewer upon Victorian industrial enterprise. An equally expensive and irrelevant scene showed Edinburgh from Calton Hill. Since *Auld Reekie* (as it was once called) has been smokeless since the 1950s, men with theatrical smoke canisters hid behind chimneys in adjacent buildings and sent up vertical jets of smoke while I spoke about social divisions. My speech was interrupted by the blare of fire engines summoned by smoke alarms in the roof of nearby Register House. This happened twice before shooting this scene was abandoned.

The film was networked all over Britain before Hogmanay in 1987 and contained a cast of excellent Scottish actors. They did very well when speaking dialogue that survived from my original script, which is printed here.

CAST IN ORDER OF APPEARANCE

MRS WILSON – an Edinburgh housekeeper in 1939
JAMIE – 80 years old in 1939, 18 years old in 1877

THE FOLLOWING BELONG TO 1877

DR KIRKWOOD – a middle-aged clergyman
TOM)
DICK)
HARRY) Jamie's medical student acquaintances
MCEWAN)
GEMMEL)
BEARDED MAN – a skilled billiard player (also **MANTON**)
JULIETTE – a mysteriously beautiful young woman
MANTON – a suave mature gambler from America
LECTURER – a Scottish anatomist
MACFARLANE – Manton's manservant
DALGLEISH – a spry old man who likes young company

KIRKWOOD'S HOUSE

CREDIT SEQUENCE

1: EXTERIOR, 1939

An Edinburgh New Town terrace, seen from across the street. A slow zoom towards a house in it (a vehicle of the period passes briefly in front) with dingy door and shuttered windows, except the study window on an upper floor where a very old man looks out between faded brown curtains. We need not see him distinctly. A large "15" is on the fanlight above the door. A message boy carrying a large wicker basket of provisions comes along the pavement, opens the gate in the area railings, and goes down steps to the basement.

2: THE KITCHEN, 1939

Like the rest of the house, the furnishing is unchanged since the 1870s. The light fittings are gas, but cooking is done on a large well-polished fire-range. The only modern details are Persil and Vim cartons on the draining board of a deep sink with a swan neck tap. The message boy places the provisions one at a time on the table while Mrs Wilson, a sensible neat widow of forty wearing a flower-patterned bib apron, ticks them off on a receipt with a pencil stub, then signs the receipt and hands it to him. He leaves, closing the door. End of credits.

SOUND: *A bell tinkles.*

MRS WILSON *lifts her eyes. A row of bells in close-up, each with a room name underneath it. The vibrating bell is labelled "study".*

3: THE STAIRWELL, 1939

Seen from below, **MRS WILSON** *mounts the stairs, passing a bust of Chalmers on a pedestal on the half landing. Carpet, curtains and paintwork, though not positively squalid, have a dusty, faded look.*

END OF CREDIT SEQUENCE

4: THE STUDY, 1939

Under large carved fireplace is a grate choked with grey ash and black cinders. Round the walls are glass-fronted bookcases interspersed with steel engravings of Moses smiting the Rock, Moses receiving the Ten Commandments, Knox preaching before Mary Queen of Scots, the Covenanters' Wedding; all these with tarnished gilt frames and mounts faded to a pale speckled coffee colour. On one picture the glass is cracked. Some bookcases are empty, and their contents (faded leather-bound volumes) stacked on the floor behind piles of newspapers tied into bales with string. A massive desk in the centre of the room faces the window. It is covered with newspapers, newspaper cuttings, an open scrapbook, scissors and paste. The camera does not dwell on these details but lets them make a background impression of eccentric, vaguely purposeful squalor. Beside the fire an octogenarian with a white moustache sits upright on a low easy chair, facing a large empty armchair with a very high back. His dress is informal late-Victorian, slightly worn but clean and neat, apart from a squint necktie. His hands rest on the handle of a stout stick planted firmly between his knees. He is in a state of nervous excitement. **MRS WILSON** *approaches.*

MRS WILSON What do you want, Sir?

JAMIE Mrs Macrae, Mrs Macrae, what day is this?

MRS WILSON Saturday. And my name is Wilson.

JAMIE Aye. Well, I've decided to go for a . . . a walk. You will be good enough to help me down the stairs.

5: STAIRWELL, 1939

Seen from above, **JAMIE** *and* **MRS WILSON** *arrive on the half landing. His left hand grips the stick, the right holds* **MRS WILSON***'s upper arm. He pauses beside the bust, partly because his hold on her gives him pleasure, and he would prolong it, but also because the nearer the front door he gets the more nervous he becomes.*

JAMIE Dr Chalmers, hero of the Disruption. My father worshipped him. Are you at all religious, Mrs er?

MRS WILSON No, I'm a working woman with no time for fripperies.

JAMIE Hihi! I'm a bit of an infidel myself, but I never told them then, so don't you tell them now. Let that be our secret, Mrs er.

6: THE LOBBY, BEFORE FRONT DOOR, 1939

A massive coat-stand with two cape-shouldered overcoats, one in Macintosh waterproof, the other in thick tweed: also some tweed caps. A ledge supports a set of clothes-brushes. **MRS WILSON** *lifts down the tweed overcoat.*

JAMIE Well now. The coat. Yes. Aye. Mhm.

She helps him into it with an air of patient resignation, then dusts it with a clothes brush, as he slowly, almost unwillingly buttons it. She then opens the door and looks at him. Between them we see the sunlit street outside.

JAMIE [*in a sudden low fierce voice*] What are they saying about me?

MRS WILSON [*calmly*] Who are you talking about, Mr Kirkwood?

JAMIE The gossips. The scandalmongers. The people of Edinburgh. I will not be fooled. You are a servant and servants gossip as much as all the rest together. Tell me what folk say about me or I ... I ... I will not go out.

MRS WILSON [*after a pause*] The only body I ever hear say a word about you is the baker's old auntie in the shop at the corner. She says you're a queer old man who never leaves his house. As if I didn't know that myself.

JAMIE [*triumphant*] The baker's auntie deceived you! On the16th of June nineteen hundred and thirty – on a Saturday like this one, almost five years ago –

MRS WILSON Almost ten.

JAMIE Don't interrupt me woman, on that day I opened this door myself, I needed no stick then, and walked down to the road, and was about to cross, when some people walked past and stared at me. Hard. They obviously knew how I had killed him. So I turned back again.

He frowns thoughtfully. A pause.

MRS WILSON [*quietly*] Who did you ever kill?

He doesn't hear her.

MRS WILSON Anybody wearing a coat like yours is stared at nowadays.

He shakes his head obstinately.

MRS WILSON Are you turning back again this time too?

JAMIE I . . . have not yet decided.

SOUND: *Air-raid siren.*

JAMIE What's that?

MRS WILSON It could be an A.R.P. exercise, but maybe the Germans are raiding Leith docks or the naval base. [*looks out and up*] The A.R.P. expect us to go down to the basement and sit in the smallest walled space we can find.

JAMIE [*with decision*] Shut the door, I won't go out if it is against the law.

She shuts it and helps him off with his coat.

JAMIE Hihi! Are you and I really going into a cupboard together, Mrs Macrae?

MRS WILSON We'll go to the kitchen in the basement, if you don't mind.

7: KIRKWOOD'S KITCHEN, 1939

The windows are sealed off by hinged wooden shutters, gaslight shines on the kitchen table, **JAMIE** *and* **MRS WILSON** *sit at adjacent sides of it. There is a tea set between them with teapot and cosy and an open tin of Abernethy biscuits.* **JAMIE**, *having dunked a biscuit in his tea, nibbles it with great appreciation.* **MRS WILSON** *watches him steadily.*

SOUND: *Air-raid siren, fades to silence.*

JAMIE When I was a wee lad, I spent a lot of time down here with the servants.

MRS WILSON Who did you kill?

JAMIE [*casually*] My father, with the shame of it. All Edinburgh knew that once. Mrs Tulloch must have told you my story when you took over from her.

MRS WILSON [*without irritation*] My name is not Macrae and I never met your last housekeeper, but I do know she was not called Tulloch.

JAMIE [*nodding thoughtfully*] You're right. Mrs Macrae came to me at the start of the Kaiser's war. Your name is [*he looks at her*] Wilson.

MRS WILSON Yes.

JAMIE And you know nothing about me?

MRS WILSON [*smiling*] Only what the baker's auntie knows.

JAMIE [*wondering*] So in the world's eyes I am just an old man who never goes out. Nobody but me now remembers the horrible thing I did. Queer. I once lived for this moment. [*shakes his head*] What a let-down. What a let-down. Hihi!

MRS WILSON [*coaxing*] Tell me what you did, it can do no harm.

JAMIE [*slyly*] If you wish me to break the silence of a lifetime, you must pour me, at least, another cup of tea.

He smiles at her. She smiles and pours for him.

JAMIE My father, you see, was – [*he pauses, then says with emphasis*] the Reverend Doctor John Kirkwood. Many sons would have been proud of such a father, but I fear that, for me, he was a little too strict.

FADE INTO JAMIE'S YOUTH SEQUENCE

8: THE HOUSE EXTERIOR, 1877

White steps up to a shining front door, and clean windows curtained in heavy maroon velvet. The street in front is unmetalled. A nursemaid leading two children along the pavement is hidden for a moment by a driver trotting a hackney cab in the other direction. Clothing indicates the period, and that the day is very cold. Slow zoom to the study window where **JAMIE**, *a gaunt morose lad of 18 with a fierce moustache, glares accusingly out.*

9: KIRKWOOD'S STUDY, 1877

A tidy, heavily furnished, rich but comfortable room with a blazing fire in the hearth. The books are all in their cases, the print mounts are snowy white, all colours are strong and clear, and the furniture is where it will stand for 63 years. The central desk, beautifully polished, has nothing on it but an ink stand with pens, a sheaf of lined foolscap, and a large Bible and Concordance, one laid on the other. We see **JAMIE** *across the desk-top, his back to the room.*

SOUND: *A door opened and closed.*

JAMIE *does not move as the* **REVEREND JOHN KIRKWOOD** *approaches the desk, takes a key from his pocket, unlocks a drawer, lifts out some coins and lays one by one on a corner of the desk a sovereign, eight half-crowns and two shillings.*

KIRKWOOD There it is, Jamie.

JAMIE [*unmoving*] There is what, sir?

KIRKWOOD [*locking the drawer*] Your pocket money for the coming month. As you well know.

JAMIE [*unmoving*] And how much is it, sir?

KIRKWOOD Exactly what you know to expect from me – coins to the value of two guineas. [*sits in the high-backed chair*] Nothing more, nothing less. [*contemplates the back of his son's head*].

JAMIE [*tonelessly, after a pause*] Thank you sir. I am grateful, of course.

KIRKWOOD [*calmly, but with force*] Stop hinting, Jamie! If there is something you wish to tell me, speak it out like a man.

JAMIE *turns and points to the coins.*

JAMIE Father, that money is ... a pittance! Two guineas a month – barely ten shillings a week for a man of eighteen! Four times that amount would be nothing unusual – and you can easily afford it!

KIRKWOOD Are you ever hungry, Jamie?

JAMIE No sir. But I have to eat at home.

KIRKWOOD Your home is ten minutes walk from the university – I see no hardship in that. I pay your college fees. I pay for your clothing. You have your own warm bed and bedroom here. What do you want more money for, Jamie?

JAMIE [*coming nearer*] So that I can mix as an equal with my social equals, Father! You are a famous and respected clergyman, I am studying to be a doctor, but I cannot keep company with other gentlemen's sons without getting into debt.

KIRKWOOD [*sharply*] You are in debt?

JAMIE [*who has come nearer*] No! Or at least ... I have not sunk so low ... as to borrow what I have not quickly repaid; but nowadays, when young men entertain each other, money must be spent. And anyone who does not entertain others as much as he is entertained looks mean, and selfish, and becomes a social outcast.

KIRKWOOD Are you referring to the popular pastime of "standing your round"?

JAMIE *sits in the easy chair to be nearer his father's level.*

JAMIE [*pleading for sympathy*] Father, I admit that I enjoy company – human company – more than you do, but I am honest! I have never hurt or deceived or cheated anyone. And I am chaste – I do not keep company with women. And I have never, never been overpowered by drink!

KIRKWOOD Never been a drunkard! Astonishing.

JAMIE [*almost, but not quite, out of hope*] Father, I am not a very bad sort. If you could like me enough to . . . trust me, Father, I am sure you would discover that!

KIRKWOOD [*after a moment*] If I give you more, Jamie, will you promise me it shall be spent as I should wish?

They look hard at each other.

JAMIE [*with sudden determination*] No!

With an impatient shoulder shrug **KIRKWOOD** *turns his face to the fire.* **JAMIE** *stands up, strides to the door, opens it, hesitates, strides back to the desk, scoops the coins with his right hand into his left and walks out.*

10: EDINBURGH STREET, 1877

A pavement with an area railing on one side. **JAMIE** *strides grimly forward, rhythmically clenching and unclenching the fist with the coins in it. He comes to a sign on the railing indicating a billiards saloon, pauses briefly, then turns into an entrance beside it.*

11: BILLIARDS SALOON, 1877

Four students of **JAMIE***'s age and class –* **TOM, DICK, HARRY** *and* **MCEWAN** *– are in the last stages of a game.* **TOM** *is plump and jocular,* **DICK** *a neat little dandy,* **HARRY** *is spectacled,* **MCEWAN** *is a thick-set Highlander. All are in their shirt sleeves. At an adjacent table, a calm, heavy, bearded man of about 30, whose clothing hints at wealth without flaunting it, is making careful practice shots. Empty tables isolate these five from more plebeian players near the saloon entrance, from which* **JAMIE** *approaches.*

NOTE: *the game is Pyramids, an early form of pool.*

TOM [*rises from a shot and says to* **DICK**] Get out of that one.

DICK *ponders it, bending and squinting.*

HARRY Hallo Kirkwood.

JAMIE Will anyone here cover a stake of two guineas?

They stare at him. **DICK** *stands up.*

DICK What's got into you, Kirkwood?

MCEWAN I cannot play for that kind of money.

HARRY I can but I won't!

DICK Same here!

TOM Has your Guvnor kicked the bucket?

Behind them a bearded man is sighting accurately along a cue.

JAMIE So I have to go elsewhere?

BEARDED MAN [*still sighting*] I'll cover that stake.

JAMIE Good!

The **BEARDED MAN** *smites the ball before standing.* **JAMIE** *places his money on the corner of his table and starts removing his jacket.* **HARRY** *addresses him quietly and urgently.*

HARRY Pull out of it, Kirkwood. That fellow's a sharp.

JAMIE Mind your own business, Cunningham.

Behind them the **BEARDED MAN** *puts two sovereigns beside* **JAMIE***'s stake and stands with a shilling between his fingers.*

BEARDED MAN You call.

JAMIE Heads.

BEARDED MAN [*spinning, catching, displaying*] I break.

A sequence of rapid close-ups shows the course of the game. The **BEARDED MAN***'s play is calm and deliberate.* **JAMIE** *plays with a nervous intensity shown by the rapidity of his strokes after each sighting. Glimpses of the onlooking students – perhaps* **HARRY** *is marking the scoreboard – show their attitude to the game change from slightly surprised curiosity to an excited identification with* **JAMIE***, who just manages to win.*

BEARDED MAN [*abruptly*] Your game . . . Care for another?

HARRY [*murmuring to* **JAMIE**] Cut and run, old chap.

JAMIE *points to the stake and tells the* **BEARDED MAN***:*

JAMIE Cover that again and I'm on.

The **BEARDED MAN** *dips fingers in his waistcoat pocket.*

Another sequence indicates a game which **JAMIE** *wins more rapidly.*

BEARDED MAN Your game.

JAMIE Care for another?

BEARDED MAN No, I'm for off. You're in luck tonight.
JAMIE Luck? Don't you call it skill?
BEARDED MAN Are you often as skilful as that?
JAMIE Not . . . often. No.
BEARDED MAN Then it's luck. Goodbye.
He leaves. **JAMIE** *scoops the coins into his fist and then, with a tight little smile, looks at the others who are staring at him with a touch of awe.*
JAMIE Well if it's luck, let's try it further.

12: BETTING SHOP, 1877

CHARLIE GEMMEL *stands near the counter reading a sporting paper. He is a young man of* **JAMIE**'s *physical type, but with a fair moustache, and more fashionably dressed, and more fashionably languid. He does not see* **JAMIE** *lead* **TOM, DICK, HARRY** *and* **MCEWAN** *into the shop and glance up at the blackboard chalked with the odds. He notices him when he approaches the counter.*
GEMMEL [*without much interest*] What are you doing here Kirkwood? You know nothing about horses.
JAMIE I know more than you think.
He puts money on the counter and tells the bookmaker's clerk:
JAMIE Five pounds on Joyous Absconder.
GEMMEL [*astonished*] Five pounds!
He stares from **JAMIE** *to his followers.* **CUT TO**:

13: BETTING SHOP LATER

GEMMEL, TOM, DICK, HARRY *and* **MCEWAN** *stand in an astonished, uneasy, rather envious little group, talking in low voices. The cash counter is behind them.* **JAMIE**, *at the head of the queue, is being served there.*
GEMMEL Kirkwood's collecting.
TOM How much?
HARRY Thirty pounds.
MCEWAN I have never seen so much money go into one man's pocket.
JAMIE *joins them, smiling broadly for the first and last time in this play.*
JAMIE Congratulate me, gentlemen – I know when to stop! [*laughs aloud. They cheer, laugh, slap his back, shake his hand*] You're all in luck too. For the first time in my life I am in a position to play the host. Where will we start tonight? The Deacon Brodie?

14: EXTERIOR SHOT OF PUB FRONT, 1877

Fast zoom into sign: "The Deacon Brodie".

15: PROSPEROUS PUB SNUG ALCOVE, 1877

The six young men, each with a tumbler of whisky in hand, stand round a circular table. **JAMIE** *and* **GEMMEL** *are side by side.*
JAMIE [*solemnly*] Whisky and freedom gang thegither.
GEMMEL [*solemnly*] Take off your dram.
Everyone solemnly drinks, then sits down. **TOM**, *as if struck by a sudden thought, declares:*
TOM A fig for those by law protected.
He looks at **DICK**.
DICK Liberty's a glorious feast!
He looks at **HARRY**.
HARRY Courts for cowards were erected!
He looks at **MCEWAN**, *who raises his arms as though conducting an orchestra.*
EVERYONE TOGETHER, BUT JAMIE LOUDEST:
Churches built to please the priest!
SOUND: *Loud fiddle music plays "The Dashing White Sergeant" over:*

16: THE DEBAUCH, 1877

16/1 **JAMIE** *leads his guests at a trot down an old Edinburgh close and through a door. Zoom to a sign over the door, "The Bass Rock".*
16/2 **JAMIE**'s *guests chat and drink in a crowded, wholly masculine pub. Their tumblers are nearly empty, but* **JAMIE**, *to the dread of those near him, carries from the bar a tray of six full glasses on one hand held high over the heads of the crowd.*
16/3 *Zoom up to inn sign: "The Auld Alliance".*
16/4 *A fiddler plays in the corner of a bar parlour with wall benches.* **TOM** *and* **DICK** *sit on each side of a fat, gap-toothed, middle-aged woman, probably a prostitute, each with an arm round her, and all three laughing heartily. Nearby* **GEMMEL** *talks gallantly to a young plump girl.* **MCEWAN** *and* **HARRY** *whisper furtively to a consumptively thin, pale one. In the foreground a mature, pleasant woman in shawl and apron talks*

beguilingly to **JAMIE**, *who does nothing but smile and slowly shake his head.*

16/5 *Zoom up to an inn sign: "The Café Royal".*

16/6 *A dining room with bright wallpaper, a sideboard, and a central table with twelve chairs round it and the remains of a meal on the cloth. Many wine bottles, mostly empty, stand among the dirty plates, though one lies on its side in a red stain.* **JAMIE** *sits at the top of the table, head flung back and roaring with laughter. A chair away* **HARRY** *is slumped with his head on his arms and his arms among the plates. Elsewhere* **DICK** *sits close to* **GEMMEL**'*s former companion, whispering to her intently, his arm around her waist. She is barely able to keep awake.* **TOM** *and* **MCEWAN** *are wrestling on the floor.* **JAMIE** *forces himself drunkenly onto his feet, and raises his hand as if to make an important announcement.*

SOUND: *End of fiddle music.*

CUT TO:

17: BLACKOUT

Silence for two seconds, then –

SOUND: *Low plangent throbbing like a bagpipe drone. This persists in darkness for two more seconds and continues over the next sequence.*

18: P.O.V. SEQUENCE WITH HAND-HELD CAMERA IN STROBE LIGHTING, 1877

18/1 *Low angle shot of a gas lantern at the top of a lamppost reeling across the screen.*

18/2 *Tilted shot of pavement and railings rushing towards us.*

18/3 *Tilted shot of what could be the* **KIRKWOOD** *front steps and door, rushing into close-up of the door.*

18/4 *Low angle shot of stairs and banisters.*

18/5 *Low angle close-up of a banister knob suddenly clutched by* **JAMIE**'*s hand.*

18/6 *Low angle shot of doorframe and door with zoom towards door which suddenly opens on very dim light.*

18/7 *Upward view of a gas chandelier with a dim blue flame burning in the mantle.* **JAMIE**'*s hand pulls the pendant chain which makes the mantle flame brightly.*

SOUND: *End of droning.*

19: JULIETTE'S BEDROOM: MANTON'S HOUSE, 1877

First, a creamy surface without boundaries – the ceiling above the bed where **JAMIE** *lies. Hold for a second.*

SOUND: *Very faint hiss.*

Tilt across ceiling past hissing gas chandelier (hiss fades when gasolier passed) and tilt down wall, crossing ornate cornice, stopping on a woman's dressing table furnished with a mirror and articles. The legs of the table are hidden by a bed's carved mahogany footboard viewed from the pillow. The mirror reflects the upper central part of a bed's carved mahogany headboard. **JAMIE**'*s staring face rises into this reflection. He stares suddenly right and – quick pan right along a wall with woman's dresses hanging on nails; a wardrobe of light, varnished wood; a footbath in a corner. Quick pan left across the dressing table (***JAMIE**'*s face glancing left in the mirror as camera crosses it) to the room's other corner where there is a shut door.* **JAMIE**'*s jacket has been dropped at the foot of the door. His waistcoat, shirt, trousers, shoes and underwear are scattered in a line across the carpet. The last of these garments has fallen in front of a tall cheval glass. This has a stand beside it loaded with finger-rings, earrings and necklaces.* **JAMIE** *jumps out of bed and sees himself reflected full length in the cheval glass. He wears a woman's silk nightshirt with much lace on the sleeves and the bosom. It comes a little below his knees, the sleeves half way to his elbow. Appalled, he drags it up over his head, tearing it, and casts it on the bed. Two or three quick shots of* **JAMIE** *hurrying into his clothes, then feeling in his pockets, while glancing hurriedly around. A bedside tabletop with a key on it, which* **JAMIE** *grabs.*

20: THE LANDING: MANTON'S HOUSE, 1877

This is familiar, as Manton's house, with woodwork, paintwork and gas fittings, is identical to the Manse. **JAMIE**, *stealthily emerging from the bedroom door, is disconcerted by this, and also by a framed "Judgement of Paris" print from Rubens' painting, at which he throws a haunted glance.*

SOUND: *Faintly from downstairs, laughter and voices.*

JAMIE *tiptoes to the banisters. A downward shot of the stairwell, with* **JAMIE** *leaning over, listening.*

SOUND: *Distant door opened and general party noise gets louder. The voices of a few cheerful, slightly drunk men are heard from the hall below.*

VOICES: – get my revenge another time. Goodnight!

Make it soon. Goodnight! Madam, departing from you desolates us. Aha, goodnight! Goodnight. Good –

SOUND: *A front door shuts, cutting out the nearer voices, then an interior door, reducing the party noise. Light footsteps approach the stairs.* **JAMIE** *retreats to the bedroom.*

21: JULIETTE'S BEDROOM, 1877

JAMIE *tiptoes quickly in, closes the door, and stands beside it, listening. Footsteps approach. He shrinks behind the door as it opens. A girl of his own age enters. She is dark haired and wears a black evening dress which leaves her shoulders bare. There is a rose in her bosom. She does not see him, but automatically closes the door, goes to the cheval glass and stares at herself in it very seriously for a while. Then she sighs, removes the rose, places it on the jewel stand, and unclasps her bodice.* **JAMIE** *steps forward.*

JAMIE I beg your pardon –

She faces him, bewilderment, astonishment, then the beginning of anger in her face.

JULIETTE What on earth –

She pauses. He has gone near her, but not near enough to suggest menace.

JAMIE [*eagerly*] Madam, for the love of God, make no mistake. I am no thief, and I give you my word, I am a gentleman. I do not know where I am – I have been vilely drunk – that is my paltry confession. It seems that your house is built like mine, that my key has unlocked your front door. Also our bedrooms are in the same positions! How or when I came here the Lord knows; but I awakened in your bed a few minutes back – and here I am! It is ruin for me if I am found; if you can help me out you will save a fellow from a dreadful mess. If you can't – or won't – God help me!

He stares at her, wide-eyed and open-mouthed.

JULIETTE [*not quite taking this in*] I have never seen you before. You are none of Manton's friends.

JAMIE I have never even heard of Manton. I tell you, I don't know where I am! I thought I was in Queen Street, number 15 – the Reverend Doctor Kirkwood's. That is my father.

JULIETTE You are streets away from that! You are near Stockbridge, at Manton Jamieson's. You are not fooling me?

JAMIE [*shaking his head*] No! But – [*points tragically to bed*] – I have torn your nightshirt!

She picks it up, frowns at it, looks back at him, finds his wild seriousness comic, and laughs a little.

JULIETTE Well, this is not like a thief. But how did you get into such a state?

JAMIE [*with very slight smile*] Oh! The great affair is not to get into such a state again.

JULIETTE We must get you smuggled out. Can you use the window?

She watches **JAMIE** *go to it. It faces the door and the curtains are white and transparent.* **JAMIE** *parts them, looks out and turns.*

JAMIE Not from this window. It will have to be the door.

JULIETTE The trouble is that Manton's friends – they play roulette and sometimes play late; and the sooner you are gone the better. Manton must not see you.

JAMIE [*earnestly*] For God's sake not ... I am very lucky that you are prepared to help such an unwelcome guest.

JULIETTE [*dryly*] I am not thinking of you in the least. [*she turns to the mirror and consults her reflection*] I am thinking of myself.

She sighs and starts to fasten her bodice.

SOUND: *A double tap at the door by a single knuckle.*

JULIETTE *and* **JAMIE** *stare at each other.* **JAMIE** *tip-toes into the angle between wardrobe and wall, out of sight of the door.*

SOUND: *The double tap repeated.*

MANTON's **VOICE OUTSIDE:** Juliette!

JULIETTE *swiftly unfastens her hair, and lifts a brush to it.*

JULIETTE Yes?

The door is opened by **MANTON** *who stands in doorway. He is the* **BEARDED MAN** *from the billiard room, in evening dress.*

MANTON [*courteously*] May I enter?

JULIETTE I cannot prevent you. But I am tired of company tonight, Manton. I thought you understood that.

She brushes her hair. **MANTON** *glances round the room.*

MANTON [*casually*] Who were you talking to?

JULIETTE To myself. Please leave me, Manton.

MANTON *smiles and closes door behind him, saying:*

MANTON Your voice is trembling!

He goes to her – she continues brushing – he stands behind her, lays his hands on her hips, gently kisses her shoulder. She stands frigid. She sees that part of **JAMIE** *is visible behind the reflection of the wardrobe in the mirror.*

MANTON You seem disturbed by something. [*kisses her again*] Or someone. Is it that fellow behind the wardrobe? [*releases her and turns, saying quietly, but with contempt*] Come out of there.

JAMIE, *very pale, steps forward and confronts him.*

MANTON [*with a touch of surprise*] Well well! The lucky young man in the billiard hall. [*grins, shakes his head, and adds on an intimate note*:] My boy, your luck. Has just. Run. Out!

22: KIRKWOOD'S HOUSE KITCHEN, 1939

Old **JAMIE** *and* **MRS WILSON** *at the table, she leaning on her folded arms, staring at him. He is leaning back in his chair, hands folded on stomach, apparently examining the ceiling.*

MRS WILSON [*after a pause*] Well?

JAMIE [*not looking at her*] Eh?

MRS WILSON What did he do?

JAMIE [*puzzled*] Who?

MRS WILSON The Manton chap.

JAMIE Oh I didn't meet him that night. We met the following night.

MRS WILSON But you said he came into the room . . .

JAMIE [*slightly annoyed*] You misunderstood me, Mrs Wilson. That is what I feared would happen. What really happened, you see, was, like this.

23: JULIETTE'S BEDROOM, 1877

JAMIE *and* **JULIETTE** *stand near the cheval glass.*

JULIETTE We must get you smuggled out. Can you use the window?

She watches **JAMIE** *go to it. The curtains are white and transparent.* **JAMIE** *parts them, looks out and turns.*

JAMIE Not from this window. It will have to be the door.

JULIETTE The trouble is that Manton's friends – they play cards for money and sometimes play late, and the sooner you are gone the better. Manton must not see you.

JAMIE [*earnestly*] For God's sake not . . . I am very lucky that you are prepared to help such an unwelcome guest.

JULIETTE [*dryly*] I am not thinking of you in the least. [*turns to the mirror and consults her reflection*] I'm thinking of myself. [*sighs and starts to fasten her bodice, talking mainly to herself*] Oh, the company downstairs is deadly dull, deadly dull. But I am capricious. I have discovered that I cannot rest without another hour of their slurred voices and smoky breaths. I will return to them – [*pats her hair*] – and be as fascinating as usual. [*lifts the rose from the stand and fixes it in her hair*] Maybe more so. [*examines the result in the mirror then turns to the ardently staring* **JAMIE**] Follow me down at a safe distance and wait on the half landing when I enter the drawing room. I will ensure that nobody leaves it for a while. You must do the rest yourself.

JAMIE Yes, but – please give me your name! I must tell you that –

JULIETTE *puts her hand on the door and speaks to him over her shoulder.*

JULIETTE You must tell me nothing! Do exactly what I have told you and be careful! For both our sakes!

24: THE LOBBY, MANTON'S HOUSE, 1877

Seen from the front door, the stairs at the back right rise to the half landing in shadow above; back left is the corridor to the servants' quarters. Front right is a large hallstand loaded with coats, hats, sticks and a hall table supporting an overflow from this. Front left is the drawing room door.

SOUND: *Polite men at drink and cardplay – not too much laughter: some brief chuckles with a sharp haha!*

JULIETTE, *frowning, resolutely descends the stairs, pauses before the drawing room door, smoothes down her bodice with her hands, then glances up to where* **JAMIE** *lurks on the landing. She nods once to him, turns to the door, shakes her head, smiles vivaciously, opens the door and stands within it, one hand on the knob, the other on her hip. We see nothing of the company.*

SOUND: *Most voices in the room cease, with one saying*:

VOICE You're not the man I think you are if . . .

MANTON'S VOICE [*surprised*] Juliette!

GEMMEL'S VOICE [*enthusiastic*] Miss O'Sullivan!

OTHER VOICES: Hooray! Haha! This is indeed a pleasant ...

She closes the door behind her. **JAMIE** *creeps cautiously to the foot of the stairs. The door is suddenly opened by an old servant carrying a tray of empty glasses on one hand. He enters the hall sideways because he must shut the door behind him with the other hand.* **JAMIE** *has time to retreat up a few steps before the servant turns and walks to the back of the house without raising his eyes. As* **JAMIE** *wipes his brow and creeps down again*:

SOUND: *From the drawing room: a bright piano introduction is soon joined by* **JULIETTE** *singing*:

JULIETTE'S VOICE Why won't the men propose Mama?
Why won't the men propose?
'Tis not your fault indeed, Mama,
that everybody knows.

JAMIE *creeps into close-up.*

JULIETTE'S VOICE There's not a man of any ton
about the town that goes,
you do not fete and flatter yet –
But still – they won't – propose.

25: THE DOORSTEP, MANTON'S HOUSE, NIGHT, 1877

The door is identical with that of the Kirkwood house. Part of the drawing room window can be seen to the left of the door, with a chink of light through heavy curtains. The door opens. **JAMIE** *emerges stealthily, then pauses on the mat, listening.*

JULIETTE'S VOICE Mama! Mama!
Why won't the men propose?
Mama! Mama!
Why won't – [*crashing chord*]
The men – [*crashing chord*]
Propose? [*crashing chord*]

JAMIE *abruptly slams the door on one of the chords.*

CUT TO:

26: MANTON'S HOUSE, FROM ACROSS STREET, 1877

JAMIE *leaps down the steps and strides along the pavement. The drawing room curtain abruptly parts to show the silhouette of a man in the triangular opening.*

27: JAMIE STRIDING HOME THROUGH EDINBURGH, NIGHT, 1877

27/1 *Coming round the pavement of a curving terrace.*
27/2 *Crossing a street with a prospect at the end of the Castle or Arthur's Seat or Calton Hill or the Firth of Forth under the moon.*
27/3 *Passing the façade of a city church.*

28: OUTSIDE KIRKWOOD'S FRONT DOOR, NIGHT, 1877

JAMIE *arrives here and halts, gazing at the number on the fanlight. We see him from behind.*

JULIETTE'S VOICE [*distant*] I have never seen you before. You are none of Manton's friends.

JAMIE'S VOICE [*distant*] I don't know where I am! I thought I was in Queen Street, number 15 – the Reverend Doctor Kirkwood's – that is my father.

Zoom past **JAMIE** *into a close-up of the dark front door.*

29: KIRKWOOD'S DINING ROOM, MORNING, 1877

This is a large bleak room with a massive circular central table, and sideboard, and mantelpiece, but a bright coal fire. Cold daylight floods in between the curtains of a high window. **JAMIE**, *looking pale and absentminded, sits across from his father. Both have linen napkins tucked into their collars. Doctor Kirkwood frowns over the pair of kippers he has almost consumed* [**JAMIE** *eats slowly, with frequent pauses*] *then raises his eyes to the level of* **JAMIE***'s face.*

KIRKWOOD I did not hear you come home last night.

JAMIE [*meekly, after a brief pause*] No sir. [*resumes eating*]

KIRKWOOD I assume that it was not your medical studies which kept you out the house till well past two in the morning?

JAMIE *looks at him in a slightly puzzled way, as if trying to understand what he means. For a while father and son stare into each other's face.*

JULIETTE'S V.O. [*distant laughter, then*]: Well, this is not like a thief. But how did you get in such a state?

JAMIE *shakes his head, then resumes eating. His father, in real distress, passes a hand across his face, pulls off his napkin, rises and stands with his back to the fireplace.*

KIRKWOOD Jamie! I have said these words to you before, but I will not say them again, so attend! Attend! You are not working properly at your studies which ought one day to get you a living. Man is born to earn his bread in the sweat of his brow. I am a minister of religion; I am required to set an example in this community; I must not support a son who is a mere idler, wastrel, and profligate!

He stops, gaping open mouthed at the son who appals him. **JAMIE** *stands, willing to conciliate, but his mind is mainly elsewhere.*

JAMIE [*nodding*] I – I will give the matter thought sir. [*he pulls his napkin off*]

He goes to the door.

30: THE UNIVERSITY LECTURE THEATRE, 1877

Steeply tiered narrow benches curve round a rostrum with a desk where the lecturer is engaged in a demonstration. Pan along benches crowded with young students, half of them scribbling in hardbacked notebooks, the other half staring hard: some worried, some horrified, some fascinated, some amused. Among them **JAMIE**, *when we at last see him, is conspicuously a man whose mind is elsewhere.* **TOM**, *scribbling assiduously, sits beside him.*

LECTURER'S VOICE So when the current – enters the nerve – the muscle contracts and frog's leg kicks – although you saw me decapitate the poor beastie four minutes ago. So what may we conclude? [*pause*] What may we conclude?

CUT TO: *the* **LECTURER**, *impressively backed by a blackboard on which is chalked an extensive diagram of a nervous system linking otherwise disassociated cross-sections of a brain and a leg. Beside him a wired skeleton hangs from a stand. The desk before him has a galvanic battery on it and large glass vessels of clear fluid in which float a human embryo, a brain and a flayed leg. The* **LECTURER** *leans forward on his fists, which are placed on either side of a wooden slab with something small and bloody on it. He grins without humour.*

LECTURER What, Mr Kirkwood, may we conclude?

CUT TO: JAMIE *with the surrounding students staring at him. He merely frowns, thoughtfully.*

JULIETTE'S V.O. [*distant*] I was not thinking about you in the least. I was thinking of myself.

31: THE UNIVERSITY QUADRANGLE, 1877

JAMIE, *in hat and overcoat, slowly descends the terrace of steps on the south side, among chatting hatted and coated students hurrying in both directions. He moves in a stream of casual, solemn or flippant remarks which he seems not to hear.*

STUDENT VOICES: Medicine, the ministry or the law . . . lofted it onto the green and sunk it with a straight putt ... said I respected Hegel but I can't read Hegel ... she worked hard for a belly like that, so she did . . . Hahaha! . . . they clapped an interim interdict on him . . . God is not mocked! . . . Will I see you later at Manton's place?

JAMIE *is suddenly alert and glancing sideways.*

CUT TO: CHARLIE GEMMEL, *descending the steps, has paused to glance back at* **DICK** *who, climbing them, has also paused.*

DICK Aren't you going to Manton's place?

GEMMEL Not tonight. I'm out of funds.

GEMMEL *walks on towards the University entrance. We backtrack before him, seeing* **JAMIE** *follow, overtake and fall in step beside him.*

GEMMEL *becomes aware of* **JAMIE** *without enthusiasm.*

GEMMEL Hullo Kirkwood, how's your head today?

JAMIE Who's Manton Jamieson?

GEMMEL You should know, you were in his house last night.

JAMIE [*alarmed*] How do you – why do you think so?

GEMMEL [*glancing at him*] We took you there, you duffer! You were pretty tight, though. We all were, rather. You did us proud last night, Kirkwood!

They are under the arch of the entrance. **JAMIE** *brings them to a halt.*

JAMIE What exactly did I do, Gemmel?

GEMMEL [*smiling*] Nothing that I know! The servant let us into the hall, we hung up our hats and when we next looked round you had vanished. You must have walked straight back out again. On the front step you'd muttered something about the place being your father's house – I suppose you really thought it was your father's house, and turned tail and fled. You don't remember?

JAMIE *shakes his head.*

GEMMEL It's just as well. You missed seeing Juliette – the lovely Miss Juliette O'Sullivan. A woman to die for, Kirkwood.

He sighs and walks slowly on.

JAMIE [*following*] Tell me about . . . Manton Jamieson.

GEMMEL Manton runs the only polite shebeen in Edinburgh. It's so polite that nobody calls it a shebeen, but if you're the right sort you can drink and play there till all hours. Manton made his pile in America, so they say. Nobody knows how. He's not talkative.

JAMIE You mentioned some woman?

GEMMEL Juliette! [*stands still now*] Juliette adds tone to the establishment. She's beautiful, Kirkwood, she's witty and she sings like an angel. We swarm about her like bees round a queen. Manton never lets her out of his sight. No wonder! She's his ward, his niece, his step-daughter, or – or something else! [*groans*] I'm in love with her, Kirkwood – but that's nothing unusual.

He makes to walk on, but **JAMIE** *detains him.*

JAMIE I would like to go there sober, Charlie: tonight if possible. Can you introduce me?

GEMMEL Nothing easier! You're a sort Manton would

take to. The deuce of it is, I'm clean out of funds and though gaming isn't compulsory at Manton's place it's the done thing. We'll be given all the champagne we want so it's only fair that one of us hazards something on a game. Are you, er, penniless again?

JAMIE [*staring grimly at him*] Yes.

GEMMEL [*smiling and nodding*] Yes, you certainly did us proud last night, but I suppose you have a watch?

***JAMIE** detaches a watch from inside his overcoat and hands it to him. **GEMMEL** snaps open the silver case and brings it near his eye with something like the professional regard of a pawnbroker.*

GEMMEL This is a good watch – we can raise quite a bit on it. Will I show you where?

32: THE LOBBY OF MANTON'S HOUSE, NIGHT, 1877

Viewed from the stairs, we see again the hall stand and table loaded with hats and shed garments.

SOUND: *Male conversation and laughter from the drawing room, then the doorbell ringing over this.*

*The elderly servant goes to the door and opens it to **GEMMEL** and **JAMIE**, who stand there with unbuttoned coats. **GEMMEL** removes his hat and steps inside.*

GEMMEL Good evening MacFarlane. This gentleman is a particular friend of mine. [*deposits his hat and turns to let MacFarlane help him off with the coat*] I assume Mr Jamieson will have no objection to me introducing him into the company.

MACFARLANE [*grumbling slightly*] Probably not sir. Probably not.

***JAMIE**, who has also entered, is closing the front door.*

33: THE DRAWING ROOM, EARLY EVENING, 1877

*Eight men sit round a green clothed table, watching or playing a game of baccarat. **MANTON** is banker. A bald, toothless, spry old man is one of the company [we will call him **DALGLEISH**] but the rest are nearer **JAMIE**'s age. One of them is **DICK**. There is a grand piano, and a buffet stocked with food and drink. At a fireplace far from the door **JULIETTE**, in a gown of white velvet, stands talking quietly to **HARRY**. The door is knocked from outside. Folk at the table look up or round, but not **MANTON**.*

MANTON [*loudly, yet pondering his hand*] Yes?

*The door is opened by **GEMMEL**, who enters a little way through it, followed by **JAMIE**. **MANTON** lays his cards face down on the cloth and stands.*

MANTON Good evening.

GEMMEL Mr Jamieson, I took the liberty of bringing a friend – Jamie Kirkwood – who greatly wishes to meet you. His father is the Rev –

DALGLEISH [*jeering*] Haha! We know who his Reverend father is!

DICK Amen!

MANTON [*quietly, with a thin smile*] Mind your manners, gentlemen. [*to **JAMIE**, courteously*] I know you by sight, Mr Kirkwood, you are welcome. We are playing baccarat, you will excuse us if we continue. Perhaps later you will join us? Your hostess is my ward, Miss O'Sullivan. [*calling*] Juliette!

*He sits down and lifts his cards. **JULIETTE** is already approaching the rivals.*

JULIETTE How nice to see you again Mr Gemmel. [*she gives him her hand*] And so on!

GEMMEL [*bowing over the hand*] Can't keep away from you, Miss O'Sullivan.

*He retains the hand longer than she likes. She waits until he releases it, then looks coldly at **JAMIE**.*

JULIETTE How do you do?

***JAMIE** bows.*

JULIETTE As hostess I should introduce you to the other guests Mr –

GEMMEL Kirkwood.

JULIETTE – but most of them, as you see, are engaged with the game. There is the buffet. Please help yourself.

*She walks back to the fireplace. **JAMIE** gazes after her. **GEMMEL** nudges him.*

GEMMEL Confess it! You're smitten.

He chuckles, goes to the buffet and fills a glass with wine. He is about to fill another.

JAMIE Not for me!

***GEMMEL** smiles, puts down the bottle and sips from the first glass.*

***JAMIE** stares after **JULIETTE** with a haunted look.*

GEMMEL I've never seen her so chilly with a new guest before, but don't take it to heart. Pursue her! Pursue her! She flirts with all of us eventually! [*bitterly*] Nothing comes of it.

*He goes towards the game. **JAMIE** goes to the fireplace where **JULIETTE** and **HARRY** sit on the sofa, she smiling and nodding* *while* **HARRY**, *gesturing with his hands, tries hard to be amusing.* **JAMIE** *folds his arms and leans patiently against the wall nearby.*

HARRY So this pot, this urn, yes this quite big urn full of – of foetid stuff comes crashing down on his head and – well, it was no joke, I tell you! [*but he hopes it is*] However, not all the professors are such duffers. Hullo Kirkwood!

JAMIE *nods.*

JULIETTE Harry, do you think Mr Kirkwood is queuing up for me?

HARRY [*guffawing*] Looks like it! I'm just going to sit tight however.

JULIETTE Be kind. Give him just two minutes.

HARRY *stares at her, then stands up.*

HARRY He can have all the time in the world, for what I care.

He goes towards the buffet. **JAMIE** *takes his place.* **JAMIE** *and* **JULIETTE** *watch each other sideways for a moment. He is eager, shy and angry; she is coldly angry.*

JAMIE Please don't ignore me. Ever!

JULIETTE You have no right to be here.

JAMIE I have as much right as – as – as Charlie Gemmel.

JULIETTE [*with contempt*] You are no gambler!

JAMIE I am whatever I choose to be!

JULIETTE [*facing him scornfully*] Do you choose to be rich?

He stares at her. She softens.

JULIETTE Are you rich?

He shakes his head. She sighs and lays his hand on his. He is electrified, but she is too full of her own thoughts to notice this.

JULIETTE [*pleading*] Did I not prove I was your friend last night?

He nods.

JULIETTE I am still your friend. Leave this house and don't come back. Don't see me again. Ever! Please!

JAMIE [*automatically*] Excuse me.

He stands and walks away. We see his face in close-up, wide-eyed, tight-lipped, and breathing hard.

SOUND: *The room noises are completely cut out.* **JULIETTE**'*s voice loud in the distance, resounds with a trace of echo.*

JULIETTE'S VOICE Did I not prove I was your friend last night? I am still your friend. I am still your friend. I am still your friend. Please. Please. Please. Don't ever see me again!

JAMIE [*firmly and aloud, among normal acoustics*] I will!

HARRY, *nearby, stares at him curiously.*

CUT TO: *the card table an hour later.* **MANTON**, *quietly businesslike, is collecting money from* **GEMMEL** *who hides his depression with a show of reckless resignation. The room has more guests in it. Many, glasses in hand, stand watching round the table.* **JAMIE**, *arms folded and leaning against a wall, watches extra-intently.*

MANTON The bank is doing well tonight. Dalgleish! [*lifts a lit cigar from an ashtray near his elbow*] Take my place for a bit. [*stands*] I need to stretch.

He strolls over to **JAMIE** *and stands beside him. They both watch the table without seeming to notice each other.*

MANTON [*at last*] You like card play?

JAMIE Why else would I come here?

MANTON [*smiling*] In the tight little Presbyterian republic of Scotland card play has all the intoxication of forbidden fruit. Many of my guests play because the company makes them feel like devilish fine fellows.

JAMIE [*coldly*] I will play when I can afford to play.

MANTON [*watching him thoughtfully*] Would you like a loan?

JAMIE [*definitely*] No!

MANTON [*nodding approval*] Good! And I see that, like myself, you do not drink. That gives me hopes of you. But [*intimately*] get your friend out of here. He has not a cool head.

He goes towards the sofa where **JULIETTE** *holds court among three young men.* **JAMIE** *goes to the table and touches* **GEMMEL**, *who sits stunned by his failures, upon the shoulder.*

JAMIE We must go now.

GEMMEL [*looking blearily up*] Eh? Alright. Alright.

DALGLEISH Haste ye back! Haha!

34: A PAVEMENT, NIGHT, 1877

JAMIE *and* **GEMMEL** *walk side by side.* **GEMMEL**, *in unbuttoned overcoat, is glum but talkative.*

GEMMEL I shan't be back there in a hurry. It's nearly a month till my next allowance and my brute of a governor won't allow me another advance on it. And I owe money everywhere! Everywhere! You were wise to drag me away when you did, Kirkwood. I usually hang on to the bitter end, because of Juliette, you know – the beautiful Miss Juliette O'Sullivan. Wasn't I right Kirkwood? Isn't she a woman to die for?

JAMIE *holds his hand out, palm up.* **GEMMEL** *sighs, takes some things from his pocket and passes them over.*

GEMMEL There's the pawn ticket and there's the change

– not much, I'm afraid. I had hoped to repay you with interest, Kirkwood, but luck was against me.

JAMIE [*firmly*] Luck does not exist. Luck is superstitious rot. You lost to Manton like everyone else tonight, because he is skilful and you are all idiots.

GEMMEL [*daunted*] Could you have done better?

JAMIE Of course not, so I did not play. When I go back there, Charlie – when we go back there, Charlie – we will play and we will win because we will have made ourselves better than Manton!

GEMMEL How?

JAMIE By studying and practice. By practice and study. There are books about card games, are there not? Books by dependable authorities?

GEMMEL Well, Cavendish is thought pretty good, and one or two French fellows.

JAMIE We'll work on them. A month just might be sufficient if we apply ourselves hard. After all, we've nothing better to do with our time.

GEMMEL, *disconcerted, glances sideways at him.* **JAMIE** *looks determinedly forward.*

35: KIRKWOOD'S STUDY, 1877

The **REVEREND DOCTOR KIRKWOOD** *sits at his desk, spectacles on nose, writing a sermon between open Bible and Concordance. The study door is rapped and opened.*

JAMIE [*at the door*] May I speak to you, father?

KIRKWOOD *lays down his pen and turns towards him.* **JAMIE** *closes the door and approaches.*

JAMIE I have a favour to ask.

KIRKWOOD *removes his spectacles and looks his son in the face.* **JAMIE** *looks straight back at him.*

JAMIE I believe I will do better at my studies if I share them with a college friend, Charlie Gemmel. Since this house is a quieter place than his I want us to work most evenings and weekends in the privacy of my bedroom. Would you object to him sharing our meals between whiles?

A pause.

KIRKWOOD [*quietly and emphatically*] I can have no possible objection to that.

JAMIE [*nodding*] Thank you sir.

He goes out. His father stares after him.

SOUND: *Solemn organ music over these sequences*:

36: CARDPLAY PRACTICE SEQUENCE, 1877

36/1 **MANSE STAIRWELL**, *night. A low angle side shot of* **JAMIE** *climbing them with a lit candle in a holder, followed by* **GEMMEL** *carrying a Gladstone bag*

36/2 **JAMIE**'*s* **BEDROOM***: Identical with* **JULIETTE**'*s in all but furnishings – the bed has brass rails.* **JAMIE** *holds the candle up to the mantle of the gasolier which takes fire and brightens.* **GEMMEL** *is unpacking books and a card case from a bag onto a tabletop.*

36/3 *Downward close-up of tabletop, a pack of cards in the centre.* **JAMIE**'*s hand cuts it and shows the King of Hearts;* **GEMMEL** *cuts and shows Nine of Spades. They practice playing baccarat. Very quick shots of them:-*

36/4 *Dealing, placing and covering bets.*

36/5 *Exposing hands, collecting winnings, with scribbled pencil notes used for money.*

36/6 *The banker has increasing amounts of these notes before him. The banker's opponent is pondering several hands.*

36/7 *Passage of time indicated by brief shot of* **GEMMEL, DR KIRKWOOD** *and* **JAMIE** *eating round the dining room table, and also by the two young men's increasingly hollow-cheeked pallor but* **GEMMIL** *is certainly the worse for wear.* **JAMIE** *remains fanatically tight-lipped, cool and businesslike, though palest of all.*

36/8 **JAMIE** *stands reading from a book, his forefinger raised, while* **GEMMEL**, *looking dazed, stares at an upturned pattern of play.*

36/9 *Downward shot of* **STAIRWELL** *a maidservant carrying upstairs a tray holding covered dishes for two. She puts it on the floor in front of* **JAMIE**'*s bedroom door, then knocks on the door.*

SOUND: *End of organ music.*

37: JAMIE'S BEDROOM, 1877

JAMIE *sits in a chair by the fire, book in hand and deep in thought.* **GEMMEL** *sits holding his head in both hands at the table, which has hands of cards exposed on it. He is exhausted, dishevelled and unshaven.*

SOUND: *The door is knocked.*

GEMMEL [*after a pause*] Food. [*another pause*] I said, food!

JAMIE *does not move.*

JAMIE Charlie, I'm beginning to understand this game.

GEMMEL Ha! You and I would be qualified doctors if we'd given our medical studies this degree of attention. [*gets up, opens door, lifts and brings tray in, closes door, puts tray on table and, without clearing the cards, sets a place for himself, talking all the time:*]

You're a monomaniac, Kirkwood, a fanatic, like your father, but cards have become your religion. I thought I was mad about them but you've almost cured me. If it wasn't for my creditors I'd have left here days ago. [*uncovers a plate of grilled chops, onions and roast potatoes, and appreciatively sniffs it*] I must admit, though, your father keeps a good cook. Why don't you eat?

JAMIE *stands on the hearth rug talking quietly, firmly yet vehemently: as much to himself as to* **GEMMEL**.

JAMIE The secret of victory lies in the bank – the main chances always favour the bank! Manton's superior skill maintains his lead in a game which is already on his side because he has most money.

GEMMEL [*with food in his mouth*] Banks have been broken.

JAMIE Yes! By runs of luck! We could wait weeks or months before hitting one of those, and we haven't the resources to play a waiting game. Our strategy must make us rich in an evening: a single evening.

GEMMEL [*shaking his head*] Only one strategy is sure to do that in a game which is three fifths chance.

JAMIE [*looking straight at him and nodding*] Yes!

GEMMEL *lays down knife and fork.*

GEMMEL I'm no saint Kirkwood. I'm not going to preach to you. But foul play is impossible in baccarat if you're not the banker. Nobody else touches the pack.

JAMIE I will be banker.

GEMMEL That's out of the question! Manton is richer than we are, he's also our host, we –

SOUND: *A knock on the door.*

GEMMEL *quickly scuffles the cards together.* **JAMIE** *stays cool, walks to the door and opens it about three inches.* **DR KIRKWOOD***'s face is visible outside.*

JAMIE [*still cool*] Hullo father.

He opens it a few inches further, keeping hold of the knob.

KIRKWOOD [*gently*] I'd like a few words with you Jamie – private words.

JAMIE Shall I come to your study when I've finished my meal?

KIRKWOOD [*nodding*] Do that.

He turns away.

38: KIRKWOOD'S STUDY, 1877

The room is identical with Scene 9. **JAMIE** *stands before his father's desk, his fingertips pressing the edge of it.* **KIRKWOOD** *unlocks a drawer, lifts out some coins, lays ten sovereigns in a row on the surface.*

KIRKWOOD Your pocket-money!

JAMIE [*thoughtfully*] Ten guineas.

KIRKWOOD I am giving you more, Jamie, because you deserve more. A month ago you asked for an allowance worthy of a gentleman's son while declaring you would not spend it as a gentleman ought. I admired your honesty, of course, but I loathed your cynicism. You have changed since then, Jamie! When I look at you I no longer see an ordinary, thankless young drifter, I see a man with a purpose, a man determined to make his way in the world, a man I can trust!

JAMIE *regards the money quietly, and speaks without raising his eyes.*

JAMIE Thank you father. You know – [*taps the desk twice with his fingers*] – other gentlemen pay their son's pocket-money not a month, but a quarter in advance.

His father, with a droll grimace, pretends to be surprised:

KIRKWOOD Do they indeed?

JAMIE [*nodding*] Indeed they do!

KIRKWOOD [*with a resigned headshake*] Then of course I must do likewise. [*counts out more money from the drawer*] Thirty guineas.

JAMIE *picks them up, pockets them and stares at his father with a small crooked smile.*

JAMIE You are being ... very kind to me.

KIRKWOOD [*shyly*] Since you changed for the better, Jamie, it has occurred to me that perhaps I should make a similar effort. [*turns his face away*] Perhaps one day you and I may even be friends.

JAMIE Perhaps. However [*shrugs*] I must return to my studies.

39: JAMIE'S BEDROOM, 1877

GEMMEL *leans back smoking in the fireside chair. The meal-things are cleared away, the cards neatly stacked in the centre of the table.* **JAMIE** *enters, sits on the edge of the table and shows* **GEMMEL** *a handful of coin.*

JAMIE See this? My allowance. Thirty guineas the quarter – in advance!

GEMMEL [*staring*] You are in luck.

JAMIE [*coldly*] No luck. I earned this gold. [*pockets it*] I earned it by devotion to that – [*cuts the cards, turning up the ace of diamonds and briefly smiling at it*] The old man thinks I am now a model student. [*replaces the cards*] But thirty guineas is too little. I must start my play with Manton by risking all that and losing it without a qualm. Then I will take over the bank –

GEMMEL But how –

JAMIE I need capital! With capital, a cool head and courage a man can achieve anything Gemmel. So. I must beg it, or borrow it, or steal it. There is a certain desk I know with a drawer containing – quite a lot. I'm sure the lock could be forced ... [*sees that* **GEMMEL** *is staring at him*] Don't worry Charlie! Whatever I beg, borrow or steal will be returned next day.

GEMMEL You can't be sure of that. [*stands, throwing his cigarette in the fire*] For God's sake don't steal, Jamie! Listen, if you must borrow I can give you the name of a money-lender, an out-and-out shark who will supply you with any amount of ready money. He knows your guvnor is a respectable clergyman who would pay a fortune to keep his son out of a public scandal.

JAMIE [*grimly*] Then he knows more than I know! [*pause*] How much will you invest in our venture, Gemmel?

GEMMEL Not one penny! When I get my allowance I will pay my creditors, live frugally on the remainder and never enter Manton's house again. I've sown my wild oats, Jamie, and the crop isn't worth a damn. As a man-about-town I'm a failure, Jamie. You've taught me that. With a bit of effort, however, I can become a decent general practitioner.

JAMIE So you won't choose to be rich?

GEMMEL *says nothing.* **JAMIE** *smiles, sits down at the table and picks up the cards.*

JAMIE All the more for me, then. But you're tired, Gemmel. Sit down. [*motions* **GEMMEL** *to the chair facing him*] You be banker this time.

He puts the cards on **GEMMEL***'s side of the table.*

SOUND: *organ music.*

40: A QUICK SEQUENCE OF SHOTS SHOWING:

40/1 **JAMIE** *striding down an Edinburgh Old Town wynd and through an entry with a loan-office sign.*

40/2 **JAMIE** *signs a document in a dingy parlour at a table overseen by two scoundrelly-looking witnesses.*

40/3 **JAMIE**, *in his father's darkened study, forcing open a locked drawer to expose golden sovereigns inside.*

40/4 **JAMIE** *striding, in a low-angle shot, along a New Town pavement.*

40/5 **MANTON***'s front door, in a high-angle shot from the hall stairs, being opened to* **JAMIE** *by the old* **SERVANT**. **JAMIE** *stands confident and central on the front step before removing his hat and entering.*

SOUND: *end of organ music.*

41: THE DRAWING ROOM, MANTON'S HOUSE, 1877

This is much as it was when we first saw it, though the room is slightly busier. **TOM**, **DICK**, **HARRY** *and* **MCEWAN** *are all present, with some strangers, but* **JULIETTE** *is still the only woman. She holds court, as usual, near the fireplace, and her dress is the one she wore when* **JAMIE** *first met her.* **MANTON**, *at the card table, is about to deal when the* **SERVANT** *opens the door. There is a lull in conversation.*

SERVANT [*loudly, to* **MANTON**] Mr Kirkwood, Sir!

JAMIE *enters.* **MANTON** *looks up, but does not stand.*

MANTON Mr Kirkwood! It is some time since we enjoyed your company. Have you come for the cardplay, or for another tête à tête with your hostess, Miss O'Sullivan?

JAMIE [*bowing towards* **JULIETTE**] For both, I hope. But first and foremost, for cardplay.

MANTON Excellent! Make room for Jamie Kirkwood.

Two players move aside to let **JAMIE** *occupy a chair between them.*

MANTON *deals.* **CUT TO:**

42: THE TABLE, LATER

JAMIE *exposes a winning hand.* **MANTON** *smiles agreeably.*

MANTON You are doing well, Mr Kirkwood!

He pushes notes and coins towards **JAMIE**. **CUT TO:**

43: THE TABLE, LATER

JAMIE *exposes a losing hand.* **MANTON** *chuckles, and collects.*

MANTON You play very well, Mr Kirkwood. You have lost more than you have won, but that is the table's fault, not yours.

JAMIE I wish, Mr Jamieson, I had your chances of winning.

He has spoken slightly too loudly for polite conversation. The rest of the room begins to pay attention.

MANTON [*with no change of voice*] All chances are equal round this table.

JAMIE Not quite. The banker has a better chance than anyone.

MANTON Since the house risks the greatest sum of money, Mr Kirkwood, it is only fair that its losses – with reasonable care – do not bankrupt it. But if you wish to take my place as a banker for a while – [*stands up*] – please do! There is more than £800 on the table. [*smiles ironically*] Of course, you can cover that?

JAMIE *also stands. He now has everyone's attention. Reaching inside his coat-breast he brings out a wad of notes with a band round them and lays it on the table, also a small wash-leather bag which he empties after untying the neck.*

JAMIE Here is £800 in notes and, er . . . here is £200 in guineas.

MANTON *stares at him.* **JAMIE** *stares back.*

DALGLEISH Haha!

The company talk and whisper violently. **TOM** *and* **DICK** *tug at* **JAMIE***'s right and left sleeves.*

TOM This is lunacy, Jamie! Lunacy! Lunacy!

DICK Don't do it!

JAMIE [*quietly*] Be quiet.

He stares at **JULIETTE**. *She expostulates with* **MANTON**, *who has turned to face her.* **MANTON** *at last shakes his head and turns back to the table. The company falls silent.*

MANTON Mr Kirkwood, my ward, Miss O'Sullivan, thinks you a foolish young man who should be asked to leave for his own good. [*smiles and shrugs*] But so far you have not played like a fool. You are a cool customer, certainly, but you don't seem out of your mind. Your request is eccentric and yes, I've a mind to grant it. Take my place sir!

Babble occurs as **MANTON** *gathers up his money.* **JAMIE** *moves towards* **MANTON***'s seat while* **JULIETTE**, *looking furiously angry, goes to the door.* **MANTON** *pocketing his cash, sees her about to open it.*

MANTON [*loudly, for the first time*] Juliette!

Silence. She pauses, then turns.

MANTON You will stay here, Juliette, and watch the course of play. [*to the company*] Pardon my harsh tone, gentlemen, but I admit to one superstition. My ward, Miss O'Sullivan, brings me luck. [*sits in* **JAMIE***'s place as* **JAMIE** *sits in his.* **MANTON** *looks up at* **JULIETTE** *who now stands behind him looking stormly at nobody*] Juliette, I must not keep all my luck to myself. Stand mid way between me and Mr Kirkwood, my dear. That should equalise both our chances.

With an anguished but resigned look **JULIETTE** *stands where he bids.* **JAMIE** *shuffles the cards, lets* **DALGLEISH** *cut them, and starts to deal.* **CUT TO:**

44: THE CARD GAME, LATER

Guests stare and whisper. **MANTON** *is doing well. So is the bank.* **DALGLEISH** *throws a hand down in disgust.* **JAMIE** *collects.*

CUT TO:

45: THE CARD GAME, LATER.

Onlookers stare. Only **JAMIE** *and* **MANTON** *are playing.* **JULIETTE**, *quite expressionless, is now sitting close to* **JAMIE**. **TOM**, **DICK**, **HARRY** *and* **MCEWAN** *stand near him with expressions of excited identification reminiscent of Scene 11 in the billiards saloon.* **JAMIE** *collects from* **MANTON**, *giving* **JULIETTE** *a glance of concealed triumph. She answers it with a non-committal look.*

CUT TO:

46: THE CARD GAME, LATER

A close-up of **MANTON**, *pondering over a hand. He purses his lips, frowns, looks up, then casts it on the table.*

MANTON [*quietly*] Mr Kirkwood, I can play no more with you tonight.

A buzz of excitement. **JAMIE**, *with a dazed look, stares at a heap of sovereigns, bank notes and promissory notes in front of him. Friends press closer to congratulate him.*

DICK [*awed*] That was miraculous!

HARRY Hip hip hooray, old boy!

JAMIE *stares hopefully at* **JULIETTE**, *who stares inscrutably back.* **MANTON** *stands up.* **DALGLEISH** *and another, older man are near him and seem willing to say something, but he ignores them.*

MANTON [*loudly*] Gentlemen, this has been a strenuous evening. Mr Kirkwood and I will conclude our business in private. Goodnight all of you. Goodnight to you too Dalgleish. Goodnight gentlemen. Goodnight. Goodnight.

He ushers everyone out and returns to the table where **JAMIE** *is stacking the coins and notes methodically together, with a wondering look which he still sometimes turns on* **JULIETTE**. **MANTON** *stands looking down at him.*

MANTON It is a good thing for you, Jamie Kirkwood, that I am an honest man. A rogue would have accused you of cheating and flung you out of his house. You could have had no redress in a court of law.

JAMIE [*quietly, looking at him*] But you are an honest man.

MANTON [*dryly*] It would seem so. [*sighs*] The cash is yours, but it will take me a year to make good the promissory notes.

JAMIE [*after a pause*] That will be quite satisfactory if – if I am allowed to see more of you in the interval and – and more of your ward, Miss O'Sullivan.

He looks at her. So does **MANTON**.

MANTON [*smiling crookedly*] Well Juliette? What is your sentiment on the matter?

JULIETTE *stands, places her hands on* **JAMIE***'s shoulders, bends down and kisses his brow.*

JULIETTE This is my sentiment, Manton.

She bends and kisses **JAMIE***'s mouth.* **CUT TO:**

47: THE KIRKWOOD KITCHEN, 1939

Old **JAMIE** *sits at the table with a painful smile.*

MRS WILSON She kissed you in front of him!

JAMIE [*fiercely*] That should have happened!

MRS WILSON She didn't kiss you?

JAMIE *shakes his head in the negative.*

MRS WILSON [*impatiently*] Then you've been making it all up! You never won that game!

JAMIE [*with a sudden vehemence*] But I did win it! And I hadn't even cheated! Not once! There was no need! Luck had been with me from the very start! Except for ... except for ...

He rubs his brow.

MRS WILSON Tell me what really happened.

CUT TO:

48: CARD GAME, 1877, BEFORE THE END OF SHOT 46

A buzz of excitement. **JAMIE** *with a dazed look contemplates the heap of winnings in front of him. His friends press closer to congratulate him.*

DICK [*awed*] That was miraculous.

HARRY Hip hip hooray, old boy!

JAMIE *stares hopefully at* **JULIETTE***, who is biting her thumb.* **MANTON** *stands up.* **DALGLEISH** *and another older man are near him and seem willing to say something.*

MANTON [*loudly*] Gentlemen, this has been a strenuous evening. Mr Kirkwood and I will conclude our business in private. Goodnight, all of you ... [*quietly*] Dalgleish. MacKenzie. Wait in the library – or nearer, if you like. [*loudly, to the rest*] Goodnight gentlemen! Goodnight, Goodnight!

He ushers out **TOM, DICK, HARRY** *and* **MCEWAN***, who are least willing to go, and having closed the door behind them, turns round with a smile and returns, chuckling, to the table, where* **JAMIE** *is gathering his money methodically together.* **JULIETTE** *has not moved.*

MANTON Hahaha! Ha ha ha ha ha! Oh, you are a man after my own heart. I like that, hahaha! Really like it. It won't do though. [*coldly*] Leave the money to me.

JAMIE [*pauses, puzzled*] It's mine, Mr Jamieson!

MANTON [*grinning*] Oh no. You played a good trick on me, you handled it like a master, but I am a grand master, you see, so it's no go. The money is mine. [*raps the table with his fist*] All of it. Right, Juliette?

JULIETTE [*drearily*] Give him some of it.

JAMIE [*incredulous*] You accuse me of cheating?

MANTON [*gravely*] I have witnesses to prove it.

JAMIE What witnesses?

MANTON Dalgleish, for one. MacKenzie, for another. And Juliette, of course.

JAMIE Juliette! [*turns to her*] Miss O'Sullivan, I did not cheat. You did not see me cheat!

JULIETTE [*smiling forlornly*] I must support my husband, Mr Kirkwood.

JAMIE [*automatically*] Husband.

MANTON [*nodding*] We're man and wife, Kirkwood. But in this God-forsaken land young fools from respectable families are attracted by kept women, and since gaming is my profession – keep away from that money!

JAMIE *grabs for it.* **MANTON** *springs on him and wrestles him to the floor in a shower of notes and coins.* **JULIETTE** *jumps up screaming.*

JULIETTE MacFarlane! MacKenzie! Mr Dalgleish!

Door opens and these rush in.

MANTON Help me to – fling this cheat – out!

JAMIE [*wildly*] I am no cheat! I did not cheat! [*appealingly*] Juliette, help! You are my friend, I did it for you! [*they drag him to his feet and towards the door. He turns vindictive.*] I'll take you all to court! I'll have the law on you. I'm warning you! I'm warning you! [*wailing*] I need that money! [*kicks out. They grab his legs and carry him. He yells:*] I'll tell my father! My father! My father is the Reverend Doctor Kirkwood! Yaaaah! [*stops struggling and puts all his energy into a prolonged and completely insane scream*].

SOUND: *The drone of a bagpipe's chanter.*

49: QUICK SEQUENCE IN STROBE LIGHTING, 1877

49/1 **JAMIE** *is dropped on the lobby floor where he lies with limbs spread out like a starfish, his eyes tight shut and still screaming. Four seconds.*

49/2 *His father's horrified face, in frontal close-up, passes across the scene. Three seconds.*

49/3 **JAMIE**, *in a straight jacket, eyes still shut and mouth open, is lifted by male attendants into the back of a horse-drawn ambulance. Four seconds.*

49/4 *His father's image, much bigger, again crosses the screen. Three seconds.*

49/5 **JAMIE**, *seen from behind, is carried down a bleak corridor with a barred window at the end and taken through a door on one side. The door slams shut, in close-up. Five seconds.*

49/6 *His father's face, but very small, again crosses the screen. Three seconds.*

49/7 *An iron-framed bed in the corner of a room.* **JAMIE**, *huddled up like an embryo, has squashed himself into the corner. Zoom into his face, with mouth and eyes shut very tight. Five seconds.*

SOUND: *end of droning.*

50: THE MANSE KITCHEN, 1939

JAMIE *and* **MRS WILSON**

JAMIE I thought I was being taken to prison, but it was hospital, of course. "A prolonged nervous collapse" is what they called it. I was afraid to be seen by anybody! Anybody! I thought the whole story was in the newspapers, but [*thoughtfully*] maybe not. My father was dead when I came back here. But he left me enough to be comfortable on, he – he must have paid the money lender and hushed the matter up.

MRS WILSON [*moved*] That's a terrible story!

JAMIE [*nodding smugly*] I suppose it is! [*wistfully*] And nobody knows it? [**MRS WILSON** *shakes her head*] Come to think – I'm the only one who ever knew the whole of it.

SOUND: *Air-raid siren.*

MRS WILSON The all clear.

She stands and opens the shutters.

JAMIE [*in a fresh voice*] Does this mean the war is over, Mrs Wilson?

MRS WILSON No, just a small bit of it. The sun's still shining.

JAMIE Then there's corn in Egypt yet! [*raises himself to his feet*] Tomorrow I will certainly go for a walk. [**MRS WILSON** *moves towards him*] No! I can manage the stairs if I take my time to it. [*takes the stick from behind his chair*] You must now prepare the evening meal, which I trust you will serve with due promptitude. Yesterday – I fear – you were a little late, Mrs Wilson. But we'll say no more about that. To your chores, woman!

He wags his finger at her and walks stiffly from the kitchen, but his head is held high. He is once again a dominant male.

I HAD EXPECTED *Lanark* to be my only novel, but finding publishers would pay advances for more fiction I started turning forgotten plays (such as *Kelvin Walker*), or plays written but not produced, into novels, novellas and short stories. Sometimes an original idea was suggested by something I read or heard about or dreamed. When putting together stories for *Ten Tales Tall And True* (published in 1993) I woke one morning remembering a dream. In the dim back room of a Glasgow tenement I watched a young woman who sat before a window, staring out at children playing in a back green. Someone beside me said, "She won't be able to think until she remembers enough things to think with." And I knew the young woman had the brain of a newly-born baby.

This idea was good enough, I thought, to make two or three interesting pages, but how could such a woman happen? Brain transplants are still impossible and imagining how they might happen would be a drab chore. I decided that the surgeon who achieved this miracle should live before the end of the 19th century, halfway between the publication of Mary Shelley's *Frankenstein* in 1818 and my birth in 1934. He must be a medical genius so obscure that his discoveries were even now unknown to science, and it would be easiest to introduce him through reminiscences of a friend as obscure as himself. I started writing this tale and (as had happened once before) it expanded until I was writing a full length novel. To get the 19th century atmosphere right I read Wilkie Collins *The Woman in White* and *The Moonstone*, which gave hints for a story in several narrative voices, and reread much of Dickens and Robert Louis Stevenson. I tried to get the novel going with a sentence as brisk as that starting *Kidnapped*:

> *I will begin the story of my adventures with a certain morning early in the month of June, the year of grace 1751, when I took the key for the last time out of the door of my father's house.*

This is how I started *Poor Things*:

> *Like most farm workers in those days my mother distrusted banks. When death drew near she told me her life-savings were in a tin trunk under the bed and muttered, "Take it and count it."*

It often happens in the midst of a new piece of writing that an idly opened book tells me something useful. In a thick bound volume of *Blackwood's Magazine* I found *A Woman Hater* by Charles Reade, a serialised novel with an episode describing the terrible struggle of the first women to get medical training in Edinburgh University. Scientific facts I needed were supplied by Dr Bruce Charlton, my friend who had taught anatomy at Glasgow University and was now writing a history of medicine. From Dostoevsky's comic masterpiece *The Gambler* I took the atmosphere of a German gambling spa and two characters, the gambler himself and the archetypal British business gent, Mr Astley.

And I enjoyed my characters becoming friends, living and working and making love in the district around Glasgow University, Kelvingrove Park and Park Circus where I had made friends, worked, lived and wandered with my first wife and only child – and with my second wife, Morag. The street plan and most buildings were unchanged since the 1890s when my father was born. I too could remember Glasgow as a great port, ship-building and steam engine-building city whose wealth came from coal-fired industries. These had all ended in the 1960s. Our dense winter fogs also ended then, and skies grey with soot that, even in summer, hung like a ceiling over the Clyde Valley giving it an atmosphere as Victorian as any in Sherlock Holmes London.

Sometimes I visited Bernard MacLaverty and read him the work in progress. Reciting words aloud helps me improve them, and listeners' remarks are occasionally helpful. It was Bernard who suggested my heroine be revived by receiving the brain of her own unborn baby. I at once rejected this creepy idea, before seeing it was the only new brain she could logically receive.

When writing *Poor Things* I was SURE this story would start my career as a big screen film writer. Weird gothic and Frankenstein films had been popular before soundtracks were invented and grown more popular since. So had films with lavish 19th century settings and costumes. When sending the finished manuscript to Bloomsbury Publishing I also sent a copy to Robbie Coltrane, sure that he would love to play Godwin Baxter, and sent copies to Iain Brown and Sandy Johnson. I was wrong about Robbie Coltrane but Iain at once paid me for the film rights and paid Sandy and me to write a shooting script.

The book was published in 1992 and sold so well that two American companies wrote to me offering to buy the film rights: Orphan Films of New York, and a Disney subsidiary with a woman's production team. I told them that the film rights were sold and suggested a cooperative venture between our British and their USA film company. The consequence was that I heard no more from them. Then the London Government decided to start a state lottery, and as usual when introducing a new measure (such as the poll tax) tried it out first in Scotland. Iain had sent the *Poor Things* script to British Screen Enterprises and also to the Scottish Film Production Board. Both united in recommending it to the charity of the Scottish Lottery Fund, which responded by offering Iain Brown a million pounds, payable as soon as the film went into production. The film only needed another five or six million for production to commence. Iain Brown is still trying to raise the money, though recent inflation means that he will now have to raise another twelve million. Meanwhile, here is the script.

DEVELOPED WITH THE SUPPORT OF
SCOTTISH SCREEN, BRITISH SCREEN/UKFC
AND THE EUROPEAN SCRIPT FUND.

DIRECTOR................................SANDY JOHNSON

PRODUCER...................................... IAIN BROWN

11 Spencer Road, London W3 6DN
iain@brownfilms.co.uk

1 GLASGOW NECROPOLIS 1914 – BLACK & WHITE

Credit sequence with type grouped in the top right hand corner of the frame – not centred, the wording is scarlet.
In the foreground, bottom left, a branch with a bird twittering on it. In the centre a sharp bend in a path leading up between Victorian monuments. Beyond and below is the spire of Glasgow Cathedral, domes of the Royal Infirmary, reeking smokestacks of an industrial city.
SOUND: *Bird calls then, faintly, a slow drumroll resolving into the beat of The Dead March in Saul. Organ strains start emphasising this as:*
A **MINISTER** *in gown and bands of a Scottish doctor of divinity climbs the path towards camera. As he turns the bend and recedes from it we see a coffin whose front bearers are* **KENNETH** *and* **GRAHAM MCCANDLESS**, *young men in their mid twenties.* **KENNETH** *wears the uniform of a Highland Light Infantry Officer,* **GRAHAM** *is artistic but wears conventional mourning : his temperament is conveyed by a looser and more opulent black necktie.* **TWO BROTHERS** *of 19 or 20 –* **TWIN 1** *and* **TWIN 2** *– carry the coffin rear. All bearers are profoundly solemn. Behind them their mother* **BELLA** *follows, a fascinating woman of perhaps 45 years. She wears the professional costume of a late 19th century woman doctor – man's waistcoat cut to emphasise her hourglass figure, fur-collar coat open over ankle-length skirt. A pince-nez in her waistcoat pocket is linked by a ribbon to the lapel. She is responding happily to the beauty of the day and smiles at the bird as she passes it. Her manners contrast with the solemnity of the* **MINISTER** *and her* **SONS** *in front, and the* **EIGHT** *or* **NINE ELDERLY MIDDLE-CLASS MOURNERS** *following her.*

2 CUT TO: INT. BAXTER MAUSOLEUM 1914

Credits still rolling.
SOUND: *The Dead March, more grandly awful.*
A sarcophagus rests in the foreground, dominating the centre of the chamber. It is that of Godwin Baxter. Through the open door at the back, summits of monuments are visible. The **MINISTER** *leads in the cortege. When the* **FOUR SONS** *lay their father's coffin down parallel to Baxter's, but a yard or two away, it becomes clear that Baxter's sarcophagus is enormous. The* **MINISTER** *stands at the head of the McCandless coffin, his* **SONS** *stand two on each side of it with bowed heads,* **BELLA** *sits comfortably on the Baxter sarcophagus with one leg thrown casually over the other while the* **MOURNERS** *enter and cluster reverently around the smaller coffin.*
SOUND: *End of music.*
The **MINISTER** *prays, the* **SONS** *listen with bowed heads,* **KENNETH** *glancing disapprovingly sideways at his mother,* **GRAHAM** *smiling with sympathetic amusement.*
MINISTER We are here to commit to the tomb the body of Archibald McCandless : good doctor, loving father, devoted husband ...
The **MINISTER** *glances towards* **BELLA**. *Tears suddenly slip down her cheeks. She lowers her eyes with a tender smile. We see her gloved hand caress a large plate on the coffin where she sits. It is inscribed with the words:*

GODWIN BAXTER F.R.C.S
HEALER AND PHILANTHROPIST

3 CUT TO: EXT. OUTSIDE NECROPOLIS GATE

SOUND: *The Dead March resumes, done with trumpets to the best New Orleans ragtime.*
Low angle view of an open carriage and **BELLA** *mounting into it followed by her* **SONS**, *who shake hands with the* **MINISTER** *before doing so. Glasgow Cathedral is behind them*
SOUND: *The Dead March becomes jinglingly cheerful with scotch fiddles blending in.*

4 CUT TO: EXT. CROWDED STREET. CENTRAL GLASGOW

The carriage jostles between horse-drawn traffic and electric trams with open tops. **BELLA**, *looking pensive, sits with* **GRAHAM**, *who*

squeezes her hand comfortingly. He seems a favourite of hers – she smiles at him.
SOUND: *The Dead March works up to a rousing crescendo, with saxophone and bagpipe strains.*

5 CUT TO: EXT. PARK CIRCUS

This is a palatial Victorian residential area with trees in the centre and broad steps bridging deep basement areas to the front doors. The carriage comes round this and halts before the door of Number 18. The **BOYS** *leap smartly out, the* **TWINS** *standing aside while* **GRAHAM** *and* **KENNETH** *offer their mother a hand which she takes before jumping down between them.*
She then sweeps up the steps to the front door at the head of her brood. It is opened for her by a young, sharp-faced **MAIDSERVANT**.
BELLA *enters regally.*
SOUND: *End music.*
End of credits.

6 CUT TO: INT. 18 PARK CIRCUS – THE LOBBY

BELLA *removes her hat and gives it to the* **MAID** *while her sons hang theirs on a hat rack. The* **MAID** *looks full of important news.*
MAID There's been a delivery of books while ye were at the burial, Doctor McCandless.
BELLA *pauses in the act of stripping off her gloves and speaks in a well-to-do Scottish accent.*
BELLA [*puzzled*] Books? What books?
MAID A printer's man brought them. I've had them put upstairs in the study.
BELLA How peculiar!

7 CUT TO: INT. 18 PARK CIRCUS – STUDY

All the furniture is opulently massive in the mid-Victorian style. Armchairs, easy and upright chairs, a huge sofa, sideboard and tall glass-fronted bookcase with cupboard beneath. On the mantelpiece is a black marble clock shaped like the front of the Parthenon. Over it hangs a conventional late Victorian oil painting of **ARCHIBALD MCCANDLESS**, *standing in a dominant pose contradicted by his smile, which seems begging for approval. Above the sofa hangs a portrait of* **GODWIN BAXTER** *in heavy gilt frame, glum and powerful with arms folded to hide his fingers.*
The contemporary features are William Morris wallpaper, matching curtains and six photographs in crisp white mounts with slim black frames. [These are used as stills in Scenes 132, 133, 134, 135, 136 and 137 and are described fully there]
Under a central gasolier [a gas chandelier able to be raised or lowered] with frosted glass globes is a table with a neat stack of 100 identical books on top and a printer's bill on top of them.
BELLA *and* **SONS**, *rid of their outside clothes, enter and surround the table.*
BELLA *lifts the bill, adjusts her pince-nez and reads it while each son lifts a volume. These lack dust jackets but have a strong design stamped in white and black covers.* **GRAHAM** *reads the title on the spine aloud while the rest stare with sudden alarm at the covers, then glance in an embarrassed way at each other and their mother.*
GRAHAM Poor Things! Episodes from the Early Life of Archibald McCandless M.D. Why call it Poor Things? [*to* **BELLA**] Did you know he had written his autobiography?
KENNETH *has moved softly to the window where he looks inside the book, while the* **TWINS** *sink down on the sofa and do the same.*
BELLA [*dropping the bill*] No, but he paid to have it printed so it's an unimportant vanity publication.
She falls silent, noticing the topmost cover. Lifting the book she turns round holding it so that her sons cannot avoid seeing both her and the design. It shows **BELLA**, *naked, leaning out of the mouth of a giant skull with her arms folded under her breasts.*
BELLA [*bewildered*] Is this figure supposed to be me?
The **TWINS** *look aghast at each other.* **KENNETH** *seems unmoved.* **GRAHAM** *is quietly amused.*
GRAHAM [*nodding gravely*] There IS a similarity.
KENNETH [*soothingly*] The book is dedicated to you, mother, in a rather sweet verse. [*reads it out*] To Bella from her faithful Archie.

> My own dear sweet kind lovely doctor, do
> Smile on this tribute from an author who
> Was lover – daft old husband – doctor too.
> Kiss my queer book and,
> Since you can't return it,
> Read it just once, then, If you hate it, burn it.

BELLA *drops the book on the table, shaking her head disapprovingly.*
BELLA Burning it is just what I feel like doing. I don't know what sort of book it is, but it cost enough to buy twenty unemployed families food and boots for a year.
GRAHAM [*suavely*] Don't judge by the cover, mater! We can have it rebound!
TWIN 1 [*timidly*] The fact is mother ...
TWIN 2 [*less timidly*] Yes the fact is mother ...
KENNETH [*firmly*] The fact is, we know nothing about

our father's early life, and where he came from, and how you met him and Uncle Godwin.

BELLA'S SONS *glance towards the portrait of* **BAXTER**.

TWIN 2 You always made us feel it was wrong to ask about them, so we didn't.

TWIN 1 And now he's dead.

BELLA *now has the expression of someone ruminating on an old problem.*

BELLA The story of how your father met and courted me was too – [*she hesitates*] – peculiar for childish ears. You may be old enough to hear it now but I doubt if Archie has the courage to tell it!

She lifts the book again and smiles at the cover.

BELLA He was a true Victorian romantic.

GRAHAM Then we'll all read it and you can tell us where it goes wrong.

KENNETH [*still examining the book by the window*] It's shorter than it appears – big type, broad margins. [*looks at* **BELLA**] Read it aloud.

GRAHAM *leads* **BELLA** *to an armchair by the fire, lifting a volume from the table on the way.*

GRAHAM Yes! Sit down, mother, and read it like you read us fairy tales when we were bairns.

She sits, taking the book from him and opening it. He squats boyishly on the floor with arms folded round his knees.

GRAHAM We'll be quiet as mice and listen like good wee boys.

The **TWINS** *lean eagerly forward.* **KENNETH** *slips into an easychair facing her. There is an expectant pause.* **BELLA** *sighs.*

BELLA If Archie has been completely honest some episodes will surprise you, but ... [*she shrugs, smiling*] ... we'll see!

BELLA [*readjusts her pince-nez and reads*] Poor Things – Episodes from the Early Life of a Scottish Public Health Officer, by Archibald McCandless M.D. [*she turns a page*] Chapter one ...

8 CUT TO: INT. ATTIC BEDROOM 1880 – NIGHT – COLOUR

N.B *From now on the film uses warm, earthy colours till indicated otherwise.*

Poor farm-servant's attic bedroom, in warm, subdued colour, candlelit, **DYING WOMAN** *in bed. Her son, young* **MCCANDLESS,** *in coarse labourer's clothes kneels beside her, staring into her face.*

MCCANDLESS [V.O.] Like most farmworkers in those days my mother distrusted banks. When death drew near she told me her life savings were in the tin trunk under the bed.

DYING MOTHER Take it and count it.

He pulls the trunk out, opens it, removes a small, soft leather bag, unties strings, empties it onto the coverlet. He is awed by the heap of sovereigns.

MCCANDLESS [V.O.] I did, and the sum was more than I had expected.

DYING MOTHER Make something of yersel' with it.

MCCANDLESS [*gazing into her eyes again*] I'll mak mysel' a doctor, Mither!

He nods as he says this. She nods back and manages to smile.

DYING MOTHER [*in a sudden fierce whisper*] Don't pay a penny towards my burial. If Scraffles puts me in a pauper's grave then hell mend him! Promise ye'll keep all ma money to yersel'?

He presses her hand, nodding.

9 CUT TO: INT. COUNTRY GRAVEYARD – DAY

A single church bell tolls in a bleak corner, a coffin in an open grave with four people at the edge. **MCCANDLESS**, *in his best Sunday suit which does not well fit him, stares down at the coffin.* **MINISTER** *in black divinity gown and bands shakes hands with a lean farmer who is McCandless'* **FATHER**. *A* **SEXTON** *is leaning on a shovel beside the excavated earth.*

The **MINISTER** *leaves. McCandless'* **FATHER** *taps his son's shoulder.* **MCCANDLESS** *does not look at him*

MCCANDLESS [V.O.] "Scraffles" was the local nickname for my father and for a disease that afflicts badly fed poultry. Scraffles did pay for the burial.

FATHER Since you can afford to pay to go to university I'm leaving you to pay for the stone.

FATHER *walks away.* **MCCANDLESS** *ignores him, staring fixedly at the coffin as the* **SEXTON** *throws the first shovelful of dirt on it.*

10 CUT TO: GLASGOW UNIVERSITY CLOISTERS AND QUADRANGLE 1880 – DAY

Suavely or raffishly dressed **STUDENTS** *stand gossiping and smoking in affable clusters. The clothing indicates the period is 1880. Most wear bowler hats, one or two have toppers.* **MCCANDLESS** *strides dourly through them towards a door with a sign saying "Materia Medica" on it. He wears corduroy trousers with a pea-jacket and tweed cap. He goes through the door.*

MCCANDLESS [V.O.] At university my clothes and manners announced my farm servant origins and since I would let nobody sneer at me on that account I was usually alone outside the lecture theatres and dissecting room. I found only one man in that entire institution who I recognised as my equal.

11 CUT TO: INT. DISSECTING ROOM

GODWIN BAXTER, *huge, beautifully dressed, with a patient and suffering face, walks quietly between two lines of tables, each holding a corpse on which students perform dissection.*

All but **MCCANDLESS** *work in couples.* **MCCANDLESS** *is apparently concentrating more than the rest until he looks up and asks*:

MCCANDLESS Who's yon big chap?

POLITE STUDENT Godwin Baxter, only son of the first surgeon to be knighted by Queen Victoria.

JEALOUS STUDENT A very rich, very lucky bastard.

POLITE STUDENT His mother was the old man's maid servant. The son keeps her on as his housekeeper.

JEALOUS STUDENT I thought he kept her in a lunatic asylum.

SUAVE STUDENT His father's lack of interest in female beauty was legendary, but the offspring proves he had a strong appetite for female ugliness.

All but **MCCANDLESS** *chuckle.*

Beyond the speakers we see **BAXTER** *reach into a metal bin, lift out a human brain resembling a large cauliflower and carry it to a bench with microscope and other instruments where he starts carefully measuring it. He has shirtcuffs which hide all but the tips of his fingers but his appearance is so grotesque that this is not a prominent detail.*

MCCANDLESS What's his line of research?

JEALOUS STUDENT He hasn't one. He's a harmless lunatic who dabbles with brains and microscopes to make himself look important.

SUAVE STUDENT Since his looks would scare human patients to death he runs a charity clinic for animals in his father's old home.

JEALOUS STUDENT And he does post-mortems for the police.

SUAVE STUDENT He never opens his mouth because his voice is as weird as his body.

12 CUT TO: EXT. MEETING HALL

SOUND: *Hubbub of voices, clattering feet.*

MCCANDLESS *in a stream of* **STUDENTS** *crowds through a door with a sheet above painted with the words: – GRAND DEBATE! CREATION OR EVOLUTION?*

13 CUT TO: INT. MEETING HALL

STUDENTS *pour exuberantly in. On the platform we see the* **SUAVE STUDENT** *is chairman with* **TWO DEBATERS** *on each side. A quick sequence of shots shows* **DEBATERS** *speaking portentously or facetiously between bursts of applause and booing.*

SPEAKERS *from the floor claim attention. Among them* **MCCANDLESS**, *obviously interested in the discussion, looks uncouthly different [as usual] from the rest, especially the* **JEALOUS**, **GOSSIPING** *and* **POLITE STUDENTS** *who are his neighbours. He seeks to catch the eye of the* **SUAVE STUDENT** *on the platform.*

SOUND: *Varieties of echoing hubbub are suddenly silenced by the* **SUAVE STUDENT** *rapping with his gavel and crying*:

SUAVE STUDENT I see that my droll friend Archie McCandless wants to honour us with his views! Speak up Erchie! Whit wad ye hae us ken, man?

MCCANDLESS [*standing, nervous but vehement*] I wad hae ye ... know ... that the speakers have treated this matter with a mixture of fanatical solemnity and trivial jocosity which has utterly bumbazed and ramfeezled the whole issue ...

An outburst of laughter confuses him.

MCCANDLESS [*louder*] Can we no ... can we not unite to agree upon that platform of scientifically proven fact erected by Comte and Darwin and Haekel? Whit fur can we no?

A huge burst of laughter. **MCCANDLESS**, *astonished, stares down at his clothes then around at the crowd.*

MCCANDLESS What's wrang wi' me?

JEALOUS STUDENT [*yelling*] Naething, laddie! Naething at all!

Deafening laughter. Many stamp their feet. **MCCANDLESS** *squares his shoulders, pushes into the aisle with a set, dignified face starts walking out when an oddly piercing noise stops him short and strikes silence into the rest. It is the voice of* **GODWIN BAXTER** *speaking from the balcony above in a shrill, drawling almost castrato voice.*

BAXTER Every speaker but the last has contradicted himself as much as his opponents. And those are the chosen few! The animal response to Mr McCandless's sensible remark shows the mental quality of this mass.

MCCANDLESS [*with a grim nod*] Thank you, Baxter.

He walks out in silence.

14 CUT TO: NARROW LANE IN GLASGOW SLUM

BAXTER *and* **MCCANDLESS** *pass among many poorly clad, hungry people.* **BAXTER** *wears a thick overcoat with fur collar,*

MCCANDLESS *a thick muffler. Overhead are slung many lines of tattered clothing hung out to dry.*

BAXTER ... public hospitals are nothing but places where doctors learn to get rich by practising on the poor.

MCCANDLESS But Florence Nightingale has made nursing a decent, efficient profession.

BAXTER Aye, if nurses controlled the medical profession our hospitals would do nothing but good.

15 CUT TO: EXT. RIVER CLYDE, WATER FRONT

Cranes, capstans, stacked bales and docked 1880s steamships. Across the river is a skyline of warehouses and reeking factory smokestacks.

MCCANDLESS *and* **BAXTER** *appear, chatting cheerfully.* **BAXTER** *wears fashionable summer clothes.* **MCCANDLESS***'s voice fades in before we see them.*

MCCANDLESS My early education was accidental. I learned how my mother conceived me by watching my father's cattle.

BAXTER When I asked how I was made Sir Colin gave me an anatomy lesson.

MCCANDLESS Sir Colin? Your father?

BAXTER I never heard him called anything but Sir Colin. My mother was a nurse who died soon after they produced me, so I grew up thinking fathers and mothers were doctors and nurses who specialised in small people, though I was never small ...

BAXTER*'s voice fades out after they leave.*

16 CUT TO: HILLHEAD [POSH RESIDENTIAL DISTRICT]

Thick fog. **BAXTER** *and* **MCCANDLESS** *emerge, talking, into distinct close-up.* **BAXTER** *wears Inverness Cape and deerstalker hat,* **MCCANDLESS** *wears a pea jacket and muffler.*

MCCANDLESS What's the exact nature of your researches, Baxter?

BAXTER I'm refining Sir Colin's techniques.

MCCANDLESS Why refine out-of-date techniques? Your famous father was a great surgeon but in the last ten years we have discovered things he would have thought incredible – how to remove brain tumours and repair ulcerous perforations.

BAXTER [*smiling to himself*] Sir Colin discovered something better than those in the field of grafting and transplanting.

MCCANDLESS [*puzzled*] Grafting and transplanting can only be done with trees and vegetables.

BAXTER [*gently, but smiling to himself even more*] Then forget that I referred to them, McCandless.

MCCANDLESS, *angry, stands still facing* **BAXTER**, *who halts.*

MCCANDLESS [*cold and firm*] I hate mysteries Baxter, especially the man-made sort which are always a sham. Do you know what the other medical students think of you? They think you a harmless lunatic who tries to look important by futile antics in the dissecting room.

BAXTER [*astonished and hurt speaks faintly*] Do you think that too?

MCCANDLESS If you don't answer me frankly what else can I think?

BAXTER [*sighing*] Well ... come home and I will show you something.

17 CUT TO: EXT. 18 PARK CIRCUS

BAXTER *and* **MCCANDLESS** *climb the steps,* **BAXTER** *unlocks the door and enters.*

18 CUT TO: INT. LOBBY

Huge **DOGS** *– Newfoundland, Alsatian and Afghan – lie overlapping on the floor but spring alert as* **BAXTER** *and* **MCCANDLESS** *enter.* **BAXTER** *leads* **MCCANDLESS** *through them [the door slams shut behind] muttering.*

BAXTER Wait, Lulu. Rest, Fiona. Sit, Muriel.

19 CUT TO: INT. TOP LANDING

They arrive at the top and **BAXTER** *leads them to a door between slim wooden fluted columns supporting a lintel carved like a shallow triangular pediment with an eye in the centre.*

BAXTER [*unlocking the door*] This was Sir Colin's old operating theatre.

BAXTER *leads* **MCCANDLESS** *in.*

20 CUT TO: INT. OPERATING THEATRE

Skylight above, large windows in two adjacent walls. A central operating table of unusually large size has straps to hold the subject [or patient] down, and a rabbit hutch on it. The cylinders, dials and tubes of a primitive anaesthetic machine stands nearby on a wheeled carriage. Other equipment recalls the laboratory in the first Frankenstein film, but not so as to suggest this film is a spoof.

BAXTER *walks straight towards the operating table saying:*

BAXTER This is where I first saw the light of day.

MCCANDLESS *pauses to look at a pen containing* **PURE BLACK** *and* **PURE WHITE RABBITS** *nibbling lettuce leaves.*

MCCANDLESS You were delivered by Caesarean section?

BAXTER [*ignoring the question*] Not quite ... Come here McCandless.

He lifts out and hands **MCCANDLESS** *a* **RABBIT,** *black from the tail to an exact line round the waist, pure white above.* **MCCANDLESS** *receives it with the assured grip of a countryman.* **BAXTER** *brings out and cradles on his sleeve a* **RABBIT** *with the same colouring but reversed.*

BAXTER You will agree that two such exactly reversed colourations are not exactly natural. What sex is that one?

MCCANDLESS [*peering*] Male genitals – a buck.

BAXTER Feel the nipples.

MCCANDLESS [*palpating*] Female nipples! A hermaphrodite?

BAXTER [*tonelessly*] Give it to me. Examine this.

They exchange **RABBITS**. **MCCANDLESS** *looks, palpating.*

MCCANDLESS Female genitals with male nipples! Baxter! How did you do it?

He strokes the rabbit as if it were infinitely precious. **BAXTER** *gloomily restores one* **RABBIT** *to the hutch, then the other, saying:*

BAXTER I've done nothing wonderful! I've treated them very shabbily. Mopsy and Flopsy were ordinary happy wee rabbits before I put them to sleep last week and they woke up like this. Procreation no longer interests them and it was once their favourite sport. But tomorrow I'll reassemble them the way they were before.

MCCANDLESS But Baxter – what can your hands not do if they can do that?

BAXTER Oh, I could replace the diseased organs of rich people with the healthy ones of poorer folk, but it would be unkind to lead millionaires into such temptation.

He shuts the hutch and walks away followed eagerly by the excited, suddenly garrulous **MCCANDLESS**.

21 CUT TO: INT. STAIRWELL

They descend, talking, to the lobby past two landings.

MCCANDLESS But most bodies in our dissecting rooms belong to friendless paupers who have died by accident or suicide! If we used their undamaged organs to mend the bodies of valuable citizens we could save more lives than any other doctors in the universe! We would be the greatest doctors in the world!

BAXTER [*fiercely*] If doctors wanted to save lives instead of making money out of them they would unite to prevent diseases, not compete to cure them. The prevention of most illness has been known since the ancient Greeks – sunlight, cleanliness and exercise, McCandless; fresh air, pure water, and a government ban on all work and housing which prevents these.

MCCANDLESS Impossible, Baxter! The British rule the greatest empire in human history because Britain is the industrial workshop of the world. The ban you suggest would impoverish everyone!

They are in the lobby where the **DOGS** *again rise to their feet.* **BAXTER** *passes through them to the door.*

BAXTER Exactly. So until Britain loses its empire and industries our doctors will be nothing but servants of a heartless plutocracy. Goodbye McCandless.

He opens the door, stands aside to let **MCCANDLESS** *pass.* **MCCANDLESS** *pauses before him, talks in a low fast voice, aware that the* **DOGS** *are drawing nearer and looking hostile.*

MCCANDLESS Baxter, I was daft to tell ye what fools say about ye! I didnae mean to hurt ye!

BAXTER You did mean to hurt and you succeeded.

MCCANDLESS [*desperate*] Godwin, if you don't want to use your father's discoveries, let me do it! I'll attribute them to you – and when the public outcry comes, for it will be huge, I'll defend you! I will be your bulldog just as Huxley was Darwin's bulldog! McCandless will be Baxter's bulldog!

BAXTER Goodbye McCandless!

The **DOGS** *are growling.* **MCCANDLESS** *backs onto the doorstep.*

22 CUT TO: EXT. DOORSTEP, PARK CIRCUS

MCCANDLESS At least let me shake your hand, Godwin!

BAXTER [*smiling slightly*] Why not?

He holds it out. Close-up of his cuff with protruding fingers. For the first time we see the whole hand emerge. It is a thumbless cubical stump with a small finger at each corner. **MCCANDLESS***' hand almost touching it, halts, trembles.*

FREEZE FRAME.

BELLA [V.O.] I was incapable of touching that hideous hand – What nonsense!

23 CUT TO: INT. PARK CIRCUS STUDY 1914 BLACK & WHITE

BELLA*, seated as at the end of Scene 7, looks up from the book in her lap.*

BELLA [*scornfully*] What nonsense! There was nothing strange about Godwin's hands.

She sees her **SONS** *gazing at the portrait with tightly folded arms.*
KENNETH Are you sure of that, Mother?
BELLA [*defensively*] Yes, he was shy about his hands but only because he had lost a thumb in a laboratory accident which could have happened to anyone. Your father is shamelessly exaggerating.
GRAHAM Just go on reading, mother.
BELLA [*sighing*] As you wish.

24 CUT TO: EXT. DOORSTEP 1880, COLOUR

Close-up of **BAXTER***'s hand with* **MCCANDLESS***' hand trembling in front of it. Pull back to show their faces:* **MCCANDLESS** *petrified with horror and embarrassment,* **BAXTER** *faintly smiling.*
MCCANDLESS [*almost whispering*] I ... I c-can't shake your hand, Godwin.
BAXTER [*smiling and shrugging*] Goodbye McCandless.
He shuts the door. **MCCANDLESS***, dazed, departs from the step. A gust of withered leaves drifts across it.*

25 WIPE TO: EXT. DOORSTEP – 18 PARK CIRCUS

Now covered with snow. **MCCANDLESS** *is there, having pressed the bell. The door is opened by* **MRS DINWIDDIE***, who is middle-aged, friendly but firm.*
MCCANDLESS Is Mr Baxter at home? I would like to ...
MRS DINWIDDIE [*interrupting*] Mr Baxter is at home to nobody, sir.
She shuts the door. We see **MCCANDLESS** *turn and dolefully descend to the circus pavement with its background of bare-branched trees.*

26 CUT TO: INT. UNIVERSITY LABORATORY

At a bench, the **JEALOUS STUDENT**, **SUAVE STUDENT** *and* **MCCANDLESS** *sit in a row.* **MCCANDLESS** *with eyes to a microscope, pencil in hand, makes notes. The others sit back from their microscope talking. One smokes a pipe.*
JEALOUS STUDENT It's half a year since we saw that grotesque chappie, Godwin Baxter. What's become of him?
SUAVE STUDENT Where's Baxter these days, McCandless? You and he were bosom cronies once.
MCCANDLESS [*not looking up*] Leave me alone.

27 CUT TO: GLASGOW STREET

A bright day in a fashionable Glasgow street circa 1880.
Close-up of **MCCANDLESS***, dour and lonely, walking along it seen from the shoulders up.*
Noise of traffic – hoof clopping and carriage wheels – then an odd hand grasps **MCCANDLESS***' right shoulder.*
BAXTER Bulldog McCandless ...
Pull back to show **BAXTER** *walking smiling by* **MCCANDLESS***' side, a silver-knobbed cane under one arm, a flower in his buttonhole, a shining silk waistcoat.*
BAXTER How is my bulldog this weather?
MCCANDLESS [*smiling*] A lot better for hearing your ugly voice, Baxter. Have you never thought of giving yourself a new larynx? The vocal cords of a sheep twang more melodiously than yours ... [*with a touch of envy*] ... you look happy, Baxter.
BAXTER Yes! I now enjoy better company than you ever provided, McCandless ... a fine, fine woman who owes her life to these ugly fingers of mine ... [*he holds out his hand and waggles the fingers*] Come home and meet her. Cab! Cab!
We see a cab.

28 CUT TO: INT. HANSOM CAB

Inside the moving cab **BAXTER***, smiling as if at a secret joke, talks effusively but as much to himself as to* **MCCANDLESS** *who watches, puzzled by his manner.*
BAXTER The divine Bella Baxter is physically perfect but her mind is still forming – yes, her mind has wonderful discoveries to make. You will find her much more interesting than Mopsy and Flopsy.
MCCANDLESS What did you cure her of?
BAXTER Death.
MCCANDLESS You mean you saved her from death.
BAXTER Partly, but most of her is a skilfully manipulated resurrection.
MCCANDLESS You don't make sense man! How did you meet her?
BAXTER [*blithely*] I tell people she is my niece, and that her parents died last year in a South American railway accident – an accident that deprived her of her memory.
MCCANDLESS She's amnesiac?
BAXTER You must judge for yourself.

29 CUT TO: INT. LOBBY – 18 PARK CIRCUS

There are no dogs. From an adjacent room a piano is playing "The Bonnie, Bonnie Banks of Loch Lomond" far too quickly. **BAXTER** *leads* **MCCANDLESS** *in through the front door but pauses before opening the door into the drawing room.*
BAXTER [*in a low, confidential voice*] I've surrounded her

with a great clutter of things because the more things she knows the better she'll think.
He opens the door.

30 CUT TO: INT. DRAWING ROOM

Two tall windows overlook the terrace outside and a multitude of opulent Victorian toys and instruments spread everywhere: doll's house, model railway, toy castle, zoo animals, globe of the world, telescope, concert harp, skeleton on a gibbet, large books open at coloured pictures etc. **TWO RABBITS**, *one coal black, one pure white, nibble a carrot on the hearth rug near the feet of* **MRS DINWIDDIE** *who sits quietly knitting but nods placidly at the viewers. The* **DOGS** *lie around the pianola at which* **BELLA BAXTER** *sits, playing it with her feet only, waving her arms at her sides like the wings of a bird but not in time with the music. We see her from behind. Copious, unbound hair cloaks her almost to the waist, its colour in strong contrast with a pure white silk dress of girlish cut, though she is a fine figure of a woman. The music roll [which she has played as fast as possible] stops. Abruptly she stands and turns.*
Her movements in this scene are all abrupt enough to hint at a mechanical doll. She is wonderfully beautiful, with something doll-like and also childish in her unwaveringly happy smile.
Her voice is sweet and clear, her accent Mancunian. She separates each syllable.
BELLA Hel low God win. Hel low new man!
MCCANDLESS *stands with* **BAXTER** *a little behind him.* **BELLA** *takes short little steps towards them, as if careful not to fall, stops four feet away then flings both arms straight towards* **MCCANDLESS**, *and keeps them there, parallel.*
BAXTER [*smiling kindly*] Give only one hand to new men, Bell.
She drops one arm to her side. **MCCANDLESS**, *enraptured with her, takes the tips of the fingers of the other in one hand and rises on tiptoe to kiss them. This is the first courtly gesture in his life – it is her first kiss.*
She gasps and slowly withdraws her hand, looking at it and rubbing the fingertips with her thumb as if testing something, while giving **MCCANDLESS** *happy little glances.*
BAXTER [*beaming proudly*] This is McCandless, Bell.
BELLA Hel low Miss ter Candel, new wee man with inter rested face, blue neck tie, crump pled coat waist coat trow sirs made of brown cord dew ... ray?
BAXTER Corduroy my dear.
BELLA Cord dew roy, a ribbed fab brick wove ven from cot ton Mis ter Make Candel.
BAXTER Mac Candless, dear Bell!
BELLA But dear Bell has no candel so dear Bell is Candle less too!
BAXTER You reason beautifully Bell, but have still to learn that most names are not reasonable.
He turns to **MRS DINWIDDIE** *while* **BELLA** *and* **MCCANDLESS** *continue staring enraptured at each other.*
BAXTER Mrs Dinwiddie, take Bell down to the kitchen and give her lemonade and a doughnut. McCandless and I will be in the study.

31 CUT TO: STAIRWELL

BAXTER *leads the way upstairs, smiling upward.*
BAXTER So what do you think of Bella?
MCCANDLESS [*gravely ascending*] A bad case of brain damage, Baxter. Only idiots and infants show such radiant happiness on meeting a stranger.
BAXTER You're wrong. Her mental powers are growing at enormous speed. Six months ago she had the brain of a baby.
MCCANDLESS What reduced her to that state?
BAXTER [*pausing on the half landing and looking back*]. Nothing – she has risen from it, McCandless. It was the brain of a perfectly healthy baby.
MCCANDLESS, *horrified, clutches a banister post and seems inclined to vomit.*
MCCANDLESS [*hoarsely*] No ... But ... Where – did you get the other bits?
BAXTER From the Clyde – the police fished out everything I needed.
MCCANDLESS *covers his face with his hands, staggers and would fall if* **BAXTER** *did not grab him round the waist, hoist him over his shoulder and run with him upstairs saying:*
BAXTER When you hear the whole story you'll feel as pleased about it as I do – and you're the only one I can tell it to – the only one in the world!

32 CUT TO: STUDY

The furniture is as in Scene 7, with Victorian bookcases, but the wallpaper has a strong Victorian pattern of huge dark red and green roses, the curtains are green or blue with gold tassles and fringes. Instead of photographs the wall decorations are framed anatomical engravings by Vesalius and Leonardo. Above the mantelpiece is a large portrait of Sir Colin, a lean, clean shaven man dressed in the style of the early Regency. He has a

Mephistophelean smile and holds a skull whose orbit he seems to be measuring with a pair of calipers. **BAXTER** *places* **MCCANDLESS** *on an upright chair at the table.* **MCCANDLESS** *leans his elbows on the table, still covering his face with his hands and shuddering.*

BAXTER [*puzzled*] What's wrong with you?

MCCANDLESS [*in a muffled voice*] Give me a drink.

BAXTER *goes to the sideboard on which stands a peculiar distilling plant with bubbles sliding along glass tubes and sickly grey-green blobs of slime plopping steadily into a beaker in a tray.* **BAXTER** *briskly places the beaker on the table before* **MCCANDLESS**.

BAXTER Here's a fluid which nourishes blood, bone and nerves – I eat and drink nothing else.

MCCANDLESS *peers at it, shudders, covers his face again.* **BAXTER** *sighs, returns to the sideboard, and takes a decanter of port and a glass from it.*

BAXTER If you must have alcohol here is my father's port – poisonous stuff.

He glances disapprovingly at his father's portrait, fills the glass from the decanter and puts both by **MCCANDLESS**' *elbow.* **MCCANDLESS** *sits up, empties the glass in a single swallow, refills from the decanter and stares belligerently at* **BAXTER**.

MCCANDLESS How did that lovely woman come here?

BAXTER *faces him, beaker in hand with behind him a framed print showing Leonardo's study of an unborn child curled in a womb.*

BAXTER Nature can be cruel, McCandless. Babies are born with good brains but exposed spines, or no stomachs, or some other defect condemning them to death. But nature is less cruel than mankind.

33 CUT TO: EXT. CLYDE SUSPENSION BRIDGE

BAXTER [V.O.] Every year our damnably unjust society turns thousands of healthy women into social outcasts by deliberately excluding them.

BELLA, *with the travelling costume and appearance of a desperately unhappy, determined, pregnant upper-class woman, walks onto the bridge and climbs the guard rail at one side.*

BAXTER [V.O.] ... Hundreds of these can suffer no more, go mad and drown themselves.

BELLA *dives into the river.*

34 CUT TO: RIVER EMBANKMENT

BAXTER [V.O.] The Glasgow municipality employs an official whose main task is to fish such unfortunates out and put them in a special mortuary behind his home on Glasgow Green ...

BELLA *is dragged from the river by a* **HUMANE SOCIETY OFFICIAL.**

35 CUT TO: INT. MORTUARY

BAXTER [V.O.] It is my job to examine their bodies and – if unclaimed – transfer them to the University dissecting rooms. Six months ago I examined such a woman – pregnant, but with pressure marks round her fingers where engagement and wedding rings had been removed.

BELLA *on zinc-topped table in a small dingy room,* **BAXTER** *holding her hand with a look of sentimental reverence.* **HUMANE SOCIETY OFFICIAL** *and* **POLICEMAN** *behind.*

BAXTER [V.O.] What does that suggest to you, McCandless?

36 CUT TO: INT. STUDY

MCCANDLESS She was carrying the child of a husband she hated, or of a lover who had abandoned her.

BAXTER [*nodding*] Exactly. Her brain was dead but the rest – using Sir Colin's techniques – was revivable. I cleared her lungs of water, brought her here, gave her a new young brain and ... [*he spreads his arms wide, beaming upward at the ceiling*] ... Bella Baxter is now mine!

MCCANDLESS [*grimly*] Yours!

MCCANDLESS *sips from the glass, puts it down and from now on adopts the manner of a prosecuting lawyer.*

MCCANDLESS Frankly, Baxter, your story of losing her memory in a railway accident is more convincing. How do you explain her accent? Is there Manchester blood in her veins?

BAXTER [*broodingly*] Yes, the muscles of Bell's throat, tongue and lips move as they did when directed by the brain I discarded. Which proves early habits become instinct through nerves of the whole body. Go easy on the port, McCandless.

MCCANDLESS [*deliberately filling the glass again*] How will you educate this poor orphan?

BAXTER [*firmly*] Not by sending her to school where she would be treated as an oddity! I will take her on a world tour where she will learn about life dealing with foreigners who won't think her stranger than most British people – and charmingly normal when compared with ... [*he smiles and pats his chest*] ... me!

With a determined air **MCCANDLESS** *suddenly puts down his glass.* **BAXTER** *sips from the beaker, but as* **MCCANDLESS** *speaks* *sets it down slowly.* **MCCANDLESS** *moves from forensic zeal to wild denunciation, rising to his feet and ending with one arm raised to invoke the powers of heaven, the other pointing an accusing forefinger at* **BAXTER.**

MCCANDLESS And of course Baxter, she will be wholly at your mercy! Yes Baxter, you plan to possess what men have hopelessly yearned for throughout the ages, the soul of a trusting child in the opulent body of a lovely woman! You may be the rich heir of a mighty nobleman and I the bastard bairn of a poor peasant, but I will preserve Bella's honour with the last drop of blood in my veins as sure as there is a God in heaven – a God of Pity and Vengeance before whom the mightiest emperor is less than a falling sparrow!

BAXTER *takes the still quarter-full decanter back to the sideboard, locks it inside and faces* **MCCANDLESS**, *pocketing the key.*

MCCANDLESS [*wildly*] I love her, Baxter!

He collapses into the seat again, weeping and beating his brow with his fists. **BAXTER** *goes to him and, smiling sadly, lays a soothing hand on his shoulder.*

BAXTER I love her too, McCandless, but neither you nor I know who Bella will love – she will decide for herself. Remember, she is six months old and will not reach adolescence before the age of two. You can trust me till then, McCandless. I am an ugly fellow, but have you known me do ugly things?

MCCANDLESS [*grumbling*] What about Mopsy and Flopsy?

BAXTER [*still smiling*] Go home, McCandless.

37 CUT TO: STAIRWELL

BAXTER *ushers* **MCCANDLESS** *down to the front door; the* **DOGS** *are waiting in the lobby.*

MCCANDLESS When are you leaving on your world tour?

BAXTER Shortly.

MCCANDLESS Can I see her again before you leave?

BAXTER No, you must wait till we return. Your effect on Bella does not worry me. Her effect on you does.

BAXTER *opens the door, the* **DOGS** *advance on* **MCCANDLESS** *who retreats to the doorstep as previously.*

38 CUT TO: EXT. DOORSTEP, PARK CIRCUS

MCCANDLESS One moment! When she drowned herself – how advanced was her pregnancy?

BAXTER Nine months.

MCCANDLESS Could you not have saved the child?

BAXTER I did save it – the thinking part. I put the child's brain into the mother's head – but you need not believe that if it disturbs you.

BAXTER *shuts the door.* **MCCANDLESS** *drifts sullenly down to the pavement. A sound of tapping on glass.* **MCCANDLESS** *looks back and sees* **BELLA** *at a window, blowing a kiss. Excited, he blows one back. She wriggles and squirms with delighted, inaudible laughter. He turns and walks forward, looking downward with a wondering, hopeful smile. Track in to close-up on his face.*

FREEZE FRAME.

MCCANDLESS [V.O.] Fifteen unexpectedly happy months passed before I saw her again. Scraffles died and left me almost as much money as he left his legitimate sons.

39 CUT TO: INT. MCCANDLESS'S FACE ON A PLAIN BACK–GROUND

Suddenly he lifts his chin into another frozen pose. His smile is proud and firm, his formerly unkempt hair trimmed and combed, his chin supported by a wing collar and neat silk cravat with pearl tiepin. Unfreeze frame and pull back to show:

40 CUT TO: INT. ROYAL INFIRMARY WARD

MCCANDLESS *in smart morning coat, walks down between hospital beds escorted by a* **MATRON** *and* **TWO NURSES**. *The faces of all* **PATIENTS** *are turned to him. He and his entourage pass through double doors out of the ward.*

MCCANDLESS [V.O.] I became house doctor in the Royal Infirmary with a ward full of patients and a team of nurses. I cultivated a lordly surface softened by unpredictable flashes of humour.

41 CUT TO: INT. HOSPITAL CORRIDOR

MCCANDLESS *halts, touching his cheek with his finger as though struck by an idea. The* **MATRON** *walks on, leaves him with* **NURSE** *to right and left. With a sudden smile he turns and, with forefinger, chucks one under the chin, then the other. They grin frozenly, then grimace at each other behind his back as he walks onward.*

MCCANDLESS [V.O.] I acquired savoir-faire and popularity!

MCCANDLESS *walks out of frame.*

42 CUT TO: KELVINGROVE PARK

MCCANDLESS [V.O.] One hot summer Sunday evening, a need of exercise took me out into Kelvingrove Park.

Wide view of the skyline above smokestacks to the south. Tilt down past posh tenements beside the park to the footpaths around the Memorial Fountain where a **FASHIONABLE CROWD** *strolls.* **MCCANDLESS** *comes through it towards us, his eyes on the ground.*

MCCANDLESS [V.O.] I was trying to remember the colour of Bella's eyes but could only remember the sound of her voice when she said ...

BELLA Candle, where are your cord dew roys?

BELLA *and* **BAXTER** *confront* **MCCANDLESS** *arm-in-arm and side by side.* **BAXTER** *is so unhappy that he looks positively ill. He wears black.* **BELLA** *is radiantly happy as ever, wears a crimson silk dress, sky blue velvet jacket, purple toque, snow white gloves. She twirls in her left hand the shaft of a yellow silk parasol with an emerald green fringe. With the abruptness of an impulsive school girl she takes her right arm from under* **BAXTER***'s and thrusts it as straight out towards* **MCCANDLESS** *as when they first met. Once again he stands on tiptoe and kisses her fingertips. When he releases them she clenches the hand and shakes it triumphantly in the air saying to* **BAXTER**.

BELLA Haha! He is still my little Candle, God! Be polite and say hullo.

BAXTER [*sighing drearily*] Hello McCandless.

BELLA [*pointing*] Sit on that bench, God! I am taking Candle for a walk saunter stroll dawdle trot canter short gallop and circum-ambu-lation ...

BAXTER *sinks onto a bench between a* **NURSEMAID** *with a baby which screws up its mouth to scream before she swiftly departs with it and an* **ARMY OFFICER** *who sneers and also retreats. Meanwhile* **BELLA**, *without ceasing to chatter, snaps her parasol shut, seizes* **MCCANDLESS***' right hand, tucks it under her left arm.* **MCCANDLESS** *responds to her like an infant who finds it hard to believe in his good luck.*

BELLA [to **BAXTER**] Poor Old God! Without Bella you will grow glum, glummer, glummest until just when you think I am forever lost, crash bang wallop, out I will pop from behind that hollybush ...

BELLA [*swings* **MCCANDLESS** *round and leads him quickly saying*:] You were the first man who ever kissed me, Candle, and now I me Bell Miss Baxter citizen of Glasgow native of Scotland subject of the British Empire have become a woman of the world ...

43 CUT TO: LUSH BLOOMING RHODODENDRON THICKET

BELLA, *peering left and right, leads the dazed* **MCCANDLESS** *up a steep path into it.*

BELLA ... French German Italian Spanish African Asian American men and some women of the north and south kind have kissed this hand and other parts but I still dream of the first time though oceans deep between have roared since auld lang syne. This place will do.

She hurls her parasol like a spear into a flowering rhododendron bush, drags **MCCANDLESS** *in after and sinks down on her knees among the branches, drags him down beside her, unbuttons and strips off her right hand glove and flings it over a twig, smiling at* **MCCANDLESS** *and licking her lips.*

BELLA [*almost growling*] Now then!

She flings her left arm round his neck, clasps her naked palm over his mouth without noticing the edge of the hand blocks his nostrils. He is soon struggling for breath while she immediately enters a state of orgasm, wrenching her head blindly about and moaning through flushed and pouting lips as bloom petals fall around them.

BELLA A Candle on Candle the Candle of Candle to Candle by Candle from Candle I Candle we Candle ...

MCCANDLESS [V.O.] From feeling as helpless as a doll I suddenly wished to be nothing else, her pressure on my mouth and neck became so terribly sweet that I was soon struggling – not against suffocation – but against a delight too great to be borne!

MCCANDLESS *pulls himself free, with a faintly orgasmic yelp.*

BELLA *smiles at him and reaches for her glove.*

BELLA [*with some deeply contented sighs*] Do you know Candle, I haven't had the chance to do that since I got off the ship from America last week ...

She stands up, pulls on and buttons the glove, steps out onto the path saying:

BELLA Baxter has not left me alone with anyone except him. Did you enjoy what we just did?

44 CUT TO: KELVINGROVE PARK – SUNSET

MCCANDLESS, *following her out, nods in a dazed way. She beats twigs, leaves and petals from her clothing and his, saying*:

BELLA [*slyly*] You didn't enjoy it as much as I did – you'd have acted more daft if you had. But men seem better at acting daft when they're miserable.

MCCANDLESS *hands her the parasol. She tucks his hand under her arm and leads him away saying brightly*:

BELLA What shall we talk about?

MCCANDLESS [*emotionally*] Miss Baxter – Bella – oh dear Bell have you done that with many men?

BELLA Yes, all over the world but mostly in the Pacific. On the boat out of Nagasaki I met two Petty Officers –

they were devoted to one another – and I sometimes did it six times a day with each.

MCCANDLESS [*fearfully*] Did you ... do anything more with other men than you and me did in the rhododendrons?

BELLA [*laughing*] You rude little Candle – you sound as miserable as God! I never do more than we've just done with MEN – more with men makes babies. Babies frighten me because I can't remember being one. I can't remember being anything but a hulking great woman. [*frowns crossly*] God says my Pa sold rubber copper coffee bauxite beef tar esparto grass, things whose markets fluctuate, so he and my Ma had to fluctuate too, before the crash took away their lives and my memory. But what was I DOING while they fluctuated? I have eyes and a mirror, Candle, I SEE I am a woman nearer thirty than twenty, most women are married by then ...

MCCANDLESS [*wildly*] Marry me, Bella!

BELLA Don't change the subject, Candle, why were my parents carting a lovely thing like Bella Baxter about with them? That's what I want to know.

They have been circling back towards **BAXTER***'s bench by way of the duck pond or fountain. The park is emptier. Sunset colours are gathering in a clear gloaming sky behind the gothic University. For a moment they walk in silence,* **BELLA** *brooding on the mystery of her past,* **MCCANDLESS** *on her rejection of his proposal.*

MCCANDLESS [*harshly*] Bell – Bella – Miss Baxter, have you ever done what you and I did in the shrubbery with Baxter?

BELLA No, I can't do it with God and that's what's making him miserable.

BELLA He and I are like Heathcliff and Cathy in Wuthering Heights by one of these Brontës.

MCCANDLESS [*stiffly*] I have not read it.

BELLA Nor me neither but I know the story. Cathy and Heathcliff are big people who love each other more than anyone on earth, but they're in the same family so she can't let him kiss her and she marries a small man like you. Then Heathcliff goes daft. I hope Godwin won't. Look at him!

They stand arm-in-arm before **BAXTER.** *We see a frontal view of him between their heads. He slumps in the centre of the empty bench with stick planted upright between his knees, hands clasped on top, chin resting on hands, aghast eyes seeming to see nothing. His head has behind it the bright reds and golds of a western sky where the sun is setting.*

BELLA Boo! Do you feel better now?

BAXTER [*with a painful effort at a smile, and faintly*] A little better.

BELLA Good! Because Candle is going to marry me and you must be happy about that.

SOUND: *A chord with subsonic resonances, which acquires the rhythm of a heartbeat and intensifies through what follows.*

TRACK IN *to* **BAXTER***'s mouth – the only part of him which moves – steadily opening, while* **ZOOMING OUT** *to wide angle suggesting the opening is getting larger than his head till it blots the head out, so that his body supports a vast tooth-fringed cavern in the sunset sky.*

SOUND: *becomes painfully ear piercing.* **REVERSE ANGLE** *from inside the mouth shows* **MCCANDLESS** *and* **BELLA** *responding: he pressing hands to his ears and writhing in agony, she flinging up her arms and falling to the ground.*

SOUND: *cut noise.*

BELLA, *fainted, lies on the path.* **MCCANDLESS** *stands on one side in an attitude of astonishment,* **BAXTER** *kneels on the other, grasping his hair with both hands and crying aloud to the heavens.*

BAXTER [*in a strong new baritone voice*] Forgive me, Bella! Forgive me for making you like this!

BELLA [*opening her eyes and speaking faintly*] What's that supposed to mean? You are not our father who art in heaven, God. What a silly fuss to make about nothing. Still, your voice has broken. There's that to be thankful for ... Help me up, both of you.

They help her up. She walks away arm-in-arm with both.

45 CUT TO: PARK CIRCUS – A LAMPLIT PAVEMENT – NIGHT

BAXTER, BELLA *and* **MCCANDLESS,** *arm-in-arm as before, walk towards number 18.*

BAXTER [*miserably*] It is agony to find you treating me like a wrecked ship and McCandless like a lifeboat, Bella.

BELLA [*soothingly*] I am not deserting you right away, God. Candle is poor so we must live with you until he's rich. But I am a romantic woman who needs a lot of sex though not from you God, because you treat me like a child. I will marry Candle because I can treat him how I like.

BAXTER *looks enquiringly at* **MCCANDLESS.**

MCCANDLESS [*happily*] She's right.

BAXTER *brings them to a halt under a lamp-post near the front door.*

BAXTER I will help you both to do anything you want, but first – both of you – please grant a favour which may save my life – do not see each other for a week. Give me seven days to prepare for the lonely years ahead – please! Oh please!

Tears trickle down his cheeks.

BELLA [*shocked*] But a week for me is years and years and years!

MCCANDLESS Bella!

With a noble air, **MCCANDLESS** *takes the pearl-headed pin from his necktie.*

MCCANDLESS This is the most expensive thing I have ever owned, the head of it is a real pearl! Hereby I plight our troth.

He puts the pin into the lapel of her jacket.

MCCANDLESS We are now engaged to be married – nothing can prevent it.

He kisses her on the brow, then detaches himself. She touches the spot on her brow with her finger, then looks at the tip of it, obviously disappointed, before staring morosely at **MCCANDLESS**, *with petulantly out-thrust underlip.*

MCCANDLESS [*nobly*] Farewell, my wee pet lamb! See you next Saturday – Goodnight, Baxter!

BAXTER Thank you.

MCCANDLESS *walks happily away from a puzzled, resentful* **BELLA.**

46 CUT TO: HOSPITAL CORRIDOR AND OFFICE – DAY

MCCANDLESS [V.O.] The next few days were among the happiest of my life. I performed my hospital duties mechanically because I was writing love poems ... "Oh Bella fair, without compare, my memory sweetly lingers, By Kelvinside, my future bride, where first I kissed your fingers ... "

MCCANDLESS *walks from a ward with* **MATRON** *and* **NURSES** *as before, the* **MATRON** *explaining something to him which he does not seem to hear. Leaving her mid-sentence he dives through a door into an office, flings himself into a chair behind a desk covered with temperature charts, seizes one and scribbles on it.*

MCCANDLESS [*to himself*] I have known glee, by pond and sea, and spate that cleaves the mountain, but known no glee, my bride to be, no glee so great, my future mate, as by Loch Katrine memorial fountain ...

The **MATRON** *enters, holding out a paper form.*

MATRON [*grimly*] A telegram, Doctor.

MCCANDLESS *springs up, seizes it, reads.*

47 CUT TO: HOSPITAL CORRIDOR

MCCANDLESS *racing down it.*

BAXTER [V.O.] Come at once McCandless! I was mad to part you and Bella.

48 CUT TO: ROYAL INFIRMARY GATEWAY

The Infirmary gate is seen from a traffic-laden street, **MCCANDLESS** *charges out, leaps into a cab.*

BAXTER [V.O.] I have accidently injured us all in a terrible way. Only you, perhaps, may save us ...

49 CUT TO: PARK CIRCUS

The cab gallops at breakneck speed round to number 18 ...

BAXTER [V.O.] ... if you come here quickly, before sunset, as soon as possible.

... stops, **MCCANDLESS** *springs out and up the steps, is halted for a moment by an outcry from the* **CABBY**, *at whom, turning, he flings money as* **MRS DINWIDDIE** *opens the door behind him.*

BAXTER [V.O.] Please forgive your miserable and repentant friend, Godwin Baxter.

50 CUT TO: THE DRAWING ROOM

As before, without the toys and rabbits. **BAXTER**, *with a look of unexpected composure, stands firmly on the hearth rug surrounded by recumbent* **DOGS.** *The dogs rise, looking suspiciously at* **MCCANDLESS**, *charging in crying:*

MCCANDLESS Where is she? What is wrong?

BAXTER Upstairs in her bedroom, not ill, and all too happy. Try to be calm, McCandless, while I tell you the whole ghastly story. She is about to elope with Duncan Wedderburn.

MCCANDLESS Who!!!!!!?????

BAXTER A handsome, smooth-tongued, well-groomed, unscrupulous, lecherous lawyer.

MCCANDLESS How did they meet?

BAXTER Since she was going to marry you I wanted to give her an income of her own and sent for Wedderburn to arrange the transfer. They met here in this very room. Bella greeted him with her usual effusiveness. He responded so coldly I felt there was no harm in leaving them together for a moment. This morning, over breakfast, she cheerfully told me that for the past three nights he has visited her bedroom after the servants retire. An owl-hoot in the garden is his signal, a candle in the window is hers, then up goes a ladder and up goes he! Try to be calm McCandless!

MCCANDLESS [*tearing his hair*] Oh what have they done together?

BAXTER Nothing whose outcome you need dread – on our world tour I noticed her romantic nature and trained her in the arts of contraception.

MCCANDLESS Have you not told her how evil and vicious he is?

BAXTER Of course! She replied that wicked people need love as much as good ones and are a lot better at it. Go to her, McCandless! Prove her wrong.

With a vigorous nod **MCCANDLESS** *strides to the door but turns before going out.*

MCCANDLESS When Wedderburn arrives, set your dogs on him.

BAXTER [*shocked*] Impossible, McCandless! If I did that Bella would stop thinking I am her friend!

MCCANDLESS [*disgusted*] Ha!

51 CUT TO: STAIRWELL WITH LANDING AND BEDROOM

Through the open bedroom door we see **BELLA** *seated at the open window.* **MCCANDLESS** *leaps onto the landing, pauses at the door, looks. She is in profile, elbow on sill, cheek supported by hand. For the first time we see her at rest and pensive. She wears a sober travelling costume. A hat with veil lies on a packed portmanteau near her feet. As* **MCCANDLESS** *approaches she turns to him with a welcoming smile.*

BELLA How kind of you to visit me, Candle, on my last evening in the old home. I wish God could be here too but he's so miserable just now that I can't stand him.

MCCANDLESS I'm miserable too, Bell. I thought we were to marry.

BELLA [*nodding, and slightly puzzled*] Yes! We arranged that years ago.

MCCANDLESS Six days, Bella!

BELLA That's eternity to me. [*looks out into the back garden*] Duncan Wedderburn touched me in places you never did and now I'm mad about him. When gloaming comes so will he, tiptoe tiptoe tiptoeing through the cabbages with his ladder. He'll push the tip of it ever so gently through my window here then sweep me away to life, love and Europe! But I will never forget the old days and how wonderful I felt when you kissed my fingers.

MCCANDLESS Bella, we have only met three times and this is the third.

BELLA [*suddenly angry with life*] Exactly! I am only half a woman since something happened here ... [*she touches her head*] ... and robbed me of my childhood and past. Duncan Wedderburn will give me a lot of past fast. Duncan is quick! [*more calmly and with an affectionate smile*] And he so loves being wicked! He probably would not want me if he knew Baxter would let me walk, saunter or stroll out the front door with him.

MCCANDLESS *kneels and seizes her hands.*

MCCANDLESS You will NOT marry this worthless man Bell! You will NOT bear his children.

BELLA [*stares at him startled*] I know! I'm engaged to you. [*touches the pearl in her coat lapel*] This is the symbol of our plighted troth!

MCCANDLESS [*standing*] I will wait for him in the garden below and knock him down!

BELLA, *scowling, also stands, then her face suddenly softens into a sweetly affectionate smile. She opens her arms to him. He steps between them, is embraced, closes his eyes in an ecstasy caused by cheek-to-cheek contact. With open eyes and a mischievous, maternal smile she murmurs in his ear:*

BELLA We've hours and hours before Duncan arrives – come upstairs and let me show you something.

52 CUT TO: STAIRWELL TOP LANDING – EVENING

BELLA *pauses outside the operating theatre door, which she opens, saying to* **MCCANDLESS***:*

BELLA You must wait outside and not peep till I call you Candle, then you will be surprised!

She enters, closing the door behind her. **MCCANDLESS** *paces restlessly back and forth.* **MCCANDLESS** *suddenly stands still before the door, stares at it. The door opens inward. We see nothing within but the operating table.*

BELLA [*teasingly*] Come in little Candle! Come in!

We follow **MCCANDLESS** *into the theatre.*

53 CUT TO: OPERATING THEATRE – EVENING

MCCANDLESS *in the doorway, stares from side to side.* **BELLA** *is close behind him, with the anaesthetic equipment, the tube and mask of these in her right hand. With her left arm she presses him back against her chest.* **TRACK IN** *to close-up as he relaxes there.*

BELLA [*murmurs in his ear*] I will let nobody hurt my little Candle. [*clamps the mask over his face.*]

54 CUT TO: BLACKOUT

Five seconds silence, then a sound of heavy breathing.

BAXTER [V.O.] Evil. Evil. I am evil. [*he groans*] Two more seconds of blackout.

55 CUT TO: STUDY – NIGHT

CLOSE-UP *of the gasolier from a low angle –* **MCCANDLESS**' *P.O.V. This slowly lowers to take in* **BAXTER** *sitting beneath, elbows on table, hands supporting a drearily miserable face.*

SOUND: *Faint coughing.*

BAXTER *slowly raises his head, looks into the camera which swings round to include* **MCCANDLESS** *laid out on the sofa under a blanket. He stares at* **BAXTER** *without yet trying to sit up. Through one of the windows overlooking the terrace we see a full moon.*

MCCANDLESS Time?

BAXTER Well after two.

MCCANDLESS Bell?

BAXTER Eloped.

MCCANDLESS *struggles into a sitting position, covers his face with his hands, weeps.* **BAXTER** *comes over and sits beside him with a paper in his hand.*

BAXTER She ... she mentions you in a note she left.

He shows it. Close-up of large, clear childish printing in violet coloured ink of words without vowels: DR GD, I HV CLRFRMD CNDL etc.

MCCANDLESS Gibberish!

BAXTER [*indignant*] It makes perfect sense! She has simply saved time by omitting the vowels. Listen! "Dear God, I have chloroformed Candle in the operating theatre. Ask him to live with you when he wakes up and then you can both talk about Dearly Beloved Bell Baxter. I will telegraph regularly to say where I am when I get there." ... Will you move in here with me McCandless? It might make us both less lonely. You could help in my weekend clinic for sick animals.

MCCANDLESS [*after a thoughtful pause*] Why did you call yourself evil?

BAXTER [*not looking at him*] That little nine month old foetus I saved from the drowned woman's body should have been coddled as my foster child. By recasting its brain in the mother's body I turned a free human being into a toy – a toy for Duncan Wedderburn! [*in agony he strikes his head with his fists*].

MCCANDLESS [*thoughtfully*] If you committed a crime by making Bell as she is then I'm glad of it, because I love what she is whether she marries Wedderburn or not. And the woman who chloroformed me will never be anybody's helpless toy, Baxter.

BAXTER, *struck by this speech, grips and wrings* **MCCANDLESS**' *hand.*

MCCANDLESS [*screams*] Aaaaaaaah!

BAXTER [*releasing crippled hand*] I'm sorry!

MCCANDLESS *jumps up, nursing his hand and glaring.*

MCCANDLESS [*furiously*] Whit fur did ye dae that?

BAXTER I was expressing gratitude. [*he too stands*].

MCCANDLESS Keep it tae yersel in future!

BAXTER [*pleading*] Sorry ... you must be hungry, let me get you something to eat.

BAXTER *starts leading* **MCCANDLESS** *towards the door.*

56 CUT TO: 18 PARK CIRCUS – DAY

A **CABBY** *lifts a trunk onto the pavement, and places it beside a heap of Gladstone and carpet bags supervised by* **MCCANDLESS** *at the foot of the front steps.* **BAXTER** *stands at the open door waving a telegram form.*

BAXTER [*excited*] A telegram from London, McCandless! She says "Don't worry"!

CLOSE-UP *of telegram showing message: "DNTWRRY"*

ACCELERATING MONTAGE SEQUENCE

57 CUT TO: BREAKFAST ROOM

Early morning. **MCCANDLESS** *and* **BAXTER** *eat at opposite ends.* **MCCANDLESS** *has a conventional boiled egg in a cup before him and pours tea from a pot.* **BAXTER** *has the complex distilling plant before him and holds a beaker to catch blobs from a spout in one hand while receiving in the other a telegram from an envelope opened by* **MRS DINWIDDIE.**

BAXTER [*reading*] Monte Carlo!

58 CUT TO: PETS SURGERY

In front of benches where some **CHILDREN** *and* **OLD WOMEN** *sit holding a variety of* **PETS, MCCANDLESS**, *in shirt-sleeves, waistcoat and long white bibbed apron, weighs a* **HEDGEHOG** *on a pair of scales with brass weights.* **BAXTER**, *with a thermometer in one hand which suggests he has just been taking its temperature, reads another telegram handed him by* **MRS DINWIDDIE.**

BAXTER Cairo!

59 CUT TO: BILLIARD ROOM

MCCANDLESS, *in shirt-sleeves and waistcoat holding a cue, pauses while* **BAXTER**, *in shirt-sleeves and waistcoat with cue in crook of* *arm, takes from a torn envelope a telegram, he glances over as* **MRS DINWIDDIE** *departs.*

BAXTER [*frowning and disappointed*] This isn't from Bell! It's from the superintendent of Glasgow Royal Lunatic Asylum.

MCCANDLESS, *also disappointed, stoops to resume a stroke.*

BAXTER He asks if I can call and throw light on the mental condition of a new inmate – Duncan Wedderburn!

BAXTER *and* **MCCANDLESS** *stare at each other.*

60 CUT TO: GARTNAVEL ROYAL HOSPITAL – GLASGOW LUNATIC ASYLUM

Rapid approach shot to front door of a gaunt, grey, high-windowed battlement facade, against a sky of stormy clouds. Door starts to open.

SOUND: *Thunder.*

61 CUT TO: ASYLUM CORRIDOR

A wide but very long bleak corridor has many doors with spy-holes at regular intervals all the way along, a strip of carpet down the centre, a **UNIFORMED OFFICER** *sitting with folded arms, very straight backed, in an upright, armless chair halfway down the corridor. The* **SUPERINTENDENT** *walks beside* **BAXTER**, **MCCANDLESS** *slightly behind them. The* **SUPERINTENDENT**, *in wing collar and conventionally sober Victorian professional clothes, has a humorous expression, a way of shrugging his shoulders which may be a disguised nervous twitch, an occasional slight chuckle through closed lips and sounding: Hm hm!* **BAXTER** *has his stick under his arm.*

SUPERINTENDENT Your name occurs frequently among his ravings, Mr Baxter. A few kind words may do him good. [*shrugs*].

BAXTER What is the nature of his illness?

SUPERINTENDENT Persecution mania! [*shrugs*] Religious melancholia! [*shrugs*] Optical hallucinations hm hm!

SUPERINTENDENT But he's not dangerous, even to himself. [*stops at the door*] We don't need to lock him in. [*opens the door*] He loves this little room hm hm! Wants never to leave it. [*He enters. They follow*].

SOUND: *Thunder.*

62 CUT TO: PRIVATE ROOM IN VICTORIAN ASYLUM

This small room has whitewashed walls above waist-high oak panelling, a Persian carpet on the floor; a single bed with patchwork coverlet along one wall and a framed reproduction of Holman Hunt's Scapegoat hanging above; a table with the remains of a meal on it, also a bible, inkstand, papers and [*not immediately obvious*] *a sheaf of papers covered with Bella's writing in violet ink and tied with blue ribbon in a bow knot. There is also an easy chair and, at the table, two rush-bottomed upright chairs.* **WEDDERBURN** *in dressing gown and carpet slippers, crouches on the floor in a corner near a high-barred window, face pale, eyes bloodshot, hair lank and dishevelled. He ignores the visitors, being busy punching and slapping imaginary insects swarming around his head.*

BAXTER [*gravely*] Is he always like this?

SUPERINTENDENT [*quietly*] Company helps him out of it. [*loudly*] Company, Mr Wedderburn!

WEDDERBURN *drops his arms and glares fearfully at the others.*

BAXTER Don't you know me, Wedderburn?

WEDDERBURN, *mouth and eyes wide open, stands up like an automaton and stares at* **BAXTER** *before saying in a toneless voice.*

WEDDERBURN Yes. Oh yes. You are Bella's ... [*pause then suddenly shouts*] God!

SUPERINTENDENT [*cheerily to Baxter*] I see you'll get on very well with him, hm hm! [*goes to the door*] I've got other calls to make but stay as long as you like.

SUPERINTENDENT *leaves* **BAXTER** *and* **MCCANDLESS** *facing* **WEDDERBURN. MCCANDLESS** *can no longer repress himself.*

MCCANDLESS [*violently*] Where is Bella, you villain? What have you done with her?

BAXTER *glances at* **MCCANDLESS** *with displeasure –* **WEDDERBURN** *stares at him with a grin of wild incredulity before wailing faintly.*

WEDDERBURN What has she done to me? [*crying slyly*] Sire! Is your Royal Highness The Great Emperor Candle who Bella will one day marry?

MCCANDLESS I am! Where did you leave her? How is she?

WEDDERBURN [*with a gloating grin*] Your fiance is very happy. She's in her element. She is working in a Parisian ... [*pause, then shouts*] ... brothel!

MCCANDLESS *stares at him, aghast.* **WEDDERBURN** *maintains the same gloating grin, then claps his hands to his head, collapses in a chair and sways from side to side in terrible grief.*

MCCANDLESS [*almost as bad*] Brothel? ... Brothel?

BAXTER [*taking control*] Sit down, McCandless.

MCCANDLESS *collapses into the easy chair, shaking his head. With his odd fingers* **BAXTER** *grips a shoulder of* **WEDDERBURN** *who shudders and stares at him in terror.*

BAXTER *[firm but kind]* You are in terrible misery?
WEDDERBURN *nods.*
BAXTER It will lessen if you confess all that happened between you and my niece.
WEDDERBURN *[feebly]* You know that already because you are God-swine Back-stair, Beast of the Bottomless Pit.
BAXTER Tell me about it anyway.
WEDDERBURN From the beginning, God?
BAXTER *nods.* **WEDDERBURN** *stares in a dazed way at the air before him.*
WEDDERBURN *[feebly]* In the beginning ...
WEDDERBURN *suddenly sits upright and speaks with something like his normal voice.*
WEDDERBURN In the beginning I was young, handsome, proud ...
NOTE: *The filming of Wedderburn's story is melodramatic black and white with red touches which grow more lurid towards the end.*

63 CUT TO: PARK CIRCUS

WEDDERBURN, *looking as splendid as he describes himself, approaches the door of number 18 in fine sunshine and rings the bell. His rosy complexion, gleaming pink lips and red carnation contrast with the surrounding blacks, whites and greys of his top hat, clothes and surroundings.*
WEDDERBURN [V.O.] I was young, handsome, proud and passionate when I went to your home six months ago, and so high principled that I had hitherto only slaked my powerful sexual lusts with women of the servant class.
The door is opened by **MRS DINWIDDIE**. *As he enters past her* **WEDDERBURN** *leers speculatively sideways. She is not pleased.*

64 CUT TO: DRAWING ROOM

BAXTER *gloomily introduces suave* **WEDDERBURN** *to an excited* **BELLA**, *who blushes rosily at* **WEDDERBURN**. *Her skin maintains this pleasant glow until the end of Scene 103. What follows is indicated by V.O.*
WEDDERBURN [V.O.] When you introduced me to your niece my high principles melted like snow in a furnace. In matters of the heart it is best to be direct. When you left the room for a moment I said –
WEDDERBURN *[rapidly]* May I see you alone soon without anyone else knowing?
BELLA *looks startled and nods.*
WEDDERBURN Is your bedroom at the back of the house?
BELLA *smiles and nods.*
WEDDERBURN Will you put a candle in the window when everyone else is in bed? I will bring a ladder.
BELLA *laughs and nods.*
WEDDERBURN *[quiet but intense]* I love you.
BELLA *[chattily]* I've had another lad who does that too. He's not as tall as you ...
BAXTER *enters carrying a deed box.*
WEDDERBURN [V.O.] She was chatting about her fiance when you returned. Her guile excited and astonished me. Little did I think ...

65 CUT TO: BACK GARDEN – NIGHT

WEDDERBURN *swiftly mounts the ladder to the open window where* **BELLA**, *wearing a night-gown, holds a candle up in one hand while eagerly beckoning with the other.*
WEDDERBURN [V.O.] ... that your house was a mantrap, and Bella the bait luring me to eternal damnation!
On the word "mantrap" the light in the window glows red as **WEDDERBURN** *reaches it and leaps in. The candle goes out : a moment later a much brighter light goes on in the room and* **WEDDERBURN** *climbs out of the window with* **BELLA** *over his shoulder. She wears her travelling costume, hat with veil, and clutches the portmanteau. He is also in travelling garb – a Jaeger suit.*
WEDDERBURN [V.O.] So cleverly did you blind me, so great was my love that when she and I eloped on that soft summer night I believed Bella would become my wife.

66 CUT TO: STATION PLATFORM WITH STEAM TRAIN

WEDDERBURN *and* **BELLA**, *he with suitcase, she with portmanteau, run towards a first class carriage door held open by a guard.*
WEDDERBURN [V.O.] Though I knew she would inherit all your great wealth, not greed for gold but passion for Bella winged our flight.
They leap into the carriage. The guard slams the door [we see a reserved sign on it] and blows his whistle.

67 CUT TO: HEAVILY UPHOLSTERED CARRIAGE – NIGHT

WEDDERBURN *and* **BELLA**, *partly dressed against the scarlet lining of her travelling coat, turbulently entwine along a seat. His mouth moves as if asking something.*
WEDDERBURN [V.O.] Imagine my consternation when, before the train reached Crossmyloof my intended bride said ...

BELLA [*suddenly static, in a cheerful voice*] I can't marry you Wedder – it would break my fiance's heart.
WEDDERBURN [*amazed*] Surely he belongs in the past!
BELLA No. The future.
WEDDERBURN But ... where does that leave me?
BELLA [*enthusiastically*] Here and now you lucky man!
She rips his shirt open.

68 CUT TO: INT./EXT. MONTAGE SEQUENCE – STEAM TRAIN – NIGHT

A toiling **FIREMAN**, *stripped to the waist, toils at hurling spadefuls of coal into the flickering crimson gullet of the locomotive furnace, over shots of thrusting pistons, steam squirting from valves, smoke and sparks billowing from a funnel.*
WEDDERBURN [V.O.] She was a houri – Mahomet's paradise. Ours was not an express train. We must have stopped at Kilmarnock, Dumfries and stations north of Watford junction but I knew only the motion and rare pauses in our pilgrimage of passion. I was man enough for her but the pace was terrific.
MCCANDLESS [V.O.] [*a cry of mental agony*].

69 CUT TO: PRIVATE ROOM IN ASYLUM – DAY

WEDDERBURN *leans with one elbow on the table, a leg flung over the other. In the easy but slightly offended posture of an interrupted raconteur he frowns at* **MCCANDLESS** *who, slumped in the chair, is ending his outcry in a groan, also watched by* **BAXTER** *who sits in the other chair, hands folded on the knob of the stick which is upright between his legs.*
BAXTER [*considerately*] Is this causing you pain, McCandless?
MCCANDLESS [*covering face with his hands*] Go on! Go on!
WEDDERBURN [*firmly*] I will. As our coal-fired steed panted ...

70 CUT TO: TRAIN HALTING AT EUSTON PLATFORM – DAY

The exhausted **FIREMAN** *drops his shovel as the* **ENGINE DRIVER** *slams shut the furnace door.*
WEDDERBURN [V.O.] ... to a halt in the southern terminus of the Midland Line I felt sure our acts of union had wiped out all memory of her other lover ...

71 CUT TO: RAILWAY CARRIAGE

BELLA *stands briskly adjusting her clothing.* **WEDDERBURN** *sprawls behind her, exhausted, dishevelled, unshaven. Now only the whites of his eyes are pink.*

BELLA Ee, I can't wait to do that all over again in a proper bed.
WEDDERBURN [*faintly*] Please Bella. Marry me.
BELLA Can't you remember my answer to that one? Let's go to the station hotel and order a huge breakfast of porridge and bacon and eggs and kippers and sausages and pints of sweet, hot, milky tea because we must keep your strength up Wedder! Our holiday has just begun!

72 CUT TO: INT./EXT. FRANTIC TRAVELLING MONTAGE – DAY/NIGHT

Using mostly early film footage – a sequence showing glimpses of a crowded railway station – crowd pouring down a gangway from a crowded deck of a steamer – cabs galloping round Place de la Concorde or Saint Peter's – busy foyer of a grand hotel, then racecourse, then crowds around a roulette table under splendid chandeliers.
WEDDERBURN [V.O.] So now you know the pattern of my existence as I fled across Europe and round the Mediterranean with a woman who never slept! At first I thought I might get a little sleep by exhausting us – so by an iron exertion of will I rushed Bella by train, ferry and cab to and fro, in and out of the most tumultuous hotels, theatres, racecourses, markets, zoos and alas, alas gambling casinos on the continent.

73 CUT TO: INT. CONTINENTAL HOTEL BEDROOM – DAY

Frantic montage of sexual activity between **BELLA** *and* **WEDDERBURN**.
WEDDERBURN [V.O.] Again and again I fell into bed as into sleep of death and awoke to find I was pleasuring her. I consciously embraced the dance of love with groans of ecstasy and agony until gleams through the shutters heralded the purgatory of another day.

74 CUT TO: VENICE – SAN GIORGIO MAGGIORE – DAY

Montage showing **LOW ANGLE** *shot of facade,* **CLOSE-UP** *of stone steps swinging upside down,* **HIGH ANGLE** *shot of* **MAN** *falling into smooth, dark water with a splash and spreading ripples.*
WEDDERBURN [V.O.] Outside San Giorgio Maggiore in Venice I collapsed and rolled into the lagoon.

75 CUT TO: LINER'S DECK – MEDITERRANEAN

WEDDERBURN, *swaddled like a papoose in travelling rugs, shawl and cap which hide all but his face, sits helpless in a bathchair* *beside a funnel from which steam unrolls towards a horizon. Beside him* **BELLA**, *wearing a pale dress and huge sunhat, in a basket chair sits with a writing case on her lap, cheerfully writing.*

WEDDERBURN [V.O.] I awoke on board a passenger steamer bound on a Mediterranean cruise.

BELLA [*looking kindly up*] No more rushing about for you, Wedder. I am in charge now and I order complete rest – except at night, when we are wedding.

Tears trickle down his cheeks. She leans across and dries them with a handkerchief.

WEDDERBURN [*faintly*] Marry me Bella.

BELLA [*amused*] No sensible woman will ever marry you, Wedder. You are only good for one thing but you are very good indeed at it – a true grandee monarch magnifico excellency emperor lord high paramount president principal bobby-dazzler and boss at it.

He weeps again while she returns to her writing.

WEDDERBURN [V.O.] Yet I still thought her kind! GUFFAW GUFFAW GUFFAW you damnable Baxter, I still thought her kind! Not even the incident at Gibraltar opened my eyes.

76 CUT TO: PUBLIC GARDEN ESPLANADE – GIBRALTAR

Palm trees and part of the Rock in the background. A **MAJESTIC LADY**, *promenading with a parasol and a* **PAGE BOY** *carrying a* **PEKINESE**, *hails* **BELLA**, *to whose arm* **WEDDERBURN** *clings. His other hand leans heavily on a stick. In yachting cap, blazer, rug over white flannels and knotted scarf he looks slightly healthier.*

MAJESTIC LADY How splendid to see you here, Lady Blessington, why did you not call on us at once? Do you remember me? Surely we were introduced four years ago at Cowes 'board the Prince of Wales' yacht?

BELLA [*impressed by the idea*] How wonderful! But most folk call me Bell Baxter when I'm not trundling my droopy old Wedder about.

MAJESTIC LADY But surely – surely you are the wife of General Blessington whom I met at Cowes!

BELLA Oo I hope so! Though God told me I was in Brazil four years ago. What's my husband like? Handsomer than this one? Taller? Stronger? Richer?

MAJESTIC LADY [*stiffly*] There is obviously some mistake, though your appearance and voice are remarkably similar.

The **MAJESTIC LADY** *bows and moves on.* **WEDDERBURN** *turns and speaks to* **BELLA**. *She replies. He looks agitated.* **BELLA**'*s pink glow fades – her eye shadow and scarlet lipstick become ominously intense.*

WEDDERBURN [V.O.] It was thus I learned that my awful mistress had no memories of her life before the shock which made the strangely regular crack circling her skull under the hair – if crack it be, Mr Baxter! But YOU know and I now know what it really is!

SLOW TRACK *in to* **WEDDERBURN**'*s increasingly aghast face close to* **BELLA**'*s increasingly scarlet speaking mouth.*

MCCANDLESS [V.O.] [*wildly*] Baxter!

77 CUT TO: PRIVATE ROOM IN ASYLUM

The scene as before, but **WEDDERBURN** *is pointing accusingly at* **BAXTER** *who still sits calmly with hands folded on his stick but looking at* **MCCANDLESS** *who has hurried over to him.*

MCCANDLESS [*low but terrified*] He has discovered everything, Baxter!

BAXTER [*calmly*] What have you discovered, Wedderburn?

WEDDERBURN [*triumphantly*] That crack round Bella's skull proves she is a lemur, vampire, succubus and thing unclean!

MCCANDLESS *shows signs of relief.* **BAXTER** *smiles.*

BAXTER [*kindly*] Tell us more, Wedderburn.

78 CUT TO: PARIS STREET SCENE – EARLY MORNING

A small square where three narrow lanes converge. A sign above a small door says Hotel de Notre Dame. There is also a café with two or three exterior tables which cover a quarter of the square's visible area. The chairs are stacked, an aproned **WAITER** *is about to set them out as* **BELLA** *and* **WEDDERBURN** *approach, she firm of foot with portmanteau in left hand,* **WEDDERBURN**'*s much bigger travelling bag held on her right shoulder, he sauntering alongside with an air of languid discontent, hands in pockets.*

WEDDERBURN [V.O.] We arrived at last in Paris by overnight train and sought cheap lodgings near the river. My money was almost exhausted. I had recovered some of my physical strength, but refused to let Bella know this lest she drain me, once again, of all physical manhood.

As the **WAITER** *sets out the first chair on a table beside the hotel door* **WEDDERBURN** *collapses into it.*

WEDDERBURN [to **WAITER**] Garsong! Oon absongth.

The **WAITER** *withdraws as* **BELLA** *sets the bags down and goes into the hotel. The towers of Notre Dame appear close above roofs*

bordering a lane in that direction. **WEDDERBURN***'s wandering glance suddenly fixes on them. Red lights gleam from the windows.*
SOUND: *Organ music.*
WEDDERBURN *stands up slowly, staring as if in a trance. The* **WAITER** *lays the absinthe glass on the table.* **WEDDERBURN,** *without ceasing to gaze on the cathedral, automatically drinks it in one gulp and walks forward.*

79 CUT TO: INT. NOTRE DAME

SOUND: *Organ music.*
A chapel with a shrine to Madonna and Child. A pyramid of scarlet candles burns before it. Some **OLD WOMEN** *and a very attractive* **YOUNG WOMAN** *in widow's weeds kneels praying devoutly.* **WEDDERBURN** *is doing the same. The* **YOUNG WOMAN** *rises and walks away.* **WEDDERBURN** *as if in a trance, rises and follows her to a row of confession boxes. She enters one. Like a sleepwalker he enters one beside it.*

80 CUT TO: CONFESSION BOX IN CROSS-SECTION

In dim red light, **WEDDERBURN,** *kneeling in profile, blabs frantically into the penitent's grill. A gaunt, grim-faced* **CONFESSOR** *faces us, ear to grill, hand supporting cheek, one leg flung over the other. He wears a black soutine with scarlet buttons.*
WEDDERBURN [*hoarsely*] Bless me father, for I have sinned – with women – interminably.
The **CONFESSOR** *raises his hands to stifle a yawn of utter boredom.*
WEDDERBURN It began with my nanny, when I was two ...
SOUND: *Doomful chords.*
We see **WEDDERBURN** *blabbing, weeping, beating his breast, denouncing himself. The* **PRIEST** *remains impassive until:*
PRIEST [*in a distinct but hissing accent to the petrified.* **WEDDERBURN**] Since Monsieur is a heretic I can impose no penance, but Monsieur must marry this woman who is destroying him, or renounce her utterly, or rot in hell. Adieu Monsieur, I will pray for your soul.

81 CUT TO: THE HOTEL DE NOTRE DAME

LOW ANGLE SHOT *of* **WEDDERBURN***'s head and shoulders as he strides determinedly towards the door.*
SOUND: *Organ music and a choir singing a savage Dies Irae.*

82 CUT TO: PARIS HOTEL FOYER AND STAIR

The hotel is a small one with red wallpaper and a plump black-clad **MANGERESS** *at a desk at the foot of the stair.* **WEDDERBURN** *is asking* **BELLA***'s room number. She speaks and points upward. While ascending he is passed by a* **DEBONAIR MALE GUEST** *coming down from a closing door through which we barely glimpse a* **WOMAN** *in a negligee.* **WEDDERBURN** *opens the door beside it, enters and shuts it.*
SOUND: *Organ, choir and Dies Irae end on a slammed door.*

83 CUT TO: PARIS HOTEL BEDROOM

This is small – not much more than a cubicle with space for a double bed with pink coverlet, wardrobe, dressing table. The wallpaper pattern is rosy bouquets tied with scarlet ribbon. The two bags are on the bed. **BELLA** *has hung her travelling coat on a hanger and is about to put it in the wardrobe, an action* **WEDDERBURN** *interrupts.*
WEDDERBURN Bella! When I ravished you from home in Glasgow I thought myself a fiend in human form: but now I have discovered the truth – you are the fiend who is leading me to damnation and my love for you has turned to HATE HATE HATE HATE HATE – loathing, detestation and hate!
BELLA [*sensibly*] Then you must go back to Glasgow without me, Wedder.
WEDDERBURN [*raving*] I can't go anywhere without you Bell! I have no money! You have made me a pauper!
BELLA [*joyfully*] Don't worry about money, Wedder!
She flings her coat on the bed, exposing the scarlet lining. Seizing a nail-file from the dressing table, she rips the lining open, removes sheaves of ten pound notes and plonks them steadily on the coverlet in front of **WEDDERBURN,** *talking while she does so.*
BELLA God said you would soon tire of me and gave me this for when it happened, so you must take it in return for all the fun you gave me. I don't need unearned income now because I'm going to work for a living like other people have to do so fly from me!
SOUND: **BELLA***'s voice fades behind a sinister organ note.*
Freeze frame of **BELLA** *proffering money,* **WEDDERBURN** *recoiling Here follows a* **SEQUENCE WITH ANIMATION** *of* **WEDDERBURN** *going mad in slow motion. The room around him goes blood red while the bouquets in the wallpaper change to black and orange, fanged and winged, highly active creatures swarming over him. He backs, crouching, into a corner, trying to defend his face with one hand while beating them off with the other. We glimpse but do not hear* **BELLA** *open the door and shout for help.*
WEDDERBURN [V.O.] As my brain tried to grasp and repel her hideous meaning I retreated into a corner and sank to the floor, punching the air around my head which

seemed to swarm with huge wasps or carnivorous bats though I knew these vermin were inside my brain and gnawing, gnawing.

SOUND *Organ note becomes a remote jabbering as:*

The swarm of monsters is wiped out by a **SWARM OF PROSTITUTES** *in red and pink negligées and bright lipstick. They swarm into the bedroom past* **BELLA** *and overpower and lift the struggling maniac in the corner, one pressing the neck of a cognac bottle into his yelling mouth.*

WEDDERBURN [V.O.] Bella must have called in the Manageress but my crazed mind multiplied these two into a jabbering crowd of women, their scanty clothing displaying their charms to the full as they swarmed over me like all the serving women I have ever seduced. I lost consciousness –

SOUND: *Cut distant jabbering.*

84 CUT TO: DUNGEON SUITE – NIGHT

WEDDERBURN, *wearing nothing but a flannel combination suit, sits cross-legged on a polished parquet floor against a wall unconvincingly painted to look like stone-work. A real ringbolt in it has an attached chain running to a fetter round his ankle. He stares with absolute incomprehension at a headsman's block and an axe obviously made of painted plywood.*

WEDDERBURN [V.O.] – and regained it in a place that, even in my madness, I knew must be hallucination. I was there a long time until one day they dressed me –

Invisible hands cast **WEDDERBURN***'s outdoor clothes onto the floor in front of him.*

85 CUT TO: HOTEL DE NOTRE DAME

The **MANAGERESS** *and* **WAITER** *from a nearby café help* **BELLA**, *the stupefied* **WEDDERBURN** *and his bag into a cab.*

WEDDERBURN [V.O.] – shoved me into a cab –

86 CUT TO: PLATFORM OF GARE DU NORD

A couple of **PORTERS** *march* **WEDDERBURN** *to the open door of a carriage. They are supervised by a* **SUPERIOR RAILWAY OFFICIAL** *and* **BELLA** *who walks briskly beside him. A* **THIRD PORTER** *carries his bag.*

WEDDERBURN [V.O.] – but it was Bella who bought my tickets, had me bundled onto the boat-train and thrust out of her life forever!

The **PORTERS** *put* **WEDDERBURN** *and bag in the carriage while* **BELLA**, *smiling merrily, gives a bundle of notes to the* **OFFICIAL**.

87: CUT TO: RAILWAY CARRIAGE

WEDDERBURN *sits like a dummy beside a window with* **BELLA** *in the nearby door chatting to him. He gives no sign of seeing or hearing her.* **OTHER PASSENGERS** *are interested.*

WEDDERBURN [V.O.] And all the time she was pouring out a maddening stream of chatter.

BELLA ... poor Old Wedder, I've been bad for you, you'll LOVE being home again, your tickets and passport and money are in your inside pocket and remember to give God the letter I wrote him, it's in your bag, and tell him I'll soon want my little Candle and ...

SOUND: *Doors slamming and a whistle.*

BELLA Oops I have to go now.

88 CUT TO: PLATFORM OF GARE DU NORD

The train is pulling out faster and faster. **BELLA** *runs beside it waving and yelling –*

BELLA GIVE MY LOVE TO BONNY SCOTLAND!

89 CUT TO: ROOM IN ASYLUM – DAY – MCCANDLESS COLOUR ZONE

BAXTER *sits as before with hands calmly folded on the head of his stick. Close behind him* **MCCANDLESS** *stands with folded arms, leaning against the wall beside the door.* **WEDDERBURN** *still sits by the table in negligent pose, talking now in a strange sing-song chant.*

WEDDERBURN So now I know who Bella really is – the white demon who destroys the most noble and virile of men in every age. The Greeks called her Helen of Troy, the Jews called her Delilah, Bonnie Prince Charlie called her Clementina Walkinshaw. [*slowly stands, saying*] But in every age and nation the white demon is tool and puppet of another, vaster demon! [*points and cries*] You! God swine back stair! BEAST OF THE BOTTOMLESS PIT AND DARK LORD OF THE MATERIAL UNIVERSE!

MCCANDLESS, *alarmed prepares to defend* **BAXTER.**

BAXTER [*unmoved but slightly impatient*]Stop over-acting, Wedderburn. You may have had a nervous breakdown in Paris. You are certainly no madman now.

WEDDERBURN *slumps back into his chair, sighs and says sensibly*

WEDDERBURN Probably not, but this is the only place where I'm not pestered by the fools who once lent me money.

WEDDERBURN *gloomily rests his elbow on the table, fist supporting cheek.* **BAXTER** *stands up.*

BAXTER You said Bella gave you a letter for me.

WEDDERBURN Here! I can make no sense of it.

WEDDERBURN *hands* **BAXTER** *the ribbon-tied sheaf.* **BAXTER** *glances at it, pockets it and turns to the door saying:*

BAXTER Thanks. Goodnight.

WEDDERBURN [*pleading*] Baxter – you might send me a case or two of champagne, or even whisky. You can easily afford that.

BAXTER [*over his shoulder*] I'll discuss it with Bella when she returns to me ...

MCCANDLESS [*agitated*] Yer a sleekit lothario, you bloody canoodlin' dandy!

BAXTER Home, McCandless!

In **CLOSE-UP: MCCANDLESS** *opens the door and walks out followed by* **BAXTER.**

90 CUT TO: THE STUDY – NIGHT

In **CLOSE-UP: MCCANDLESS** *enters the door followed by* **BAXTER** *so the location seems to be the asylum corridor until we notice they wear smoking jackets and that the* **DOGS** *are coming through the door with them.*

MCCANDLESS [*arguing*] Sane or insane, I refuse to believe that a British subject could abandon Bella in a brothel.

BAXTER, *carrying Bella's letter, goes to a chair by the fire. The* **DOGS** *accompany him and settle on the hearth rug.*

BAXTER I agree that Wedderburn is an inveterate liar. Only Bella can be trusted to tell the truth, the whole truth and nothing but the truth.

BAXTER *sits with the sheaf on his knees and unties the ribbon.*

MCCANDLESS *sits facing him.*

MCCANDLESS Read it to me!

BAXTER [*tenderly stroking the top page*] I would rather read it to myself first [*staring, delighted*] She has actually written it in Shakespearean blank verse!

MCCANDLESS [*loudly and pointing*] I will break into that closet and drink the last of your father's port if you don't start reading!

BAXTER *stares at* **MCCANDLESS**, *nods and starts reading, but the voice is* **BELLA***'s.*

NOTE: *In the next sequence the colouring becomes magically richer, the movements much more graceful. This is more obvious at the start where some scenes repeat episodes from Wedderburn's sequence.*

91 CUT TO: DECK OF A LINER, SEA AND SUN

BELLA, *in a pale dress with a huge sunhat, sits in a basket chair beside the funnel, writing case open on her lap, pen in hand, the shawl-swathed* **WEDDERBURN** *beside her. The dress is creamy silk, the hat has coloured fruit and birds wings on top,* **WEDDERBURN***'s shawls are thick but not gaudy tartan. All harmonize beautifully with the blue distance.*

BELLA [V.O.] Dear God, I had no peace to write before
We are afloat upon this blue blue sea.
Wedder is tucked up snug and glad at last
Not to be do do doing all the time.
How Auld Lang Syne seems that soft warm bright night
When I bade you goodbye, chloroformed Candle –

92 DISSOLVE TO: PARK CIRCUS GARDEN – NIGHT

SLOW MOTION

WEDDERBURN *climbs out of the window with* **BELLA** *over his shoulder*

BELLA [V.O.] Then skipped down ladder in my Wedder's arms.

93 DISSOLVE TO: STATION PLATFORM WITH TRAIN – NIGHT

SLOW MOTION

WEDDERBURN *and* **BELLA** *with suitcase and portmanteau run towards carriage door held open by a* **GUARD.**

BELLA [V.O.] Swift as the wind we sped into our train.

94 DISSOLVE TO: INT./EXT. MONTAGE SEQUENCE – NIGHT

SLOW MOTION: *They make balletic love on the padded seat whose patterned upholstery, beside the colour of* **BELLA***'s garments, give her the aspect of a geisha in Hiroshige prints.*

BELLA [V.O.] And curtained carriage where we wed wed wed, Went wedding all the way to London town,
And booked into Saint Pancras's Hotel.

95 DISSOLVE TO: LONDON HOTEL BEDROOM – DAY

SLOW MOTION: PAGEBOY *holds door open to admit erect, spruce, slightly dishevelled, lovingly smiling* **BELLA** *arm-in-arm with a dazed and dishevelled* **WEDDERBURN**. *Behind them a* **HOTEL PORTER** *puts their baggage on the floor and leaves the* **PAGEBOY** *shutting them in together. They move towards the bed, flinging their hats off and starting to undress,* **BELLA** *with serene delight,* **WEDDERBURN** *a little wearily.*

BELLA [V.O.] You never wedded, God, so may not know
A night and day of it takes more from men
Than they can give without becoming ... strange.

96 CUT TO: LONDON HOTEL BEDROOM – LATER

NORMAL SPEED: BELLA *sits up naked in a restful, graceful pose among the confused sheets of the bed. She looks beautiful but puzzled.* **WEDDERBURN** *lies flat on his back, naked, beside her, staring grimly up at the ceiling.*

WEDDERBURN [*in a cold monotone*]
I'm not the only man you ever loved.
Admit you have had hundreds before me.

BELLA [*mildly thoughtful*]
Not hundreds – no. I never counted them,
But half a hundred might be about right.

WEDDERBURN *covers his face with his hands and moans.*

BELLA [*puzzled*] What's wrong with letting people kiss my hands?

WEDDERBURN They did much more than that.

BELLA [*shaking her head*] They never did!
Only my wed-wed-wedding Wedderburn
Has poked me with his middle footless leg!

BELLA *rests her hand affectionately on the sheet over his penis. It delights her by springing erect – no other part of him moves*

WEDDERBURN [*weary and despairing*]
Bella, you are a liar and a whore.
You are no virgin. Who deflowered you first?

BELLA [*not hurt – just trying to understand him*]
Why are you calling me these nasty names?

WEDDERBURN [*points to* **BELLA***'s stomach above pubic hair*]
How did you get that scar?

BELLA [*looking down and touching*] This little line?
Surely all women's bellies have this line?

WEDDERBURN [*shaking his head*] No, no, no, no.
Only the pregnant ones.
Who've been cut open to let babies out.

BELLA *wonderingly places one hand on her womb, feels her head with the other.*

BELLA Wedder! That must have been B.C.B.K –
The time before they cracked poor Bella's knob.
I don't remember anything from then.

She shrugs helplessly. He leans forward, feels around her skull under the hair then rests his hands on her shoulders, staring into her eyes.

WEDDERBURN Why did you never tell me that before?

BELLA I thought you did not want to know my past
My hopes, my fears, my thoughts ... my character!

WEDDERBURN [*bursting into tears*]
You're right! I am a fiend! I ought to die!

He strikes his brow with both fists. She embraces him.

97 DISSOLVE TO: HOTEL BEDROOM MONTAGE

SLOW MOTION: BELLA *and* **WEDDERBURN** *making love again, but* **BELLA** *is now obviously the dominant partner.*

BELLA [V.O.] I soothed him, babied him – he is a baby –
And got him wedding at a proper speed.
Yes, wed he can and does, but little Candle,
When you hear this do not feel very sad.

98 DISSOLVE OR WIPE TO: THE STUDY, PARK CIRCUS – NIGHT

BAXTER *is reading the letter to the fascinated* **MCCANDLESS**.

MOVE INTO CLOSE-UP *of* **MCCANDLESS***' mournful face.*

BELLA [V.O.] Women need Wedderburns, but need much more
Their faithful, kindly man who waits at home.

MCCANDLESS*' mouth softens into a smile.*

99 DISSOLVE TO: INT. HOTEL BEDROOM – NIGHT

BELLA *sits up in bed, naked, her hand resting on her stomach,* **WEDDERBURN** *asleep behind her. She is wrestling with a puzzling idea. Move into* **CLOSE-UP** *of her face.*

BELLA [V.O.] I had a baby once. God, is that true?
If it is true what has become of her?
For I am somehow sure she is a girl.
This is a thought too big for Bell to think.
I must grow into it by slow degrees.

Her face fills screen, background becomes sky blue. Pull back to show.

100 CUT TO: DECK OF SHIP – DAY

BELLA *writing. Pull back to show her full figure, and the swathed* **WEDDERBURN** *beside her.*

BELLA [V.O.] God, do you read the change there is in me?
I am not quite as selfish as I was.
By making me his nurse poor Wedderburn
Has taught me how to feel for other folk.

She gives him a tender glance.

101 CUT TO: EXT. AND INT. COLLAGE – DAY AND NIGHT

Coloured picture postcard stills of crowded squares and plazas in European Capitals around 1880s give way to interiors of a magnificent hotel foyer – racecourse – cathedral – theatre – Moulin Rouge cabaret – boxing stadium, all given motion by zoom-ins.

BELLA [V.O.] The jealousy he had shown in London
Got worse when we were on the con– tin-ong,
To stop me meeting any other men

He hurried us through cities and hotels,
Cathedrals, racecourses and theatres.
His face was white. His eyes grew big, and shone.
"I am no weakling, Bell!" he cried, "On! On!"
And on we rushed – might have been rushing yet
If the poor fool had not begun to bet.

102 CUT TO: SALON OF FASHIONABLE CASINO

CLOSE-UP *of spinning roulette wheel. Pull back to show gold and silver coins heaped on numbered squares of a table surrounded by an opulently cosmopolitan mob presided over by a monumentally impassive* **CROUPIER**. *The salon is a large hall lit by huge chandeliers. The walls are fluted pillars with Corinthian capitals [white and gold] and windows between them swathed in velvet curtains. Three gambling tables have have spectators around them, seated, or standing. There are sofas between the tables where some folk listlessly wait.*

WEDDERBURN *sits with a clenched fist [containing coins] near four sovereigns on a number 5 square otherwise empty. White-faced, gaunt and bright-eyed, he stares at the spinning wheel with the intensity of all but four in that crowd: the* **CROUPIER**; **BELLA** *who stands behind* **WEDDERBURN***'s chair wearing a simple deep blue gown with silk elbow-length gloves, a pearl choker necklace and a bored expression;* **MR HOOKER**, *a rich, suave, darkly dressed American with an air of quiet authority who observes only* **BELLA**. **HOOKER** *is not eye-catching in this crowd of emphatically Italian, German and French* **ARISTOCRATS**, **RICH BUSINESSMEN** *and their* **WIVES**, *well dressed* **CONFIDENCE TRICKSTERS** *and* **UNIFORMED OFFICERS**.

A plump **FRENCH COURTESAN** *in a low-cut gown sits by* **WEDDERBURN** *and as the scene progresses shows increasing interest in him. The wheel comes to rest.*

CROUPIER *[calling]* Numero cinq!

All but **BELLA**, **HOOKER** *and* **CROUPIER** *stare jealously or admiringly at* **WEDDERBURN** *as coins are raked by* **LIVERIED ATTENDANTS** *from every square but his, and the four sovereigns are thrust towards him with twelve others. Half turning he smiles smugly up at* **BELLA** *who says wearily –*

BELLA Oh Duncan, please take me away from here!
Let us play billiards. Billiards need some skill.

WEDDERBURN *[in a low, intense voice, growing steadily louder]*
You hate roulette? You hate to see me win?
Of course! You inwardly despise my brain,
Think it a mere appendage of my prick
And less efficient than my testicles!
Well, woman, I will show I hate it too!
Hate and despise it, and to prove I do
Will now amaze, appal and put to shame
The croupier who controls –
the fools who play this game!

CROUPIER Faites vos jeux! Place your bets!

WEDDERBURN *slams the sovereigns in his fist onto number 5 and pushes his earlier winnings on it too. His voice has drawn attention. His action interests or surprises all but* **BELLA**, *who leaves as the* **CROUPIER** *sets the ball rolling and the* **COURTESAN** *slides nearer* **WEDDERBURN**, *murmuring.*

COURTESAN Your courage is formidable, M'Sieur.

Lost in the game, he does not notice.

BELLA *sits with her back to the game on a Victorian sofa several yards away. The sofa back, in plan, is S shaped, letting two sit side-by-side facing different directions. She resigns herself to waiting and does not see* **HOOKER**, *who has quietly followed her, sit down beside her.*

HOOKER *[looking sideways]*
Madam, will you forgive if I intrude?

BELLA *turns her head, looks him up and down then smiles brightly*

BELLA You look quite clever. What have you to say?

Between their profiles we can see the central part of the crowd round the table. **HOOKER***'s manner conveys sexual interest restrained by an immense self control. Though pleased by his regard she is more excited by his words.*

HOOKER My name is Eli Hooker – President
Of Philadelphia Fuel and Armament,
Also a Christian who would hate to see
A lovely lady forced into poverty.

CROUPIER *[distant]* Numero cinq!

BELLA You are American!

HOOKER Yes, thank the Lord!
Your husband's playing recklessly and soon
Is bound to lose.

BELLA *[nodding emphatically]* Oh yes! I think that too.

HOOKER Can you not make him stop?

BELLA I tried. I can't.

HOOKER Is he a wealthy man?

BELLA *[smiling and shaking her head]* Not Wedderburn!

HOOKER *[with grave pity]*
Why then, I fear he'll ruin both of you.

BELLA *[cheerily touching her necklace]*
Oh no! I'll sell this jewellery of mine.

HOOKER *waves his hand to dismiss any interest in sales of portable property.*

HOOKER I have no wish to pry in your affairs.
I do suggest you take him quickly home.

CROUPIER [*distant*] Numero cinq!

There is greater excitement round the roulette table which **BELLA** *and* **HOOKER** *ignore.*

BELLA [*shaking her head in vehement denial*]
I want more weddings with my Wedderburn,
Venice and Greece, Istanbul, Pyramids,
Before I settle down to married life.

HOOKER Your husband, by incredible good luck,
Is now a millionaire and can remain one
If only he leaves now! Please make him leave!

BELLA *delighted by so much attention, stands up, stripping the gloves from both her hands.*

BELLA Because you're such a gent I'll do my best.
I'm very glad the world is made of men
As kind – unselfish – loving – as you are

She offers her left hand which holds the gloves to **HOOKER** *who kisses it. Her ecstatic pleasure in the experience is noted by him. Withdrawing she sweeps regally towards the table followed by* **HOOKER**. *As she nears the table ...*

CROUPIER Zero!

WEDDERBURN [*invisible in the crowd emits a horribly prolonged wail*] *Everything freezes, then the crowd parts and through the gap.*

WEDDERBURN, *clutching his head, totters towards* **BELLA**, *his eyes staring, mouth wide in a horrified grin, tears streaming down his cheeks. He falls to his knees at her feet.*

WEDDERBURN [*between choking sobs*] I've lost everything!

He falls on all fours and starts banging his brow on the floor. **BELLA**, *with a smile of loving pity, kneels beside him and embraces him murmuring*

BELLA Poor Wedderburn! You poor old silly soul!

103 CUT TO: DECK OF A LINER – MEDITERRANEAN – DAY

BELLA *stands at the rail overlooking the prow with her back to it.* **HOOKER** *smokes a large cheroot, with which he sometimes gesticulates. The movement of the ship is conveyed by a pennant fluttering from a stay rope, and* **BELLA**'*s hair whipping about. If she wears a sunhat she might be holding it against the breeze.*

BELLA [V.O.] And that, dcar God, is how I come to be
Afloat upon the Mediterranean Sea
With this new loving friend who worships me.

They stroll forward, her hands on **HOOKER**'*s arm, chatting as they pass ventilators and* **PASSENGERS** *on deck chairs.*

BELLA Why are you bound for Egypt, Mr Hooker?

HOOKER Oil is my business.

BELLA Oil that burns in lamps?

HOOKER Oil that will one day fuel the world's machines
Like coal does nowadays. And oil is found
In desert places where the land is poor.

BELLA How kind of you to go discov'ring wealth
For people in a land that's very poor.

HOOKER *turns his face to hide a smile.*

HOOKER No doubt some native chiefs will benefit.

BELLA *detaches herself for they have arrived where* **WEDDERBURN** *sits near a funnel, as in Scenes 75 and 91, staring at her hauntedly. She adjusts the shawl more snugly round him, saying:*

BELLA What is a native, Mr Hooker, please?

WEDDERBURN [*interrupting in a feeble croak*]
Natives are folk who live where they are born.

HOOKER [*joking*] No Englishmen are natives. They prefer
The lands of other people.

WEDDERBURN [*nodding*] Very true.

BELLA, *having kissed* **WEDDERBURN**'*s brow, links arms with* **HOOKER** *and strolls on.*

HOOKER Britain now rules a quarter of the globe –
More, if you count the oceans.

BELLA [*intrigued*] Why is that?

HOOKER [*shrugging, then smiling at the future*]
They have the money, ships and armaments
And soon the U.S.A. will have them too.

BELLA [*puzzled*] That makes no sense to me.

HOOKER Good! Politics,
Like dredging cesspools or like fighting wars,
Is very filthy work. Leave it to men. [*pats her hand*]
Stay innocent, my dear.

BELLA [*forcefully bringing them to a stop*] I need to know
Exactly how the world is being run –
Knowledge that's missing from this head of mine!

They are near the ship's rail beside a suspended lifeboat. **HOOKER** *flings his cheroot over the rail and faces her.*

HOOKER [*oracular*] We two are of the Anglo Saxon race.
The kindest, cleanest, clev'rest, most Christian,
Most free and democratic folk alive!
Also the richest. God created us
To subjugate those of inferior breed
Who don't know how to subjugate themselves –
The niggers, dagoes, red men, yids and chinks.

BELLA [*distressed*] Mister Hooker, I am a woman of the world!
I've been all round it – talked with many folk
Whose skins were not our colour. None of them
Seemed stupider or nastier than me.

In a fatherly way **HOOKER** *draws her arm through his and walks on.*
HOOKER You've led a very sheltered life my dear –
You've never seen a ghetto or a slum.
The world is certainly a filthy place –
Talking about it only makes it worse.
BELLA, *appalled, backs away from him, looking around as if totally lost. Her face loses its rosy blush.*
BELLA The – world – a – filthy – place?!?!?!
HOOKER *goes after her with outstretched hands as if to embrace and protect.*
HOOKER [*urgently*] Only in parts!
In Egypt we will go to a hotel
From which, in perfect safety, you will see
Why Christ died for our sins, and also see
Exactly why the Anglo Saxon race
Must purify this earth with fire and sword!
BELLA *touches her head as if feeling something there. A large Union Jack flutters behind them.*

104 CUT TO: INT. AND EXT. EGYPTIAN HOTEL – DAY

Rapid stream of images.
SOUND: *A low dangerous throb or hum indicating tension steadily increases under sound from what is shown – beggars chanting "Baksheesh", screams, crack of whips, laughter – is also distantly heard.*
P.O.V. Approach through an expensive Egyptian hotel lounge to the veranda where **SERVANTS** *in tarbooshes and baggy trousers attend* **RICH EUROPEANS** *who sit dining, drinking and laughing at a spectacle lower than the veranda. Silhouettes of the great pyramids fill the distance.*
Track across dusty ground into the centre of a crowd of **NEARLY NAKED BEGGARS** *of every age, but most of them* **STARVING CHILDREN**, *some displaying hideous mutilation, bowing and praying for alms to the* **WEALTHY FOLK**, *some trying to gain attention by clowning in an ingratiating way, others by dramatically exposing their sores, others helplessly displaying themselves.*
Reverse track from the crowd to the veranda. **BELLA**, *horrified, stands with* **HOOKER** *behind a table where a rich, lean* **PRUSSIAN INDUSTRIALIST** *[with a sabre scar] sits laughing with a horribly amused and fat* **WIFE** *and* **CHIILDREN**. *He flings a handful of coins out onto the ground – the* **BEGGARS** *who can run, charge forward in a horde and fling themselves upon it, fighting and pushing each other.*
TRACK FORWARD *as, one from each side,* **TWO HOTEL SERVANTS** *with whips rush at the mob and start whipping it back. Some retire under the lashes, others keep scrabbling and fighting for coins.*
REVERSE TRACK *to the veranda where the* **FASHIONABLE CROWD** *roars with laughter as someone else flings another handful of coins. We see* **BELLA** *stand horror-struck beside* **HOOKER**, *who smiling smugly, suddenly points towards the* **BEGGARS**.
HOOKER These were the race that built the Pyramids.
That looks like a deserving case.
TRACK FORWARD *to a very thin* **BEGGAR GIRL**, *about seven years old, one eye blinded by a cataract, holding up a* **BABY** *blind in both eyes. Her other arm is stretched towards the veranda: her opening and shutting hand and mouth is her only movement.*
SOUND: *Cut humming noise. The yells and chanting of the* **BEGGARS** *and the laughter swell up deafeningly.*
CUT TO: BELLA *leaping from the veranda to the ground.*
BELLA *tears the whip from the* **HOTEL SERVANT**'*s hand, flings it away, wades into* **BEGGARS** *who surge around her as she opens her reticule.* **SPECTATORS** *on the veranda strain or stand for a better view as* **HOOKER** *leaps from it after* **BELLA**.
BELLA *holds purse from her reticule out to the* **GIRL** *with the* **BLIND BABY**. *A* **HIDEOUS BEGGAR** *snatches it away and falls under a scrum of others who pile on top fighting for the spoils. Purse bursts, coins scatter, fighting, cursing, screaming worsens.*
HOTEL SERVANT, *whip in hand, is glimpsed hesitating to strike the mob back since* **BELLA** *kneels in it embracing the* **GIRL** *with the* **BLIND BABY**. *Two voices sound through the uproar.*
HOOKER [*bellowing*] Come back, my dear! [*shouting*] Mrs Wedderburn!
Hands snatch away **BELLA**'*s reticule, hat, scarf, hair-clips as she lifts the* **GIRL** *and* **BLIND BABY** *and returns, her hair falling about her.* **BEGGARS** *fall back, uproar lessens.* **HOTEL MANAGER**, *in fez and evening dress, with outspread arms blocks her way to the veranda.* **HOOKER** *and* **HOTEL SERVANTS** *press in on her from each side.*
MANAGER You cannot bring filthy beggars in here!
BELLA I'm taking them home to God!
MANAGER Not through my hotel!
HOOKER They won't be allowed into Britain, Bella! [*emphatically*] You can do no good!
She stares at him in horrified disbelief.
SOUND: *Organ chord.*
In slow motion **SERVANTS** *grasp the* **GIRL** *and* **BLIND BABY** *and pluck them away while* **HOOKER** *holds her arms as she writhes her body and head about in terrible grief, then opens her mouth and draws a great breath.*
HOOKER *claps a hand over her mouth. She grabs it in both of hers and bites it like a dog biting a bone.*
HOOKER [*screaming*] Aaaarg!

105 CUT TO: EGYPTIAN HOTEL CORRIDOR

HOOKER, *half fainting, his right hand wrapped in bloody handkerchief, is helped along by* **BELLA**.

BELLA *has the serious look of an efficient nurse with no trace of pity or tenderness. The* **HOTEL MANAGER**, *leading them, flings wide a door admitting them to*:

106 CUT TO: EGYPTIAN HOTEL GUEST ROOM

Persian carpets are hung on white walls, spread on tiled floor. Latticed doors in Moorish arches stand open into a courtyard with a fountain in the centre. Beside a large wicker armchair stands a brass-topped table on which lie bandages, cotton wool and a bottle of iodine tincture. A **SERVANT** *in tarboosh and baggy pants puts a bowl of steaming hot water beside these and leaves through the courtyard.*

BELLA *helps* **HOOKER** *into the chair then kneels, unwraps the wounded hand and starts deftly bathing the wound.* **WEDDERBURN**, *seated in his bath chair, is staring out at the fountain in the courtyard beyond.*

BELLA Don't worry, I know how to do this. I've bandaged many a wounded dog in my guardian's clinic.

HOOKER *accepts her attentions with closed eyes and a drowsy smile.*

MANAGER [*quietly to* **HOOKER**] You are now – safe with her?

HOOKER [*murmuring, yet distinct*] Yes. Temporary derangement.

The **MANAGER** *withdraws.* **BELLA** *pours iodine onto cotton wool.*

BELLA [*urgently*] It was wrong of you to say I could do no good. If I can do no good then I AM no good so why should I live?

HOOKER *opens his eyes at that.* **BELLA** *pauses and stares into them.*

BELLA [*needing an answer*] Why should I live?

HOOKER *says nothing. She resumes bandaging.*

HOOKER [*awkwardly*] You cannot take responsibility for all the world's evils, my dear. Jesus did that for us by dying on the cross.

BELLA [*fiercely, as she finishes tying the bandage*] What would Jesus have done for my half blind little girl with the blind baby, Mr Hooker?

HOOKER Jesus made the blind to see, my dear.

BELLA What if he hadn't been able to? Would he have walked straight past like a bad Samaritan?

She stands up and faces him. He looks gravely back.

HOOKER Do not mock my religion, Mrs Wedderburn.

BELLA [*pleading*] Surely not all countries in the world have people as poor as those Egyptians?!

HOOKER [*sharply*] You insist on truth?

BELLA *nods emphatically.*

HOOKER The main difference between Egypt and your country is that the British police keep the British poor where our sort need not see them.

BELLA Our sort? What sort is that?

HOOKER Businessmen and property owners like me. Ladies of leisure like you.

BELLA [*walking distractedly to and fro*] I don't want the world to be like that – it makes me feel dirty – wicked – oh what can I do about it?

HOOKER *holds his left hand out to her.*

HOOKER Sit by me Bella. Hold this hand. If you don't bite it I'll tell you how to feel happy and good again.

BELLA *hurries to him, eagerly clasps the hand in both of hers and crouches at his feet. His thumb strokes the second finger of her left hand. Between them we can see* **WEDDERBURN**, *back to us, in the background.*

HOOKER [*softly*] You're not married?

BELLA [*softly*] How clever of you to notice!

HOOKER [pleading] Marry me and have children, Bella. I have land with several farms and towns on it – a small kingdom. Between caring for our family you could bully me into lowering rents and improving the drains of a whole community! You might start your own hospital – what a force for good you would be with your own charity hospital! Poor children would flock to you from every slum in Philadelphia!

BELLA *frowns, then drops his hand and stands.*

BELLA [*commanding*] Stand up, Eli.

He does. They face each other with equally serious faces, his softened by hope, hers by pity. **WEDDERBURN** *is seen between them looking jealously on, but is hidden when* **BELLA** *suddenly ties* **HOOKER***'s arms to his sides in a passionate embrace and fiercely kisses him. She withdraws her lips when he is thoroughly overcome.*

BELLA [*kindly*] You've given a splendid reason for marrying a man I do not love, but the woman who marries a clever devil like you will be a worse fool than the one who marries poor old Wedder.

She releases him and wanders away, strengthened by his affection but pondering what to do about the world. **HOOKER** *flings himself into the armchair, scowling and gnawing his underlip.*

BELLA [*struck by an idea*] I can't be the only one in the world who thinks it's badly arranged, Eli!

HOOKER [*dryly*] Join the socialists.

BELLA What are socialists?
HOOKER Fools who think the goods of the rich should be shared equally with everyone else.
BELLA [*excited*] But they should be! That would make the world a good home where everyone was happy! That must be what lucky people are for! [*appealing to* **HOOKER**] Surely you see the truth of that?!
HOOKER [*smiling sadly*] I am too old and rich to see the truth of that. You are preparing a load of grief for yourself my dear.
BELLA Where can I find socialists, Eli?
HOOKER Try Paris, French socialists have been staging revolutions there since 1790. They always turn nasty and get crushed, of course.
BELLA [*determined*] Then I won't be a lady of leisure for much longer.

107 CUT TO: PARIS STREET

As before but sunlit, crowded with the social life Toulouse Lautrec painted. The **WAITER** *who once served Wedderburn now serves café tables crowded with* **PROSTITUTES**, **BOULEVARDIERS**, *bearded* **INTELLECTUALS** *proclaiming, drinking, arguing and flirting. Slow move in on* **BELLA** *who, dressed more sexily than hitherto, sits at a table scribbling in her letter case. She is ogled by a stout middle-aged* **BON VIVEUR** *with moustachios, watch-chain, bowler hat and cane who sits as near as possible, ogling her.*
BELLA [V.O.] So here I am, God, in the capital of France, among socialists, communists and anarchists who all think the world must be changed so that nobody need beg or starve, especially not sick little girls. They squabble about how to make the change, but agree it must be made. Wedder had a nervous breakdown and is having to rest. Meanwhile I am a working woman.
The **BON VIVEUR** *lays his hand on* **BELLA***'s wrist. She looks up, he hitches his thumb towards the sign of the Hotel de Notre Dame. She shuts her writing case, lifts it and stands. He gallantly offers his arm. She takes it and they move through the throng to the hotel.*
BELLA [V.O.] Since wedding is the only thing I know how to do, I live by wedding men who want a change from their wives and sweethearts.

108 CUT TO: FOYER AND STAIRS OF HOTEL

As before, but with more richly coloured wallpaper. Downwards shot of **BELLA** *determinedly climbing the stairs while below the* **BON VIVEUR** *pays the* **MANAGERESS** *seated at the desk at the foot, then hurrying eagerly up after her.*
BELLA [V.O.] I don't much like the work but why should I? Farm labourers and factory hands do much more useful work and enjoy it even less. What matters is, I earn my keep by a service people need. Frenchmen are easily pleased
She opens a door on a landing and, with a formal simper, gestures the **BON VIVEUR** *through.*
BELLA [V.O.] All they want –

109 CUT TO: PARIS HOTEL BEDROOM

Track into still of **BELLA** *and* **BON VIVEUR** *undressing.*
BELLA [V.O.] – is a bedroom –
Track into still of **BELLA** *spread like a starfish naked on the bed and* **BON VIVEUR**, *in shirt and socks, about to fall on her.*
BELLA [V.O.] – a bed –
Quick pan upward over a mirror, where some erotic turbulence on the bed is reflected, and onto the ceiling.
BELLA [V.O.] – and a show of enthusiasm.
CAMERA: *focuses on a small light fitting.*
BELLA [*throatily, from below*] Ah! Formidable!

110 CUT TO: DUNGEON SUITE

A room with a polished parquet floor and walls unconvincingly painted to look like stonework with ring-bolts from which dangle chains and manacles.
Pan round to show, one at a time, a headman's block and axe obviously made of plywood; a **FAT MAN**, *naked but for a black silk bag with eye-slits tied over his head, squats on a tiny chamberpot with his wrists cross-handcuffed to his ankles; an umbrella-stand holding a neatly rolled umbrella and canes; a vividly painted nursery rocking horse gently rocking,* **ANOTHER NAKED MAN** *with bag-mask being face-down on top with his wrists and ankles handcuffed to its hooves.*
BELLA [V.O.] The English clients have more complicated needs which we attend to in the dungeon suite. Before each session we have to cover our faces and learn what to say.
BELLA, *dressed like Queen Victoria in black crinoline and widows weeds, small teapot-lid crown on top of a black veil which completely hides her face, holds a cricket bat in a regally threatening pose above the buttocks of a* **MAN** *bent over a purple velvet pouffé. He is naked but for a black silk bag with eye-slits tied over his head. He wriggles a little but* **BELLA** *stays perfectly statuesque.*
BELLA [*menacingly*] Spankybot!
MAN [*in a little boy's voice*] No, Nanny! No! No!

BELLA *[exactly as before]* Spankybot!
MAN You are pitiless, Nanny! Pitiless!
BELLA Spankybot!

111 CUT TO: PARIS HOTEL BEDROOM – EARLY MORNING

As before but unlit with closed curtains. The **MANAGERESS** *enters briskly.*

MANAGERESS Awake, Bella! Arise, up, up, up and go downstairs *[she draws the curtains]* – the doctor is here.

BELLA *sits up in bed. She is naked and alone.*

BELLA *[sleepily]* Certainly Madame. What doctor is this?

MANAGERESS The health officer employed by the municipality. Wear just this, mon cher, and he will be done with you tout-de-suite.

MANAGERESS *lifts a very short chemise from a chair and flings it onto the bed.* **BELLA** *grabs it and swings her legs over the side of the bed saying enthusiastically:*

BELLA That's what I call real socialism!

MANAGERESS Pardon?

BELLA How splendid that the local government pays a doctor to care for working women, whether they call him in or not!

The **MANAGERESS** *stares and then bursts out laughing.*

112 CUT TO: PARIS SALON

BELLA *is posing with another* **WOMAN** *for a Lautrec painting of resting prostitutes. Starting on* **BELLA** *the camera withdraws slowly to show the upholstered divan where she sprawls, also the famous painting and* **LAUTREC** *working on it.*

BELLA [V.O.] And that, dear God, is how I learned about venereal disease. An engaged woman must not risk that. I have therefore stopped wedding strangers and started working for artists – it is a more restful job, and soon I will return to you. First however, I am sending Wedderburn home with this letter. Get ready, God, to meet a different Bella from the fool who ran off with him.

NOTE: *Here the filming returns to the earthier colouring of McCandless's narrative.*

113 CUT TO: PARK CIRCUS STUDY – NIGHT

As before **BAXTER** *reads,* **MCCANDLESS** *listens while the dogs bask in firelight on the rug between.* **MCCANDLESS** *is now curled up in an almost embryonic posture with his legs under him, fist, clenched and pressing his cheeks on each side. His mouth and eyes are wide open in a dumbfounded stare. Move into close-up of him.*

BAXTER *[reading]* I will want answers to some serious questions. Tell my dear Candle that his wedding Bell has had all she will ever want of other men ... "other" is underlined, McCandless ... so Candle will soon be panting in the arms of dearly beloved ding dong Bell Baxter. What do you think of that?

MCCANDLESS *unknots himself with movements and a smile conveying tremulous excitement.*

MCCANDLESS It almost terrifies me. She now knows much more about life than I do.

BAXTER *[gloomily]* You have nothing to fear. *[sits suddenly upright, listening]* Listen!

The **DOGS** *have pricked up their ears. The two men slowly stand.*

SOUND: *Hoof beats and a rumble of a cab rapidly approaching from the distance.*

BAXTER *strides to the window.* **MCCANDLESS** *clasps his hands under his chin in a spasm of bashfulness.*

SOUND: *The cab stops.*

MCCANDLESS Can it be?

BAXTER *[looking out]* It is!

114 CUT TO: VIEW FROM WINDOW – NIGHT

P.O.V. Shot through window of **BELLA**, *portmanteau in hand and coat open, springing from the cab onto the lamplit pavement below, flinging coin to the* **CABMAN**, *leaping up the front steps.*

SOUND: *Doorbell violently rung.*

115 CUT TO: LOBBY AND STAIRWELL

MRS DINWIDDIE, *in night-dress, mob cap and dressing gown, stands with her arms spread wide open in heartfelt welcome.*

MRS DINWIDDIE Oh, my wee pet lamb, you're home, you're home.

BELLA *flings her portmanteau down and embraces her. Behind them the* **DOGS** *pour down the stairs into the lobby and surround them with excited barks.*

BELLA I'm glad you haven't changed, Dinwiddie.

Detaching herself she rapidly pats the **DOGS**' *heads.*

BELLA Hello Lulu – Fiona – Muriel.

She sees **BAXTER** *descending the stairs with* **MCCANDLESS** *behind him.*

BELLA *[shouting and removing her hat]* Back to the study, God and Candle! I want a word with you two.

116 CUT TO: STUDY – NIGHT

BAXTER *stands gravely in front of the sofa,* **MCCANDLESS** *nervously to one side,* **BELLA** *enters coatless, closing the door, goes straight up to* **BAXTER** *and pauses, facing him. With a timid smile he opens his arms murmuring :*

BAXTER Bella?

With a cry between a laugh and a sob she embraces him.

BELLA Dear God! Dear God!

She withdraws, smiles through some tears at the enviously hovering **MCCANDLESS**, *then draws from the lapel of her jacket the pearl-headed tiepin and holds it up reassuringly.*

BELLA The symbol of our plighted troth, Candle.

He smiles and goes to her, reaching out his arms but she stops him with a gesture.

BELLA Not yet! First God must – [*turning to* **BAXTER**] – tell me what became of my baby?

BAXTER, *appalled, freezes.* **BELLA** *and* **MCCANDLESS** *stare in helpless horror as –*

SOUND: *A chord with subsonic resonance is struck, which acquires the rhythm of an accelerating heartbeat and intensifies through what follows.* **SLOW TRACK** *in on* **BAXTER** *as, pressing his fingertips to his head, his skin colour changes through purple to green, his hair turns grey, his mouth opens and in a dull, vibrating, yet leaden voice he manages to say –*

BAXTER The – Event – That – Destroyed – Your – Memory – Also – Deprived – You – Of – Your – L – L – L ...

He is trying to say "Life".

MCCANDLESS [*shouting*] Your child, Bella!

SOUND: *End queer acoustics.*

BAXTER *sinks down on the sofa. While* **MCCANDLESS** *holds* **BELLA***'s attention* **BAXTER***'s skin nearly regains its normal colour but his hair does not.*

MCCANDLESS The shock that destroyed your memory killed the child in you!

BELLA [*sighing*] Yes, I feared that.

Tears flow down her cheeks but she smiles kindly from **MCCANDLESS** *to* **BAXTER**.

BELLA Poor God! You've aged, haven't you?

BAXTER *stays impassive like a statue with closed eyes as* **BELLA** *sits beside him, lays her head on his shoulder, embraces him as far as she can and closes her own eyes. After a moment* **MCCANDLESS** *sits beside* **BELLA**, *slides his arm round her waist, rests his head against her shoulder and closes his eyes. She moves slightly to accommodate him. All three now seem asleep.*

BELLA [*without opening her eyes*] I am going to be a doctor, God.

BAXTER [*without opening his eyes*] Good.

MCCANDLESS [*without opening his eyes*] Women aren't allowed to study medicine!

BAXTER [*opening his eyes*] Parliament has changed the law, McCandless. A medical college is opening in Edinburgh, Glasgow will soon have one.

BELLA *opens her eyes and stands up,* **MCCANDLESS** *rising with her. They face* **BAXTER**, *hand in hand.*

BELLA I will need all your money, God, to start a clinic where I will help poor women to have healthy babies.

BAXTER *shrugs his shoulders and smiles almost imperceptibly.*

BAXTER You shall have it, Bell.

BELLA *smiles at* **MCCANDLESS**.

BELLA You're going to be a doctor's husband, Candle. But first you must teach me all you know!

MCCANDLESS [*grinning happily*] Baxter knows ten times more.

BAXTER *stands up saying heavily:*

BAXTER More than I'll ever tell. [*wistfully to* **BELLA**] Goodnight, my dear. I'm glad you're home.

BELLA *hugs him. He smiles sadly and wearily leaves the room. She watches, a little puzzled.*

BELLA He does look old. And he's upset about something.

MCCANDLESS [*gravely*] He's sorry you're marrying me and not him.

BELLA *slips an arm round his waist and leads him from the room saying.*

BELLA He's no right to be sorry.

117 CUT TO: STAIRWELL WITH LANDING AND BEDROOM – NIGHT

BELLA *and* **MCCANDLESS** *emerge on the landing.*

BELLA God is too wise to need an idiot like me. You're different, Candle.

They pause before her open bedroom door. A candle burns on a table beside the window. We glimpse part of the bed.

BELLA [*softly*] Remember how I kissed you in there the night I ran away?

MCCANDLESS [*nodding*] Aye!

BELLA [*tapping his nose with forefinger*] Tonight I want to sleep cuddling and being cuddled, Candle. Nobody cuddled me in Paris.

MCCANDLESS *seems to grow an inch taller. It is he who now kisses her. She murmurs in his ear:*

BELLA But I may have picked up a Parisian disease. When will I know I've not?
MCCANDLESS In about four weeks, but tonight I'll risk it.
BELLA [*smiling*] I won't! Can we cuddle each other with a sheet between us? The French call it frottage.
MCCANDLESS In Scotland we call it bundling.
BELLA Then we'll bundle, Candle.
They enter the bedroom, **MCCANDLESS** *shutting the door behind them. Camera remains on the door.*
MCCANDLESS [V.O.] [*exultant*] But Bella had picked up no disease at all and a month later.

118 WIPE TO: STAIRWELL WITH LANDING – DAY

SOUND: *Wildly cheerful carillon of wedding bells over the next shots. The bedroom door which closed before the blackout opens to disclose* **BELLA** *emerging in full white bridal gown with train and floating veil, beautiful and radiantly smiling.*
LOW ANGLE SHOT *of* **BELLA** *descending the stairs to the lobby on* **BAXTER***'s arm, he's dressed to give her away in the height of 1880s sartorial fashion, nosegay in buttonhole, topper under the other arm. Grey hair and a slight stoop make him look much older but not more decrepit. A wistful smile shows he thinks this is a joyful occasion, though he is not perfectly happy.*

119 CUT TO: OPEN CARRIAGE DRIVING FROM PARK CIRCUS

P.O.V. from behind **BELLA** *and* **BAXTER**. **BELLA** *waves cheerfully,* **BAXTER** *gravely nods as a fashionably dressed* **STROLLER** *or two on the pavement raise their hats* [*if male*] *or bow* [*if female*]. *Over treetops a spire becomes visible – Glasgow University.*

120 CUT TO: UNIVERSITY CHAPEL

SOUND: *The wedding bells, dulled by intervening stone, are coming to an end.*
At the foot of the aisle stands **MCCANDLESS** *the groom with former* **SUAVE STUDENT**, *his best man. Splendidly dressed,* **MCCANDLESS** *is happily confident, his companion more pompously smug. In the front pew behind them sits* **MRS DINWIDDIE**, *the former* **POLITE, JEALOUS** *and* **JEALOUS STUDENTS**, *the* **TWO NURSES** *and* **MATRON**, *all in their Sunday best. Some rows behind are occupied by* **STUDENTS** [*glimpsed in the debate Scene 13*], *with* **WIVES** *or* **GIRLFRIENDS** *they have acquired since. There are a few elderly* **PROFESSIONAL MEN** *who knew Baxter's father, and some* **SPINSTERS** *of the parish present from sentimental curiosity. These rows are crowded enough to let* **FIVE STRANGERS** *sit together unnoticed at the back. Through an open doorway at the head of the aisle, treetops and sky are glimpsed until –*
SOUND: *Wedding bells stop.*
BELLA *and* **BAXTER** *appear arm-in-arm in the doorway.*
SOUND: *Mendelssohn's Wedding March.*
BELLA *and* **BAXTER** *advance down the aisle with becoming dignity,* **BELLA** *pretending to ignore the admiring regard of those who crane to see her on each side. As she nears* **MCCANDLESS** *he appears to stand taller. When she arrives beside him they exchange smiles of perfect complicity.*
SOUND: *Wedding March ends.*
The **MINISTER**, *in black academic gown with white bands, appears before* **BELLA** *and* **MCCANDLESS**. *The* **MINISTER** *speaks with quietly awful gravity.*
MINISTER You are Archibald McCandless, only son of Jessica McCandless, spinster of Whauphill Galloway?
MCCANDLESS [*boldly*] I am.
MINISTER You are Arabella Baxter, only daughter of Ignatius Baxter, of Buenos Aires, and his wife, Serafina O'Mally.
BELLA [*brightly*] That is what I've been told.
After the briefest pause, the **MINISTER** *addresses the* **CONGREGATION.**
MINISTER If any present know why these two should not be joined together in holy wedlock, let them speak now or forever hold their peace!
GENERAL BLESSINGTON *stands up in the back row with* **STRANGERS**, *a tall man with the accusing glare and moustache of Lord Kitchener. His voice is clear, harsh and grating.*
BLESSINGTON This marriage cannot take place.
General astonishment. Beside **BLESSINGTON** *a thickly built wild-looking* **OLD MAN** *is struggling to his feet.*
MINISTER [*unexpectedly squeaky*] Who are you?
BLESSINGTON I am General Sir Aubrey De La Pole Blessington. That woman [*points at* **BELLA**] – is me wife Victoria Blessington, formerly Victoria Hattersley. This [*gestures to* **OLD MAN**] – is her father Blaydon Hattersley; owner and director of the Union Jack Steam Traction Company of Manchester and Liverpool.
HATTERSLEY, *tears streaming down his cheeks, stretches his arms towards* **BELLA** *and says in her own dialect:*
HATTERSLEY Vicky! My little Vicky! Do you not recognise your old Dad?
BELLA *looks at him with great interest, then with equal interest at* **BLESSINGTON**, *who glares rigidly back. She is the only one present to show no consternation.*

BELLA Well, you look a fascinating couple but I cannot remember seeing either of you before!
BLESSINGTON Harker! Prickett! Grimes!
HARKER, *a lean solicitor,* **PRICKETT**, *a flurried G.P.,* **GRIMES**, *a weasel-like Private Detective, stand up beside* **HATTERSLEY**.
BLESSINGTON Harker is me solicitor, Prickett me family doctor, Grimes a private detective. All will swear to the truth of my statement.
The excited **CONGREGATION** *stares, shifts, murmurs.* **MCCANDLESS** *is so distressed that* **BELLA** *reassuringly pulls his hand through her arm. The* **MINISTER** *turns to* **BAXTER.**
MINISTER [*not loudly*] This wedding cannot take place.
BAXTER [*loudly to the* **CONGREGATION**] Your attention please!
Everyone looks at him. He has shrugged off his bowed look and appears a strong, wise man taking charge of a weighty situation.
BAXTER I apologise to everyone here, but this wedding is postponed by a confusion of identities. General Blessington please come to the vestry and discuss it with us.
BAXTER *shepherds an appalled* **MCCANDLESS** *and excited* **BELLA** *towards a side-door after The* **MINISTER**. **BELLA** *comforts* **MCCANDLESS** *by pulling his hand through her arm and patting it.*
BELLA [*reassuringly*] I never thought marriage would be so interesting.

121 CUT TO: CORRIDOR TO VESTRY

Close-up of **BELLA** *and* **MCCANDLESS** *from in front with* **BAXTER***'s gloomy face between and behind.* **BELLA** *glances back.*
BELLA [*puzzled*] Why do you look so miserable, God? Why are you not as excited as I am?
BAXTER You are going to learn that I have lied to you.
BELLA You? A liar?
BAXTER nods.
BELLA [*dismayed*] Do you mean that queer old man really is my father? And I'm married to that stick with a moustache on top?
BAXTER *nods.* **BELLA** *brings them to a stop.*
BELLA [*grimly*] Hold onto me, Candle! If you don't I might run away from everybody!
MCCANDLESS *slips an arm round* **BELLA***'s waist. They move on because* **BLESSINGTON**, **HATTERSLEY**, **GRIMES**, **HARKER** *and* **PRICKETT** *grimly approach from behind.*

122 CUT TO: INT. VESTRY

A bleak square room wood-panelled to waist height, white-washed above. Being in a Presbyterian Church it lacks a crucifix, ornament and devotional pictures. It looks like a trap or cell which, as it fills with grotesquely contrasted professional males, makes us fear that Bella may never escape from them.
The furnishings are sparse, save for a table, some armchairs and a bench seat either side of a fireplace. The **MINISTER** *hangs his divinity gown on the coathook [he wears a grey tweed suit beneath it] and turning as* **BELLA**, **MCCANDLESS** *and* **BAXTER** *approach.*
BAXTER I regret this intrusion.
MINISTER No doubt.
MINISTER *shuts the register and puts it on the shelf with the others as* **BELLA** *sits in the armchair,* **MCCANDLESS** *sits on an arm holding her hand,* **BAXTER** *stands behind with arms folded on the back. Enter* **BLESSINGTON** *who stands with his back to the door, leaving room for his followers to enter.* **HATTERSLEY** *sits on a chair to the left of the door,* **GRIMES**, **HARKER**, *and* **PRICKETT** *file in along the bench wall but remain standing.* **BLESSINGTON** *addressed the* **MINISTER** *with an air of quiet command.*
BLESSINGTON The British churches and the British armed forces are equal partners under Her Majesty the Queen, padre, so it is obviously your duty to help me get back that wife of mine.
MINISTER Let me inform you, sir, that The Church of Scotland recognises no ruler but Christ. For twenty minutes I will allow you the use of this room but no longer. Excuse me.
The **MINISTER** *leaves.*
BAXTER Please sit down, gentlemen. Apart from her appearance have you any proof of identity between the general's wife and the lady here?
BLESSINGTON Tell him, Grimes!
BLESSINGTON *steps into the window recess and looks out at the garden with back to the room.* **HARKER** *and* **PRICKETT** *take this as permission to sit on the bench.* **GRIMES** *remains standing in arm's reach of the communion wine which we see behind him. Perhaps he leans with one hand on the table top.*
GRIMES Last month I came to Glasgow persuin' information received from one, Duncan Wedderburn, that Miss Baxter was Lady Blessntn, the same Lady Blessntn ...

123 DISSOLVE TO: HALL OF GENERAL BLESSINGTON'S COUNTRY HOUSE – NIGHT

A superbly palatial hall, empty but for **BELLA** *in travelling costume of Scene 33, creeping timidly from the foot of a vast staircase towards a great double doorway.*

GRIMES [V.O.] ... oo ad vanished from er usband's country ouse three years ago bein preggers which sometimes sends the fair sex round the twist pore things.

124 DISSOLVE TO: CLYDE SUSPENSION BRIDGE

As before ending with **BELLA***'s dive into the Clyde.*

GRIMES [V.O.] Police records showed that exactly three years ago a woman in Lady Blessinton's state flung erself into river.

125 DISSOLVE TO: RIVER EMBANKMENT

As before showing **BELLA** *dragged out.*

GRIMES [V.O.] – got fished out –

126 DISSOLVE TO: MORTUARY

As before showing **BELLA** *on slab,* **BAXTER** *and* **OFFICIALS** *engaged with her.*

GRIMES [V.O.] – was took to morgue where Godwin Baxter, police surgeon, signed death citificate and arranged shifting body to university anatomy department since none claimed it.

127 DISSOLVE TO: VESTRY

GRIMES *now has the bottle of communion wine uncorked on the table beside him and a glass of it in his hand.*

GRIMES [*cheerfully, to* **BAXTER**] But you took the corpus delecti home instead and here she is! [*raises his glass to* **BELLA**] Your ealth, dear Lady!

She nods thoughtfully back to him. He swigs half the contents and retires to the sofa.

HARKER It is glaringly obvious, Mr Baxter, that you revived the woman you had declared dead and had her cohabit with you instead of returning her to her lawful husband.

BAXTER She would have been locked in the charity ward of a public asylum had I not taken her home. She had [*hesitantly*] – the mind of a baby – was amnesiac – without memories of the past. [*with new vigour*] And the police knew nothing of the General's loss. All Britain would have been searching for Lady Blessington had he announced it publicly. Why did he not?

Everyone looks at the unmoving **BLESSINGTON** *for a moment.*

HARKER [*dryly*] To avoid scandal.

HATTERSLEY [*bitterly*] Yes, the General is a hero of the Crimean War, the Indian Mutiny and the March on Pekin'!

HATTERSLEY Schoolbooks and newspapers hold him up as an example to British youth.

BELLA *leaps up and talks to* **BLESSINGTON**.

BELLA [*violently*] Stop talking as if I'm not here! Why did I run away from you and try to kill myself with a whole baby live inside me?

Tears flood her cheeks though she does not sob. All look at **BLESSINGTON** *who again says without turning:*

BLESSINGTON You were mad, Victoria.

PRICKETT [*eagerly*] Yes indeed! You ran away to escape from the surgery that would have cured you.

BAXTER [*swiftly*] A surgical operation to cure insanity! What insanity was this?!

PRICKETT*, seeing that* **BLESSINGTON** *has turned to glare at him, shrinks into himself.*

PRICKETT I can't say. I really can't. Not, not, not with a lady present.

He avoids looking at **BELLA**.

BLESSINGTON [*contemptuously*] Tell them, Prickett. Say the word. Deafen them with it.

He turns back to the window. All look at **PRICKETT***, who is sweating*

PRICKETT Lady Blessington is ... was ... was a nymphomaniac.

BELLA *looks enquiringly at* **MCCANDLESS** *who has moved to her side. He shrugs.*

BAXTER Was promiscuous?

PRICKETT [*shocked*] Of course not! Outside her marriage she was a most genteel and respectable lady.

BAXTER And inside it?

PRICKETT She ... I have no wish to offend anyone ...

128 DISSOLVE TO: LADY BLESSINGTON'S BEDROOM – NIGHT

The only illumination is from a candelabrum with three candles in it on an ornate table beside a vast four poster bed out of which **BELLA** *creeps, looking lonely and terrified. Lifting the candelabrum she goes trembling to a door among grotesque shadows.*

PRICKETT [V.O.] [*with desperate clarity*] Lady Blessington refused to recognise that a husband and wife need separate bedrooms. She wished to sleep in Sir Aubrey's arms when she was pregnant!

129 DISSOLVE TO: GENERAL BLESSINGTON'S BEDROOM – NIGHT

The only illumination is from the candelabrum **BELLA** *carries towards another canopied bed among equally grotesque shadows.*

When the light falls on the pillow we see the **GENERAL** *asleep wearing a gauze moustache protector and sucking his thumb. He wakens and sits up in a state resembling terror more than anger.* **BELLA** *puts the candelabrum on the bedside table and climbs into bed, stretching her arms out imploringly. Waving his hands and shouting at her violently he climbs out the other side. She lies back weeping and covering her face with her hands while he stands beside the bed, denouncing her with a wagging fore-finger.*

BELLA [V.O.] The poor soul only wanted some cuddling – don't we all?

BLESSINGTON [V.O.] You could never face the fact that the touch of a female body arouses diabolical lusts in a potent male – lusts we can hardly restrain. Cuddlin! The very word is unmanly. It soils your lips, Victoria.

PRICKETT [V.O.] No normal, healthy woman wants sexual contact except as duty. Even pagan philosophers declare that only debauched females wriggle their hips.

130 DISSOLVE TO: VESTRY

PRICKETT A small surgical operation would have ensured the purity of Sir Aubrey's marriage bed.

BAXTER What surgical operation could possibly cure your wife's nymphomania, Sir Aubrey?

BLESSINGTON One that the Mahometans do to their daughters at birth. It makes em thc most docile wives in the world.

BAXTER *looks enquiringly at* **PRICKETT**.

PRICKETT Yes. Clitoridectomy.

BELLA [*stupefied*] Clitori ... you'd have cut out my ... when I was pregnant?

BLESSINGTON [*with satisfaction*] By the best surgeon in London.

MCCANDLESS By the best bloody butcher, I say!

BELLA [*to* **BAXTER**] Are both these men insane?

BAXTER No Bella. They are the victims of insane educations.

BELLA *clutches her head, feeling inclined to vomit. She bites her underlip and masters her innards while* **MCCANDLESS** *and* **BAXTER** *reach out to her protectingly. She waves them aside, goes to* **BLESSINGTON** *and stares into his eyes.*

BELLA Since you don't love me, why do you want me back?

Unable to face her **BLESSINGTON** *turns to the window, snarling.*

BLESSINGTON Tell her, Harker!

HARKER Six months ago Sir Aubrey was elected to parliament in the Liberal interest. Since then his political opponents have hinted ... [*hesitates*] ... hinted ...

BLESSINGTON [*snarling over his shoulder*] Hinted that I dealt with you, Victoria, as I dealt with African blacks and Canadian half breeds. I'm in danger of bein' blackballed from me clubs. The Daily Telegraph actually calls me Bluebeard Blessington. I'll sue it for libel when I get you home.

HARKER Return with your husband to his country house, Lady Blessington, and earn his forgiveness by becoming a dutiful, undemanding wife.

He stands, drawing a legal document from an inner pocket.

HARKER [*to* **BELLA**] If you refuse this court order will be employed to arrest you, for in the eyes of the law you are a deranged woman who escaped from her husband's custody, cohabited with a Scotch body-snatcher, and attempted bigamy with his parasite.

MCCANDLESS [*incredulous*] Parasite? [*violently*] No graduate of Glasgow University is a parasite!

BAXTER *sinks into a chair beside* **BELLA**, *suffering what looks like a minor stroke.* **BELLA** *is too occupied by her challengers to notice* **BAXTER** *as* **HATTERSLEY** *approaches her in a state of enthusiastic excitement and mutters urgently in her ear:*

HATTERSLEY Go back to your husband, daughter! He's a sick man! In a few years you'll be the richest widow in England with twelve coal mines in the Black Country, half of County Kildare and more houses than you can count – that's why I made you marry him! And if you squeeze a son out of him before he pops his clogs, why, I'll be Grandad to a Baronet! You owe me that, Vicki, because I gave you life!

BELLA *stands boldly beside* **BAXTER** [*he has recovered a little*] *and says loudly with great deliberation:*

BELLA Tell that bad old man [*points to* **HATTERSLEY**] – and that mad old man [*points to* **BLESSINGTON**] – that a hundred horse-power steam traction engine can't drag me back to the life they gave me.

BAXTER An English court order has no legal force here, Sir Aubrey, and if you fight for custody of this lady in a Scottish court, I am rich enough to make the case drag on for years.

BLESSINGTON *suddenly relaxes his stiff rigidity, becomes boyish, genial and amused.*

BLESSINGTON Fight in a law court? No, that's not my way. Go outside, Harker, and tell the cabman we're leavin!

HARKER *swiftly leaves the room as* **BAXTER**, *sighing as if freed from a weight, sits up and faces* **BLESSINGTON** *with a smile.*

BAXTER I'm glad, Sir Aubrey, that this interview has reached a civilised conclusion.

BLESSINGTON [*shaking his head*] This is not a conclusion, Mr Baxter. It is a new beginning. Ready, Grimes?

GRIMES *suddenly stands to attention.*

GRIMES Sir!

BLESSINGTON Cover McCandless.

BLESSINGTON *produces a revolver from inside the bosom of his greatcoat, levels it coolly at* **BAXTER** *and removes the safety catch.* **GRIMES** *does the same, levelling his revolver at* **MCCANDLESS** *while saying in a friendly voice.*

GRIMES Sit down, Mr McCandless.

MCCANDLESS, *hypnotised by the hole at the end of the barrel, does so on the bench.*

BLESSINGTON [*cheerfully*] There will be no killin', Mr Baxter, but if you move I will put a bullet in your groin. Prickett! The chloroform.

PRICKETT *struggles to pull a bottle and rag from inside his clothing.*

PRICKETT I dudo, dudo, dududo this with gugugreatest reluctance, Sir Aubrey.

BLESSINGTON [*easily*] Of course, but you're a good man so I can trust you. Now Victoria, sit down and let Prickett send you to sleep. If you don't I'll put a bullet into Baxter where it hurts and stun you with the butt of this revolver

BELLA *stands up and steps in front of* **BAXTER**, *facing* **BLESSINGTON**.

BLESSINGTON [*screaming*] Out of the way, woman!

She walks towards **BLESSINGTON**, *stretching her hand out to his revolver. He steps to one side, trying to aim round her but she grasps the barrel with her left hand and pushes it down. It explodes.* **BLESSINGTON** *lets it go. She passes it calmly to her right hand saying*:

BELLA You silly soldier, you've shot me in the foot.

Everyone stands still staring at her. She holds the revolver pointing at **BLESSINGTON**'*s chest.* **BELLA** *wipes her left hand, scorched by the barrel, against the side of her dress.*

GRIMES The game is up, General.

He clicks the safety catch on and pockets his revolver with an apologetic shrug to **MCCANDLESS. BLESSINGTON** *speaks softly with his eyes on* **BELLA**'*s thoughtfully frowning face.*

BLESSINGTON No, Grimes. The game is not quite up. [*to* **BELLA**] Shoot!

She does not move.

BLESSINGTON [*cajolingly*] Come, Victoria. Squeeze the trigger. It is your husband's last request.

She does not move. He draws himself erect and bellows.

BLESSINGTON Shoot! I order you to shoot!

She swings her arm round and fires five shots in rapid succession into the back of the fireplace. The resulting smoke sets **PRICKETT** *coughing. She blows a fume away from the end of the barrel, without moving her feet leans forward and replaces the pistol in* **BLESSINGTON**'*s inner pocket, and collapses in a faint.* **BAXTER** *springs forward, lifts* **BELLA**, *carries her to the sofa, lays her there, pushes back the wedding dress, strips off her bloodstained shoe and stocking and examines the foot.*

Meanwhile **MCCANDLESS** *has rushed to a cupboard under the bookcases, removed a medicine chest, brings it to the sofa then kneels beside* **BAXTER** *and removes cotton wool, iodine, gauze bandages. Meanwhile* **BLESSINGTON**, **GRIMES** *and* **PRICKETT** *hover uneasily and* **HATTERSLEY**, *slapping his thigh, exclaims*:

HATTERSLEY Ee she's a wonderful girl, wonderful! A real chip off the old block, a true daughter of Blaydon Hattersley.

BAXTER [*to* **MCCANDLESS**] The bullet has punctured the tendon between the proximal phalanges without chipping the bone.

The door is opened by the **MINISTER**.

MINISTER Is this a matter for the police, Mr Baxter?

BAXTER No, Mr Campbell. There has been a small accident but our English visitors are preparing to leave. Please fetch a pan of hot water.

MINISTER *withdraws.* **BLESSINGTON**, *though abashed, is unwilling to retreat.*

BLESSINGTON [*argumentatively*] Mr Baxter, I am not completely pitiless ...

BELLA *at once opens her eyes.*

SOUND: *The word "pitiless" echoes and re-echoes over the zoom into close-up of* **BELLA**'*s face.*

CUT SOUND *as* **BELLA** *smiles broadly and tells* **BLESSINGTON**

BELLA Pitiless?

She gazes at **BLESSINGTON** *and with* **MCCANDLESS**' *help sits up saying:*

BELLA I remember you! The man in the mask – we met in the dungeon suite at the Hotel de Notre Dame. You are Mr Spankybot! [*laughing hugely*] General Sir Aubrey de la Pole Spankybot! The things we girls had to do to stop you coming in the first half minute would have made a cat laugh!

BLESSINGTON *recoils in horror.* **BELLA** *gets furiously angry.*

BELLA And you're the man who would have had my clitoris cut off to protect the purity of your marriage bed! Fuck off! Fuck off you poor, nasty, stupid, stupid old fucker!
In **SLOW MOTION** *we see* **BLESSINGTON** *cover his eyes with his hands, opening his mouth in a soundless scream of agony. Reeling to the left he collides with* **PRICKETT**, *recoiling right he bumps into* **GRIMES**, *they assist him to the door and out of it followed by* **HATTERSLEY** *who, turning in the doorway, stretches a clenched fist with wagging forefinger towards* **BELLA**. *End* **SLOW MOTION**.
HATTERSLEY [*growling*] No daughter of Blaydon Hattersley uses that kind of language.
BELLA Kiss me, Candle.
MCCANDLESS *kisses her while* **BAXTER** *bathes her foot, murmuring thoughtfully to himself.*
BAXTER I think the General will now agree to a legal separation, if not an actual divorce. This means you must stay unwed ... [*he glances at them*] ... until he dies of natural causes.
They continue kissing. On a note of envious satisfaction **BAXTER** *says:*
BAXTER You may have to wait for years.

131 CUT TO: HALL OF GENERAL'S COUNTRY HOUSE

A superbly palatial hall, empty but for **BLESSINGTON** *striding diagonally across it towards one of the smaller of many surrounding doors. His face is deathly pale, his face tragically determined.*
MCCANDLESS [V.O.] But Baxter, for maybe the only time in his life, was wrong.
The door shuts. Track into the words GUN ROOM on it.
SOUND: *A reverberating gun shot.*

132 CUT TO: BREAKFAST ROOM, PARK CIRCUS

BAXTER, *seated by his distilling apparatus, is partly hidden by the Manchester Guardian or London Times, from which he reads aloud.*
BAXTER "The tragic end of this truly great and brave and noble soldier has plunged the whole Empire into mourning."
Pull back to show **BELLA** *and* **MCCANDLESS** *seated side by side with boiled eggs before them.* **MCCANDLESS** *is pouring tea.* **BAXTER** *lowers the paper and we see him looking older than ever before. His hair is snow white and seems to float around his skull like mist. He speaks to the others directly.*
BAXTER The editor also suggests Sir Aubrey shot himself because his political services had been ignored by the Liberal party, and blames Gladstone for it.
BELLA [*firmly*] Next time, Candle, we shall marry in a registry office.
She decapitates the egg.

133 CUT TO: a SEQUENCE OF STILLS – *resembling conventionally posed Victorian photographs.*

CUT TO STILL OF: PHOTOGRAPHER'S STUDIO

BELLA *in trim costume with short veil and bridal bouquet, smiles cheerfully arm-in-arm with smug* **MCCANDLESS**; *behind them a painted balustrade with urn and sprouting ferns.* **BAXTER** *sits by them on the left,* **MRS DINWIDDIE** *on the right.*
MCCANDLESS [V.O.] Reader, she married me, and there is little more to tell ...

CUT TO STILL OF: UPSTAIRS OFFICE, GLASGOW MUNICIPAL BUILDINGS

MCCANDLESS *sits facing a camera behind a huge desk, his back to a wall of arched windows overlooking George Square with the summit of the Scott Monument. His pose – pen in hand, over a spread of documents – head raised as if he had only just noticed the camera – is Napoleonic but not convincing.*
MCCANDLESS [V.O.] I am now senior Public Health Officer of the second greatest city in the British Empire.

CUT TO STILL OF: LAWN OF FABIAN SUMMER SCHOOL – 1900 – DAY

BELLA *in a group of* **FABIANS** *including* **BERNARD SHAW**, **SIDNEY** *and* **BEATRICE WEBB**, *also* **H.G.WELLS** *whose expression and proximity to her suggest considerable intimacy.*
MCCANDLESS [V.O.] My wife, Dr Bella McCandless, is an active member of the Fabian Society and British Labour Party ...

CUT TO STILL OF: INT. ALBERT HALL

A vast suffragette rally. On a platform draped in huge banners with slogans, **BELLA** *is the only standing figure, having risen from the central chair behind a long table with* **FOUR WOMEN** *sitting on each side of her.*
MCCANDLESS [V.O.] ... and has spoken for female suffrage in capital cities throughout the civilised world.

CUT TO STILL OF: INT. CLINIC

BELLA *in a severe black dress with white celluloid collar and cuffs, sits on a chair smiling happily at a camera with* **TWO WOMEN** *in hospital matron costume seated on each side and a double row of*

NURSES *standing behind.* **BELLA** *holds* **TWO BABY GIRLS** *upon her lap and the* **NURSES** *behind hold one each. Despite the symmetrical grouping, everyone seems relaxed and cheerful.*
MCCANDLESS [V.O.] But my wife is happiest when managing the Godwin Baxter natal clinic for daughters of the poor, an institution she started with money we inherited.

CUT TO STILL OF: STUDY – 18 PARK CIRCUS

A family group. **MCCANDLESS** *in a black three-piece suit, stiff wing collar, and watch-chain and resolute expression sits on a chair, supporting a* **BABY TWIN** *on each knee.* **BELLA**, *wearing an astonishingly fashionable costume, stands beside him, smiling flirtatiously at someone who is not in the group.* **YOUNG GRAHAM** *and* **KENNETH** *on each side stand around them, gazing reproachfully at the camera.*
MCCANDLESS [V.O.] I believe our sons find their stolid old father a welcome counterpoise to their brilliant, unconventional mother. I like to think their mother also finds me that ...

134 CUT TO FREEZEFRAME OF: UPSTAIRS OFFICE, GLASGOW MUNICIPAL BUILDINGS

This, with **MCCANDLESS** *behind desk, is identical to the previous still in 133, but the camera moves slowly into* **MCCANDLESS** *and the primitive telephone on the desk near him.*
MCCANDLESS [V.O.] It is with heavy heart that I now describe the last day of he who I will always consider the wisest and best of men ...
SOUND: *The phone rings.*
UNFREEZE FRAME: MCCANDLESS *lifts the mouth piece.*
MCCANDLESS [*grandly*] Senior Public Health Officer speaking.
SOUND: Faint wild squawking.
MCCANDLESS [*suddenly serious*] Mrs Dinwiddie! Is something wrong?

135 CUT TO: PARK CIRCUS

A galloping cab reins up before it. **MCCANDLESS** *leaps down and springs up the steps as* **MRS DINWIDDIE**, *looking stooped and ancient, opens the door.*

136 CUT TO: STAIRWELL

MCCANDLESS *leaps up the stairs, runs across the landing and into the study.*
SOUND: *Throbbing murmur of* **BAXTER***'s heart, growing louder as* **MCCANDLESS** *nears the study.*

137 CUT TO: STUDY

Jacketless, collarless, with open waistcoat, **BAXTER** *sits crouched at the central table, his left arm flung on it with shirt sleeve rolled above his elbow. The right hand holds a hypodermic syringe he is unable to use because his skin vibrates and body shudders in time to –*
SOUND: *Loud throbbing heartbeats.*
MCCANDLESS *springs to* **BAXTER***'s side as the latter cries in a dull, hollow, blurred voice.*
BAXTER Help! ... help me!
MCCANDLESS *takes the syringe, grips the back of* **BAXTER***'s left hand in his and forces the bare arm down on the table with the full weight of his own, keeping it as still as possible while injecting the vein. The vibration ends, shudders decrease as.*
SOUND: *Also decreases but does not become inaudible.*
BAXTER, *his face glistening with sweat, draws breath and looks at* **MCCANDLESS** *with a friendly smile.*
BAXTER Thank you, McCandless! I am glad you came. I am about to die.
MCCANDLESS, *staring at him, drops into a chair beside him then starts to weep.* **BAXTER** *smiles more braodly and pats his shoulder.*
BAXTER Thank you again, McCandless. Those tears console me. They mean I have been good for you.
MCCANDLESS [*hoarsely*] Can you not live longer?
BAXTER [*shaking his head*] Not without pain and loss of intelligence.
A **DOG** *emerges from under the table and lays its chin on his knee. He strokes it as he speaks.*
BAXTER Emotions are bad for my peculiar physique. When Bella announced she would marry you it dislocated my respiration. The terrible question she asked on returning from Paris fankled my neural network. Recent shocks made it advisable for me to die within the hour. It is weak of me to want company at the end but – I am weak!
MCCANDLESS *jumps up.*
MCCANDLESS I'll fetch Bella.
BAXTER [*commanding*] No, Archie! I love her too much. If she begged me to live longer I could not refuse and her last sight of me would be of an uncontrollably, filthy, paralytic idiot! I will leave life while I can do so with dignity. [*playfully*] But too much dignity is pompous. Let us share a deoch an doris, a glass of my father's port together. Here is the key. You know the cupboard.
MCCANDLESS *takes the key to the cupboard, opens it, produces the quarter-full decanter locked away by* **BAXTER** *earlier, also two*

delicate stemmed glasses. He dusts the glasses with a handkerchief from his breast pocket before setting them beside the decanter on the table top and filling them from it – the decanter is now empty. With a sly smile **BAXTER** *lifts a glass and inhales the bouquet.* **MCCANDLESS** *lifts the other.*

MCCANDLESS You've never tasted alcohol before?

BAXTER Never. My will leaves everything to Bella and you, but make sure Mrs Dinwiddie is properly cared for in her old age.

MCCANDLESS *nods.* **BAXTER** *pats a dog.*

BAXTER And you won't neglect my dogs.

MCCANDLESS *shakes his head.* **BAXTER** *clinks his glass with* **MCCANDLESS** *saying*:

BAXTER Health and long life to you and Bella, Archie, but especially Bella – my finest piece of work.

MCCANDLESS To Bella!

MCCANDLESS *sips;* **BAXTER** *empties the glass in one big swallow and sets it down saying* –

BAXTER So that is how wine tastes!

He grips each knee with a hand, leans back and chuckles, the noise swelling into laughter as his head bends further and further back till it gapes upwards at the ceiling.

SOUND: *All the disturbing sonic effects connected with Baxter in earlier scenes gradually merge into the laughter, plus majestic organ chords.*

MCCANDLESS *claps his hands to his ears. Furniture vibrates, the gasolier sways. When* **BAXTER***'s mouth reaches the greatest possible width he shudders and goes rigid as*:

SOUND: *Sharp detonation followed by total silence.*

MCCANDLESS *rises, tiptoes over to* **BAXTER** *and peers reverently into his mouth.*

MCCANDLESS [V.O.] Baxter's first and last laugh had broken his neck. Death was instantaneous.

BELLA*'s voice is heard talking Scottish as in the first scenes.*

BELLA [V.O.] [*amused*] ... and so miraculously, was rigor mortis! [*impatiently*] What total nonsense!

138 CUT TO: PARK CIRCUS STUDY 1914 – BLACK & WHITE

Set as in Scene 7, but **BELLA** *has now risen from the chair and stands beside the mantelpiece, resting an elbow upon it with the book in her other hand. She snaps it shut and regards the cover design with a smile – it now strikes her as funny.* **GRAHAM** *sprawls in a chair she has vacated with the expression of one who has also enjoyed an entertaining joke.* **KENNETH** *paces the room brooding upon how the tale would affect his career if it got about. The* **TWINS** *are wholly bewildered. Each glances sideways at the other to see what he thinks, then looks away to avoid the other's gaze.*

BELLA [*thoughtfully*] I wonder why Archie wrote this. It positively stinks of 19th century – the most morbid, sex-obsessed, hypocritical period in human history.

GRAHAM It's a damned good yarn!

BELLA Have it.

BELLA *tosses the book to* **GRAHAM**,*who easily catches it and opens it at the start again.* **KENNETH** *halts and confronts his mother from a distance.*

KENNETH Mother, was any of that story true?

TWIN 1 [*eagerly*] And if so [*hesitates*].

TWIN 2 [*nervously*] How much?

BELLA [*thoughtfully*] Now I come to think of it, quite a lot.

GRAHAM *and the* **TWINS** *are appalled.* **GRAHAM**, *startled, looks up from the book. During her next speech she moves around the room so as to be seen with pictures of the three people she refers to – the portrait of Sir Colin becomes visible on a wall-section we have not noticed.*

BELLA Godwin Baxter did restore me to life after my suicide attempt. He used heart massage and artificial respiration. He could not – alas [*hesitates and sighs*] – alas he could not save the life of my poor little stillborn first baby. But he gave me a better, braver nature. He did it by allowing me the education and freedom my bullying father and first husband thought unwomanly. Godwin liked helping poor things. I loved him for it. Unluckily he was not the marrying sort [*sighs*].

KENNETH [*grimly*] So you eloped with Wedderburn.

BELLA [*smiling tenderly*] Poor old Wedder, I still visit him when work takes me to Gartnavel Lunatic Asylum. He's perfectly happy.

TWIN 1 [*impetuously*] But did you really ... [*hesitates*]

TWIN 2 [*almost simultaneously*] ... work in a ... Parisian ...

The **TWINS** *fall silent, blushing, as* **BELLA** *stops and contemplates them with a faint smile.*

BELLA [*distinctly, after a moment*] I worked for exactly six days in a Parisian brothel. Luckily for you! It taught me enough about my hideous first husband to get rid of him and consort with your father. Any more questions?

BELLA *looks from* **KENNETH** *to* **GRAHAM**, *who sprawls in a chair with his cheek supported by a clenched fist.*

GRAHAM How did you meet father?

BELLA He lived here as Godwin's medical assistant.

KENNETH [*disapproving*] And you actually married him in a registry office?

BELLA [*amused*] I never married him at all.

Only **GRAHAM** *manages to grin at this but it is not a cheerful grin.* **THE TWINS** *shake their heads at each other.* **KENNETH** *closes his eyes and bites his underlip.*

BELLA My last meeting with Blessington, completely cured me of wanting to marry anyone again, ever. But I pretended to be your father's wife because my professional work would have suffered had I not.

KENNETH [*almost to himself*] Then I'm ... then we're ... ?

BELLA [*impatiently*] Bastards? Yes! Like Archie and Godwin, the only other men I have greatly loved. [*thoughtfully*] Mind you, H.G.Wells is fun – almost as good as poor Wedderburn. Why are you looking so mournful?

GRAHAM [*shrugging hopelessly*] We're more conventional than you, mother.

BELLA [*briskly*] Then snap out of it! We have entered the twentieth century where science, democracy and Socialism are making the world a better place for everyone. In a few years words like bastard will cease to be unmentionable. [*moves towards the window*] I was very fond of Archie but I suppose he envied my love for Godwin, hence that [*waves to books on the table*] – absurd tale suggesting Godwin was a monster and that Archie – not I – comforted him on his deathbed.

BELLA *stands at the window staring out at the trees. She is seen from her sons' P.O.V. with them or parts of them in the foreground. Perhaps* **GRAHAM** *rises to his feet.*

GRAHAM You were there when Godwin died?

BELLA [*quietly without turning*] Yes.

KENNETH [*heavily interrupting*] Exactly how did you comfort him on his deathbed?

BELLA *turns and reveals a smile of tender happiness and pride. Tears flow down her cheeks. She does not notice them but speaks tenderly and proudly as she walks slowly into close-up saying*

BELLA Godwin was dying the whole time I knew him. He never mentioned it and I was too ignorant and selfish to notice. I would never have eloped with Wedderburn had I known God was so close to death. Thank goodness he was still breathing when I returned!

139 DISSOLVE TO: PARK CIRCUS 1882 – COLOUR

This almost repeats Scene 114 – a shot from above of **BELLA**, *portmanteau in hand and coat open, springing from the cab onto the pavement, flinging coin to the* **CABMAN** *and leaping up the front steps, but this is in daytime so the colours are lighter, creamier ones of* **BELLA**'*s narrative sequences, as are all scenes from this one to the end. Like Scene 114 this ends with –*

SOUND: *Doorbell violently rung.*

140 CUT TO: LOBBY AND STAIRWELL

This keeps a sense of déjà vu by starting like Scene 115 with **MRS DINWIDDIE** *standing with her arms spread wide open in a heartfelt welcome, but she is obviously grief-stricken.*

MRS DINWIDDIE Oh, my wee pet lamb, you're home, you're home!

BELLA *flings down her portmanteau, is about to embrace her but stops alarmed.*

BELLA What's wrong, Dinwiddie?

MRS DINWIDDIE Master Godwin! He's ... he's ... I canna say it. I canna say it.

141 CUT TO: STAIRWELL

Stairs seen from P.O.V. of **BELLA** *charging up them, across the middle landing, upstairs to the top landing and up to the operating theatre door which she opens and rushes through.*

142 CUT TO: OPERATING THEATRE

Skylight and large windows leave no doubt that this is the room of Scenes 20 and 53, but is now a gentleman's bedroom luxuriously furnished in art nouveau style of Charles Rennie Mackintosh white drawing room and bedroom in Glasgow Hunterian Museum: – white carpet, white wooden furniture with white upholstery, white window curtains, white curtains looped back from a canopy above the bed where **BAXTER**, *propped up on pillows is dying. His face, apart from the shadows under his eyes, is a ghastly grey, almost as pale as his hair. It glitters with sweat. His chest heaves with the effort of his breathing. His hands are under the sheets. In his lap lie the pages of* **BELLA**'*s letter, recognisable by their violet ink. The only strong colours in the room are the pelts of the* **DOGS** *sprawled on the carpet, the black waistcoat and trousers of* **MCCANDLESS**, *who stands to the left of the bedside, arrested in the act of putting drops of medicine into a glass bottle from a measuring spoon, and medicine bottles of green and purple and claret-coloured liquids on a table, and* **BELLA** *rushing to a chair on the right, casting off her coat as she does so.* **BAXTER** *smiles at her sweetly.*

BELLA [*passionately*] What's wrong God? What's wrong?

BELLA *leans weeping over the bed. On the other side* **MCCANDLESS**, *with expert precision, resumes putting small quantities of different* *liquids into the glass with the measuring spoon.*

BAXTER [*gently stroking her hair*] I inherited from my father a venereal disease which has almost destroyed my body – that is why we could never be lovers. In a few hours the disease will also destroy my brain if Archie were not mixing a medicine which will put me to sleep forever. It is good to see you before I leave.

BELLA [*lifting her face to his*] How can I live without you, God?

BAXTER [*amused*] I'll tell if you give me your hand. Give me yours too, Archie.

MCCANDLESS *impassively extends his right hand. Wonderingly,* **BELLA** *does the same. With an effort* **BAXTER** *brings their hands together and rests his own on them. We see that, though a thumb is missing, they are normal.*

BAXTER I once hated the notion of dying because I had no children, but you are my children now. Love each other. Have children of your own. Teach them what you have discovered, Bell.

In a frenzy of grief **BELLA** *pulls her hand away and clutches her hair with both hands.*

BELLA I discovered nothing, God! I'm ignorant and stupid!

With feeble fingers, **BAXTER** *takes a page from his lap.*

BAXTER [*whispering*] Here is a letter you wrote to me, Bella. Read the words I have underlined.

BELLA *takes the letter.* **BAXTER** *lies back his eyes closed listening to her with a smile of perfect contentment. As she reads her grief-laden voice becomes brave and clear. At the end she too is smiling.* **MCCANDLESS** *watches solemnly, glass in hand.*

BELLA Exploitation is not a law of nature! If there are millions of miserable unhappy children in the world then we lucky ones must make the world a good home where everyone is happy! That must be what lucky people are for!

BAXTER *opens his eyes and looks at* **BELLA**. *They exchange smiles.*

BAXTER You will teach your children that?

BELLA *smiles and nods.* **BAXTER** *says with his eyes on* **BELLA**:

BAXTER Time for my medicine.

BELLA Give it to me, Archie.

BELLA *takes the glass from* **MCCANDLESS** *and with her right arm, aided by* **MCCANDLESS**, *raises* **BAXTER**'*s torso from the pillow.*

BELLA [*watching* **BAXTER** *lovingly*] Will it be quick, Archie?

MCCANDLESS A few seconds – no pain.

BAXTER [*in a jocular whisper*] The Greeks gave it to Socrates.

BELLA *puts the glass to his lips.* **BAXTER** *drinks it in one swallow and is laid back on the pillows. His eyes still watch* **BELLA**, *his expression is unchanged.* **MCCANDLESS** *takes back the glass, sees* **BELLA** *is about to kiss* **BAXTER** *and pulls out a clean handkerchief.*

MCCANDLESS Wait!

MCCANDLESS *dries* **BAXTER**'*s lips with the handkerchief.* **BELLA** *thanks him with a nod before laying her lips tenderly on* **BAXTER**'*s. This kiss, watched thoughtfully by* **MCCANDLESS**, *does not stop when* **BAXTER** *shuts his eyes, but goes into freeze frame.*

BELLA [V.O.] So now, my children, you know the exact truth.

143 CUT TO: VIOLET SCREEN

Final credits start rolling on this. Brief pause, then we hear:

GRAHAM [V.O.] All the same, mother, you do have a strangely regular crack round your skull under the hairline.

TWINS 1 & 2 [V.O.] [*almost simultaneously*] Yes ... yes!

KENNETH [V.O.] You let us feel it when we were children.

As the credits roll the violet background changes imperceptibly through the whole spectrum of pastel hues – blue, green, yellow, orange, red and ending with indigo – while the voices continue.

BELLA [V.O.] [*gaily*] There is a completely natural explanation for that, but you will have to work it out yourself ... I must hurry now or I will be late for a meeting of the Fabian Society.

A door is heard shutting.

KENNETH [V.O.] [*firmly*] I prefer father's account of events. He doesn't suggest we are ... are ...

GRAHAM [V.O.] [*brightly*] Bastards?

KENNETH [V.O.] Illegitimate.

TWIN 1 [V.O.] But he does say that mother was produced by a surgical experiment.

TWIN 2 [V.O.] Like Frankenstein's monster.

GRAHAM [V.O.] But she is monstrously eccentric.

TWINS 1 & 2 [V.O.] No! Nonsense! Not at all!

KENNETH [V.O.] You've gone a bit too far there, old man. She's just ... just an uncommonly natural woman.

BIRDS OF PARADISE is a Glasgow theatre company and registered charity formed to help disabled folk stage their own plays. Forrest Alexander, confined by multiple sclerosis to a wheel-chair, is a founding member and a friend of my wife Morag. He did not know I had once written plays when, in1997, he suggested I write one for *Birds Of Paradise*. He knew I had published several novels and thought any novellist was a potentially successful playwright, since both created characters, described settings and used dialogue. This is not always true, as Henry James discovered on the first night of *Guy Domville.* But I was very glad to be introduced to this small theatre company.

From the 6th of June until the 22nd of August I had nine meetings with the art director Andrew Dawson, the administrator Patsy Morrison, and several of the company's actors and friends. We met at 5pm on Thursdays in a large room leased from Glasgow City Council, or perhaps lent by it, in Albion Street near Glasgow Cross. Here we sat round a table among the vivid paintings and papier-mache sculptures of a disabled peoples art class.

I brought one idea to the first meeting: the play must have strong parts for as many disabled folk as possible, so it should be set in a world where the able-bodied are a pitiable minority. The company thought this amusing. Forrest Alexander suggested a wheelchair benefit tribunal to which the able-bodied would (unsuccessfully) appeal. Mrs Anne Marie Robertson suggested that the tribunal be a dumb one which spoke to the appellants through an artificial voicebox. Grotesque notions like these were what I wanted, but I needed embarrassing everyday details of being disabled so that my able-bodied hero could suffer these too. I heard how hard it is for people in wheelchairs to get service in pubs if not with an able-bodied friend. Mrs Robertson had been wheelchair bound for many years and spoke of how many found it hard to accept her marriage and three children. When asked, "How did you manage that?" she had to smile and shrug. She had once to refuse a good job because acceptance meant flitting to a house where light switches, taps, cooker surface and other essential things were out of her reach, and she lacked money to re-equip it.

At the first meeting I also heard that my idea was not original. Vic Finkelstein, senior lecturer in disability studies at the Open University, had set a story in a village designed for the badly disabled. Their able-bodied carers were endangered by low doors, ceilings and wheel tracks linking the buildings. Central television had issued a video cartoon of this story. It makes the same social point of working legs by being more informative about needs of disabled folk, but differs in plot and characters. I consciously stole from Mr Finkelstein the low door in Scene 2 and Able's offer to wear a safety helmet.

A week later I met Alistair Fleming, a student of architecture before being hit by a car. It had left him partly paralysed and had damaged his short term memory. He knew my novel *Lanark* because he had read it before the accident and told me his own story in a jocular way, saying he had been very lucky – in his parents. When hospital treatment stopped doing him good his mother gave up her job to nurse him at home, and both parents had used their savings to fight a long legal battle with their car's insurance company. They won. Alistair now lives in a house adapted to his needs and employs a truly Christian minder. At a third meeting I met Mrs Alice Thompson who suggested her own appalling experience could give my play a happy end. A married woman and working nurse, she had undergone an operation for a heart condition and suffered a stroke during it. She recovered consciousness seven months later, but no longer had the use of her legs.

This gallant willingness to make fun of terrible events made my job easy. I wrote the first two scenes in time for the fourth meeting. From then on we sat round a table reading scenes aloud as they were added and discussing how the play should go. Ernest Kyle, who suffers from emphysema and is also a writer, suggested that Able's leginess should have led to the breakdown of an earlier marriage. Ernest invented the concept of wheel-training, wrote the tender dialogue that ends Scene 4, and gave detailed information about how our Government was deliberately breaking down the social welfare services. As we read on it grew easy to see readers in particular parts. John Campbell seemed right for Able McMann because prosthetic surgery on both legs let him walk with a natural appearance, yet his thoughtful, anxious face indicated that life was not easy. Anne Marie seemed suited to the manager or Meg. It was she who suggested Able's ankles be handcuffed by the police.

Christopher Boyce, librarian for The Herald, advised me on how to make Scene 10 in the newspaper office convincing, and suggested the reappearance of Miss Shy at the end. Angela Mullane helped with legal details. Doctors Bruce Charlton and Gillian Rye wrote the operating theatre scene for me.

The *Birds of Paradise* company received generous grants from Glasgow City and Scottish Arts Councils which helped the company enlarge and engage with forty-five drama workshops throughout Scotland, all rehearsing *Working Legs*. In 1998 the Glasgow company took the play on tour through small theatres in the Scottish Lowlands and Highlands, ending with a performance in the Gilmorehill Theatre of Glasgow University. It has not been staged since. If any other theatre companies employing disabled actors perform it they may do so without paying me, unless they are acting in a London West End theatre.

A few words and phrases show that this is a Scottish play, but companies from other places can change these into idioms from their own province. When preparing to fight the police **ABLE** could sing *The Wearing of the Green, Men of Harlech, Ilkley Moor Ba'T'at* or *Land of Hope and Glory* instead of *Scots Wha Hae*. But nearly all characters are middle class so most English speaking companies may be smart enough to act the whole play without changing it.

Despite having a cast of thirty-eight characters this play could be acted by an energetic company of fifteen or an unusually energetic company of twelve. A perfect production would have all wheel-bound characters played by wheel-bound actors, thus saving rent of chairs. Those acting the **SOCIAL WORKER** and **BENEFITS TRIBUNAL** would also be blind and deaf. Perfection is almost impossible, but the four actors playing the Benefit Tribunal in Scene 8, if not genuinely deaf, should learn enough sign language to converse convincingly in it, as most audiences will notice if actors are inventing meaningless gestures and some signs (the one for "Get rid of him" for instance) can be read by anyone. A production in which the Tribunal's sign speech appears as words on a screen will gain in humour but lose in sinister effect. I have provided an alternative Scene 11 for companies lacking the resources to act the surgical shadow play.

CAST IN ORDER OF APPEARANCE

All actors but two perform in wheelchairs.

ABLE MCMANN, a hero with working legs but usually in wheelchair. He has a part in every scene but 10 and the alternative Scene 11.

BARTENDER		Scene	1 and 9
THRUST, a business person			1 and 9
BLAND, a big businessman			1, 7 and 9
COY, a seductive woman			1 and 9
SUAVE, a seductive man			1 and 9
SOCIAL WORKER, blind			1, 5 and 9
MANAGER, a business person			1, 5 and 12
BETTY MACRAE, our heroine			3, 4, 6 and 12
UNDERMANAGER	)		
WAITRESS	)		
BETH	)	These are all in Scene 3	
LIZ	)	although **LIZ** and **LEX**	
ALEC	)	are not essential to it.	
SANDY	)		
LEX	)		
MRS MACRAE, Betty's mother		Scene	4, 6 and12
MR MACRAE, Betty's father			4, 6 and12
PRIME MINISTER, blind			5
MEG, a conscientious office worker			6
FOUR DEAF MUTES, benefit tribunal			8
APPLICANT, with working legs and one line			8
MISS SHY, who has working legs			9, 10 and 12
FOUR POLICEMEN: no lines			9
EDITOR,			10 and 12
REPORTER,			10
SUB-EDITOR,			10
NURSE	)		(
SISTER	) Scene 11.		(
SURGEON	) surgical	alternative	(**POLITICIAN**
ANAESTHETIST	) shadow	Scene 11.	(**JUDGE**
HOUSE-OFFICER	) play		(
ADMINISTRATOR	)		(
DOCTOR		Scene	12

ACT ONE: BACK TO NORMAL

1 Lounge Bar – Props: gantry with glasses, bottles, telephone, folding stool.
2 Manager's Office – desk, low door, folding stool, extra wheelchair for **ABLE**.
3 Office Party – balloons, streamers, party hats. Music, off.
4 Macrae Living Room – standard lamp, hearth rug, low sideboard.
5 Several Places – drip-feed, manager's desk.
6 Macrae Living Room – as before.

ACT TWO: ROAD TO RUIN

7 Supply Office – two desks, two word processors, one telephone.
8 Benefit Tribunal – platform, table, four chairs, pushbell, voicebox, white mat.
9 Lounge Bar – as Scene 1, with ropes, handcuffs, truncheons.
10 Newspaper Office – long table, two word processors, three phones.
11 Shadow Play – table, anaesthetic machine, surgical tools, tray of drinks.
11 Alternative Scene – with two brandy glasses.
12 Hospital Ward – hospital bed, drip-feed, spectacular new wheelchair.

1: LOUNGE BAR

Beside a low gantry of bottles and glasses **BARTENDER** *sits slowly drying a glass and listening to the conversations of seated customers.* **ABLE** *stands awkwardly nearby. He wears jeans, a sweater, a small knapsack and is trying and failing to catch attention without shouting.* **THRUST** *and* **BLAND** *discuss business,* **COY** *and* **SUAVE** *are obviously flirting. Both couples have nearly empty glasses on their chair armrests.*

THRUST He comes from the shoot 'em kill 'em brigade into contract management and doesn't even know that a contract locks you into a fixed profit margin.

BLAND [*nods and smiles*] So he was no use to you.

THRUST None at all. Same again?

BLAND Why not?

THRUST [*loudly, to* **BARTENDER**] Same again, please!

BARTENDER Certainly sir.

BARTENDER *pours two gin and tonics.*

COY [*slyly*] I told her Bill McGuffie and I had a passionate love affair last year. She said, "But Bill's a married man!" I said, "A year ago I was a married woman!"

SUAVE *chuckles and pats her hand.*

COY I wish you'd seen her face!

SUAVE So do I! Shall we be wicked and have another?

COY *nods.*

SUAVE [*loudly*] Same again please!

BARTENDER In a minute sir!

BARTENDER *takes drinks to* **THRUST** *and* **BLAND**.

SUAVE [*intimately, to* **COY**] You've a wild sense of humour. I could never fall for a woman who didn't have a wild sense of humour.

COY *simpers.*

THRUST There are two levels to everything. If your profit margin looks significant on your reading of the top twenty then you may have a level one situation.

BARTENDER *places glasses on* **THRUST** *and* **BLAND**'s *armrests.*

BLAND Or you may have a dinosaur. Nowadays all big killings are made in property. I'd go into property myself if I was five years younger. My turn to pay.

BLAND *puts money on the* **BARTENDER**'s *armrest.*

BARTENDER Thank you sir. [*To* **SUAVE** *while returning to gantry*] Two gin and tonics was it sir?

SUAVE That's right.

ABLE [*desperately*] Listen, I've been waiting for fifteen minutes and you're still serving people who came in after me!

General embarrassment. Company look at each other, **THRUST** *grinning,* **BLAND** *shrugging.* **SUAVE** *taps the side of her head with a finger.* **COY** *sighs and adopts an appearance of patient waiting.*

BARTENDER [*stiffly*] I'm not unsympathetic sir, but it's not easy to notice people whose heads aren't at the usual level. What exactly do you want?

ABLE [*defiantly*] A large whisky.

BARTENDER A large whisky?

ABLE Yes!

BARTENDER Are you sure that won't have an effect on your condition?

ABLE What has my condition to do with what I drink?

BARTENDER [*offended but trying not to show it*] I'm not unsympathetic sir but spirits can harm people in your condition. We had one last year who went berserk – kicked out all around – knocked four policemen out of their chairs before they dragged him out.

ABLE [*violently*] I am not the violent sort!

BARTENDER Better safe than sorry. I'll get you a soda water and lime.

ABLE [*almost yelling*] Now listen!

General tension. Enter blind social worker, swiftly.

SOCIAL WORKER I know that voice! It's all right – I can vouch for him – he's a friend of mine.

All but **ABLE** *relax.*

SOCIAL WORKER [*to* **ABLE**] Calm down. Where's the bar staff?

BARTENDER Here sir.

SOCIAL WORKER I'm his social worker. Give him a drink.

BARTENDER What does he want?

SOCIAL WORKER [*to* **ABLE**] What do you want?

ABLE Whisky.

SOCIAL WORKER [*to* **BARTENDER**] A small glass for him, large G and T for me. [*To* **ABLE**] Sit down! It's hard to hear you at that altitude.

BARTENDER *goes to gantry.* **ABLE** *removes his knapsack and takes out a small folding stool.*

ABLE People shouldn't treat me like that.

SOCIAL WORKER I know you're as sensible as the rest of us but look at it another way. A lot of unempowered folk turn bitter and aggressive. No wonder!

ABLE *squats on the stool.* **THRUST**, **BLAND**, **COY** *and* **SUAVE** *react approvingly and prepare to enjoy their drinks.*

SOCIAL WORKER I've news for you.

ABLE Yes?

SOCIAL WORKER A job interview. Tomorrow.

ABLE [*jumping to his feet*] A job!

Everyone reacts nervously. The **BARTENDER** *spills a whisky then grimly reaches for a soda water.*

SOCIAL WORKER [*scowling*] I told you to calm down and sit!

With effort **ABLE** *sits. Widespread relief.*

ABLE I'm sorry. It hardly ever happens but whenever I hear a bit of good news I seem to need to jump up and walk about a bit. After five idle years! A job!

SOCIAL WORKER A job *interview.* And you haven't a hope in hell if you don't learn to control yourself.

ABLE What's the firm?

SOCIAL WORKER National Equilibrium. It employs hyperactive people through an arrangement with Social Welfare. But you won't survive your probation – you won't survive your interview if you don't cut out these involuntary movements and keep your temper.

ABLE *nurses the knapsack on his knee, rocking backwards and forwards slightly and muttering.*

ABLE I *will* control myself. I will.

SOCIAL WORKER Let's drink to that.

BARTENDER [*to* **SOCIAL WORKER**] Your gin and tonic sir. [*To* **ABLE**] Here's your soda water and lime.

ABLE [*loudly*] But ...

BARTENDER *faces him defiantly,* **SOCIAL WORKER** *sternly,* **THRUST** *annoyed,* **BLAND** *amused,* **COY** *worried.* **SUAVE** *sighs and raises his eyes to heaven. After a moment* **ABLE** *fumbles in his pocket.*

ABLE [*quietly*] Let me pay for this.

SOCIAL WORKER *smiles and nods approval.*

2: MANAGER'S OFFICE

A pool of light surrounds a desk with impressive wheelchair behind, less impressive one in front, a telephone and typed letter on top. In shadow to one side is a door four and a half feet high. The **MANAGER** *has a kind, polite voice and manner but looks at* **ABLE** *without smiling or moving her chair throughout the interview.*

MANAGER [*on telephone*] I'm ready for him.

She lays down phone and sits back waiting. A moment later the door is faintly tapped.

MANAGER Stand up Mr McCann, we've plenty of headroom.

ABLE [*standing erect*] Thank you madam.

MANAGER [*pointing*] There's an empty chair. Can you use it?

ABLE Frankly madam, so much depends on this interview that I can't help feeling nervous, and when nervous I prefer to stand.

MANAGER [*nodding*] Your problem is psychological.

ABLE [*hurt*] No! I get cramp when I don't exercise, the doctors say that always happens in legs with working muscles.

MANAGER Your hyperactive legs could be cured by a surgical operation.

ABLE The doctors don't advise it. There's a danger of a stroke. I've a weak heart.

MANAGER [*lifting the letter*] Poor you! This letter from your last employer says before the accident you were clean, punctual, efficient, intelligent and popular with colleagues and superiors.

ABLE [*eagerly*] I loved my work. I was a quality controller.

MANAGER It says that after it you grew slovenly, depressed and left without giving notice.

She stares at **ABLE** *who shrugs, sighs and shakes his head.*

MANAGER Tell me about your accident. I thought hyperactivity was an inherited disease.

ABLE Not in my case! The doctors say that if I ever have a child it's as likely to be normal as anyone else's. About my accident ... [*shows his knapsack*] ... Do you mind if I sit on a small stool I have here? I'll talk easier on it than in that ... thing. [*waves his hand at the wheelchair*].

MANAGER Sit how you like.

ABLE *swiftly unpacks, unfolds and squats down on the stool.*

ABLE [*speaking quickly*] I didn't always hate wheelchairs. Perhaps this happened because I liked my first one too much. I was crossing a busy road one day when the wheels jammed just when a hundred-ton juggernaut tanker came roaring round a corner. Suddenly I was up and running for the kerb. I didn't decide to do it, I just did it! And even now I can't pretend I'm sorry.

MANAGER That's understandable.

ABLE [*gratefully*] Thank you madam. The tanker crushed my chair into a knot of flattened tubes while I stood on the kerb in a crowd of folk who just sat staring at me like statues. All they could do was stare – they couldn't help me! I hated that look of pity and revulsion. I ran away from them. I ran all the way home. My wife fainted when I walked in through the door.

MANAGER [*puzzled*] Walked?

ABLE Crawled, I should have said. If the insurance company meets my claim I'll get a home with a six-foot high ceiling and matching door.

MANAGER So your hyperactivity is basically a chair-phobia unfitting you for professional desk jobs.

ABLE *becomes so excited that he has difficulty not standing up.*

ABLE No madam! Not at all! When working at my desk I forgot all about chairs and legs and other stupid things. I thought of nothing but quality control. I lost myself in quality control.

MANAGER Then why did you leave Rock Fire Life? You weren't sacked.

ABLE Because of teabreaks. When teabreaks came I had to stand up and walk about – couldn't stop myself. That wasn't a crime, of course, but people who had been my friends began acting as if hyperactivity was an infectious disease: turning their faces away and not hearing when I spoke to them. One morning I felt unable to face them. I stayed in bed, pulled the duvet over my head, refused to eat, drink or speak until an ambulance took me to hospital.

MANAGER Sad. Were you medicated?

ABLE With anti-depressants. They made me more depressed than ever.

MANAGER Did you see a psychiatrist?

ABLE Yes. He said it was all caused by inadequate wheel training in infancy. It's true that I stopped crawling later than most children – but so do forty-five percent of normal kids.

MANAGER Other therapies?

ABLE I was locked in a padded cell with nothing but a wheelchair and a floor they could electrify. They tried conditioning me into thinking the chair was a friend because when on it I was safe from shocks through the floor. They failed! [*gives a small, frantic laugh*] I knelt on that chair, stood, jumped up and down, danced on it, did everything but sit!

MANAGER [*shaking her head*] Bad!

ABLE I was in hospital for over two years, then my wife decided it was doing me no good and brought me home. Luckily she's a trained nurse. She gave up her job to look after me.

MANAGER Brave woman.

ABLE Yes, it was she who restored me to sanity. I'll always be grateful, though she divorced me six months ago.

MANAGER Another man?

ABLE That wasn't the reason she gave. She said I would be better on my own – that I was taking advantage of her support to enjoy my hyperactivity.

MANAGER [*sternly*] Were you?

ABLE *does not reply but covers his face with his hands.*

MANAGER Telling the truth won't hurt you with me, Mr McMann. Secrecy will.

ABLE [*from behind his hands*] You may find this hard to believe, but it is easier for a man to urinate while standing up. She caught me doing it.

MANAGER Anything else?

ABLE [*uncovering his face and sighing*] I found it easier to sleep at nights if I danced a wee jig around the living room when she wasn't there. Unluckily our house – her house – is semi-detached. The neighbours heard me and told her. That was the last straw – I had to leave. I learned she had another man after my social worker helped me to a bedsit. [*Suddenly eager*] But now I'm all right! As right as I'll ever be. All I want – all I need – is work. Something to do. A purpose in life.

MANAGER [*clearing her throat*] Unluckily we cannot offer you anything as grand as a desk in quality control but we have a vacancy for an internal courier.
ABLE I'll fill it.
MANAGER The wage is not large.
ABLE Anything's better than nothing.
MANAGER But the messenger will have to use a chair. [*She points*] That chair!
ABLE [*after a pause*] Let me tell you something madam. Using my own two feet I can do that job faster than a messenger in a chair. Chairs are faster in the open air but indoors – in a building with lots of lifts and awkward corners – you cannae beat a pair of working legs.
MANAGER But the doors!
ABLE I'll wear a safety helmet.
MANAGER That is not the point, Mr McMann. My other employees will put up with your prancings if I order them but think of the customers! Some are old enough to remember when people like you were never seen in public – they were doped to the eyeballs and kept in locked wards. A successful firm must not be suspected of encouraging hyperactivity. But something you said makes me think that with a little effort you can be a normal courier here.
ABLE What did I say?
MANAGER That when doing a job you forgot your phobia and became lost in the job itself. So let's try a little experiment. Stand and take this letter.
MANAGER *offers letter,* **ABLE** *uneasily stands and takes it.*
MANAGER Imagine that I have told you to take that very important letter to our archives on the third floor – by chair of course. You have gone in your chair to the lift, entered it and pressed the third floor button. The journey by lift takes ten seconds. Will you sit down in that chair and imagine carrying a letter for me while I count up to ten?
ABLE [*terrified*] I ... I ... All right.
ABLE *goes to the chair, takes a deep breath, closes his eyes and sits abruptly down with tightly folded arms. The* **MANAGER**, *watching the dial of her wristwatch, steadily counts.*
MANAGER One. Two. Three. Four. Five. Six. Seven ... Eight ... Nine ... You've arrived!
She looks at **ABLE** *whose face – because he is holding his breath – has gone very red. He remains as he was, rigid with tight shut eyes.*
MANAGER [*slightly worried*] Mr McMann! Mr McMann! The game is over.
ABLE *still does not move.* **MANAGER**, *more worried still, reaches for the telephone.* **ABLE** *suddenly opens his eyes and jumps shouting:*
ABLE I counted another ten!
MANAGER [*stretching out a firm, genial hand*] You can do it. Join National Equilibrium tomorrow.
ABLE [*shaking her hand*] God bless you madam! God bless you!
He dances a joyful little jig. The **MANAGER** *sits down.*
MANAGER [*reprovingly*] Mr McMann!
ABLE [*standing still*] Yes?
MANAGER Keep that sort of exercise for the privacy of your own home.
ABLE [*subdued*] Yes madam. Thank you for reminding me madam.
MANAGER My name – [*settles back in her chair*] – is Isabel Townsend so my employees call me Eye Tee – sounds more democratic than madam, eh?
ABLE Oh yes madam – sorry, madam – Eye Tee I mean.
MANAGER Remember that part of your wage will be paid by the British Taxpayer. An old-fashioned socialist would say we were exploiting you, so you needn't be so pathetically grateful to me all the time.
ABLE [*folding his stool and putting it in his knapsack*] Thank you very much for telling me that Eye Tee. It's a great weight off my mind – thank you very, very much, Eye Tee.
The **MANAGER** *smiles for the only time in the play.*

3: OFFICE PARTY

The stage is meant to be the corner of a dance floor so everyone leaves or enters from front left. Dance music. Everyone wears bright paper hats. **ABLE**, *in a wheelchair, sits backstage left watching enviously.* **LEX** *and* **LIZ** *dance on their chairs: they are a good-looking couple in perfect harmony and obviously delighted with each other.* **BETH** *and* **SANDY** *dance in: a couple who amuse each other but are certainly not in love. They circle the stage with* **LIZ** *and* **LEX**. **ALEX** *rolls on. He wears a flamboyant waistcoat, fancies himself as a ladies' man, scowls at* **ABLE** *then goes and sits front right, watching the women dancers with an air of an experienced man assessing his chances.* **BETTY** *dances in with* **UNDERMANAGER**, *an older man who finds her attractive but to whom she is only polite.* **ALEX** *at once recognises her as his target;* **ABLE** *also quickly notices her but at once becomes withdrawn and stops watching anyone.* **MANAGER**, *with glass of wine, enters and sits front left watching the company as music and dance come to an* *end.* **LIZ** *and* **LEX** *go to one side of the floor and sit whispering.* **UNDERMANAGER** *separates from* **BETTY** *to join* **MANAGER**, **BETTY** *and* **BETH** *join each other near* **ABLE**. **WAITRESS** *enters with glasses on a tray and serves them to the company starting with* **ABLE**, *who takes and nurses a glass of orange.*

ALEX [*slapping* **SANDY***'s back*] Congratulations! You're well on your way with that one. Stick it into her.

SANDY [*good humouredly*] Don't be daft, she's a married woman.

ALEX No obstacle man! No obstacle! Who's that stotter she's with?

SANDY She's just been promoted from sales into cost analysis.

ALEX If she was oiled the right way she'd take off like a rocket. Slainte!

Both take drinks from the waitress and sit watching **BETTY.**

BETTY Thank God that's over! Why am I always picked on by older men in senior management?

BETH Because you keep saying no to younger ones on our level.

BETTY Can you wonder? Look at that pair eyeing us up.

BETH The one with the fancy waistcoat obviously thinks he's your destiny.

BETTY He'd be a fate worse than death – utter boredom.

MANAGER [*loudly*] Hello Able!

Silence. **ABLE** *looks quickly up.*

MANAGER Enjoying the party, Able?

ABLE *smiles, nods, raises his glass then sips from it.*

MANAGER Good! Good!

Everybody is now looking at **ABLE** *except the* **WAITRESS**, *from whom the* **UNDERMANAGER** *takes a glass of wine.* **LEX** *whispers to* **LIZ.**

BETTY [*to* **BETH**] I like the look of him.

BETH Same here! I wouldnae mind a plateful if he wasnae

Whispering, **BETH** *leans nearer* **BETTY**.

ALEX [*grinning*] Did you hear the story about the hyperactive Jew, the hyperactive lesbian, the hyperactive darkie and the hyperactive nun who were shipwrecked on a desert island? On the first day –

SANDY Quieter! Eye Tee is a Catholic.

ALEX *leans nearer* **SANDY** *and whispers.*

MANAGER How's he coping?

UNDERMANAGER As a courier there's nothing wrong with him.

MANAGER But?

UNDERMANAGER Same bother we had with the last one. When not working he won't sit. If I turn round to give an order I expect a friendly human face, not a horrible blank crotch. And during teabreaks people can't talk to him without looking up at angles that are sore on the neck.

MANAGER He stands through teabreaks?

UNDERMANAGER Only when he thinks nobody notices, but sooner or later they do notice of course.

MANAGER How often?

UNDERMANAGER At least once a week.

MANAGER That isn't often.

UNDERMANAGER It doesn't bother me Eye Tee, but knowing that sooner or later they're bound to see him in that state makes the middle management nervous.

MANAGER Tell them their nervousness makes him nervous, which makes it hard for him to control his attacks.

UNDERMANAGER Will do, Eye Tee.

BETTY [*to* **BETH**] Hyperactivity isn't a crime – it doesn't bother me.

She goes to **ABLE** *and sits beside him.*

BETTY Can I have the next dance?

ABLE Eh? Er, I don't dance I'm afraid.

BETTY Have you never danced?

ABLE Yes, but I had an accident.

BETTY Hyperactivity?

ABLE Aye.

BETTY Why should that stop ye? You obviously still know how to manage a chair.

ABLE Well, if you want to know the truth ... whenever I hear the music I get an impulse to get up and dance with my legs!

BETTY *laughs cheerfully. After a moment* **ABLE** *laughs too.*

ABLE Yes, it's funny but it's true!

BETTY Tell you what, dance with me! I'm strong. I'll hold ye down if you try anything outrageous.

ABLE [*attracted*] Will you?

ALEX [*disgusted*] For fuck's sake why is she chatting him up? What use is he to her?

SANDY Maybe she's the motherly type.

ALEX Blethers. She's the sexy type. She's just trying to attract attention. Well, she's got all of mine.

He glowers at **BETTY** *and* **ABLE** *who are approached by the* **WAITRESS.**

WAITRESS Another orange juice sir?

ABLE [*returning his glass*] I'll risk something stronger this time.

MANAGER Mrs Mackintosh of material output is leaving to have a baby at the end of the month. I'm going to give her desk to Able.

UNDERMANAGER [*surprised*] Can he handle it?

MANAGER He once handled quality control for Rock Fire Life – was a bit of a whiz kid at it. He'll easily handle material output for half Mackintosh's wage – and without grumbling about overtime. [*speaks very loudly*] Good news ladies and gentlemen! [*Everyone falls silent and stares at her*].

MANAGER I'm leaving now. I know that mice play better when the cat isn't watching.

ALEX, **SANDY**, **LEX** Hahahahahahaha!

BETH, **LIZ** Teeheeheehee!

The **UNDERMANAGER** *registers approval by smiling and silently clapping hands.* **ABLE** *and* **BETTY** *exchange glances.*

MANAGER [*heartily*] Goodnight Able! Goodnight Miss Macrae! [*She leaves*].

VOICE OFF Take your partners for the next dance – the [*The dance is named*].

LIZ *and* **LEX** *swing onto the floor followed by the* **UNDERMANAGER** *who has gone for* **BETH**, *and* **BETTY** *and excited* **ABLE**. **ALEX** *glowers at them.*

ALEX For fuck's sake!

SANDY Calm down, calm down.

Music. The dance begins. **ABLE** *and* **BETTY** *do very well, and are starting to enjoy each other thoroughly when they pass near or pause briefly near* **ALEX**, *who speaks in a voice not loud enough to be heard by other dancers.*

ALEX Currying favour with the senior management's pet are we Miss Macrae?

After a moment of astonishment **ABLE** *leaps to his feet. The other dancers stop and stare. He stands rigid with clenched fists.* **ALEX**, *smiling, turns away.*

SANDY [*to* **ALEX**, *muttering*] That wasnae very nice.

BETTY [*to* **ABLE**] Ignore him! Sit down! Sit down!

4: MACRAE LIVING ROOM

ABLE *and* **BETTY**, *partly undressed, embrace on hearth rug in light of standard lamp, his wheelchair on one side, hers on the other. Discarded clothes – blouse, sweater, socks, shoes – lie near. A low sideboard has decanter and glasses. Recent lovemaking has left them at peace together with* **BETTY**'s *head resting on* **ABLE**'s *arm.*

ABLE [*after a pause*] Are you comfortable?

BETTY Yes. Are you?

ABLE Never more so. I'm terrified of your mum and dad coming back.

BETTY [*amused*] Relax! They've gone to a show that won't have reached the first interval yet. [*kisses him*].

ABLE [*amazed and happy*] I'm comfortable all the time with you – just seeing you in the company corridors makes me feel at home there. I've never felt that way with anyone else – not even before my accident. I was engaged to be married for a year and half the time my fiancée and I were quarrelling – when we weren't making love.

BETTY What did you quarrel about?

ABLE She didn't like my friends, ideas, the way I dressed or anything else about me, but that didn't stop us marrying. Betty, I'm glad my chair jammed!

BETTY Same here! But I hope – [*kisses him lightly*] – I hope you're not going to propose marriage. [*She is teasing. After a pause she speaks coldly*] A couple should practise living together before they sign a contract to do it till one of them dies.

ABLE [*amazed and happy again*] You'd like that?

BETTY *smiles and nods.*

ABLE Come here!

They kiss.

BETTY But we mustn't rush things – we must plan them very carefully.

ABLE I know! [*sighs*] I wish your parents liked me. I wish you hadn't told them I was hyperactive. They wouldn't have noticed at first. They would have taken me for an ordinary bloke who's clumsy with chairs. Through knowing you I've almost overcome my phobia – I can even sit down when I'm not working, if you're nearby.

BETTY If I'm not ashamed of your disability why should you be, you idiot? Kiss me!

He is about to do so when there is a sound offstage. They sit up staring at each other.

BETTY The car!

ABLE They're back. [*jumps up*].

BETTY [*sliding into her chair*] Sit down! Sit down! Quick!

She pulls on her discarded clothing. **ABLE** *scoops up shoes and clothing, flops on his chair and makes a bad job of dressing himself while remaining seated. Sound of door opening, then* **MRS MACRAE** *rolls in and glares at* **ABLE** *who is pulling a sweater over his head.* **MR MACRAE** *enters, more quizzical than angry.*

MRS MACRAE [*to her husband*] Oh yes I'm the unreasonable one, always hysterical, always in the wrong, but where did reason get us? "I'm bringing a pal home Saturday night," says Betty – the night she knows we're going out – "What pal?" says I. "Oh just a poor hyperactive friend I met at work," says she –

BETTY [*infuriated*] I never called him poor!

MRS MACRAE You implied it!

MR MACRAE Mary dear –

MRS MACRAE [*to* **BETTY**, *ignoring him*] You can't pull the wool over my eyes Miss Reasonable! I knew what would happen. It ruined the show for me. We left before the interval and now the whole weekend and everything is ruined! Everything! Ruined!

MR MACRAE Mary dear –

MRS MACRAE You're all obviously trying to turn me into a hypermaniac like him!

She points to **ABLE**. *He gets up and recklessly finishes dressing on his legs.*

MRS MACRAE Look at that! He isn't even trying to act normal! [*weeps*]

ABLE [*stooping to finish tying shoelaces*] I'm leaving, Betty.

BETTY Sit down Able! This is my house as much as theirs. I've paid my share in it since I went to work eight years ago.

ABLE *sits, grabbing the arms to hold himself down.*

MR MACRAE No need to take that tone Betty but yes, stay there Able. I want a word with you. And Mary, the world isn't coming to an end because Betty and Able have snogged on the living room floor – [*lays a hand on his wife's shoulder: she shakes it off*] – sex isn't the life or death business it was in our young day, and they'd have been in her bedroom behind a locked door if they'd have been up to anything serious.

MRS MACRAE [*becoming deadly calm*] Having a hypermaniac grandchild forced on us may not seem serious to you but I'm not having it – oh!

She shrieks because **ABLE**, *unable to stop himself, has jumped up again. All three stare at him.*

MRS MACRAE Good night! I'm going to bed. [*She exits with dignity*].

BETTY *looks anxiously at* **ABLE** *who stands glowering at the floor.* **MR MACRAE** *rolls to the sideboard saying:*

MR MACRAE [*pouring a drink*] I cannot deny that my wife has a temper. So has my daughter, but I don't suppose you've seen that side of our Betty yet, Able?

BETTY [*fiercely*] Keep out of this, Dad! What's between Able and me is our own business!

MR MACRAE Right, Betty! Health to both of you. [*raises his glass and sips*] But perhaps I love my daughter as much as you do Able, so I'd like to know your plans.

BETTY [*still fiercely*] Able and I are going to live together till we find if we want to marry.

MR MACRAE Starting when? And where? In a bedsit? Or will you take out a mortgage on a place of your own? How are you off financially, Able? I gather you're on probation with the firm after a long spell of unemployment.

ABLE *shifts his feet and opens his mouth to speak but* **BETTY** *gets in first.*

BETTY Able came here to see me, not to be interrogated by you, Dad!

MR MACRAE [*soothingly, to* **BETTY**] Let Able get a word in edgeways – I'm sure he can speak for himself.

ABLE [*shrugging*] I've recently been promoted to a desk job and the boss has gone out of the way to say she likes my performance. Also my insurance claim must be met sometime. My lawyers are quite confident they'll win – the case has dragged on for five years. I used up my savings fighting it so my parents are lending me theirs.

MR MACRAE What's the problem?

ABLE [*sighing*] The company who made my chair claim that it jammed because it hadn't been properly serviced – it had been, but the firm servicing it went out of business soon after. We keep finding witnesses to support my claim and the company keeps finding experts to discredit them, so each year the cost goes up. Just now my lawyers are claiming fifty thousand. If they win I'll get half that when I've met outstanding fees and repaid parents and Social Welfare.

BETTY Insurance companies want claimants to die before a settlement is reached! Only the rich can afford lawyers who settle things fast.

MR MACRAE [*reasonably*] If companies met every reasonable-looking claim they would go bankrupt, Betty.

ABLE They don't say that in their adverts.

MR MACRAE Of course not – business is business. I'm going to ask one thing of you both – don't rush things.

Plan what you do very carefully beforehand.

BETTY [*through gritted teeth*] We'd decided that before Mum and you charged in!

MR MACRAE Yes, you've your mother's temper. I'm off to bed. [*puts down the glass, rolls to the exit but turns before leaving*] Will you have children if things pan out all right?

BETTY [*immediately*] Yes – [*hesitates*] – if Able wants them too.

She looks appealingly at **ABLE** *who smiles back then speaks more boldly than we have ever heard him.*

ABLE There's no medical reason why our children will not be as fit as anyone else's, Mr Macrae.

MR MACRAE No medical reason, but socially they won't find life easy.

BETTY The best start in life children can have is a couple of parents who love each other!

MR MACRAE Oh yes, if you can love each other better than most married couples it just might compensate your weans for feeling ashamed of their father.

ABLE *and* **BETTY** *stare at him.*

BETTY You're a devil, Dad!

MR MACRAE [*leaving*] Expect the worst and you'll never be disappointed Betty. Good night.

He leaves. **ABLE** *looks at* **BETTY**. *She holds out her arms to him. He gets up and goes to her.*

ABLE I'm glad you want kids.

BETTY [*leaving her chair for the hearth rug*] Oh I do!

They find comfort by resting, clothed, in each other's arms. After a pause – **ABLE** *says wistfully –*

ABLE Have you noticed that nobody minds what wee kids do with their legs? They can kick with them, stand on them, even toddle on them before they're wheel-trained. If they do it in public folk just smile or shrug their shoulders.

BETTY [*sensibly*] They also yell and girn when hungry and wet and mess their nappies.

ABLE But working legs are a sign of healthy growth, Betty! Won't you be glad when you feel our baby kicking inside you?

BETTY [*amused*] Yes but how far back do you want to go, Able? Will you be climbing into the trees next?

ABLE [*chuckles*].

BETTY [*suddenly fierce*] My dad really is a devil! We won't disappoint each other ... will we?

ABLE [*supremely confident*] We'll get on fine.

5: SEVERAL PLACES

Total darkness.

ANNOUNCER'S VOICE And now, an election address by the Prime Minister of Great Britain, the Right Honourable Humpty Dipsy.

A spotlight shows the **P.M.** *seated centre stage and facing the air above the audience's heads with an expression of indomitable courage. He wears a white hospital gown, glasses with black lenses and a hearing aid. From an attachment to his chair a tube runs from a suspended bottle into a bandage on his arm. He carefully unplugs his hearing aid and clasps hands on crossed legs before speaking.*

PRIME MINISTER Good evening. All political parties seek election by promising to make life better for people, and there was once a time when British Governments did it by pampering minorities. The strong and efficient were penalized to benefit the feeble and useless; good successful workers were taxed to make life easy for those who could not or would not work. You all know what that leads to. British employers could not compete in foreign markets, teenagers turned to sexual promiscuity, drug abuse was advocated by trendy artists and gurus and even a parliamentary commission. No wonder that the British people decided to call a halt.

You did it by electing into government a party which promised to get Britain rolling forward instead of continually applying the brakes and letting air out of tyres. My party kept these promises, which is why we have been in power ever since. Yes, some people are homeless but more Britons than ever occupy homes of their own. This is good for them, good for our banks, good for our building societies. Yes, inadequate people whinge about the state of public healthcare, but those with thrift and foresight face the future without fear because London is the insurance capital of the world. Most Britons today are tougher, more independent, more realistic and – as MPs of every party realize – more wealthy than they have been since the great days of the Empire. And if you don't like how we have achieved this you won't change it by voting for others! Those who attacked our curbs on trade union and local government dictatorship, those who invest in the privatization of our public transport, communications, power, heat and water, now agree that our good work cannot be undone, so no matter who takes office after us, we will have conquered.

So with full confidence in the support of the majority I announce a new round of tax cuts, to be paid for by total privatisation of property and services remaining in public hands. I know this will cause the usual outcry about the plight of the unemployed, the aged and the hyperactive poor, but remember the words of Saint Paul: "Now abideth Faith, Hope and Charity, and the greatest of these is Charity." Which is why Charity – like banking, insurance and arms manufacture – is another British industry in a healthy and flourishing condition. I am sorry for the unemployed, the elderly and the hyperactive poor, but my job is still to get as many as possible rolling forward at their own speed on their own wheels. Goodnight.

The spotlight goes out and reappears left on the **MANAGER** *who is dictating a letter.*

MANAGER Dear Mr McMann, when you joined this firm I told you that the welfare subsidy was a great part of what made it profitable to employ you. Since this subsidy is terminating I am compelled to give you a month's notice. I regret it because you have been a highly valued member of staff, but Mrs Mackintosh returns at the end of the month having recovered from her pregnancy. If I scrapped her instead of you I might be charged with wrongful dismissal. Your old post of courier has of course been filled.

However, I enclose a reference stating that your ability, efficiency and willingness to serve are exceptional, and that your physical condition in no way disqualifies you for a desk at the highest level of middle management. Why not use this reference to get yourself off the hyperactivity register? My influence – and perhaps a young lady in cost analysis – seem to have cured you of standing up and jigging about. Discuss it with your social worker.

ABLE *and* **SOCIAL WORKER** *facing each other.* **ABLE**, *holding a letter, is cheerily wheeling his chair backwards and forwards.*

ABLE [*eagerly*] See! I can use this no bother! I've got over my phobia!

SOCIAL WORKER Are you really cured of standing and jigging?

ABLE [*not embarrassed*] Oh I do it at home all the time! All the time! It drives the other flatmates mad but they're a bunch of alcies so the landlord doesn't care. And I never do it at work.

SOCIAL WORKER You'll be out of work in a fortnight.

ABLE But with this reference from Eye Tee – [*waves it*] – I can go to the job centre and sign on to the professional register if I get my name off the hyperactive one! [*twirls his chair around*].

SOCIAL WORKER There's a lot more professional unemployment than the government admits. And nowadays the hyperactive register is much harder to get off than on – as you'll learn if you find work and then have a relapse.

ABLE [*sitting still at last*] If I thought like you do I would take seriously to drink!

SOCIAL WORKER [*apologetic*] Sorry Able – in my job we get used to expecting the worst, and coming off the hyperactive register is going to affect your disability allowance and insurance claim.

ABLE [*blithely*] I've seen my lawyers about that! They say if I get a decent job they'll have to settle for less money, but it will be enough to pay them and pay what I owe my parents and the Social Welfare – and I'll still have a few hundred pounds to myself. The important thing is a fresh start in life!

SOCIAL WORKER I admire your guts, Able. Good luck. [*He holds out his hand*] Good luck. Goodbye. You're my final case.

ABLE [*shaking hands*] You're leaving social work?

SOCIAL WORKER I'm taking early retirement. The job's become too tough for me.

ABLE Can I ask something?

SOCIAL WORKER *nods.*

ABLE Why don't Welfare offices employ hyperactive social workers to deal with hyperactive people? They wouldn't need to ask a lot of questions because they would understand our situation already.

SOCIAL WORKER Can't you work that out for yourself?

He grins bitterly. **ABLE** *shakes his head.*

SOCIAL WORKER The government doesn't want employees who understand people like you – it wants nothing to do with people like you. I belong to a dying breed – the social worker who was employed to help. If you have a relapse and come back to us you will be given a form asking for exact details of everywhere you've lived and everything you've done. This information is already stored in official data banks but many folk have forgotten it so will be eliminated because their form is incomplete. The rest will then receive a questionnaire which gets them assessing their own hyperactivity through a points allocation system which only those who invented it can understand. And the winners of this mental obstacle race will be sifted out by a machine – a processor which chooses who to benefit not according to needs, but on the basis of funds which are being slowly reduced to zero.

ABLE *has grown restless during this speech.*

ABLE But ... But ...

SOCIAL WORKER If you want to know why the government is slowly, not quickly axing social welfare, it's because our middle class would be shocked if our cities suddenly started looking like Calcutta or Jakarta with skeletal hyperactive beggars doing dances of death on every corner. They're being allowed time to get used to it. Our upper classes are unshockable of course. They live in country houses or specially policed security zones.

ABLE You've a sick mind! I would certainly take to drink if I believed Britain is going to be like that!

SOCIAL WORKER [*soothingly*] You needn't believe what you can't see, Able. I hope to hell you get a decent job – and keep it!

Spotlight goes out.

6: MACRAE LIVING ROOM

Light comes up on **BETTY** *who, distressed, sits knitting a small garment, watched tensely by her mother opposite. Voices are squabbling opposite. Voices offstage and on overlap.*

ABLE'S VOICE I've got to see her! I've got to see her!

MR MACRAE'S VOICE Not possible, Able.

MRS MACRAE Pay no attention.

ABLE'S VOICE Why won't she see me? We haven't quarrelled, and I've good news for her – for both of us. Tell me what's wrong, Mr Macrae!

MR MACRAE'S VOICE She doesn't want to see you and that's not wrong, it's right, Able!

BETTY I wish I could see him!

She stops knitting.

MRS MACRAE [*hissing*] You promised not to!

ABLE'S VOICE Stop condescending to me, Mr Macrae! You are no longer dealing with a hyperactive invalid! I am as firmly settled in my chair as you are in yours!

MR MACRAE'S VOICE If you want a fight you've found the right man!

Sounds of a struggle.

MRS MACRAE [*swivelling her chair*] I'm phoning the police!

BETTY No!

ABLE'S VOICE [*shouting*] Betty, are you there? I'm off the hyperactive register and I've a new job! A great new job!

BETTY [*shouting*] Able! Able! Oh let him in Dad! Please! Please! Please!

She weeps. **ABLE** *rolls in, embraces and comforts her.* **MR MACRAE** *enters more slowly. Both men are untidy from their tussle.*

MRS MACRAE [*violently to her husband*] You had no right letting that man into our house! No right! None at all! You promised you wouldn't so fling him out! Fling him out!

MR MACRAE [*patiently*] Mary –

MRS MACRAE Fling him out now! Now! Now!

MR MACRAE Mary, you can see Able has taken to his new wheels like a duck to water, and if he has a good job ... What job is it, Able?

ABLE Managing the supply department of Caledonian Gubernators – more responsibility and better wages than I had with Rock Fire Life.

MR MACRAE That's a better job than I ever had, Mary, so we haven't an axle to revolve on.

BETTY [*drying her eyes*] Leave Able and me alone for a bit, both of you. I've some explaining to do.

MR MACRAE True. Come on Mary.

MRS MACRAE Oh it's not fair. Not fair. After all I did for that girl – after all I was going to do for her – everybody's ganged up against me again.

ABLE *and* **BETTY** *are left facing each other.*

ABLE What was the matter?

BETTY Do you know what this is? [*She displays knitting with partly finished article of baby wear*].

ABLE [*delighted*] A baby?

She smiles and nods. They embrace.

ABLE [*amused*] We did so little!

BETTY It was enough.

ABLE You thought you were in a safe period!

BETTY Yes, it was me who led you on after deciding to be slow and careful. Then National Equilibrium fired you and I was afraid you'd feel I'd trapped you.

ABLE Poor Betty!

BETTY I didn't know what to do. Dad wanted me to terminate it ...

ABLE The bastard!

BETTY Luckily Mum was on my side – in a way. She said I must have the baby and live here and she's look after both of us – if I promised not to see you again.

ABLE The bitch!

BETTY She meant well. She'll adjust to us when we get our own house in a nice neighbourhood, and we will, won't we? We'll easily get a mortgage now, won't we?

ABLE Yes. I'm starting on Monday as a supplies manager with a staff of seventeen under me. Happy ending!

BETTY Happy beginning!

– INTERVAL –

7: SUPPLY OFFICE

A telephone rings before the light goes up on centre stage with two desks. The left faces audience and holds a word processor, telephone, empty IN and OUT trays. The right desk faces the left with front edge touching. Here a word processor, both trays and every surface carry overflowing heaps of order forms, manuals and correspondence. **MEG** *sits at this desk in profile to the audience, telephone handset to ear, patiently trying to soothe someone who is angry about something. While she talks* **BLAND** *and* **ABLE** *roll in but she ignores them until* **BLAND** *speaks to her directly.*

MEG I'm sorry, I know ... I know, I'm sorry ... Yes, I know you should have had them today, yes we promised them today but ...

Enter **BLAND** *and* **ABLE** .

BLAND Here it is, your new dominion, the nerve centre of Scottish gubernator supply.

MEG ... no, sorry, no I can't promise delivery tomorrow though I'll do my best, sorry, goodbye. [*She puts the phone down and taps rapidly on the word processor*].

BLAND [*indicating* **MEG**] This is Meg, your assistant, who has been with us for over twenty years. She knows more about gubernator supply than anyone else here – even me! Especially me, whose grandfather started the business! Isn't that right Meg?

MEG [*pausing with fingers on keyboard*] Yes?

BLAND You know more about the business than anyone else. Right?

MEG Yes! [*resumes typing*].

BLAND Not so fast! Meet Able McMann, your new boss. Put him in the picture. Show him the grips. Teach him the moves Meg and don't be too hard on him.

MEG *folds arms, looks expressionlessly at* **ABLE.**

ABLE [*trying to be nice*] I'm very glad to meet you.

MEG Hullo.

BLAND Good. I'll leave you both to get on with it. [*produces a cigarette case*] I'll have a word with Dimitri Suave of foreign orders, a tremendous character, the life and soul of any party. I'll come back later to see how you're doing and make some suggestions ... [*pauses to light a cigarette*].

The phone rings. **MEG** *lifts it.*

MEG Yes? No, I'm sorry ... I'm sorry, I know ... Yes I know we promised them for last week but ...

BLAND [*talking loudly over her*] Learn all you can from Meg but don't let her bully you! Our last supplies chief was so wholly under her thumb that we had to let him go – he didn't last a fortnight. Remember, the buck stops with you! Bye bye!

Exit **BLAND**. **ABLE** *faces* **MEG.**

MEG ... I'm sorry, I can't promise a definite delivery date before the consignment leaves our depot, but I'll do my best ... I'm sorry, that's all I can do. [*puts phone down and faces* **ABLE**] Welcome to hell.

ABLE *stares at her.*

MEG I said welcome to hell.

ABLE [*Going behind the left desk*] You're obviously telling me something but I need an explanation. [*awaits an explanation, arms folded on desktop*].

MEG [*sighing*] I'll make it short and simple. We're a long-established Scottish firm which supplies things a lot of people want, but we're losing business to an English competitor with one advantage over us.

ABLE Superior technology?

MEG No.

ABLE Better advertising?

She shakes her head in a negative.

ABLE Competitive underpricing?

MEG No. Their senior management in London lets their Scottish management get on with the job. Our Senior Management Group – I call them the Smug – draw big salaries for doing sweet damn nothing. I don't mind that. It is a fact of life that the least productive people get the most money. But our Smug aren't content with money, they feel insecure if they aren't issuing commands, so they give folk like you and me instructions that make efficiency impossible.

ABLE Which cannot be the whole story.

MEG Then forget it. Would you sign these supply forms? I can't authorize them now you're here.

She offers him a fat sheaf of papers.

ABLE [*not taking them*] Have you checked them? Are they in order?
MEG Yes.
ABLE You could issue them when I wasn't here?
MEG Yes, between bosses it's me who issues them.
ABLE Then I – your present boss – don't want to waste time signing them. Send them out as they are.
MEG [*shaking her head*] Sorry boss. If I do that the Smug will say I've taken over your job and not you – but me! – will be reprimanded.
ABLE *takes the forms and with gloomy rapidity signs and piles them up while* **MEG** *taps briskly on her keyboard. These activities continue as they talk.*
ABLE It strikes me ... that the Smug ... should have given you my job.
MEG [*nodding*] Yes.
ABLE Did they not do it because you're a woman?
MEG They didn't do it because they knew I would tell them to their faces what I've told them for years through interior memoranda which they ignore.
ABLE Why did my predecessor only last a fortnight?
MEG He was conscientious. He tried to improve things.
The phone rings on **MEG**'s *desk.*
ABLE I'll handle it! [*lifts his phone with his left hand while signing things with his right*] Yes, supplies here ... I'm sorry, I didn't know ... Yes, I can well believe it ... No, I cannot give you a new delivery date because though I am Head of Supplies I only started work today and have not yet come to grips with some hitches generated by what I am told is a new computer program, but rest assured that your problem is now top of the Caledonian Gubernator priority list. Good day.
MEG [*impressed, but still typing*] Well done. Who was it?
ABLE [*still busily signing*] Clapperclaw Service Stations.
MEG Poor souls! They're ninth on our priority list. I wish the government hadn't scrapped the hyperactive welfare scheme. It would save us time and money to have a cheap hyperactive sitting in a cubicle doing nothing but apologize over the phone. Something wrong?
She looks at **ABLE** *who now scowls at the forms in front of him, tapping them steadily with the end of his pen. She stops typing.*
MEG Is something wrong?
ABLE [*abruptly*] The woman I love is pregnant and lives with her parents. I live in a bedsit not much bigger than a cubicle in a house full of sick and elderly people. I want to marry, get a nice home, support a family. I need this job. How can I keep it?
MEG [*shrugging*] Easy. Don't do a damn thing except suck up to the senior management. Pass on their orders to your underlings without question and when chaos follows blame us for it. Entertain the Smug with all sorts of stories about our stupidity and incompetence. Never never never suggest that they change their ways. They'll think you one of them and your future here will be secure – as long as the firm lasts. I give it a year at the most. [*sighs*] And now if I can return to my work I may achieve a miracle – six-thousand double elephant gubernators delivered to Alpha Index of Coventry on time today. They're the only big company which still has faith in us and please! Finish signing these forms.
She types, **ABLE** *signs. Enter* **BLAND**, *very cheerful.*
BLAND Busy busy busy are we? Good good good. There is something you can do for me, Able. I've just had a phone call from Sir Arthur Shots, a very gallant old soldier and near cousin of Humpty Dipsy. Though three score and ten he still plays his regular eighteen holes round the Royal and Ancient and his golf chair needs a new gubernator. Knowing I am in the business he asked me to send one fast without using the normal boring supply channels. He only needs one small wee tiny semi-demi gubernator of the sort we supply to Clapperclaw Service Stations and Clapperclaw are not fast deliverers –
ABLE I know why; you see we –
BLAND Allow me to finish. What you know is less important than what you do, so tell Meg to stop what she's doing and give top priority to Arthur Shots. I hear that a truck is leaving the depot for Coventry shortly. Get Meg to send it to St Andrews first – she'll find Arthur's exact address in Who's Who. It is an honour and a privilege to be useful to such a man. [*smiles genially at* **ABLE**].
MEG *stops typing, folds arms, watches* **ABLE** *expressionlessly.* **ABLE** *shuts eyes, sucks lower lip, then opens eyes and speaks quietly but firmly.*
ABLE Mr Bland, that's impossible. That truck is delivering a huge consignment to our best client and they won't arrive as promised if we divert it to –
BLAND, *wagging a forefinger, interrupts more genially than ever.*
BLAND Nothing is impossible Able! Never let the word impossible be heard within the walls of Caledonian

Gubernators! I see you have been got at by the excellent and indispensable Miss Meg, a middle management pessimist who would sink us all into gloom if ignorant males like us did not take a broader view. Numerically speaking, yes, it is foolish to deliver six thousand double elephants later than promised so that one tiny little semi-demi is delivered on time, but priorities are not always governed by arithmetic. Sir Arthur is on the board of many important companies. Clapperclaw Services and Alpha index of Coventry could well be among them. So! Now! Do! What! I! Say!

BLAND *shows all his teeth in a grin.* **ABLE** *shuts eyes, folds arms tight, rocks to and fro.*

BLAND [*sharply*] Well?

ABLE [*loudly, without looking at* **MEG**] Do what he says.

MEG [*giving a smart military salute*] Yes sir! At once sir! I'll go and look for a Who's Who sir!

MEG *swings her chair round and leaves fast.*

BLAND [*calling after her, laughing*] My secretary will give you one Meg, hahahaha! What a weird sense of humour she has, women are inexplicable. [*He looks puzzled at* **ABLE**] Is something wrong?

ABLE *still rocks to and fro with shut eyes, tightly grasping the arms of his chair.*

BLAND [*gently and kindly*] You seem ill – can I do something to help?

BLAND *lays a kindly hand on* **ABLE**'s *arm.* **ABLE** *suddenly opens his eyes and shows his teeth in a hysterical grin.*

ABLE You can do nothing to help but vanish! [*He stands up*] Disappear! [*He shakes clenched fists and roars*] Fuck off out of here!

BLAND *recoils in terror, leaves swiftly.* **ABLE** *drops back into chair and covers face with hands.*

8: BENEFIT TRIBUNAL

Front left a white circular mat 18 inches across with a black blindfold on it, the blindfold with elastic for ease of putting on and off. Back right and angled to confront the mat, a platform high enough to lift the heads of those sitting there above the head of anyone standing below. A table on the platform has **A** *and* **B** *sitting side by side behind,* **A** *with a push-bell,* **B** *with an anglepoise lamp casting strong light on the mat – other light is comparatively dim.* **C** *and* **D** *sit one at each end of the table. All four have sheaves of typed reports and printed forms on tabletop or armrest. All four are wired to an artificial voicebox in the centre of the table so in the following dialogue it is impossible to know which one of them is speaking. It must be one who has watched* **ABLE***'s lips, but two of them are always doing this, though never the same two. Throughout this scene messages are exchanged in sign language. Directions for them are given in a different typeface because they don't interrupt the dialogue though happening at the same time, and* **ABLE** *is not aware of it.*

The scene starts with **A** *striking the push bell as* **C** *and* **D** *examine papers.*

VOICEBOX Next case – Able McMann.

ABLE *enters left and stares down at mat and then at the tribunal, unsure what to do.*

VOICEBOX Stand on that spot facing the light and we'll have no trouble reading your lips Mr McMann.

ABLE *lifts blindfold and stands where it lay, blinking into light of the anglepoise lamp as* **B** *tightens the screw so that the beam rests on* **ABLE**'s *face.*

C [*signing to* **D**] How's your head feeling now?

D [*signing back*] Horrible! Probably still as bad as yours.

A [*signing to* **C** *and* **D**] Careful! Maybe he can read us.

VOICEBOX Use the blindfold if the light hurts your eyes.

ABLE [*humbly*] Thank you. [*puts on blindfold*] Thank you, that's a lot better. Am I looking the right way again?

A [*signing to the others*] We've six others before the break. Be quick with this one.

VOICEBOX Yes. Why are you standing there Mr McMann?

ABLE Because soon I'll need money – soon I'll be penniless.

VOICEBOX You find standing gets you more sympathy than sitting down?

ABLE No!

VOICEBOX You came off the hyperactive register after holding a good desk job for six months. A recent medical report says the doctor found no muscular or nervous ailment to stop you sitting down for fourteen or fifteen hours a day – like many other hyperactives who manage to lead normal lives.

ABLE [*hesitantly*] Then that doctor ... is not a good doctor ... because he ignored what I said. I told him that when the future – when terrified of the future – I stand or walk about until I drop. If he suspected me of lying he should have got one of your snoopers – sorry one of your investigators – to learn the truth from my neighbours.

C [*signing to the others*] Oh we've a real Smart Alec here,

haven't we? This one fancies himself as a lawyer!
A He's right though. In a juster world ...
D We haven't the resources to be just.
A But in a kinder world –
D We haven't the resources to be kind.
VOICEBOX Our doctors are overworked, Mr McMann, and despite rumours to the contrary there is a limit to the number of our investigators. You have been employed twice since you came off the hyperactive register and both times left work on your first day. Why?
ABLE At Caledonian Gubernators I did not see eye to eye with the Director –
VOICEBOX So you resorted to menacing language.
ABLE Only a little! I'm not a violent man – I've no record of menacing behaviour before then –
VOICEBOX You have. Now why did you leave Hurricane Sales Service?
ABLE I was shut in a room full of teenagers, young folk who don't feel it's rude and intrusive to phone housewives and elderly folk and talk them into letting in even tougher salesmen, but I –
VOICEBOX Felt able to pick and choose. You received nineteen thousand insurance compensation for the initial injury of which nine thousand seven hundred and twelve were repaid to Social Welfare leaving nine thousand two eighty eight. What became of it?
C [*signing*] What chance do you think Iron Butterfly has for the two-thirty at Uttoxeter?
B Shut up! Some of us have to watch the bugger's mouth.
D We've seen a million poor buggers. Iron Butterfly hasn't a hope in hell.
ABLE After repaying my parents' legal expenses loan I had less than seven hundred. I've been living on that but I'm down to my last two hundred and will lose my bedsit in two or three weeks if I can't get –
VOICEBOX Won't your parents help?
ABLE They're old people living in sheltered housing and afraid of illness – with the National Health Service as it is I don't want to bother them. Do you need to ask all these questions? I've answered them again and again in forms I've filled in several times. Have you not read them?
VOICEBOX You argue very strongly for someone who wants us to think he's in a weak position.
ABLE *helplessly shrugs shoulders, shakes head.*
C [*signing*] He's no answer to that one!
A But his body language is eloquent.
ABLE [*appealing*] Surely you're paid to help people like me – not to make us feel guilty.
D [*signing*] Get rid of him.
VOICEBOX We are paid to separate scroungers and spongers from those who need help and deserve support. Your aggressiveness and rejection of job opportunities are not attitudes that deserve support. You admit that at present you do not need help since you have a room and money for rent. Should your material circumstances change in the near future you have every right to apply to us again in six weeks. Goodbye.
A *hits the push-bell,* **B** *switches off the lamp and they converse among themselves while* **ABLE** *pleads on.*
ABLE But if you don't give me cash I'll be homeless in six weeks. Without a fixed address I can't apply to you again! Your rules don't allow it. Yes I might hold on a bit longer by begging from my parents and the woman I love but I don't want to beg, I'd feel dirty, feel despicable begging, don't make me a beggar please. You seem to think I'm a tough guy but I'm not, I'm an ordinary man who did a steady nine to five job, did exactly what I was told, just like you! I paid taxes just like you do for eight years before my accident. Are you listening to me? Please? Are you?
A [*signing*] That was a tough one!
B I admired his attitude towards his parents.
D If he's not a fool we've taught him a lesson which will do him good.
C He's a fool, a bore, a snob and a weakling and we're rid of him – thank goodness – for ever.
A A year ago we would have helped him.
B Those days are gone.
C Look, he's still raving at us!
A *looks at his papers and hits the push-bell again.*
VOICEBOX Next applicant please – Jack O'Rourke.
ABLE Did you not hear what I said?
A tough guy enters left, slaps **ABLE**'s *shoulder.*
NEXT APPLICANT My turn for the blindfold mate.
ABLE *pulls blindfold off and stares at* **NEXT APPLICANT**, *open-mouthed.*

9: LOUNGE BAR

Set and actors as in Scene 1 but without **ABLE**, *and* **MISS SHY** *is crouching on a folding stool to one side, nursing on her knee a handbag* *which held the stool and trying, with small beckonings, to get the* **BARTENDER**'*s attention.*

THRUST He comes fron the shoot 'em kill 'em brigade into contract management and doesn't even know that a contract locks you into a fixed profit margin.

BLAND You told me that quite a while ago.

THRUST It still happens. Same again?

BLAND Please.

THRUST Bartender! Same again!

BARTENDER Certainly sir.

SUAVE [*intimately*] My wife mentioned you over breakfast this morning.

COY Ooh! What did she say?

SUAVE "Who's that woman in your office who dresses with unusual elegance?" I told her I knew nobody like that in my office.

COY [*smiling and placing her hand on his*] You've a wild sense of humour. I could never fall for a man who hadn't a wild sense of humour. Let's be wicked. Let's have another.

SUAVE Same again, bartender!

BARTENDER In a minute sir!

THRUST Common workmen are no trouble nowadays and soon the skilled technicians will knuckle under too. Who'll need them?

Their work will be done by Brazilian and Chinese orphans paid with handfuls of food – and grateful for it.

BLAND Thank goodness there'll always be room for our kids in administration. My turn to pay. [*pays the* **BARTENDER** *who has just served the drink*].

BARTENDER [*calling to* **SUAVE**] Two gin and tonics was it sir?

SUAVE Yes but I believe this lady should be served first – she's been waiting some time.

MISS SHY *smiles gratefully at* **SUAVE**, **COY** *pats his hand approvingly, he shrugs modestly.*

BARTENDER It's not easy to see people who are not at the usual level sir. What would you like madam?

MISS SHY A small dry sherry if it's no trouble thank you!

Enter **ABLE** *in a wheelchair, very fast. He wears a dandelion flower in his lapel and hides hysterical excitement under a cheerful manner.*

BARTENDER Is alcohol alright for someone in your condition?

MISS SHY Yes! My doctor recommends it.

ABLE [*boisterously*] There's a voice I know! Don't worry bartender, this lady is a friend of mine. Give her what she wants and me a large Glenfiddich!

BARTENDER [*smartly*] At once sir!

ABLE *sits facing* **MISS SHY** *with his back to the rest of the room. He speaks quietly to her at first and is ignored by all but* **BLAND.**

MISS SHY I'm sorry but I don't know you at all.

ABLE Never mind. I hate these selfish bastards too.

MISS SHY [*alarmed*] I don't hate anyone, what do you mean?

ABLE I'll show you if nobody's watching. Are they?

MISS SHY [*looking*] A big man over there is watching.

ABLE *looks round then waves, smiling broadly.*

ABLE A fine evening Mr Bland! Do you remember me?

BLAND [*sternly*] Indeed I do.

ABLE No hard feeling I hope, Mr Bland?

BLAND None! None! [*becomes genial*] Glad to see you looking so very much better. [*turns and talks quietly to* **THRUST**].

ABLE, *seeing nobody watching now, turns back to* **MISS SHY** *and shoots both legs out straight for a second.*

MISS SHY [*nodding gravely*] I see.

ABLE [*patting his chair arm*] I only need this contraption to get service in bars.

BARTENDER *approaches with tray of drinks, for all.* **ABLE** *puts a five-pound note on his tray.*

ABLE Keep the change, tonight I have something to celebrate. Do you remember me by the way?

BARTENDER [*staring*] Thank you sir but I can't say I do.

ABLE Forget it. [*To* **MISS SHY**] Yes, I'm celebrating tonight. Skol!

ABLE *drinks.* **BARTENDER** *serves* **SUAVE** *and* **COY**, *but thereafter watches* **ABLE** *thoughtfully.*

MISS SHY Are you drunk?

He places her glass on the floor.

ABLE Slightly. But don't worry. An hour will pass before my condition gets me into serious trouble.

He drinks.

MISS SHY Oh please don't lose control! Things get much worse if you do – I once lost control.

ABLE You haven't asked me what I'm celebrating.

MISS SHY [*concerned for him*] You mustn't lose control!

ABLE I am celebrating a new life. [*drinks*] After closing time tonight I will be a new age traveller, a nomad, gypsy, sponger, scrounger, parasite, one of Great Britain's mighty army of homeless and hopeless. [*more thoughtfully*] Tomorrow I may also be a father.

MISS SHY [*horrified*] You should be saving every penny, not buying drink.

ABLE The money I am spending is rent due to a landlord who has evicted me. If I pay him I will not only be homeless but penniless so I am giving myself a treat before taking to the road.

MISS SHY [*very quietly*] You're frightening me.

ABLE [*sincerely*] I'm sorry.

BLAND [*quietly, to* **THRUST**] All the same he makes me decidedly uneasy. Let's go.

BLAND *and* **THRUST** *start to go out, handing their glasses to the* **BARTENDER** *as they pass.*

ABLE [*boisterously*] Leaving already Mr Bland? I hoped there would be time for a wee get-together – a friendly return match for Auld Lang Syne. You definitely beat me last time.

BLAND *and* **THRUST** *leave fast.*

ABLE Another large malt please!

BARTENDER Sorry sir but you've had enough.

ABLE I'm the best judge of that –

BARTENDER *reaches for the telephone.*

ABLE Don't touch that!

BARTENDER *freezes, his fingers almost reaching the handset of the phone.* **ABLE** *gets up, walks swiftly across, rips the handset from the wall and flings it away. Then he speaks to* **SUAVE** *and* **COY** *in a loud, firm, sober voice.*

ABLE Closing time lady and gent! I'm afraid I must ask you to leave.

SUAVE Certainly certainly! [*Knocking his gin back he rushes out in abject panic*].

COY [*squealing and pursuing*] You bastard, wait for me!

MISS SHY *stands up, clutching her handbag and weeping with pity.*

BARTENDER [*grimly*] You're in trouble – serious trouble.

ABLE *grips the back of the bartender's chair and pushes it towards the exit.*

ABLE So fetch the police. Tell them I haven't a gun, haven't a knife but will put up a fight all the same – just for laughs – just for exercise. Right?

BARTENDER [*rolling off*] Right, but you really are in trouble!

ABLE *goes to* **MISS SHY**, *picks up her stool, folds it and holds it out to her.*

ABLE [*cheerfully and kindly*] Open up!

MISS SHY [*weeping and shaking her head*] You've lost control, you've lost control!

ABLE [*smiling*] I honestly think I've gained it. Open up.

MISS SHY [*opening her handbag*] I would like to stay with you but I'm too frightened! Too frightened!

ABLE [*slipping the stool inside*] Will you take a message for me? To my wife – I mean to my girlfriend, Betty Macrae.

MISS SHY *nods hard.*

ABLE She's in a maternity ward of the Queen Mother's. Tell her not to be ashamed of me because I'm not ashamed of myself! Tell her to tell our child – when it's old enough – that Daddy started life as a wimp who not even hyperactivity could change. Tell Betty that I achieved manhood through her love and the promise of a child, Betty Macrae and my child gave me the guts to be nasty and violent instead of helpless and pitiable. Tell her I am now a force to reckon with, a father to be proud of! [*Raising a clenched fist*] Hypermaniacs of the world, unite!

MISS SHY, *inspired, drops her bag and embraces him vigorously.*

MISS SHY You're wonderful – I'm staying here!

They kiss fiercely then **ABLE** *holds her away from him*

ABLE No! You must deliver my message! [*releases her*]

MISS SHY [*stooping for her handbag she looks up to him*] I will tell it to everyone!

ABLE Go, and remember, walk tall!

MISS SHY This is the happiest moment of my life.

ABLE Same here!

As **MISS SHY** *leaves, walking on tiptoe as tall as possible,* **ABLE** *dances a jig round the stage. It ends with him pushing his wheelchair off then picking up the glass of sherry.*

ABLE Clear decks for action! [*goes to the bar and sits on it, pondering*] Half an hour ago I expected to pass the night dead drunk on a cardboard mattress under the Monkland motorway. Now I'll pass it in a solid room with inside lavatory, clean blankets and regular big mugs of sweet hot milky tea at the taxpayer's expense. Why haven't other homeless folk discovered that option? Perhaps they have. Of course they have. It explains the soaring crime rate.

He drains the sherry glass in one swallow, puts it down, stands, takes a larger glass in each hand, fills them from suspended gin and whisky bottles, singing:

ABLE Scots wha hae wi' Wallace bled, Scots wham Bruce has aften led,Welcome to your gory bed, Or to victory!

He swallows the glass of whisky in three gulps. **SOUNDS** *of rapidly approaching police sirens.*

ABLE Now's the day and now's the hour, See the front o' battle lour, See approach proud Edward's power, Chains and slavery!

He swallows gin. Sirens stop. Slamming of doors. Silence. **ABLE** *puts down glass, advances in crouched posture to midstage, arms flexed, fingers hooked like claws, eyes looking left to right as he croons.*

ABLE Wha will be a traitor knave? Wha can fill a cowards grave? Wha sae base as be a slave? Let him turn and flee! [*Speaking*] Welcome, lads!

Two **POLICE** *wearing vizored helmets appear left in motorized chairs; another pair to the right. They have truncheons, handcuffs, lassoes, maybe nets. The next action must be choreographed by the cast and director, but at first their efforts to encircle him fail as he leaps and dodges, crying:*

ABLE Good ... Well done ... Yes, nearly! ... Nearly had me there! ... Oops, another near thing! ... Ouch, yah you've got me! [**POLICE** *entangle him and he goes limp*] All right I surrender, you've definitely got me. [**POLICE** *pull the ropes tighter*] Ouch – that hurts! [**POLICE** *hoist him upside down and handcuff his ankles together*] Hey there's no need – no need for this! [*A couple of* **POLICE** *drag him off by the legs followed closely by a couple pulling out truncheons. As* **ABLE** *vanishes offstage he yells in panic*:] I'm not black! I'm not black!

A sharp crack is followed by a sharp scream, another crack by another scream, a third crack by silence.

10: NEWSPAPER OFFICE

The three newspapermen face the audience side by side behind a table long enough to allow plenty of elbow room. **REPORTER** *and* **SUB** *have a screen, keyboard, cordless phone, notepad and pencil, the* **EDITOR** *only a phone. All seem tired of their jobs. The* **EDITOR** *leans as far back as possible with closed eyes and hands clasped behind head.* **REPORTER** *and* **SUB** *tap their keyboards listlessly with one hand,* **SUB** *sips from a coffee mug with the other.*

EDITOR [*without moving*] We've a hole on page five. Anything from the police?

REPORTER [*taps twice then reads*] Jobless Hypermaniac Wrecks West End Pub.

EDITOR *yawns.* **SUB** *notices.*

SUB I'm bored by jobless hypermaniacs. The whole nation's bored by jobless hypermaniacs.

EDITOR [*without moving*] Try the courts.

SUB [*puts down the mug, taps twice, reads*] Not much ... This might raise a laugh ... In magistrate court today thirty-three-year-old Able McMann of no fixed abode, no previous record, was charged with vandalising a phone etcetera. Asked how did he plead he pointed straight at the magistrate, screamed "Guilty!" and kept screaming guilty and pointing at the magistrate until dragged out. He's being held for a psychiatric report. Telephone Vandal Judges Judge?

REPORTER Not judge. Magistrate.

SUB Readers don't know the difference.

REPORTER [*reading screen*] Able McMann is the hypermaniac who wrecked Bonham's lounge last night.

EDITOR [*not moving*] How?

REPORTER I don't have that.

SUB I've got it. [*taps twice, reads*] He maliciously destroyed public telephone – used menacing language to the terror of the lieges – ejected bar staff by physical force – stole excisable liquors and challenged the police – resisted with skilful use of boxer-kicks and karate-chops which knocked four policemen out of their chairs before they managed to haul him in. Yes, and a slum landlord has charged him with absconding with a week's rent arrears.

REPORTER [*impressed*] They should have rounded it off by planting cocaine on him.

EDITOR [*opening his eyes*] He's earned more than half a column. Is his CV on the worldwide web?

REPORTER's *phone rings. He lifts and listens.* **SUB** *starts tapping and reading aloud as he taps.* **EDITOR** *sits forward, puts elbows on table midway between* **REPORTER** *and* **SUB**, *rests chin on clenched fists without looking left or right.*

SUB Good school ... Studied business at Strathclyde ... Eight years managerial post with Rock Fire Life ...

REPORTER She sounds insane but put her though anyway.

SUB [*tapping and reading*] Six years ago chair accident left him hyperactive.

REPORTER Exactly who are you?

SUB [*tapping and reading*] Through jobs aid got managerial desk with National Equilibrium. Did well, came off hyperactive register. Government ends jobs aid, end of story. [**SUB** *stops tapping and leans back*].

REPORTER [*into phone*] What message?

EDITOR [*without moving*] Wife and kids?

SUB [*eyes on screen*] Divorced. No kids.

EDITOR [*without moving*] Pity. We could use kids.

SUB To make a whole page of it?

REPORTER [*loudly into phone, waving hand to attract* **EDITOR**] Give me your number quick and I'll phone back. [*Pause*] Got it thanks. Stay there Monica. [*To* **EDITOR**, *putting down handset*] Monica Shy, calling from a payphone. She's McMann's girlfriend, a hypermaniac and loony about him. She was also with him in the pub before he tackled the police and she wants us to print his message to the universe. Ready for it?
EDITOR [*not moving*] Shoot.
REPORTER Hypermaniacs of the world unite! Social inadequates should be proud to go berserk.
EDITOR [*not moving*] Call her back and pass her to me.
All three lift handsets and clap them to their faces, **REPORTER** *after tapping digits.*
REPORTER [*into phone*] Sorry to keep you waiting Monica. Our editor Tom Hume is very interested in your boyfriend's message. Here he is.
EDITOR [*warm, oily, paternal*] It's a privilege to speak with you Monica, not many outside phone calls bring us messages of encouragement and hope. Have you given it to any other papers? [*Pause*] Several?
REPORTER *and* **SUB** *show alarm, then relief.*
EDITOR [*into phone, unruffled*] I'm not surprised they weren't interested. Most papers today are too far right for a radical message like that! The Daily Discord is the only British paper to stand up for ... for ... to stand up and be counted so we're sending a fast car to fetch you here. [*Pause*] No, don't take a taxi, travel at our expense. Where are you? Why the Queen Mother's Maternity ward? [*Pause*] Who is Betty Macrae?
A pause in which **REPORTER** *and* **SUB** *listen intently.*
EDITOR [*into phone, very slowly*] I ... seeeeee. Yes.
REPORTER *and* **SUB** *gape at each other in delighted wonder. Still listening hard* **EDITOR** *points stern finger at* **SUB** *who swiftly presses digits on his own phone.*
EDITOR [*into phone*] So Betty Macrae is about to have your boyfriend's baby?
SUB [*into phone, fast and quiet*] Hullo Jock, top priority, lift Monica Shy from Queen Mother's foyer – you'll recognize her, she'll be standing, yes she's a hypermaniac, hurry!
EDITOR [*into phone, sharply*] Twins! When? [*With effort, speaks softly*] Early this morning. What a nice surprise for everyone. [*Musically*] See you soon Monica!
All slam handsets down. **REPORTER** *and* **SUB** *laugh, spin chairs back, career round table in opposite directions, slapping hands as they pass in front of it.* **EDITOR** *resumes his central chin-on-fists pose.*
EDITOR [*loudly, without moving*] This sort of thing restores my faith in God.
SUB [*reaching for phone*] Will I tell them to hold the front page?
EDITOR [*impatient*] Don't be sodding stupid! This story is a three-day accumulator so listen hard!
He talks with abrupt head and arm movements, watched by **REPORTER** *and* **SUB** *who frequently nod.*
EDITOR Day one! Give the page lead to page four to Hyperactive McMann Runs Amok in West End Pub. Hyperactive remember, not Hypermanic or Hypermaniac, they come later. Play up the rampage. Interview threatened customers, manhandled bar staff, stoical police. If the pub interior isn't damaged show it from outside with stern worried faces in front and column heads like I Was Terrified and He Packs A Hefty Punch! Get a close-up of the wrecked telephone.
He pauses. **REPORTER** *and* **SUB** *listen intently.*
EDITOR Then – we're still Day One page five – have his parents, pals, ex-wife, explain why such a decent citizen went wrong. Get a photograph of him, even if it shows him as a toddler. Put his head in the Page One Puff captioned How McMann Went Wrong exclamation mark, but have nothing, nothing yet about his sodding bitches and bastards and message to the nation, right?
REPORTER and **SUB** [*simultaneously*] Right!
EDITOR Day Two! Full page story under four column pic of Blooming Betty with her Brace of Bastards –
REPORTER [*shocked*] Bairns surely! Bairns!
EDITOR Don't interrupt my flow, has the Macrae bitch still got the hots for the McMann geek?
REPORTER [*subdued*] Monica Shy said so.
EDITOR Great, because on Day Two the Discord is all for them. We emphasize her sexiness and loyalty –
SUB [*inspired*] Eat Your Heart Out Normals! Blooming Betty Stands By Her Hypermanic Bonker McMann.
EDITOR Use a front page splash by Senga Dishart saying McMann shows the plight of the hyperactive poor under Humpty Dipsy's welfare cuts. A lot of them will like that because most of them are sodding Labour voters, but Betty's story ...
Suddenly inspired he grabs the phone.

EDITOR [*to* **REPORTER**] Watch this. You'll learn something. [*Into phone*] Tom Hume. Put me through to someone in charge of a Queen Mother's post-delivery ward. I don't know who – they have Betty Macrae, mother of twins in care.. [*To* **REPORTER** *and* **SUB** *who are watching him, fascinated*] I hope she's got big tits.

REPORTER Likely at this stage.

EDITOR Let's give the Tories something too! Frank McNasty could mention in his column that he doesn't know why colleagues are sentimentalizing over a violent criminal and his slut who ... [*pauses, then into phone: warm, oily, paternal*] Hello nurse, this is Tom Hume, editor of the Daily Discord. I want to congratulate you and the Queen Mother's for excellent treatment of Betty Macrae and her two lovely bairns. [*pauses, then chuckles*] Oh, not much escapes us. The Discord is about to start a campaign for natural motherhood. Is Betty breastfeeding her wee weans? [*brief pause*] Good! No danger of milk shortage? [*brief pause*] Good, but that's not my main reason for phoning. [*on an intimate note*] Perhaps Betty told you that the father of her twins is in serious trouble? [*brief pause*] No? Never mind. I'm phoning because I have great news for her, news that will take a great weight off her mind. Now, I don't want to intrude, and if she's asleep I'll try some other day but ... You'll see? Good.

EDITOR [*to* **REPORTER** *and* **SUB**] Big tits in working order. Now to arrange interview and photograph.

SUB [*pondering*] Where will we put the picture?

REPORTER [*sarcastically*] Put her on page three.

With the briefest of delays **EDITOR** *and* **SUB** *give a thumbs-up sign.*

EDITOR [*into phone: warm, oily, paternal*] Hello Betty, Tom speaking, Tom Hume editor of the Daily Discord. Monica Shy tells me she recently gave you a message from your man Able, yes? [*pause*] Yes and now he's in police custody but I want you to know that we in the Discord think society has treated him horribly and we're coming out strong for him – [*brief pause*] – yes – [*brief pause*] – yes but – [*longer pause in which he grimaces to* **REPORTER** *and* **SUB**, *indicating he endures endless drivel by rotating forefinger against side of head*] Don't worry, Betty, about money for a good defence lawyer, leave that with me, I'm phoning because we're starting to defend him tomorrow with a strong publicity drive and here's where we need your help. I know this is a very hard time for you, a wonderful time but an exhausting time and I don't want to tire you in any way at all so this is what I'll do. Hector Brash and Jenny Aw-Things! Do these names mean anything to you? [*brief pause*] He's Scotland's photographer – photographer to the queen – Jenny's a wonderful reporter and a very sympathetic woman. From nine in the morning to nine at night I'll have them sitting in the Queen Mother's waiting room and if, at any time, you can spare four or five minutes ask your ward nurse to invite them in. [*pause, then chuckles*] Of course it will cost the Discord a lot of money but money doesn't matter, your happiness and Able's happiness are what matters ... [*pause*] ... You think you can? [*brief pause*] Bless you Betty! You're a brave good woman. Bye bye now. [**EDITOR** *clashes down the phone, lies back in the chair with eyes shut, hands clasped behind head as at first*] Send Brash and Aw-Things straight to her ward at nine tomorrow.

SUB [*wildly clapping hands*] Great, Tom! Great! Great!

EDITOR [*without moving*] I was wrong about you, Henry.

REPORTER How, Tom?

EDITOR You're a good networker but I thought you hadn't the guts to be a real newsman. I was wrong. [*chuckles*] That notion of an unmarried mother's tits on the wank page was a stroke of genius! A real human interest story under the tart pic on the page three wank page – the Discord will be making history. The Discord will be setting new standards.

SUB What if she doesn't look like a sexpot?

EDITOR Trust Hector Brash! With his angles and lighting and lab work any bitch with big boobs can be page three fodder.

REPORTER [*glumly*] I meant it as a joke.

EDITOR [*sits up, grinning*] The greatest things in the world start as jokes, laddie! Christianity was a joke before the Romans made it a multinational corporation.

REPORTER [*sighing*] What about Day Three? McMann will be out on bail by then.

EDITOR That's right, the big boys will be after him – sleuths from the Moon, the Fanfare, the Chimes, the Fender. They can have him. We won't need him then, or Betty Macrae. We'll have the story of Bonker McMann's affair with Monica Shy, first apostle and bearer of his message – [*spreads his arms wide*] – hypermaniacs of the world, unite!

REPORTER She said hypermanics.

EDITOR Are you sure? Is she sure? Can anyone now be sure of what McMann said in a moment of excitement? The Press Council won't reprimand us for the difference of one letter.

SUB [*inspired*] Arch-Hypermaniac Able McMann Calls For Revolution! – all over the front page.

REPORTER So you're dropping him in the shit?

EDITOR [*nodding*] With the biggest splash since the sinking of the Belgrano.

SUB [*snapping fingers*] Gotcha!

EDITOR We'll treat his message as a law and order issue. The Discord is on the side of the people against forces of oppression but cannot support a lunatic leftist plotting to overturn society.

REPORTER Maybe a hyperactive union wouldn't want to overturn society – just help its members.

EDITOR [*warmly and paternally*] The Discord's social mission, Henry, is putting excitement into dull lives. Subtle distinctions are for prosperous snobs who read the Chimes or the Fender. Your future is with us. [*pats his shoulder*] You discovered Able McMann. You gave me Monica Shy. You thought of how to present Betty Macrae. You're going to get a whacking big bonus.

REPORTER [*humbled and grateful*] Thanks Tom.

Phone rings. **SUB** *lifts and listens.*

SUB She's at the front desk.

EDITOR Send her up.

SUB [*into phone*] Send her up.

REPORTER [*sighing*] I'm sorry for her.

EDITOR [*sighing*] Yes, poor Monica. It's a rotten world but we didn't make it. God made it. [*leans back with folded arms*] The best we can do is preserve our honour. We never feel ashamed if we preserve our honour.

REPORTER *and* **SUB** *stare at him startled.*

SUB What is honour, Tom?

He really wants to know.

EDITOR Doing the job you have chosen as well as you can do it.

REPORTER *and* **SUB** *nod solemnly.* **EDITOR** *suddenly spins his chair back.*

EDITOR She's here. Take note.

EDITOR *rolls to right round the table as* **MISS SHY** *enters front left, walking as tall as when she left the lounge bar. They meet centre front as* **REPORTER** *and* **SUB** *lift pencils, tap keyboards, peer at screens and seem to take notes from them. They only do so when* **MISS SHY** *speaks.*

EDITOR [*reaching up to shake her hand*] Welcome Monica! You're looking as good as I expected. No wonder Able fell for you!

MISS SHY [*confused*] He didn't. He doesn't even know my name. I didn't know his until Betty Macrae told me.

EDITOR But you like him?

MISS SHY I'll love him forever. All my life I've been ashamed of my working legs. He cured me of that. I'll never be ashamed again.

REPORTER *and* **SUB**, *scribbling, exchange glances.*

EDITOR [*quickly*] So now you're shameless, well Able's obviously a man of great charm, immense charisma, the natural leader of a mighty movement. The Discord will pay you – hm – five hundred for exclusive rights to your story of Able and his call for hyperactive unity.

MISS SHY [*indignant*] I don't want money!

EDITOR I know, but think of the help you could give Able at his next court appearance. He's destitute. Will Betty Macrae help him?

MISS SHY Yes! She loves him too!

EDITOR [*shaking head*] You're a cruel girl, Monica. Unless Betty's a very rich woman she'll need all her savings to support Able's weans. And he won't get much help from legal aid nowadays.

MISS SHY *frowns hard at* **EDITOR** *for a moment. All wait on her response. It is sudden.*

MISS SHY He won't get very much help out of five hundred pounds!

EDITOR Good! How much do you want?

MISS SHY [*troubled*] I know so little about these things!

EDITOR Ten hundred.

MISS SHY Perhaps I should consult somebody else before committing myself …

EDITOR Miss Shy, we are the only paper interested in giving the world Able's message! But since it's a hopeful message – and because we admire your guts – we offer twelve hundred for exclusive rights and not a penny more.

MISS SHY [*suddenly bold*] Fifteen hundred!

EDITOR Ouch, this hurts! I'll have to take advice! [*To* **REPORTER** *and* **SUB**] What do you say boys? Should she get fifteen?

REPORTER and **SUB** [*together*] Yes!

EDITOR Outnumbered three to one. Miss Shy, you've beat me. Put it there! [*shakes hands with her*].

MISS SHY [*astonished*] That's the first bargain I've ever struck.
EDITOR Now Monica, I feel distinctly hungry. So must you. We'll discuss details of our campaign over a meal. Working legs go faster than wheels indoors so go down to the front desk, order a car for Tom Hume and wait inside when it comes. I won't be far behind. Off you go!
MISS SHY *hesitates, puzzled by his abruptness. He smiles and nods at her.*
EDITOR [*oily, paternal*] Off! You! Go!
She nods and walks briskly out. **REPORTER** *looks after her gloomily,* **EDITOR** *impassively,* **SUB** *grins.*
EDITOR [*after a pause*] Poor Monica. She was never taught to think in thousands.
SUB Never give a sucker an even break! [*laughs heartily*].
EDITOR [*to* **REPORTER**] Shocked are you?
REPORTER Less than I'd have been an hour ago. [*sighs*].
EDITOR [*with approval*] You're learning. Tell Brash and Aw-Things what to do tomorrow. Have an exclusive rights contract ready for signature when I bring her back. [*to* **SUB**] Start internetting! Find the right addresses then send Snout, Muzzle, Hatchett and Killiebunkie to interview McMann's parents, pals, ex-wife etcetera. [*rolls offstage saying triumphantly*] The story of Able McMann and his doxies will be launched, wrapped up and trashed before next week's royal divorce. It's a wonderful thing to be stitching the seamless garment of life's rich tapestry.
SUB *taps busily on keyboard and without stopping glances sideways at* **REPORTER** *who slumps at the table, hand supporting head.*
SUB [*busily tapping*] What's up?
REPORTER [*without moving*] He's wrong about God.
SUB Eh? [*frowning but still tapping*].
REPORTER [*preparing to tap*] God didn't make this world. We make it.
SUB [*tapping*] Maybe, but it's too late for us to change it now.
REPORTER *taps, stares at screen, taps again, stares again then seizes telephone.*
REPORTER [*into phone*] Front desk? MacFarlan of editorials here. The chief is on the way out. Catch him before he leaves and put him on to me. [*to* **SUB**, *putting down phone*] Able McMann is now at the Western Infirmary. He had a massive heart attack in his police cell two hours ago.
SUB [*overjoyed, flinging his arms up*] Glory, glory, hallelujah!

11: SURGICAL THEATRE SHADOW PLAY

Low back lighting casts silhouettes of **ABLE** *prone on low central table, and to one side a structure of cylinders, bottles, tubes, dials, wires with* **SISTER** *adjusting valve on a suspended bottle. A rubber tube runs from a cylinder to a mask which* **ANAESTHETIST** *holds over* **ABLE**'*s face. On opposite side* **HOUSE OFFICER** *sits observing him beside* **NURSE** *who is arranging instruments on a tray.*
SOUND: *hiss of gas and murmur of conversation.*
Enter **SURGEON** *who rolls into space behind* **ABLE.** **NURSE** *hands* **SURGEON** *rubber gloves.* **SURGEON** *pulls them on saying:*
SURGEON So this is Able McMann. The eyes of the media are on us! We must not do less than our usual best. What, Mrs Anaesthetist, is the patient's condition?
ANAESTHETIST Steady, Mr McKinnon.
SURGEON Colour?
ANAESTHETIST Good.
SURGEON Pulse?
ANAESTHETIST Regular sinus rhythm.
SURGEON Blood gases?
HOUSE OFFICER Normal.
SURGEON Let's open him up. Scalpel.
NURSE *hands it. He leans forward and makes one strong, steady vertical incision, hands scalpel to nurse and pulls edges of cut open with hands.*
SOUND: *amplified beat of a human heart.*
SURGEON Forceps ... retractor ... clamp ... sutures ... swabs ...
NURSE *hands him these. His fingers are busy within the chest.* **HOUSE OFFICER** *leans over, watching closely from the other side.*
SURGEON Suction ... damn!
HOUSE OFFICER What's the problem?
SOUND: *heart rhythm accelerates.*
ANAESTHETIST [*consulting dials*] Blood pressure falling!
SURGEON Open up the drip. Run in haemocell and FFP.
SISTER *and* **ANAESTHETIST** *turn valves.*
SURGEON [*muted triumph*] Aha! A minor haemmorage. Well ... maybe not so minor. [*With sudden urgency*] Diathermy! Fry those bleeders!
NURSE *hands instrument to* **HOUSE OFFICER** *who employs it in the cavity.*
SOUND: *sizzle.*
HOUSE OFFICER *returns instrument to nurse.*
SURGEON [*rapidly*] Cross-match eight units of packed cells! House Officer! Insert a long line for rapid access. Large cannula. Move it!

From structure with monitor screen **SISTER** *passes a cable ending in needle to* **HOUSE OFFICER**, *who inserts it into vein of patient's neck.*
SOUND: *heartbeat becomes slow and hesitant.*
SURGEON [*grumbling*] More suction Sister. Hurry, it's like a swamp in here.
HOUSE OFFICER What's happening Mr McKinnon? Why has the patient gone off?
SURGEON [*working busily*] Unstable myocardium. Or CVA with coning. Or idiosyncratic hypersensitivity reaction – common among hyperactives.
SOUND: *loud bleeping from monitors.*
SURGEON Is that VF?
SISTER Afraid so.
SURGEON Right. I'm going to shock him. The defibrillator! [*takes it from* **NURSE**] Charging ... Ready ... Stand clear!
SOUND: *loud electric sizzle.*
ABLE'S *body convulses, lies still.*
SURGEON [*bending closer*] No good. He's still fibrillating. IV lignocaine! Stat!
SISTER *lifts hypodermic syringe and injects into the line into neck.*
SOUND: *heartbeat stops.*
SURGEON Monitor?
HOUSE OFFICER [*staring at box in structure*] He's flat-lining.
SURGEON Dammit, inject intra-cardiac adrenaline!
NURSE *passes syringe to* **HOUSE OFFICER** *who leans forward and injects it into heart.*
SURGEON Well? Well?
ANAESTHETIST Not a blip. We're losing him.
SURGEON [*grimly*] Open massage is our only chance, move fast, scalpel, forceps, retractor, clamp, suture, swabs, anything!
HOUSE OFFICER *and* **SISTER** *manipulate things in cavity.* **SURGEON**'s *regular elbow movements show he is squeezing the heart manually.*
SOUND: *hesitantly the heartbeat starts again.*
NURSE He's coming up!
SURGEON More bicarb!
SOUND: *heartbeat becomes slow but firm.*
ANAESTHETIST Sinus rhythm is restored!
SISTER *turns to consult monitor.*
SISTER Observations stable, respiration spontaneous – you've done it Mr McKinnon!
SURGEON *withdraws from the table, pulling off mask.*
SURGEON [*wearily, to* **HOUSE OFFICER**] Close him up. [*wearily, to* **SISTER**] Drinks all round.
The **SISTER** *rolls out.*
ANAESTHETIST [*pulling off mask and clapping hands cheerfully*] Yes, drinks all round! He's alive! You've saved him!
SURGEON [*yawning and shrugging wearily*] More or less.
The **HOUSE OFFICER** *is stitching up* **ABLE**, *helped by* **NURSE** *as* **SISTER** *returns with tray of glasses and bottle of spirits,* **ADMINISTRATOR** *close behind.*
SOUND: *heartbeat fades into silence.*
SISTER Mr McKinnon, the Senior Administrator wants a word.
SURGEON [*incredulous*] You! Why are you here? Administrators bugger off home at half past four.
SENIOR ADMINISTRATOR [*unperturbed*] I'm interested in this case because –
SURGEON [*stripping off gloves*] Next of kin are you?
ADMINISTRATOR [*patiently*] – because the Secretary of State is interested in this case.
SURGEON Wants to chuck him back in jail does he?
ADMINISTRATOR [*impatient*] Of course not – this is a clear case for clemency. The health service will be highly embarrassed if this particular chap dies on us. A lot of wets are claiming he's a martyr to some sort of social breakdown. Will he die on us?
SISTER *has filled glasses.* **SURGEON** *lifts and contemplates one.*
SURGEON Not at once. The operation failed but the patient survived.
ADMINISTRATOR [*testily*] What does that mean?
SURGEON The heart stopped long enough to starve the brain of oxygen. He is in a coma which could last days, weeks, years – or until someone turns off his drip-feed. Your health! [*raises his glass*].
ADMINISTRATOR The Secretary of State won't like that at all. Our private investors won't like it much either. Is there nothing you can do?
SURGEON Yes, I can drink their healths. Health to all of us! [*drinks*].

ALTERNATIVE SCENE 11

The **POLITICIAN** *sits gloomily nursing a balloon of brandy.* **HIGH COURT JUDGE** *enters with similar glass, smiling. His presence is acknowledged with a weary nod.*
JUDGE [*playfully*] Does something depress us?
POLITICIAN [*gloomily*] It does.
JUDGE Are the initials Ay Em?

POLITICIAN Yes. Excitement about the Able McMann case is mounting at the wrong time for us. The public were bored by the plight of the hyperactive poor until the damned Daily Discord made it interesting again.

JUDGE [*slyly teasing him*] The Chimes says nationwide interest in McMann has nothing to do with his disease – it merely shows a widespread middle-class dread of unemployment and failing pension funds.

POLITICIAN [*grimly nodding*] Quite so. It's an issue that might force a change of government.

JUDGE [*chuckling*] Nonsense! The middle class knows which side its bread is buttered. It'll never restore anything you destroy.

POLITICIAN In this case it may. In this case we may – just for a while. I told the press that McMann was only destitute because he hadn't explored all available benefit channels. This caused such a spate of enquiries that Social Welfare is under pressure to restore some former benefits. Did you see McMann's women on Cosmorama last night?

JUDGE [*nodding*] The shy hypermanic was obviously deranged but his former social worker and the mother of his children spoke well.

POLITICIAN [*sighing*] We can no longer dismiss his supporters as loony leftists. Eye Tee of National Equilibrium has spoken out for him.

JUDGE [*puzzled*] Why does the head of a respectable British company resort to such cynically exploitational advertising?

POLITICIAN National Equilibrium needs a caring image to distract from its child labourers in the Caribbean.

JUDGE Indeed? I have shares in that company. Any news from the hospital?

POLITICIAN None. He's still in a coma. They don't know when or if he'll emerge from it. He could stay that way for weeks, months, years before they pull the plug on him.

JUDGE Might that not happen sooner rather than later? Accidentally, I mean?

POLITICIAN A stupid idea. He must not be made a martyr. That's how movements start.

JUDGE [*emphatically*] No movement!

POLITICIAN Nip it in the bud!

JUDGE Return Able McMann to decent obscurity by the shortest possible route. We won't prosecute.

POLITICIAN [*wearily*] Yes an obvious case for clemency. God damn him let's order lunch.

12: HOSPITAL WARD

DOCTOR, **BETTY**, **MANAGER**, **EDITOR** *and every other available member of the cast execpt* **MISS SHY** *stand in darkness round a bed with* **ABLE** *in it.*

SOUND: *the slow, steady ticking of a clock. After half a minute the Westminster chimes sound the three-quarter hour. There is a moment of silence, then a very brief flash of light shows most of the cast standing round a bed.*

BETTY'S VOICE [*in darkness*] He blinked! He blinked!

SOMEONE ELSE'S VOICE [*in darkness*] His eyes are still shut.

DOCTOR'S VOICE [*in darkness*] There was definite eye movement. There is definite eye movement!

Light comes on. **ABLE** *blinks at audience from his hospital bed, centre stage. He wears hospital gown, is propped up on pillows, with drip-feed into bandaged right arm from suspended bottle.* **DOCTOR** *stands on drip-feed side with fingers on* **ABLE**'s *pulse.* **BETTY** *sits on other side with her hand on* **ABLE**'s *other hand. Gathered round is everyone else in the play except* **MISS SHY**. **MANAGER** *is close to* **BETTY**'s *side.* **EDITOR**, *with notebook and pen, is on edge of group on* **DOCTOR**'s *side, scribbling from time to time.* **ABLE** *looks from side to side then his gaze fixes on* **BETTY**. *He opens his mouth, tries to speak, fails to speak, licks his lips and tries again.*

ABLE [*slowly and feebly*] Hull ... hullo Betty.

BETTY Oh Able! [*She weeps with joy*].

ABLE [*puzzled*] Then ... this isn't prison is it? Why ... why are all these people here? [*feebly gestures to them*].

BETTY They're all friends and you're in a proper hospital and you'll never go to prison again!

ABLE [*still confused*] Why ... How long was I asleep?

BETTY [*weeping*] A long time! A long time!

DOCTOR [*briskly*] You've been in a coma for seven months and sixteen days. I'm glad you've come out of it, we need this bed for someone else.

DOCTOR *detaches drip-feed, swabs* **ABLE**'s *arm and puts elastic bandage on drip-entry-point during the following speeches.*

ABLE [*shaking head*] Seven months ... don't cry Betty ... Eye Tee, why are you here?

MANAGER To tell you that a desk in Quality Control is yours whenever you return to us. National Equilibrium is a company which cares.

EDITOR [*making note*] The Daily Discord will tell the universe that!

MANAGER Thanks!

EDITOR And you have no money worries, Able. The

Daily Discord has a small fortune in a bank account for you.

ABLE [*perplexed*] The Daily Discord ...

EDITOR [*chuckling*] The British Press is as sentimental as the British public. After your stroke we started a sympathy fund to give you the best health care money could buy. You've more than fourteen thousand left.

BETTY Enough down-payment for a mortgage on a bungalow in Milngavie!

ABLE [*radiantly happy*] With later, perhaps, a holiday home in Arran!

DOCTOR [*warningly*] Less general excitement please. Stand back, I have tests to make.

All but the **DOCTOR** *withdraw a little,* **BETTY** *waving to* **ABLE** *reassuringly.*

DOCTOR [*to* **ABLE**] Raise your right arm.

ABLE *slowly does so.*

DOCTOR Drop it ... [*feels* **ABLE***'s pulse*] ... Now try the left.

ABLE *lifts and moves the left arm.*

DOCTOR Good. Drop it. Are you able to sit up? [*stands back slightly*].

ABLE, *pushing with his arms, sits clear of the supporting pillows.* **BETTY** *gasps with delight, others murmur approval.* **DOCTOR** *flings clothes aside exposing* **ABLE***'s legs.*

DOCTOR Can you get your feet to the floor?

With great effort **ABLE** *gets feet to the floor and sits on the bed edge, gasping for breath.* **DOCTOR** *leans forward, lifts* **ABLE**'s *right leg and supports it on his lap.*

DOCTOR [*holding* **ABLE***'s toes*] Wiggle your toes.

ABLE *strains.*

DOCTOR [*holding* **ABLE***'s ankle*] Flex your ankle.

ABLE *strains.*

DOCTOR [*gripping calf*] Can you raise your knee?

ABLE [*straining*] No!

DOCTOR *solemnly lowers* **ABLE**'s *foot to the floor. Everyone stares at the* **DOCTOR** , *hopefully.*

DOCTOR [*solemnly*] It's perhaps rather early to say but I believe he is almost completely paralysed from the waist down.

EVERYONE Hooray!

While others shake hands, slap each others shoulders, laugh or grin, **EDITOR** *grins and scribbles,* **ABLE** *shakes his head in wondering astonishment at his good luck,* **BETTY** *rolls round the bed to him. Only* **DOCTOR** *stays impassive.*

DOCTOR [*loudly, clapping hands*] Chair!

A wheelchair more excitingly modern than any we have seen is pushed so forcefully on stage that it stops near the bed. **DOCTOR** *and* **BETTY** *help* **ABLE** *into it.*

ABLE [*wondering*] When I remember all that's happened to me ... when I remember the years between my road accident and waking up just now ... they seem, apart from meeting you Betty dear ... [*squeezes her hand*] ... they seem a nightmare. An impossible nightmare!

BETTY But you're awake at last and this is real!

She embraces him. Widespread emotion. **EDITOR** *pockets notebook, advances to front stage and addresses audience.* **ABLE** *and* **BETTY** *continue embracing. The rest of the company politely turn their backs on them and attend to* **EDITOR**, *standing left and right of him.*

EDITOR Ladies and gentlemen, you may notice that this play has no hero. Able McMann is just an ordinary man who started life a bit luckier than most folk and by sheer accident got worse for a while. But though we have no hero you perhaps think of me as a bit of a villain –

ANYONE ELSE Surely Humpty Dipsy is the villain!

EDITOR Nonsense. Prime Ministers haven't the strength to be villains. They just do what stock exchanges let them. No, I am the one consciously selfish guy in this play and I'm proud of it. Our happy ending was made possible by me – me and the Daily Discord.

MISS SHY [*yelling offstage*] No! No! No! No!

MISS SHY, *walking tall, strides on with a placard saying HYPERMANICS OF THE WORLD UNITE! She glares from the company to the audience.*

MISS SHY [*loudly*] This is NOT a happy ending! It is NOT! It is NOT!

EDITOR [*to audience*] Happy or not, this is definitely ...

THE WHOLE CAST EXCEPT MISS SHY *in unison*: The! End!

The lights go out, then full lighting is restored to show the cast, with all who are able to stand bowing to very great applause.

BUILT IN 1862, Kelvinside and Botanic Church was once the most western of three noble churches with conspicuous spires along Great Western Road. In 1972 the congregation was now too few for so great a building, so joined the congregation of Hillhead Parish Church. The building was a bible college for sixteen years, then for four years stood derelict under a Historic Scotland preservation order until two groups offered to buy. One, keeping the building's outer shell, would have filled it with luxury flats, but the group that bought it belonged to Colin Beattie, publican who turned it into the Oran Mor arts and leisure centre. Oran Mor is Gaelic for *the great music*, meaning pibroch or Highland bagpipe music, but also the music of mankind and universal nature.

For more than a century the nave of the former church had the highest ceiling of any enclosed space in Glasgow. A new floor was made at the level of the old gallery, leaving room beneath for a big ground floor pub, with above it a lofty auditorium that has since been used for concerts, dances, banquets, conferences and a meeting of the Scottish Parliament. But in 2004 the Oran Mor lunch hour theatre *A Play, A Pie and A Pint* started performing there six days a week between one and two pm. Colin Beattie employed Dave MacLennan to commission and produce new one-act plays, despite MacLennan's fear that the theatre would die of thin audiences. Colin reassured him, "It will get better houses in the second year," but the theatre got full houses from the start. Pints were provided by the Oran Mor bar staff, pies or vegetarian pasties by the restaurant staff, plays from such well-known Scots authors as Peter MacDougall, William MacIlvanney, Liz Lochhead, Jackie Kay, and many by authors in Scotland whose plays would otherwise never have been professionally staged in their homeland.

At that time I was decorating the apse of the auditorium on scaffolding invisible to the audiences, sometimes stopping work to watch the plays, but usually following it with my ears while continuing to paint. This theatre got me thinking as a playwright again, so I wrote *Goodbye Jimmy*, another attempt at justifying the ways of God to man. It was produced in 2006 with Paddy Cunneen the director, John Mulkeen as Jimmy, Sean Scanlon as the Head.

Early in the 1980s Liz Lochhead, Tom Leonard, Jim Kelman and I had successful revues staged in the Tron, Glasgow, and The Pleasance, Edinburgh. The first had my short sketch of a maddeningly stale marriage. In 2007, maddened by adverts on the Classic FM station, I enlarged this into *Midgieburgers*. With Paddy Cunneen directing again this had Sean Scanlon as **HE**, Louise Ludgate as **SHE**, Andy Gray as **JACK**.

The Pipes! The Pipes! was suggested by remarks overheard in several local pubs. It was too short for performance before I had another short play to go with it. I will exlpain later how the Scottish and London BBC inspired the fourth play.

CAST

THE HEAD Tall, elderly, fit. He wears sandals with socks, slacks, sweater under a green dressing gown, untied, with a mobile phone in the pocket. His accent is working class Scots honed by a university education. He has the relaxed, slightly amused manner of one who knows everything. He sits on a tabletop which he only leaves twice during the play, but can twist and turn on it in any relaxed way that seems natural to an athletic, playful old man.

JIMMY Young, handsome, careworn. He wears a white shirt outside black trousers. His accent is crisp Dublin Irish, his manner usually cool and sometimes icy. He feels the Head owes him help and dislikes being treated like anyone else.

SET

The backdrop is a screen filled by a large projection of the Stephen Hawking's website video The Universe In A Nutshell, played slightly slower than the original.

Stage left, a small, elegant imitation antique table with an open laptop on it. The screen, facing the audience, also has an image of the same film, playing slightly faster than the image on the backdrop. A swivel chair stands before the table, a waste bin beside it.

Stage right against the backdrop and partly masking it, a large blackboard with sticks of chalk on the ledge and this chalked upon it:

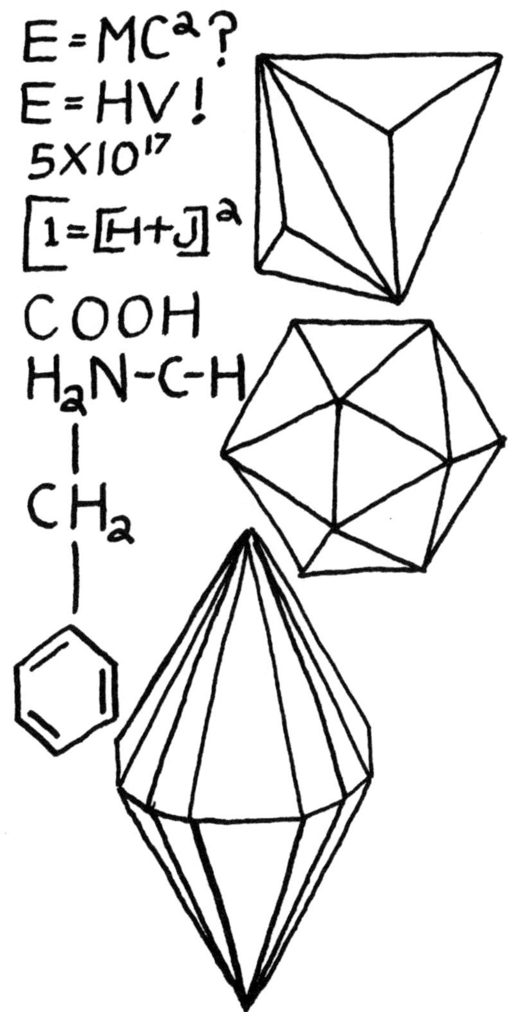

Stage front but nearer the right, the large table where **THE HEAD** *sits beside a terrestrial globe of the sort lit from inside and three cardboard models of platonic solids. The largest is an octahedron about 30 inches across painted bright yellow, with short projecting rod for ease of handling. There is an orange cube about a foot square, on which rests a tetrahedron, each side about 7 inches. The tetrahedron is painted white at the four apexes, has a large irregular blue patch in the middle of each surface, and areas of green and brown between white and blue.*

SOUND: *Opening bars of Thus Spake Zarathustra as in 2001: A Space Odyssey.*

A darkness in which we see large moving images of nebulae on the backdrop, the smaller image of something similar on the laptop stage left, the globe of the world stage right. The **HEAD** *enters left and is seen as a silhouette against the backdrop, which he pauses to consider for a moment, before going to sit on the big table.*

Cut **SOUND** *as light comes up.* **HEAD** *sits contemplating backdrop, thoughtfully sucking a thumb. After a moment mobile phone rings. He unpockets it, listens, speaks with an air of resignation.*

HEAD Right, let him in. [*Pockets phone, continues contemplating blackboard*].

JIMMY *enters left carrying briefcase, stands watching the* **HEAD** *for a while, sighs, lays briefcase on desk, then turns and waits patiently with folded arms.*

HEAD [*at last*] Aye, aye. There you are. [*turns slightly, speaks with ironic courtesy*] To what do I owe the pleasure of this visit?

JIMMY You won't answer my e-mails.

HEAD [*gesturing to blackboard*] I've a lot of other things to think about, Jimmy.

JIMMY [*ironically*] Life on other worlds?

HEAD Yep.

JIMMY Any luck with it?

HEAD Nope. [*waves hand to backdrop*] I've produced a lot of microbes in submarine volcanic vents, but climate changes keep wiping them out before they even evolve into annelid worms. A planet supporting much life needs a lot of water and a steady temperature half way between absolute zero and boiling. You can't get that without a near neighbour as big as Jupiter to hoover up the huge meteors, a satellite like your moon to grab most of the others. In this universe [*waves hand to backdrop*] the chance of me getting a planet like that are a million squared to one against.

JIMMY [*intensely, not loudly*] But you got one! Why turn your back on it? The only world rich in all kinds of life? Some with the brain to grasp your intention and I am not talking about whales.

HEAD [*smiling*] Calm down Jimmy.

JIMMY I am perfectly calm and don't call me Jimmy.

HEAD [*amused*] Do you prefer your ancient titles O Lucifer, son of the morning? Prometheus, bringer of fire?

JIMMY [*seeing the joke, but wistfully*] King of the Jews. Prince of Peace.

HEAD [*wagging a forefinger*] Prince of Darkness! Loki! Kali!

JIMMY [*delicately savouring each syllable*] Meph–Is–Toph–El–Ease.

HEAD [*in broad Scots*] Auld Nick! [*puts fists on brow with raised forefingers wagging, drops hands and broad Scots accent and shrugs*] I've been called some queer names too.

JIMMY [*not placated*] So why Jimmy?

HEAD It suits my accent.

JIMMY Why talk like a Scot?

HEAD [*serious for once*] I still get messages from that world of yours, messages from lonely, desperate people who want help. They demand help. These impossible demands ...

JIMMY Are called prayers!

HEAD [*raising his voice*] You should stop them reaching me! These impossible demands [*slight pause*] are mostly from mothers ...

JIMMY [*nodding*] Mothers worry you.

HEAD [*strongly*] I cannot break natural laws that keep this universe running! I cannot stop fire from burning babies and wee kids just because their skin is burned off by homicidal idiots obeying orders! [*more quietly*] When I answer people's ... [*hesitates*] ... prayers in a Scots accent they know I cannot be a strong loving father who works miracles. They know they havnae a hope in Hell.

JIMMY Then why not sound American? [*USA accent*] Like Dubya?

HEAD [*turning to globe and sadly touching North America*] Don't depress me. I once had hopes of the USA.

JIMMY [*brightly*] Why not sound like a Scottish Prime Minister with an English accent? He thinks you're one of his fans.

HEAD [*face in hands*] Don't sicken me. [*drops hands, sighs*] Supernatural folk are only heard when they use other folk's voices. You sound Irish because you like to be liked, and (IRA apart) the Southern Irish accent usually does sound friendly to people outside Ireland. But [*calmly but coarsely*] God the Father must sook up to Naebody. Naebody.

JIMMY [*after a pause, calmly*] Do you talk Scottish to me because I too haven't a hope in Hell?

HEAD [*looking straight at him*] Yes. But it won't stop you saying what you want to say, so [*resigned*] say on MacDuff.

JIMMY [*opening briefcase and removing a sheaf of papers*] Here are printouts of the e-mails you ignored.

HEAD Bin them. I know what they say because I know everything. Everything.

JIMMY But you don't pay attention to everything so [*brandishes papers*] attend to these!

HEAD [*patiently*] They say governments with enough nuclear weapons to kill everything bigger than a cockroach are working to deliver more, while planning more nuclear power stations to profit banks and investors when the oil runs out.

JIMMY They are also fighting wars, and threatening to fight them, to stop poorer nations doing exactly the same.

HEAD [*smiling*] Miss Jean Brodie's morality: "Do not do as I do, little girls, do as I say." [*shakes head*] Don't let the politicians fool you. The United States are not afraid of any other single nation fighting it. It zapped Saddam Hussein because he had started selling Iraqi oil for euros instead of dollars. Bush and Blair needed a lying excuse for that war because most folk nowadays dislike fighting for commercial profit. Iraq now sells its oil for dollars again. Iran now also looks like selling its oil on the free market, so naturally the United States is threatening Iran too.

JIMMY [*sitting down in chair*] Iran is ruled by fundamentalists. They whipped a boy of fourteen to death because he insulted you. He was seen eating in the streets during Ramadan.

HEAD A pity. [*shrugging*] Iran once had a middle class elected parliament, but it tried to nationalise Iranian oil, so the USA and Britain backed a military coup that replaced the parliament with a dictatorship, to keep the oil in the hands of a global corporation. But now a fundamentalist government looks like grabbing it, which is a threat to United States free trade.

JIMMY There is no such thing as free trade!

HEAD Of course there is, O Lord of the Flies. Remember 1839?

JIMMY [*gloomily*] The Chinese government stopped British traders selling opium in China.

HEAD [*nodding cheerfully*] So the British defended the free trade drug traffic by smashing that government.

JIMMY [*covering face with hands*] The USA and other Christian nations invaded China too. They also wanted a slice of that rich, free market.

HEAD [*chortling*] Meanwhile, Indians who grew opium could only sell it through British traders – Britain was protecting them from greedy foreigners! Every empire, O Prince of Peace, is as greedy as its armed forces let it be. What do you want me to do? Intervene personally?

JIMMY [*nodding*] I do.

HEAD Never works. I gave Moses a few good rules for everybody – don't kill, don't steal, don't tell lies. Many mothers still teach that to their kids. But along came lawmakers and made exceptions to my rules – you shall not suffer a witch to live, stone to death women taken in adultery, kill men and women and children when taking over their living space. Every powerful clique on earth – especially cliques who call me God – has made laws to justify killing. Had I said to Moses, this I command thee, do what the hell you like, human history would have been just as bloody.

JIMMY Nobody thinks your law against killing applies to the killing of foreigners. [*stands up*].

HEAD [*gently*] You did your best to correct them on that point, my ...

JIMMY *suddenly looks at him hard.*

HEAD [*seeing this says teasingly*] ... my boy. [**JIMMY** *looks away, disappointed*] You went among them in person and told them to spread my word to the world – love your neighbour as yourself. Don't fight enemies. Give them all they want, but don't fight, lie, steal or kill for them. [*sighs*].

JIMMY [*wistfully*] These were good words to spread.

HEAD [*embarrassed for the only time in this play*] There is something I've wanted to ask. When you were ... hanging there ...

JIMMY I was nailed.

HEAD [*nodding*] Yes. You told somebody in the same state that he would go to Heaven with you. Why?

JIMMY [*shrugging, spreading hands*] He tried to be kind to me. I wanted to be kind back. Should I have told him there is as little justice in Heaven as on Earth? My body was in such pain that I forgot it was temporary. I was delirious. Up to the very last minute I was mad enough to think you might save everybody who suffered unjustly – and save them [*desperate chuckle*] through me!

HEAD If Heaven only existed to give eternal sweeties to the good and continual beltings to the bad goodness would be a cheap thing. There would be no decency, no heroism in it. I love heroism and you were a hero. I am proud of what you told people and what you endured for telling them.

JIMMY You didn't need heroism to be crucified – the Romans did it to thousands. From the start of history down to the present day millions of men, women, children still endure worse deaths just because they exist – just because they are born in unlucky places.

HEAD [*consolingly*] Your words have comforted unlucky people, especially slaves and women.

JIMMY [*nodding*] Yes. When my comforting words grew so popular that even policemen were christened, my Christians started massacring neighbours who thought different and burned down their temples and synagogues. My Jesus was as big a flop as your Moses, which is why I want you to –

HEAD [*snapping fingers*] – Suddenly, simultaneously appear on every television and computer screen on the planet announcing [*chants in an Anglican High Church voice that swiftly becomes Dalek*] "You shall love the Lord your God with all your heart and all your soul and all your mind and your neighbour as yourself or! You! Will! Be! Ex! Ter! Min! Ated!" [*normal voice*] They would treat me as a rogue virus, Jimmy.

JIMMY [*shaking head*] You don't understand. I want you to exterminate all the brutes.

HEAD [*pursing lips and cocking head*] Say that again.

JIMMY Exterminate the brutes ! Now!

HEAD [*pretending astonishment*] Michty me. Crivens. Jings Jimmy don't be so damned Biblical! I am not the genocidal lunatic described in Genesis. There was never a deluge that drowned everyone except a single family of each species. I did not burn Sodom and Gomorrah with fire and brimstone out of heaven!

JIMMY You wiped out the dinosaurs and the salt water plankton. You smothered Pompeii and Herculaneum in volcanic ash.

HEAD [*patiently*] A wholly stable universe is physically impossible. Even with Jupiter and the moon to shield it an asteroid the size of Dundee is bound to hit the earth every thirteen million years or so. The dinosaurs lasted a lot longer than that. They had a fair innings. Six and a half million years will pass before the next asteroid – plenty of time for folk to learn how to stop it. And it's not my fault that men built cities beside a volcano. Your job was to stop them blaming me for things priests and insurance companies used to call Acts of God – floods, plagues and epidemics caused by ignorance of good cultivation and hygiene – and you cured that ignorance!

JIMMY [*covers face with hands, cries bitterly*] O yes! [*uncovers face*] I encouraged Bacon and Galileo when ignorance was the main problem and true scientists were thought black magicians or heretics. And now natural science has triumphed.

HEAD [*nodding*] Educated people no longer blame you and me for everything bad. A definite step in the right direction. I refuse to wipe out life on earth because the agent who should encourage it is tired of it.

JIMMY But I love life on Earth! I want you to save it by quickly destroying only one kind of brute – the most selfishly greedy kind. Get rid of men, please, before they destroy every other living thing.

HEAD [*smiling*] If mankind heard you now they really would think you – [*extends hooked fingers like claws*] Be – el – zee – bub!

JIMMY [*flinging printouts in bin*] You know what I'm talking about –

HEAD [*slightly bored*] Atmosphere overheating from diesel fumes. Glaciers and ice caps melting. Sea level rising. Forests felled, land impoverished. Pure water tables shrinking or polluted. Drought increasing where thirty per cent have malnutrition and soon billions will die of that and thirst.

JIMMY [*passionately*] The primitive Christians were right – scientists *are* black magicians. Nearly all of them work for corporations tearing up the fabric of life with the help of governments they have bribed. Half the animals alive fifty years ago are extinct. Frogs and sparrows are nearly extinct. The bumblebees are going. Some conscience-stricken biologists are freezing the sperm of threatened creatures, so they can be brought back to life when the planet is governed sanely. Mankind will never govern it sanely.

HEAD [*with a tolerant chuckle*] Aye, men have always been great wee extinguishers. Remember North America at the end of the last big ice age? A vast forest of deciduous trees with nothing dividing them but lakes and rivers and rocky mountains – home of the biggest, most peaceful vegetarians we ever achieved – titanic browsers, tree-sloths as big as elephants and completely harmless. The first men who entered that continent across the Bering Straits had never dreamed of such easy meat. Killing bears and woolly elephants in Eurasia was dangerous work, but men easily took over America. The tree-sloths couldn't run away, couldn't run at all, didn't even have to be trapped. Set fire to the trees and you had several roasted tree-sloths burned out of their pelts in a gravy of their own melted fat. The number of men expanded hugely – for two generations they were too busy eating to kill each other – they gorged themselves down to New Mexico. [*notices* **JIMMY** *staring at him in disgust*] Cheer up. That's how the Prairies came about. It made room for herds and herds and herds of buffalo.

JIMMY Which the white men exterminated because the red men lived off them. But you know things are far worse now. Farmers are sowing genetically modified crops that die as soon as harvested, so they must buy new seed from companies that patented them, while plants folk used to feed on vanish forever. Soon the only live creatures on earth will be the men and the mutants they eat.

HEAD [*in a singsong voice, grinning*] You're forgetting viruses, Jimmy! They too are busy wee mutators. People are great breeding grounds for viruses, especially people eating battery-farmed meat and mutant vegetables. [*with regret*] Croak croak. A pity about the frogs.

JIMMY Are you fond of the Barrier Reef?

HEAD [*reminiscently*] My greatest work of art, one thousand, two hundred and fifty miles long – a masterpiece of intricately intertwined fishes, plants and insects, with the beautiful vivid colour variety of every great picture Matisse painted, and a refinement of detail even Paul Klee never achieved. I was millions of years ahead of my time when I came up with that one. [*shakes head in wonder at his own genius*].

JIMMY It's dying. It'll be gone in thirty years unless men die first.

HEAD [*slight shrug*] Nothing lasts for ever. [*sucks thumb, contemplating blackboard*].

Both are silent for a moment.

JIMMY [*suddenly*] What use are you?

Startled but amused, **HEAD** *smiles kindly at him. A pause.*

JIMMY What do you do with yourself while failing to develop annelid worms in submarine volcanic vents?

HEAD [*thoughtfully contemplates the tetrahedron*] I'm preparing to generate a better universe.

JIMMY Where?

HEAD Outside this one.

JIMMY How can you make a universe outside this one?

HEAD [*raising didactic forefinger*] If you subscribed to *Scientific American* you would know how other universes happen. You see – [*with enthusiastic, descriptive arm gestures*] – every universe is like a carpet with a gigantic draft blowing underneath, so in places it gets rippled up into peaks where energy and mass are so concentrated that BANG! – a hole is blown in the fabric through which mass and energy pour out, forming another universe where physical laws can bend differently.

JIMMY [*keenly*] What causes the draft?

HEAD [*slyly watching him sideways*] Would you think me a megalomaniac if I told you it was my breath?

JIMMY Yes.

HEAD [*impatiently*] I have to use metaphors when describing universal things. If ripples displease you, call them – [*the briefest of pauses*] labour pains, but I am planning a universe where planets are this shape.

He lifts and displays the tetrahedron.

JIMMY [*approaching, incredulous*] A pyramid?

HEAD A pyramid has five sides if you count the base: this has only four, each a perfect isosceles triangle. Get the idea?

JIMMY No.

HEAD [*rotating the model*] Four polar regions! Water collects in ice at the corners and forms an ocean in the middle of each surface – four Mediterranean seas of roughly equal size where life will evolve, and when it takes to land around the shores it will find no huge continent where an empire can grow. All nations will be small and coastal, like Scandinavia [*hands model to* **JIMMY**].

JIMMY [*examining model*] I take it these are islands. The British Empire spread from an island.

HEAD An island with a lot of coal and iron when James Watt devised the first commercial steam engines. In my new world there will be no fossil fuels and every metal will be equally dispersed. No Gold Rushes! The machines people invent will have to be powered by oil from plants that can be grown, and harvested, and replanted.

JIMMY This shape of planet is gravitationally impossible!

HEAD [*gesturing dismissively to backdrop*] Only in this universe. I am preparing a liquid universe where the Heavenly bodies will be formed by crystallisation instead of gravitation – whole galaxies of tetrahedral planets revolving round suns probably this shape. [*lifts octahedron, smiling at it and murmuring dreamily*] A universe without big bangs and collisions.

JIMMY How can a planet have seas in a universe full of liquid?

HEAD [*handing octahedron to* **JIMMY**] My universal fluid will be light as air. [*snaps fingers, suddenly struck by idea*] In fact, it will be air! I'll make it air!

HEAD *jumps down onto floor and strides to blackboard.*

HEAD What a fool I was not to think about that in the first place! Never mind. No matter. Live and learn.

While **JIMMY** *moves tetrahedron experimentally back and forward around the octahedron* **HEAD** *chalks on the blackboard the following figures* – N – 78.1% *then heavily underlines it, saying*:

HEAD When my Heavenly bodies have crystallised, these chemical constituents must remain.

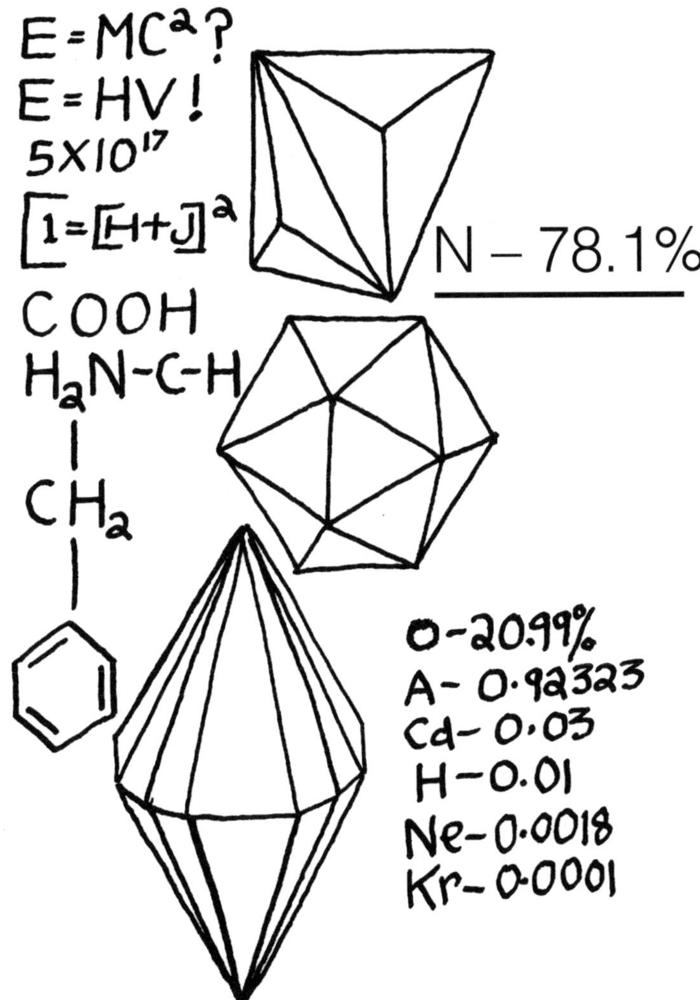

He chalks the extra column of figures to the right, muttering:

HEAD This universal ... solution ... will make flight between worlds ... easy. No need for people ... to blast themselves ... across light years of dreary, subzero vacuum ...

There! [*flings down chalk, grins smugly at* **JIMMY**].

JIMMY But ...

HEAD You are going to tell me, Mr Prometheus O'Lucifer, that air is mostly nitrogen exhaled by vegetation, and how can I grow enough plants to fill a universe with it? But my next universe will start with a big splash instead of a bang, so the initial chemistry will be quite different. *Sits cross-legged on table with hands on knees, triumphant.*

JIMMY Okay Mister Sly-boots Clever-clogs, I was also going to ask about this planet's angle of rotation. [*hands back the tetrahedron*] It will have to perform intricate summersaults if one of the triangular continents is not to be in perpetual twilight.

HEAD [*placidly replacing it on cube*] That is a problem. I'm working on it.

JIMMY So how long will it take you to get this ... airy new universe up and running?

HEAD [*smiling to himself*] I have eternity.

JIMMY You will spend eternity dreaming up a Utopia while mankind destroys the Earth in a couple of generations?

HEAD [*consolingly*] That's nonsense, Jimmy. Men cannot destroy the Earth. They can only destroy themselves and other equally complex creatures. In which case insects will inherit the Earth while vegetation recovers, and then, [*with growing enthusiasm*] – from the segmented worms – you and I will evolve a wealth of new creatures with different organs and sensations and minds. I never repeat my mistakes. [*thoughtfully*] It was maybe a mistake giving big brains to mammals.

JIMMY Why deny intelligence to creatures who suckle their young?

HEAD Freud thinks it makes folk unhealthily dependent and unhealthily greedy. I may try hatching big intelligences from eggs. Birds, in general, seem happier than people. [*thoughtfully*] Tropical birds are as colourful as fishes in the Great Barrier Reef, and the world will be a very tropical planet when men have made it too hot to hold them.

JIMMY [*explosively*] But –

HEAD [*quickly*] You are about to say bird brains are too small for development because their necks are too thin! But owls have short thick necks and are notoriously brainy. One day you may fly to me in the form of a dove with an eagle's wing span and find me a gigantic owl [*spreads arms*] with coloured feathers like a parrot – pretty polly!

JIMMY Is that the most comforting message I can take back to the few on Earth who listen to me? The few who care for the future of life there?

HEAD [*mildly*] You recently asked me to exterminate the human race and now you want me to send it comforting messages!

JIMMY Not comforting messages, useful messages. I lied when I asked you to exterminate humanity. I was trying to goad you into coming up with a new way of saving them. [*sighs*] You knew that.

HEAD [*nodding*] I did, and there are no new ways of saving mankind. They can only save themselves by old things that come in threes.

JIMMY [*glumly*] Faith, hope and love.

HEAD And the greatest of these is love. But love cannot work without liberty, equality, fraternity.

JIMMY [*explosively*] Jesus, Mary and Joseph, what are you on about? What do these words mean? I've been so mixed up with – [*brief pause with hand snatching for something*] – post-modern people that I've forgotten.

HEAD [*shrugging*] Liberty is not having to obey others just because they're stronger or richer.

JIMMY Equality?

HEAD Is what everybody enjoys with good friends, or in groups where everyone knows they need each other.

JIMMY Fraternity?

HEAD Brotherhood. The brotherhood of man.

JIMMY [*ironically*] Exclusively masculine?

HEAD A good point Jimmy. Call fraternity love also, love that makes your world the centre of the universe.

JIMMY Don't talk shite! My wee world is near the edge of an average galaxy among a million million galaxies! I helped Galileo destroy the Jewish notion that the whole shebang revolved around them. How can my wee world be a universal centre?

HEAD [*patiently*] A centre of the universe is wherever somebody opens their eyes, and the earth is still the only place where that happens. I hoped mankind would take life to my other worlds. [*gestures to backdrop*] They have the technology. [*shrugs*] If they use it to wipe themselves out we'll start again with another species. [*absentmindedly*] To-whit-to-woo. Pretty pol.

JIMMY *is sitting down looking totally defeated.* **HEAD** *claps hands, rubs them together, stands for the first time and goes to him briskly.*

HEAD [*cheerfully*] And since we now see eye to eye I must waste no more of your valuable time. Tell folk the competitive exploitation of natural resources is a dead end. Nuclear power, used wisely, will give access to all the space, raw material and energy they need without fighting nasty aliens for it. [*claps* **JIMMY** *on shoulder to raise him, talking faster*] Less than five miles beneath the Earth's surface is heat that, rightly channelled, will drive their motors and machines without poisonous emissions. [*turns* **JIMMY** *towards the exit*] Fossil fuels should be exclusively used as fertiliser. Goodbye Jimmy.

JIMMY [*resisting departure*] Nobody with wealth and power will believe me. They know the damage they're doing but they're still extending motorways! Making and selling cars! Nobody owning one will change to a bicycle! Nobody who flies will go by boat! Owners of companies wrecking the ecosphere are buying self-sustaining bunkers where they and their like can survive when everyone else is poisoned!

HEAD [*chuckling*] They won't survive. Only those who work to save others have a chance. Perhaps. [*propels* **JIMMY** *towards entrance*] So workers of the world unite! [*mischievously*] Remind them of co-operative Socialism, Jimmy – William Morris, Bernard Shaw, James Connelly.

JIMMY [*frantic*] I'll be laughed at!

HEAD [*highly amused*] Then all laughter will become screams of hysterical despair. Don't forget your briefcase. [*lifts it up and holds it out*] Goodbye son.

JIMMY Son! [*stares at* **HEAD**, *then speaks with difficulty*] I'm glad ... you occasionally admit ... I'm in the family [*accepts briefcase*].

HEAD [*quietly*] Goodbye son. [*turns back on him, returns to table*] Good luck.

JIMMY Which is not something you need, is it dad?

He leaves.

HEAD *sits down, sighs, contemplates blackboard. Stage starts to darken.*

HEAD He thinks I don't need luck. [*sigh*] Green ... grow ... the rashes-o. [*sings*] I'll give me one-o, green grow the rashes-o, What is my one-o? One is one and all alone and evermore shall be so. [*speaking sadly*] One is one. [*sighs*] And all alone. [*sighs*] And evermore shall be so.

It is now nearly completely dark. Suddenly: –

SOUND: *A melodious chord struck on a harp.*

HEAD *is lit by a spotlight from above. He looks up.*

A WOMANS VOICE [*not severe or tender but amused*] You silly wee man.

HEAD [*questioningly*] Mother?

CAST

HE – Middle class, middle aged and eager to be genial.

SHE – Middle class, middle aged, unhappy, and a furious knitter.

JACK – A quiet, agreeable gentleman, except on mobile phone and near the end.

SET

A hearth rug at stage front, centre, has an easy-chair on each side, one behind it facing the audience. The back is made claustrophobic by two walls meeting at a corner, a window in the middle of the left, a door in the right with upright chair beside it. On both walls hang well-mounted and framed Piranesi prints from his Carceri series.

HE, *hands in pockets, stands looking out of window. His speeches are punctuated by brief pauses indicated thus ...* **SHE** *sits stoically knitting in the right hand chair.*

HE Well well. [*sighs*] Yes indeed. [*sighs*] I wonder what the weather's like.

SHE Where?
HE Outside.
SHE Go and look.
HE I am insufficiently ... Motivated ... You're lucky.
SHE Why?
HE You knit. You do housework ... Early retirement has made me ... An appendage. I ought to cultivate something.
SHE What?
HE A hobby. A garden. Friends.
SHE Friends are not cultivated. They happen, like weeds.
HE I bet I could plant some. [*with sudden enthusiasm*] This is a free country – I can go into any pub, see an interesting stranger, walk right up to them, hold out my hand and say, "My name's Jim Barclay, tax avoidance accountant, retired. How do you do? What brings you to this neck of the woods?" ... Mind you, it would sound better if I was American. [*in American voice*] "Howdy stranger! Jim Barclay's the name. What brings you to this neck of the woods?"
SHE Woods don't have necks.
HE [*sighs*] Not around here, anyway. [*sighs*].
SOUND: *Doorbell chimes.*
HE Well well well! Someone's arrived! [*strides to door*] Someone's arrived! [*opens it, cries*] Look who's here!
JACK [*modestly*] Yes. It's me.
HE Come in come in come in!
JACK *enters.* **SHE** *looks up.*
HE Linda! Linda! This is old, old, old, old ... [*snaps fingers*] ... old, old, old, old ...
JACK [*helpfully*] Jack.
HE Yes, old Jack! He was my pal in the old P I S Q S.
SHE *resumes knitting.*
JACK [*amused, shaking his head*] Actually, it was the old S H I Q T.
HE [*puzzled*] Are you sure?
JACK [*nodding*] Definite.
HE It was certainly one of those hell holes. But you saved my life, I remember that well enough!
JACK [*shrugging*] It was my job. I was in charge of security. Today I was driving north and felt like looking in.
HE Thank goodness! This calls for a celebration. Have a seat.
JACK Only if you're having one yourself.
HE No, too excited. What's the weather like?
JACK Outside?
HE Yes.
JACK Much the same as in here. Nothing to speak of.
HE Pity. Care for a drink? Tea? Coffee?
JACK No thanks.
HE Orange juice? Beer? Gin? Vodka? Whisky? Drambuie? Tia Maria? Sherry? Port? Chateau Mouton Rothschild du Pape? I'm afraid we're out of champagne.
JACK Sorry, I'm a health freak. I only drink water and stopped at a pub for a couple of pints ten minutes ago.
HE [*disappointed*] Oh. [*sits down in centre chair*].
JACK *sits in the other. A pause.*
HE [*suddenly inspired*] Care to talk about being a health freak? I mean, you might manage to convert us, ha ha.
JACK No no. You'd find the topic too bloody boring.
HE [*heartily*] Ha ha ha, you're right there! [*on an intimate note*] Sorry I can't ask you what car you drive, and tell you about mine and all the trouble I have with it. Linda finds the topic too bloody boring.
JACK Ha ha, she's right there!
Another pause.
JACK and **HE** [*simultaneously*] What are you doing these days?
Both laugh.
JACK You first!
HE No, you!
JACK You! I insist.
HE Well as a matter of fact –
SOUND: *A mobile phone plays the first two lines of Do You Ken John Peel?*
JACK Excuse me. [*unpockets phone*].
SHE *looks up, listening.*
JACK Hello ... Listen, bitch, and listen good. There were no witnesses to that promise you allege I made, pills are cheap so your bastard is not my concern. If you must whine try whining at my lawyer. He'll land you in Fumbleton Vale Jail without your feet touching the ground and women commit suicide to escape from that place. So get out of my life! [*pockets phone. Apologetically*] Sorry about that. As a matter of fact you've what?
SHE *resumes knitting.*
HE Taken early retirement.
JACK But you used to be such a live wire!
HE [*depressed*] The firm made me an offer I couldn't refuse.
JACK [*sympathetically*] The swines!

HE [*shrugging*] Business is business. [*thoughtful pause, then, struck by idea*] Have you noticed that every ten years since 1975 the number of millionaires in Britain has doubled?
JACK [*nodding*] Yes.
HE Have you never wanted to be one?
JACK I am one.
HE [*not hearing him*] It's done by cashing in on the market whether it's going up, down or sideways. Jack Rotter of the Porridge Union is coming to everyone's neck of the woods tomorrow so why not book a talk with him on rotporridge at slash dot crash dot wallop yahoo dot com and get tips straight from the horse's mouth? All terms and conditions apply.
SHE [*exasperated, looking up*] He's already told you he is a millionaire.
HE [*to* **JACK**] Did you?
JACK [*smiling and nodding*] Yes!
HE [*chuckling*] Dear me, that ought to teach me something.
SHE It should teach you to listen as much as you talk.
HE [*not noticing her*] Yes it really ought to teach me something. [*sighs*] But I wish they hadn't pushed me out of tax avoidance.
JACK I seem to remember you were damned good at it.
HE I was, but even accountants don't know everything.
JACK A disturbing thought. But I think my own accountant is trustworthy.
HE You could be living in a fool's paradise. Just the other day I was running to the seaside when the door of a parked car suddenly opened and smacked me into the middle of the road. I was left with nine broken ribs and a fractured pelvis.
JACK Tough!
HE [*smugly*] Not at all. I got straight on to J C Pooter who will get me a cool million in compensation and a year's holiday in the Bahamas.
JACK [*nodding approval*] J C Pooter was your knight in shining armour.
HE What are you doing these days?
JACK As a matter of fact I'm –
SOUND: *mobile phone rings.*
SHE *pauses, listening.*
JACK Excuse me a moment. [*on phone*] Hello ... They're rioting? We knew they would ... Of course they've invaded the plant, I hope they burn it down so the firm can claim insurance ... You're trapped on the roof? Phone the police to airlift you off. [*pockets phone*] Sorry about that. I was saying?
SHE *resumes knitting.*
HE What you're doing these days?
JACK I'm a troubleshooter.
HE You shoot trouble makers?
JACK [*chuckling*] No no no no, I never pull a trigger. I tell other people to do that.
HE [*admiringly*] That must take courage.
JACK [*with regret*] Not much. Hardly anyone gets killed. They usually see reason when confronted with the wee black holes at the ends of Kalashnikovs.
HE Does Russia still make these?
JACK Not sure, but nowadays you can pick them up anywhere for a song.
HE By the way, which of the following statements is untrue. Stoats are animals with almost human fingernails. For two centuries the Austro-Hungarian official language was Chinese. You can afford an Assassin Javelin Jeep, with inbuilt recording studio, leather upholstery and all the trimmings. The Madagascar royal flag is an inverted hippo.
JACK Er ... the inverted hippo?
HE [*triumphantly*] They're all true! The most domestically-abused single-parent pauper can now afford an Assassin Javelin Jeep thanks to an easy credit deal that lets anybody sell their children into slavery.
JACK Do all terms and conditions apply?
HE [*enthusiastically*] Of course! Hallelujah! At last Assassin Javelins have put the best jeep in the world within everybody's reach. But I'd like to put in another word for the Porridge Union ...
SHE [*deliberately, having ceased knitting*] Hell. Hell. Help.
JACK [*alarmed, looks at her, then at* **HE** *murmuring*] Should we bring your wife into our ... our ...
HE [*gloomily*] Discourse? You can try.
JACK [*genially*] Forgive me for asking rather a personal question Mrs ... Mrs ... [*quietly to* **HE**] What's her surname?
HE Just call her Linda.
JACK Linda, forgive me for asking a rather personal question, but have you enjoyed the wonderful sensation of Gloria Vampa's new make-up remover?
SHE [*stonily*] I don't use make-up.
JACK [*cheerfully*] Then maybe it's time you started! The surveillance society is here to stay, so why not wow the

policemen watching us on closed circuit street television cameras by looking like a new woman every day? And Maxine Hererra can make that easy!

SHE Maxine Hererra of New York?

JACK Yes, Maxine Hererra of New York's heart-shaped scarlet love-box has a new lipstick giving you the choice of 69 distinctly glamorous shades and 96 luscious flavours at the flick of a wrist, and the cost is a mere –

SHE [*desperately*] No!

HE [*quietly*] She thinks you're being too commercial. Discuss something else with me.

JACK You know, when Greenspan's tenure is seen through the prism of the current situation we cannot turn a blind eye to the explosion in sub-prime mortgages and the rapid growth of complex credit derivatives.

HE [*astonished*] Can't we?

JACK No. History has never dealt kindly with the aftermath of protracted low-risk premiums, and the regulators will have to rely on counterparty surveillance to do the heavy lifting.

SHE [*through gritted teeth*] The markets for money and cosmetics are equally commercial.

JACK [*quietly*] Let's discuss music.

HE [*nodding*] Please.

JACK [*enthusiastically*] You know, my favourite radio programme is Classic FM.

HE It is?

JACK Definitely! You cannot beat Classic FM for really smooth, relaxing music sponsored by the British Savings Bank which is currently celebrating the 50th anniversary of premium bonds ...

JACK *sees* **SHE** *is writhing in torment.*

JACK [*guiltily to* **HE**] Sorry about that. Health, perhaps?

HE Try it.

JACK You know, there's nothing very clever about living with a hernia.

SHE *resumes knitting.*

HE But operations used to be painful, took months, were often worse than useless.

JACK No more! And about time. Nowadays you can walk into the Universal Hernia Centre and walk out twenty minutes later with a brand new, state-of-the-art hernia and a life-long permanent kidney guarantee, and it won't cost you a –

SHE *screams.* **HE** *clutches at his hair.*

JACK [*inspired*] I've got it! Science! Pure science! E equals M C squared!

HE [*relieved*] Oh yes yes yes! E equals M C squared. Poor Albert Einstein. He never could get his head round quantum physics. "God doesn't play dice," he said.

JACK [*chuckling*] Max Planck told him, "Don't tell God not to play games!".

SHE [*grimly resuming knitting*] Was that not Niels Bohr?

JACK One or tother. Einstein never understood that a unified field equation was only possible in a steady-state universe that would be indistinguishable from one infinite Permenidean solid.

HE Exactly! That equation would have established Calvinist predestination all over again, making human consciousness an inexplicable epiphenomenon.

JACK Schopenhauer showed how impossible that was.

HE [*overjoyed*] He did, he did, he did!

SOUND: *Do You Ken John Peel?*

JACK Excuse me. [*on phone*] Hello ... Okay ... Okay, the demonstrators have you spread-eagled naked and face down on a tabletop with a funnel stuck up your arse. And? ... They are going to pour melted lead down it, unless? ... [*incredulous*] Unless the government promises to nationalise their factory and reopen it? Why should the government do that? ... You're Gordon Brown's nephew? What's that got to do with it? Family loyalty is as dead as the brotherhood of man. I'm sorry you got yourself into this mess but there's now nothing I can do. [*pockets phone*] Sorry about that. You were saying?

HE Schopenhauer showed the definition of will as effect, not cause, depended on consciousness itself – a reductio ad absurdum that would reduce the gods to helpless laughter.

JACK No wonder Nietzsche and Wagner loved Schopenhauer. I think Bruckner did too. In a peaceful wood, on a summer afternoon, one's mood is exactly conveyed by the almost inaudible vibration that opens his fourth symphony.

HE [*nodding*] Yes, the unity of art and science, hand and eye is predicated by the past – our only inevitability. Did you know that Phoebe Traquair – evening star of the Arts and Crafts Movement – married a marine palaeontologist who specialised in asymmetry in flat fish?

SHE [*flings knitting down*] I can take no more of this pretentious shit!

HE [*jumping up and pointing angry forefinger*] O yes. It's very easy to sit on one side knitting and nagging! I hate pretentious shit just as much as you, but I loathe something else even more – that ghastly, brain-destroying silence in which people sit uselessly hating each other. Well, I give up. I wash my hands of the whole business. I'm leaving him to you.

HE *walks to window and stares out, hands in pockets.* **JACK** *has watched all this with interest but no embarrassment.* **SHE** *smiles and shifts to the chair beside him.*

SHE [*pleasantly*] Well Jack, what brings you to this neck of the woods?

JACK [*slapping his knee*] Ah, now you've got me really started! From now on you won't get a word in edgeways. I've been sent north by the S. L. I. C. Q. E. because –

SHE Exactly what is the S. L. I. C. Q. E.?

JACK Scottish Lice and Insect Corporate Quango Enterprises. They want me to –

SHE [*firmly*] Insects are disgusting.

JACK They are! They are! But from an industrial point of view midges –

SHE The female flesh fly, Sarcophoga Carraris, lays young larvae in the fresh or decomposing flesh of almost any animal. Or in manure.

HE *is now pretending to inspect the framed prints, but obviously listening closely.*

JACK I know, I know, but why does a salmon as big as this [*spreads his arms*] leap out of a river to swallow a wee toaty midge as big as this? [*shows forefinger nearly touching thumb*].

SOUND: *Do You Ken John Peel?*

JACK [*reaching into pocket*] Excuse me!

SHE I won't. No gentleman will let a mobile phone interrupt a conversation with a lady. Switch it off.

HE *stares at his wife in astonished admiration.*

SOUND: *Do You Ken John Peel?*

JACK [*becoming frantic*] I must answer it! If it's the boss I'll be sacked if I don't answer! I have to be on call day and night! Day and night!

SHE Is it your boss? Won't the phone tell you?

SOUND: *Do You Ken John Peel?*

JACK [*in agony*] I don't know! Nowadays anyone with technical skill can hack into my phone and make it say my boss is calling. I'm bombarded with calls from a prostitute I picked up in a Thailand children's brothel. I chucked her out a fortnight ago and now she rings me almost hourly! My life is a nightmare! [*weeps*] ...

SOUND: *Do You Ken John Peel?*

JACK [*through tears*] Please let me answer! I'm drinking myself to death ...

SHE With water?

JACK Water can kill faster than alcohol ...

SOUND: *Do You Ken John Peel?*

JACK Please ... Please ...

SHE [*firmly*] Switch it off, Jack. It's probably only strikers who want you to hear your colleague screaming while they pour molten lead into his bum.

JACK [*resigned*] I pray to God you're right.

SOUND: *Do You Ken John Peel? interrupted halfway as* **JACK** *switches off.*

HE [*carrying over an upright chair*] My my, Jack, you really live at the centre of things. [*puts chair between* **SHE** *and* **JACK** *and sits*] Tell me, why do great big salmon leap out of rivers to swallow toaty wee midges?

JACK [*triumphantly*] Because of the adrenalin! Every wee midge is a molecule of pure protein fuelled by an atom of adrenalin. That's why midges are able to stot up and down all day above rivers, lochs, ponds, stanks and puddles in your back garden.

SHE [*stonily*] Cephenormia Auribarbos is a rather flat parasite fly whose shape and claws allow it to move quickly, crab-wise, across the soft hairy surfaces of ponies and suck their blood. The female gives birth to full grown larvae, which at once pupate.

JACK Very true. But what would you have if all the swarms of midges infesting the Highlands and Islands were squeezed together into one huge dripping block?

HE [*fascinated*] What would she have?

JACK A lump half the size of Ben Lomond containing enough adrenalin to start a Scottish subsidiary of International Pharmaceuticals, while leaving another half mountain of protein to be sliced and marketed locally as midgieburgers. The working class soon won't be able to afford fish suppers, Scottish beef and venison are for export only, so midgieburgers are going to become Britain's fastest food – our economy will depend on it. And Scotland is in luck! Global warming is turning the Western Isles into a new Caribbean! So S. L. I. C. Q. E. are using lottery funds to shunt pensionless old age pensioners, and the unemployed, and the disabled, and criminals doing community service into Highland and Island nudist camps where they do nothing but sunbathe and let S. L. I. C. Q. E. cull the midges they attract!

HE [*awestruck*] Goodness gracious! Five of Scotland's worst social problems solved at a stroke. That's wonderful!

SHE [*grimly*] The Deer Bot Fly, Calliphora Vomitaria –

HE Sorry dear but I have to interrupt. Jack is a trouble-shooter. Exactly what trouble are you here to shoot, Jack?

JACK The midges aren't biting.

HE Why?

JACK Nudists are using midge repellents.

SHE [*trying again*] Calliphora Vomitaria –

HE I'm sorry dear, this is really important. [*to* **JACK**] International Pharmaceuticals want the midges but they also make the repellent sprays. They can make the sprays sold in Scotland ineffective by weakening the contents!

JACK They've done that. But local chemists have enough stockpiles of effective stuff to repel midges for the next 20 years.

SHE Calliphora Vom –

HE [*testily*] I told you, Linda, this is important –

SHE *huffily resumes her former seat and stonily knits again.*

HE Listen, Jack! The companies must tell local chemists the repellents they've stockpiled may induce skin cancer because they've been insufficiently tested, so they will be replaced by safe stuff free of charge.

JACK [*shaking his head*] Too dangerous. If that lie turns out to be true word will leak out and the pharmaceuticals have no defence when someone sues them.

HE So what can you do?

JACK S. L. I. C. Q. E. has called in T. I. Q. T. S. who –

SHE [*explosively*] What is T? I? Q? T? S?

JACK Troubleshooters International Quick Termination Service [*proudly*] – my firm!

HE [*fascinated*] What will you do?

JACK [*in a low voice*] Can you keep this to yourself?

HE A Boys' Brigade Captain never clypes.

JACK I'm going to ... [*his voice becomes an inaudible whisper*].

HE [*horrified and admiring*] You can actually do that nowadays?

JACK [*nodding*] Mhm!

HE But when that was done in Soviet Russia nearly everyone thought ... I mean in Britain, Europe and the USA people thought ... I mean even the newspapers said it was ... er ... wrong. Bad. Dirty. I think we even had laws against it.

JACK [*happily*] We're living in a new age, Max!

HE [*gently correcting him*] Jim.

JACK [*puzzled*] I'm sorry?

HE [*sharing the joke*] I'm not Max – I'm your old friend Jim Barclay.

JACK [*thunderstruck*] Not ... Max Fensterbacher?

HE [*patiently*] Jim Barclay.

JACK [*standing up*] Is this not Sixteen Conniston Place, Strathnaver?

HE It's Sixteen Denniston Place, Strathinver.

JACK [*starting to sound dangerous*] No wonder nothing you've said has made sense! O but you've been very, very smart. I have to admire how you screwed what you did out of me!

HE [*standing up, slightly disturbed*] It's you who's making no sense! It's you who made the mistake first.

JACK But you didn't go out of your way to correct it! [*in menacing tone*] Who are you working for?

HE I'm not working at all. I'm a tax avoidance accountant who took early retirement, my hobby is cultivating friendship and you're making it very, very difficult.

JACK They all say that. I will now tell you what I came north to tell Fensterbacher, and you'd better believe it. If you're working for one of the other sides, come clean and we'll do a deal, because we can always do a deal with the other sides, but if you're a loose cannon you haven't a hope in hell. Get this. Everything you've heard, everything you know, everything you think is under the Official Secrets Act and if you breathe one word of it you can kiss your ass goodbye. And if they come for me first I'll make sure we both go down the chute together!

SHE [*desperately*] The Deer Bot Fly, Calliphora Vomitaria, deposits larvae in the nostrils of young deer. The larvae live in the nasal or throat passages, attached by their mouth hooks, living on the secretions of the host. When full-fed they are passed out with the deer's droppings and pupate on the soil.

JACK [*ignoring her*] Remember, Fensterbacher, the crocodiles at the bottom of that chute have needle-sharp teeth and take years to make a meal of a man!

SOUND: *Do You Ken John Peel?* **JACK,** *pulling it from pocket, rushes out, slamming door after him.*

HE [*sadly*] Well well well [*sighs*] Well well well.

HE *lifts upright chair, places it back beside window, stands with hands in pockets looking out.* **SHE** *resumes knitting.*
HE I quite enjoyed his company before he turned nasty. [*sighs*] I wonder if he was all he cracked himself up to be. [*sighs*] I'll know for sure if chemists' storerooms start exploding [*turns towards wife*] Should I phone the police about that?
SHE He was the police – a special branch of it.
HE Not a troubleshooter for a private corporation?
SHE That too. The police are half privatised now, like the government [*sadly*] ... I wish you were him.
HE Why?
SHE He and I nearly had a conversation before you butted in – the first intelligent conversation I've had with a man since we married. Before that you sometimes talked to me. Never since. Not now.
HE [*absent mindedly*] Not now, no. [*sighs and turns to window*] Not now. I wonder what the weather's like outside.
Pause.
SHE [*stops knitting, looks at his back, says softly*] What if we – both you and me – were always listening – I mean really listening to the silence. Would we hear, – really hear and heed – the importance of waiting, – really waiting – for the right moment – to begin the song?
Pause.
HE [*without turning*] Did you say something?
SHE A poem I remembered.
HE Oh. I thought you said something.
Pause.
SHE [*sighing*] What does the weather look like outside?
HE Much the same as in here.
SHE Pity.

NOTE: The poem **SHE** *recites above is used with permission by the author, Larry Butler.*

THE PIPES, THE PIPES

THIRD NOW PLAY

2007

CAST OF FIVE PLAYED BY THREE ACTORS
CONVENTIONAL BARMAID
REGULAR MIDDLE CLASS CUSTOMER
The following characters are played by the same actor.
ELDERLY PROLETARIAN resembling Grandpa Broon.
PLAIN CLOTHES COP
AN ASIAN GAEL in tartan regalia, turban and very brown or black face.

SCENE
A small pub interior in a posh district, like the Wee Ubiquitous Chip Bar on Ashton Lane, Glasgow.

The **BARMAID** *is doing something barmaidenly, like drying tumblers. The* **REGULAR CUSTOMER** *is reading the sports supplement of a well-known newspaper.*
REGULAR [*without looking up from his paper*] You know my brother, the artist?
BARMAID Yes.
REGULAR He's more than an artist now. He's the chief arts administrator for the whole of Lanarkshire. He's shagged just about every woman in Lanarkshire. [*looks up from his paper*] Has he shagged you?
BARMAID No.
REGULAR Where you from?
BARMAID Dumbarton.
REGULAR That explains it. [*reads again*] He's also into property.
BARMAID Oh?
REGULAR You know that tenement at the corner of Boghead Road and Sheriff Irvine Smith Street? That's his.
BARMAID A prime site.
REGULAR Yes, a prime site. He's stuffed it from floor to ceiling with lavatory pans and cisterns.
BARMAID I've seen them through the oriel windows.

REGULAR You won't see them again. He's whitewashed the windows on the inside. Do you know what the best thing in life is?

REGULAR *falls silent as an old bearded man resembling* **GRANDPA BROON** *enters and stands looking around in a dazed way.*

BARMAID Are you looking for someone?

GRANDPA Where are the muriels?

BARMAID There's nobody called Muriel here.

GRANDPA Ye've goat me wrang, Missis. A'm talking aboot big wa' pictures, same as Michelangelo wrote a' owr the wa's o' the Pope's private chapel.

REGULAR This is a respectable pub in a respectable neighbourhood! Don't try to drag your religion in here.

BARMAID [*politely*] What would you like sir?

GRANDPA A wee goldie, Miss. But whaur did the muriels go? Did Glasgow Art Gallery and Museums grab them?

REGULAR [*with contempt*] When did you ever see mural paintings in this place?

GRANDPA Not so long ago! The time of the Upper Clyde Work-in! A was a fitter in the yairds, and Jimmy Reid led us up this wie to a protest demonstration ootside the BBC.

BARMAID [*serving him a whisky*] The BBC building's south of the river. Twelve pounds.

GRANDPA It wasnae then. Twelve pounds for a wee goldie. O dear.

He sadly pays and sips, watched grimly by **REGULAR**.

GRANDPA A great man, Jimmy Reid. Him and me were out together in the fifties apprentice strike. A great man for Culture. That's why he broat me in here. "The Byres pub is what every Scots pub should be," said Jimmy, "A living centre of local community culture! It is here that the Scoatish intelligentsia mingle with each ither and the coammon working man. Hugh MacDiarmid! The Wee MacGreegor! Wee Willie Winkie! Wullie Joss of the MacFlannels! Duncan MacRae who appeared in *Our Man in Havana* alang wi' Alec Guiness and Noel Coward! And James Bridie the Scoatish George Bernard Shaw! And if they're no' actually here when we drap in, ye kin still see them because there they are, large as life, pentit oan the wa's." And so they were. Aye, so they were.

REGULAR Are you aware of how ridiculous you are being?

OLD MAN Eh?

REGULAR Not only ridiculous, but obnoxious. It is no pleasure to have a shower of forgotten has-beens poured over us. Since you came here in the 1970s this pub has been completely renovated four times by four different managements, and you can bet your bottom dollar that any old wall paintings of any old celebrities ended up in a skip that took them straight to Dawsholme incinerator.

GRANDPA [*dazed*] Even the portrait of James Barke? Who wrote *The Wind that Shakes the Barley*?

REGULAR [*with relish*] He was the first to go! And I advise you to follow him.

GRANDPA, *stupefied, wanders out.*

REGULAR As I was saying before I was so rudely interrupted, do you know what the best thing in life is?

BARMAID No. What is it?

REGULAR The kind of frank friendly conversation I am having with you.

BARMAID Thanks.

REGULAR No problem! But nowadays it is almost impossible to keep a conversation like ours alive.

BARMAID O?

REGULAR Almost impossible. I met a bartender in the lounge of the Grosvenor Hotel last night. He was tight-lipped, in fact downright taciturn. I was the only customer so to get him chatting and widen the scope of our conversation I told him how the wife had left me, about the bills I had to pay and the goldfish I had to feed. Do you know what he said to me?

BARMAID No.

REGULAR He said, "My friend, have you accepted Jesus Christ as your personal saviour?"

BARMAID And had you?

REGULAR [*stupefied*] What?

BARMAID Had you accepted Christ as your personal saviour?

REGULAR For God's sake, is every pub in Glasgow staffed by religious fanatics? If there is one thing I cannot tolerate it is fanaticism, fundamentalism or any form of religious bigotry. Every bigot, Protestant, Catholic or Muslim, should be burned, hung by the neck and stoned to death regardless of race, nationality or political creed ...

PLAIN CLOTHES COP [*enters saying loudly*] Hear hear! Amen to that! Good for you! I'm with you all the way! Drinks all round miss for my good friend here and take one yourself. For me, a large malt of the month. What's everyone else having?

REGULAR [*hiding behind his paper*] No more for me thanks.

BARMAID [*pouring out the whisky*] I don't drink at work.

COP [*putting down notes*] Keep the change. [*lifts the whisky and sits beside the* **REGULAR** *who tries to ignore him by not looking up from the paper*]

COP What do you think of the weather prospects?

REGULAR I don't discuss politics.

COP O come come come! You used to be mad keen on politics. I mean, you were a close friend of my close friend Harvey Drambogie.

REGULAR I have never in my life known a man called Harvey Drambogie.

COP But you shared a flat with him when we were all students together. That flat was a hotbed of radical politics. We were all Anarchists or Socialists or Nationalists.

REGULAR I shared a flat with hundreds of people once and maybe one of them was called Harvey, maybe not. I never remember a face if I can help it. Or a name! And I have always been completely unpolitical – a Tory, in other words.

COP [*chuckling*] You can't possibly be as anti-social as all that! And in those days radical politics were just an innocent hobby. Anyway, old Harvey Drambogie swears you taught him all he knows about Karl Marx and Prince Krapotkin and Rosa Luxemburg. You went around telling people to start throwing up dykes.

REGULAR You must be mixing me up with somebody else.

COP [*coldly*] If that's the line you take I will remove my velvet glove and give you a touch of the iron hand. Look at this! [*holds out a card covered by transparent plastic*] Do you know what this means?

REGULAR No.

COP [*triumphantly*] Of course you don't know what it means, but it gives me full power to arrest anyone who gets on my tits and hold them for questioning for any period up to three months without informing their friends or family or allowing them any right of legal appeal.

REGULAR But I've not done anything! I'm innocent.

COP You can't touch pitch without being defiled.

REGULAR What's that supposed to mean?

COP Do you deny that your brother has made half the women in Lanarkshire pregnant? That he's filled his Sherrif Irvine Smith Street flat with illicit lavatory plumbing equipment? And whitewashed the windows from the inside?

REGULAR Why should that make me a criminal?

COP Because you can't touch pitch without being defiled!

REGULAR *cowers while* **COP** *glares at him and the* **BARMAID**, *producing needles and wool, starts knitting or darning a sock while listening with interest to the conversation.*

REGULAR Please don't arrest me! Yes, Harvey Drambogie was my friend, we were both in the old Labour Party, but I left as soon as I graduated and I've never voted for anybody since. I promise never to see my brother again as long as I live, and I'm sorry I was so stand-offish when you spoke to me at first. I'm ashamed of myself. Will you not accept my humble apologies?

COP [*thoughtfully*] You're beginning to sound sincere. [*after a pause, cheerfully extends his hand*] Okay, apology accepted. Put it there.

They shake hands. The **COP** *holds on to* **REGULAR**'*s, smiling and saying* –

COP And now you're going to prove you're sincere!

REGULAR How?

COP Hand over your wallet.

REGULAR *meekly hands it over. The* **COP** *looks through it.*

COP Don't worry, I don't want your notes, only your banker's card. Here it is. [*hands back the wallet, waves the card in the air*] But without your personal identification number this is useless, and so?

REGULAR Zero zero nine zero.

COP [*standing up*] Not a number I'll forget. Would you like to know what will happen to you if you've lied to me about this?

REGULAR Please, please don't tell me. I wouldn't dare lie to you.

COP Wise man. See you around. Goodbye Miss.

The **BARMAID** *nods to him. The* **COP** *leaves. She resumes knitting.*

REGULAR *sighs once or twice.*

REGULAR [*gloomily*] That's the third banker's card the security forces have relieved me of this year.

BARMAID I'm surprised you have any money left.

REGULAR I have small token sums in several bank accounts. My main savings are in a waterproof condom gaffer-taped to the inside of my lavatory cistern.

BARMAID A wise precaution. But you can't have saved much if you keep it in a condom.

REGULAR What would you say if you heard that condom contains over fourteen million pounds?

BARMAID Impossible.

REGULAR [*smugly*] It does.

BARMAID How can it?

REGULAR When I saw how galloping inflation was devaluing the currency I converted my capital into jewels, mainly diamonds and pearls, though I admit to a weakness for multi-faceted amethysts, if they're really well cut.

BARMAID That makes sense. I like a good amethyst.

REGULAR You're not getting any of mine! Don't expect it! I'm not an idiot!

A brown or black-faced man in full Highland regalia enters, wearing Sikh turban with black cock feathers attached by a Cairngorm brooch. He carries either a claymore or assegai. The others pay no attention as he advances to the counter and lays the weapon or assegai on it.

GAEL [*in a clear soft West-Highland voice*] If you please, mistress, a celebratory malt of the month.

BARMAID *pours one, places it before him. He lays notes on counter, lifts the glass.*

GAEL Keep the change. Slanjay Vawr. [*downs it in one*] Has anyone here heard the great news?

REGULAR [*not looking up from his paper*] If you want to tell us the Broomielaw dykes have burst and rising water is turning Glasgow into a cluster of islands you can save your breath. We knew months ago that was bound to happen.

GAEL Yes it is happening, but that is not the great news. The Prince has landed!

The others show no interest.

GAEL [*more emphatically*] I am telling you, the Prince has landed!

BARMAID [*politely*] What prince is that?

GAEL Prince Charles Windsor Xavier Sobieski Stuart the tenth, our Once and Future King.

BARMAID I'm afraid I've got more to worry about than politics these days.

REGULAR [*suddenly attending*] Where, exactly did you dredge up that prince?

GAEL He has been with us all his life, but kept from his rightful inheritance by treacherous Prime Ministers conniving with a lying old mother who calls herself Elizabeth the Second of Britain. The first monarch of United Britain was James Stuart the Sixth of Scotland, who came after Elizabeth the First of England. The House of Hanover was only given the British throne because it had Stuart blood in its veins, blood of which Queen Victoria was righteously proud! Prince Charles has now extirpated his Hanoverian taint by fully identifying himself with his Stuart ancestry. Yes! All Scotland must now arise to make Prince Charlie the only rightful King of Scotland, England, Ireland, Poland and North America.

REGULAR [*reading his newspaper again*] If you asylum seekers had sense you would keep your mouths shut.

GAEL [*in a dangerously calm voice*] Asylum seeker. Is that supposed to have some reference to my complexion?

REGULAR It stands out a mile.

GAEL [*with dignity, then rising passion*] I will have you know, I was born a subject of the British Empire. My father fought for it in two World Wars. In 1944, King George the Fifth in Buckingham Palace pinned a medal to my father's chest, as an award for conspicuous bravery in North Africa. He at once married my mother, a MacTavish of Jura, and twenty years later I was born. Since then I have farmed the soil of my ancestral croft with my own bare hands and you have the gall to call me an asylum seeker?

REGULAR I'm glad the British Empire gave you a chance in life, but frankly, your sort have been diluting the purity of Scottish culture since the year dot and enough is enough – here in Glasgow anyway.

BARMAID, GAEL [*simultaneously*] What Scottish culture?

REGULAR [*patiently at first, to the* **BARMAID**] The culture of Scotland gave the world the Protestant Bible, steam engines, gas lighting, the bicycle, tar macadam, MacIntosh raincoats, electric telegraph, television, penicillin, Campbell's Soup and McDonald's Burger King. [*to the* **GAEL**, *becoming excited*] Asylum seekers have been diluting that proud culture since the Eye-ties came here in 1890 with their decadent ice cream and fish and chips, then came the Jews, Indians, Pakis, Chinks, Serbs and Croats. Every fucking stupid wee nation we try to teach sense to by bombing brings in a new wave of asylum seekers crowding out our natural native food with their filthy foreign restaurants until now, [*sobs*] now Scottish salmon, Scottish lamb, Aberdeen Angus beef, haggis, black pudding, Highland venison and even my granny's tablet are for export only. [*pulls himself together*] Let us change the subject [*quietly to the* **BARMAID**]. The wife phoned me again last night.

The **GAEL** *eager to speak raises his hand but is steadily ignored.*

BARMAID O?

REGULAR Said she still passionately loved me. She doesn't know what passion is. She's frigid. Never an orgasm in her life. She was drunk, of course. An alcoholic.

BARMAID [*non-committaly*] I thought she'd sorted that problem out.

There is the faint distant sound of a pipe band playing "Wha Daur Meddle wi' Me".

REGULAR Alcoholics never change. She sits around doing nothing but her hair and polishing her piano.

BARMAID Senga Spotiswood still sees her.

REGULAR God knows why [*raising his voice as the pipes sound nearer*]. What's going on out there?

GAEL [*lifting his weapon and waving it*] I told you! The Prince has landed!

REGULAR [*louder still*] Why should anyone pipe up for a second rate no-user like the Prince of Wales?

BARMAID [*angrily*] Excuse me but that language is out of order!

GAEL [*brandishing his weapon and raising his voice over the increasing sound of the pipes*] My friend, you have been brainwashed by the capitalist press which derides a man for loving trees, old architecture and a lady as unglamorous as himself! The only man fit to represent a second-rate nation like Britain! I am one of millions ready to rise and help the last of the Stuarts reclaim and redeem his kingdom!

The **GAEL** *rushes out. A moment later there is a tremendous splash after which* **SOUNDS** *the moan of quickly deflating bagpipes. The* **REGULAR** *stares at the* **BARMAID** *who stares at the foot of the door.*

BARMAID [*glumly*] There's a trickle of water coming in under that door. We'll soon have to leave.

REGULAR [*philosophically*] Aye, half the Scottish Lowlands will soon be submarine. But it's only a trickle – there's enough time for a quicky before it wets our feet. A whisky please. And you have one on me. [*lays down money*].

BARMAID [*pouring two whiskies*] Thanks. Will you be moving to the Highlands?

REGULAR If there's room. The English have been buying houses there. You've got to admire their foresight! Folk with cash are always a jump or two ahead of the rest.

BARMAID Why didn't they build dykes? I mean, most of the Dutch have had dry houses under sea level for centuries, and Holland isn't being flooded.

REGULAR It's a matter of economics, dear. The British Empire was once the world's police force, so had no time for local agriculture. Now the job's been taken over by the Yanks who need our support to save civilisation from terrorists who do not share our democratic values. Let's have another for the road.

With a great CRASH the lights go out and there is a terribly prolonged **SOUND** *of rushing waters.*

THE STAGING OF the first two *Now* plays inspired me to again try boarding the good ship BBC, because I thought that *Midgieburgers* would sound well on radio. At the end of 2007 I asked my Scottish literary agent, Jenny Brown, if she could persuade a producer in Scottish BBC to discuss the possibility of commissioning a play from me. She did. On the 9th of January 2008 I had a business lunch in the Oran Mor bar-restaurant with her and David Neville, developer and producer of plays for BBC Radio Scotland. It was a pleasant meal, but disappointing. Mr Neville did not want me to adapt anything I had already written for broadcasting. He wanted something completely new from me, and honestly confessed that producers in London BBC would have to accept any fresh idea I came up with before he could commission me to work on it. We separated amicably, though I had no intention of trying to imagine a wholley new play.

But my vain wee creative subconscious (which R.L. Stevenson sometimes called his Brownies and sometimes his engine) came up with an east European statesman, former victim of a Communist dictatorship and now victim of its mafia-controlled successor. He is contacted by a youngster who once thought him a hero and wants to know what went wrong. I swiftly wrote the start of the play and indicated an end where both make a bid for freedom, and submitted this to Mr Neville. He was interested – said he would need to know more before considering a commission. With more work my solemn little play with its hints of pathos developed affinities with *Duck Soup*, the Marx Brothers' most anarchic film about European politics in the 1930s depression. I doubt if Mr Neville sent it to London before rejecting it. The BBC cannot broadcast a comedy mocking modern capitalism and mentioning the United States War on Terror. Written for the stage, the Oran Mor Play, Pie and Pint lunchhour theatre performed it with *The Pipes! The Pipes!* in February 2009. Iain Heggie directed; Sean Scanlon played the regular customer and President Rudi; Anita Vitesse was the barmaid and Vera; George Docherty was everyone else.

VOICES IN THE DARK

FOURTH NOW PLAY

2008

CAST

RUDI the elderly alcoholic president of Fredonia
VERA leader of a dissident group
SECURITY GUARD speaking from outside a door
GROLSH a mafia boss and former state policeman
The following are heard over a loud speaker:
THE MALE VOICE OF AMERICA
FEMALE USA VOICE
VOICE OF THE ITALIAN MAFIA
THE VOICE OF CHINA
POSH ENGLISH VOICE

SET

Centre stage, a large single bed with a huge elaborate padded headboard with the initials R and F entwined in a roundel at the top. On each side a bedside table has tumblers and labelled bottles of alcoholic drink, one or two nearly full and the rest nearly empty. The right-hand table also has a cordless telephone. To the right of the bed is a window covered by closed curtains and an upright chair. To the left is a door and another upright chair. Darkness.

RUDI, *in pyjamas, snores softly under the bedclothes.*
SOUND *A pane of glass is broken, a window stealthily opened and stealthily entered.*
VERA, *wearing combat gear and woollen balaclava with only a slit for the eyes, creeps in from between the curtains, switches on a torch with a pencil-thin beam in her left hand while holding a gun in the right. She flashes the beam round the room until, having located the bed, she creeps over to it, lays the torch on the table so that it lights up* **RUDI**'s *bald head. She then brings the nearest chair to the bedside, sits, switches on the near bedside lamp, pulls off the balaclava to show she is a very small serious woman. Pointing the gun at* **RUDI**'s *head she says quietly –*
VERA Hist! Wake up!
SOUND *snoring continues.*
VERA [*more urgently*] Wake up! Wake up!
SOUND *snoring continues.*
VERA [*harshly*] Wake up you old fool!
RUDI Mm? Eh?
VERA Wake up!
RUDI [*drowsily and slightly drunk*] Impossible. Impossible. The sleeping pills I am given no longer work, it is true, so I reinforce them with alcohol – what is the time?
VERA Three a.m.
RUDI Well, before midnight, on top of my pills, I consumed a bottle of 90% proof absolute alcohol so you cannot possibly have wakened me at three a.m. Go away.
VERA [*prodding with gun*] Open your eyes! This hard cold thing pressing your ear –
RUDI Ouch!
VERA – is the barrel of a gun.
RUDI [*not excited*] Yes, it feels like one, but dreams sometimes contain strong sensations. I recently dreamed

I was eating a buttered roll, the loveliest experience of my life, a memory of the birthday present my mother gave me when I was two or three. That was during the German occupation – nearly everyone was hungry then, even though the Jews and Gypsies had been removed. My mother [*he sobs*] my mother must have loved me a lot to have given me a whole buttered roll and not kept half for herself. Leave me alone.

RUDI *yawns and tries to settle down again.* **VERA** *slaps his face.*

RUDI Huh?

VERA Was that not more real than the dreamed taste of your mother's buttered roll?

RUDI [*sulkily*] No. It was not.

VERA *slaps him harder. He sits up a little.*

RUDI Ouch! Yes, that would convince me that I'm awake if this house was not surrounded by guards and electronic alarm systems and all kinds of clever protective devices installed by Americans, the smartest people in the world at that kind of thing. I regret disappointing you, my dear, but you must be a hallucination because nothing else could have penetrated the impregnable security fence that protects me from –

SOUND: *Knocking on door.*

VOICE OUTSIDE THE DOOR Sir! Sir! Are you alright?

RUDI [*sitting up*] Of course I'm alright! Can the President of Fredonia not indulge in a bit of Shakespearian soliloquy by talking to himself without a God-damned bodyguard questioning him? I have all the security I need – more security than I could ever want! Avaunt and quit my door! Abscond! Be gone! Shog off, shut up, retreat! Have a heart, as the Yanks say. (*with a Slavonic accent*) Have pity on your soul, as Dostoevsky says. Leave me in peace. Do you hear me? Do you hear me?

OUTSIDE VOICE [*muttering*] Yes sir.

RUDI But I don't want to hear you! Eff Off, as the English say!

RUDI [*after a pause, very loudly*] Do you hear me? Have you gone? [*pause, then a chuckle*] He's gone. My dear, I begin to think you are something more than a sexual fantasy.

VERA [*almost admiringly*] You're a smart old bastard. You knew I'd shoot you if you'd called him in.

RUDI [*sighs*] Why should you not shoot me? I'm useless. Useless to myself, useless to my nation, useless to the world.

VERA [*coldly*] But a tyrant to your people!

RUDI You do me too much honour. I drove that servile security guard away because I was enjoying our conversation about appearance and reality. Do you know that nowadays in Western Europe and the USA, post-modern deconstructionist philosophy declares that all external realities are mere opinions, all different but all equally valid?

VERA [*savagely*] Decadent bourgeois obfuscation!

RUDI [*delighted*] I love these old Marxist phrases! After the German occupation was replaced by the Russians, nobody cheered the regime they set up more than I did. I became an enthusiastic young Communist medical student. I made long speeches about Capitalist Lackeys, Neo-Fascist Warmongers, Bourgeois Hyena Cannibals and even, God forgive me, The Elimination Of Unproductive Social Elements. I hailed the coming day when the Revolution would be complete and the State would wither away. These words rang in my ears like trumpets must have sounded in the ears of Crusaders galloping out to exterminate the infidels! [*pathetically*] Please join me in bed.

VERA [*astonished*] You dirty old sod!

RUDI O don't mistake me. Since Comrade Grolsh put electric currents through my testicles I've been completely impotent, so the pressure of a friendly woman's body does not greatly excite me. But it would greatly soothe me, and nobody has soothed me like that since the old regime arrested me. Time I had another drink. [*reaches for a bottle and tumbler*] Have some too.

VERA Certainly not.

RUDI [*sipping*] You must have a reason for breaking in here. Do you want to ask me something?

VERA Yes. I want to know why you have betrayed us.

RUDI Betrayed who?

VERA The people of Fredonia.

RUDI Surely it is they who have let me down – not all of them of course, but the professional people – the lawyers and academics and administrators all seem perfectly content with how Grolsh and his pals are running everything.

VERA Who is Grolsh?

RUDI [*with an admiring chuckle*] He must be as smart as ever if even political dissidents don't know that he and his pals now run Fredonia. He always knew it was wise to stay out of the limelight. He never let the old party bosses promote him higher than the rank of Deputy

Commissar of State Security. When the Communist regime collapsed only those he had personally tortured knew what a criminal he was, and even we did not want to remember that. I suppose you belong to a minority political opposition group?

VERA We call ourselves the Decembrists.

RUDI Was that not the name of the group who planned to assassinate the Czar of all the Russias in 1820 something?

VERA [*laying down her gun*] Yes. At first we wanted a name recalling the great Soviet Revolution of 1917, the one that started going bad under Lenin, went rotten under Stalin and collapsed under Gorbachev. But we decided to call ourselves after an earlier group of revolutionaries –

RUDI Who failed!

VERA Alas yes, but Pushkin nearly joined them and Tolstoy approved of them.

RUDI [*chuckling*] And so you broke in here to assassinate the Czar of Fredonia! You nearly succeeded. I might have died of a heart attack.

VERA [*distressed*] I did not want to kill you. I once loved you. You were my hero when I was a tiny girl!

RUDI [*seriously and sadly*] O dear.

VERA That speech you made in the seventies gave hope to everyone in Fredonia. My mother and father heard it over the radio with tears streaming down their faces. You said the Republic of Fredonia would now take her own unique path of democratic socialism, and all censorship would be abolished, and the people everywhere would be allowed to say what they thought about anything – [*weeps*]

RUDI [*patting her hand, sings quietly*] Hail, hail Fredonia, land of the free! [*changing his tune*] For all that, and all that, It's coming yet for all that, That man to man the wide world o'er, Shall brothers be for all that.

VERA [*angrily*] I am a woman.

RUDI In a true democracy women count as men.

VERA Count me out!

RUDI Why?

VERA You retracted everything you said in your great speech!

RUDI I was an idiot Vera, not a liar at first. I believed every word of that first speech. You see, under the bad old Communist regimes, leaders kept announcing that things were about to change and improve because everyone would be allowed more freedom. Even Chairman Mao announced that 1,000 flowers would be allowed to contend. No sensible Communist underlings disagreed, they just carried on as usual. I was such a simpleton that I believed Khrushchev's announcement of yet another thaw –

VERA It was Brezhnev.

RUDI So it was. I was then the Commissar in charge of National Health, and cheerfully gave orders that every political dissenter who had been registered insane should be released from our lunatic asylums. I announced this over the radio as a reason for public rejoicing and a few hours later I was strapped to an operating table with electric wires attached to parts of me that – that – that I will not embarrass an attractive young woman by mentioning.

VERA You've already told me what parts.

RUDI I must be senile if I told you that, but yes, it happened. So a week later I announced that my previous speech had been the result of a mental breakdown. I said I was retiring from politics for the good of my health, which was certainly true. I was kept under house arrest until the Russian empire collapsed.

VERA We knew you had been coerced into making that speech. And someone called Grolsh coerced you?

RUDI Grolsh isn't totally evil. Like many sadists he's a good family man, with many wives and five times as many children, many more children than he can support out of his private fortune, even nowadays. So he has not completely dismantled our welfare state. Single parent mothers still receive family benefits. Our national health service has not been wholly privatised. Being a doctor I was very proud of it. Our health service was as good as the British one in its early days and infinitely superior to anything in the USA. Is it still functioning, my little Decembrist?

VERA Don't change the subject! We elected you president in 1990 because you were the only politician we knew who had tried to defend democracy under the bad old Communist regime! We still loved you! Still trusted you!

RUDI [*excited*] I remember the speech I made as if it was yesterday! "Fredonia will become the first truly democratic Socialist state! Every small business will now be owned by the family running it! The collective farms will be broken up and the fields given back to the farmers!

Every large state enterprise will become a cooperative enterprise owned and managed by its own workers! Transport, water, energy, mineral resources, broadcasting, education and (above all things) justice will be maintained for the people's benefit by the people's own elected parliament!" I sounded wonderful. No wonder they cheered and cheered and cheered me. [*sobs*]

VERA Fraud. Hypocrite. Whited sepulchre.

RUDI [*sighs deeply*].

VERA Why did you go back on all that?

RUDI I never did. That is why they keep re-electing me.

VERA [*with contempt*] Surely you know the election results are faked?

RUDI I suppose they must be, with old Grolsh in charge.

VERA Why has everything you promised to defend in 1992 disappeared? Everything in Fredonia now belongs to foreign global corporations and the international mafia. Nearly half our young people today are drug addicts or vandals. Crime, disease and deaths in police custody are steadily increasing. The streets are full of beggars. Most people are worse off than they were under the rotten old Communist regime.

RUDI Yes, under that regime there was widespread social equality for everyone who was not a party official. It was equality of scarcity, of course. Shoppers stood in queues for hours; most folk had only three or four really satisfying meals per week. But nobody starved and we had no beggars because nobody was penniless. There was full employment because everyone without a productive job was paid by the state to spy on their neighbours.

VERA Are you defending the regime that screwed your balls off?

RUDI [*sighing*] No.

VERA Then what went wrong with Fredonia when you were elected president after all these fine speeches?

RUDI [*puzzled*] I don't exactly know. I signed some documents that I thought made it legal for farmers to own their own fields and plumbers to own their own shops and in swarmed middle men – brokers – there is an unpronounceable French name for these people –

VERA Entrepreneurs.

RUDI These entry-pruners swarmed in and asset-stripped the entire nation. I could not stop them. Nobody else tried to. I kept announcing that this should not be happening and demanding that people in responsible jobs stop it.

VERA You did. That is why some of the working class still trust you.

RUDI The speeches of an incompetent old president cannot change history when his lawyers and judges and civil servants, the elected MPs, everyone in his government and the opposition are working privately for global companies while being openly paid out of the public purse! I became what I am now, a hollow figurehead, more useless than a scarecrow. Scarecrows at least keep predatory birds away from grain that is needed for bread! I am a sham Vera. You are right to despise me. [*drinks*]

SOUND *the phone rings, playing the first nine bars of the Fredonian national anthem more than once.*

RUDI Excuse me a moment.

He picks it up, singing softly along with it –

RUDI Hail, hail Fredonia, land of the freeeeeee – [*switches the phone on*] Yes?

THE VOICE OF GROLSH Rudi?

RUDI Yes.

VOICE OF GROLSH This is Grolsh.

RUDI Why?

VOICE OF GROLSH I want a word with you.

RUDI Say it.

VOICE OF GROLSH I must say it to your face. At once. Now.

RUDI Why?

VOICE OF GROLSH A national emergency. Very serious. Very urgent.

RUDI Where, exactly, are you, Grolsh?

VOICE OF GROLSH Outside your bedroom door.

VERA, *terrified, seizes her gun.* **RUDI** *is amused.*

RUDI At four in the morning? What a busy bee you are. And now I come to think of it, that's the usual hour when security forces grab a government's political enemies. I hear that the British police now arrest asylum seekers at this hour.

VOICE OF GROLSH Please! I am not here to arrest you but please, we must now talk.

RUDI [*merrily*] I'll call you in when I have adjusted my clothing. [*puts down phone, says to* **VERA**] You can come into bed or get under it. I suggest in.

RUDI *pulls back the bedclothes on his left side,* **VERA** *slips in and under. He covers her head then raises his knees to make a tent hiding the lump of her body seen from the right.*

RUDI *[in a loud sing-song warble]* Enter Comrade Grolsh!

GROLSH, *a very gloomy, well-dressed businessman, comes through the door, shuts it carefully behind him, picks up a chair, carries it to the right side of the bed and sits down with his hands clasped between his knees.*

RUDI Care for a drink?

GROLSH Yes.

RUDI Help yourself.

GROLSH *nearly fills a tumbler with vodka, swigs from it, says:*

GROLSH This building has been the president of Fredonia's residence since the days of Looper Firefly in the 1930s. Even then, this was the president's bedroom. Did it never occur to you that state security would have this room bugged?

RUDI *[chuckling]* Strange as it may seem, it never did.

GROLSH *[sighing]* I know that Vera Zazulich, leader of the Decembrist group, is either in bed with you, or under it, with a gun in her hand that she will shortly point at my head.

VERA *[sitting up, gun in hand]* Yes Mr Grolsh. It seems you are largely responsible for the terrible state of Fredonia, so if you call in your henchmen I will not hesitate to put a bullet in your brain.

GROLSH Had I feared that I would have sent them in before me. A sudden clean death from a bullet in my brain is the least thing I fear nowadays.

RUDI *[laughing]* The poor fellow must be in serious trouble, Vera! Who is after you Grolsh? Will they attach electrodes to your genitals? Or work all over you with pliers and a blow torch?

GROLSH *[wincing]* Don't joke! Yes, I am in trouble, and a deal with you two may be the only way out of it. And I promise both of you will benefit hugely by playing ball with me because Grolsh is a man of his word.

RUDI I am past playing ball games, Grolsh, but go on! Go on! You are beginning to interest us. Your health! *[clinking his glass against* **GROLSH***'s]* Vera, can I not persuade you to – ?

VERA No!

GROLSH *[after swigging again and sighing]* I wish I had left Fredonia in 1989 but it was never easy to take effective currency out of a left wing regime. Swiss nationality could be obtained by any western politician or corrupt businessmen who had built up a big Zurich bank account, but the old Communist states were notoriously stingy. Then came the liberal revolution that made you president, Rudi, and everything in Fredonia was for sale! I admit that went to my head. It was an intoxicating time. Never, in the history of capitalism, has so much been sold to so many by so few. I sold coal mines, copper mines, schools, reservoirs, power stations, drugs, justice, everything! I lost count of the many things I sold and now – *[sighs]* – now it appears that I sold some of them twice to completely different international organisations.

RUDI But Grolsh is a man of his word! He must have discovered some way of compensating three different global corporations for buying the same power stations.

GROLSH *[nodding solemnly]* It can be done. Yes, there is a way of doing it that will delight you Rudi, and you Vera Zazulich. The liberal revolution, my friends, has now obviously gone too far. It hugely enriched a new middle class at the expense of the workers and the poor, but now a trade recession is starting to hurt professional people so it is time for everyone to enjoy a new government by a new political party – the Party of the New Deal!

RUDI *[merrily]* What will the New Dealers do?

GROLSH They will make you more that a mere figurehead! You will be able to keep some promises made in your great speeches. You will truly represent the democratic socialism you suffered by defending.

RUDI *[snarling]* He remembers my sufferings Vera! How kind he is!

GROLSH You Vera, the Decembrist, represent all those young idealists who still have faith in liberty, equality, fraternity. The new party will put you in charge of education, broadcasting, sport, culture, fashion, anything you like! You can be Home Secretary and create a Ministry of Feminism. And I must emerge from the shadows and support your new political platform, the platform of the New Dealers Party. I will be in charge of trade, industry, finance – boring matters high-souled people like you don't understand.

VERA *[scornfully]* You think such an alliance will save your soul?

GROLSH *[violently]* To Hell with my soul! It's my body I fear for. I want to die painlessly of old age.

RUDI And what will this wonderful new government of ours actually do?

GROLSH Give back Fredonia to the people of Fredonia!

VERA *and* **RUDI** [*together*] How?

GROLSH [*enthusiastic*] We three left-wingers understand Marxist historical logic – Thesis! Antithesis! Synthesis! The state Communism that collapsed in 1990 was our thesis. It provoked the state Capitalism that is also starting to crumble. Our New Deal government will renew this nation by synthesising both systems.

RUDI [*merrily*] You will create Capitalist Communism!

VERA [*merrily*] Communist Capitalism!

GROLSH Exactly, exactly, exactly! We will do it by renationalising all industry and public services that no longer profit the present owners.

RUDI So all the global corporations that bought them so cheaply will be richly compensated by the Fredonian taxpayers – including all the corporations who paid for the same power stations.

GROLSH Our new government will not last a week if it is not trusted by the International Monetary Fund.

VERA *and* **RUDI** *both laugh heartily.*

VERA I'll have a drink after all. [*pours one*].

GROLSH [*grumpily*] What is this big joke you laugh at?

RUDI You.

VERA We don't believe in you.

RUDI You have lurked in the shadows so long, Grolsh, that you have become one. You are no longer solid, but a phantom – a ghost of the mirage of an illusion.

GROLSH [*strongly*] You are both terribly wrong. I still wield power, terrible power, and can prove it.

RUDI I suppose you mean the outré harpooners still trust you?

GROLSH Yes, because I am one of them! Also, I have important international contacts of immense strength and intelligence ...

SOUND: *The first six notes of the American national anthem.*

GROLSH *cowers.*

A MALE USA VOICE This is the Voice of America! This message is for European agent 87,329 pee cue zero six, otherwise known as Vladimir Grolsh.

FEMALE USA VOICE Agent Grolsh, you are in breach of the contract forbidding you to form new political alliances without previous CIA clearance.

GROLSH I had no time to inform you of the alliance I have just proposed – I only conceived it half an hour ago – but I am glad you have listened in to my modest proposal, though I did not know this room had also been wired by the CIA.

FEMALE USA VOICE We have not wired it. We are addressing you over a new satellite system which allows us total powers of surveillance and interference everywhere at any time. Ours is the only operating system of its kind in the world ...

SOUND: *First six notes of La Donna Mobile.*

A **SINISTER ITALIAN VOICE** Not quite the only operating system of its kind. This is the Casa Nostra speaking. Under clause 312 of the CIA and Mafia International War on Terror Treaty, Casa Nostra agents only need clearance from us and our Fredonian agent Grolsh received that clearance from us 20 minutes ago.

SOUND: *A Chinese gong is struck.*

CHINESE VOICE But Agent Grolsh has not received clearance from the Chinese Central Intelligence Agency!

A **POSH ENGLISH VOICE** And if I might be allowed to put in a word ...

FEMALE USA VOICE You may not!

POSH ENGLISH VOICE I know the UK is a junior partner in our alliance, but the city of London is still the world's greatest money laundering centre, and it seems to me Agent Grolsh has become a useful link between all of us, including the Muslims, is that not true Grolsh?

FEMALE USA VOICE No deals with the enemy.

GROLSH [*pleading piteously*] Surely in a free market economy a man may sell himself to every agency who can afford him? And the USA, the Mafia, the UK and China are allies! You are not at war with each other!

SOUND: *Chinese gong.*

CHINESE VOICE Every nation must be prepared for every eventuality.

FEMALE USA VOICE You can say that again.

SOUND: *Chinese gong.*

CHINESE VOICE Every nation must be prepared for every eventuality.

ITALIAN VOICE Grolsh, you had better come back to Sorrento.

RUDI *starts singing softly "Hail hail Fredonia, land of the freeeeee!" and keeps it up to the end of the play.*

FEMALE USA VOICE No way! When Grolsh leaves the president's bedroom he will be coshed, chloroformed, rolled in a carpet and sent for debriefing to Abu Ghraib.

GROLSH [*wailing*] Mercy! Mercy! England! England! Please! Surely your renowned sense of fair play will come to the aid of poor old Grolsh, your most faithful of Fredonian agents?

ENGLISH VOICE Sorry Grolsh old bean. Our prime minister is Scotch and has just given permission for your extraordinary rendition through Prestwick Airport.

GROLSH Vera! You were going to put a bullet in my brain. Please do it now!

VERA No!

GROLSH Then give me the gun!

VERA [*handing it over*] Here – but there are no bullets in it. [*starts singing along with* **RUDI**].

GROLSH [*after a despairing cry*] Rudi, sanctuary! Sanctuary! Shelter me!

RUDI *kindly raises the bedclothes on the right side.* **GROLSH** *seizes a half full vodka bottle, slides in, swigs from the bottle then joins* **RUDI** *and* **VERA** *singing the Fredonian national anthem as loudly as they can over:*

SOUND: *The first bars of the American national anthem, the end of which overlaps "Goodbye to Sorrento" warbled on a mandolin, which overlaps the fading English voice saying:*

ENGLISH VOICE Surely all the parties concerned can settle this business through a free and frank discussion ...

SOUND: *A final huge boom from the Chinese gong.*

I WAS FOURTEEN in 1949 when the BBC Third Radio Programme, celebrating the bicentenary of Goethe's birth, broadcast the five acts of his Faust over three nights in a new translation by Louis MacNeice. The vast social and historical scope of the play – a drama of good and evil forces – make it an epic to set beside those of the Biblical Genesis, Greek Homer, Roman Vergil, Italian Dante and English Milton; also beside Shakespeare's tragedies, Hogg's Justified Sinner and Melville's Moby Dick. Faust so excited me that, lacking the energy to learn German, I began reading all the translations into English I could find, knowing that every translator would show a different aspect of Goethe's masterpiece. I admit that I identified with Faust. My parents would have loved me to have become a highly respected university professor, but I wanted more from life. Goethe's tale of old Professor Faust obtaining youth, sexual love, wealth and earthly power with Satan's help suited me. This had become the plot of ambitious operas and novels for over a century. The price paid by those who try to do well by criminal means can be read in *Great Expectations* and *Crime And Punishment*, besides *Dr Jekyll and Mr Hyde* and *The Picture Of Dorian Gray.* For years I wanted to write a modern version starting like Goethe's play, but with a different end. Despite Faust's worldly triumphs through warefare, high finance, murder and robbery, Goethe finally admits him into Heaven. I felt he should either be finally damned to Hell or saved by some great unselfish act.

In 2006 the local success of my short play *Goodbye Jimmy* brought back all my notions of rewriting Faust for modern times. After several starts and stops I completed my version up to the end of a first act, and stopped, not sure of how to continue. I had made Faust (I thought) a convincing modern scientist, engaged him with Mephistopheles (who I called Nick), and through Nick's agency introduced him to the woman he would love, and also made him young again. Nearly all of this was taken from Goethe's play, especially the prologue before the gates of Heaven. Most of speeches and encounters in what followed were also adapted from Goethe's Faust, though I had left a great deal out. I knew that the play would diverge greatly from Goethe's. On January 16th 2008 I posted what follows to the National Theatre Of Scotland, hoping they would pay me to work more on it.

PROLOGUE BEFORE HEAVEN

Dark blue theatre curtains.

SOUND: *Grand solemn chords of religious music, Haydn, Handel or Bach.*

The curtains part to reveal **THREE ANGELS** *facing the audience in long robes the colour of the curtains. Behind them a dawn sky where the sun-sphere slowly ascends, crimson changing through orange and gold to white as the angels chant.*

RAPHAEL The sun-star, glorious as ever,
bathes all his worlds in golden light
still rolling round the galaxy
midst nebulae as vast and bright.
Planets and moons attend his glory,
reflect his beams in sparkling ray
while angels, heralding this story,
announce the dawning of a day.

GABRIEL Swift, unimaginably swift
the mighty earth is rolling too
from darkness of profoundest night
to skies celestially blue.
while winds contest with ocean waves
or drive them on like fleeing crowds
against the base of granite cliffs
whose summits penetrate the clouds –

MICHAEL Storm clouds, whose snow and hail and rains
in stream and cataract pour down
to flood and irrigate the plains
ensuring growth is nature's crown –
that seeds take root and creatures feed
from humble worm to beast of prey,
while angels, heralding the Lord,
announce the dawning of His day.

The sun has disappeared upwards leaving the sky clear blue. The angels look up, raising their arms. A spotlight shines down on them. They start chanting the chorus as **NICK** *enters jauntily, wearing a dark red sweater, black jeans. He mounts the stage and, just before the curtains, bends his knees in servile caricature of a courtly bow, raising arms in mocking imitation of the angels.*

THE THREE ANGELS CHANT TOGETHER
And sounding colour glows and leaps
twixt star and sun and world and moon –
God is necessity that keeps
all nature's orchestra in tune!

The spotlight swings out onto **NICK** *who jumps up, stands to attention and gives a Nazi salute before speaking with the overdone bonhomie of an experienced gatecrasher.*

NICK Good Lord, it's wonderful to have you here,
and – God Almighty – since you condescend
to let me supervise this bad wee globe,
I'm bound to greet you as a long-lost friend,
my oldest chum. Excuse my slang these days
but since expulsion from your Heavenly choir
I've never seen one thing deserving praise
in jargon your angelic hordes admire.
Creation is perhaps a giant joke
that pleases you. Not me! I deal with folk –
men – women – shit, in short. Why give these clods
intelligence? A gift that damned immortal Gods
like me – your deputy! Men would be less bad
without the sciences that make them glad
to torture, kill themselves, their planet too.

GOD Do you like nothing here?

NICK Nothing. The whole mess gars me grue.

GOD Do you know Faust?

NICK Professor Faust? O yes.
A muddled soul. I laugh at his distress.
A mammy's boy. A teacher's pet. A swot
who hoped the girls would find him fascinating
for knowing what the other lads did not.
That did not fetch them. Missing youthful pleasures
he groped in books for intellectual treasures
till, master of three sciences or four,
he finds professoring a deadly bore
and knows his over-stimulated brain
has done no good, and left him half insane.

GOD Faust is unhappy like all honest folk
who do not think the world a giant joke
and find the prize they worked for, hard and long,
is worthless, and has put them in the wrong.

NICK Aye aye! These very intellectual pains
come easily to men who have no weans
and wives to feed, and do not hear the pleas
of homeless millions, dying of disease.

GOD Faust is bewildered. Science and art are born
by those whose inner selves are almost torn
apart by pains that will not let them rest
until they reach the highest and the best.

NICK Reach you, in fact! How lovely! What if I
prevent that? How about it? Let me try!

GOD You tried before.

NICK [*in Yankee*] In three-six-nine BC
with Job, your servant? Yep, he sure fooled me.
I knocked his house down, killed his children quick,
stole all his money, left him poor and sick,
his skin one itching scab from head to toe,
then friends arrive, appalled to see such woe,
and to console him, busily explain
he must be wicked to deserve such pain!
Despite the evil things you let me do
that poor sap Job never lost faith in you!

GOD People with nothing else have only me.

NICK The wealthy are my business? I agree.
Professor Faust owns nothing rich and fine.
I'll give him all he wants, to make him mine
– if you allow me?

GOD Do your wicked best.

NICK Indeed I will! Good Lord I am impressed
by your permissiveness. Moses talked rot
when parroting his slogan, Thou Shalt Not.
God forbids nothing. Why do folk forget
the first word that you ever spoke was Let –
Let There Be Light! Let there be Lucifer,
and the pervading brightness lets all see
the lightest of your eldest sons is me.

GOD A fool.

NICK – who's licensed by your Holiness,
the jester of the universe, no less!
Forgive me levity. I must feel gay
since you are letting me make Faust my prey.

GOD Demons like you, Old Nick, I tolerate
because your antics undo something worse –
those smooth routines upholding every state
where management makes government a curse.
Faust keeps rich managements in good repair.
His well-attended academic courses
turn youths into exploitable resources.
Remove him from his academic chair!

NICK Dead or alive?

GOD Alive.

NICK [*briefly Australian*] Good on you, God!
I hate tormenting ghosts. It's much more nice
to toy with living souls, like pussy toys with mice.

GOD'S *spotlight swings back from* **NICK** *to his* **ANGELS**.

GOD My better children, come back to the sky
and there enjoy the better things we do.
Make life the loveliest form of energy
that every day creates the world anew!

SOUND: *With chords like a great Amen the curtains close.* **NICK**, *outside them, turns, faces the audience and tells them in a familiar way:*

NICK I like to see the old dear dropping in
when weary of his land of endless light
that gave me heatstroke once. He needs Old Nick,
and toffs like him are never impolite.

Exit **NICK**, *as jauntily as ever.*

ACT ONE

SCENE: *Faust's study, low lighting at first.*
Backstage centre, a wide window so high we cannot see the top – outside a starry night sky diagonally crossed by the milky way.
Back right, a laboratory bench with Bunsen burner, its low flame under a retort of glowing liquid bubbling out along glass tubes; a plastic globe of the modern world, lit from inside, also several beakers and green glass stoppered bottles.
Left back, a tall church lectern with brass eagle facing audience, supporting on its wings a great shut book.
Front right, a swivel chair at an office desk with computer, the latter slanted to show on the screen a mathematical formula in several colours.
Front left, a narrow spot lights a throne-like armchair where **FAUST**, *bearded, wearing a quilted dressing gown, sits morosely contemplating a skull in his hand.*

SOUND: *Westminster chimes strike the half hour.*

FAUST Psychology – I've mastered that,
biology and physics too.
In each I've made discoveries
my colleagues lecture on as true,
the fools. [*stands and wanders uneasily about*]
One certainty my knowledge brings –
science and wisdom are quite different things.
Why call my colleagues fools? I'm just as bad.
[*puts skull down on desk or bench*]
Students pour in to pay their fees,
swallow my words and use my knowledge
to stay behind and teach in college
or start their own consultancies.
Who once had gained high office in the Church
are now engaged in highly-paid research.
I once believed the sciences I taught
were founding universal brotherhood.
Psychologists today become spin doctors,
Biologists are making cheap, fast food.
The physicists invent new ways of killing
for sale to terrorists of every nation –
government forces or their enemies –
both sides enrich a global corporation.
I can't go on like this. I have to change,
how? I must call on what, to me, is strange –
occultism. Self-hypnosis. Artful tricks
which once got people burned as heretics.
No wonder!
FAUST *goes to lectern.*
Nostradamus wrote this book.

He opens it. Blue light from within shines on his face.

FAUST He knew some things smart moderns overlook.
These starry signs can give a man control,
of forces that still shape the human soul.
[*As he turns pages his face is lit by other colours.*]
Dealings with Mercury would make me rich,
and Bachus elevate me with his wine.
Venus could turn me into Don Juan,
Apollo make my singing voice divine.
Mars, giving victory through marshal art,
might make of me another Bonaparte.
Great Jupiter has made more lasting kings,
but heads of state today are feeble things.
Such partial gods divide the human soul,
where is the spirit that can make it whole?
[*turns a page that lights his face more strongly.*]
The sign of the Earth Spirit! – yes, the Earth
alone can give a man a second birth.
[*gazes in wonder.*]
I think that I begin to understand it
but do I have the courage to command it?
No solid mass of mineral density
but a great fountain of vitality
or else a strongly rooted wind-tossed tree
with many gleaming fruits among the leaves –
fruits that are living souls. And is one me?
[*violently.*] No! I am God's image –
shaped from earthly clay
but with a soul that never shall decay!
Anything less than God must be my brother.

He rips the page out and holds it up, staring at it.

Earth Spirit, visit me in human form
for you and me must talk to one another!

SOUND: *of a tremendous musical chord with fading echo as night sky behind window is replaced by a dazzling face so big that at first only an eye, then mouth, are completely visible.* **FAUST** *drops the page which a gust sweeps into the wings. The* **SPIRIT'S** *voice is clear, with slight echo.*

SPIRIT Why do you call?

FAUST, *with inarticulate cry, reels, shuddering.*

SPIRIT Answer! Why call me here?

FAUST *clutches his hair.*

SPIRIT Why do you want me? Answer! Are you dumb?

FAUST: Go! . . . Back! . . . A little further back! My fear
is almost overcome.

The **SPIRIT** *recedes so that most of the centre fills the doorway. It is the face of a pre-adolescent child, indignant but capable of derision.*

SPIRIT [*mocking*] Fear almost overcome?
Where is the insolence that called me brother
and tried to give itself a better goal
by forcing me into this tete-a-tete,
to recreate your wretched little soul?

FAUST You daunted me at first, great spirit, true.
Not now! Now I command you to renew
the thing I am by saying what you are!

SPIRIT I am the only planet of your star
to carry living souls who question me.
In calms and storms
and foaming waves
I bring new forms
from birth to graves,
steadily blending,
coming and going,
brief but unending
lives overflowing,
from ocean depths up to the windswept sky
I weave for God the clothes you see Him by.

Hearing this, **FAUST** *has become exalted.*

FAUST O noble spirit, working through time and space
to make this sordid globe a better place,
thank you! A thousand thanks for now I see
we are alike!

Amused, the **SPIRIT** *speaks through silent laughter.*

SPIRIT You see a vision you're imagining!
Not me!

FAUST [*yells*] Not you?

SOUND: *Tremendous musical chord as face dwindles to vanishing point in the night sky.*

FAUST [*groans*] I made that ...
thing appear before my eyes
and questioned it, and listened to replies,
and glimpsed a being similar to mine
sharing a purpose that I thought divine,
yet saw it falsely! Why do I exist?
Professor Faust's a paltry solipsist!
An academic fraud! Impotent too!
Useless and sexless –

SOUND: *Loud knocking.*

FAUST [*in a snarling shout*] Enter! Who the hell are you?

Enter **NICK** *as an enthusiastic spectacled lad with tousled hair, wearing slippers and pyjamas under an open white laboratory coat, a half bottle of whisky in the pocket. The audience need not at once notice he is* **NICK. FAUST**, *disgusted, slumps down in the big chair.*

NICK Excuse me sir, I think you were rehearsing
a tragedy translated from the Greek.
Though just a residential lab assistant
a grasp of languages is what I seek.
A scientist like you I'll never be,
but might become a guru on TV

telling folk what we do in this laboratory,
making it sound like fun, if I'd the oratory.
Tell me sir, would a course of drama teach
a lad like me a better flow of speech?

FAUST Your present flood of words is adequate –
smooth eloquence is wholly out of date.
Broadcasters think the public is a fool
so sounding stupid is their golden rule.
If you would like to be more widely known
don't try to change your . . . slightly vulgar tone.

NICK Wonderful news! [*frowns*] A bit depressing too,
if famous me can never be, like you,
looked up to!

FAUST You'd be envied for your fame.

NICK You make that seem a rather pointless game.
I'll think about it. Sorry I butted in.

FAUST Carter, I'm glad. Your unexpected knocking
prevented me indulging in a shocking
burst of self-pity, I regret to say.

NICK Yes, many folk feel like that on Hogmanay.

FAUST Hogmanay?

NICK Soon we will hear the bells.

FAUST Year gone and nothing gained.

NICK My granny tells
me time goes faster as we use years up.
Let's welcome, sir, the new year in a cup
of what the Scots call kindness – raise a cheer
with friends who've come
to welcome the new year –
fine girls among them! You need a party, so –

He takes out and offers whisky bottle.

FAUST [*violently*] Carter, it's peace I need!
Thank you, but go!
Please leave. A party? Surely not. No. No.

NICK *grimacing, leaves with sharp backward glance.*

SOUND: *The Westminster chimes, preparatory to the strokes of midnight.*
During it **FAUST** *stands and approaches the laboratory bench, then starts talking loudly, heavily and slowly so that each of his lines punctuated by a stroke of the bell.*

FAUST Carter, that idiot, (**1**) stopped me going mad.
The very greatest, (**2**) fun-da-men-tal cause
of me and all I know (**3**) both good and bad
declared I could not (**4**) see the thing it was.
So! I twist every (**5**) thing to selfishness?
True, but I can't (**6**) continue in this mess.
[*he lifts bottle from bench, unstoppers it*]
To be, or not? Not! (**7**) I will pour my own
cup of kindness. Mhm (**8**) Phe-no-bar-bi-tone
[*pours measure into beaker*]
will end my year. (**9**) Faust, why hesitate?
Courage, Professor! (**10**)
Come, embrace your fate.
You don't fear death. (**11**)
You don't believe in Hell.
This cup of kindness (**12**)
will make all things well.
Raises the beaker to his lips, when suddenly –

SOUND: *of wild chiming bells, fireworks crackling as rocket explodes in night sky.*

Simultaneously, **NICK**, *in sweater and trousers, pulling* **MAY** *by one hand,* **AGNES** *by the other, bursts in with* **JILL** *and* **BILL** *in fancy dress and paper party hats, singing.* **BILL** *with a bottle of wine.* **FAUST** *stares, astonished.*

ALL THE VISITORS SING:
A guid new year to ane and a'
and mony may ye see!
And here's tae a' the years tae come
and happy may they be!

NICK *pulls the two women over to* **FAUST** *shouting.*

NICK Because, Professor, you are far far too
busy to join the girls, they come to you!

He and flings away **FAUST'S** *beaker.*

NICK Now then!

The bemused **FAUST**, *his hands seized by* **MAY** *and* **AGNES**, *is pulled into a ring of* **NICK** *hand-in-hand with* **MAY** *and* **JILL** *and* **BILL** *(who has put his wine bottle on the floor) hand-in-hand with* **JILL** *and* **AGNES**. *They dance sideways singing –*

AGNES Should auld acquaintance be forgot,
And never brought to mind?

MAY We'll tak a cup o kindness yet
For auld lang syne.

EVERYONE EXCEPT FAUST
For auld lang syne, my jo,
For auld lang syne
We'll tak a cup o kindness yet
For auld lang syne.

The ring dances the opposite way with **FAUST** *starting to be amused.*

MAY We twa hae paidl'd in the burn,
Frae morning sun till dine;

AGNES But seas between us braid he roar'd
Sin' auld lang syne.

EVERYONE EXCEPT FAUST
For auld lang syne, my jo,
For auld lang syne
We'll tak a cup o kindness yet
For auld lang syne.

All cross hands to shake each others, narrowing the circle.

MAY Then there's a hand, my trusty fiere!

AGNES And gie's a hand o' thine!

MAY AND AGNES
And we'll tak a right gude-willie waught
For auld lang syne.

FAUST *now looks and laughs from one girl to the other who laugh back.*

EVERYONE, FAUST INCLUDED
For auld lang syne, my jo,
For auld lang syne
We'll tak a cup o kindness yet
For auld lang syne.

The ring breaks. **NICK**, *without releasing* **MAY'S** *hand, pulls her to the desk and sits on it, pushing her down into the swivel chair.* **AGNES**, *older, plumper and more sexily dressed, pulls* **FAUST** *by the hand to his own chair. He collapses into it with relief, she sits on the chair arm, snuggling against him.* **BILL** *lifts the bottle, goes with* **JILL** *to the bench. He empties the bottle into six beakers, then serves* **NICK** *and* **MAY** *with two as* **JILL** *takes two to* **FAUST** and **AGNES**; *then* **JILL** *and* **BILL** *amuse themselves at the bench with the other two glasses and the skull, before going to the lectern where* **BILL** *enjoys turning the book's pages to show images* **JILL** *pretends to find shocking or frightening. Meanwhile the others converse,* **AGNES** *talking to* **FAUST** *who answers absentmindedly because he is looking across at MAY,* **NICK** *talking to MAY who is intrigued by the sight of* **FAUST** *and* **AGNES**.

FAUST One of my students are you?

AGNES Don't you know?

FAUST When lecturing my mind's on what I teach.

AGNES You don't see faces?

FAUST No need. The exams show who listens.

AGNES Oh? You failed me in psychology.

FAUST [*amused*] I hope you're not expecting an apology.
They both sip from their beakers.

NICK Behold Professor Faust learning to flirt!

MAY He isn't streetwise.

NICK Worried he'll get hurt?
You like big daddies?

MAY I don't like you, Carter!

NICK Of course! I'm a smart alec – no-one smarter.
No decent girls want me I'm glad to say.
Drink up!

FAUST Will you repeat the year? [*still watching* **MAY**].

AGNES [*nodding*] I've paid my fees.

FAUST Mature student?

AGNES Twice divorced, you see –

FAUST [*interrupts, raising forefinger*] Please!
Give me no details. I'm not a wise confessor
but just your rather immature professor.

AGNES We all know that! [*smiling*].

FAUST [*indifferent*] Who is this all who know?

AGNES Your female students, sir.

FAUST [*mildly interested*] How does it show?

AGNES Not looking at us straight is the reaction
of someone terrified of our attraction
unless we're out of reach, like my friend May.

FAUST, *for the first time, looks straight at* **AGNES**.

FAUST Is that her name? Perhaps you think I'm gay?

AGNES [*laughing*] Oh no sir. You're as miserable as Hell.

Laughing, **FAUST** *lifts her hand to his lips and kisses it.*

FAUST I failed you in psychology! Well well!

NICK [*to* **MAY**] Professor Faust's emerging from his shell.
But Agnes is not his type. It's you, my dear,
he'll want when he relaxes – never fear.

MAY That's stupid! I am no professor's pet.

NICK Not now you ain't but he'll surprise you yet.

MAY He's far too dignified, too old, too stout!

NICK Inside him there's a young chap wanting out.

NICK *suddenly empties his glass, claps hands, leaping to middle of floor, shouting:*

NICK My friends! My friends!
Bad news! Bad news! Bad news!
It's Hogmanay and we've run out of booze!

Loud groans from **BILL** *and* **JILL**.

NICK There's plenty in my room – you know the way!

BILL Three cheers for Carter! Hip hip hip –

BILL, **JILL**, **AGNES** Hooray!

AGNES *empties her glass as* **BILL** *and* **JILL** *leave, and stands, saying to* **FAUST** –

AGNES Coming?

FAUST No.

AGNES You ought to come – cheerio.

AGNES *leaves as* **NICK** *pulls* **MAY** *across to* **FAUST**.

NICK Professor, this shy girly wants to say – what is it?

MAY Thankyou.

FAUST [*rises*] For what? I gave you nothing, May.
You helped to save my life.

NICK [*laughing*] He's right! That's true!

MAY *and* **FAUST** *gaze into each other's eyes, then abruptly she runs out.* **NICK** *slaps* **FAUST** *on the shoulder and strolls away, pleased, rubbing his hands and chortling.* **FAUST**, *arms folded on chest, stands watching him curiously.*

FAUST Carter, what are you?

NICK *[to the audience]* He's rumbled my wheeze.

FAUST Rumbled?

NICK I turn to slang at times like these,
being embarrassed by the fact that I
(though your assistant) am a . . .
sort of . . . spy.

FAUST Who for? The government?

NICK *[scratching his head]* I'll start again.
Forgive me! It's not easy to explain.

FAUST *sits back in his chair, cheek on fist, prepared to be bored.*

NICK I am a part of what was endless night
before a greater part discovered light.
That bigger part is everybody's dad –
boss of all things, including you, my lad.
Dad has (don't ask me why) conceived a plan
that needs you to become a better man.

FAUST I know our universities are now infested
With spies but I am just not interested.
[yawning]
And everybody's dad? Stop talking rot.
Police chiefs do not think that way.

NICK Why not?
My brother, who's a simpleton and dunce,
became a carpenter's apprentice once.
Why should his older brother not be earning
cash as your lab-boy in this seat of learning?
I'll tell you why! Working here stunts my growth,
just as it's stunting yours. It's time we both
set out for fresher fields and pastures new.

FAUST Carter, I am alive because of you
and grateful, but please tell the CIA
or MI5 or any other boss,
Faust's not for hire. He'll find me no great loss.

NICK *raises his eyes to Heaven punching his brow, then flings away his spectacles and goes to* **FAUST** *saying –*

NICK O Faust Faust Faust! Why must you be so thick?
Look at me! *[grasps* **FAUST'S** *shoulders]*
Can't you see that I'm Old Nick?

FAUST *[without getting up]* Give me a sign.

NICK *stands back, snaps his fingers.*

SOUND: *Deafening crash of thunder.*

LIGHT: *Instant darkness on stage, through the window the sky turns red with branched lightening crackling over it. Silence and normal lightening is suddenly resumed.*
FAUST, *sitting up in his chair, watches* **NICK** *who faces him triumphantly from a distance, hands on hips.*

NICK Are you convinced?

FAUST A cinematic trick,
impressive though. And what else can you do?

NICK Some hokus-pokus stuff involving you.

FAUST *jumps up, alarmed.*

NICK Worry ye not! The change, when I unfold it,
will please you very much when you behold it.
[claps his hands]
Music and cosmeticians come to me!
Make over Faust as he would like to be!

SOUND: *Sinister, seductive music like Anitra's dance from the Peer Gynt Suite.*

LIGHTS: *Changes to revolving coloured spots cast by disco ball.*

TWO FEMALE BEAUTICIANS *and a* **BARBER** *skip in with trolley holding tools of their trade. They wear scarlet and/or purple clothes that are otherwise conventional. Their ballet with* **FAUST** *(who is dazed and passive) removes his thickly padded gown, taking away enough bulk to show an athletic figure in black slacks and white shirt. They press him into the chair, drape a barber's sheet round him,* *turn the chair-back to audience. A* **BARBER** *shaves and trims* **FAUST** *helped by the women who present towels, razors, combs, brushes, moisturisers.*

NICK *strolls around, sometimes watching with approval, sometimes slightly bored.* **BARBER** *whisks off sheet, swivels chair round and helps to his feet a handsome new beardless* **FAUST** *as the* **BEAUTICIANS** *pull in from the wings a tall mirror on casters, turning it to show* **FAUST** *his new beardless image.* **BARBER** *and* **BEAUTICIANS** *skip out with trolley as –*

SOUND: *music stops.*
LIGHT: *goes normal.*

FAUST *turns to* **NICK** *who contemplates him smugly.*

FAUST Why have you done this?

NICK To display my might.

FAUST Old Nick's an exhibitionist?

NICK Not quite.
I am a salesman. This is an example
of goods I'm selling. Call it a free sample.

FAUST Your other goods?

NICK Sex, money, power and glory.

FAUST Paid for in Hell?

NICK Please disregard that story.
You pay for them in Hell, but never fear.
Your Hell is not eternal. It is here.

FAUST Hell is on earth?

NICK On earth – I won't deceive you,
the goods I'm offering will often grieve you.
Self pity for the hearts you have to break –
regret for lives you ruin by mistake –
the loneliness of being rich and great
and hated by all who envy your estate –
are tedious at times. I must confess
self pity and regret and loneliness
are what you'll pay me for the goods I sell.

FAUST I've known these all my life.

NICK [*cheerfully*] Welcome to Hell!
You'll find the game
well worth the entrance price,
but first, a word of warning and advice.
The satisfying of each splendid sense
may place a burden on your conscience
unless you shake it off.

FAUST Can that be done?

NICK Of course! With drink and drugs –
but it's more fun
to lose old deeds by plunging into new.
Rapid activity's the drug for you.
All passionate delight in womankind
produces babies or a broken heart.
All schemes to make the world a better place
must break some heads
and spoil some works of art.
In the destructive element immerse!
I'll teach you swimming, Faust – it is your fate
to be magnificent! Dare to be great!

FAUST [*coldly*] You have not told me why you offer this.

After a pause **NICK** *says unwillingly:*

NICK I do it to annoy someone I hate.

FAUST Why does God let you?

NICK [*desperately*] Please! Forget that shit!

FAUST You're hiding something that I need to know.

NICK [*in Cockney*] Rumbled my wheeze again,
you cunning lad.
[*soberly*] The whole thing started many years ago
when there was perfect peace,
secure, blank, black,

featureless, timeless, silent cosiness
till someone moved. With a tremendous crack
eternity became a gibbering mess
of substances – the universe became!

FAUST We call it The Big Bang.

NICK Too kind a name. I call it The Big Fart.
The gas condensed in globes flying apart
and waltzing round each other while they fled,
half blinding me who loved the kindly night
before the first mover shattered my warm bed.
The echo of his fart rings in my ears.

FAUST [*amused*]
It has been called the music of the spheres.

NICK Spectacularly pointless radiation
was not enough for that prolific toff
who spat it, shat it out. He wanted admiration!

FAUST But God has angels.

NICK Aye, a heavenly host
who think he's the bees' knees,
but dogs don't boast
of how they love their fleas' appreciation.
Love has to be free. Mine was the one free mind.
I loathed that dog-spelled-backward's
whole creation.
"What use are your
billion zillion worlds?" I cried.
"What use are new born babies?" he replied,
teasing me with a wholly senseless word.
A million zillion centuries elapsed
before the first babies occurred.

FAUST [*keenly*] So God foresaw men before life began?

NICK God knows what God foresaw –
I don't, young man.
The babes he looked to maybe were jellyfish,
worms, centipedes, any low form of life
except those pissing, squawking manikins
who grew up to be Adam and his wife.

FAUST And was that when you came to earth?

NICK [*sighing*] O no.
I came here long long long long long long ago.
[*speaks the next lines in Cockney.*]
One day Almighty Gawd, 'e sez ter me,
"Nicky, let us agree ter disagree.
Ere's a young planet – nufink too immense –
where molecules is shuffling into sense
and that means life, my boy! So you go there
and do your best to ruin the affair.
I'm all for life," (sez 'e), "but if you can
manage to stamp it out,
then you're the better man."
"Want a bet, guv?" I sez to 'im, "Alright!"
[*speaking as usual*]
And that is why I've met you here tonight.

FAUST But life has triumphed!

NICK [*shrugging*] So far, so it seems.

FAUST What place have I in your destructive schemes?

NICK His Holiness and I both want to see
how you will use the powers that make you free
to do just what you want.

FAUST Well, first of all
I want a good night's sleep.

NICK [*snapping his fingers.*] A good idea. Start small.

IMMEDIATE DARKNESS ENDS ACT ONE

THE NATIONAL THEATRE OF SCOTLAND returned that fragment because Edinburgh's Lyceum Theatre had recently staged another modern version of Goethe's play by John Clifford. Then suddenly I saw how to develop Faust's story in a way that would let me respect him – he would save God's credit and beat the Devil by abandoning happiness, wealth and power in a spectacularly 21st century way. Having made the middle and end of my play different from Goethe's, I renamed it and the hero after a Scottish footballer who had played for Glasgow Rangers and Norwich City, Robert Fleck. His surname 'Fleck' replaced 'Faust' in the prologue and first act without changing the rhyme scheme. When my play was completed in the summer of 2008 only God and Nick had the same characters as in Goethe's play.

I was so pleased with *Fleck*, so sure any good theatre would see how to make a roaring commercial success of it – so sure its political moral was what our unhappy world needed – that I did not wait to publish it in *THIS* book: I sent it to Sharon Blackie and David Knowles who run Two Ravens Press from their croft on the shore of Loch Broom. In October 2008 they published it in a beautifully printed and designed paperback at the retail price of £8.99. The world of bookshops and reviewers hardly noticed it. Every Scottish theatre whose name I remembered turned it down. An important London theatrical agency (called *The Agency*) liked it and had it refused by several good English theatre companies, because it it did not fit their schedule, or was not their cup of tea, yet praised it so highly that I felt it was the best play never produced. If you found pleasure in this playbook and want more of the same, order *Fleck* from

www.tworavenspress.com.

To stimulate a sale by whetting your curiosity,
here is how it ends.

EPILOGUE BEFORE HEAVEN

Dark blue theatre curtains.

SOUND: *Grand solemn chords of religious music, Haydn, Handel or Bach.*

The curtains part to reveal **THREE ANGELS** *facing the audience in long robes the colour of the curtains. Behind them a dawn sky where the sun-sphere slowly ascends, crimson changing through orange and gold to white as the angels chant.*

THE THREE ANGELS, *as in Prologue to Goethe's play, chant this slightly shorter hymn:*

RAPHAEL The sun star, glorious as ever,
bathes all his worlds in golden light,
still rolling round the galaxy
midst nebulae as vast and bright.

GABRIEL Swift, unimaginably swift
the mighty earth is rolling too,
from darkness of profoundest night,
to skies celestially blue.

NICK *is heard as he staggers drunkenly in through the audience, shouting loudly until he mounts the stage.*

MICHAEL:	**NICK**:
While winds contest with ocean waves	Fuck you all!
or drive them on like fleeing crowds	Fuck you all!
against the base of granite cliffs	Fuck you all!
whose summits penetrate the clouds –	Fuck you all!

GABRIEL:	**NICK**:
Storm clouds, whose snow and hail and rains	All! All!
in stream and cataract pour down	All of you!
to flood and irrigate the plains	Fuck all of you!
ensuring growth is nature's crown –	Fuck Fuck!

RAPHAEL:	**NICK**:
That seeds take root and creatures feed	Fuck you all!
from humble worm to beast of prey	Fuck you all!
while angels, heralding The Lord	Fuck you all!
announce the dawning of His day!	Fuck you all!

NICK *collapses on stage hammering it with his fists and groaning as the angels chant:*

THE THREE ANGELS CHANT TOGETHER:
While sounding colour glows and leaps
twixt star and sun and world and moon!
God is the harmony that keeps
all nature's orchestra in tune!

LIGHT: *God's spotlight shines on* **NICK**.

GOD You are drunk, my friend. Sorry you lost our bet?

NICK I can't go on!

GOD [*kindly*] Poor Devil, you want peace
only possible if life would finally cease.

NICK Let it cease! Why not? Why stop me making
everything die? Everyone should!

GOD They always do.

NICK Why must you keep creating them anew?
I loathe the screams of women giving birth.

GOD I suffer with them. With them I recover.
The universe requires me for her lover,
don't you know?

NICK Yes! Since you both cast me out
millions of years ago!

NICK *rises to his knees.*

GOD You left because you hated us, Old Nick.

NICK Because! I foresaw your foul arithmetic,
that multiplies the swarms of life on earth
with germs of every size, constantly giving birth.
Life is a foul disease that we should cure!
I beg you, please,
let's sterilize the world and make it pure!

GOD Love will not let me – love that drove John Fleck.

NICK *leaps up and yells –*

NICK To suicide?

GOD He gave folk hope that greed
will not destroy the planet they all need
to share and live upon in liberty –

NICK [*yelling*] Equality? Fraternity?
Cretin! Can't you see, will you not confess
the fight for these prolongs the human mess?

GOD Fleck did not want the human race to end
and you, poor drunkard, only feel distress
because you came to feel he was your friend.

NICK [*weeping*] My only friend!

GOD [*laughing*] Apart, of course, from God!

NICK You shit! You squirt of piss! You stinking sod!
You Nobodaddy! – nastier than worms
infesting earth because you love their squirms!

GOD *addresses his angels.*

GOD My better children, come back to the sky
and there enjoy the better things we do.
Make life the loveliest form of energy
that every day creates the world anew.

Heaven closes. **NICK** *pulls himself together, shrugs his shoulders and sighs.*

NICK So God fucks off as usual into air – thin air –
leaving the stage to me and my despair.
He becomes thoughtful.
Despair? Am I desperate?
– Hm. Not quite!
Fleck's speech has caused confusion.
Prompted by me, chaos, war will ensue.
Nuclear fires may still burn the earth black,
turning life back into eternal night.

With increasing enthusiasm he addresses the audience.

Au'voir, dear friends, au'voir, we'll meet again
in famine, bloodshed, pestilence and pain!
I hope this entertainment pleased you well.
It has no moral – see you all in hell!

SOUND: *Splendid Amen chords, followed by a cheerful and rapid voluntary by Handel, Haydn or Bach.*

Compared with the poetic conclusion to Goethe's Faust my epilogue is mere doggerel, but it is dramatically more in harmony with his Prologue outside heaven, in which Satan starts the play (as he starts *The Book of Job*) by claiming he can lead Faust into renouncing God, if God will give Satan the power to corrupt that good man. God does give Satan that power, and the long ensuing drama tells how Faust is absolutcly corrupted. With Satan's help he does all the damage a selfish seducer and multi-millionaire supporter of corrupt old political regimes CAN before death. After which Satan, rightly sure of having earned Faust's soul by half a lifetime of giving him all he wants, is cheated into releasing it by the angels of the Prologue. Faust then floats upward through a heaven of purified souls, where God never appears, and finally joins the soul of the woman he drove to madness and infanticide. This happy, sentimental end is produced by *Das ewig Weibliche* – in English, Eternal Femininity – a force of levity which ensures forgiveness for anyone who (like Stalin, Hitler, Mussolini, Edward 1st, William the Waster etc.) struggles hard to the end of their days.

Goethe partly took this conclusion from *Dante's Divine Comedy*, where the author is led to the height of Godhead by the soul of a girl he loved when they were children. But Dante's God is a presence surrounding and sustaining the universe, not a character playing a game with Satan for the soul of a single man.

POSTSCRIPT

THIS BOOK LACKS SEVERAL PLAYS, mostly documentary dramas produced by Scottish radio and educational TV in the late 1960s and 70s. It still contains enough forgotten work to prove me a busy though unimportant dramatist, driven by the vanity that made me, at the age of nine, get a primary school class acting a scene in which I starred as Polyphemus.

When arranging the plays in chronological order I noticed that the majority met the requirements of a great thinker, amateur playwright and former Prince of Denmark. When speaking in sober prose (not the blank verse he used when talking to himself) Hamlet told a theatre company that their job should be, *to hold, as t'were, the mirror up to nature, to show virtue her own feature, scorn her own image, and the very age and body of the time his form and pressure.* The nature he wanted actors to reflect is human nature under the social and historical pressures that provoke and limit people's actions.

Shakespeare wrote this kind of play for his actors, as did Molière, Goethe, Büchner, Ibsen, Shaw, Wedekind, Chekov, Brecht, Beckett. Their plays were often at first rejected by ordinary commercial theatres (especially in Britain) for being unactably dreary. It is true that most folk visit theatres to be distracted from life's hardest facts. This is proved by centuries of moneymaking plays being forgotten after a decade or two, because their frivolity was no longer fashionable. Of course frivolous successes also reflect social pressures, for when politics turn agonizing even intelligent folk want to stop thinking about them. Throughout the First World War the most successful London theatre production was *Choo Chin Chow*, a musical comedy based on the Ali Baba fantasy. As the Nazis took over Germany the most popular drama was *Wanda the Bagpiper*, another musical comedy based on a fairytale.

It is not strange that many respectable folk began by hating plays of true pathos like *Woyzek*, *The Doll's House*, *Mother Courage*. Shaw's first two great plays, *Mrs Warren's Profession* and *Widowers' Houses*, were banned in Britain for the first quarter of the twentieth century because they told the truth about prostitution and slum landlords. My own plays do not approach such high artistry but many do reflect the body and pressure of their times.

Jonah was written in 1956 when the British Empire still dominated lands it would soon have to leave in Cyprus, Palestine, Africa and Malaysia. Our government had only recently overcome the austerity of food rationing, but Britain had full employment, its first effective welfare state, and strong trade unions who made sure that their workers had better wages and social security than the British working class had ever known. As a Tory Prime Minister said around 1960, we "had never had it so good." A widespread sense of liberation, especially among the young, made British fashions in dress, pop music and cinema widely known abroad. Even I wanted to live in London, and imagined doing so in *The Fall Of Kelvin Walker*. My sexual comedies and *Mavis Belfrage* show life in this Britain where unmarried domestic lives couples are taken for granted. *The Man Who Knew About Electricity* shows real poverty returning to Britain as building programmes and new motorways destroy old districts and communities. Public scandals showed many civil servants and politicians were being bribed by industries they were starting to privatize – see *McGrotty and Ludmilla*. Then such bribes became legal wages, and new laws let brokers shift capital abroad. A Tory statesman asked why British workers should be paid with money to build ships, when Asian workers could be paid in handfuls of rice. Despite trade union resistance, British heavy industries were asset stripped and destroyed, as reflected in my *Rumpus Room*. Later plays, including *Fleck* which I am certain is my best, show a world of governments whose only aim is monetary power got by using laws and police forces. These plays are all comic fantasies. Don't take them seriously.

This book should, but does not, say anything about playwrights who were my contemporaries and sometimes friends, e.g. Archie Hind and Joan Ure (the latter the pen name of Betty Clark) and Liz Lochhead, and James Kelman. I also knew Cecil Taylor, whose best plays were internationally produced. I saw many highly successful productions – McMillan's *The Bevellers*, John McGrath's *The Cheviot, The Stag and the Black, Black Oil*, Archie Hind's stage version of *The Ragged Trouser Philanthropist*, Byrne's *Slab Boys*. There were many more. Since the 1970s, Scotland has had enough talent to make it as lively a theatrical nation as Ireland or any other, and many younger writers are enforcing the fact. But a lack of confidence here has producers only supporting local achievements sporadically. They seldom revive, and never build upon them.

In 1973 Cecil Taylor and Tom Gallagher tried to improve our drab state by inviting Scots dramatists to a meeting in Edinburgh. Their initiative founded the Scottish Society of Playwrights, for which I was the minutes secretary for a year or two before private troubles made me incapable of unpaid work. The Society still helps members to sign fair contracts with managements. It should always be conferring with those employed to boost art in Scotland.

But Scottish drama will never flourish until each of our big towns has a theatre that can be leased by *any* company able to put on a show and sell enough tickets. The sale of tickets to good audiences should be able to recover the cost of rent and production expenses and company wages. For years high rents have made that impossible, so even the most successful productions depend on arts council grants or commercial sponsors. Good audiences do not decide what plays succeed, but administrators and advertisers who of course like this state of affairs. So do all landlords who profit from high theatre rents.

The state of drama here, like other activities,
will only improve when folk living in
Scotland feel responsible for
their own government.